Michael Cooper's

B...

Guide

to New Zealand

Wines

2005

Hodder Moa Beckett

A catalogue record for this book is available from the National Library of New Zealand.

ISBN 1-86971-012-6

Text © Michael Cooper 2004
The moral rights of the author have been asserted.

Design and format © Hodder Moa Beckett Publishers Limited 2004

Published in 2004 by Hodder Moa Beckett Publishers Limited
[a member of the Hodder Headline Group]
4 Whetu Place, Mairangi Bay, Auckland

Designed and produced by Hodder Moa Beckett Publishers Limited
Typeset by Jazz Graphics, Auckland
Printed by Griffin Press, Australia

All rights reserved. No part of this publication may be reproduced or transmitted in any
form or by any means, electronic or mechanical, including photocopying, recording, or any
information storage and retrieval system, without permission in writing from the publisher.

'This is the most comprehensive guide available on New Zealand wines, written by the most accomplished of local wine writers ... Overall, a must-have book which will give the wine lover many hours of pleasure.'
– *The Press*

'Cooper doles out bouquets and brickbats in equal proportions, without fear or favour ...'
– *Winepress*

'Michael Cooper's book is indispensable, edition by edition.'
– *New Zealand Listener*

'If you have any interest in local wines, or have a few bottles stashed away, buy this book.'
– *Next*

'As a practical buying tool, this book is five-star value for money.'
– *New Zealand Herald*

'The best of the publications that regularly appraise New Zealand wines.'
– *Hawke's Bay Today*

Michael Cooper is a leading authority on New Zealand wine, with 30 years' experience of researching and writing about the subject. In the 2004 New Year Honours, he was appointed an Officer of the New Zealand Order of Merit for services to wine writing.

The author of 26 books and hundreds of magazine and newspaper articles, Cooper has several major literary awards to his credit, including the Montana Medal for the supreme work of non-fiction at the 2003 Montana New Zealand Book Awards, won by his authoritative *Wine Atlas of New Zealand*. He is wine editor of New Zealand's foremost food and wine magazine, *Cuisine*, and chairman of its New Zealand wine-tasting panel.

In 1977 Michael Cooper obtained a Master of Arts degree from the University of Auckland with a thesis entitled 'The Wine Lobby: Pressure Group Politics and the New Zealand Wine Industry'. A full-time wine writer since 1991, he is chairman of judges at the New World Wine Awards and an international wine ambassador for New Zealand Trade and Enterprise.

Cooper's other works include *Classic Wines of New Zealand*, *The Wines and Vineyards of New Zealand*, which ran to five editions and was the bible of the industry for many years, *Michael Cooper's Buyer's Guide to Imported Wines* and *Pocket Guide to Wines of New Zealand*. He is also the New Zealand consultant for Hugh Johnson's annual best-selling *Pocket Wine Book*.

Contents

The Winemaking Regions of New Zealand

Area in producing vines 2005 (percentage of national producing vineyard area)

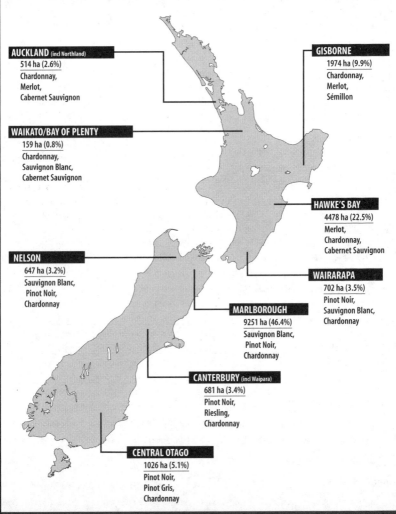

AUCKLAND (incl Northland)
514 ha (2.6%)
Chardonnay,
Merlot,
Cabernet Sauvignon

WAIKATO/BAY OF PLENTY
159 ha (0.8%)
Chardonnay,
Sauvignon Blanc,
Cabernet Sauvignon

NELSON
647 ha (3.2%)
Sauvignon Blanc,
Pinot Noir,
Chardonnay

GISBORNE
1974 ha (9.9%)
Chardonnay,
Merlot,
Sémillon

HAWKE'S BAY
4478 ha (22.5%)
Merlot,
Chardonnay,
Cabernet Sauvignon

WAIRARAPA
702 ha (3.5%)
Pinot Noir,
Sauvignon Blanc,
Chardonnay

MARLBOROUGH
9251 ha (46.4%)
Sauvignon Blanc,
Pinot Noir,
Chardonnay

CANTERBURY (incl Waipara)
681 ha (3.4%)
Pinot Noir,
Riesling,
Chardonnay

CENTRAL OTAGO
1026 ha (5.1%)
Pinot Noir,
Pinot Gris,
Chardonnay

These figures are extracted from the *New Zealand Grape and Wine Industry Statistical Annual 2003*, published by New Zealand Winegrowers. Between 2004 and 2006, the area of producing vines is expected to expand from 18,112 to 20,877 hectares, a rise of 15 per cent.

Preface

'You can't possibly have tasted all the wines in the book,' several people have suggested to me in the past year. With over 2000 New Zealand wines on the market, how could anyone taste the lot?

It's easy. Most days, I spend an hour before lunch swirling, sniffing, sipping and spitting between six and 10 wines. If you spread that over a year, the task of tasting 2000 wines doesn't look tough at all. And there's no prize for guessing my favourite part of the working day!

When you consult the *Buyer's Guide* or magazine tasting articles, or scan the results of wine shows, always remember that wine-tasting is inherently subjective. Three experts on a panel only occasionally come up with identical scores. A Chardonnay that tastes 'fresh and vibrantly fruity' to one judge 'lacks complexity' to another. A Pinot Noir praised by one panellist for its 'firm tannins and structure to age' may be marked down by another for being 'over-extracted and tough'.

The marathon, all-day tastings organised by magazines and competitions favour wines that can stand out in a crowd – blockbuster wines, robust and high in alcohol, strongly oaked and sometimes slightly sweet (which adds smoothness). Wines with finesse and delicacy – the sort that may well be the most enjoyable to drink – are often overshadowed in big tastings by more powerful, upfront wines.

So I like to taste wines in different ways. Blind tasting eliminates the preconceptions we all have, based on a wine's price and reputation, but tasting a wine with its label exposed, over a meal, lets you really get to grips with its personality. I once asked André Lallier, of Champagne Deutz, whether he entered his wine in shows. 'You can't understand my wine in 30 seconds or a minute,' he replied. 'To get to know it properly, you need an evening.'

The tasting notes in this book have been gathered from a multitude of tastings – usually, but not always, without food; often 'blind', but frequently not; sometimes as part of a panel; sometimes not. By the end of the year – during which the wine itself has been evolving – I have often tasted the same wine several times. The notes published in the *Buyer's Guide* reflect the nature of all these tasting formats, and I hope they are strengthened by it.

— *Michael Cooper*

2004 Vintage Report

It was the bumper harvest that had to happen. New Zealand's exploding vineyard area until recently failed to produce a proportional surge in wine output, due to a run of low-cropping seasons. But in 2004 the vines yielded according to expectations, producing a total harvest of 166,000 tonnes of grapes. Apart from 2002 – the previous record harvest of 118,700 tonnes – the 2004 crop was more than twice as big as any previous vintage in New Zealand.

The record 2004 harvest was gathered from a producing vineyard area of 18,112 hectares – far ahead of the 15,800 hectares cropping in 2003, 13,787 hectares in 2002 and 11,648 hectares in 2001. Yields were the other key factor. With the exception of 2002, the vines' average yields had plummeted over the past five seasons, from 8.9 tonnes per hectare in 1999 to just 4.9 tonnes per hectare in 2003. (The weather, the changing mix of grape varieties and regions, and a growing awareness of the link between wine quality and crop levels all contributed to the decline in yields.) In 2004, however, the vines' average crop leapt to 9.17 tonnes per hectare – the highest since 1998.

It was a record crop for most grape varieties, above all Sauvignon Blanc and Pinot Noir. At 67,773 tonnes, the Sauvignon Blanc harvest nearly doubled the old record (36,742 tonnes in 2002) and formed 42 per cent of the total vintage. The Pinot Noir crop of 20,145 tonnes also nearly doubled the previous record (10,402 tonnes in 2002). The Chardonnay, Merlot, Riesling, Sémillon and Pinot Gris harvests also exceeded past records, although Cabernet Sauvignon dipped slightly below 2002 and 1998.

In terms of regional output, Marlborough, Hawke's Bay and Gisborne were again the key players, producing 92 per cent of the national harvest (up from 88 per cent in 2003). A whopping 57 per cent of all New Zealand wine flowed from Marlborough in 2004, ahead of Hawke's Bay (19 per cent) and Gisborne (16 per cent). Nelson was the largest of the smaller regions (2.7 per cent).

Despite a wild early spring, with endless overcast days sprinkled with rain and wind, frost damage was far more localised than in 2003. Matua Valley, which owns vineyards in Auckland, Gisborne, Hawke's Bay and Marlborough, reported that 'bud-burst was very even throughout and over all varieties'. Weather conditions during the vines' flowering were favourable in most regions, laying the foundations for a large crop.

Summer was a season of extremes. Regions stricken by drought in January experienced unusually cool temperatures and record rainfall in February. That month, a major storm battered the country when a burst of cold air from the Antarctic collided with moist air from a weak tropical low. Of the wine regions, the Wairarapa was the worst affected.

In dramatic contrast to February, March was markedly drier than average in most parts of the country, which reduced the threat of disease. March and April were both cooler than normal. 'In many areas this led to the vintage being slightly later than normal,' said the industry body, New Zealand Winegrowers, 'but the benefit has been that growers have been able to give the grapes plenty of "hang time", [producing] very good flavours in the grapes'. According to Joe Babich, 'with the Indian summer it turned out a very good vintage across the regions – Auckland, Gisborne, Hawke's Bay and Marlborough'.

Northland

Northland bucked the national trend with a small grape crop of 144 tonnes, well below the 182 tonnes picked in 2003 and the record 2002 harvest of 186 tonnes.

'Cold, strong south-westerlies in early spring slowed bud-burst,' reported Okahu Estate at Kaitaia, 'then gave way to an extended fine period to establish good growth, flowering and fruit set.' A severe dry spell during late autumn and early summer was broken by heavy rains in late January, and February proved exceptionally wet, with a total rainfall four to five times the average.

March, however, was notably dry. Okahu Estate experienced 'a glorious, long, sunny autumn, with cool nights promoting excellent sugar levels. We got lovely, ripe fruit across the board – our Merlot, Cabernet Franc and Syrah all came in at 24 brix.'

Auckland

Auckland's vineyards yielded a bumper crop of 1497 tonnes of grapes, more than double the 2003 crop of 715 tonnes, although slightly less than the regional record of 1526 tonnes, set in 2002.

'Bud-burst was up to two weeks late on most blocks,' reported grower spokesman Steve Nobilo. On Waiheke Island, Te Whau Vineyard experienced 'excellent weather during flowering and fruit set'. But after a dry early summer, February brought the highest rainfall on record.

'It was the worst February in memory, with so much rain,' says Milan Brajkovich of Kumeu River. Nobilo also described February as 'an absolute shocker, but the wind helped to counter the wet weather; disease pressure throughout the season was virtually non-existent'. Brick Bay, at Matakana, also reported a growing season 'with very little humidity, largely because our weather patterns came from the south-west, rather than the north'.

After a dry autumn, the predictions were for high-quality wines. 'The wet weather in February had an effect on the earlier-ripening Chardonnay,' said Goldwater Estate, on Waiheke Island. 'But March and April were unusually dry, allowing us to extend our harvest dates ... [We achieved] excellent depth in the reds.'

'You know it's a good season when Cabernet Sauvignon ripens well,' declared Nobilo, 'and this year it is great, with nice, ripe blackcurrant flavours.' Pinot Noir was the most affected by the February rains, says Milan Brajkovich, 'but our Chardonnay, Pinot Gris, Merlot and Malbec couldn't be better, in terms of yield and quality. Chardonnay wasn't high in sugar, but it shows good flavour intensity.' Brajkovich rates Kumeu River's Chardonnay crop as highly as the excellent 2002, 'although it's not as good as [the outstanding] 2000'.

Waikato/Bay of Plenty

Waikato winemakers harvested only 457 tonnes of grapes – less than in the frost-affected 2003 vintage (497 tonnes) and far less than in 2002, which yielded a bumper crop of 932 tonnes.

Spring frosts were less of a concern than in recent years, according to grower spokesman Ross Goodin, at Te Kauwhata, but from the last week of January to the end of February 'the weather was atrocious. The rain was extensive, there was a great deal of cloud and heat summation was down dramatically.' The region's total summer rainfall was more than double the average.

Although March was relatively dry, fogs slowed ripening in some areas and 'downy mildew created major problems', according to *New Zealand Grapegrower* magazine.

'While there has been some very good quality Chardonnay and Sauvignon Blanc, generally acids have been very high,' reported Goodin.

Gisborne

'The most pleasing' vintage in James Millton's vast experience (stretching back to 1984) yielded a total crop of 25,346 tonnes of grapes – Gisborne's second-largest ever, just behind 2002 (26,587 tonnes) and far ahead of 2003 (14,350 tonnes). Some outstanding wines are likely.

In spring, September was wetter and warmer than usual, and October wetter but cooler. 'Bud-burst occurred about the usual time on the early varieties and was generally considered to be good,' reported Warwick Bruce, Gisborne vineyards supervisor for Allied Domecq Wines NZ.

High humidity and heavy rain in January and February 'had grape-growers concerned,' admits the Gisborne Winegrowers Society, but an 'exceptionally dry' March and April delivered a top vintage. A Gisborne grower who monitors botrytis bunch rot concluded that 'the 2003–04 growing season has had the lowest total hours of botrytis risk of the six years assessed'.

The harvest (12 days later than normal, according to Bruce) climaxed a cool growing season, which boosted flavour development in the berries. 'Our Gisborne Chardonnay is as clean as a whistle,' declared Ross Spence of Matua Valley.

James Millton enthused that 'vivid, ripe-fruit flavours, coupled with higher acidities, have given us ripe fruit requiring little winemaker input'. Tairawhiti Polytechnic, which operates its own vineyard and runs a wine industry certificate course, reported processing 'excellent Gewürztraminer, Riesling and Sauvignon Blanc ... [and] impressively ripe Viogniers'.

Hawke's Bay

From a frost-stricken 10,832 tonnes in 2003 to 30,429 tonnes in 2004 – that extraordinary production leap sums up the bumper 2004 vintage in Hawke's Bay, also described by Paul Mooney, winemaker at Mission Estate Winery, as 'the best overall vintage for quality since 1998'.

'The timing of bud-burst was normal,' says Peter Cowley of Te Mata Estate, 'and a warm spring ensured a good and very even flowering.' November was wetter than usual but after lighting his heat-pots six times, Alwyn Corban of Ngatarawa Wines reported 'no frost damage'.

After a mild, dry early summer, by mid-January staff at Trinity Hill were busy 'trimming and tucking the lusty growth which resulted from rain between Christmas and New Year'. January was warmer than average, but '20 January onwards saw horrific winds and a fair bit of rain, necessitating lots of canopy retucking and net replacements,' says John Kemble, of Kemblefield Estate.

In February, gale-force winds stripped leaves off vines (especially those on exposed hill sites) and snapped off posts, but the total rainfall was only slightly above average, according to Vidal and Mission.

March, according to Gordon Russell of Esk Valley Estate, was 'cool' and 'unexpectedly sunny'. By late March, Merlot and Cabernet Sauvignon were seven to 10 days behind normal, says grape-grower spokesman Chris Howell, but 'once the weather cleared, things went like a rocket'.

Cold nights in early April activated windmills and triggered helicopter call-outs, but by mid-April Gordon Russell reported a highly successful vintage: 'It's just tremendous, very similar to 2002 but maybe better again.' Jeff Clarke, chief winemaker at Allied Domecq Wines NZ (formerly Montana), praised his company's Hawke's Bay Chardonnay as 'the best for several years. Better than 1998 and 2002, due to higher acids.' Russell agreed, describing Esk Valley's Chardonnay crop as 'robust, high in alcohol, but with remarkable acidity levels, due to the cool temperatures of March'.

Clarke summed up Allied Domecq's red-wine crop as 'stunning. It's better than 2002, without a doubt, and the average quality of our Merlot and Cabernet Sauvignon is higher than in 1998.' Grant Edmonds, of Sileni Estates and Redmetal Vineyards, views 2004 as a 'fantastic year for Merlot and Cabernet Franc, with dense purple/black colours [and] super-ripe raspberry and blackberry jam flavours'.

Wairarapa

There'll be plenty of Wairarapa wine from 2004. At 2820 tonnes, the total crop more than doubled the 1311 tonnes of grapes harvested in 2003, and easily surpassed the previous record of 2022 tonnes, set in 2002.

Spring frosts caused little damage. Weather conditions during the vines' flowering in early December were 'warm and settled' according to Nga Waka, 'resulting in a successful set and large crop'. Dry River noted 'unusually rampant growth early in the season', necessitating plenty of leaf-plucking to keep the vines' vegetative growth in check.

Summer, however, brought more than double the normal rainfall. Early summer was dry and hot (a total fire ban was imposed in January, after temperatures topped 30°C), but February was a washout. Some districts received four to five times their usual February rainfall; the region suffered its worst floods in a century; and Martinborough's February sunshine hours reached an all-time low.

In autumn, the weather reverted to a more normal pattern, 'with close to average rainfall but cooler than average temperatures, which delayed the start of harvest by two weeks,' says Nga Waka. The total growing season, however, was wetter and warmer than usual, and one winemaker reported widespread botrytis bunch rot, especially in Sauvignon Blanc.

After declaring that 'all varieties reached our normal ripening targets, albeit at higher than usual acid levels, the legacy of lower sunshine hours', Nga Waka summed up its quality overall as 'good to very good'.

Nelson

With a record crop tucked away in Nelson's wineries but predictions of variable wine quality, grape-grower spokesman Philip Woollaston described the 2004 vintage as reminding him 'of the ancient Chinese curse: may you live in interesting times'.

For the second year in a row, Nelson harvested a larger crop than any of the other 'small' regions. The total harvest of 4563 tonnes of grapes was a record, well ahead of the previous high of 3149 tonnes, posted in 2003.

In spring, a generally wet September and October caused 'a later bud-burst this season, but good, even growth', according to a grower in the Moutere hills. November and December were both sunnier and drier than average. 'Fine, breezy, warm weather has given us the most uniform and quick flowering ever,' reported a grower on the Waimea Plains.

A hot, but wet and cloudy, January led into a wet, cold February. 'The vegetative growth has been greater than in previous years and we have done much more leaf-plucking,' noted a Waimea Plains grower in late February. Despite the plentiful February rainfall, the unusually low temperatures reduced the threat of botrytis bunch rot.

After a favourable March, the weather deteriorated in late April. 'It will be a mixed bag of results,' declared one of the region's top winemakers. 'Our Sauvignon Blanc looks lovely and the big surprise was how beautifully ripe our Malbec has got,' enthused one grower on the Waimea Plains in late April. 'We won't even try to pick our Shiraz, though.'

Another grower in the Moutere hills reported 'good, clean fruit apart from a little botrytis in the Sauvignon' and 'some diluted character in Pinot Noir and Chardonnay'. At Kahurangi Estate, some of the crop's brix (grape sugar) levels were 'high, some just right and some low'.

Marlborough

Over half (57 per cent) of all New Zealand wine from 2004 will flow from Marlborough, where the bumper harvest almost equalled the 2002 and 2003 vintages combined. The region's crop of 92,581 tonnes of grapes far outstripped the previous record of 54,496 tonnes, set in 2002.

In spring, October and November were both cooler but slightly sunnier than average. 'We have had a beautiful bud-burst,' reported grape-growers' spokesman Stuart Smith. Framingham noted 'some early season frost impact [mostly in the southern valleys] although not as widespread as 2003'.

December was dry, sunny and the hottest since 1990. 'The week of 11–17 December, when much of the Sauvignon Blanc on the central Wairau Plains was in flower, was very warm,' said HortResearch, which reported 'very good pollination and fruit set'. The pattern of warm, dry weather continued into mid-summer; January was the hottest since 1986.

February, however, was cloudy, cool and wet. Marlborough recorded its lowest February sunshine total since the 1930s and almost three times its usual rainfall. 'Towards the end of the month, the weather went to the extreme,' observed Claire Allan of Huia. 'Gale-force winds snapped wooden and steel posts alike … The rain has pumped the berry size up to some of the biggest I've seen (bar 1995), but there are surprisingly few split berries.'

The cool temperatures of late summer continued into autumn, slowing ripening. March, although extremely sunny and dry, was also the coolest since 1996. April was also slightly sunnier than usual, but mean temperatures stayed well below the long-term average.

'The rather cool end to the season made it difficult to ripen some of the substantial crop,' admitted one grower. Another winery owner described 'large crops of unripe fruit still on the vines around the valley at the end of April'. According to the *Marlborough Express*, several wine companies declined growers' fruit that failed to meet their quality and ripeness standards. 'This year could be a warning to growers that taking advantage of a productive year with large crops will not always pay off,' declared Ant Mackenzie of Spy Valley.

Most predictions were for good-quality wines from 2004. Framingham reported 'elegant wines with concentrated, ripe flavour profiles and good acid structures'. 'If anything, the last few years have been atypical,' Mackenzie believes. 'This year the grapes were a bit more typical with higher acid levels.' John Buchanan, of Mount Riley, described the company's Marlborough wines as 'the best ever'.

Sauvignon Blanc, says Simon Waghorn of Whitehaven, will be 'up and down. It depends on sites and crop levels. The flavours are pretty typical, with plenty of tropical fruit.' Waghorn also reported 'very, very good Chardonnay, with high alcohol and good fruit weight'.

Joe Babich praised his Marlborough Pinot Noir as 'the best yet'. Patrick Materman of Allied Domecq also enthused that 'Pinot Noir stood out, with lifted fruit flavours and soft tannins'.

Canterbury

There'll be more Canterbury wine around from 2004 than any previous year. The total crop of 2825 tonnes set a new regional record, virtually doubling the 2003 harvest of 1422 tonnes.

In spring, the vines escaped significant frost damage. After a wet, windy September and cold early October, bud-burst was later than usual, but a hot early summer produced a quick, successful flowering. 'The extremely warm and windy late spring and early summer resulted in a great fruit set,' reported Waipara Springs.

After the driest December in the region's history, a January heatwave created an extreme fire risk. Waipara was unaffected by the storms that ravaged much of the country in February, according to Ivan Donaldson of Pegasus Bay, 'and that's true of the rest of Canterbury too. But it was cooler than we'd like in February.'

A cool, wet March made 'canopy management a major task on many blocks', according to *New Zealand Grapegrower*. 'Some growers who over-cropped their vines found their sugar [ripeness] levels below expectations,' admits one leading winemaker. 'Some of those grapes were not harvested.'

Kym Rayner of Torlesse was excited by the vintage, reporting 'good colour and flavour in the reds, and varieties such as Riesling, Gewürztraminer and Pinot Gris all had good aromatics'. However, another top winemaker was more cautious. 'It was very successful in Waipara, especially for reds. But this has been very dependent on not overcropping.'

Central Otago

Jack Frost shifted south in the past year, ravaging Central Otago vineyards at the start and end of the growing season. Despite the region's exploding vineyard area, its 2004 harvest only totalled 1439 tonnes of grapes – 21 per cent less than in 2003 and the smallest crop since 2000.

'WILD is how we would describe spring!' declared Black Ridge at Alexandra. 'We've had gales of nor'westers, followed by sharp, cold southerlies that bring snow to the hills and the anxieties of frost. In between there have been wonderfully warm days ...'

In November, severe frosts played havoc with young vines around the region, especially those on the most vulnerable, flat sites. 'The biggest frost, on 13 November, wasn't forecast,' says a leading winemaker. 'Temperatures plummeted to –4°C and we had nothing in place to protect the vines. Many vineyards have since upgraded their monitoring systems.'

December and January were hot and dry. 'Temperatures sizzled,' reported Black Ridge, 'with day after day of clear blue skies, incredible heat and no rain ... our irrigation system was working overtime to keep [the vines] happy.' In late summer, however, the weather turned exceptionally cold and wet. 'It was the coldest February at Gibbston since 1940,' declared one grower. Another vineyard in the sub-region recorded five times its normal February rainfall.

As harvest approached, frosts struck again, especially in the Gibbston area. One grower, expecting 10 tonnes of grapes, picked 0.4 tonnes.

Despite the devastation, some growers are predicting good wine. 'The quality of the grapes was fine, particularly the aromatics,' says Heather McPherson of Olssen's, at Bannockburn. Peregrine harvested Pinot Noir and Pinot Gris at Northburn at a very ripe 26 brix. 'We'll only make 5000 cases of 2004 Pinot Noir, compared to 8000 cases in 2003,' says Greg Hay of Peregrine. 'But its quality will be as good as the 2003, or possibly better.'

Trends in the Wine Market

As the tidal wave of wine from the record 2004 harvest floods onto the market, many winemakers are worrying: who will drink all the wine?

Less than half the wine we drink is home-grown. Imports of bottled and bulk wine rose last year, overwhelmingly from Australia. Local winemakers are not expecting to claw back a significant share of their domestic market, because most imported wines sell for under $12 a bottle – a price segment in which New Zealand's small wineries, due to their high production costs, cannot compete.

Despite this country's international acclaim for the variety, the biggest-selling Pinot Noir in New Zealand by value in the quarter to June 2004 was from across the Tasman – Wyndham Estate Bin 333 ($15). The most popular Riesling was also Australian – Jacob's Creek ($12).

Supermarkets, which now control almost 60 per cent of New Zealand's total wine sales, report that in the year to mid-2004 the average price paid for a bottle of white wine was $11.08. Of every 100 bottles of white wine purchased in supermarkets, only one cost more than $20. (Wines are now commonly launched with a 'recommended retail price' in the $20.95 to $22.95 range, with the obvious intention of being 'discounted' to the fast-growing sub-$20 category.)

Chardonnay dominates the white-wine market, accounting for 45 per cent by value of all bottled white-wine sales. However, the big mover is Sauvignon Blanc, on 36 per cent, which even outsells Chardonnay in the $15 to $20 category.

Riesling is the third-largest-selling bottled white wine, with a steady 9 per cent share of the market. Pinot Gris, although increasingly fashionable, still accounts for only 2 per cent of bottled white-wine sales in supermarkets. During the past year, supply shortages of many New Zealand Pinot Gris have led to a surge in imported labels.

For a bottle of red wine, the average price paid in supermarkets is even lower than for white – $10.42. Cabernet Sauvignon-based reds and Shiraz (Syrah) account for 65 per cent of the market, but their sales are expanding slowly.

Merlot, the second-fastest-growing red variety (with sales up 29 per cent by value in the past year), now accounts for 18 per cent of the total bottled red-wine market. Demand for Pinot Noir (with 8 per cent market share) is rising even faster. In the past year, supermarket sales of Pinot Noir soared by 39 per cent.

Rosé is still classified by wine marketers as a 'niche' product, but last year the sales of pink wine more than doubled.

Best Buys of the Year

Six irresistible bargains, including the overall winner of the Best Buy of the Year award, are featured here.

Most wines offer a level of quality that is roughly in line with their price – in other words, reasonable value. A few, however, will surprise and delight you by exceeding your price-based expectations.

The wines featured here all offer brilliant value and, at the time of publication in late 2004, were readily available. Don't miss them.

Best Buy of the Year

Villa Maria Cellar Selection Merlot/Cabernet Sauvignon 2002
(★★★★★, $21.95)

In the Merlot and Cabernet Sauvignon sections of *Cuisine*'s 2004 tasting of New Zealand reds, five wines achieved a maximum five-star rating. Four of the wines command a retail price of $40 – in line with what you'd expect to pay for a distinguished, local, 'Bordeaux-style' red. The fifth, however, is widely available at $21.95.

When I encountered Villa Maria Cellar Selection Merlot/Cabernet Sauvignon 2002 in the tasting, I jotted down: 'Bold, inky hue. Warm and concentrated. Mouthfilling body, with sweet fruit characters. Deep plum/spice flavours and good structure. Will age well. 18.5/20.' When the wine's identity was revealed, I was not surprised. The dark, densely packed 2000 vintage of this Hawke's Bay red was the Best Buy of the Year in the 2003 edition of the *Buyer's Guide*, proving that this mid-priced wine consistently offers brilliant value.

Cuisine's panellists are not the only judges to rate the wine highly. At the 2004 New Zealand Wine Society Royal Easter Wine Show, it scooped a gold medal and the Champion Merlot or Merlot Blend Trophy.

If you ask Alistair Maling, group winemaker for Villa Maria, why the wine is so good, he stresses that the Cellar Selection red is 'basically treated like one of our Reserves. The vines are low-yielding, the grapes were hand-picked and 2002 was a fantastic season, with hot summer days and no rain issues. You could harvest when you wanted.'

Grown in the company's Ngakirikiri and Omahu Gravels vineyards in the Gimblett Gravels district, the fruit was hand-picked into trays and transported to Villa Maria's Auckland winery. The grapes from 15 blocks within the vineyards (differentiated by soil type, vine age, pruning techniques, clones and grape varieties) were crushed and fermented separately, 'which gives us huge flexibility at blending time,' says Maling, a Master of Wine.

During the ferments, the skins were hand-plunged into the juice four or five times daily, to maximise tannin and colour extraction. Most New Zealand reds are oak-aged for one year, but the Cellar Selection spent 18 months in French (85 per cent) and American oak barriques (30 per cent new). 'The extra time promotes a better integration of the fruit, oak and tannins,' believes Maling.

At the final blending session, held for the Cellar Selection and Reserve ranges, assessing the reds was a challenge in itself, 'due to the deep black colours of the wines and their high quality of concentration, tannin and structure'. The final blend of varieties for the Cellar Selection red was 80 per cent Merlot, 18 per cent Cabernet Sauvignon and 2 per cent Malbec.

Compared to Villa Maria's Reserve reds, sold at twice the price, the Cellar Selection is based on slightly heavier-cropping vines and is aged in a lower proportion of new oak barrels. 'The tannins tend to be a bit softer, so it's more enjoyable in its youth,' says Maling.

Given the surging popularity of Pinot Noir in New Zealand, are Bordeaux-style reds such as the Cellar Selection underrated by many wine lovers? Maling – who drinks a lot of the Cellar Selection himself – believes so. 'It's a matter of perception. Pinot Noir has been more in the limelight, so consumers will pay more for it.'

Over 6000 cases of Villa Maria Cellar Selection Merlot/Cabernet Sauvignon 2002 were produced – enough to distribute the wine widely in New Zealand and overseas. 'In our export markets, we get the best response in the UK,' reports Maling. 'They really understand Bordeaux-style reds there.'

And when is the best time to drink his sturdy, flavour-crammed, bargain-priced red? 'It's drinking well now,' says Maling, 'but needs another year to really settle down. And you can mature it with confidence for at least six more years; maybe even longer.'

Other Shortlisted Wines

Corbans Marlborough Riesling 2003
(★★★★, $13.95)

This Riesling is far better than you'd expect for $13.95. At that modest price, most wines lack depth, but this beauty is scented and lively, with strong yet delicate flavours, a sliver of sweetness and mouth-watering acidity.

Most Marlborough Rieslings are fuller-bodied – with about 12.5 cent or even 13 per cent alcohol – but Corbans' wine is only 11 per cent. Perfumed and intense, it won a silver medal at the 2004 New World Wine Awards.

My tasting notes read: 'Light lemon/green hue. Attractive, floral scents. Gently sweet, light and lively, with citrusy, appley flavours showing good delicacy. Lovely harmony, with immediate appeal.' As a drink-young quaffer, this is hard to beat.

Villa Maria Private Bin Marlborough Sauvignon Blanc 2004

(★★★★, $15.95)

For a Sauvignon Blanc of four-star quality, you normally have to pay just under $20. At around $16, you can choose between lots of labels, but almost all lack the intensity of the higher-priced wines. This wine is a rare exception.

Grown in the Wairau and Awatere valleys, in its youth it is simply bursting with flavour. Mouthfilling (13.5 per cent alcohol), fresh and vibrant, with rich, ripely herbaceous flavours and crisp, racy acidity, it's a finely balanced and immaculate wine, already delicious. If you're looking for an excellent but affordable Sauvignon Blanc for this summer, look no further.

Morton Estate White Label Hawke's Bay Chardonnay 2002

(★★★★☆, $16.95)

This is a wonderful bargain. The sort of powerful, high-flavoured Chardonnay many wineries ask twice the price for, it won a gold medal at the 2004 New World Wine Awards.

Long recognised as one of the best-value New Zealand Chardonnays, the 1994 vintage of this Hawke's Bay classic (sold at $16.95) won the Best Buy of the Year award in the 1995 edition of the *Buyer's Guide*. I praised it then as 'a five-star Chardonnay at a three-star price'. Almost a decade later, the price hasn't changed, making the 2002 vintage an irresistible buy.

Harvested ripe at an average of 24 brix, it was fermented and lees-aged for 14 months in French and American oak barriques, and 15 per cent of the final blend went through a softening malolactic fermentation. Weighty, rich and soft, it has oodles of stone-fruit, grapefruit and toasty oak flavours in a bold, lush style with sweet fruit characters, finely balanced acidity, a creamy texture and great harmony.

You can cellar it for a year or two, but it's delicious right now.

Fusion Sparkling Muscat

(★★★★, $13)

If you make a top Asti-style bubbly in New Zealand, few people take notice. Dry wines are most in demand, so producers of sparkling wine look to the classic Champagnes of France for their inspiration, rather than the seductively light, sweet and soft Asti Spumantes of northern Italy.

Wine snobs may peer down their noses at sweet, frothy sparkling wines, but the Soljans winery in West Auckland has come up trumps with an irresistible Asti Spumante look-alike. Delightfully perfumed, Fusion Sparkling Muscat is fresh, vivacious and light (only 9 per cent alcohol) with the rich, sweet flavours of ripe Muscat grapes, grown in Gisborne.

Winemaker Mark Compton shows he hasn't lost his touch since he worked on Bernadino Spumante at Montana in the 1980s. At the 2004 Winewise Small Vignerons Awards in Australia, the judges awarded Fusion a gold medal and trophy, praising it as 'a beautiful expression of the Italian Moscato/Asti Spumante style [which] would hold its own against the best of them'.

Vidal Estate Merlot/Cabernet Sauvignon 2002
(★★★★☆, $19)

A gold medal red for under $20 is a bargain by any standards. Awarded gold at the 2003 Air New Zealand Wine Awards, this fragrant, sturdy Hawke's Bay wine didn't score quite that highly when I tasted it blind (18 out of 20, on both occasions, with 18.5 needed for gold or five stars), but it came extremely close.

In July, I jotted down: 'Richly coloured, with toasty oak aromas. Tight-knit, with good complexity and concentration of cassis, spice, coffee and nut flavours. Youthful, with firm tannins.'

A Merlot-based blend with 21 per cent Cabernet Sauvignon and 9 per cent Malbec, it was grown in four vineyards and matured for 16 months in French and American oak casks. Delicious from the start, with low acidity (5.8 grams/litre) giving it a welcome warmth and roundness, it's an upfront style (due to the Malbec and American oak influences), showing far greater depth and personality than most sub-$20 reds.

Where to Buy Your Wine

Where do you buy wine? From the supermarket, your local wine store, directly from the winery?

Wine retailing is big business. The grocery trade sold over 42 million litres of wine in the year to mid-2004, worth $472 million. Thousands of other retailers, from specialist wine stores to the 'booze barns' plying beer, spirits and wine, are also competing for your custom.

To sell wine to the public, you need a licence. A host of licences existed until 1990, each with its own labyrinth of rules governing the types of products that could be stocked, hours of opening, minimum purchase volumes, and so on. Those arbitrary restrictions were abandoned in 1990 and replaced by a much-simplified off licence, which put those who retail wine on a legislative equal footing.

In August 1990, the Devonport New World in Auckland became the first new food store allowed to sell wine in more than 30 years. Around the country, New Zealanders leapt at the chance to buy a bottle of Chardonnay with their bread, meat and vegetables, and today the grocery trade commands an almost 60 per cent share of the total retail wine market.

For wine buyers, supermarkets offer convenience, a good selection of popular brands and competitive, often sharp prices. If you know the wine you want and it's widely available, a supermarket is usually an easy, cheap place to buy it. But don't expect to find a wine expert hovering in the aisles, eager to advise you on the best wine to accompany your hapuku, or the differences between two Sauvignon Blancs that caught your eye.

Specialist wine stores lack the bulk buying power and 'grab-and-run' convenience that have led to the runaway success of supermarket wine departments. By promoting wines that are not found in supermarkets, the specialists are able to avoid price comparisons. In order to clearly differentiate themselves from their grocery rivals, the leading independents offer such inducements as skilled advice, home delivery, regular, themed wine tastings, and an eclectic and stimulating array of labels.

A cheap and highly enjoyable way to buy wine is directly from the wineries. Sometimes you will meet the owner or winemaker (at least at the small producers); you can often buy older vintages and rare, limited-production wines never released to the wine trade; prices are usually lower than in the shops; and you can usually taste before you buy. But beware: a wine always tastes at its irresistible best at the winery, while you are chatting with the winemaker in a romantic vineyard setting.

Mail-order and emailed newsletters can keep you in touch with favourite wineries around the country. Most new wineries lack the output (and promotional budget) to satisfy the needs of supermarkets, and also face intensifying competition to get onto the shelves of the independent wine stores. Selling directly to the public (over the winery counter, by mail order or through the vineyard restaurant), can be critical to the survival of new wineries. Giving a winery visitor a memorable experience can create an enduring emotional link to a brand.

Solicited through flyers often inserted in newspapers and magazines, thousands of New Zealanders join 'wine clubs', which are in fact large-scale commercial enterprises. The clubs' chief appeal is to novice wine buyers, who after nominating their preferred grape varieties and price range receive on a regular basis a mix of wines chosen on their behalf. Club membership averages about four years, by which time most wine drinkers feel sufficiently confident to enter a shop and handle their own purchasing.

The wine clubs offer convenience and good customer service, but many of the wines are sold under the clubs' exclusive brands, eliminating the competition that encourages sharp pricing. I have often encountered the wines in blind tastings, and rarely found they offer superior value.

If it's value you want, rather than convenience, try the auction system. Several thousand cases, from overstocked wineries, wine distributors or retailers, can go under the hammer at a single auction. Webb's, in Auckland, says that 'wine sold at auction will typically sell for about half of its normal price; sometimes less'.

Classic Wines of New Zealand

A crop of one new Super Classic (Pegasus Bay Riesling), four Classics (all promoted from the Potential Classics category), and 10 Potential Classics, together with five deletions (of labels no longer at the very top of the tree), are the features of this year's revised list of New Zealand wine classics.

What is a New Zealand wine classic? It is a wine that in quality terms consistently ranks in the very forefront of its class. To qualify for selection, each label must have achieved an outstanding level of quality for at least three vintages; there are no flashes in the pan here.

By identifying New Zealand wine classics, my aim is to transcend the inconsistencies of individual vintages and wine competition results, and highlight consistency of excellence. When introducing the elite category of Super Classics in 1998, I restricted entry to wines that have achieved brilliance in at least five vintages (compared to three for Classic status). The Super Classics are all highly prestigious wines, with a proven ability to mature well (even the Sauvignon Blancs, compared to other examples of the variety).

The Potential Classics are the pool from which future Classics will emerge. These are wines of outstanding quality that look likely, if their current standards are maintained or improved, to qualify after another vintage or two for elevation to Classic status. All the additions and elevations on this year's list are identified by an asterisk.

An in-depth discussion of New Zealand's greatest wines (what they taste like, how well they mature, the secrets of their success) can be found in my book *Classic Wines of New Zealand* (Hodder Moa Beckett, 1999), which grew out of the *Buyer's Guide*'s annually updated list of New Zealand wine classics.

ꙮꙮꙮSuper Classics

Chardonnay
Ata Rangi Craighall
Clearview Estate Reserve
Kumeu River Kumeu
Kumeu River Mate's Vineyard
Morton Estate Black Label
Neudorf Moutere
Te Mata Estate Elston

Gewürztraminer
Dry River

Pinot Gris
Dry River

Riesling
Dry River
*Pegasus Bay

Sauvignon Blanc
Cloudy Bay
Hunter's
Hunter's Winemaker's Selection (prev. Oak Aged)
Palliser Estate

Sweet Whites
Dry River Selection & Late Harvest Sweet Wines
Villa Maria Reserve Noble Riesling

Cabernet Sauvignon-predominant Reds
Goldwater Cabernet Sauvignon & Merlot
Stonyridge Larose Cabernets
Te Mata Estate Coleraine Cabernet/Merlot

Merlot
Esk Valley Reserve Merlot-predominant blend

Pinot Noir
Ata Rangi
Dry River
Martinborough Vineyard

ᚱᚱClassics

Chardonnay
Babich Irongate
Church Road Reserve
Cloudy Bay
Coopers Creek Swamp Reserve
Dry River
Esk Valley Reserve
Martinborough Vineyard
Montana Ormond Estate
Palliser Estate
Pegasus Bay
*Sacred Hill Riflemans
Vidal Reserve
Villa Maria Reserve Marlborough
Wither Hills Marlborough

Chenin Blanc
Millton Te Arai Vineyard

Riesling
*Felton Road
Palliser Estate

Sauvignon Blanc
Grove Mill Marlborough
Isabel Marlborough
Lawson's Dry Hills Marlborough
Nga Waka
Seresin Marlborough

Villa Maria Reserve Clifford Bay
Villa Maria Reserve Wairau Valley
Wither Hills Marlborough

Sweet Whites
Ngatarawa Glazebrook Noble Harvest Riesling

Bottle-fermented Sparklings
Deutz Marlborough Cuvée
Pelorus

Branded and Other Reds
Esk Valley The Terraces
*Unison Selection

Cabernet Sauvignon-predominant Reds
Brookfields Reserve Vintage Cabernet/Merlot
*Newton/Forrest Cornerstone Cabernet/Merlot/Malbec
Te Mata Estate Awatea Cabernet/Merlot
Vidal Reserve Cabernet Sauvignon-predominant

Merlot
C.J. Pask Reserve

Pinot Noir
Felton Road Block 3
Fromm La Strada Fromm Vineyard
Gibbston Valley Reserve
Neudorf Moutere
Palliser Estate
Pegasus Bay

Syrah
Mills Reef Elspeth
Stonecroft

Potential Classics

Branded and Other White Wines
Cloudy Bay Te Koko

Chardonnay
**Fromm La Strada Clayvin Vineyard
Millton Clos de Ste Anne
**Ngatarawa Alwyn
Seresin Reserve
Te Awa
Trinity Hill Gimblett Road

Gewürztraminer
Cloudy Bay
**Lawson's Dry Hills
Stonecroft
Te Whare Ra

Riesling
Neudorf Moutere
Villa Maria Reserve Marlborough

Sauvignon Blanc
**Framingham Marlborough
Montana Brancott Estate
Saint Clair Wairau Reserve
Whitehaven Marlborough

Sweet Whites
Cloudy Bay Late Harvest Riesling

Bottle-fermented Sparklings
Elstree Cuvée Brut
Nautilus Cuvée Marlborough

Branded and Other Reds
Babich The Patriarch
**Benfield & Delamare
Te Awa Boundary
**Tom

Cabernet Sauvignon-predominant Reds
Mills Reef Elspeth Cabernet/Merlot
Mills Reef Elspeth Cabernet Sauvignon

Merlot
Matua Valley Ararimu Merlot/Cabernet Sauvignon
**Sacred Hill Brokenstone
Villa Maria Reserve Merlot
Villa Maria Reserve Merlot/Cabernet Sauvignon

Pinot Noir
Greenhough Hope Vineyard
Isabel Marlborough
Kaituna Valley The Kaituna Vineyard
Neudorf Moutere Home Vineyard
Pegasus Bay Prima Donna
**Peregrine Central Otago
Seresin
**Villa Maria Reserve Marlborough
Wither Hills Marlborough

Syrah
**Te Mata Estate Bullnose

*New Classic, **New Potential Classic

Cellar Sense

Who doesn't relish the idea of a personal wine cellar, packed with vintage wines maturing slowly to their peak? Yet surveys have shown that most wine in New Zealand is drunk on the day it is bought and the proportion cellared for more than a year is tiny. So much for cellaring – we love contemplating it, but few of us actually do it.

It *is* worth the effort. To enjoy wine at the height of its powers, when its flavour is at its most complex, harmonious and downright enjoyable, you need to lay it down (in the case of screw-capped wines, standing upright is fine) for a few years. Keeping a stock of wine in the house is convenient and also economical: you can buy by the case at lower prices and it's the cheapest way to obtain mature vintages.

Which wines most repay cellaring? First, forget the idea that all wines improve with age. Much New Zealand wine is best drunk young, especially unoaked Sauvignon Blanc, which is typically at its aromatic and zesty best within 18 months of the vintage. Modest quality, low-priced Rieslings, Gewürztraminers, Pinot Gris and Chardonnays, specifically made for early consumption, after a year or two typically lose the fresh, vibrant fruit characters that are the essence of their appeal. Only superior examples of a few classic grape varieties blossom in the bottle for several years.

Chardonnay, Riesling, Pinot Noir, and Cabernet Sauvignon and Merlot-predominant reds should be the mainstays of your cellar. Chardonnay from top producers usually has the weight and richness to flourish for three or four years (the 2002s should be drinking well during 2005); fine quality Riesling improves even longer. Premium-quality Pinot Noir, Merlot and Syrah should also flourish for at least three to five years. Top vintages of the best Cabernet Sauvignon-based reds from Hawke's Bay and Waiheke Island benefit from at least five years' cellaring and can age gracefully for a decade.

A sprinkling of other New Zealand varietal wines will add interest and diversity to your cellar: good Pinot Gris and Chenin Blanc (especially), Gewürztraminer, barrel-aged Sauvignon Blanc, Viognier and Sémillon will age well for at least a couple of years and often a lot longer.

Build your cellar in the coolest, darkest place you can find in (or under) the house. Start by buying full or half cases of your favourite wines, and monitor their development by broaching a bottle every six months or so. Many people with cellars make the mistake of keeping their wines too long. You'll get more pleasure from your wine when it's still a bit too young than when it's faded and dull.

Cellaring Guidelines

Grape variety	Best age to open
White	
Sauvignon Blanc	
(non-wooded)	6–18 months
(wooded)	1–3 years
Gewürztraminer	2–3 years
Viognier	2–3 years
Chenin Blanc	2–4 years
Sémillon	2–4 years
Pinot Gris	2–5 years
Chardonnay	3–5 years
Riesling	3–10 years
Red	
Pinotage	1–3 years
Malbec	1–3 years
Cabernet Franc	1–4 years
Merlot	2–5 years
Pinot Noir	2–5 years
Syrah	2–5 years
Cabernet Sauvignon	3–7+ years
Cabernet/Merlot	3–7+ years
Other	
Bottle-fermented sparklings	3–5 years

Vintage Charts 1994–2004

	Auckland	Gisborne	Hawke's Bay	Wairarapa	Nelson	Marlborough	Canterbury	Otago
WHITES								
2004	6	6	5–6	5	5	6	3–6	3
2003	5–6	4	3–4	6–7	5–6	5–6	4–6	5
2002	6	7	6	6	6–7	4–6	4–7	5–7
2001	3–5	4	4–5	6–7	6–7	6–7	6	4–6
2000	7	5	6	5–7	5–6	5–7	3–6	4–5
1999	6	5	5–6	5–7	5–6	6–7	5	5–6
1998	4–7	6	6	6–7	6–7	5	6	6–7
1997	5	5	4–6	6–7	6–7	6	5–6	4–5
1996	6	6	4–6	6–7	5	6	3–6	4–5
1995	4	4	3–7	5–6	2–4	2–3	6–7	5
1994	6	6	6–7	6	5–6	5–6	4	4

	Auckland	Gisborne	Hawke's Bay	Wairarapa	Nelson	Marlborough	Canterbury	Otago
REDS								
2004	5–7	6	5–6	5	5	5	4–7	4
2003	4–6	4	3–4	6–7	5–6	5–6	4–6	5
2002	6	7	5–6	4–6	5–7	4–7	4–7	6–7
2001	4–5	4	4	5–7	6–7	5–7	7	6
2000	7	5	5–7	5–7	5–6	5–7	4–6	4
1999	6	4	4–6	6–7	6	5–6	5–7	6
1998	4–7	6	7	6–7	6	6–7	6	6–7
1997	4–5	4	4	6	6–7	5	5–6	5–6
1996	6	5	4	7	5–6	4	4–6	5
1995	4	2	5–7	6	2–4	2–3	6–7	6
1994	6	6	5–6	6	5	5	4	5

7=Outstanding 6=Excellent 5=Above average 4=Average 3=Below average 2=Poor 1=Bad

Note: these vintage charts are compiled with input from two leading winemakers in each region. They also reflect my general impressions of what counts most: what's in the glass.

How to Use This Book

It is essential to read this brief section to understand how the book works. Feel free to skip any of the other preliminary pages – but not these.

The majority of wines have been listed in the book according to their principal grape variety. Lawson's Dry Hills Marlborough Sauvignon Blanc, for instance, can be located simply by turning to the Sauvignon Blanc section. Non-varietal wines (with names that do not boldly refer to a grape variety or blend of grapes), such as Cloudy Bay Te Koko or Crossroads Talisman, can be found in the Branded and Other Wines sections for white and red wines.

Most entries are firstly identified by their producer's names. Wines not usually called by their producer's name, such as Drylands Marlborough Sauvignon Blanc (from Nobilo Wine Group) or Oyster Bay Marlborough Chardonnay (from Delegat's), are listed under their most common name.

The star ratings for quality reflect my own opinions, formed where possible by tasting a wine over several vintages, and often a particular vintage several times. THE STAR RATINGS ARE THEREFORE A GUIDE TO EACH WINE'S OVERALL STANDARD IN RECENT VINTAGES, rather than simply the quality of the latest release. However, to enhance the usefulness of the book, in the body of the text I have also given a QUALITY RATING FOR THE LATEST VINTAGE OF EACH WINE; sometimes for more than one vintage.

I hope the star ratings give interesting food for thought and succeed in introducing you to a galaxy of little-known but worthwhile wines. It pays to remember, however, that wine-tasting is a business fraught with subjectivity. You should always treat the views expressed in these pages for what they are – one person's opinion.

The quality ratings are:

★★★★★	Outstanding quality (gold medal standard)
★★★★☆	Excellent quality, verging on outstanding
★★★★	Excellent quality (silver medal standard)
★★★☆	Very good quality
★★★	Good quality (bronze medal standard)
★★☆	Average quality
★★	Plain
★	Poor
No star	To be avoided

These quality ratings are based on comparative assessments of New Zealand wines against one another. A five-star Merlot/Cabernet Sauvignon, for instance, is an outstanding-quality red judged by the standards of other Merlot/Cabernet Sauvignon blends made in New Zealand. It is not judged by the standards of overseas reds of a similar style (for instance Bordeaux), because the book is focused solely on New Zealand wines and their relative merits.

Where brackets enclose the star rating on the right-hand side of the page, for example (★★★), this indicates the assessment is only tentative, because I have tasted very few vintages of the wine. A dash is used in the relatively few cases where a wine's quality has oscillated over and above normal vintage variations (for example ★ – ★★★).

Super Classic wines, Classic wines and Potential Classic wines (see page 22) are highlighted in the text by the following symbols:

Super Classic   Classic   Potential Classic

Each wine has also been given a dryness-sweetness, price and value-for-money rating. The precise levels of sweetness indicated by the four ratings are:

DRY	Less than 5 grams/litre of sugar
MED/DRY	5–14 grams/litre of sugar
MED	15–49 grams/litre of sugar
SW	50 and over grams/litre of sugar

Less than 5 grams of sugar per litre is virtually imperceptible to most palates – the wine tastes bone-dry. With between 5 and 14 grams, a wine has a hint of sweetness, although a high level of acidity (as in Marlborough Sauvignon Blancs, which often have 4 to 7 grams per litre of sugar) reduces the perception of sweetness. Where a wine harbours over 15 grams, the sweetness is clearly in evidence. At above 50 grams per litre, a wine is unabashedly sweet.

Prices shown are based on the average price in a retail wine outlet (as indicated by the wine producer), except where most of the wine is sold directly to the public, either over the vineyard counter or by mail order.

The art of wine buying involves more than just discovering top-quality wines. The greater challenge – and the greatest satisfaction – lies in identifying wines at varying quality levels that deliver outstanding value for money. The symbols I have used are self-explanatory:

–V	=	Below average value
AV	=	Average value
V+	=	Above average value

The ratings discussed thus far are all my own. Many of the wine producers themselves, however, have also contributed individual vintage ratings of their own wines back to the 1990s and the 'When to drink' recommendations. (The symbol

WR indicates Winemaker's Rating, and the symbol **NM** alongside a vintage means the wine was not made that year.) Only the producers have such detailed knowledge of the relative quality of all their recent vintages (although in a very few cases, when the information was not forthcoming, I have rated a vintage myself). The key point you must note is that EACH PRODUCER HAS RATED EACH VINTAGE OF EACH WINE AGAINST HIS OR HER HIGHEST QUALITY ASPIRATIONS FOR THAT PARTICULAR LABEL, NOT AGAINST ANY ABSOLUTE STANDARD. Thus, a 7 out of 7 score merely indicates that the producer considers that particular vintage to be an outstanding example of that particular wine, not that it is the best quality wine he or she makes.

The 'when to drink' (**Drink**) recommendations (which I find myself referring to constantly) are largely self-explanatory. The **P** symbol for PEAKED means that a particular vintage is already at, or has passed, its peak; no further benefits are expected from aging.

Here is an example of how the ratings work:

Pegasus Bay Riesling   ★★★★★

This is very classy stuff. Estate-grown at Waipara, in North Canterbury, at its best it is richly fragrant and thrillingly intense, with concentrated flavours of citrus fruits and honey, complex and luscious. The 1995, 1998, 2000, 2001 and 2002 vintages are all memorable. The 2003 (★★★★★) was hand-picked, whole-bunch-pressed, cool-fermented with cultured yeasts in stainless steel tanks and bottled early. Gorgeously perfumed and intense, it's a fleshy, distinctly medium wine (19 grams/litre of residual sugar) with zingy acidity, a powerful surge of lemon, apple and apricot flavours and a slightly honeyed richness. A lovely aperitif.

Vintage	03	02	01	00	99	98	97	96	95	MED $23 V+
WR	7	7	6	7	6	6	5	4	6	
Drink	04-13	04-12	04-11	04-10	04-09	04-07	P	P	P	❦ ❦ ❦

The winemaker's own ratings indicate that the 2003 vintage is of outstanding quality for the label, and is recommended for drinking between 2004 and 2013.

Describes 'Classic' status, ranging from
❦ ❦ ❦ for Super Classic,
❦ ❦ for Classic to
❦ for Potential Classic.
This is a wine that in quality terms consistently ranks in the very forefront of its class.

Dry-sweetness rating, price and value for money. This wine is medium in style, with sweetness clearly evident (15–49 grams/litre of sugar). At $23 it is above average value for money.

Quality rating, ranging from ★★★★★ for outstanding to no star (–), to be avoided. This is generally a wine of outstanding quality.

White Wines

Branded and Other White Wines

Richmond Plains Escapade, Dog Point Vineyard Section 94, Karikari Estate Silver Cloud, Hatton Estate Gimblett Road EC2 – in this section you'll find all the white wines that don't feature varietal names.

Lower-priced branded white wines can give winemakers an outlet for grapes like Chenin Blanc, Sémillon and (until recently) Riesling, that are otherwise hard to sell. They can also be an outlet for coarser, less delicate juice ('pressings'). Standing out from the bewildering array of varietal wines, strong, distinctive brands like White Cloud (New Zealand's answer to Blue Nun) have been hugely successful in attracting supermarket customers.

Some of the branded whites are quaffers, but such wines as Cloudy Bay Te Koko, Clearview Endeavour and Craggy Range Les Beaux Cailloux are highly distinguished.

Babich Fumé Vert – see Babich East Coast Sémillon/Chardonnay

Black Ridge Otago Gold   ★★☆

The Alexandra winery's estate-grown white for summer quaffing is typically pale, floral and light, its citrusy flavours harbouring a distinct splash of sweetness. Blended from Breidecker (principally) and other varieties, and vintage-dated since 2001, it's an enjoyable drop, but the big wineries churn out this sort of wine cheaper.

> MED $12 AV

Clearview Endeavour   (★★★★★)

Launched from the 2002 vintage (★★★★★) in a 1.5-litre magnum sold at $200, the Hawke's Bay winery's 'super-premium' Chardonnay was promoted as 'New Zealand's highest-priced white wine'. Based on the 'pick of the fruit', given a full, softening malolactic fermentation and matured for two years in new French oak barriques, it's a 'more oxidative' style than his famous Reserve Chardonnay, says winemaker Tim Turvey. It's a strapping (14.5 per cent alcohol) wine, beautifully rounded and rich, with deep, ripe stone-fruit, butterscotch and toast flavours. There is no 2003.

> DRY $200 (1.5L) -V

Cloudy Bay Te Koko   ★★★★★

Te Koko o Kupe (the oyster dredge of Kupe) is the original name for Cloudy Bay; it is also the name of the famous Marlborough winery's innovative, oak-aged Sauvignon Blanc. The 2001 vintage (★★★★) was fermented with indigenous yeasts and matured on its lees for 18 months in French oak barriques (10 per cent new), with full malolactic fermentation. Bright, light lemon/green in hue, with a slightly rustic, earthy bouquet, it pushes the boundaries even further away from the aromatic Marlborough norm than the outstandingly rich, complex and harmonious 2000 (★★★★★). Full-bodied and rounded, with grapefruit and subtle oak flavours, it's a tightly structured and refined wine, but slightly more restrained and less beguiling than the 2000.

Vintage	01	00	99	98	97	96
WR	6	6	5	5	5	5
Drink	04-06	04-05	P	P	P	P

> DRY $36 AV

Craggy Range Les Beaux Cailloux (★★★★★)

The debut 2001 vintage (★★★★★) is an unusually complex Hawke's Bay Chardonnay, with loads of personality. Based on first-crop, ultra low-yielding Gimblett Gravels vines, it was fermented with indigenous yeasts, lees-aged for over a year in French oak barriques (80 per cent new), with full malolactic fermentation, and bottled without fining or filtering. High-priced but very classy, it shows great texture, mouthfeel and depth, with a complex, earthy rather than fruity bouquet, layers of grapefruit, peach and slight butterscotch flavours, finely balanced acidity and a rounded, rich finish.

Vintage	01	
WR	7	**DRY $60 AV**
Drink	05-09	

Dog Point Vineyard Section 94 (★★★★)

Looking for 'texture, rather than rich aromatics', winemaker James Healy and his partner, Ivan Sutherland (both former Cloudy Bay stalwarts), fermented and lees-aged their debut 2002 vintage (★★★★) Sauvignon Blanc in seasoned oak casks. Grown in Sutherland's Dog Point vineyard (for which 'Section 94' was the original survey title) and fermented with indigenous yeasts, it's a fragrant, youthful Marlborough wine with lovely, well-ripened, tropical and citrus fruit flavours, a subtle oak influence and crisp, balanced acidity.

DRY $33 -V

Glenmark Waipara White ★★☆

Pale, crisp and floral, this North Canterbury wine tastes like the Müller-Thurgau it basically is, with other grapes (including Breidecker, Sauvignon Blanc and Pinot Gris) accounting for 20 per cent of the blend. The 2001 vintage (★★☆) is light, with clean, lemony, appley flavours and a gently sweet finish.

MED $12 AV

Hatton Estate Gimblett Road EC2 ★★★

Designed as 'a delightful aperitif', the 2003 vintage (★★★☆) is made from clone 15 Chardonnay grapes (EC2 stands for 'Experimental Chardonnay 2'), grown in Gimblett Road, Hawke's Bay. Produced 'in the Chablis style' (read: without oak), it's a tangy wine with fresh, strong, lemony, appley aromas, good mouthfeel and depth of crisp, vibrant, citrusy flavour and a dry, slightly flinty finish.

Vintage	04	03	02	
WR	7	7	7	**DRY $22-V**
Drink	04-07	04-05	P	

Karikari Estate Silver Cloud (★★☆)

Grown on the Karikari Peninsula, in the Far North, the 2003 vintage (★★☆) is a blend of virtually identical proportions of Chardonnay, Viognier and Sémillon. It's a full-bodied wine with ripe, stone-fruit characters, but in its youth was overpowered by toasty oak.

DRY $27 -V

Richmond Plains Escapade (★★☆)

Grown organically in Nelson, the 2003 vintage (★★☆) is a blended white wine, offering slightly sweet, lemony flavours, pleasantly fresh and crisp.

MED $16 -V

Rippon Hotere White   ★★☆

Cultivated on the shores of Lake Wanaka in the Southern Alps, this wine is made 'for summer drinking, not sipping'. Blended from such varieties as Müller-Thurgau, Breidecker and Chenin Blanc, it is typically a pale, light, appley, fractionally sweet wine, crisp and clean but lacking any real flavour depth. A solid quaffer, it's a bit high-priced for what it delivers.

MED/DRY $14 -V

St Aubyns Dry White   ★★

This bottom-rung Villa Maria wine is ideal when you simply want a glass of no-fuss, off-dry white with reasonable body and flavour and a modest price-tag. The non-vintage blend of New Zealand and Australian wine I tasted in mid-2004 (★★) was floral and light, with fresh, citrusy, appley flavours and a fractionally sweet (7 grams/litre of sugar) finish.

MED/DRY $8 AV

St Aubyns Medium White   ★★

Villa Maria's low-priced quaffer is blended from New Zealand and Australian wines. The non-vintage wine I tasted in mid-2004 (★★) was a distinctly medium style (20 grams/litre of residual sugar) with smooth, slightly honeyed flavours in a very easy-drinking style.

MED $8 AV

St Helena Bernice   (★★★★)

The 2002 vintage (★★★★) is the best wine I've tasted lately from this long-established Canterbury producer. Made from Pinot Blanc grapes, harvested at an ultra-ripe 27 brix (the highest sugar content since planting 22 years ago), with some noble rot, it was matured on its yeast lees for six months, but not oak-aged. Softly mouthfilling, with lovely richness of peachy, slightly spicy and honeyed flavour, gentle acidity and a slightly sweet (12 grams/litre of residual sugar) finish, it has an Alsace-like weight and structure, and is already a delicious mouthful.

Vintage 02
WR   7
Drink   04-06

MED/DRY $22 AV

Schubert Tribianco   ★★★☆

The 2002 vintage (★★★☆) is a distinctive Martinborough dry white, blended from Chardonnay, Pinot Gris and Müller-Thurgau. Fermented both in tanks and seasoned French oak hogsheads and puncheons, it's a bone-dry style, fresh and full-bodied, with citrus, pear and spice flavours, moderate acidity and some nutty, leesy complexity. A flavoursome wine with lots of interest, it's likely to be at its best during 2004–05. The 2003, reduced by frosts to one-third its normal volume, is Schubert's only white wine from the vintage.

Vintage 02   01   00
WR   6   6   5
Drink   04-08 04-07 04-06

DRY $20 -V

White Cloud   ★★

From Nobilo, this has long been popular in supermarkets. A non-vintage wine based on Gisborne Müller-Thurgau, sweetened with Muscat Dr Hogg juice, it is an easy-drinking, gently sweet style (12 grams/litre of residual sugar), at its best fragrant, grapey and flavourful. The wine I tasted in mid-2004 (★★) was clean and crisp, with light, lemony, appley aromas and flavours, but lacked real freshness and zing.

MED/DRY $9 AV

Breidecker

A nondescript crossing of Müller-Thurgau and the white hybrid Seibel 7053, Breidecker is rarely seen in New Zealand. There were 20 hectares recorded as planted in 2002, but in the 2003 national vineyard survey, there is no trace of the variety. Its early-ripening ability is an advantage in cooler regions, but Breidecker typically yields light, fresh quaffing wines, best drunk young.

Hunter's Breidecker ★★★

This Marlborough wine is made 'for those who are new to wine'. Grown in the Wairau Valley, it is typically fresh and floral, light and lively, with ripe, slightly sweet flavours of lemons and apples in a very charming style, easy to gulp.

Vintage	04	
WR	5	MED $13 AV
Drink	05	

Chardonnay

New Zealand Chardonnay has yet to make the international impact of our Sauvignon Blanc, accounting for 11 per cent of wine exports by volume, compared to 65 per cent for Sauvignon Blanc. Our top Chardonnays are excellent, but so are those from several other countries in the Old and New Worlds.

The most prominent recent overseas success was by Matariki Hawke's Bay Chardonnay 2002, which scooped the trophy for champion wine of the show at the 2004 Cool Climate Wine Competition, staged in Melbourne but open to wines from cool-climate regions around the world. For the third year in a row, Matariki won the trophy for the best Chardonnay.

There's an enormous range of New Zealand Chardonnays to choose from. Almost every winery in the country makes at least one; many produce several and the big wineries produce dozens. The hallmark of New Zealand Chardonnays is their delicious varietal intensity – the leading labels show notably concentrated aromas and flavours, threaded with fresh, appetising acidity.

The price of New Zealand Chardonnay ranges from below $10 to $200 per bottle (for a magnum of Endeavour, from Clearview Estate, reviewed in the Branded and Other White Wines section). The quality differences are equally wide, although not always in relation to their prices. Lower-priced wines are typically fermented in stainless steel tanks and bottled young with minimal oak influence; these wines rely on fresh, lemony, uncluttered fruit flavours for their appeal.

The 2002 and subsequent vintages have brought a surge of unoaked Chardonnays, as winemakers with an eye on overseas markets strive to showcase New Zealand's fresh, vibrant fruit characters. However, as Stephen Brook, a UK wine writer, put it: 'They tend to be fairly simple wines ... so I think they have a limited place in the market.' Without oak flavours to add richness and complexity, Chardonnay handled entirely in stainless steel tanks can be plain, or even boring. The key to the style is to use well-ripened, intensely flavoured grapes.

Mid-price wines may be fermented in tanks and matured in oak casks, which adds to their complexity and richness, or fermented and/or matured in a mix of tanks and barrels. The top labels are fully fermented and matured in oak barriques (normally French, with varying proportions of new casks); there may also be extended aging on (and regular stirring of) yeast lees and varying proportions of a secondary, softening malolactic fermentation (sometimes referred to in the tasting notes as 'malo'). The best of these display the arresting subtlety and depth of flavour for which Chardonnay is so highly prized.

Chardonnay plantings have been outstripped in the past few years by Sauvignon Blanc, as wine producers respond to overseas demand, and in 2005 will constitute 19.2 per cent of the bearing vineyard. The vines are spread throughout the major wine regions, particularly Marlborough (where almost 30 per cent of the vines are concentrated), Hawke's Bay (where it is the number two grape, just behind Merlot), and Gisborne (where it now accounts for well over half of all plantings).

Chardonnays of exciting quality are flowing from all of New Zealand's key wine regions, from Auckland to Otago. Of the three dominant regions, Gisborne is renowned for its deep-scented and soft Chardonnays, which offer very seductive drinking in their youth; Hawke's Bay yields sturdy wines with rich grapefruit-like flavours, power and longevity; and Marlborough's Chardonnays are leaner but stylish and mouth-wateringly crisp.

Chardonnay has often been dubbed 'the red-wine drinker's white wine'. Chardonnays are usually (but not always) bone-dry, as are all reds with any aspirations to quality. Chardonnay's typically mouthfilling body and multi-faceted flavours are another obvious red-wine parallel.

Broaching a top New Zealand Chardonnay at less than two years old is infanticide – the best of the 2002s will offer excellent drinking during 2005. If you must drink Chardonnay when it is only a year old, it makes sense to buy one of the cheaper, less complex wines specifically designed to be enjoyable in their youth.

125 Gimblett Road Chardonnay (★★★★)

The powerful 2002 vintage (★★★★) is the first release from the Blake Family Vineyard in Gimblett Road, Hawke's Bay. Fermented with indigenous yeasts and matured in new French oak barriques, and bottled without fining or filtering, it's a weighty, richly flavoured wine with ripe, citrus and stone-fruit characters, but in its youth was slightly dominated by a strong, toasty oak influence.

DRY $28 AV

Akarua Central Otago Chardonnay ★★★★

This is consistently one of the region's best Chardonnays. Fermented and matured for 10 months in French oak barriques, the 2003 vintage (★★★★) is a mealy, full-bodied wine (14 per cent alcohol) with deep grapefruit and biscuity oak flavours and slightly buttery, limey characters in a complex style with good harmony.

Vintage	03	02	01
WR	6	6	6
Drink	04-09	04-08	04-05

DRY $25 AV

Akarua Unoaked Chardonnay ★★☆

The 2003 vintage (★★☆) of this Central Otago wine was handled in stainless steel tanks. It's a lemony, appley wine, full-bodied (14 per cent alcohol), fresh and lively, with a sliver of sweetness (6.6 grams/litre of residual sugar) to balance its natural crispness. Simple, easy drinking.

Vintage	03	02
WR	6	5
Drink	04-06	04-05

MED/DRY $22 -V

Alana Estate 15 Series Chardonnay (★★★)

Pale yellow, the 2002 vintage (★★★) is a fresh, tightly structured Martinborough wine with citrusy, appley fruit characters, well-integrated oak and a slightly green, high-acid finish.

DRY $39 -V

Alana Estate Martinborough Chardonnay ★★★★

This winery produces consistently stylish Chardonnays that mature well. Hand-harvested at 24 brix and fermented and matured for nine months in French oak barriques (30 per cent new), with malolactic fermentation and lees-aging, the 2002 vintage (★★★★) is a fleshy, finely balanced wine, rich and lively, generous and supple, with satisfying body, well-ripened, citrusy fruit characters showing good concentration, subtle oak and good acid balance. Skilfully made wine, worth discovering.

Vintage	02	01	00	99	98	97
WR	7	6	6	7	6	5
Drink	04-08	04-07	04-05	04-05	P	P

DRY $29 AV

Alexandra Wine Company Ferauds Chardonnay   ★★★☆

This Central Otago wine is consistently enjoyable. The 2002 vintage (★★★☆), matured for 11 months in
French oak barriques (30 per cent new), is a flavoursome and toasty wine with mealy, creamy aromas, ripe-
grapefruit characters, firm acidity and good potential.

Vintage	02	01	00	99
WR	5	6	5	5
Drink	04-06	04-05	P	P

DRY $21 AV

Allan Scott Marlborough Chardonnay   ★★★★

This label began as a fruit-driven style, but in recent years has shown greater complexity and is now
consistently satisfying. The 2002 vintage (★★★☆), 50 to 60 per cent barrel-fermented, offers fresh, strong,
citrusy flavours and well-integrated oak, with a slightly buttery finish. It's drinking well now.

Vintage	02	01	00	99	98
WR	6	7	6	6	7
Drink	04-06	04-05	04-05	P	P

DRY $22 V+

Allan Scott Prestige Chardonnay   ★★★★☆

The debut 1998 vintage (★★★★★) was a robust, soft, lush Marlborough wine and the 1999 (★★★★★)
was memorable, with layers of peachy, figgy, nutty flavour. The 2000 (★★★☆) was crisp and toasty, but
less ripe and concentrated. Barrel-fermented and given a full, softening malolactic fermentation, the 2001
vintage (★★★★) is a mealy, generous wine, big-bodied (14 per cent alcohol), with rich, peachy, citrusy
flavours and toast and butterscotch characters adding complexity.

Vintage	01	00
WR	7	7
Drink	04-08	04-06

DRY $32 AV

Alpha Domus AD Chardonnay   ★★★★☆

The tightly structured 2001 vintage (★★★★) was grown in Hawke's Bay and fermented and matured in
French oak barriques (60 per cent new). Pale gold, with an oaky, minerally bouquet, it's a crisp, robust,
high-flavoured wine, citrusy and toasty, with excellent intensity. The 2002 (★★★★) is also toasty,
minerally and rich.

Vintage	01	00	99	98	97	96
WR	5	6	7	6	6	5
Drink	05-06	04-06	04-05	P	P	P

DRY $33 AV

Alpha Domus Hawke's Bay Chardonnay   ★★★

This Hawke's Bay wine is basically a fruit-driven style with fresh, citrusy and appley flavours to the fore
and a smooth finish. The 2003 vintage (★★★) is fresh, vibrant and lemony, with gentle oak and lees-aging
characters adding a touch of complexity. The 2004 (★★★) has strong peachy, buttery flavours.

Vintage	02	01	00
WR	6	7	7
Drink	04-07	04-06	04-05

DRY $18 AV

Amor-Bendall Reserve Gisborne Chardonnay   ★★★

The 2002 vintage (★★★) is a fleshy, warm and generous wine, but by 2004 was showing a slight loss of
freshness. The 2003 (★★★) has a fruit-driven bouquet and lemony, appley flavours, not complex but well-
balanced, fresh and lively.

DRY $25 -V

Amor-Bendall Unoaked Gisborne Chardonnay   ★★★☆

Past vintages have been attractive, and so is the 2002 (★★★). Light yellow, it's a fresh, tight, lemony, appley
wine with crisp, appetising acidity and good flavour intensity.

DRY $18 AV

Artisan Waiohika Estate Chardonnay (★★★☆)

The debut 2002 vintage (★★★☆) of this Gisborne wine was grown in the Waiohika Estate vineyard and barrique-fermented. Smooth and ripe, with fresh, attractive grapefruit and stone-fruit flavours, gentle acidity and a slightly buttery finish, it shows very good balance and depth.

DRY $23 AV

Ascension Matakana Chardonnay ★★★

Designed as an 'earlier-drinking style', the 2003 vintage (★★★) was handled in American (principally) and French oak casks (25 per cent new). Light/medium yellow in hue, it's a citrusy, tightly structured wine with a strong, toasty oak influence. Still youthful, with plenty of flavour, it offers good drinking through 2005.

DRY $22 -V

Ascension The Ascent Reserve Matakana Chardonnay ★★★★

Estate-grown, the 2003 vintage (★★★★) was hand-harvested and fermented and lees-aged (with weekly lees-stirring) for 11 months in French oak barriques (33 per cent new), with 25 per cent malolactic fermentation. It's a top effort for the difficult season – fragrant, ripe and generous, with strong yet delicate citrus and stone-fruit flavours, mealy, nutty complexities, a creamy texture and good cellaring potential. Drink 2005–06.

DRY $29 AV

Ashwell Chardonnay (★★★★)

Fragrant and toasty on the nose, the 2002 vintage (★★★★) is a fleshy Martinborough wine with substantial body, strong, ripe, stone-fruit flavours and a creamy texture. The 2003 has had 'minimal' exposure to oak.

Vintage	03
WR	5
Drink	08-09

DRY $25 AV

Askerne Hawke's Bay Chardonnay ★★★★☆

Estate-grown on the banks of the Tukituki River, north of Te Mata Peak, this little-known wine has shown steadily rising form. Offering great value, the 2002 vintage (★★★★☆) has a forthcoming, toasty, mealy bouquet. A finely textured wine, tight and elegant, full-bodied and slightly creamy, it offers ripe-grapefruit and biscuity oak flavours showing excellent depth and structure. There is no 2003.

Vintage	03	02	01	00	99	98	97
WR	NM	6	6	NM	6	5	5
Drink	NM	04-07	04-05	NM	P	P	P

DRY $20 V+

Ata Rangi Craighall Chardonnay ★★★★★

A consistently memorable Martinborough wine, since the 1996 vintage it has scaled great heights, with notable weight, richness, complexity and downright drinkability. Made from a company-owned block of low-yielding, Mendoza-clone vines in the Craighall vineyard, it is hand-picked, whole-bunch pressed and fully fermented in French oak barriques (25 per cent new). The 2003 vintage (★★★★★) is viewed by the winery's owners as 'the most elegant Chardonnay we have ever produced'. Enticingly fragrant and sturdy (14 per cent alcohol), with great depth of lush stone-fruit, butterscotch and toast flavours, it is opulent and finely structured in its youth. Showing lovely power and concentration, combined with obvious cellaring potential, it's as good as New Zealand Chardonnay gets.

Vintage	03	02	01	00	99	98	97	96
WR	7	7	7	7	7	7	7	7
Drink	04-07	04-05	04-05	P	P	P	P	P

DRY $38 AV

Ata Rangi Petrie Chardonnay   ★★★★

This single-vineyard wine is grown by Neil Petrie at East Taratahi, south of Masterton. It's not in the same class as its Craighall stablemate (above), but the price is lower. The 2002 vintage (★★★★), matured for a year in French oak barriques, has ripe peach/melon aromas leading into a fresh, creamy palate with rich peach and grapefruit characters, a distinct touch of butterscotch and a well-rounded finish. It's a full-flavoured wine with strong drink-young appeal. Due to frosts, there was no 2003.

Vintage	03	02	01	00	99	98
WR	NM	7	7	7	7	7
Drink	NM	04-06	04-05	P	P	P

DRY $25 AV

Auntsfield Cob Cottage Marlborough Chardonnay   ★★★☆

The 2002 vintage (★★★★) is a mouthfilling (14 per cent alcohol), well-rounded wine, fresh and elegant, with sweet fruit characters and rich grapefruit and peach, slightly buttery flavours showing very good harmony and depth. The crisper 2003 (★★★☆) is distinctly buttery, fresh and vibrant, with grapefruit, lime and toasty oak flvours and a smooth finish.

DRY $29 AV

Awanui Marlborough Chardonnay   ★★★☆

Sold by mail-order wine clubs, the 2003 vintage (★★★★) is fleshy and generous, citrusy and creamy, with sweet fruit characters, balanced oak adding complexity and a dry, rounded finish.

DRY $22 -V

Babich East Coast Unoaked Chardonnay   ★★★

This sharply priced wine is grown in three North Island regions – Hawke's Bay, Gisborne and Auckland. In the past it was fully oak-aged, but from 2000 onwards was only partly handled in wood, and the 2002 vintage (★★★☆) was processed entirely in tanks. A full-bodied, citrusy, lively wine with fresh, vibrant fruit aromas and flavours and a dry finish, it's a fruit-driven style – with style. Retasted in mid-2004, it's maturing very gracefully.

Vintage	02	01	00	99	98
WR	7	6	7	7	7
Drink	04-06	04-05	P	P	P

DRY $15 V+

Babich Gimblett Gravels Chardonnay   (★★★☆)

Launched from the 2002 vintage (★★★☆), this elegant Hawke's Bay wine was designed as a sort of junior Irongate. Refined and youthful, it was fermented and lees-aged in a mix of tanks (30 per cent) and seasoned French oak barrels (70 per cent), with no malolactic fermentation. Showcasing its fresh, ripe, grapefruit-like flavours, with subtle oak and lees characters adding richness, it's a minerally, well-structured, quietly classy wine with a fully dry finish.

Vintage	02
WR	7
Drink	04-09

DRY $20 AV

Babich Irongate Chardonnay ★★★★★

Now Babich's flagship Chardonnay, after the phasing out of The Patriarch Chardonnay (last made in 2000). A stylish, taut wine, Irongate is typically leaner than other top Hawke's Bay Chardonnays, but a proven performer in the cellar. It is based on intensely flavoured, hand-picked fruit from the shingly Irongate vineyard in Gimblett Road, west of Hastings, whole-bunch pressed, fully barrel-fermented and lees-matured for up to nine months. Malolactic fermentation is rare. The 1992, 1995, 1996, 1998 and 2000 vintages are outstanding. The small-volume 2001 vintage (★★★★☆) has a youthful, minerally bouquet leading into a tightly structured palate with deep flavours of grapefruit and nuts and the steely finish typical of the label. It's more expressive in its youth than some past vintages, but bound to mature well for several years.

Vintage	01	00	99	98	97	96	95	94	DRY $33 V+
WR	6	7	7	7	6	7	7	7	
Drink	04-07	04-08	04-07	04-06	P	04-05	P	P	

Babich Winemakers Reserve Chardonnay ★★★

Grown at Fernhill in Hawke's Bay, and fermented and lees-aged (with regular stirring) for 10 months in French oak barriques, the 2001 vintage (★★☆) is a light/medium gold wine, toasty and slightly honeyed, with a crisp finish. Crisp and slightly austere, it lacks the rich, sweet fruit flavours of a top year.

Vintage	02	01	00	99	98	DRY $20 -V
WR	7	6	7	7	7	
Drink	04-10	04-05	04-05	P	P	

Beach House Hawke's Bay Chardonnay ★★★★☆

The 2000 vintage (★★★★) was impressively ripe and concentrated, and the 2002 (★★★★★) is even better. Grown on the coast at Te Awanga, it's a seductively powerful, creamy-rich wine with sweet, ripe-citrus and stone-fruit flavours shining through. Barrel-fermented and lees-aged, it is robust and mealy, with good flow through the palate and a finely textured, sustained finish. A great buy.

DRY $22 V+

Bilancia Chardonnay ★★★★

Pronounced 'be-larn-cha' (Italian for balance, harmony), this Hawke's Bay wine is made by Warren Gibson (winemaker at Trinity Hill) and his partner, Lorraine Leheny. The 2002 vintage (★★★★☆) was grown at Glencoe Station, 10 kilometres south of Maraekakaho, fermented with indigenous yeasts, and lees-aged for 15 months in French oak barriques (50 per cent new), with full malolactic fermentation. It's a very elegant and harmonious wine, full-bodied and fresh, with grapefruit and peach characters, integrated oak and a hint of butterscotch. A refined, cool-climate style with a fully dry finish, it should respond well to cellaring.

Vintage	02	01	00	99	98	97	DRY $34 -V
WR	7	NM	6	6	6	5	
Drink	04-07	NM	04-06	P	P	P	

Birchwood Chardonnay (★★★)

Sold exclusively in supermarkets, the 2002 vintage (★★★) was blended from Gisborne and Hawke's Bay grapes. It's a crisp, lemony wine, fresh and clean, with more flavour depth than you'd expect at its modest price.

DRY $12 V+

Black Barn Barrel Fermented Chardonnay ★★★★

Grown on the Havelock North hills and fermented and matured in French oak barriques (50 per cent new), the 2003 vintage (★★★★) is a substantial, ripe-tasting Hawke's Bay wine, peachy and citrusy, with a strong but not excessive seasoning of toasty, nutty oak. Full-bodied and creamy, it offers considerable complexity and cellaring potential.

Vintage	03
WR	5
Drink	05-06

DRY $31 -V

Black Barn Hawke's Bay Unoaked Chardonnay ★★★

A drink-young style, the 2003 vintage (★★★☆) is a full-bodied and smooth Hawke's Bay wine, peachy and well-rounded, with a fractionally off-dry finish. Offering fresh, ripe-fruit flavours, showing good delicacy and richness, it's very easy to enjoy and a fine example of the style.

DRY $21 -V

Black Estate Waipara Chardonnay ★★★★

Estate-grown in North Canterbury, the 2002 vintage (★★★★) was fermented in French oak barriques (one-third new). It's a fleshy, rich wine with strong grapefruit, peach and fig flavours wrapped in quality oak and a creamy, rounded mouthfeel. The creamy-soft 2003 (★★★★) again shows a strong 'malo' influence, with good body and intensity of grapefruit and nut flavours. Enjoyable young, with lots of character.

Vintage	03	02	01
WR	7	6	5
Drink	05+	P	P

DRY $29 AV

Black Ridge Chardonnay ★★★

This Alexandra wine is generally attractive and one of the Central Otago region's more affordable Chardonnays. The 2002 vintage (★★★) is a more wood-influenced style than earlier releases; 90 per cent of the blend was fermented in new oak barrels and 50 per cent was barrel-aged. Quite forward in its appeal, it's full-bodied and fresh, with lemony, appley, gently biscuity flavours showing good depth and a dry, rounded finish.

DRY $23 -V

Brajkovich Kumeu Chardonnay – see Kumeu River Village Kumeu Chardonnay

Brightwater Vineyards Nelson Chardonnay ★★★☆

Grown by Gary and Valley Neale at Hope and made by Sam Weaver, the 2002 vintage (★★★) was mostly handled in tanks, but a third of the blend was fermented and lees-aged for 14 months in French oak barriques. It's a flavoursome, citrusy and slightly honeyed wine, moderately complex, with a firm, crisp finish.

Vintage	02	01	00	99
WR	6	6	6	6
Drink	04-07	04-06	P	P

DRY $21 AV

Brookfields Bergman Chardonnay ★★★

Named after the Ingrid Bergman roses in the estate garden, in most vintages this wine is grown alongside
the winery at Meeanee. Hand-picked, whole-bunch pressed and fermented and matured on its yeast lees
for eight months in French and American oak casks, the 2002 (★★★) is a fleshy, upfront style with good
body and depth of peachy, buttery flavour. The 2003 (★★★), from a frost-affected season, is a blend of
Hawke's Bay and Gisborne grapes, oak-aged for eight months. Likely to mature well, it has fresh oak
aromas leading into a fresh, youthful palate with firm acidity, some mealy, biscuity complexity and a tight
finish.

Vintage	03	02	01	00	99	98
WR	7	7	6	6	7	7
Drink	06-08	04-05	04-06	04-05	P	P

DRY $18 AV

Brookfields Marshall Bank Chardonnay ★★★★☆

Brookfields' top Chardonnay is named after proprietor Peter Robertson's grandfather's property in Otago.
Grown in a vineyard adjacent to the winery at Meeanee and fermented in all-new French oak barriques, it
is typically a rich, concentrated, strongly oak-influenced Hawke's Bay wine with peachy, toasty, buttery
flavours, lush and complex. The 2002 vintage (★★★★) is big-bodied, rich and rounded, with strong, well-
ripened stone-fruit characters seasoned with toasty oak and a creamy-smooth finish. Due to frost damage,
there is no 2003.

Vintage	02	01	00	99	98	97	96
WR	7	7	7	7	7	7	7
Drink	05-07	04-07	04-07	04-06	04-05	P	P

DRY $30 AV

Burnt Spur Martinborough Chardonnay (★★★☆)

The peachy, slightly creamy 2002 vintage (★★★☆) was hand-picked and fermented and lees-aged for 11
months in French oak barriques (30 per cent new), with a full, softening malolactic fermentation. Straw-
hued, it offers stone-fruit and butterscotch flavours, balanced acidity and good depth.

DRY $26 -V

Cabbage Tree Vineyard Chardonnay (★★★☆)

The soft, peachy 2002 vintage (★★★☆) was grown in Martinborough and fermented and lees-aged for
10 months in new and one-year-old French oak barriques. Light gold, it's a fleshy wine with very good
depth of ripe stone-fruit flavours, balanced acidity and a smooth finish.

Vintage	01
WR	6
Drink	04-06

DRY $28 -V

Cable Bay Waiheke Chardonnay ★★★☆

The debut 2002 vintage (★★★☆) is building up well with age. Blended from six sites and fermented and
matured for eight months in French oak barriques (30 per cent new), with no use of malolactic
fermentation, it's a tightly structured wine with crisp grapefruit and fig characters and good weight. The
2003 (★★★☆) is a refined, peachy, biscuity, mealy wine with good intensity and a freshly acidic finish.
Open mid-2005+.

Vintage	03	02
WR	6	7
Drink	04-08	04-07

DRY $33 -V

Cairnbrae Chieftain Chardonnay (★★★☆)

An unoaked Marlborough wine, the 2003 vintage (★★★☆) has fresh, lemony aromas leading into a
vibrantly fruity, crisp palate with strong, citrusy flavours and a hint of passionfruit. It's a well-balanced dry
wine, offering good value.

DRY $17 V+

Canadoro Martinborough Chardonnay   ★★★☆

A little- known but characterful Martinborough wine. Maturing well, the powerful 2001 vintage (★★★★) is a strapping wine (14.6 per cent alcohol), soft and creamy, with strong peach, butterscotch and toasty oak flavours, showing good harmony.

Vintage	01	00	99	98	97	96	DRY $29 -V
WR	7	7	NM	7	6	5	
Drink	04-06	P	NM	P	P	P	

Canterbury House Waipara Chardonnay   ★★☆

Most vintages of this North Canterbury wine have been solid but unmemorable, with a very restrained oak influence, straightforward, lemony, appley flavours and a firm acid spine.

DRY $19 -V

Carrick Central Otago Chardonnay   ★★★☆

From a region that often struggles with Chardonnay, this wine is typically one of the best. The 2003 vintage (★★★☆), grown on the Cairnmuir Terraces at Bannockburn, was fermented and matured in French oak barriques (16 per cent new). A mouthfilling wine with toasty, mealy, slightly buttery flavours woven with fresh acidity, it's worth cellaring. (I have also tasted a classy Extended Barrel Maturation Chardonnay 2002 (★★★★☆), oak-aged for 18 months, with excellent intensity of elegant, cool-climate fruit characters, impressive harmony and a creamy, rounded finish.)

Vintage	03	02	01	DRY $24 AV
WR	6	6	7	
Drink	04-08	04+	P	

Chard Farm Closeburn Chardonnay   ★★★

The winery's second-tier Chardonnay is typically a fresh, vibrant Central Otago wine with appetising acidity. The 2002 vintage (★★★), a blend of Bannockburn, Gibbston and estate-grown grapes, was handled entirely without oak. Full-bodied and tangy, with lemony, limey, slightly leesy and nutty flavours woven with fresh acidity, it's a drink-young style.

Vintage	02	01	00	99	98	DRY $20 -V
WR	6	6	5	5	6	
Drink	04-05	P	P	P	P	

Chard Farm Judge and Jury Chardonnay   ★★★★

Named after a rocky outcrop overlooking the Kawarau River (Central Otago) vineyard, since 1994 this wine has been a blend of estate-grown (the best slopes) and Bannockburn (the best clones) fruit. The 2002 vintage (★★★☆) was fully barrel-fermented, but new oak was excluded from the recipe. It offers strong citrusy flavours woven with fresh acidity, a seasoning of toasty oak and the slight herbal influence typical of the region's Chardonnays. Judge and Jury clearly rewards cellaring.

Vintage	02	01	00	99	98	97	96	DRY $31 -V
WR	6	6	5	6	6	5	5	
Drink	04-07	04-05	P	P	P	P	P	

Charles Wiffen Marlborough Chardonnay   ★★★☆

Charles and Sandy Wiffen own a vineyard in the Wairau Valley, but their wine is made at West Brook in Auckland. The 2003 vintage (★★★) was matured for 10 months in new and seasoned French oak barriques, with some lees-stirring and malolactic fermentation. Light yellow, it's a full-bodied, citrusy, toasty, slightly buttery wine with moderate complexity and a smooth finish.

DRY $22 AV

Church Road Chardonnay ★★★☆

This typically mouthfilling and rich Chardonnay is made by Allied Domecq Wines (NZ) at the Church Road Winery. It is usually a Hawke's Bay wine, but the 2003 (★★☆), from a frost-affected season, is a blend of Marlborough (51 per cent), Gisborne (37 per cent) and Hawke's Bay (12 per cent) grapes. Matured for six months on its full yeast lees, with regular stirring, in French oak barriques (one-third new), it's a fresh, vibrant wine, lemony, appley and crisp, but relatively simple, lacking its usual weight, ripeness, complexity and richness.

Vintage	03	02	01	00	99	98	97	96
WR	5	6	6	7	6	7	6	6
Drink	04-06	04-06	P	P	P	P	P	P

DRY $22 AV

Church Road Cuve Series Chardonnay ★★★★☆

This rare wine is the result of Allied Domecq's decision to produce 'a more Burgundian, less fruit-driven, less oaky' style of Hawke's Bay Chardonnay than its lush, relatively fast-developing Church Road Reserve wine. It is typically hand-picked, whole-bunch pressed, fermented and matured for a year in French oak barriques and given a full, softening malolactic fermentation. The 2002 vintage (★★★★) is currently very toasty, reflecting its maturation in 40 per cent new oak barrels (in future, the proportion of new oak will be reduced to 25 per cent). Light yellow, it's a tightly structured, mouthfilling wine with concentrated, ripe, grapefruit-like flavours, mealy, minerally complexities and a slightly creamy texture. The finish is crisp and youthful, suggesting good cellaring potential.

Vintage	98
WR	7
Drink	P

DRY $33 AV

Church Road Reserve Chardonnay ★★★★★

This opulent wine is based on the 'pick' of Allied Domecq's Hawke's Bay Chardonnay crop (always the shy-bearing Mendoza clone, but not always grown in the same vineyard). Given more skin contact than its Ormond Estate Chardonnay stablemate from Gisborne, and therefore more forward, it is fully fermented in French oak barriques (44 per cent new in 2002), and stays on its yeast lees for the total time in barrel (up to 10 months) with fortnightly lees-stirring. There was no 2001. Harvested at 24 brix and made without malolactic fermentation, the 2002 vintage (★★★★★) is deliciously soft, creamy and substantial (14 per cent alcohol), with integrated oak and a powerful surge of rich, ripe-grapefruit and stone-fruit flavours. A top vintage, it's already delicious.

Vintage	02	01	00	99	98	97	96
WR	7	NM	7	6	7	NM	7
Drink	04-06	NM	04+	P	04-05	NM	P

DRY $35 AV

🍇🍇

C.J. Pask Gimblett Road Chardonnay ★★★☆

For her second-tier Chardonnay, chief winemaker Kate Radburnd emphasises Hawke's Bay's citrusy fruit characters ('the fruit should shine through') fleshed out with restrained wood. The 2002 vintage (★★★★), one of the best yet, shows greater complexity than most of its predecessors and was partly barrel-fermented. Instantly appealing, it is fresh and vibrant, with citrusy, slightly biscuity aromas and flavours, subtle oak handling and a creamy-smooth finish. Good weight, delicacy and length. Due to Jack Frost, there is no 2003.

Vintage	03	02	01	00	99	98	97	96
WR	NM	7	NM	6	7	6	6	7
Drink	NM	04-08	NM	P	P	P	P	P

DRY $22 AV

C.J. Pask Reserve Chardonnay   ★★★★

Grown in Gimblett Road, Hawke's Bay, this wine has shown good, occasionally outstanding, form since the 1994 vintage. Based on the company's oldest Chardonnay vines, planted in 1984, it has usually been fermented and matured in all-new French oak barriques, giving it a strong wood influence. The fragrant 2002 vintage (★★★★☆) shows a finer fruit/oak balance than some past vintages, in a rich, mouthfilling and harmonious style with deep, grapefruit-like flavours and a slightly creamy, long finish. There is no 2003.

Vintage	02	01	00	99	98	97	96	DRY $35 -V
WR	7	NM	7	7	6	6	7	
Drink	04-07	NM	04-06	04-05	04-05	P	P	

C.J. Pask Roy's Hill Chardonnay   ★★★

The 2003 vintage (★★★) of this Hawke's Bay wine is C.J. Pask's only Chardonnay from the frost-afflicted season. Not oak-aged, it's a fresh, fruit-driven style with vibrant, citrusy flavours, finely balanced and refreshing.

Vintage	03	02	DRY $15 V+
WR	6	6	
Drink	04-08	04-06	

Clearview Beachhead Chardonnay   ★★★

This small Hawke's Bay winery has a reputation for powerful Chardonnays, and in some years its second-tier label is no exception. The 2003 (★★★☆) was fully fermented in one and two-year-old French and American oak casks (past vintages have been partly handled in tanks), and half the blend went through a softening malolactic fermentation. It's a fresh, lively, peach and butterscotch-flavoured wine with very good flavour depth and crisp acidity enlivening the finish. 'I drink it at home all the time,' says winemaker Tim Turvey.

Vintage	03	02	DRY $22 -V
WR	5	6	
Drink	04-06	04-06	

Clearview Reserve Chardonnay   ★★★★★

For his premium Chardonnay label, Te Awanga winemaker Tim Turvey aims for a 'big, grunty, upfront' style – and hits the target with ease. It's typically a hedonist's delight – an arrestingly bold, intense, savoury, mealy, complex wine with layers of flavour. Based on ultra-ripe fruit (always hand-harvested at 24+ brix), it is fermented in predominantly new French oak barriques (80 per cent in 2003), lees-stirred weekly, and about 25 per cent of the final blend undergoes a softening malolactic fermentation. The 1994 and subsequent vintages have all matured superbly. Due to frosts, the small volume 2003 vintage (★★★★) is a 50/50 blend of Te Awanga and Esk Valley grapes. A crisp, youthful wine, slightly minerally and honeyed, it shows good intensity, but lacks the power of this label at its finest.

Vintage	03	02	01	00	99	98	97	96	DRY $35 AV
WR	6	6	7	7	7	6	6	6	
Drink	04-10	04-10	04-10	04-08	04-07	04-06	04-07	P	🍇🍇🍇

Clearview Unwooded Chardonnay   ★★★

This Te Awanga, Hawke's Bay wine is a tank-fermented style, simple but full-flavoured. The 2003 vintage (★★★) was matured on its yeast lees and 20 per cent went through a softening malolactic fermentation. It's a vibrantly fruity wine, weighty, tight and slightly minerally, with a sliver of sweetness (5 grams/litre of residual sugar) balancing its fresh acidity.

Vintage	03	02	MED/DRY $20 -V
WR	5	5	
Drink	04-06	04-05	

Clearwater Vineyards Waipara Chardonnay   (★★★☆)

The pale yellow 2003 vintage (★★★☆) is flavoursome, buttery and toasty, with a strong oak influence. Harvested in early May at 22.5 brix, it was fermented and lees-aged for 10 months in French oak barriques (30 per cent new). A slightly limey wine, cut with fresh acidity, it shows some complexity and richness, and should be at its best mid-2005+.

DRY $33 -V

Clifford Bay Marlborough Chardonnay   ★★★

A single-vineyard Awatere Valley wine, made in a fresh, lively, fruit-driven style. Partly French oak-fermented, the light yellow 2002 vintage (★★★) is citrusy and slightly limey, with a subtle oak influence and smooth, slightly buttery finish.

Vintage	02	01	00	99	98
WR	6	6	6	6	6
Drink	04-06	04-05	P	P	P

DRY $19 AV

Cloudy Bay Chardonnay   ★★★★★

A powerful Marlborough wine with an arresting concentration of savoury, lemony, mealy flavours and a proven ability to mature well over the long haul (at least four years and up to a decade). The grapes are sourced from nine estate vineyards and growers' vineyards in the Wairau and Brancott valleys. All of the wine is fermented (with some indigenous yeasts) in French oak barriques (20 to 25 per cent new) and lees-aged in oak for 15 months, and in the 2002 vintage, most went through malolactic fermentation. Softer, more immediately approachable than the steely, biscuity 2001 vintage (★★★★☆), the 2002 (★★★★★) is already delicious. A generous, sturdy wine (14 per cent alcohol) with a silky texture, it possesses concentrated grapefruit, nut and slightly minerally flavours that build to a rich, creamy, buttery-smooth finish.

Vintage	02	01	00	99	98	97	96
WR	6	6	6	6	6	6	6
Drink	04-08	04-07	04-06	P	P	P	P

DRY $34 V+

Collards Blakes Mill Chardonnay   ★★★

A good drink-young style, Collards' lightly oaked wine is named after the old Blakes Mill settlement, now the site of the company's Rothesay Vineyard in West Auckland, where most of the grapes are grown. It is oak-aged, says Bruce Collard, 'for flavour and style enhancement, rather than any noticeable oakiness'. The 2002 vintage (★★★) is an enjoyable, fruit-driven style, fresh, lemony and gently wooded, with plenty of flavour and a crisp, dry, slightly nutty finish. Ready.

Vintage	04	03	02	01	00	99	98
WR	6	NM	6	6	7	6	7
Drink	05-06	NM	04-05	P	P	P	P

DRY $13 V+

Collards Hawke's Bay Chardonnay   ★★★★

This is Collards' middle-tier Chardonnay label and in favourable years it offers excellent value. Finely balanced for current drinking, the 2002 vintage (★★★★) is a creamy-smooth, fresh and vibrantly fruity wine with ripe, grapefruit-like characters to the fore, subtle use of oak and a deliciously rounded and harmonious finish.

Vintage	04	03	02	01	00	99	98
WR	NM	NM	7	NM	6	6	7
Drink	NM	NM	04-05	NM	P	P	P

DRY $19 V+

Collards Rothesay Vineyard Chardonnay   ★★★★☆

Collards' flagship white is grown in Bruce and Geoffrey Collard's Rothesay Vineyard at Waimauku, in West Auckland. It is typically mouthfilling, richly flavoured and rounded, with sweet, ripe-fruit characters and impressive harmony. The 2002 vintage (★★★★☆) shows impressive weight and strong, ripe-grapefruit and pear flavours, gently seasoned with French oak. Fresh, vibrant and finely balanced, it builds to a powerful finish.

Vintage	03	02	01	00	99	98	97	96
WR	NM	7	6	7	6	7	7	7
Drink	NM	04-05	P	P	P	P	P	P

DRY $30 AV

Coniglio Hawke's Bay Chardonnay   (★★★★★)

Launched by Morton Estate in 2001 at $80, Coniglio is one of New Zealand's most expensive Chardonnays. A Rolls-Royce version of the company's famous Black Label Chardonnay, it's an arresting wine, powerful and concentrated, but now seems fully developed. Grown in the cool, elevated Riverview vineyard at Mangatahi, Hawke's Bay, it was fermented and lees-aged for 11 months in all-new French oak barriques, with no malolactic fermentation. Richly fragrant and refined, with layers of grapefruit and nut flavours, good acid spine and a wonderfully rich, resounding finish, it has matured very gracefully, but is now just starting to dry out. There is no 1999 or 2001, but the label reappears from the 2000 and 2002 vintages.

Vintage	02	01	00	99	98
WR	7	NM	6	NM	7
Drink	04-07	NM	04-06	NM	P

DRY $80 AV

Coopers Creek Fat Cat Chardonnay – see Fat Cat Chardonnay

Coopers Creek Hawke's Bay Chardonnay   ★★★☆

Coopers Creek's middle-tier Chardonnay is typically an upfront style, hard to resist in its youth. The very small volume (only 250 cases) 2003 vintage (★★★☆) was for the first time fermented and matured entirely in French oak barriques (rather than the usual American) because it was a potential Swamp Reserve (see below). Creamy and mealy, it shows good complexity, with a savoury, rounded finish, but lacks the fruit intensity to rate more highly.

Vintage	03	02	01	00	99	98	97	96
WR	5	6	6	7	6	6	6	6
Drink	04-06	04-05	04-05	P	P	P	P	P

DRY $18 V+

Coopers Creek Limited Release Gisborne Chardonnay   (★★★)

Sold by mail-order wine clubs, the 2003 vintage (★★★) is an attractive, drink-young style with peach and butterscotch aromas and flavours in a well-rounded style, fresh and flavoursome.

DRY $20 –V

Coopers Creek Limited Release Marlborough Chardonnay   (★★★)

The 2003 vintage (★★★) is a clearly varietal, uncomplicated wine with fresh-fruit aromas leading into a vibrant, skilfully balanced palate with lemony, lively flavours. (Sold by mail-order wine clubs.)

DRY $20 -V

Coopers Creek Reserve Gisborne Chardonnay   (★★★★☆)

Made from 'super-ripe' (25 brix) grapes grown in the McLaurin vineyard, on the Slope of Gold, the 2002 vintage (★★★★☆), the first of this label, is Gisborne Chardonnay at its best. Fermented and aged for nine months in French (mostly) and American oak casks, with full malolactic fermentation, it's a fat, concentrated wine, sturdy (14.5 per cent alcohol), with strong, sweet fruit flavours of grapefruit and fig and a deliciously rounded finish.

Vintage	03	02
WR	NM	6
Drink	NM	04-06

DRY $25 V+

Coopers Creek SV Chardonnay   ★★★★

The SV (Single Vineyard) Chardonnay sits immediately below the top Swamp Reserve Chardonnays in the Coopers Creek range. The 2002 vintage (★★★★), the first since 1999, is a Marlborough wine, based on second-crop Wairau Valley vines. Fully French oak-fermented, it's a richly alcoholic wine (14.5 per cent), with well-ripened grapefruit, fig and pear flavours cut with fresh acidity, a distinct touch of butterscotch and good intensity.

Vintage	03	02	01	00	99	98	97
WR	NM	6	NM	NM	7	7	6
Drink	NM	04-05	NM	NM	P	P	P

DRY $24 V+

Coopers Creek Swamp Reserve Chardonnay   ★★★★★

Based on the winery's best Hawke's Bay Chardonnay fruit, this is typically a lush, highly seductive wine with a finely judged balance of rich, citrusy, peachy fruit flavours and toasty oak. The 2002 vintage (★★★★★) was made from a 'tiny, tiny' crop of grapes in the company's Middle Road vineyard at Havelock North. Fully fermented and matured for nine months in French oak barriques (new and one-year-old), it's a robust (14 per cent alcohol) and concentrated wine with sweet, ripe-fruit characters, rich flavours of peach, grapefruit, toast and butterscotch and a long, well-rounded finish. A classic example of the style, it's maturing superbly. There is no 2003.

Vintage	03	02	01	00	99	98	97	96
WR	NM	6	NM	6	6	6	6	6
Drink	NM	04-06	NM	04-05	P	P	P	P

DRY $29 V+

🍇🍇

Coopers Creek Unoaked Gisborne Chardonnay   ★★★

Coopers Creek recently stopped wood-aging its popular, moderately priced Gisborne wine, but the recipe still includes maturation on its yeast lees. The 2003 vintage (★★☆) is slightly honeyed, with fractionally off-dry passionfruit and peach flavours in a smooth, easy-drinking style. Winemaker Simon Nunns says the 2004 will be a step up: 'It's so ripe, with some substance.'

Vintage	04	03	02	01
WR	6	5	7	5
Drink	04-06	04-05	P	P

DRY $16 AV

Corazon The Collective Chardonnay   ★★★

The 2003 vintage (★★★) is a single-vineyard (Waiohika Estate) Gisborne wine, fermented and lees-aged for eight months in French oak barriques. It's advanced for its age, with light-medium yellow colour, peachy, buttery, toasty, slightly honeyed flavours and a rounded finish. Fat and full-flavoured, it offers plenty of character, but is likely to be at its best during 2004-05.

Vintage	03	02
WR	5	6
Drink	04-06	04-06

DRY $23 ·V

Corbans Chardonnay ★★★

Grown in the Patutahi district of Gisborne, the 2003 vintage (★★★) was mostly handled in tanks, but about 30 per cent of the blend was fermented and lees-aged for three months, with weekly stirring, in seasoned French oak barrels. It's an attractive citrusy, appley wine, fairly simple but very fresh and lively, with crisper acidity than the 2002 vintage (★★☆) and some mealy, buttery touches.

Vintage	04	03	02	01	00	99
WR	6	6	6	NM	NM	6
Drink	04-06	04-05	P	NM	NM	P

DRY $14 V+

Corbans Cottage Block Marlborough Chardonnay ★★★★☆

The 2002 vintage (★★★★) is a creamy-smooth style with ripe, citrusy fruit characters. Whole-bunch pressed, it was fermented and lees-aged for 10 months in French oak casks (50 per cent new), and given a softening malolactic fermentation. A very harmonious wine, forward in its appeal, it offers grapefruit, butterscotch and biscuity oak flavours, showing good complexity.

Vintage	02	01	00	99
WR	6	7	NM	7
Drink	04-08	04+	NM	P

DRY $33 AV

Corbans Private Bin Hawke's Bay Chardonnay ★★★

Opened in 2004, the 1999 vintage (★★), not released until 2002, was muted and slightly piquant, although showing some underlying complexity and depth of grapefruit and nut flavours. The 2002 (★★★★), matured in French oak barriques (45 per cent new) is far superior. Light yellow in hue, it is smooth and ripe, with sweet fruit characters of grapefruit and peach, oak richness and impressive delicacy and depth. Delicious drinking from now onwards.

Vintage	02
WR	6
Drink	04-06

DRY $25 -V

Corbans Private Bin Marlborough Chardonnay (★★★★)

The instantly appealing, creamy-smooth 2001 vintage (★★★★) was fermented and matured on its yeast lees in French oak barriques (45 per cent new), and two-thirds of the blend had a softening malolactic fermentation. Toasty and mealy on the nose, it's a full-flavoured wine with generous melon and grapefruit characters, good savoury, nutty complexity and a rich, rounded finish.

Vintage	01
WR	6
Drink	04-05

DRY $25 AV

Cottle Hill Chardonnay ★★★

The 2002 vintage (★★★☆) is a good buy. Grown in Northland and matured for nine months in French and American oak, it is full-bodied, with balanced acidity and very good depth of citrusy, slightly mealy and buttery flavour, gently seasoned with toasty oak. It's a tightly structured wine, maturing well.

Vintage	02
WR	6
Drink	04-07

DRY $19 AV

Covell Estate Estate Chardonnay ★★

Grown near Murupara, in the inland, eastern Bay of Plenty, the non-vintage bottling (★★) I tasted last year was a lightly oaked, golden wine with a restrained bouquet and slightly buttery flavours threaded with firm acidity. (There is also a 2002 Barrel Fermented Chardonnay.)

DRY $14 -V

Crab Farm Chardonnay ★★★☆

High-flavoured, the robust, peachy and creamy-smooth 2002 vintage (★★★☆) from this Hawke's Bay winery was oak-aged for 10 months. The 2004 (★★★☆) is an unoaked style, big-bodied (14.5 per cent alcohol), with fresh-fruit aromas. It's a buoyant fruity wine with very good depth of grapefruit, apple and lime flavours, very crisp and lively.

Vintage	04	DRY $17 V+
WR	6	
Drink	04-05	

Craggy Range Dijon Clones Chardonnay (★★★★)

Offering delicious drinking from now onwards, the 2002 vintage (★★★★) was grown in Martinborough and fermented and matured in French oak barriques (50 per cent new.) Light yellow/green, it's a fleshy, elegant wine with ripe-grapefruit characters, well-integrated oak, good harmony and a slightly buttery, creamy, rounded finish.

Vintage	02	DRY $45 -V
WR	6	
Drink	07	

Craggy Range Gimblett Gravels Vineyard Chardonnay ★★★★

In terms of vineyard and cellar work, the 2003 vintage (★★★☆) is 'the most challenging wine we have ever made,' reports Craggy Range. Fermented and matured in French oak barriques (48 per cent new), it's a pale lemon/green, Chablis-like wine with fresh, lemony, appley aromas and flavours, hints of biscuit and butterscotch, some savoury complexity and a crisp, minerally finish. Leaner than the 2002 (★★★★☆), it's still youthful; open mid-2005+.

Vintage	03	02	DRY $26 AV
WR	5	6	
Drink	06	04-06	

Craggy Range Les Beaux Cailloux – see the Branded and Other White Wines section

Craggy Range Seven Poplars Vineyard Chardonnay ★★★★☆

Grown on the banks of the Tutaekuri River in the lower Dartmoor Valley, this is typically a refined wine with lovely depth of flavour. The 2002 vintage (★★★★), based on 14-year-old vines, was fermented (with a 50/50 split of indigenous and cultured yeasts) and lees-aged for eight months in French oak casks (50 per cent new), with full malolactic fermentation. Light yellow, it's an excellent example of the Hawke's Bay regional style, fresh and mouthfilling, with rich, peachy, creamy, toasty flavours. It's arguably less intense than the 2001 (★★★★☆), but softer and more forward. There is no 2003.

Vintage	03	02	01	00	99	DRY $29 V+
WR	NM	7	5	6	5	
Drink	NM	04-06	04-05	P	P	

Craggy Range Te Muna Road Chardonnay ★★★★

The powerful ('not for the faint-hearted', in the winery's words) 2002 vintage (★★★☆) is a strapping (14.5 per cent alcohol) Martinborough wine, fermented and lees-aged, with regular stirring, for 14 months in French oak barriques (half new). It's an upfront style, softly mouthfilling, peachy, buttery and rounded, but advanced for its age and slightly dominated by toasty oak. Delicious in its youth, the 2003 (★★★★☆) is light yellow, with rich, butterscotch aromas. It makes a powerful statement on the palate, with sweet fruit delights, refined acidity, toasty oak and lush, stone-fruit flavours, showing lovely freshness and delicacy. Drink now to 2006.

DRY $29 AV

Crossroads Collectors' Edition Chardonnay   (★★★★)

Showing lovely harmony, the 2002 vintage (★★★★) of this Hawke's Bay wine is a ripe, peach, lemon and toast-flavoured wine with excellent fruit/oak balance and a soft, lingering finish. Grown at Ohiti Estate, inland from Fernhill, it was whole-bunch pressed and fermented in mostly seasoned French oak barriques, with fortnightly lees-stirring. Drink 2005–06.

DRY $30 -V

Crossroads Destination Series Chardonnay   (★★★☆)

The debut 2002 vintage (★★★☆) is described on the label as a 'fruit-driven' style, but the wine shows clear oak and malolactic fermentation influences. Matured for eight months in French and American oak, it's a weighty, smooth and creamy Hawke's Bay wine with grapefruit, pear and butterscotch flavours showing very good depth and harmony and some complexity. Drink now onwards.

Vintage	02
WR	6
Drink	04-08

DRY $24 AV

Culley Marlborough District Chardonnay   (★★★)

Produced by Neill Culley, a partner in the Cable Bay winery on Waiheke Island, and sold by mail-order wine clubs, the 2003 vintage (★★★) is a crisp, youthful, Chablis-like wine with fresh, appley, lightly oaked flavours.

DRY $19 AV

Culley Waiheke Island Chardonnay   (★★★☆)

Neill Culley is co-owner and winemaker at Cable Bay, on Waiheke Island. Produced for mail-order wine clubs, the 2003 vintage (★★★☆) is a mouthfilling, tightly structured wine with firm acidity woven through its peach, butterscotch and toast flavours, which show very good depth. Worth cellaring.

DRY $30 -V

Daniel Schuster Petrie Vineyard Selection   ★★★★

Grown at Rakaia in Mid Canterbury, south of Christchurch, this is typically a Chablis-like wine with cool-climate freshness and crisp, savoury, concentrated flavours. The 2002 vintage (★★★★) was harvested from low-yielding vines (5 tonnes/hectare), handled in French oak barriques (20 per cent new), and given extended lees contact and stirring. The bouquet is citrusy and mealy; the palate weighty and slightly buttery, with rich, sweet fruit characters and firm acid spine. (There is no 2003 and the 2004 will not be released until early 2006.)

Vintage	04	03	02	01	00	99	98
WR	7	NM	6	7	7	7	7
Drink	07-09	NM	04-06	04-07	04-06	04-05	04-05

DRY $30 -V

Dashwood Marlborough Chardonnay   ★★★

Vavasour's second-tier Chardonnay is a drink-young style with fresh, buoyant fruit flavours and appetising acidity. The 2003 vintage (★★★), a blend of Wairau Valley and Awatere Valley grapes, was mostly fermented and lees-aged in stainless steel tanks, but 30 per cent was handled in French oak barriques. Light yellow/green, it's a smooth, lemony, slightly honeyed wine, fresh and vibrantly fruity, with a touch of oak and moderate complexity.

Vintage	03	02	01	00	99	98
WR	6	7	7	6	6	6
Drink	04-05	P	P	P	P	P

DRY $17 AV

Delegat's Hawke's Bay Chardonnay ★★★

For Delegat's bargain-priced, lower-tier Chardonnay, the goal is to 'let the fruit do the talking', with wood relegated to a minor role. Fermented in stainless steel tanks and then matured for six months in seasoned oak, the 2002 vintage (★★★☆) is deliciously fleshy and smooth, with ripe-fruit characters to the fore and a rich, rounded finish. The 2003 (★★★) is more wood-influenced than usual, because it includes a barrel-fermented portion originally earmarked for the Reserve Chardonnay label (not released from 2003). Pale yellow, it's a citrusy, nutty, slightly buttery, flavoursome wine with a firm, crisp finish.

Vintage	03	02	01	00	99	98	DRY $15 V+
WR	5	6	5	6	5	6	
Drink	04-05	04-05	P	P	P	P	

Delegat's Reserve Chardonnay ★★★★

The launch of Delegat's $20 Chardonnay from the 1997 vintage was instantly successful. A deliciously easy-drinking style with a lot of class, it is fermented and matured in French oak barriques (25 per cent new), with 'intensive' lees-stirring. Fragrant, buttery and complex on the nose, the 2002 vintage (★★★★) is a fleshy, finely crafted Hawke's Bay wine, still youthful, with well-ripened grapefruit, peach and pear flavours, gently seasoned with toasty oak, and a rich, rounded finish.

Vintage	03	02	01	00	99	98	DRY $20 V+
WR	NM	7	6	7	7	7	
Drink	NM	04-05	P	P	P	P	

Delta Marlborough Chardonnay ★★☆

Sold by mail-order wine clubs, the 2002 vintage (★★☆) is a crisp, citrusy, appley wine that lacks real complexity and depth. The 2003 (★★★) is fresh and vibrant, with strong, citrusy aromas and flavours in a simple but lively style.

DRY $20 -V

Dog Point Vineyard Marlborough Chardonnay (★★★★★)

The highly refined 2002 vintage (★★★★★) reflects the talents of winemaker James Healy and viticulturist Ivan Sutherland, both ex-Cloudy Bay. Fermented and matured for 20 months in French oak barriques (25 per cent new), with full malolactic fermentation, it's a pale yellow, fragrant, ripe and savoury wine with citrusy, slightly buttery and toasty flavours, good acid spine and lovely harmony, delicacy and richness. Drink 2004–05.

DRY $33 V+

Domaine Georges Michel
Golden Mile Marlborough Chardonnay ★★★

Named after 'the central route of the Rapaura area', the 2002 vintage (★★★☆) is a fruit-driven style, French oak-aged for eight months. Full-bodied, fresh and vibrant, with ripe, pineappley characters, appetising acidity and a fractionally off-dry finish, it's a highly enjoyable, drink-young style. The 2003 (★★☆) is crisp and slightly minerally, but slightly lacks freshness and delicacy.

Vintage	02	DRY $22 -V
WR	6	
Drink	04-06	

Domaine Georges Michel La Reserve Chardonnay ★★★☆

The 2002 vintage (★★★☆), grown at Rapaura, was tank-fermented and then matured for nine months in new French oak barriques, with regular lees-stirring. It's an elegant wine, fresh and lively, with grapefruit-like fruit characters, finely integrated oak and a crisp finish.

Vintage	02	01	00	99
WR	7	7	6	6
Drink	04-07	04-06	P	P

DRY $29 -V

Drylands Marlborough Chardonnay ★★★☆

No longer carrying the Selaks brand, this popular wine is made by Nobilo. Fermented and matured in French and American oak casks, with regular lees-stirring, it is a drink-young style, typically punchy and vibrant. The 2003 vintage (★★★☆) shows toasty oak on the nose in an upfront style with fresh, citrusy flavours, some barrel-ferment complexity and very good depth and texture.

Vintage	03	02	01	00	99	98
WR	7	7	7	7	7	7
Drink	04-06	04-05	P	P	P	P

DRY $20 AV

Dry River Chardonnay ★★★★★

Elegance, restraint and subtle power are the key qualities of this distinctive Martinborough wine. It's not a bold, upfront style, but tight, savoury and seamless, with rich grapefruit and hazelnut flavours that build in the bottle for several years. Based on low-cropping (typically below 5 tonnes/hectare) Mendoza clone vines, it is hand-harvested, whole-bunch pressed and fermented in French oak barriques (averaging 24 per cent new). The proportion of the final blend that has gone through a softening malolactic fermentation has never exceeded 15 per cent. All delicacy and restraint in its youth, the 2002 vintage (★★★★☆) is finely poised, fresh and vibrant, with beautifully ripe grapefruit, melon and nut flavours and a rounded finish. It needs at least another year or two to break into full stride. The 2003 (★★★★★), from a very low-cropping season, is youthful, immaculate and intense, with a light lemon/green hue and rich grapefruit and peach flavours, threaded with fresh acidity. It's a beautifully poised wine with finely integrated oak and a minerally streak, already quite expressive, but with obvious potential; open 2006+.

Vintage	02	01	00	99	98	97	96
WR	7	7	7	7	7	7	6
Drink	04-09	04-07	04-05+	04-07	04-05	P	P

DRY $36 AV

🍇🍇

Equinox Hawke's Bay Barrel Fermented Chardonnay ★★★

The 2003 (★★★) was fermented and lees-aged for nine months in French oak barriques (30 per cent new), with partial malolactic fermentation. It's an upfront style (like the past vintages) with plenty of lemony, slightly honeyed and toasty flavour, and a crisp, minerally finish.

Vintage	03	02	01
WR	5	5	5
Drink	04-06	04-05	P

DRY $22 -V

Esk River Hawke's Bay Chardonnay ★★☆

The 2002 vintage (★★☆) from the winery formerly called Linden Estate is golden and quite developed for its age, with peachy, toasty, slightly honeyed flavours. Grown in the Esk Valley, the 2003 (★★☆) was half tank-fermented; the rest was fermented and matured for nine months in French oak casks. Yellow-hued, it's a crisp, toasty wine, advanced for its age, that lacks real fruit sweetness and depth.

DRY $19 -V

Esk River Reserve Chardonnay   ★★★☆

The pale gold, fleshy, richly flavoured 2002 vintage (★★★★) from the Hawke's Bay winery previously known as Linden Estate was grown in the Esk Valley and fermented and matured for nine months in French oak barriques (new and one-year-old). It's an upfront style, full-bodied and rounded, with sweet fruit delights and deep stone-fruit and toast flavours. The 2003 (★★★) is straw-hued, with strong butterscotch and toast aromas. It lacks the softness and richness of the 2002, but offers plenty of crisp, peachy, mealy flavour.

DRY $26 -V

Esk River Unoaked Chardonnay   (★★☆)

The 2004 vintage (★★☆) is a blend of Hawke's Bay and Gisborne grapes. Fresh fruit aromas lead into an easy-drinking wine with vibrant, lemony, appley flavours, simple but lively.

DRY $15 AV

Esk Valley Hawke's Bay Chardonnay   ★★★★

Given its affordable price, most recent vintages of this 'black label' wine have been unexpectedly classy. From a difficult season, the 2003 (★★★☆) is skilfully balanced for early drinking. Grown mostly in vineyards around the Bay View and Eskdale districts, which escaped the frosts, it was fermented and lees-aged for eight months in French and American oak barriques, with full malolactic fermentation. Pale yellow, with citrusy, slightly limey, toasty, buttery flavours, it's a fresh, crisp, tightly structured wine with good weight and depth.

Vintage	04	03	02	01	00	99	98
WR	7	6	7	6	7	6	6
Drink	04-07	04-06	04-06	04-05	P	P	P

DRY $20 V+

Esk Valley Reserve Chardonnay   ★★★★★

Since 1994, this has emerged as one of the most distinguished Chardonnays in Hawke's Bay. The 2002 vintage (★★★★★) is a beauty – highly fragrant and softly structured, with substantial body (14.5 per cent alcohol), gentle acidity and layers of peach, grapefruit and butterscotch flavours, complex and deep. Grown at Bay View, the 2003 (★★★★☆) is a single-vineyard wine, based on the Bernard 95 clone of Chardonnay, from Burgundy. Low-cropped, whole-bunch pressed, fermented and lees-aged for 10 months in French oak barriques (half new), and given a full malolactic fermentation, it's a concentrated, tightly structured wine, mouthfilling (14 per cent alcohol), with fresh acids underpinning its rich, citrusy, peachy, limey, biscuity flavours. A classy, refined wine, it's worth cellaring to 2006+.

Vintage	03	02	01	00	99	98
WR	6	6	NM	6	7	6
Drink	04-08	04-06	NM	04-06	04-06	P

DRY $33 V+

Fairhall Downs Marlborough Chardonnay   ★★★☆

Grown in the Brancott Valley, this single-vineyard wine is designed as a 'robust, fruit-driven style with a subtle hint of oak', but in fact the wood influence is quite strong. Matured for eight months in French and American oak, the 2003 vintage (★★★) has lifted, sweet oak aromas leading into a creamy, moderately complex palate with citrusy, appley flavours and a fractionally off-dry, smooth finish.

Vintage	03	02	01	00	99	98
WR	6	6	6	6	6	6
Drink	04-09	04-07	04-06	04-05	P	P

DRY $20 AV

Fairmont Estate Block One Chardonnay 2001   ★★★☆

Grown at Gladstone, south of Masterton, in the Wairarapa, the 2001 vintage (★★★☆) has 'a rich, citrusy, toasty bouquet, quite voluminous. The palate is smooth and rich, with peachy, lemony flavours, a hint of butterscotch and a soft finish. The 2002 (★★★★) is even better. Vibrant, citrusy and toasty, it's a weighty wine with excellent depth of ripe-grapefruit flavours, complexity and a well-rounded finish.

DRY $24 AV

Family Block McKenzie Vineyard
Marlborough Chardonnay   (★★★)

The 2003 vintage (★★★), sold by mail-order wine clubs, is an attractively fleshy, smooth wine with good weight and plenty of flavour, ripe and vibrantly fruity.

DRY $20 -V

Family Block Searle Vineyard Gisborne Chardonnay   (★★☆)

Sold by mail-order wine clubs, the 2003 vintage (★★☆) is a crisp, lemony wine, simple and slightly tart.

DRY $20 -V

Fat Cat Gisborne Chardonnay   ★★★

Fat Cat is made by Purr Productions of Huapai – a division of Coopers Creek. The goal is 'a fat, alcoholic wine with lots of oak – a wine that's just what the name suggests' (an unspecified portion of the proceeds goes to the SPCA). The 2003 vintage (★★☆) is a mouthfilling, peachy wine with assertive, toasty, nutty American oak characters. If you like woody Chardonnay, this is for you.

Vintage	04	03	02	01	00
WR	6	5	6	6	6
Drink	04-07	04-06	P	P	P

DRY $15 V+

Felton Road Barrel Fermented Chardonnay   ★★★★☆

This impressive Bannockburn wine typically possesses greater richness than most other Central Otago Chardonnays. The 2003 vintage (★★★★) was fermented with indigenous ('wild') yeasts in French oak casks (15 per cent new). Light yellow, it's a mouthfilling wine with peachy, toasty flavours threaded with fresh acidity and excellent complexity and intensity. Drink now or cellar.

Vintage	03	02	01	00	99	98
WR	6	7	7	6	6	6
Drink	04-09	04-08	04-05	P	04-05	P

DRY $30 AV

Felton Road Chardonnay   ★★★☆

The 2003 vintage (★★★☆) was handled entirely without oak, but malolactic fermentation and lees-aging were used to add complexity. Estate-grown at Bannockburn, in Central Otago, it's a pale yellow/green, vibrantly fruity wine with good body, plenty of lemony, appley, slightly nutty flavour and a fresh, crisp finish. A fruit-driven style with considerable class.

Vintage	03	02	01	00
WR	6	6	6	6
Drink	04-09	04-08	04-05	P

DRY $22 AV

Fiddler's Green Waipara Chardonnay   ★★★★

The 2002 vintage (★★★★) is a youthful, elegant wine, very fresh and crisp, with vibrant, ripe-fruit characters of peach and grapefruit, mealy, oaky complexities and a hint of butterscotch. Fermented and matured for 10 months in French oak barriques (30 per cent new), the 2003 (★★★☆) is pale straw, with delicate, ripe, citrusy, slightly appley flavours seasoned with biscuity oak and a creamy texture. A cool-climate style, it should be at its best 2005+.

Vintage	03	02	01
WR	6	6	6
Drink	05-07	04-06	04-05

`DRY $29 ·V`

Fierte Marlborough Chardonnay ★★★

The generous 2003 vintage (★★★☆) shows cellaring potential, with very good depth of ripe, citrusy, gently oaked flavour, fresh, tangy and youthful. (Sold by mail-order wine clubs.)

`DRY $19 AV`

Firstland Marlborough Chardonnay (★★☆)

Fermented in tanks and oak-aged for nine months, the 2002 vintage (★★☆) is a pale, youthful, uncomplicated wine with lemony, appley flavours, fresh and crisp.

`DRY $23 ·V`

Floating Mountain Aquilon Chardonnay (★★☆)

The 2003 vintage (★★☆) from Waipara winemaker Mark Rattray is a blend of Waipara and Nelson grapes. Matured for 10 months in seasoned oak barrels, it's a slightly honeyed wine with a crisp, green-edged finish.

`DRY $21 ·V`

Floating Mountain Mark Rattray Vineyard Waipara Chardonnay ★★★★

Mark Rattray's Chardonnays are typically powerful and lush. Barrel-matured for 10 months, the slowly evolving 2002 vintage (★★★☆) is weighty (14.5 per cent alcohol), with good intensity of fresh, ripe, citrusy fruit flavours and a fractionally off-dry, crisp finish.

Vintage	02	01
WR	6	5
Drink	04-06	04-05

`MED/DRY $25 AV`

Forrest Marlborough Chardonnay ★★★★

John Forrest favours a gently oaked style, looking to very ripe grapes and extended lees-aging to give his wine character. The 2002 vintage (★★★★) was 50 per cent wood-aged (in French and American oak casks); the rest was handled in tanks. Stylish and finely balanced, it offers vibrant, citrusy flavours of moderate intensity, well-integrated oak, some mealy complexity and good length.

Vintage	02	01	00	99	98	97	96
WR	6	6	5	6	6	5	5
Drink	04-07	04-05	P	P	P	P	P

`DRY $20 V+`

Forrest Vineyard Selection Chardonnay ★★★★

This is a more heavily oaked Marlborough wine than its stablemate (above) – the weighty, peachy, biscuity, smooth-flowing 2001 vintage (★★★★) was 100 per cent barrel-aged. The 2002 (★★★★) has lifted, mealy, barrel-ferment aromas. The palate is mouthfilling and citrusy, with a strong oak influence and good freshness and delicacy.

Vintage	02	01
WR	6	6
Drink	04-08	04-07

`MED/DRY $29 AV`

Fossil Ridge Nelson Chardonnay ★★★★

Grown by the Fry family in the Richmond foothills, this is a consistently impressive wine. The 2002 vintage (★★★☆) has creamy, sweet oak aromas, good weight, and ripe-grapefruit and toast flavours, with fresh acidity and some mealy complexity.

DRY $25 AV

Foxes Island Marlborough Chardonnay ★★★★☆

This richly flavoured, skilfully balanced Chardonnay is produced by John Belsham, a senior wine judge and vastly experienced winemaker. The 2002 vintage (★★★★☆) was fully fermented in French oak barriques (60 per cent new). Rich, creamy and rounded, it's a mouthfilling, tightly structured and yet highly approachable wine with vibrant, peachy, citrusy, biscuity flavours showing lots of barrel-ferment complexity and a distinct touch of butterscotch. There is no 2003.

Vintage	03	02	01	00	99
WR	NM	7	6	6	5
Drink	NM	04-06	04-05	P	P

DRY $34 AV

Framingham Marlborough Chardonnay ★★★★

Framingham is best known for Riesling, but the Chardonnays are always attractive and the 2003 vintage (★★★★) offers good value. Half the blend was handled in tanks; the rest was fermented in French oak barriques (25 per cent new), with lees-aging and malolactic fermentation. It's an elegant, harmonious and well-rounded wine with ripe, citrusy fruit characters shining through, buttery, nutty characters adding a touch of complexity and excellent mouthfeel, depth and texture.

Vintage	03	02	01	00
WR	6	6	6	5
Drink	04-07	04-05	04-05	P

DRY $22 V+

Francis-Cole Hawke's Bay Chardonnay ★★★

Simon Lampen's wine was previously marketed under the St Francis brand. The full-flavoured 2002 vintage (★★★) was matured for 14 months in French and American oak casks, and 60 per cent went through a softening malolactic fermentation. Yellow-hued, it's a soft, peachy, toasty, creamy wine, full-bodied, slightly honeyed and forward.

Vintage	02
WR	6
Drink	04-08

DRY $25 -V

Fromm La Strada Chardonnay ★★★★☆

The Fromm style is very different to the fresh, fruit-driven style of most Marlborough Chardonnays. Fully fermented with indigenous yeasts in French oak barriques (10 per cent new, to achieve a 'modest' wood influence), and barrel-aged for over a year, it is given a full, softening malolactic fermentation. The 2002 vintage (★★★★☆) is full of character and very harmonious. Grown at two sites (including the company-owned Clayvin vineyard) in the Brancott Valley, it's a fragrant, softly mouthfilling wine (14 per cent alcohol) with rich, grapefruit-like flavours gently seasoned with nutty oak and a creamy-smooth, lasting finish.

Vintage	03	02	01	00	99	98	97
WR	5	6	6	6	5	NM	4
Drink	04-07	04-07	04-06	04-05	P	NM	P

DRY $40 -V

Fromm La Strada Clayvin Vineyard Chardonnay ★★★★★

Fromm's premier Chardonnay, grown on the southern flanks of the Wairau Valley, was previously labelled Reserve, but since the 2001 vintage has been called Clayvin Vineyard (the clay soils, says winemaker Hatsch Kalberer, give 'a less fruity, more minerally and tighter character'). The pale straw 2002 vintage (★★★★★) is a wine of real individuality. Fermented with indigenous yeasts and matured for 22 months in French oak barriques (none new), it is powerful and bone-dry, with rich, stone-fruit flavours and a long, tautly structured finish. Deep and minerally, with a very restrained oak influence but notable structure and personality, it shows great cellaring potential.

Vintage	03	02	01	00	99	98	97	96	DRY $50 AV
WR	5	6	7	6	7	6	NM	7	
Drink	05-09	05-10	04-09	04-08	04-06	P	NM	04-08	

Gibbston Valley Greenstone Chardonnay ★★☆

Oak is not part of the recipe, but this is typically a fresh, vibrant wine with appetising acidity in a distinctly cool-climate style. The 2004 vintage (★★☆), blended from Marlborough and Central Otago grapes, offers crisp, lively, appley flavours in a simple but enjoyable style, pricey at $20.

Vintage	04	03	02	01	00	DRY $20 -V
WR	5	5	5	5	5	
Drink	04-06	04-05	04-05	P	P	

Gibbston Valley Reserve Chardonnay ★★★★

One of the top Central Otago Chardonnays, this is a far more complex wine than its Greenstone stablemate (above). The citrusy, subtle 2003 vintage (★★★☆) was fermented and lees-aged for 11 months in French oak barriques (15 per cent new), with full malolactic fermentation. Light yellow/green, it has biscuity, lemony aromas leading into a fresh, weighty palate showing good intensity of grapefruit, apple and butterscotch flavours, well-integrated oak and a crisp, flinty finish.

Vintage	03	02	01	00	99	DRY $32 -V
WR	6	7	6	6	7	
Drink	04-10	04-08	04-07	04-06	04-08	

Giesen Marlborough Chardonnay ★★★

With its standard Chardonnay, Giesen aims for 'elegance rather than power'. The 2002 (★★★) is creamy and slightly nutty, with a strong 'malo' influence. It is less vibrantly fruity than most of the region's Chardonnays, but shows some crisp, grapefruit-like characters.

Vintage	03	02	01	00	99	98	DRY $17 AV
WR	7	7	6	7	5	5	
Drink	04-06	04-06	P	P	P	P	

Giesen Reserve Barrel Selection Marlborough Chardonnay ★★★☆

The 2002 vintage (★★★★) is one of Giesen's finest Chardonnays yet. Youthful lemon/green, with creamy, 'malo' aromas, it's a full-bodied, finely balanced wine with grapefruit, pear and toast flavours showing excellent complexity and depth. It should be long-lived.

Vintage	02	01	DRY $22 AV
WR	7	7	
Drink	05-07	04-06	

Gladstone Wairarapa Chardonnay   ★★★★

Typically a soft and creamy wine, delicious in its youth. Half tank, half barrel-fermented, the 2002 vintage (★★★★) has good depth of fresh, lively peach and grapefruit flavours threaded with crisp acidity, some biscuity complexity and a seductively smooth finish.

Vintage	02	01	00	99	98
WR	6	6	NM	6	5
Drink	04-07	04-06	NM	P	P

DRY $23 V+

Goldridge Premium Reserve Marlborough Chardonnay   ★★★

The 2002 vintage (★★★☆) from this Matakana-based producer is a softly mouthfilling wine with plenty of peachy, slightly toasty flavour, a slightly creamy texture and well-rounded finish.

DRY $19 AV

Goldridge Premium Reserve Matakana Chardonnay   ★★★

The 2002 vintage (★★☆) is a crisp, toasty, flavoursome wine, but lacks fragrance and fresh, ripe-fruit characters. Past vintages, such as the richer and moderately complex 2000 (★★★☆), were more rewarding.

DRY $19 AV

Goldwater Roseland Marlborough Chardonnay   ★★★★

Typically a finely scented, weighty, vibrantly fruity wine with well-ripened, tropical-fruit characters and subtle use of oak in a moderately complex but highly attractive style. The 2003 vintage (★★★☆) was fermented and 'raised' on its yeast lees in French oak barriques (15 per cent new). Pale straw, with a slightly biscuity bouquet, it's mouthfilling and dry, with fresh, smooth, lemony, slightly mealy flavours showing good depth. Drink 2004–05.

Vintage	03	02	01	00	99	98
WR	6	7	7	7	7	7
Drink	04-07	04-06	04-05	P	P	P

DRY $20 V+

Goldwater Zell Chardonnay   ★★★★☆

Grown in the hillside, clay-based Zell vineyard on Waiheke Island, this is a rich, complex wine with the ripeness and roundness typical of northern Chardonnays. The 2002 vintage (★★★★☆) was hand-picked, whole-bunch pressed and fermented with indigenous yeasts in French oak casks (20 per cent new), with partial malolactic fermentation. Fleshy and well-rounded, with ripe flavours of stone-fruit, grapefruit and figs and a creamy texture, it's a classy wine, unfolding well with bottle-age.

Vintage	03	02	01	00	99
WR	6	7	6	7	7
Drink	04-08	04-08	04-06	04-05	04-05

DRY $30 AV

Gravitas Oaked Marlborough Chardonnay   ★★★★☆

Gravitas is the label of expatriate Kiwi Martyn Nicholls, whose company, St Arnaud's Vineyards, owns 30 hectares of vineyards in Marlborough. Fermented with indigenous yeasts, the 2002 vintage (★★★★☆) is strapping, lush and minerally, with lovely intensity of peach, butterscotch and nut flavours, mealy and very harmonious. The 2003 (★★★) is also stylish – a full, rich style with strong grapefruit and oak flavours. Softly textured, it offers mealy, biscuity complexities and impressive delicacy, harmony and length.

DRY $30 AV

Gravitas Unoaked Marlborough Chardonnay   (★★☆)

The 2003 vintage (★★☆) is a fresh, crisp, simple wine with citrusy, appley aromas and flavours. A solid but plain wine, it lacks the weight, complexity and richness of the top label (above).

`DRY $20 -V`

Greenhough Hope Vineyard Chardonnay   ★★★★☆

Only produced in top years, this powerful wine is estate-grown at Hope, in Nelson. Some vintages have been fermented in tanks and new French oak barriques; others (including the 2003) were fully barrel-fermented. The 2003 (★★★★) was made with indigenous (50 per cent) and commercial yeasts, restrained (17 per cent) use of new oak and 80 per cent malolactic fermentation. Pale, with a complex bouquet, it is tight and youthful, with a creamy yet crisp palate offering concentrated stone-fruit and grapefruit characters, nutty, minerally complexities and lots of personality. It needs time; open mid-2005+.

Vintage	03	02	01	00	99	98
WR	5	7	6	NM	NM	6
Drink	05-06	04-06	04-05	NM	NM	P

`DRY $30 AV`

Greenhough Nelson Vineyards Chardonnay   ★★★☆

This is a consistently attractive wine. The 2003 vintage (★★★☆) was hand-harvested, whole-bunch pressed and fermented in a mix of tanks (40 per cent) and French and American oak barrels (15 per cent new), with 25 per cent malolactic fermentation. An upfront style with a creamy, sweetly oaked bouquet, it's a full-bodied, moderately complex wine with strong, citrusy, slightly limey flavours, creamy and toasty.

Vintage	03	02	01	00	99	98
WR	5	7	6	6	5	5
Drink	04-05	04-05	P	P	P	P

`DRY $22 AV`

Grove Mill Innovator Croft Chardonnay   (★★★)

Named in honour of Peter Croft, a founder and long-serving director of the Marlborough winery, the 2002 vintage (★★★) was made from 'a specially selected parcel of ripe fruit', fermented and lees-aged for four months in tanks and French oak casks, and bottled young. Restrained on the nose, it is lemony, with good weight, some interesting minerally characters and a slightly austere, high-acid finish.

`DRY $24 -V`

Grove Mill Marlborough Chardonnay   ★★★★

Typically an attractive, skilfully balanced and flavoursome wine with well-integrated oak and fresh, crisp acidity. The 2002 vintage (★★★☆) was mostly (90 per cent) tank-fermented, but 10 per cent of the blend was French oak-fermented and half was matured in oak casks (20 per cent new). It's a tight, elegant wine, only moderately complex but offering fresh, grapefruit-like flavours with good delicacy and depth.

Vintage	02	01	00	99	98
WR	7	6	6	6	6
Drink	04-08	04-05	P	P	P

`DRY $23 V+`

Gunn Estate Skeetfield Chardonnay   (★★★☆)

The 2002 vintage (★★★☆) is the first since the established Gunn Estate brand was purchased by Sacred Hill. Grown in Hawke's Bay and fermented and matured for a year in French oak casks (new and one-year-old), it's an upfront style, deliciously drinkable in its youth, with ripe, faintly honeyed, stone-fruit characters, toasty oak and a well-rounded finish.

Vintage	02
WR	7
Drink	04-07

`DRY $25 -V`

Gunn Estate Unoaked Chardonnay   ★★☆

Produced by the fast-growing Hawke's Bay company Sacred Hill, the 2003 vintage (★★☆) is a solid but simple, slightly honeyed wine with moderate depth and a rounded finish. A blend of Gisborne and Hawke's Bay grapes, it's an easy-drinking style.

DRY $16 -V

Hanmer Junction, The, Unwooded Chardonnay   (★★★)

The 2002 vintage (★★★) of this Waipara wine was matured on its yeast lees for 10 months in tanks. Enjoyable in its youth, it offers plenty of fresh, crisp, citrusy flavour, with a sliver of sweetness (4.6 grams/litre) to smooth the finish.

Vintage	02
WR	6
Drink	P

DRY $16 AV

Hawkesbridge Marlborough Chardonnay   (★★☆)

Sold by mail-order wine clubs, the 2003 vintage (★★☆) is a fresh and crisp but simple wine with lemon and green-apple flavours showing moderate depth. (I have also tasted a taut, lemony, minerally Hawkesbridge Sophie's Vineyard Chardonnay 2003 (★★☆), which lacked real ripeness and richness.)

DRY $20 -V

Heron's Flight Barrique Fermented Chardonnay   ★★★☆

At its best, this Matakana Chardonnay is a classy wine with good weight and strong, ripe-fruit characters wrapped in toasty oak. Fermented and matured for a year in one-year-old French oak casks, it is typically generous, with very good depth of grapefruit and nut flavours.

DRY $27 -V

Heron's Flight La Volée Unoaked Chardonnay   ★★★

This tank-fermented Matakana Chardonnay typically offers good depth of melon and citrus fruit flavours in a simple but enjoyable style, with fresh acidity keeping things lively.

DRY $18 AV

Herzog Marlborough Chardonnay   ★★★★☆

At its best, this is a notably powerful, complex wine with layers of peach, butterscotch, grapefruit and nut flavours and a long, rounded finish. The 2002 vintage (★★★★) was lees-aged for a year in French oak barrels. It's a robust wine (14 per cent alcohol) with well-ripened, sweet fruit characters, strong grapefruit and peach flavours and a creamy, slightly off-dry finish. Tasted in its youth, it looked a logical candidate for the cellar.

Vintage	02	01
WR	6	6
Drink	04-10	05

MED/DRY $39 -V

Highfield Marlborough Chardonnay   ★★★★☆

A consistently classy wine. French oak-fermented and lees-aged, the stylish 2002 vintage (★★★★☆) has a youthful lemon/green colour and rich, inviting bouquet. It's a beautifully poised wine, big-bodied and creamy-smooth, with strong grapefruit and peach characters woven with fresh acidity and a seasoning of toasty oak. Maturing well, it's a good drink-now or cellaring proposition.

Vintage	02	01	00	99	98
WR	6	7	6	6	5
Drink	04-06	04-06	P	P	P

DRY $32 AV

Himmelsfeld Moutere Chardonnay ★★★☆

This rare Nelson wine is grown in Beth Eggers' vineyard in the Upper Moutere hills, near the Tasman Bay winery. Handled in American and French oak, it is typically creamy and mouthfilling, with peachy, toasty, smooth flavours showing good depth and complexity.

DRY $26 -V

Huia Marlborough Chardonnay ★★★★

The stylish 2002 vintage (★★★★) was hand-harvested in the Huia and Taylor vineyards, whole-bunch pressed and fermented with indigenous yeasts in French oak casks. Creamy and smooth, with ripe-grapefruit flavours delicately seasoned with oak, it shows excellent weight, roundness, complexity and depth, with a tight finish. It's drinking well now, but should mature gracefully.

Vintage	02	01	00	99
WR	7	6	6	7
Drink	04-07	04-05	04-05	P

DRY $25 AV

Huntaway Reserve Gisborne Chardonnay ★★★★

This former Corbans label, now an Allied Domecq (NZ) brand, is made in a high-impact, creamy-rich style, delicious in its youth. From a top vintage, the 2002 (★★★★☆) was harvested (20 per cent by hand) at 23 brix, and fermented and matured for nine months, with weekly lees-stirring, in French (85 per cent) and American oak barriques. Very creamy and toasty on the nose, it's an upfront style, ripe and smooth, with good intensity of tropical-fruit characters seasoned with toasty oak. Maturing well, it delivers great value.

Vintage	02	01	00	99	98
WR	7	NM	7	6	7
Drink	04-06	NM	P	P	P

DRY $20 V+

Hunter's Marlborough Chardonnay ★★★★☆

Finesse is the key attribute of this consistently immaculate wine, which places its accent on fresh, vibrant, searching, citrusy flavours, overlaid with subtle, mealy barrel-ferment characters. About 40 per cent of the blend is fermented and lees-aged in new French oak barriques (medium toast); the rest is tank-fermented and then matured in one and two-year-old casks. It is a proven performer in the cellar. Delicious now, the 2001 vintage (★★★★☆) is a typically great buy. Fragrant, with grapefruit and butterscotch aromas, it has sweet fruit delights, with ripe, peachy, citrusy flavours, a gentle, biscuity oak influence and a smooth, creamy texture.

Vintage	02	01	00	99	98	97	96
WR	5	6	6	5	6	6	5
Drink	04-07	04-06	04-05	04-05	P	P	P

DRY $22 V+

Hunter's Single Vineyard Marlborough Chardonnay (★★★★)

The 2002 vintage (★★★★) was barrel-fermented and oak-aged for 19 months. The bouquet is lifted, fresh and attractive, with integrated fruit and wood; the palate is tightly structured, with fresh, strong, lemony, slightly toasty flavours that linger well.

DRY $25 AV

Hyperion Helios Chardonnay ★★★

The 2003 vintage (★★★) of this Matakana wine was estate-grown, hand-picked, whole-bunch pressed and fermented and lees-aged for five months in French oak casks. Light-medium yellow, it's a full-bodied wine with strong peachy, biscuity, slightly honeyed flavours, showing considerable complexity. Drink now or cellar briefly.

Vintage	03	02	01	00
WR	5	7	6	7
Drink	04-07	04-07	04-06	P

DRY $25 -V

Hyperion Selene Chardonnay   ★★☆

Labelled as a straight Chardonnay (unlike past vintages, labelled as a Chardonnay/Pinot Gris blend), the 2002 vintage (★★☆) of this unoaked Matakana wine is a medium-dry style, offering easy, no-fuss drinking. It's a full-bodied wine with lemony, appley, slightly spicy flavours and a smooth finish. There is no 2003.

Vintage	03	02		MED/DRY $20 ·V
WR	NM	4		
Drink	NM	P		

Isabel Marlborough Chardonnay   ★★★★☆

This prestigious producer is after 'a tight, restrained style [in] a deliberate move away from the somewhat overbearing, heavily oaked and fruity wines currently in vogue'. It is one of the region's most distinguished Chardonnays – notably complex and minerally rather than fruity, with very impressive subtlety, vigour and length. Based on well-established Mendoza vines, it is fermented with a mix of indigenous and cultured yeasts in new and seasoned French oak barriques (60 per cent) and tanks (40 per cent), and given a full, softening malolactic fermentation. Tasted in late 2004, the light yellow 2003 (★★★☆) was very youthful, with citrusy aromas and a slightly flinty, minerally palate with fresh, crisp, grapefruit and toast flavours, lacking the richness of past vintages. Open 2006+.

Vintage	03	02	01	00	01	99	98	97	96	DRY $30 AV
WR	7	6	7	7	6	5	5	5	4	
Drink	05-06	05-09	05-09	04-08	04-07	04-06	04-05	P	P	

Jackson Estate Chardonnay   ★★★☆

Although best known for its classy Sauvignon Blanc, this Marlborough producer's Chardonnay is consistently enjoyable. It is grown in the heart of the Wairau Valley and French oak-aged for 10 months. The 2002 vintage (★★★☆) is a fruit-driven style with good body and ripe-grapefruit flavours, lightly seasoned with biscuity oak. A very harmonious wine with fresh acidity and a slightly creamy finish, it's already drinking well. (The barrel-fermented Reserve Chardonnay has been phased out [last vintage 1999], but an Unoaked Chardonnay was launched from 2003.)

Vintage	02	01	00	99	98	DRY $20 AV
WR	5	7	6	6	6	
Drink	04-06	04-05	P	P	P	

Jackson Estate Unoaked Chardonnay   (★★★)

A good example of the style, the 2003 vintage (★★★) is a pale, youthful Marlborough wine, crisp and weighty, with good depth of citrusy, appley flavours threaded with fresh acidity.

Vintage	03	DRY $17 AV
WR	5	
Drink	04-05	

Julicher Martinborough Chardonnay   (★★★)

The barrel-fermented 2003 vintage (★★★) is very soft and creamy. Made by Chris Buring, it has toasty, buttery, 'malo' aromas leading into a fleshy, grapefruit and apple-flavoured palate with some mealy complexity.

Vintage	03	DRY $26 ·V
WR	5	
Drink	04-08	

Julicher Unoaked Chardonnay   (★★★)

Grown on the Te Muna Terraces at Martinborough and made by Chris Buring, the 2002 vintage (★★★) is yellow/green in hue with a fleshy, weighty palate (14 per cent alcohol). Buttery, creamy characters hold sway, with a smooth finish.

Vintage 02
WR   4   DRY $20 -V
Drink   04-07

Kahurangi Estate Heaphy Series Moutere Chardonnay (★★★★)

Sold by mail-order wine clubs, the 2003 vintage (★★★★) is a good buy. A full-flavoured Nelson wine, it shows good freshness and intensity of ripe, tropical-fruit characters, with toasty oak adding complexity and a rounded finish.

DRY $21 V+

Kahurangi Estate Mt Arthur Chardonnay   ★★★★

Named after the highest peak in Kahurangi National Park, the robust 2003 vintage (★★★★) is promoted as a 'big wine, like the mountain itself'. Grown in the Upper Moutere hills and fermented and matured for seven months in oak barrels (new and two-year-old), it's a powerful wine (14.5 per cent alcohol) with toasty oak aromas and lush, concentrated stone-fruit flavours. An upfront style, fleshy and creamy, it's quite forward; drink now onwards.

Vintage 03
WR   5   DRY $25 AV
Drink   05-08

Kahurangi Estate Moutere Chardonnay   ★★

The 2002 vintage (★★☆), a lightly oaked Nelson wine, offered crisp grapefruit and green apple flavours, with a touch of biscuity oak, but also showed a slight lack of freshness and vibrancy. The pale straw, full-bodied 2003 (★★), both tank and barrel-fermented, is similar.

Vintage 03
WR   5   DRY $21 -V
Drink   05-08

Kahurangi Estate Unwooded Chardonnay   ★★★

The 2003 vintage (★★★) of this full-bodied Nelson wine is a good example of the unoaked style. Hand-picked, whole-bunch pressed, and cool-fermented and lees-aged in tanks, it's a crisp, lemony, appley wine, full-bodied, fresh and lively, with good depth of flavour.

Vintage 02
WR   4   DRY $18 AV
Drink   04-05

Kaikoura Unoaked Marlborough Chardonnay   ★★★

The bright, light yellow/green 2002 vintage (★★★☆) was grown in four Wairau Valley vineyards and handled entirely in stainless steel tanks. With its mouthfilling body (14 per cent alcohol) and ripe, tropical-fruit flavours, it would be quite at home in a tasting of Australian Chardonnays. Still drinking well, it has lots of character, with a rounded, dryish rather than bone-dry finish.

DRY $18 AV

Kaimira Estate Brightwater Chardonnay ★★★★

Top vintages of this Nelson wine are classy. Estate-grown and fermented and matured for 10 months in French oak barriques (30 per cent new), the pale gold 2003 (★★★☆) is slightly advanced for its age, in a softly mouthfilling, creamy style with strong peach, butterscotch and toast flavours. Drink now onwards.

Vintage	03	02	01	00	DRY $22 V+
WR	6	6	6	6	
Drink	04-07	04-05	P	P	

Kaimira Estate Nelson Chardonnay ★★★

Fermented and lees-aged in tanks, with 'light' oak treatment, the 2002 (★★★) is a crisply mouthfilling wine with slightly creamy and mealy characters and decent depth of ripe, peachy fruit flavours. There is no 2003, but the label returns from the 2004 vintage.

Vintage	02	01	00	DRY $18 AV
WR	5	4	6	
Drink	04-05	P	P	

Kaimira Estate Unoaked Chardonnay ★★★

In its infancy, the 2003 vintage (★★☆) was so lively and green-edged you could almost mistake it for a brisk, limey Sauvignon Blanc. Grown in the Moutere Hills, the 2004 (★★★) is fresh, vibrant and full-bodied (14 per cent alcohol), with ripe-citrus fruit and melon flavours and a slightly sweet, crisp finish. As a drink-young style, it's very appealing.

MED/DRY $16 AV

Kaituna Valley Canterbury
The Kaituna Vineyard Chardonnay ★★★★

Grown on Banks Peninsula, this is a consistently characterful and enjoyable wine, priced right. The 2002 (★★★★) is weighty, with rich, peachy, slightly toasty flavours and a finely balanced finish. The 2003 vintage (★★★☆), harvested at 23 brix, was fermented in French oak barriques (55 per cent new), with 70 per cent malolactic fermentation. It's a slightly cheesy, strongly 'malo'-influenced wine with mouthfilling body, good depth of peach and grapefruit flavours, and a soft, creamy texture.

Vintage	03	02	01	00	DRY $20 V+
WR	5	5	6	5	
Drink	04-07	04-06	04-06	04-05	

Kaituna Valley Marlborough
The Awatere Vineyard Chardonnay ★★★★

Grown in Grant and Helen Whelan's vineyard in the Awatere Valley and fermented and matured for a year in French oak barriques, this is a classy wine with great drinkability. The 2002 vintage (★★★★) is full-bodied (13.9 per cent alcohol) and vibrant, with fresh acidity, ripe, peachy, citrusy flavours shining through, slight mineral and butterscotch characters and a bone-dry finish.

Vintage	02	01	00	DRY $24 V+
WR	7	6	6	
Drink	04-06	04-05	P	

Karaka Point Vineyard Chardonnay (★★★☆)

Grown at Waiau Pa, south of the Manukau Harbour in South Auckland, the 2002 vintage (★★★☆) is a characterful, distinctive wine, mouthfilling and ripe, with concentrated, fresh peach and pear flavours, a buttery 'malo' influence and savoury, spicy oak adding complexity.

DRY $25 -V

Karikari Estate Reserve Chardonnay   (★★★☆)

From New Zealand's northernmost vineyard and winery, the 2003 vintage (★★★☆) is an auspicious debut. Made by Kim Crawford, it was fully barrel-fermented, with 100 per cent malolactic fermentation. Bright lemon/green, with fragrant toast and butterscotch aromas, it's a weighty wine with ripe, peachy, citrusy flavours, strongly seasoned with oak. It should mature well.

Vintage   03
WR   5   DRY $30 -V
Drink   04-06

Kathy Lynskey Godfrey Reserve Chardonnay   (★★★☆)

The 2003 vintage (★★★☆) of this Marlborough wine was fermented and lees-aged for 10 months in French oak casks (40 per cent new), with full malolactic fermentation. It's a strongly wooded style but already drinking well, with butterscotch characters and a soft, creamy texture.

DRY $35 -V

Kathy Lynskey Wairau Peaks Marlborough Chardonnay ★★★★

This is a consistently impressive wine. The 2002 vintage (★★★★) was estate-grown, harvested at 24 brix, fermented with indigenous and cultured yeasts in French oak barrels and lees-aged in wood for 10 months. It's a fragrant, generous, grapefruit and toast-flavoured wine showing good concentration, a delicious softness of texture (boosted by more than 4 grams per litre of residual sugar) and strong upfront appeal.

Vintage	02	01	00	99
WR	6	6	7	6
Drink	04-05	P	P	P

DRY $29 AV

Kawarau Estate Chardonnay   ★★☆

Grown organically near Lowburn, in Central Otago, this is a fruit-driven style – 10 to 15 per cent of the blend is fermented in old French oak casks, with the rest handled entirely in stainless steel tanks. At its best, it is lively, crisp and vibrant. The 2003 vintage (★★☆) is fruity and fresh, with straightforward, citrusy, appley flavours.

DRY $19 -V

Kawarau Estate Reserve Chardonnay   ★★★☆

Grown organically at Lowburn, north of Cromwell in Central Otago, this is a consistently satisfying, full-flavoured wine. The 2003 vintage (★★★) was fermented and matured in French oak casks (20 per cent new), with full malolactic fermentation. Fresh and full-bodied, it's a harmonious wine with a slightly creamy mouthfeel and good depth of grapefruit and lime flavours.

Vintage	03	02	01	00	99	98
WR	5	6	4	5	4	5
Drink	04-06	04-06	P	P	P	P

DRY $24 AV

Kemblefield The Distinction Chardonnay   ★★★★

Previously labelled Hawke's Bay Chardonnay (the 2000 vintage was marketed under both names), this is the key wine in the Kemblefield range. Estate-grown in the slightly elevated, relatively cool Mangatahi district, it is French oak-fermented and matured on its yeast lees for up to 14 months. The 2002 vintage (★★★★) was handled in 50 per cent new oak casks, with partial malolactic fermentation. Light yellow, with toasty oak aromas, it's a robust (14 per cent alcohol), creamy wine with strong stone-fruit, toast and butterscotch flavours and good complexity. Delicious drinking now onwards.

Vintage	02	01	00	99	98	97	96
WR	7	NM	7	7	7	7	6
Drink	04-07	NM	04-05	P	P	P	P

DRY $27 AV

Kemblefield Winemakers Signature Chardonnay ★★★

This is the Hawke's Bay winery's bottom-tier Chardonnay, despite its upmarket name. It is a further source of confusion that the words 'Winemakers Signature' appear solely on the back label, with winemaker John Kemble's signature on the front. Estate-grown at Mangatahi, tank-fermented and 'lightly' oaked, the 2002 vintage (★★★) is an attractive wine with vibrant fruit characters, peachy, citrusy and tangy. Showing good freshness and drive, it's a highly enjoyable drink-young style.

DRY $17 AV

Kerr Farm Limited Release Kumeu Chardonnay ★★☆

The 2002 vintage (★★☆) was estate-grown in West Auckland and fermented in French and American oak casks (30 per cent new). Yellow-hued, it's maturing solidly, with ripe, peachy flavours, slightly toasty and creamy, in a rounded, northern style. Verging on three stars.

Vintage	02	01	00
WR	7	6	7
Drink	04-07	04-05	04-05

DRY $25 -V

Kim Crawford Doc's Block Chardonnay ★★★☆

Sold only at the cellar door, the 2003 vintage (★★★★) is a sturdy, softly structured Hawke's Bay wine with toasty oak aromas, ripe, citrusy, biscuity flavours and a creamy-smooth texture. It's a big wine with some complexity and good length.

Vintage	03
WR	4
Drink	05-07

DRY $20 AV

Kim Crawford Doc's Block Hawke's Bay Chardonnay (★★★)

Weighty and creamy, with fullness of body and buttery, oaky flavours, the 2002 vintage (★★★) has plenty of drink-young appeal.

DRY $25 -V

Kim Crawford Marlborough Unoaked Chardonnay ★★★

Given a full, softening malolactic fermentation, this is an enjoyable drink-young style. The 2004 vintage (★★★) shows a strong 'malo' influence, with pronounced butterscotch characters and a peachy, fractionally off-dry (4 grams/litre of residual sugar) finish.

Vintage	04	03	02	01	00	99	98
WR	7	6	6	6	6	5	6
Drink	05-08	04-08	04-05	P	P	P	P

DRY $20 -V

Kim Crawford Te Awanga Vineyard Hawke's Bay Chardonnay ★★★

The developed 2001 vintage (★★☆) is golden, with firm acidity and honeyed, botrytis characters showing. Likely to be much longer-lived, the clearly superior 2002 (★★★★) is weighty and generous, with peach, butterscotch and toasty oak flavours in an upfront style. Its ripe-fruit flavours are slightly overpowered by oak, but the wine has good mouthfeel and plenty of character.

DRY $30 -V

Kim Crawford Tietjen/Briant Gisborne Chardonnay ★★★★☆

Made in an upfront style, this is typically one of Gisborne's boldest Chardonnays, with rich, ripe citrus/melon flavours, strongly laced with oak. Lush and soft, the 2002 vintage (★★★★) was grown in the Tietjen and Briant vineyards, fermented in American oak barriques (half new) and given a full malolactic fermentation. It's a seductive style showing excellent body and flavour depth, with well-ripened fruit characters, heaps of sweet, toasty oak, mealy, biscuity complexities and a creamy-smooth finish.

Vintage	02	01	00	99	98	DRY $30 AV
WR	7	NM	5	NM	7	
Drink	05-06	NM	P	NM	P	

Kim Crawford Unoaked Chardonnay (★★★)

Offering plenty of drink-young charm, the 2004 vintage (★★★) is a more vibrant, less obviously 'malo'-influenced wine than its unoaked Marlborough stablemate (above). A regional blend, it has fresh, fragrant fruit aromas and flavours, with lively grapefruit and peach characters and a rounded (4 grams/litre of residual sugar) finish.

Vintage	04	DRY $16 AV
WR	6	
Drink	05-06	

Kina Beach Vineyard Reserve Chardonnay (★★★★☆)

The powerful, lush 2003 vintage (★★★★☆) was harvested at a soaring 26.8 brix in Dave and Pam Birt's vineyard at Kina Beach, on the coast at Nelson, and made on their behalf by John Kavanagh. Matured for 11 months in new and one-year-old French oak barriques, it is pale yellow, with a highly fragrant bouquet of stone-fruit and toasty oak. A bold style, with commanding mouthfeel and excellent freshness and concentration, it is already full of character, but should be at its best during 2005–06.

DRY $30 AV

Kirkpatrick Estate Unwooded Chardonnay (NR)

Tasted just before bottling (and so not rated), the 2004 vintage from the Gisborne winery previously called Shalimar Estate is a fresh and vibrant, slightly sweet wine with ripe, pure fruit flavours of melons, limes and pears.

MED/DRY $16 V?

Koura Bay Mount Fyffe Chardonnay ★★★

Named after the peak overlooking the town of Kaikoura, this Marlborough wine is fermented in contact with American oak 'beans', rather than barrel-fermented, and matured on its yeast lees in tanks. The pale 2003 vintage (★★☆) is crisp and simple, with lemony, appley flavours that lack any real richness and complexity.

Vintage	03	DRY $20 -V
WR	7	
Drink	04-07	

Kumeu River Kumeu Chardonnay   ★★★★★

One of the country's most celebrated Chardonnays, this is typically a superbly constructed West Auckland wine, rich and powerful, with beautifully interwoven flavours and a seductively creamy texture. The key to its outstanding quality lies in the vineyards, says winemaker Michael Brajkovich: 'We manage to get the grapes very ripe.' Grown at five sites around Kumeu, fermented with indigenous yeasts and lees-aged (with weekly lees-stirring) in Burgundy oak barriques (typically 20–25 per cent new each year), the wine also normally undergoes a full malolactic fermentation. The 2003 vintage (★★★★☆) is from a low-cropping year – only 2200 cases were produced, instead of the usual 5000 cases. The bouquet is rich and nutty; the palate tight and refined, with deep grapefruit-like flavours and firm acidity giving a minerally, flinty character. It's a less lush, more tautly structured wine than the 2002, worth cellaring to mid-2005+.

Vintage	04	03	02	01	00	99
WR		7	6	7	6	7	6
Drink	06-09	05-07	05-08	04-06	04-06	04-06

DRY $36 AV

Kumeu River Mate's Vineyard Kumeu Chardonnay   ★★★★★

This extremely classy single-vineyard wine is Kumeu River's flagship. It is made entirely from the best of the fruit harvested from Mate's Vineyard, planted in 1990 on the site of the original Kumeu River vineyard purchased by Mate Brajkovich in 1944. Strikingly similar to Kumeu River Kumeu Chardonnay, but slightly more opulent and concentrated, it offers the same rich and harmonious flavours of grapefruit, peach and butterscotch, typically with a stronger seasoning of new French oak. For winemaker Michael Brajkovich, the hallmark of Mate's Vineyard is 'a pear-like character on the nose, with richness and length on the palate after two to three years'. The 2003 (★★★★★) is as usual slightly bolder than the Kumeu River Chardonnay, in a very Burgundian style with deep, minerally, citrusy flavours threaded with firm acidity and a taut, slightly creamy finish. It's a concentrated and immaculate wine, worth cellaring to 2006+.

Vintage	04	03	02	01	00	99
WR		7	6	7	6	7	6
Drink	06-10	05-08	05-08	04-06	04-06	04-06

DRY $47 AV

Kumeu River Village Kumeu Chardonnay   ★★★

Kumeu River's lower-tier, drink-young wine, in the past sold under the Brajkovich brand, is made from heavier-bearing clones of Chardonnay than the Mendoza used for the top wines and is normally fermented with indigenous yeasts in a mix of tanks (principally) and seasoned French oak casks. However, due to the tiny crop, the 2003 vintage (★★★☆) was fully barrel-fermented. Light yellow, it's a slightly creamy wine with firm acidity and grapefruit, biscuit and butterscotch flavours showing very good depth and considerable complexity. Drink 2004–05.

DRY $18 AV

Lake Chalice Block Two Marlborough Chardonnay   (★★★)

Despite the name, the 2002 vintage (★★★) was grown in several vineyards in the Wairau Valley. It was made in the same style (and at the same price) as the Vineyard Selection Chardonnay, but grown at different sites. Both tank and barrel-fermented, with full malolactic fermentation, it's a very easy-drinking wine with ripe, citrusy flavours, some leesy complexity and a creamy-smooth finish.

Vintage	02
WR	6
Drink	04-06

DRY $20 -V

Lake Chalice Flight 42 Unoaked Chardonnay   (★★☆)

A drink-young style, the 2004 vintage (★★☆) of this Marlborough wine was tank-fermented and 40 per cent of the blend went through a softening malolactic fermentation. Fresh and vibrant, it's a fractionally off-dry wine with a slightly creamy texture and straightforward, citrusy, appley flavours showing decent depth.

Vintage	04
WR	6
Drink	04-07

DRY $19 -V

Lake Chalice Marlborough Chardonnay   ★★★☆

This 'black label' wine is typically fresh and creamy, with drink-young appeal. Grown in several Wairau Valley vineyards and both tank (70 per cent) and barrel-fermented, with full malolactic fermentation, the 2003 vintage (★★★) is pale, with creamy, 'malo' aromas. Full-bodied and rounded, with fresh, lemony, appley flavours and a distinct touch of butterscotch, it's already drinking well.

Vintage	03	02	01	00	99	98
WR	6	6	7	7	6	7
Drink	04-07	04-05	P	P	P	P

DRY $20 AV

Lake Chalice Platinum Marlborough Chardonnay   ★★★★☆

This typically lush, rich and complex wine is estate-grown in the Falcon vineyard, hand-picked, whole-bunch pressed, fermented in French oak barriques (half new), lees-aged for eight months and given a full malolactic fermentation. It typically offers strong, nutty, mealy flavours and a very creamy texture in a fragrant, full-blown Chardonnay style. The 2002 vintage (★★★★) is weighty, with concentrated, ripe, citrusy, mealy, buttery flavours showing good complexity and fresh acidity. Due to frosts, there is no 2003.

Vintage	03	02	01	00	99	98
WR	NM	7	7	7	7	7
Drink	NM	04-07	04-06	04-05	04-05	P

DRY $28 V+

Landmark Estate Gisborne Chardonnay   (★★★)

From a long-established West Auckland winery, the 2002 vintage (★★★) is a simple but skilfully made wine, pale yellow, with fresh, citrusy aromas and crisp, lively, lemony flavours.

DRY $20 -V

Lawson's Dry Hills Marlborough Chardonnay   ★★★★

This is typically an impressively ripe and robust wine with concentrated, peachy, toasty, buttery flavours. The bright yellow 2001 vintage (★★★★) was grown in the Wairau Valley, harvested at 24 brix and fermented in new to four-year-old French oak barriques (10 per cent was handled in tanks), with partial malolactic fermentation. Maturing well, it possesses punchy, well-ripened grapefruit and toast flavours, now starting to round out, with a backbone of fresh acidity and substantial body.

Vintage	02	01	00	99	98
WR	6	6	6	6	5
Drink	04-06	04-05	P	P	P

DRY $25 AV

Lawson's Dry Hills Unoaked Chardonnay   (★★★☆)

Enjoyable from the start, the 2004 vintage (★★★☆) was grown in Marlborough and cool-fermented in tanks, with extended lees contact and stirring. It's a mouthfilling wine (14 per cent alcohol) with peach and butterscotch characters holding sway, plenty of flavour and a smooth, dryish (5 grams/litre of residual sugar) finish.

MED/DRY $19 V+

Leaning Rock Chardonnay   ★★☆

Grown at Alexandra, in Central Otago, and partly French oak-fermented, the 2003 vintage (★★★) is a lemony, appley, fruit-driven style, clean and fresh, with good body, subtle oak and a crisp, slightly buttery finish.

Vintage	03	02	01	00	99
WR	6	NM	NM	NM	5
Drink	04-06	NM	NM	NM	P

DRY $22 -V

Le Grys Unwooded Chardonnay   (★★★)

Produced by Mud House Wine Company, the 2002 vintage (★★★) is fresh and light, with lemony, appley, rounded flavours. It lacks real complexity and concentration, but is enjoyable in a simple, fruit-driven style.

DRY $20 -V

Lincoln Heritage Barrique Fermented Chardonnay   ★★★☆

Made in a rich, strongly oak-influenced, upfront style, Lincoln's middle-tier Chardonnay is dedicated to Patricia, daughter-in-law of the founder, Petar Fredatovich. The 2003 vintage (★★★☆) was grown in the Parklands Estate vineyard in Gisborne and fermented and lees-aged for eight months in French oak barriques, 15 per cent new (past releases were handled in American oak). A youthful, fragrant wine with very good depth of grapefruit, peach, butterscotch and oak flavours, it's a slightly more restrained style than past vintages, likely to age well.

Vintage	03	02
WR	6	6
Drink	04-09	04-07

DRY $19 V+

Lincoln Heritage East Coast Unoaked Chardonnay   ★★☆

Lincoln's bottom-tier Chardonnay (in the past called Winemakers Series) delivers fresh, simple fruit flavours and a smooth finish. Tasted prior to bottling (and so not rated), the 2004 vintage is a tank-fermented and lees-aged Gisborne wine, fresh and vibrant, with plenty of ripe, rounded flavour.

Vintage	04
WR	6
Drink	04-07

DRY $15 AV

Lincoln Reserve Chardonnay   (★★★★)

The rich, rounded 2002 vintage (★★★★) replaced the President's Selection label (last made in 2000) as Lincoln's top Chardonnay. Grown in Chris Parker's vineyard at Gisborne and fermented and matured for a year in French oak barriques, it has toasty oak aromas leading into a fleshy, creamy-smooth palate with ripe-fruit flavours of peach, fig and grapefruit and a touch of butterscotch. A softly textured wine, it shows good concentration. Tasted prior to bottling (and so not rated), the 2004 is a promising, single-vineyard Hawke's Bay wine with elegant fruit characters and good intensity.

Vintage	03	02
WR	NM	6
Drink	NM	04-07

DRY $29 AV

Lincoln Winemakers Series Chardonnay   ★★☆

Lincoln's bottom-tier Chardonnay offers fresh, simple fruit flavours and a smooth finish. The 2002 vintage (★★☆), grown in Gisborne and faintly oaked (5 per cent of the blend was wood-aged), is crisp, fruity and lively, delivering no-fuss, moderately priced drinking.

Vintage	02	01	00
WR	6	6	6
Drink	04-05	P	P

DRY $14 AV

Longridge Vineyards Chardonnay ★★★

Part of the Allied Domecq (NZ) portfolio, this wine showcases fresh, ripe-fruit characters, with a delicate oak underlay. The 2003 vintage (★★★), 90 per cent fermented in French and American oak casks (the rest was handled in tanks), is a blend of Gisborne (80 per cent) and Hawke's Bay grapes. Fresh, citrusy and slightly biscuity, it's an easy-drinking wine with a sweet oak influence and a smooth finish.

Vintage	02	01	00	99	98
WR	6	NM	7	7	7
Drink	P	NM	P	P	P

DRY $15 V+

Longview Estate Barrique Fermented Chardonnay (★★☆)

Estate-grown just south of Whangarei, the 2000 vintage (★★☆) was matured for 16 months in French oak casks. It's a full-bodied, creamy, assertively wooded wine with ripe, melon-like fruit flavours, but when re-tasted in 2004 looked past its best.

Vintage	00
WR	5
Drink	04-05

DRY $19 -V

Longview Estate Unwooded Chardonnay ★★★

This Northland winery has produced attractive unoaked ('timber-free', as the winery puts it) Chardonnays since 1998. Estate-grown just south of Whangarei, the 2002 vintage (★★☆) is a solid wine, full-bodied, crisp, lemon and appley, but less aromatic and vibrantly fruity than in top years.

Vintage	02
WR	5
Drink	P

MED/DRY $18 AV

Loopline Vineyard Wairarapa Chardonnay ★★☆

Grown at Opaki, just north of Masterton, the 2002 vintage (★★★) was fermented and matured for nine months in French oak casks. It's a mouthfilling wine with a distinctly buttery bouquet, ripe peach and grapefruit flavours, strong butterscotch and toast characters and a fresh, crisp finish.

Vintage	02	01
WR	6	6
Drink	04-06	04-06

DRY $25 -V

Mahi Twin Valleys Vineyard Chardonnay (★★★★☆)

Mahi is the personal label of Seresin Estate winemaker, Brian Bicknell. Complex and richly flavoured, the 2003 vintage (★★★★☆) was grown in the Fareham Lane district, where the Waihopai Valley meets the Wairau Valley, and fermented with indigenous yeasts in French oak barriques. Light yellow, with stone-fruit and toast aromas, it's a weighty, rounded wine with sweet fruit delights and lush flavours of peaches, toast, honey and butterscotch. Drink now onwards.

Vintage	03
WR	6
Drink	04-07

DRY $30 AV

Mahurangi Estate Mahurangi Chardonnay ★★★

Mahurangi Estate lies near Warkworth, north of Auckland. Fermented and lees-aged for six months in one and two-year-old oak barriques, the 2003 vintage (★★★) is light yellow, with grapefruit, peach and toast flavours and a slightly creamy texture. It's quite advanced for its age; drink 2004–05.

DRY $18 AV

Main Divide Canterbury Chardonnay   ★★★

The Main Divide range is from Pegasus Bay. The 2002 vintage (★★☆) is a golden, full-bodied, fairly
developed wine with peach, butterscotch and honey flavours, suggesting some botrytis influence. The 2003
(★★★) was barrel-fermented, lees-aged and given a full, softening malolactic fermentation. Pale yellow, it's
a mouthfilling wine with good depth of peach, grapefruit and slight honey flavours, showing some
complexity and richness.

Vintage	03	02	01	00	99
WR	6	6	7	6	6
Drink	04-08	04-07	04-05	P	P

DRY $20 -V

Margrain Martinborough Chardonnay   ★★★★☆

This is typically a powerful, sophisticated wine with rich fruit wrapped in toasty, nutty oak and impressive
weight and depth. French oak-fermented and wood-aged for 10 months, the 2003 (★★★★) is from an
ultra low-cropping vintage (1.5 tonnes/hectare). Light yellow, it is fragrant, tight and slightly minerally, with
fresh acidity woven through its grapefruit, peach and toast flavours. It needs time; open 2006+.

Vintage	02	01	00	99	98
WR	6	6	6	7	6
Drink	04-06	04-06	04-05	04-05	P

DRY $32 AV

Marlborough Wines Limited Chardonnay   (★★)

The 2003 vintage (★★) is a very light and plain wine with simple, lemony, appley flavours.

DRY $17 -V

Marsden Black Rocks Chardonnay   ★★★

This Kerikeri, Bay of Islands wine has shown varying form. Fermented and matured for a year in American
(60 per cent) and French oak casks (30 per cent new), the 2002 vintage (★★★) is a golden, robust, very
oaky wine. The bouquet is toasty; the palate is creamy and full-flavoured, with some concentration and
potential to develop, but also rather heavy-handed use of wood.

Vintage	02
WR	5
Drink	05

DRY $30 -V

Marsden Estate Chardonnay   ★★★

Estate-grown at Kerikeri, in the Bay of Islands, and fermented in French and American oak casks, the 2002
vintage (★★★☆) of this Northland wine is a strongly wooded style with lots of character. It shows good
body and fruit ripeness, with plenty of peachy, toasty flavour.

Vintage	02	01
WR	5	4
Drink	04-05	P

DRY $22 -V

Martinborough Vineyard Chardonnay   ★★★★★

Mouthfilling, peachy, citrusy and mealy, this classic wine is typically powerful and harmonious, with
concentrated flavours and rich, savoury characters. Made entirely from fruit grown on the gravelly
Martinborough Terrace, including the original Mendoza clone vines planted in 1980, it is fully fermented
(with use of indigenous yeasts since 1997) and lees-aged for a year in French oak barriques (25 to 30 per
cent new), with full malolactic fermentation. Fragrant, complex and harmonious, with excellent depth, the
2002 vintage (★★★★☆) is creamy and substantial, slightly minerally and nutty, with ripe, sweet fruit
flavours of grapefruit and well-integrated, biscuity oak. A tightly structured wine, it shows strong
personality.

Vintage	03	02	01	00	99	98	97	96	DRY $33 V+
WR	7	6	7	6	7	7	6	7	
Drink	04-09	04-07	04-06	04-05	P	P	P	P	🍇🍇

Matahiwi Estate Nelson Unoaked Chardonnay   (★★★)

From a Wairarapa-based winery, the debut 2004 vintage (★★★) was grown at two Nelson sites, on the Waimea Plains and in the Moutere hills. It's a summer-drinking wine, fresh and slightly off-dry (4 grams/litre of residual sugar), with lively, peachy, citrusy flavours and good ripeness, depth and weight.

Vintage	04	DRY $17 AV
WR	7	
Drink	04-07	

Matakana Estate Chardonnay   ★★★★

Estate-grown north of Auckland, this is typically a stylish wine with ripe, mealy, biscuity flavours and impressive complexity. Fermented and lees-aged in French oak barriques, the 2002 vintage (★★★★) has a slightly creamy texture, strong stone-fruit flavours and substantial body.

DRY $29 AV

Matariki Aspire Chardonnay   ★★★☆

The citrusy, minerally 2002 vintage (★★★☆) was grown in the company's Gimblett Gravels and Havelock North vineyards. Very vibrant, crisp and flavoursome, it shows moderate complexity and good freshness and vigour. Due to frosts, the 2003 (★★★) was blended from Gimblett Gravels (50 per cent) and other, bought-in Hawke's Bay grapes, and fermented and lees-aged in a mix of tanks and seasoned oak barrels. It's a full-flavoured, fairly high-acid wine, fresh and crisp, with citrusy, slightly limey and buttery flavours and a subtle twist of oak.

Vintage	03	02	DRY $20 AV
WR	6	7	
Drink	6	7	

Matariki Hawke's Bay Chardonnay   ★★★★

This is a consistently rewarding wine. It is grown in Gimblett Road (principally), with a smaller portion of fruit cultivated in limestone soils on the east side of Te Mata Peak giving 'a flinty, lime character'. Fermented and lees-aged in French oak barriques (40 per cent new), the 2002 vintage (★★★★☆) is a slightly minerally, intense wine with firm acid underpinning its fresh grapefruit and toast flavours. It's a rich and complex wine, highly expressive.

Vintage	02	01	00	99	98	DRY $27 AV
WR	7	6	7	7	7	
Drink	04-09	04-07	P	P	P	

Matariki Reserve Chardonnay   ★★★★☆

This Hawke's Bay wine is grown at the company's sites in the Gimblett Gravels and at Te Mata Peak (see above) and fermented (partly with indigenous yeasts) in predominantly new (90 per cent in 2002) French oak barriques. The youthful, lemon-hued 2002 vintage (★★★★) is a crisp, slightly minerally wine with grapefruit and ripe-herb flavours showing excellent complexity and richness.

Vintage	02	01	00	DRY $36 -V
WR	7	6	7	
Drink	04-09	04-07	04-05	

Matawhero Reserve Chardonnay ★★★☆

The quality of this Gisborne label has varied. At its best, the wine is rewardingly robust, complex and rich-flavoured, and can mature well, but some vintages have looked tired. Fermentation with indigenous yeasts and full use of malolactic fermentation gives a less fruit-driven style than is the norm with Gisborne Chardonnay.

DRY $29 -V

Matua Valley Ararimu Chardonnay ★★★★☆

This is Matua Valley's premier Chardonnay, as its price underlines. It is usually based on low-cropped, hand-picked grapes (all clone 15) at Judd Estate in Gisborne, and fermented and matured, with regular lees-stirring, in French (mostly) and American oak barriques (40 per cent new in 2003). The 2001 vintage (★★☆), grown in the Petrie vineyard, near Masterton, was disappointing in 2004 – lemony and austere. Marking a return to form, the 2002 (★★★★★), again grown at Judd Estate, is a classic Ararimu – a powerful, fat, oily wine with rich grapefruit and toast characters. Still youthful, the 2003 vintage (★★★★☆), grown at Judd Estate, is a stylish, mouthfilling and complex wine with ripe tropical-fruit, butterscotch and toasty oak flavours that build to a rich, sustained finish.

Vintage	03	02	01	00	99	98
WR	7	7	7	7	6	6
Drink	04-10	04-07	04-08	04-05	P	P

DRY $45 -V

Matua Valley Eastern Bays Chardonnay ★★★

This moderately priced wine is a fruit-driven style, fresh and crisp, with lees-aging and a touch of French and American oak adding depth. Immediately appealing, the 2003 vintage (★★★), blended from Gisborne and Hawke's Bay grapes, is a medium to full-bodied, crisp dry wine with plenty of fresh, vibrant, tropical-fruit flavour. A good all-purpose white.

Vintage	03	02
WR	5	4
Drink	04-07	P

DRY $16 AV

Matua Valley Judd Estate Chardonnay ★★★★

Grown in the company-owned Judd Estate vineyard in Gisborne, this is a consistently delicious, softly mouthfilling, vibrantly fruity wine with considerable complexity. Over the past few years, its volume has gone down while the price and quality have moved up. The 2003 vintage (★★★★) was fermented and matured for 10 months, with lees-stirring, in French oak barriques (one-third new). Light yellow, it's a subtle, creamy wine with concentrated grapefruit and tropical-fruit flavours, finely balanced, biscuity oak and a rich finish.

Vintage	03	02	01	00	99
WR	6	7	6	6	5
Drink	04-08	04-07	P	04-05	P

DRY $29 AV

Matua Valley Matheson Chardonnay ★★★☆

At its best, this is an excellent buy. It is grown in the company's Matheson Vineyard at Maraekakaho, in Hawke's Bay, and the 2003 vintage (★★★☆) was fermented and lees-aged for 10 months in French oak casks (one-third new), with a small percentage of malolactic fermentation. It's a bold, light yellow wine with strong, toasty oak aromas. Peachy, slightly buttery and creamy, it's an upfront, early-drinking style with loads of flavour.

Vintage	03	02	01	00	99	98
WR	5	7	6	6	6	7
Drink	04-07	04-07	P	04-05	P	P

DRY $19 V+

Matua Valley Settler Series Chardonnay ★★☆

The low-priced, fruit-driven 2003 vintage (★★★) is a blend of New Zealand (51 per cent) and Australian wines, made with 'a little oak and a creamy, yeast autolysis character'. Fresh, ripe and peachy, it's a full-bodied, flavoursome wine with some creamy, toasty, buttery notes, a smooth (fractionally off-dry) finish and more personality than you'd expect for $12.

Vintage	04	03	02
WR	4	5	4
Drink	04-06	04-05	P

DRY $12 AV

Melness Chardonnay ★★★

Grown at the Melness home vineyard and two other North Canterbury sites, the golden, honeyed 2002 vintage (★★☆) shows a clear botrytis influence, giving the impression of slight sweetness. French oak-fermented, it's a full-bodied, peachy and toasty wine for current consumption. The 2003 (★★★) is pale gold, mouthfilling and creamy, with peach, butterscotch and slight honey flavours showing good depth.

Vintage	03	02	01	00	99	98
WR	6	5	5	6	5	6
Drink	04-08	04-07	04-05	P	P	P

DRY $22 -V

Mill Road Hawke's Bay Chardonnay ★★☆

Morton Estate's bottom-tier, unwooded Chardonnay offers lively, citrusy fruit characters in an uncomplicated style. The 2002 vintage (★★☆) is fresh, clean and simple, with lemony, appley flavours and a crisp finish.

Vintage	02
WR	6
Drink	04-06

DRY $13 AV

Mills Reef Chardonnay ★★★

Mills Reef's bottom-tier Chardonnay is an easy-drinking Hawke's Bay wine, partly oak-matured, with some softening malolactic fermentation. The pale yellow, youthful 2003 vintage (★★★) is a fleshy, well-balanced wine with grapefruit and butterscotch flavours and a slightly creamy, rounded finish.

Vintage	02	01	00	99	98
WR	7	6	5	7	7
Drink	04	P	P	P	P

DRY $16 AV

Mills Reef Chardonnay Cooks Beach (★★☆)

Hand-harvested at 23.1 brix in the Shakespeare Cliff vineyard at Cooks Beach, on the Coromandel Peninsula, the 2004 vintage (★★☆) is a very lightly oaked wine with fresh, clean fruit aromas and flavours. It's a medium-bodied wine with grapefruit and pear characters and a very smooth finish.

DRY $16 -V

Mills Reef Elspeth Chardonnay ★★★★☆

Mills Reef's flagship Chardonnay, named in honour of owner and winemaker Paddy Preston's mother (who died in 2003), is consistently rewarding. It is grown in Mere Road, in the Gimblett Gravels district of Hawke's Bay, hand-picked and fully French oak-fermented, with about 60 per cent of the final blend put through malolactic fermentation. The 2002 vintage (★★★★★) is a very sophisticated wine with a complex, nutty, minerally bouquet. Tightly structured, elegant and intense, with beautifully harmonious grapefruit, fig and butterscotch flavours, it is weighty, dry and persistent. An understated, rather than brash, style, it should be long-lived. There is no 2003.

Vintage	03	02	01	00	99	98
WR	NM	7	6	7	6	6
Drink	NM	04-06	P	P	P	P

DRY $30 AV

Mills Reef Reserve Hawke's Bay Chardonnay ★★★★

Mills Reef's middle-tier Chardonnay. Fermented and matured in French oak casks, it is usually fine value. The 2003 (★★★★) offers fresh, strong, citrusy fruit characters, with good acid spine and a tight, slightly buttery and biscuity finish. An elegant, well-structured wine with some mealy complexity and considerable richness, it should mature well.

Vintage	03	02	01	00	99	98
WR	6	7	6	7	5	7
Drink	04-07	04-05	P	P	P	P

DRY $20 V+

Millton Clos de Ste Anne Chardonnay ★★★★★

Millton's memorable flagship Chardonnay, only made in top vintages (1992, 1995, 1998, 2002, 2004) is grown in the steep, north-east-facing Naboth's Vineyard in the Poverty Bay foothills, planted in loams overlying sedimentary calcareous rock. Fermented in all-new French oak barrels, then matured in older casks, it is deliberately not put through malolactic fermentation, 'to leave a pure, crisp mineral flavour'. The 2002 vintage (★★★★★) is stunning. Notably powerful, with a streak of minerality running through its stone-fruit and nut flavours, which show great depth, it's an unusually complex, distinctive, special wine. It's built to last (up to 10 years, according to James Millton), but its exceptional richness and harmony also give early appeal. There is no 2003.

Vintage	03	02	01	00	99	98	97	96	95
WR	NM	7	NM	NM	NM	7	NM	NM	7
Drink	NM	04-11	NM	NM	NM	04-07	NM	NM	P

DRY $45 AV

Millton Gisborne Chardonnay Opou Vineyard ★★★★

This is Millton's middle-tier Chardonnay, in the past labelled as Barrel Fermented Chardonnay. Grown organically and fermented in French oak barriques (mostly old), it is typically soft and ripe, with peach and citrus fruit flavours and mealy, oaky characters adding richness in a very harmonious style with good mouthfeel and loads of personality. The 2002 (★★★★), given a full, softening malolactic fermentation, is fleshy and very smooth, with ripe peach, grapefruit and butterscotch flavours showing good harmony and concentration. There is no 2003.

DRY $22 V+

Millton Gisborne Vineyards Chardonnay ★★★

This is a drink-young style with its accent on ripe-fruit flavours and 'minimal' use of oak. The 2003 (★★★), estate-grown in the Riverpoint, Opou and Te Arai vineyards, offers fresh, lively tropical-fruit flavours, with a crisp, fractionally off-dry finish. The characterful 2004 vintage (★★★☆), fermented in tanks and barrels, is mouthfilling and crisp, with very good depth of peach, melon and lime flavours and a touch of complexity.

Vintage	04	03
WR	7	5
Drink	04-06	P

DRY $17 AV

Mission Chardonnay ★★★

Hawke's Bay winemaker Paul Mooney certainly knows how to make Chardonnay taste delicious at just a few months old, and his wine has shown distinct quality advances in recent vintages. The pale lemon/green 2003 vintage (★★★) is a tank-fermented, lees-aged blend of Hawke's Bay (70 per cent), Marlborough and Nelson grapes. Fresh, simple and vibrantly fruity, it's clean and well made, with grapefruit and apple flavours and a smooth, slightly creamy finish. (The 2004 vintage is a regional Hawke's Bay wine.)

DRY $15 V+

Mission Jewelstone Chardonnay   ★★★★★

Arguably Mission's greatest wine to date, the 2002 vintage (★★★★★) was grown at Patangata, in Central Hawke's Bay, fermented and matured for nine months in French oak casks (45 per cent new), and given a full, softening malolactic fermentation. Beautifully scented, with highly concentrated grapefruit and stone-fruit flavours, buttery, oaky complexities, fresh acidity and a rich, rounded finish, it's a strikingly good, very refined wine that could have easily justified a much higher price. There is no 2003.

Vintage	03	02	01	00	DRY $28 V+
WR	NM	6	5	5	
Drink	NM	04-07	04-05	P	

Mission Reserve Chardonnay   ★★★★

For Mission's middle-tier Chardonnay, the style goal is a wine that 'emphasises fruit characters rather than oak, but offers some of the benefits of fermentation and maturation in wood'. It is usually grown in Hawke's Bay, but from a frost-devastated season, the pale lemon-hued 2003 (★★★☆) was made from bought-in Marlborough grapes, and fermented and lees-aged for nine months in French oak barriques (22 per cent new). A fresh, gently oaked wine with plenty of ripe, peachy, citrusy, slightly toasty flavour, a distinct touch of butterscotch and well-rounded finish, it's very attractive in its youth.

Vintage	03	02	01	00	99	DRY $21 V+
WR	4	5	5	5	6	
Drink	06	04-05	04-05	P	P	

Mission Unoaked Chardonnay   (★★★☆)

The debut 2002 vintage (★★★☆) was grown at Patutahi, in Gisborne, and clearly reflects the region's outstanding vintage. Ripely scented, it's a weighty wine with good depth of fresh, tropical-fruit flavours and a seductively smooth finish.

DRY $15 V+

Moana Park Barrique Fermented Chardonnay   ★★★

The 2002 vintage (★★★☆) is an upfront style of Hawke's Bay wine, grown in the Dartmoor Valley and fermented in French oak barriques (half new). Biscuity, toasty aromas lead into a strongly oaked but generous wine with ripe-grapefruit/peach flavours, some mealy notes, and good body and depth.

DRY $19 AV

Moana Park Pascoe Series Chardonnay   (★★☆)

An unoaked style, the 2004 vintage (★★☆) was grown in Hawke's Bay. Enjoyable young, it's fresh and vibrant, with grapefruit, lime and apple flavours, lively and smooth.

DRY $14 AV

Moana Park Vineyard Tribute Dartmoor Valley Chardonnay   (★★★)

The golden, barrel-fermented 2003 vintage (★★★) shows developed colour for a young wine. It's mouthfilling and full-flavoured, with peach, honey and toast characters showing good depth, but unlikely to be long-lived. Drink 2004–05.

DRY $20 -V

Montana Gisborne Chardonnay ★★★

This hugely popular Chardonnay ('New Zealand's favourite since 1973', according to the back label) is typically an undemanding wine, fresh, fruity and smooth, although recent vintages are slightly more complex than the simple wines of the past, with some barrel fermentation and malolactic fermentation and a light seasoning of American oak. Tasted just prior to bottling (and so not rated), the 2004 vintage is full-bodied and well-rounded, with fresh, ripe citrus and tropical-fruit flavours and a hint of oak.

Vintage	04	03	02	01	00	DRY $15 V+
WR	6	5	7	4	6	
Drink	04-05	P	P	P	P	

Montana Ormond Estate Chardonnay ★★★★★

This is the flagship Gisborne Chardonnay from Allied Domecq (NZ), made for cellaring (more so than its Hawke's Bay equivalent, Church Road Reserve Chardonnay). Grown in the company's Ormond Estate vineyard, it is mostly (but not entirely) hand-harvested, whole-bunch pressed, fermented in French oak barriques (43 per cent new in 2002) and matured on its yeast lees, with regular stirring, for 10 months. The powerful 2002 vintage (★★★★★) is fragrant, with substantial body (14 per cent alcohol), concentrated, ripe, tropical-fruit flavours, plenty of toasty oak and a deliciously creamy texture. With bottle-age, it has blossomed into a very classy mouthful. There is no 2003.

Vintage	03	02	01	00	99	98	DRY $29 V+
WR	NM	7	NM	7	6	7	
Drink	NM	04-10	NM	04-06	P	P	🍇🍇

Montana Renwick Estate Chardonnay ★★★★☆

This is Allied Domecq's top Marlborough Chardonnay. It is typically a tight, richly flavoured wine with citrusy characters and firm acidity in cooler years and creamy, tropical-fruit characters in warm years. The youthful, lemon/green 2001 vintage (★★★★☆) was hand-harvested, mostly in the Renwick Estate vineyard, whole-bunch pressed, and fermented and matured for 10 months in French oak barriques (40 per cent new), with 25 per cent malolactic fermentation. It's a refined, citrusy, concentrated wine with strong grapefruit and nut flavours, creamy, minerally elements and a firm, crisp finish.

Vintage	01	00	99	98	97	96	DRY $24 V+
WR	7	6	7	7	7	6	
Drink	04-07	04-06	04-06	P	P	P	

Montana Reserve Marlborough Chardonnay ★★★★

A proven winner. The smooth, harmonious and deliciously full-flavoured 2000 (★★★★★) won the Best Buy of the Year Award in the 2002 *Buyer's Guide*. Grown in Allied Domecq's Renwick Estate and Brancott Estate vineyards, the 2003 vintage (★★★☆) was fermented and lees-aged for nine months in French and American oak barriques (30 per cent new), with 25 per cent malolactic fermentation. It's an upfront, moderately complex wine, fleshy and sweetly oaked, with grapefruit, apple and butterscotch flavours, smooth and creamy. Most vintages have matured well.

Vintage	03	02	01	00	99	98	DRY $20 V+
WR	6	6	7	7	7	7	
Drink	04-07	04-06	04-05	P	P	P	

Morton Estate Black Label Hawke's Bay Chardonnay ★★★★★

Grown at the company's cool, slightly elevated Riverview Vineyard at Mangatahi, this is one of the classiest of all New Zealand Chardonnays. It's typically a powerful wine, robust and awash with flavour, yet highly refined, with beautifully intense citrusy fruit, firm acid spine and the structure to flourish with age. It is fully barrel-fermented, and given the wine's concentrated fruit characters, the French oak barriques are 80 per cent new. Released at three and a half years old, the enticingly fragrant 2000 vintage (★★★★★) is a very elegant wine with a youthful, light-medium yellow/green hue. Very typical of the label, it has a commanding mouthfeel and vibrant, rich grapefruit and nut flavours, with mealy, minerally complexities and a tautness, delicacy and intensity that promises further development in the bottle. There is no 2001, but the 2002 vintage is in the wings.

Vintage	02	01	00	99	98	97	96	95	94	
WR	7	NM	7	NM	7	NM	6	6	6	DRY $35 AV
Drink	04-08	NM	04-06	NM	P	NM	P	P	P	

Morton Estate Boar's Leap Hawke's Bay Chardonnay   ★★★

Named after a limestone cliff near the Riverview vineyard in Hawke's Bay and made without any wood-aging, the 2002 vintage (★★★☆) is a satisfying example of the fruit-driven Chardonnay style. Buoyantly fruity, it has fresh, citrusy flavours, showing considerable richness, appetising acidity and good body (reflecting a high alcohol level of 14.5 per cent).

Vintage	04	
WR	5	DRY $17 AV
Drink	04-06	

Morton Estate Coniglio Chardonnay – see Coniglio
Hawke's Bay Chardonnay

Morton Estate Riverview Hawke's Bay Chardonnay   ★★★★

Grown at the same site at Mangatahi as the famous Black Label Chardonnay, and fermented and lees-aged for a year in French oak barriques, the 2001 vintage (★★★☆) is more developed than some past releases (especially the stylish 2000). Light gold, with a toasty, slightly honeyed bouquet, it offers grapefruit, peach and toast flavours, with some mealy complexity. Full-flavoured and characterful, it's ready now.

Vintage	01	00	99	98	97	
WR	5	7	6	6	6	DRY $20 V+
Drink	04-05	04-05	P	P	P	

Morton Estate Three Vineyards
Hawke's Bay Chardonnay   ★★★★

The 2000 vintage (★★★★), released in 2004, was grown mostly at Tantallon, Morton's warmest vineyard, down on the Heretaunga Plains (which gives 'a more tropical, fruit-forward style'). Fermented and matured in French oak barriques, with partial malolactic fermentation, it has a youthful, light yellow/green hue and a bouquet mingling ripe fruit with biscuity oak. Fresh and mouthfilling, it's a softly structured wine with sweet fruit characters, strong peach, melon and butterscotch flavours, some minerally touches and good complexity. Probably at its peak, it offers fine value.

Vintage	01	00	
WR	5	6	DRY $19 V+
Drink	04-05	04-06	

Morton Estate White Label Hawke's Bay Chardonnay   ★★★☆

Morton Estate's best-known Hawke's Bay Chardonnay is typically a fairly rich wine with citrusy fruit and gentle wood flavours. The top-flight 2002 vintage (★★★★☆) was harvested ripe (at an average of 24 brix), fermented in French and American oak barriques, and lees-aged in oak for 14 months, with 15 per cent malolactic fermentation. Bright, light yellow/green, it's deliciously weighty and well-rounded in a classic regional style with generous, ripe stone-fruit flavours to the fore, mealy, toasty characters adding richness and a creamy-smooth texture. A very harmonious wine with oodles of flavour, it's as satisfying as many $30 Chardonnays and one of the Best Buys of the Year.

Vintage	02	01	00	99	98	97	96	
WR	7	5	6	6	6	5	6	DRY $17 V+
Drink	04-07	04-05	04-05	P	P	P	P	

Morton Estate White Label Private Reserve
Hawke's Bay Chardonnay   ★★★☆

The 2001 vintage (★★★☆), released in 2004, is a strapping wine (with a soaring alcohol level of 15 per cent). Bright yellow/green, with a fragrant, toasty bouquet, it's a full-flavoured wine with grapefruit, peach and toast flavours, slight honey characters and some mealy complexity. Drink now onwards.

Vintage	01
WR	6
Drink	04-05

DRY $19 V+

Morworth Estate Barrel Selection Chardonnay   ★★★☆

The 2002 vintage (★★★☆) from this small Canterbury-based winery was grown in Marlborough and matured for 10 months in French oak barriques. Showing aging potential in its youth, it is citrusy, slightly toasty and creamy, with fresh acidity enlivening the finish.

DRY $24 AV

Moteo Terroire Reserve Chardonnay   ★★☆

The 2002 vintage (★★★) of this Hawke's Bay wine ('terroire' is the winery's own spelling) is the best yet. Grown at Moteo, in the Omarunui Valley, hand-picked at 24 brix, and fermented with indigenous yeasts in French oak casks (40 per cent new), it was lees-aged in barrels for 10 months, with full malolactic fermentation. The bouquet is biscuity and mealy; the palate is robust (14.4 per cent alcohol) and rounded, with slightly honeyed, stone-fruit flavours and a strong, toasty oak influence. Drink now.

DRY $22 -V

Mount Cass Vineyards Waipara Valley Chardonnay   ★★★

The 2001 (★★★☆) showed good depth and harmony, with lively grapefruit and peach flavours, balanced acidity and mealy, toasty characters. The 2002 vintage (★★★) was fermented in French oak barriques (half new), with 80 per cent malolactic fermentation. Light yellow, it's a full-bodied, slightly honeyed wine with fresh acidity and some complexity and richness.

Vintage	02
WR	6
Drink	04-06

DRY $19 AV

Mountford Estate Chardonnay   ★★★★☆

In top vintages, this rare Waipara wine offers splendidly rich melon, grapefruit and quality oak flavours, with a commanding mouthfeel. The 2002 (★★★★★) was hand-harvested, whole-bunch pressed and fermented and lees-aged for more than a year in French oak barriques (30 per cent new), with full malolactic fermentation. Light yellow, it's a powerful, opulent wine with strong, toasty oak on the nose and palate, coupled with lush, peachy fruit characters. Oily and highly concentrated, it's a powerful, opulent wine with tremendous depth of stone-fruit and butterscotch flavours. Drink now to 2005.

DRY $39 -V

Mount Michael Central Otago Chardonnay   ★★★★

Estate-grown on a site overlooking Cromwell, this is a consistently successful wine, one of the region's finest Chardonnays. Fermented and lees-aged (with weekly lees-stirring) in French oak barriques (30 per cent new), with partial malolactic fermentation, the 2003 vintage (★★★★) is an elegant wine, citrusy and crisp, with subtle oak, good intensity and a finely balanced, lingering finish.

Vintage	03	02	01	00
WR	6	6	6	5
Drink	04-07	04-06	P	P

DRY $23 AV

Mount Riley Marlborough Chardonnay   ★★★

Mount Riley is named after the dominant peak in the Richmond Range, on the northern flanks of the Wairau Valley. The 2003 vintage (★★★☆) was fermented in tanks (60 per cent) and oak barriques (25 per cent new). A smooth, fractionally off-dry wine (4 grams/litre of residual sugar), it shows good body and depth of citrus fruit and melon flavours, with subtle oak and a touch of butterscotch. It's an easy-drinking style with some richness.

Vintage 03	
WR 6	**DRY $18 AV**
Drink 04-06	

Mount Riley Seventeen Valley
Marlborough Chardonnay   ★★★★☆

The 2002 vintage (★★★★☆), blended from Wairau Valley vineyards, was fermented and matured in French and American oak barriques. Still youthful in colour, with a refined, citrusy, biscuity fragrance, it displays concentrated peach and grapefruit flavours woven with toasty oak. An elegant wine with a rich, creamy mouthfeel and fine acidity, it's maturing well.

Vintage 02	
WR 7	**DRY $30 AV**
Drink 04-08	

Moutere Hills Nelson Chardonnay   ★★★

This is a fruit-driven style with a touch of complexity, fermented in a 50/50 split of tanks and barrels. Maturing well, the 2002 vintage (★★★☆) is fresh and full-bodied, with plenty of citrusy, peachy, slightly toasty flavour and a crisp, tight finish. The 2003 (★★★) is similar – lemony and lively, with crisp, vibrant fruit flavours and hints of oak and butterscotch.

Vintage 02	
WR 6	**DRY $24 -V**
Drink 04-06	

Moutere Hills Reserve Nelson Chardonnay   (★★★☆)

The 2002 vintage (★★★☆) is one of the finest Chardonnays yet from this small Upper Moutere producer. It's an exuberantly oaked wine, full-bodied, with loads of peachy, toasty, buttery, slightly honeyed flavour in a very full-on style. The wood handling is a bit heavy-handed, but there's lots of character here.

Vintage 02	
WR 7	**DRY $29 -V**
Drink 04-05	

Mt Difficulty Central Otago Chardonnay   ★★★☆

Grown at Bannockburn, this is typically a vibrantly fruity wine with subtle use of oak. The 2002 vintage (★★★☆) was 50 per cent oak-fermented; the rest was handled in tanks. Very fresh and buoyant, it's a distinctly cool-climate style with lively acidity, plenty of lemony, slightly nutty flavour and a crisp, flinty finish.

DRY $29 -V

Mudbrick Vineyard Chardonnay   ★★★☆

The 2002 vintage (★★★☆) was grown on Waiheke Island and fermented initially in stainless steel tanks, then in one and two-year-old French oak barriques. Light gold, with good weight and strong peach and lemon flavours, it's a fairly lush wine, gently wooded, slightly honeyed and well balanced for early drinking.

Vintage	02	01	00	
WR	6	5	5	**DRY $29 -V**
Drink	04-05	P	P	

Muddy Water Waipara Chardonnay   ★★★★☆

This is consistently one of Canterbury's finest Chardonnays. The refined 2002 vintage (★★★★☆) has a slightly nutty, complex bouquet, rich butterscotch and minerally characters, fresh, balanced acidity and a long finish. From a very low-yielding, frost-affected season, the 2003 (★★★★☆) was whole-bunch pressed, fermented with indigenous yeasts and lees-aged for 11 months in French oak barriques (10 per cent new), with full malolactic fermentation. Youthful, light lemon/green, it's a very stylish wine with grapefruit and apple fruit flavours to the fore, mealy barrel-ferment characters, subtle oak, a minerally streak and a crisp, slightly creamy finish. Showing impressive complexity, it offers excellent drinking now onwards.

Vintage	03	02	01	00	99	98	97
WR	5	6	7	6	5	6	5
Drink	04-06	04-07	04-07	04-05	P	P	P

DRY $29 V+

Mud House Marlborough Chardonnay   ★★★

The 2002 vintage (★★★☆) is a moderately complex style, French oak-aged for eight months, with toasty oak aromas and fresh, citrusy fruit flavours. Full and soft, it's a skilfully balanced wine with a slightly creamy texture. The 2003 (★★★) is fresh and citrusy, but shows only moderate complexity and depth.

DRY $23 -V

Murdoch James Martinborough Chardonnay   (★★★☆)

An unoaked style, but not labelled as such, the 2003 vintage (★★★☆) was harvested at 24 brix and fermented dry. It's a mouthfilling wine (14 per cent alcohol) with fresh, vibrant grapefruit and peach flavours, showing balanced acidity and very good depth.

Vintage	03
WR	5
Drink	05-07

DRY $25 -V

Mystery Creek [Blue Label] Chardonnay   (★★★☆)

The words 'Blue Label' do not appear on the 2002 vintage (★★★☆), but the label is partly blue, and the winery promotes it under that name, so that's how it's listed here. Grown in the Waikato and not oak-aged, it's youthful in colour, with good body and roundness. Drinking well now, it's a tight, elegant wine with ripe, peachy, citrusy flavours showing very good depth and a slightly creamy finish.

DRY $16 V+

Mystery Creek Chardonnay   ★★☆

Toasty and rounded, the pale yellow 2002 vintage (★★☆) is a blend of Waikato and Gisborne grapes with ripe, citrusy, buttery flavours, now tasting fully developed. The 2003 (★★☆) is a barrel-fermented Auckland wine. Light straw in hue, it's a mouthfilling, slightly honeyed wine, peachy and toasty, with crisp acids on the finish. It's quite forward; drink now to 2005.

Vintage	02
WR	4
Drink	04-05

DRY $20 -V

Mystery Creek Reserve Chardonnay   ★★★

The weighty 2002 vintage (★★★) was made from Waikato and Gisborne fruit, fermented in mostly new French and American oak barriques, with full malolactic fermentation. Pale gold, it offers plenty of peachy, toasty flavour, now quite mature. Made from Auckland grapes and barrel-fermented, the 2003 (★★★) is light yellow, with toasty wood aromas. It's a big, mouthfilling, peachy, oaky wine, slightly oak-dominated but high-flavoured, in a very upfront style.

Vintage	02	
WR	5	DRY $28 -V
Drink	04-06	

Nautilus Marlborough Chardonnay ★★★★

This stylish wine offers fresh, strong, citrusy flavours and finely integrated oak. It is fermented in a mix of barrels (typically 50 to 75 per cent) and tanks. The 2002 vintage (★★★★) is tightly structured, with fresh, crisp grapefruit-like characters and a subtle, nutty oak influence in an elegant, fruit-driven style that should mature well.

Vintage	03	02	01	00	99	98	
WR	7	7	6	6	6	6	DRY $27 AV
Drink	04-07	04-06	04-05	P	P	P	

Neudorf Moutere Chardonnay ★★★★★

Superbly rich but not overblown, with arrestingly intense flavours enlivened with fine acidity, this rare, multi-faceted Nelson wine enjoys a reputation second to none among New Zealand Chardonnays. Grown in clay soils threaded with gravel at Upper Moutere, it is hand-harvested from old Mendoza clone vines, whole-bunch pressed, fermented with indigenous yeasts and lees-aged for a year in French oak barriques (typically about half new, half one-year-old). The 2003 vintage (★★★★★) is a magisterial wine. Light yellow, with a biscuity, mealy fragrance, it's notably robust (14.5 per cent alcohol), with bold, peachy, nutty flavours showing exceptional depth. Weighty, tightly structured and creamy, with the delights of sweet, ripe fruit and good acid backbone, it's a beautifully harmonious wine that should last for ages, but is already a great mouthful.

Vintage	03	02	01	00	99	98	97	96	
WR	6	6	6	6	6	7	6	6	DRY $50 AV
Drink	04-14	04-13	04-10	04-09	04-08	04-08	04-07	04-05	🍇🍇🍇

Neudorf Nelson Chardonnay ★★★★

Overshadowed by its famous stablemate (above), this regional blend is an excellent Chardonnay in its own right. The elegant, concentrated 2002 vintage (★★★★) was grown at four sites on the Waimea Plains and at Upper Moutere, and was fermented with indigenous yeasts in French oak casks (30 per cent new). The straw-hued 2003 (★★★★) is powerful, with loads of personality. Showing good richness and complexity, it possesses deep peach, melon and butterscotch flavours, with a minerally streak and tight finish. Drink now or cellar.

Vintage	03	02	01	00	
WR	6	6	6	7	DRY $28 V+
Drink	04-12	04-11	04-07	04-06	

Ngatarawa Alwyn Reserve Chardonnay ★★★★★

Estate-grown in Hawke's Bay and fermented and lees-aged in French oak barriques, with no use of malolactic fermentation, this is an arrestingly bold, highly concentrated wine. It usually takes three years to reveal its full class and complexity (the golden, peachy, toasty 1998 is just past its peak, but still offers lots of pleasure). The 2002 vintage (★★★★★) is a notably complete wine, with impressive weight, highly concentrated grapefruit, fig and nut flavours and lovely harmony, richness and roundness. Based on seven-year-old, clone 15 vines and fermented in medium-toast barrels (70 per cent new), it's an absolutely classic regional style – powerful and rich, with a lasting finish.

Vintage	02	01	00	99	98	
WR	7	NM	6	7	6	DRY $35 AV
Drink	05-07	NM	04-05	P	P	

Ngatarawa Glazebrook Chardonnay ★★★☆

Ngatarawa's second-tier Chardonnay label, named after the Glazebrook family, formerly partners in the Hawke's Bay venture, is partly fermented in new and older French and American oak barrels, with some malolactic fermentation. There is no 2001 or 2003. The 2002 vintage (★★★☆) is plump and smooth, with substantial body and peach, grapefruit and butterscotch characters in a moderately complex style, flavoursome and well-rounded.

Vintage	03	02	01	00	99	98	97	96
WR	NM	6	NM	6	7	6	6	6
Drink	NM	04-06	NM	04-05	P	P	P	P

DRY $22 AV

Ngatarawa Stables Chardonnay ★★★

Ngatarawa's lower-tier Chardonnay is an easy-drinking style. The 2003 vintage (★★☆) is a 'lightly oaked' blend of Hawke's Bay, Gisborne, Marlborough and Nelson grapes. Medium-bodied, it displays fresh, lemony, appley aromas and flavours, with a touch of sweetness (6 grams/litre of residual sugar) to balance its crisp, lively acids.

Vintage	03	02	01	00	99	98
WR	6	5	6	6	6	6
Drink	04-05	04-06	04-05	P	P	P

MED/DRY $16 AV

Nga Waka Home Block Chardonnay (★★★★★)

The 2002 vintage (★★★★★) is a striking mouthful. A single-vineyard Martinborough wine, based on 15-year-old Mendoza clone vines, it was hand-picked at over 24 brix, whole-bunch pressed, and fermented and lees-aged for 10 months in French oak barriques (half new), with 70 per cent malolactic fermentation. Light lemon/green, with a fragrant, biscuity, mealy bouquet, it's an authoritative, multi-faceted wine, notably weighty and concentrated, with tightly structured grapefruit and toast flavours, a fresh, minerally character and great personality. (The 2003 vintage, oak-aged longer than the 2002, is described by winemaker Roger Parkinson as 'outstanding'.)

Vintage	02
WR	6
Drink	04+

DRY $35 AV

Nga Waka Martinborough Chardonnay ★★★★

Following the launch of the flagship label (above), the price of this consistently rewarding wine has been trimmed from $30 to $25. The 2002 vintage (★★★★) was fermented and lees-aged for 10 months in French oak barriques (20 per cent new), and 20 per cent of the blend went through malolactic fermentation. Light-medium yellow/green, with a youthful, biscuity bouquet, it is fresh and intense, with strong citrusy flavours, a touch of butterscotch and firm acid spine. Mouthfilling and minerally, with good acidity, it should mature well.

Vintage	02	01	00
WR	6	6	7
Drink	04+	04-06	04-05

DRY $25 AV

Nikau Point Reserve Hawke's Bay Chardonnay (★★★☆)

In case you were wondering, the 'One Tree Hill Vineyards' in small print on the label is a division of Morton Estate. The debut 2000 vintage (★★★☆), hand-picked and French oak-fermented, offers good value. It's an elegant style with lively melon and grapefruit characters, some mealy, oaky complexity and good acid spine.

Vintage	01	00
WR	5	6
Drink	04-05	P

DRY $17 V+

Nobilo Fall Harvest Chardonnay ★★☆

Grown in Gisborne, this is a dryish rather than bone-dry style, designed for easy drinking. The bright and punchy 2002 vintage (★★★) offers fine value. Smooth and full, with clean, ripe-peach and melon fruit characters and a slightly buttery finish, it's not a complex wine, but offers some richness. There is no 2003.

Vintage	04	03	02	
WR	5	NM	5	MED/DRY $13 AV
Drink	04-06	NM	04-05	

Nobilo Fernleaf Chardonnay ★★☆

Designed for easy drinking, the 2002 vintage (★★★) is a fleshy, creamy Gisborne wine, not complex but offering good depth of grapefruit-like flavours. It's a full, ripe, slightly honeyed wine in a forward style offering great value. There is no 2003.

Vintage	04	03	02	
WR	5	NM	5	MED/DRY $13 AV
Drink	04-06	NM	P	

Nobilo Icon Chardonnay ★★★★☆

Nobilo's middle-upper tier Chardonnay has been drawn from various regions since the first 1996 vintage, but the outstanding 2002 (★★★★★) is a blend of Gisborne and Hawke's Bay grapes. Fermented (partly with indigenous yeasts) and matured for 10 months, with weekly 'batonnage' (lees-stirring) in French oak barriques (new and one-year-old), and given a full, softening malolactic fermentation, it's a light yellow, softly seductive wine and a great example of the upfront, strongly oaked style. Fleshy and smooth, with loads of ripe, peachy, toasty flavour, it has great immediacy and drink-young appeal.

Vintage	02	01	00	99	
WR	7	7	6	NM	DRY $24 V+
Drink	04-06	P	P	NM	

Nobilo Poverty Bay Chardonnay ★★★☆

Top vintages are deliciously weighty, harmonious and well-rounded. French and American oak-aged, the fleshy, beautifully harmonious 2002 (★★★★☆) was a wonderful bargain and the Best Buy of the Year in the 2004 *Buyer's Guide*. From a difficult growing season, the 2003 (★★★) is less fragrant, rich and ripe but still enjoyable, with citrusy, pineappley, slightly toasty flavours and a smooth finish.

Vintage	03	02	01	00	99	
WR	6	6	6	7	7	DRY $16 V+
Drink	04-06	04-05	P	P	P	

Nobilo White Cloud Chardonnay – see White Cloud Chardonnay

Northrow Marlborough Chardonnay ★★★★

Made by Villa Maria for on-premise (restaurant) consumption, the debut 2002 vintage (★★★★) is pale yellow, with a scented, mealy, sweetly oaked bouquet. Smooth, ripe-peach/melon flavours hold sway, with creamy, butterscotch-like characters giving a high level of drinkability. French oak-aged for 10 months, the 2003 (★★★★) is lush, high-flavoured, toasty and creamy, with fresh underlying acidity.

DRY $22 V+

Odyssey Gisborne Chardonnay   ★★★

Odyssey is the personal label of Rebecca Salmond. A drink-young style, handled in a mix of tanks and
seasoned oak casks, it's typically a crisp, fruit-driven, often slightly honeyed wine, flavoursome and smooth.
The 2002 vintage (★★★) is a simple but well-made wine with fresh, crisp, lemony flavours.

Vintage	03	02	01	00	99	98	
WR	NM	5	5	6	5	5	DRY $18 AV
Drink	NM	04-06	04-05	P	P	P	

Odyssey Iliad Reserve Chardonnay   ★★★★☆

Top vintages, such as the 2000 (★★★★★) and 2002 (★★★★★), are Gisborne Chardonnay at its finest.
The 2003 (★★★★), hand-harvested in the Kawitiri vineyard, was fermented and lees-aged for a year, with
minimal stirring, in French oak barriques (predominantly new). Light lemon/green, it's a refined, fragrant
wine with strong grapefruit, fig and peach flavours wrapped in toasty, biscuity oak. Tightly structured, with
firm acid spine, it's less fleshy and soft than the best vintages, but equally sophisticated, with a long, crisp
finish.

Vintage	02	01	00	
WR	6	5	6	DRY $30 AV
Drink	04-08	04-05	04-05	

Ohinemuri Estate Waihirere Reserve Chardonnay   ★★★

The 2002 vintage (★★★☆) was 80 per cent barrel-fermented, and half the final blend underwent a
softening malolactic fermentation. Verging on four-star quality, it's a mouthfilling wine with beautifully
ripe, melon/grapefruit flavours seasoned with biscuity oak, good delicacy and depth and a rounded finish.
Drink now or cellar.

Vintage	02	
WR	6	DRY $23 -V
Drink	04-08	

Okahu Estate Clifton Chardonnay   ★★★☆

The 2002 vintage (★★★☆) was produced from Hawke's Bay and Te Kauwhata grapes. Fermented and
lees-aged for nine months in American and French oak barriques, and given a full malolactic fermentation,
it has strong drink-young appeal. Pale straw, it is smooth and creamy, with ripe, peachy fruit characters, a
hint of butterscotch and a strong, toasty oak influence.

Vintage	02	01	00	99	98	
WR	6	6	6	4	7	DRY $22 AV
Drink	04-06	04-05	P	P	P	

Okahu Estate Clifton Reserve Chardonnay   ★★★★

The lush, high-flavoured 2000 vintage (★★★★☆) is a blend of Northland (Okahu), Auckland (Te Hana)
and Hawke's Bay grapes. Fermented and lees-aged for 15 months in new and one-year-old American
(predominantly) and French oak barriques, with 60 per cent malolactic fermentation, it is fleshy, fragrant,
smooth and concentrated, with rich, ripe, peachy fruit characters seasoned with sweet, toasty oak. The
2002 (★★★) is citrusy and crisp, but not highly concentrated, and when tasted blind in 2004 was
overshadowed by its cheaper stablemate (above).

Vintage	00	99	98	97	96	
WR	7	6	7	5	7	DRY $30 -V
Drink	04-07	04-05	04-05	P	P	

Okahu Estate Ninety Mile Unoaked Chardonnay   (★★★)

The 2002 vintage (★★★) is a full-bodied, smooth Gisborne wine with a lemon-scented bouquet, ripe, vibrantly fruity flavours and a well-rounded finish.

Vintage   02
WR   6
Drink   04-06

DRY $19 AV

Okahu Estate Shipwreck Bay Chardonnay   ★★★

A fruit-driven style, 25 per cent oak-aged, the 2002 vintage (★★☆) is based mainly on grapes grown at Wellsford, north of Auckland. It's a crisp, lemony, appley wine, but lacks a bit of charm and richness.

Vintage   02   01   00
WR   6   6   7
Drink   04-05 P   P

DRY $17 AV

Old Coach Road Nelson Chardonnay   ★★★

The pale gold, slightly honeyed 2002 vintage (★★★☆) from Seifried is a great buy. Grown in Nelson and 40 per cent barrel-fermented, with full malolactic fermentation, it has toast, pineapple and butterscotch aromas leading into a mouthfilling, rich, slightly creamy palate. It's an upfront style, generous and long. The 2003 (★★★), American oak-aged, is light yellow/green, with slightly honeyed aromas and flavours, sweet oak characters and plenty of fresh, smooth, citrusy flavour.

Vintage   03   02   01
WR   6   7   6
Drink   04-07   04-05   P

DRY $16 AV

Old Coach Road Unoaked Nelson Chardonnay   ★★☆

Seifried Estate's low-priced Chardonnay typically appeals for its freshness and vigour. The 2003 vintage (★★☆) is citrusy and moderately flavoursome. It's a high-alcohol style (14 per cent), with a sliver of sweetness (4 grams/litre of residual sugar) smoothing the finish.

Vintage   04
WR   6
Drink   05-06

DRY $13 AV

Olssen's Barrel Fermented Chardonnay   ★★★☆

Maturing well, the 2001 (★★★★☆) is a robust Central Otago wine. It shows excellent complexity and weight, with rich grapefruit flavours and buttery, mealy, toasty characters. The 2002 vintage (★★★☆) was hand-picked and fermented and matured for 10 months, with weekly lees-stirring, in French oak barriques (20 per cent new). Displaying bright, youthful, green-tinged colour, it's a distinctly cool-climate style, fresh, vibrant and punchy, with tight, citrusy, appley flavours seasoned with quality oak and crisp acidity.

Vintage   01
WR   5
Drink   04-06

DRY $27 -V

Olssen's Charcoal Joe Chardonnay   ★★★☆

Named after a nineteenth-century goldminer, the 2002 (★★★☆) was grown at Bannockburn in Central Otago, and fermented and matured in French oak barriques (40 per cent new). It's a lemony, distinctly cool-climate style with some complexity, cut with fresh acidity. The youthful, lemon/green-hued 2003 vintage (★★★) is a full-bodied wine (14.5 per cent alcohol), with creamy, buttery aromas and flavours, coupled with citrusy, appley fruit characters, and lively acids on the finish.

Vintage 03
WR   6   DRY $32 -V
Drink 05-10

Olssen's The Bannockburn Club Chardonnay   ★★★

Showing good freshness and vigour, this is an unwooded style from Bannockburn, in Central Otago. The 2003 vintage (★★★) is full and fresh, with good weight and crisp, clearly varietal flavours of lemons, apples and grapefruit.

Vintage 03
WR   4   DRY $20 -V
Drink 04-06

Omaka Springs Estate Marlborough Chardonnay   ★★★

The latest vintages of this moderately priced wine are the best. The 2002 (★★★☆) is full-bodied and buttery-smooth, with good depth of fresh, citrusy flavour and a soft, creamy mouthfeel.

DRY $16 AV

Omaka Springs Estate Winemaker's Selection Chardonnay   (★★★★)

Drinking well now, the 2002 vintage (★★★★) of this Marlborough wine is ripely scented and fleshy, with finely balanced acidity and loads of citrusy, toasty, well-rounded flavour.

DRY $20 V+

One Tree East Coast Unoaked Chardonnay   (★★★)

Made by Capricorn Wine Estates (a division of Craggy Range) for sale in restaurants and New World and Pak 'N Save supermarkets, the 2003 vintage (★★★) is an unoaked blend of Gisborne (principally) and Marlborough grapes. Light yellow/green, it's an uncomplicated style, fleshy and soft, with ripe, tropical-fruit flavours showing good freshness and harmony.

DRY $17 AV

Opihi South Canterbury Chardonnay   ★★☆

The 2003 vintage (★★☆) was grown inland from Pleasant Point, near Timaru. Fermented in a mix of tanks and barrels, it was matured for 10 months in seasoned French oak barriques, with some lees-aging and malolactic fermentation. A medium-bodied wine, crisp, appley and green-edged, it lacks real ripeness and richness, but is fresh and lively.

Vintage 03
WR   5   DRY $18 -V
Drink 04-05

Oyster Bay Marlborough Chardonnay   ★★★☆

Made by Delegat's, this wine sets out to showcase Marlborough's pure, incisive fruit flavours. Earlier vintages were 75 per cent barrel-fermented, but since 2002 this has been cut back to 50 per cent, to achieve a more fruit-driven style. Nevertheless, all of the final blend spends some time in casks, with 'heaps' of lees-stirring, but malolactic fermentation played no part in the recipe. The 2003 vintage (★★★☆) offers fresh, cool-climate varietal flavours of lemons and apples in a crisp, vibrant style with good mouthfeel and texture.

Vintage	03	02	01	00	99	98	DRY $20 AV
WR	6	7	6	6	6	7	
Drink	04-05	P	P	P	P	P	

Palliser Estate Martinborough Chardonnay ★★★★★

Rather than sheer power, gracefulness, delicacy and finesse are the key attributes of this classic Martinborough wine. A celebration of strong, ripe, citrusy fruit flavours, it is gently seasoned with French oak, producing a delicious wine with subtle winemaking input and concentrated varietal flavours. It is barrel-fermented and lees-aged for nine months, but not lees-stirred, and the percentage of new wood is kept fairly low. Some use of indigenous yeasts and partial malolactic fermentation are also part of the recipe. Showing lovely freshness, the 2003 vintage (★★★★☆) is a rich, opulent wine with finely balanced acidity and concentrated grapefruit-like flavours wrapped in quality oak.

Vintage	03	02	01	00	99	98	DRY $30 V+
WR	7	6	6	7	6	7	
Drink	05-08	04-07	04-06	04-05	P	P	

Palliser Pencarrow Chardonnay ★★★☆

Pencarrow is Palliser Estate's second-tier label, fermented and lees-aged in American and French oak casks. A blend of Martinborough and Marlborough grapes, the light yellow 2003 vintage (★★★) is lemony and smooth, with moderate complexity and depth.

Vintage	03	02	DRY $17 V+
WR	5	6	
Drink	04-05	P	

Passage Rock Barrel Fermented Chardonnay ★★☆

The 2002 vintage (★★★) is a very upfront style (winemaker David Evans' goal is to make 'a big, luscious style of Chardonnay'). A single-vineyard Gisborne wine, it is peachy, buttery, toasty and faintly honeyed, in a full-flavoured style that would have benefited from less exuberant use of oak.

Vintage	02	DRY $22 -V
WR	5	
Drink	P	

Passage Rock Unoaked Chardonnay ★★★

The 2002 vintage (★★★) from this Waiheke Island winery is a single-vineyard, Gisborne wine. Handled entirely in tanks, it's a fresh, vibrant style with mouthfilling body (14 per cent alcohol), ripe citrusy, appley flavours, balanced acidity and a rounded finish.

DRY $17 AV

Pegasus Bay Chardonnay ★★★★★

Strapping yet delicate, richly flavoured yet subtle, this sophisticated wine is one of the country's best Chardonnays grown south of Marlborough. Muscular and taut, it typically offers a seamless array of fresh, crisp, citrusy, biscuity, complex flavours and great concentration and length. Estate-grown at Waipara, it is based entirely on the shy-bearing Mendoza clone, whole-bunch pressed, fermented with indigenous yeasts, given a full, softening malolactic fermentation and matured for a year on its yeast lees in barrels (French oak, 25 per cent new in 2003). The 2003 vintage (★★★★), from a very low-cropping season, is a weighty and concentrated wine, peachy, mealy and toasty, with firm acid spine. Robust, with a slightly honeyed richness, it is still unfolding; open mid-2005+.

Vintage	03	02	01	00	99	98	97	96	DRY $33 V+
WR	6	6	6	5	7	6	6	6	
Drink	04-10	04-09	04-08	04-06	04-08	04-06	P	P	

Peregrine Central Otago Chardonnay   ★★★☆

Fermented in a mix of stainless steel tanks and French oak barriques, the 2003 vintage (★★★★) is very skilfully made. Fragrant and full-bodied (14.5 per cent alcohol), it's a fresh, vibrant, cool-climate style with excellent depth of peach, grapefruit and biscuity oak flavours and a crisp, lively finish.

Vintage	03	02
WR	5	5
Drink	04-05	P

DRY $23 AV

Phoenix Gisborne Chardonnay   ★★★

Most of the Pacific winery's wines are labelled 'Phoenix'. The 2002 vintage (★★) was grown in the Butler vineyard and 60 per cent barrel-fermented, in American (two-thirds) and French oak; all of the blend was lees-aged. It's a robust but slightly dull wine, lacking real freshness and charm. I far prefer the Opaheke Chardonnay (below).

Vintage	02	01	00	99	98
WR	6	5	6	5	6
Drink	P	P	P	P	P

DRY $17 AV

Phoenix Opaheke Chardonnay   (★★★☆)

The youthful, tightly structured 2002 vintage (★★★☆) was grown in South Auckland, lees-aged and 50 per cent barrel-fermented. Fresh and lively, with grapefruit, peach and slightly nutty and minerally aromas and flavours, it should age well.

DRY $16 V+

Pleasant Valley Yelas Marlborough Chardonnay   (★★★☆)

The 2003 vintage (★★★☆) is an attractive and finely balanced, fruit-driven style. Skilfully made, it is very fresh and buoyant, with lively, lemony flavours showing very good depth, a hint of butterscotch and a well-rounded finish. Verging on four stars.

DRY $20 AV

Ponder Marlborough Chardonnay   (★★★)

Sold by mail-order wine clubs, the 2003 vintage (★★★) is slightly honeyed, with crisp lemony, appley flavours showing decent depth.

DRY $20 -V

Pond Paddock Chardonnay   (★★☆)

Grown in Martinborough and fermented in four-year-old oak casks, the 2003 vintage (★★☆) is a pale wine with lemony, appley aromas and flavours, a buttery, creamy influence and a crisp finish. It's a solid wine, but lacks real complexity and richness.

Vintage	03
WR	5
Drink	04-05

DRY $18 -V

Pukeora Estate San Hill Chardonnay   (★★)

Grown near Hastings and made at the Pukeora Estate winery at Waipukurau, one hour south of Napier, the 2002 vintage (★★) is a light-bodied wine (11 per cent alcohol), aged briefly in new American oak barriques, with full malolactic fermentation. Light yellow, with a very oaky bouquet and flavour, it's a wood-dominated wine with lemony fruit flavours beneath and a crisp, dry finish.

DRY $15 -V

Ransom Barrique Chardonnay ★★★

Grown at Mahurangi, north of Auckland city, at its best this is a stylish wine with rich fig/melon flavours, fleshed out with subtle mealy, nutty characters. The developed 2002 vintage (★★☆) was fermented and matured for 10 months in a mix of new and used French oak barriques. Golden, with a buttery, honeyed bouquet, it's a sturdy, peachy, toasty, obviously botrytis-influenced wine, with lots of flavour, but probably not for cellaring.

Vintage	02	01
WR	6	5
Drink	04-07	P

DRY $26 -V

Revington Vineyard Chardonnay ★★★★☆

Typically a classy Gisborne wine with mouthfilling body and rich peach and grapefruit flavours in a complex, powerful style, although botrytis has restricted its aging ability in lesser years and in 2003 frost wiped out production. The assertively oaked 2002 vintage (★★★★) was harvested at 23.5 brix and fermented and matured in French oak barriques (75 per cent new). Light yellow, it is richly fragrant and mouthfilling, with beautifully ripe, citrusy, peachy flavours, sweet fruit delights, a strong toasty oak influence and a rounded finish.

Vintage	02
WR	7
Drink	05+

DRY $26 V+

Ridgeview Estate Chardonnay (★★☆)

Grown at altitude on Waiheke Island and barrel-fermented, the crisp, yellow-hued 2002 vintage (★★☆) looked promising in its youth, with plenty of citrusy, slightly mealy and buttery flavour, but by 2004 had lost a bit of freshness and vibrancy.

DRY $34 -V

Rimu Grove Nelson Chardonnay ★★★

Grown in the Moutere hills, the 2002 vintage (★★★) was hand-picked, whole-bunch pressed and French oak-fermented. Light yellow, with citrusy aromas, it's a Chablis-like wine with crisp, lemony flavours showing some elegance.

DRY $28 -V

Rimu Grove Reserve Chardonnay (★★★☆)

The 2001 vintage (★★★☆) is full of character. A blend of estate-grown fruit from Mapua and Brightwater (Waimea Plains) grapes, it was hand-picked and whole-bunch pressed, and 87 per cent was fermented and lees-aged for 10 months in French oak barriques (15 per cent new), with 30 per cent malolactic fermentation. Pale yellow, it's a tightly structured, slightly creamy, full-bodied wine with firm acidity and good flavour concentration.

DRY $28 -V

Rippon Chardonnay ★★★

Grown on the shores of Lake Wanaka, in Central Otago, this is typically a steely, Chablis-like wine with fresh, lingering, citrusy, appley flavours and a strong undertow of acid.

DRY $29 -V

Riverside Dartmoor Chardonnay   ★★☆

This Hawke's Bay wine is typically a drink-young style with straightforward, lemony flavours. The 2003 vintage (★★☆), fermented in barrels (40 per cent) and tanks, is light yellow, with crisp, citrusy, slightly honeyed flavours. A solid but simple wine, priced right.

Vintage	03	02
WR	5	6
Drink	04-05	P

DRY $15 AV

Riverside Stirling Reserve Chardonnay   ★★★★

Grown in the Dartmoor Valley of Hawke's Bay, top vintages of this wine are fragrant, intense and refined. Fermented and matured in new and seasoned French oak barriques, the 2000 (★★★★) is a beautifully harmonious wine with strong, ripe, citrusy fruit characters overlaid with biscuity, spicy oak. Fleshy and slightly buttery, it shows good complexity.

Vintage	00	99	98
WR	7	6	6
Drink	04-05	P	P

DRY $28 AV

Rockburn Central Otago Chardonnay   ★★★

The 2002 vintage (★★★) is a crisp, lemony, nutty, green-edged wine with some flavour richness. The 2003 (★★★) was grown at Lowburn (82 per cent) and Gibbston and mostly handled in tanks; 13 per cent of the blend was oak-aged. Lean, appley and crisp, in a distinctly cool-climate style with some savoury complexity and good freshness and vigour, it's a slightly austere wine, but elegant and tightly structured.

DRY $28 -V

Rongopai Reserve Gisborne Chardonnay   (★★★★)

The creamy-smooth 2002 vintage (★★★☆) was grown at the Glencoe Estate vineyard and 75 per cent barrel-fermented (in new and older casks), with full malolactic fermentation. Sweetly oaked, it offers ripe grapefruit and peach flavours, slightly figgy and nutty, with a strong butterscotch influence and good depth. Drink now or cellar.

DRY $20 V+

Rongopai Seasonal Chardonnay   (★★☆)

A drink-young style, the 2003 vintage (★★☆) is a 50/50 blend of Te Kauwhata and Gisborne grapes, 'lightly oaked'. Fresh and crisp, it's a youthful wine with lemony, appley flavours showing decent depth.

DRY $17 -V

Rongopai Ultimo Chardonnay   (★★★)

The 2002 vintage (★★★) is a Gisborne wine, fermented and matured for 18 months in French (80 per cent) and American oak casks (40 per cent new). Light yellow/green, with a toasty, biscuity bouquet, it shows good weight, freshness and depth of grapefruit-like flavours, but the fruit is overpowered by heavy-handed use of oak.

DRY $36 -V

Rymer's Change Chardonnay   (★★★)

A fruit-driven style from Te Mata Estate, the 2004 vintage (★★★) is a Hawke's Bay wine, whole-bunch pressed, tank-fermented and briefly matured (for three months) in seasoned French and American oak barrels. Fresh, full-bodied and rounded, with vibrant, delicate, grapefruit and melon flavours, it shows good texture and weight. Fine value.

Vintage	04
WR	7
Drink	04-06

DRY $15 V+

St Francis Hawke's Bay Chardonnay – see Francis-Cole
Hawke's Bay Chardonnay

St Jerome Unoaked Chardonnay   (★★☆)
The non-vintage wine (★★☆) on the market in 2004 is a blend of Gisborne and Marlborough grapes.
Light yellow, it's a crisp dry wine, tight and lemony, but slightly lacks fragrance and freshness.

DRY $16 -V

Sacred Hill Barrel Fermented Chardonnay   ★★★★
A typically delicious, outstanding value wine, sturdy, with rich, ripe, tropical/citrus fruit flavours fleshed out
with mealy, lees-stirred characters and toasty oak. The lovely 2002 vintage (★★★★☆) is a Hawke's Bay
blend of Ohiti Valley and estate-grown, Dartmoor Valley fruit, whole-bunch pressed and fermented and
matured for six months in French and American oak barrels. It's a classic regional style, showing ripe-
grapefruit and stone-fruit characters, well-integrated toasty oak, a hint of butterscotch and a rich, rounded
finish. The 2003, from a frost-devastated vintage, is a Marlborough wine, but 2004 brings a return to
Hawke's Bay.

Vintage	03	02	01	00	99	98
WR	6	7	6	6	6	5
Drink	04-06	04-05	P	P	P	P

DRY $20 V+

Sacred Hill Riflemans Chardonnay   ★★★★★
Sacred Hill's flagship Chardonnay is typically powerful yet elegant, with striking intensity. The memorable
2002 vintage (★★★★★), grown in the cool, inland, elevated Riflemans vineyard in the Dartmoor Valley,
was hand-picked, whole-bunch pressed, and fermented with indigenous yeasts in French oak barriques (75
per cent new), with 50 per cent malolactic fermentation. Sturdy and rich, yet also extremely refined, it is
weighty, complex and tightly structured, with a powerful surge of citrusy, mealy, minerally flavours
threaded with fresh acidity and a resounding finish. Hawke's Bay (and New Zealand) Chardonnay doesn't
come any better than this.

Vintage	02	01	00	99	98	97
WR	7	6	5	6	5	7
Drink	05-09	04-08	04-06	04-05	04	P

DRY $35 AV

Sacred Hill Whitecliff Estate Unoaked Chardonnay   ★★★
A fresh, smooth, flavoursome Chardonnay, made in a drink-young style. It is typically crisp and lively, with
ripe, citrusy flavours and a slightly creamy finish. The 2003 vintage (★★☆), grown in 'East Coast' regions,
is a fresh, simple, lemony, crisp wine with moderate depth.

DRY $17 AV

Saddleback Central Otago Chardonnay   (★★☆)
Launched from 2003 (★★☆), this is a second-tier wine from Peregrine; 'fruit is paramount and oak a
visitor only'. Grown in the Wentworth vineyard at Gibbston, it was mostly handled in tanks (less than 10
per cent was matured in four-year-old French oak barriques). Light yellow, with green apple aromas, it is
full-bodied (14.5 per cent alcohol), with slightly herbal fruit characters, a strong buttery influence and crisp,
firm acidity.

DRY $22 -V

Saint Clair Explorer Chardonnay   (★★★)

Grown in Marlborough's Brancott Valley, the slightly creamy 2002 vintage (★★★) was two-thirds barrel-fermented and lees-aged for eight months. Pale lemon in hue, it's an elegant, middleweight style with citrusy aromas and flavours, rounded and ready.

DRY $21 -V.

Saint Clair Marlborough Chardonnay   ★★★☆

Neal Ibbotson produces a smooth, full-flavoured wine with strong drink-young appeal. The 2003 vintage (★★★) was 50 per cent fermented and lees-aged for seven months in new and older French and American oak casks (the rest was handled in tanks), and half the final blend went through a softening malolactic fermentation. It's a fresh, full-bodied wine with peachy, appley flavours and a touch of sweet oak in a moderately complex style with good weight, texture and depth.

Vintage	03	02	01	00	99	98
WR	6	6	6	6	6	7
Drink	04-06	04-05	P	P	P	P

DRY $20 AV

Saint Clair Omaka Reserve Chardonnay   ★★★★☆

A proven show-stopper, this is a fat, creamy Marlborough wine, weighty and rich, in a strikingly bold, upfront style. The 2002 vintage (★★★★☆) was fermented and lees-aged for 10 months in American oak casks (50 per cent new). Weighty and crisp, with sweet oak aromas, grapefruit and peach fruit characters and a sliver (4 grams/litre) of sweetness, it's slightly less seductive than the fleshy, lush, creamy-soft 2001 (★★★★★), but still powerful and rich.

Vintage	02	01	00
WR	7	7	7
Drink	04-06	04-06	P

DRY $29 V+

Saint Clair Unoaked Chardonnay   ★★★

Offering very easy drinking, this is typically a fruity Marlborough wine with simple but attractive tropical/citrus flavours. It is cool-fermented in tanks and full malolactic fermentation is used to 'add complexity and soften the acidity'. The 2003 vintage (★★☆) is a pale, light-bodied wine with appley, limey flavours and a crisp, fractionally sweet (5.4 grams/litre of residual sugar) finish.

Vintage	03	02	01	00
WR	6	6	7	6
Drink	04-06	04-06	P	P

MED/DRY $18 AV

Saint Clair Vicar's Choice Chardonnay   (★★★)

Oak-aged for four months, the 2004 vintage (★★★) is very attractive in its infancy – not complex, but flavoursome, ripe and smooth. Grown in Marlborough, it is fresh and vibrantly fruity, with ripe melon, grapefruit and pear flavours and a well-rounded finish.

Vintage	04
WR	5
Drink	04-06

DRY $17 AV

Saints Gisborne Chardonnay   ★★★☆

'Chardonnay is all about pleasure,' says the back label – and Allied Domecq's delicious wine delivers the goods. From one vintage to the next, this seductively smooth wine is one of the country's top Chardonnay bargains. It is typically grown in the company's vineyards at Patutahi and Ormond, and fermented and matured for six months in French (two-thirds) and American oak barriques (20 per cent new). The 2002 vintage (★★★☆) is an upfront, creamy-smooth wine with lifted, toasty oak aromas and a deliciously well-rounded palate with strong, ripe-peach/melon flavours and a buttery finish. There is no 2003.

Vintage	03	02	01	00
WR	NM	6	5	7
Drink	NM	04-06	P	P

DRY $17 V+

Sanctuary Marlborough Chardonnay ★★★

A fruit-driven, 'lightly' oaked wine from Grove Mill that drinks well within a few months of the vintage. Buoyantly fruity, the 2003 vintage (★★★) was mostly tank-fermented, with some malolactic fermentation, oak maturation and lees-aging. A full-bodied and rounded wine, it has citrusy, slightly limey flavours, fresh acidity and a dry, well-balanced finish.

Vintage	03	02	01
WR	7	7	6
Drink	04-05	P	P

DRY $15 V+

Schubert Hawke's Bay Chardonnay ★★★☆

Grown in Gimblett Road, the 2002 vintage (★★★☆) was fermented and aged for 10 months on its full ('gross') lees in French oak barriques and puncheons (50 per cent new), and then matured for another four months on its fine lees. Fresh and youthful, with the slight leanness typical of many of the district's Chardonnays, it's a citrusy, leesy, nutty, slightly limey wine, bone-dry, with lively acidity and good length. There is no 2003, but the label returns from 2004.

Vintage	03	02	01	00
WR	NM	6	NM	6
Drink	NM	04-10	NM	04-07

DRY $25 -V

Seifried Nelson Chardonnay ★★★☆

The quality of this wine has risen sharply in recent years. The 2002 vintage (★★★★) was grown at Rabbit Island and 60 per cent was fermented and matured for 12 months in year-old American oak barriques; the rest was fermented in tanks. The two portions were then aged for a further 10 months in three-year-old casks. It's a fleshy wine with excellent depth of peach, pineapple and toast flavours, a soft, creamy texture and impressive richness and harmony. The 2003 (★★★☆), French oak-aged, is also finely balanced, with strong, peachy, toasty flavours, a hint of butterscotch and a slightly creamy texture. Drink now or cellar.

Vintage	03	02	01	00	99	98
WR	6	7	6	6	6	6
Drink	04-08	04-06	04-05	04-06	P	P

DRY $19 V+

Seifried Winemaker's Collection
Barrique Fermented Chardonnay ★★★★

This is a bold style, at its best concentrated and creamy-rich, with lashings of flavour. The 2002 vintage (★★★★), a weighty Nelson wine grown at Rabbit Island, was fermented and lees-aged for a year in American oak casks. It's a powerful, lush wine with toasty aromas, a rich, ripe, strongly oaked palate and excellent body and flavour depth. The light lemon/green 2003 (★★★★) spent a year in new American and French oak barriques, emerging rich and toasty, with deep grapefruit and butterscotch flavours in a richly fragrant, upfront style.

Vintage	03	02	01	00	99	98
WR	6	7	7	7	6	7
Drink	04-08	04-07	04-06	04-06	04-05	P

DRY $30 -V

Selaks Founders Reserve Hawke's Bay Chardonnay   (★★★★★)

The beautifully rich 2002 vintage (★★★★★) was hand-picked in the Pearce vineyard and fermented and lees-aged for 10 months in new and one-year-old French oak barriques, with full malolactic fermentation. Light yellow/green, with a very forthcoming, lush, toasty bouquet, it's a weighty, tightly structured and complex wine with a seamless array of stone-fruit, butterscotch and nutty oak flavours, deliciously ripe and rounded.

Vintage	02
WR	7
Drink	04-05

DRY $27 V+

Selaks Founders Reserve Marlborough Chardonnay   ★★★★☆

The bold, classy 2003 vintage (★★★★☆) was hand-picked in the Woolley vineyard and fermented – with some use of indigenous yeasts – and lees-aged for 10 months in new and one-year-old French oak casks, with full malolactic fermentation. The bouquet is toasty and oaky; the palate is mouthfilling and generous, with warm, tropical-fruit flavours showing excellent intensity and a well-rounded finish. Fleshy and creamy, it's a very upfront style, arguably over-oaked, but offers lovely depth and immediacy.

Vintage	03	02	01
WR	7	NM	7
Drink	04-06	NM	P

DRY $27 V+

Selaks Premium Selection Chardonnay   ★★★☆

The 'standard' Chardonnay from Selaks usually shows a touch of class, and the 2003 vintage (★★★) is a good buy. A blend of Marlborough and Gisborne grapes, it was mostly handled in tanks, with some barrel-fermentation and full malolactic fermentation. It's a very fresh and lively wine with strong, citrusy, slightly buttery and honeyed flavours.

Vintage	03	02	01	00	99	98
WR	7	7	7	7	7	6
Drink	04-06	P	P	P	P	P

DRY $16 V+

Seresin Chardonnay   ★★★★

This stylish Marlborough wine, estate-grown near Renwick, is designed to 'focus on the textural element of the palate rather than emphasising primary fruit characters'. It is typically a finely balanced, full-bodied and complex wine with good mouthfeel, ripe melon/citrus characters shining through, subtle toasty oak and fresh acidity. The 2002 vintage (★★★★) was fermented (mostly with indigenous yeasts) in a mix of tanks and French oak barriques, with 60 per cent malolactic fermentation. Still youthful, it is a satisfyingly full-bodied, slightly creamy wine with strong grapefruit and peach characters, mealy, nutty, leesy characters adding complexity, and excellent depth and harmony. Due to frosts, there is no 2003.

Vintage	03	02	01	00	99	98
WR	NM	6	7	6	6	6
Drink	NM	04-08	04-07	04-07	04-05	P

DRY $24 V+

Seresin Chardonnay Reserve   ★★★★★

Finesse is the keynote quality of this classy Marlborough wine. Estate-grown at Renwick, hand-picked, French oak-fermented with mostly indigenous yeasts and lees-aged in oak for over a year, it is typically a powerful wine, toasty and nutty, with citrusy, mealy, complex flavours of great depth. The light yellow 2002 vintage (★★★★★) is a softly mouthfilling, concentrated wine with peach, citrus and butterscotch flavours showing a slightly honeyed richness. It's an opulent wine, now in full stride.

Vintage	02	01	00	99	98
WR	6	7	6	5	6
Drink	04-09	04-08	04-06	04-07	04-06

DRY $34 V+

Shepherds Point Chardonnay (★★★)

Made by the Mudbrick winery, the 2002 vintage (★★★) is based on first-crop vines at Onetangi, on Waiheke Island. Fermented initially in stainless steel tanks, then in seasoned French oak casks (where it was also matured on its yeast lees), it's a more woody wine than you'd expect (given the vinification details), with good body and crisp, dry, peachy, citrusy flavours. A moderately complex style, it needs time; open 2004 onwards.

DRY $29 -V

Shepherds Ridge Marlborough Chardonnay (★★★★)

The great-value 2002 vintage (★★★★) from Wither Hills was harvested at 24.6 brix, and fermented and lees-stirred for 10 months in French oak barriques, with 25 per cent malolactic fermentation. Fleshy and ripe, with generous tropical-fruit flavours underpinned with lively acidity, it's deliciously vibrant and rich in a softly textured, upfront style with loads of character.

Vintage	03
WR	7
Drink	05-09

DRY $20 V+

Sherwood Estate Marlborough Chardonnay (★★★☆)

The 2003 vintage (★★★☆) offers great value. Harvested at 22 brix and fermented in a 50/50 split of tanks and barrels, it's an elegant wine, full-bodied and fresh, with grapefruit and apple flavours, a hint of oak, and finely balanced acidity. Drink 2004–05.

DRY $16 V+

Shingle Peak Marlborough Chardonnay ★★★

Until recently, this wine was labelled solely as Shingle Peak, but now features the Matua Valley logo as well. It is typically a fresh, fruit-driven style with well-integrated oak and a smooth finish. The 2003 vintage (★★★☆) was fermented initially in tanks, then in barriques, and oak-aged for 10 months, with some lees-stirring and 10 per cent malolactic fermentation. Already enjoyable, it's a fresh, flavoursome, citrusy and slightly creamy wine with balanced toasty oak and good depth and harmony.

Vintage	03	02	01	00	99	98
WR	6	6	5	6	5	6
Drink	04-07	04-06	P	P	P	P

DRY $17 AV

Sileni Cellar Selection East Coast Chardonnay ★★★☆

Designed for early drinking, the 2003 vintage (★★★) was blended from Gisborne and Hawke's Bay grapes, and partly barrel-fermented. A full-bodied, fruit-driven style, it is fresh and vibrant, with plenty of crisp, citrusy, peachy flavour, slightly buttery and honeyed, moderate complexity and a smooth finish.

Vintage	03	02	01
WR	7	7	7
Drink	04-07	04-06	P

DRY $22 AV

Sileni Estate Selection The Lodge Chardonnay ★★★★☆

This is Sileni's middle-tier Chardonnay, estate-grown in Hawke's Bay. It gets the works in the winery – whole-bunch pressing, fermentation with indigenous yeasts in French oak barriques (a high percentage new), full malolactic fermentation and lengthy maturation on gross lees, with frequent lees-stirring. Drinking beautifully now, the 2002 vintage (★★★★☆) is richly scented, with a youthful lemon/green hue. It's a mouthfilling, very ripe wine with deep grapefruit and peach flavours, slightly buttery and toasty, and a soft, lasting finish.

Vintage	02	01	00	99
WR	6	NM	7	6
Drink	04-08	NM	04-06	04-05

DRY $34 AV

Sileni EV Chardonnay   (★★★★★)

'EV' stands for 'exceptional vintage', and the 2002 (★★★★★) is on a grand scale. Estate-grown in Hawke's Bay and barrel-fermented, with 100 per cent malolactic fermentation, it's a light straw, strapping wine (14.5 per cent alcohol) with hugely concentrated, sweet fruit flavours of peaches and apricots and mealy, toasty complexities. With its commanding mouthfeel and great overall richness, it's a hedonistic wine, offering delicious drinking from now onwards.

Vintage   02
WR   6   DRY $60 AV
Drink   05-09

Sleeping Dogs Chardonnay   ★★☆

Grown in Roger Donaldson's vineyard at Gibbston, in Central Otago, and produced on his behalf by contract winemaker Dean Shaw, the 2003 vintage (★★☆) is pale yellow, with a slightly rustic bouquet and crisp, tight, lemony, austere flavours.

DRY $20 -V

Soljans Barrique Reserve Chardonnay   ★★★☆

The 2002 vintage (★★★☆) of Soljans' top Chardonnay, grown in Hawke's Bay, is fresh, vibrantly fruity and creamy, with grapefruit and pear flavours and integrated oak. It's a finely balanced wine, drinking well now.

DRY $20 AV

Soljans Hawke's Bay Chardonnay   ★★☆

The 2002 vintage (★★☆) is a fruit-driven style, not wood-aged, but one-third of the blend went through a softening malolactic fermentation. Fresh and lively, with smooth, ripe, citrusy flavours, it's a no-fuss wine for current consumption.

DRY $16 -V

Solstone Chardonnay Premier Selected   (★★★★)

Grown at Te Horo, on the Kapiti Coast, the 2003 vintage (★★★★) was fermented in a 50/50 split of tanks and barrels, and fully matured in French oak casks for seven months. Weighty (14.25 per cent alcohol), rich and softly textured, with excellent concentration of stone-fruit flavours, slightly buttery and honeyed, it's a style departure – a slightly sweet Chardonnay with 13 grams per litre of residual sugar. Judged as such, it's very successful.

Vintage   03
WR   6   MED/DRY $24 V+
Drink   05-08

Spencer Hill Coastal Ridge Nelson Chardonnay   ★★★★☆

American Phil Jones built his Chardonnay reputation with a series of rich, creamy-smooth wines under the Tasman Bay label, based principally on Marlborough grapes. Now he's exploring the Chardonnay potential of his elevated, early-ripening Coastal Ridge vineyard, 7 kilometres north of Nelson city. The debut 2001 vintage (★★★★★) was enticingly fragrant, notably soft and rich, with great power and presence through the palate. The 2002 (★★★★) is full-bodied, with strong, ripe flavours of peach, grapefruit and lime coupled with strong butterscotch and toast influences. It's an impressive wine, but in its youth tighter and less seductive than the 2001.

Vintage   02   01
WR   6   7   DRY $37 -V
Drink   04-08 04-05

Springvale Unoaked Chardonnay   ★★☆

Grown at Alexandra, in Central Otago, the 2002 vintage (★★★) is a simple style but fresh and crisp, with lemony, lively fruit characters to the fore.

DRY $21 -V

Spy Valley Marlborough Chardonnay   ★★★☆

The attractive 2002 vintage (★★★★) was harvested at over 24 brix in the Johnson Estate vineyard in the Waihopai Valley, and fermented and lees-aged for a year, with some use of indigenous yeasts, in French oak barriques (30 per cent new). Fresh, sturdy (14 per cent alcohol) and harmonious, it offers strong grapefruit and apple flavours and nutty oak complexities, with a creamy-smooth finish. The skilfully crafted 2003 (★★★☆) is fresh and full-bodied, with very good depth of ripe, toasty, moderately complex flavours and a smooth finish.

Vintage	03	02	01	00
WR	6	6	6	5
Drink	04-07	04-06	04-06	04-05

DRY $20 AV

Squawking Magpie Gimblett Gravels Chardonnay   ★★★☆

Squawking Magpie is the label of Gavin Yortt, co-founder of the Irongate vineyard in Gimblett Road, Hawke's Bay. Also grown in Gimblett Road, the 2002 vintage (★★★☆) was hand-picked, whole-bunch pressed and fermented and lees-aged for 11 months in new French oak barriques. Fresh, nutty and creamy, it's a high-alcohol style (14.5 per cent) with crisp, appley, lemony flavours, tight and youthful.

DRY $33 -V

Squawking Magpie The Chatterer Chardonnay   (★★★)

The 2002 vintage (★★★) was grown in Hawke's Bay and partly French oak-fermented, and 90 per cent of the blend went through malolactic fermentation. It's a much more forward style than its stablemate (above), fleshy and creamy, with citrusy, appley flavours showing moderate complexity. Drink now.

DRY $20 -V

Staete Landt Marlborough Chardonnay   ★★★★

The 2002 vintage (★★★★) of this single-vineyard wine, grown in the Rapaura district, was hand-picked at 24.7 to 25 brix, whole-bunch pressed and fermented with some use of indigenous yeasts in French oak barriques (25 per cent new). Wood-aged for 15 months, with lees-stirring and full malolactic fermentation, it possesses rich, ripe, citrusy fruit flavours, integrated biscuity wood and a distinct touch of butterscotch. It's an elegant, concentrated and tightly structured wine, with a long finish.

Vintage	02
WR	5
Drink	04-06

DRY $28 AV

Stafford Lane Nelson Chardonnay   (★★★☆)

Based on 14-year-old vines, the 2003 vintage (★★★☆) was mostly tank-fermented and matured, but a small percentage was barrel-aged. It's a fresh, well-balanced wine with tropical and citrus fruit flavours, a sweet, toasty oak influence and a crisp, dryish rather than bone-dry finish.

Vintage	03
WR	7
Drink	04-09

MED/DRY $20 AV

Stonecroft Chardonnay   ★★★★☆

Hawke's Bay winemaker Alan Limmer aims for a 'restrained style of Chardonnay with elegance and complexity which ages well'. His wine also has impressive weight and flavour richness. The 1994 vintage, opened in 2004, was golden, toasty and honeyed – past its best but still alive. The 2003 vintage (★★★☆), fermented with indigenous yeasts and lees-aged for 10 months in French oak barriques, reflects the frost-affected, ultra low-cropping (1.25 tonnes/hectare) season. Being a high-acid year, 50 per cent of the blend was put through a softening malolactic fermentation, compared to the usual 10–15 per cent. Fragrant and biscuity on the nose, it's a tight, youthful wine with grapefruit and butterscotch flavours and a dry, crisp finish, but lacks the generosity and fruit ripeness of top vintages.

Vintage	03	02	01	00	99	98
WR	5	7	6	7	6	6
Drink	05+	04-10	04-10	04-10	04-06	04-05

DRY $25 V+

Stoneleigh Marlborough Chardonnay   ★★★

Made by Allied Domecq (NZ), this wine typically has fresh, cool-climate, appley aromas, good weight, crisp, vibrant lemon/apple flavours and a subtle oak and lees-aging influence. Handled in French and American oak casks, the 2003 vintage (★★★) is smooth and slightly creamy, with ripe, citrusy, appley flavours tinged with sweet oak, and good body and roundness.

Vintage	03	02	01	00	99	98
WR	6	6	6	6	6	6
Drink	04-07	04-06	P	P	P	P

DRY $19 AV

Stoneleigh Vineyards Rapaura Series Marlborough Chardonnay   ★★★★

The 2001 vintage (★★★★) is a deliciously full-flavoured and finely balanced wine, peachy, citrusy, mealy and toasty, drinking well now. The fragrant, harmonious 2002 (★★★★) was fermented and lees-aged for 10 months in new to two-year-old French oak barriques, with 50 per cent malolactic fermentation. Light yellow, it shows excellent depth of grapefruit, biscuit and butterscotch flavours, vibrant, harmonious and rich.

Vintage	03	02	01	00	99
WR	6	6	7	NM	7
Drink	04-08	04-07	04-05	NM	P

DRY $23 V+

Stony Bay Chardonnay   ★★★

From the Matariki winery in Hawke's Bay, the 2002 vintage (★★★) has lots of drink-young appeal. Handled in French oak casks (50 per cent) and stainless steel tanks, it has ripe melon and citrus fruit characters, cut with fresh acidity, and a slightly buttery finish.

Vintage	02
WR	7
Drink	04-05

DRY $20 -V

Stonyridge Row 10 Chardonnay   ★★★★☆

Only 40 cases were produced of the highly impressive 2000 vintage (★★★★☆), sold exclusively at the Waiheke Island winery. It's a strapping, very mouthfilling wine with beautifully ripe, melon-like fruit characters seasoned with fine-quality oak. The 2002 (★★★★☆) was fermented and matured in French oak barriques (two-thirds new). Pale straw, with a complex bouquet of grapefruit, nuts and quality oak, it's a highly concentrated wine with figgy, nutty flavours, interesting minerally touches and loads of personality. It should mature well.

Vintage	02
WR	7
Drink	04-06

DRY $49 -V

Stratford Martinborough Chardonnay ★★★★☆

Strat Canning (winemaker at Margrain Vineyard) also produces a consistently rewarding wine under his own Stratford label. The 2002 vintage (★★★★) was fermented and matured for 11 months in French oak barriques. It's a tight, youthful, elegant wine, built for cellaring, with strong citrusy and nutty flavours, minerally, crisp, dry and long.

Vintage	02	01	00	99	98
WR	6	6	6	6	6
Drink	04-07	04-06	04-05	04-05	P

DRY $32 AV

Sunset Valley Chardonnay (★★★)

Pale yellow, the 2002 vintage (★★★) of this Nelson wine is full and citrusy, with ripe, grapefruit characters, a bare hint of sweetness and good depth.

DRY $19 AV

Tasman Bay Vintage Special Selection Chardonnay ★★★★

American Phil Jones has built a glowing track record since his first Tasman Bay Chardonnay flowed in 1994. Seductively soft, rich and creamy-smooth, it is a hugely drinkable wine in its youth – it is typically irresistible at only 18 months old and peaks within two or three years. It is fermented entirely in stainless steel tanks, with full malolactic fermentation, and is not barrel-aged; instead, Jones immerses French and American oak staves in his wine. The 2003 vintage (★★★☆), blended from Nelson and Marlborough grapes, is moderately complex, with sweet, toasty oak aromas leading into a creamy, high-flavoured wine with ripe-fruit characters, fresh acidity and a fractionally off-dry, smooth finish.

Vintage	03	02	01	00	99	98
WR	6	6	6	7	6	6
Drink	04-07	P	P	P	P	P

DRY $18 V+

Te Awa Chardonnay ★★★★★

The 1996, 1998, 2000 and 2002 vintages (★★★★★) of this Hawke's Bay wine (until 2002 labelled Te Awa Farm Frontier Chardonnay) have all been very classy. Hand-harvested in the Gimblett Gravels district, whole-bunch pressed, and fermented and lees-aged for over a year in French oak barriques (30 per cent new), it displays intense grapefruit and nut characters, with excellent weight, texture and harmony. Winemaker Jenny Dobson rates the 2002 vintage (★★★★★) as her best yet; I rank it alongside the equally outstanding 2000. A very refined wine with a youthful, light lemon hue, it has lovely intensity of delicate sweet fruit flavours of peach and grapefruit, woven with biscuity, buttery, mealy characters. A classy young wine on the rise, it's a classic cellaring style.

Vintage	02	01	00	99	98	97	96	95
WR	7	6	7	6	7	NM	6	6
Drink	04-08	04-08	04-06	04-05	P	NM	P	P

DRY $30 V+

Te Awa Farm Longlands Chardonnay ★★★☆

Estate-grown in the Gimblett Gravels district of Hawke's Bay, this is typically a moderately complex wine, full-flavoured and rounded. The 2003 vintage (★★★) was fermented and lees-aged for 10 months in French and American oak casks (15 per cent new). A tight, youthful wine, it's crisp, vibrant and lemony, with slightly nutty, mealy characters and a firm acid spine.

Vintage	03	02	01	00	99	98
WR	5	7	7	7	7	6
Drink	04-06	04-06	P	P	P	P

DRY $20 AV

Te Kairanga Castlepoint Chardonnay ★★

The 2003 vintage (★★) is a slightly sweet style based on Gisborne and Wairarapa grapes, and includes 25 per cent Sauvignon Blanc in the blend. It's a smooth wine (7 grams/litre of residual sugar), not oak-aged, with slightly honeyed flavours offering simple, easy drinking.

Vintage	03	02
WR	6	5
Drink	04-06	04-05

MED/DRY $14 -V

Te Kairanga Gisborne Chardonnay ★★★

This is typically a drink-young style with fresh, vibrant fruit characters and restrained oak. The 2003 (★★☆), 30 per cent barrel-fermented, reflects the difficult year. Yellow-hued, it is developed and slightly honeyed, with lemony, fairly simple flavours and a crisp finish. The much fresher and more stylish 2002 (★★★☆) is still drinking well.

Vintage	03	02	01	00
WR	6	5	NM	5
Drink	04-06	04-05	NM	P

DRY $20 -V

Te Kairanga Martinborough Chardonnay ★★★★

Te Kairanga's second-tier Chardonnay. The elegant 2002 vintage (★★★★) was fermented and lees-aged for 10 months in French oak casks (20 per cent new), with 15 per cent malolactic fermentation. Fresh and vibrant, it has citrusy fruit flavours to the fore, with slightly creamy and nutty characters adding some complexity and a smooth, lingering finish. Due to frosts, there is no 2003.

Vintage	03	02	01	00	99	98
WR	NM	7	7	7	NM	5
Drink	NM	04-05	04-05	P	NM	P

DRY $25 AV

Te Kairanga Reserve Martinborough Chardonnay ★★★★

In top years, this is a distinguished wine with searching flavours and authoritative acidity. The 2003 vintage (★★★★) was harvested at 23.5 brix and fermented and lees-aged for eight months in French oak barriques (20 per cent new), with 25 per cent malolactic fermentation. Light yellow/green, with a biscuity bouquet, it offers strong, citrusy, appley flavours, threaded with crisp acidity. An elegant, more finely balanced wine than some past vintages, it's tight-knit and minerally, with a long finish.

Vintage	03	02	01	00	99	98
WR	7	NM	7	7	7	5
Drink	04-07	NM	04-06	04-05	04-05	P

DRY $30 -V

Te Mania Estate Reserve Chardonnay ★★★★☆

Typically a powerful, generous wine with heaps of oak seasoning rich, concentrated, ripe-fruit flavours and a creamy-smooth texture. The 2003 vintage (★★★★) was fermented and matured for 10 months in French oak casks (40 per cent new). Nutty oak aromas lead into a weighty Nelson wine with a strong surge of grapefruit and toast flavours and a creamy-rich finish.

Vintage	03	02	01	00
WR	7	7	6	7
Drink	05-08	04-07	04-06	P

DRY $28 V+

Te Mania Nelson Chardonnay ★★★

Lightly oaked in tanks, the vibrant 2003 vintage (★★★) is an easy-drinking, medium-bodied wine with fresh, ripe, tropical-fruit flavours to the fore and a smooth finish.

Vintage	03	02	01	00	99	98
WR	6	6	6	5	6	6
Drink	04-07	04-06	04-05	P	P	P

DRY $19 AV

Te Mata Elston Chardonnay ★★★★★

One of New Zealand's most illustrious Chardonnays, Elston is a stylish, intense, slowly evolving Hawke's Bay wine. At around four years old, it is notably complete, showing concentration and finesse. The grapes are all grown in the Havelock North hills, and the wine is fully French oak-fermented and goes through full malolactic fermentation. The 2002 (★★★★★) is a wonderfully fragrant wine, creamy and nutty, with a distinct touch of butterscotch. The palate is weighty and well-rounded, with ripe-grapefruit and peach flavours, mealy, toasty characters adding complexity and lovely depth and harmony. It's drinking well now.

Vintage	03	02	01	00	99	98	97	96
WR	7	7	7	7	7	7	7	7
Drink	05-09	05-08	05-07	04-07	04-05	04-05	04	04

DRY $36 AV

Te Mata Estate Woodthorpe Chardonnay ★★★☆

This Hawke's Bay wine is based solely on the Mendoza clone of Chardonnay, cultivated at the company's Woodthorpe Terraces site in the Dartmoor Valley. Fermented in a mix of tanks and barrels, with full malolactic fermentation and barrel-aging, the 2003 vintage (★★★★) shows excellent depth, with sweet, ripe-grapefruit characters enriched with biscuity oak and some barrel-ferment complexity. It's a very harmonious wine, offering attractive drinking through 2005.

Vintage	03	02	01
WR	6	7	7
Drink	04-07	04-06	04-05

DRY $22 AV

Terrace Road Marlborough Chardonnay ★★★

Terrace Road is a Cellier Le Brun brand, reserved mainly for still (non-sparkling) wines, but also appearing on a mid-priced bubbly. The 2003 vintage (★★★☆) is already drinking well, with ripe, citrusy, toasty aromas and a full-bodied, slightly creamy palate showing good freshness and intensity.

DRY $19 AV

Te Whare Ra Chardonnay ★★★

Estate-grown at Renwick in Marlborough, the pale 2003 vintage (★★★) is a lightly oaked, high-alcohol wine (14.5 per cent), with fresh, ripe flavours of pineapples, lemons and apples and a touch of butterscotch on the finish. It's a crisp, simple, 'fruit-driven' style, already enjoyable.

Vintage	03	02	01
WR	6	6	5
Drink	04-07	04-06	04-05

DRY $18 AV

Te Whare Ra Duke of Marlborough Chardonnay ★★★☆

With winemaker Allen Hogan at the helm, Te Whare Ra produced distinctive, muscular, peachy-ripe Chardonnays. The wine went through a rough patch a few years ago, but the wine has been back on form since 1999. Already enjoyable, the 2002 vintage (★★★★), based on the Mendoza clone, was fermented and matured on its gross lees in French oak casks, with partial malolactic fermentation. Slightly honeyed on the nose, it's a powerful and weighty (14 per cent alcohol) wine with ripe-peach and fig flavours showing some lushness and a moderate degree of complexity.

Vintage	02	01	00
WR	6	7	5
Drink	04-12	04-06	04-06

DRY $25 -V

Te Whau Vineyard Chardonnay ★★★★☆

Typically a very classy Waiheke Island wine with grapefruit and fig-like fruit characters showing good concentration, nutty oak and a long, finely poised finish. Fermented and matured for eight months in French oak barriques (one-third new), the 2003 (★★★★★) is impressively weighty and seamless. Still youthful, it possesses deep peach and grapefruit flavours, with mealy, biscuity complexities and the warmth and roundness typical of northern Chardonnays. Rich, ripe and highly refined, it should age well.

Vintage	03	02	01	00	DRY $34 AV
WR	7	7	6	7	
Drink	04-08	04-05	P	P	

Three Hands Wairau Valley Chardonnay (★★☆)

Sold by Caro Wines, an Auckland retailer, the 2002 vintage (★★☆) shows some fruit sweetness and richness, but is also slightly piquant.

DRY $20 -V

Tiritiri Chardonnay Reserve ★★★☆

Duncan and Judy Smith's tiny (0.27-ha), organically managed vineyard is in the Waimata Valley, 25 kilometres from the city of Gisborne. French oak-fermented and lees-aged for 10 months, the 2002 vintage (★★★★) has a light gold colour, developed for its age. Fleshy and forward, with strong stone-fruit flavours seasoned with toasty oak, it's creamy and full of character, and maturing solidly. Frosts wiped out the 2003 crop.

Vintage	02	01	00	99	98	DRY $30 -V
WR	7	5	NM	5	6	
Drink	06-07	04-05	NM	P	P	

Tohu Gisborne Chardonnay ★★★☆

Barrel-fermented, with full malolactic fermentation, the 2003 vintage (★★★☆) is a medium-weight wine with lemony, appley fruit characters and a toasty, creamy influence. Fresh and crisp, with plenty of flavour, it offers good value.

DRY $19 V+

Tohu Gisborne Reserve Chardonnay ★★★☆

The 2002 vintage (★★★★) was hand-picked and French oak-fermented. A youthful wine, full-bodied and ripe, with peachy fruit characters seasoned with toasty oak, it is fresh and full-flavoured, offering excellent drinking.

Vintage	02	DRY $25 -V
WR	5	
Drink	04-06	

Tohu Unoaked Chardonnay ★★★

As a drink-young style, the 2002 vintage (★★★☆) worked well, with ripe, stonefruit flavours showing very good depth and a creamy-smooth finish. The 2003 (★★☆) is on a lower plane. Pale, it's fresh and clean, with moderate depth of lemony, appley, slightly honeyed flavour.

DRY $18 AV

Torlesse Canterbury Chardonnay (★★☆)

The vibrantly fruity 2002 vintage (★★☆) was grown in Waipara and other parts of Canterbury and 25 per cent barrel-fermented, but most of the wine was handled in tanks. It's a medium-bodied wine, fresh and citrusy, with a slightly limey, appetisingly crisp finish. Priced right.

Vintage	02	DRY $15 AV
WR	7	
Drink	04-06	

Torlesse Waipara Chardonnay   ★★★☆

The pale gold 2002 vintage (★★★★) is a barrel-fermented wine, mouthfilling, with ripe, peachy, toasty flavours, nutty, creamy and rounded. It's a high-flavoured style, showing good harmony and richness. Drink now onwards.

Vintage	02	01	00	99	98
WR	6	7	6	6	6
Drink	04-07	04-07	04-05	P	P

DRY $21 AV

Trinity Hill Gimblett Road Chardonnay   ★★★★★

The flagship Chardonnay from John Hancock is a very stylish, intense and finely structured wine that often needs two or three years to show its class. Grown in the Gimblett Gravels district of Hawke's Bay, it is hand-harvested, whole-bunch pressed, and fermented and matured on its yeast lees in French oak barriques. The fleshy, generous 2002 vintage (★★★★☆) was picked at 24 to 26 brix in four vineyards and barrel-aged (in 47 per cent new casks) for 16 months, with (for the first time) full malolactic fermentation. Already delicious, with a fragrant, toasty, creamy bouquet, it's a more open, forthcoming wine in its youth than some past vintages, offering rich grapefruit, melon and toast flavours and a well-rounded, lingering finish.

Vintage	04	03	02	01	00	99	98
WR	5	NM	6	5	6	7	6
Drink	05-10	NM	04-08	04-06	04-06	04-05	04-05

DRY $30 V+

Trinity Hill Shepherd's Croft Chardonnay   ★★★☆

The words 'by John Hancock' emblazoned across the label leave you in no doubt this Hawke's Bay wine is made by the high-profile winemaker who built his reputation at Morton Estate. The 2002 vintage (★★★☆), French oak-aged for a year, is a fresh, crisp, citrusy wine with a touch of complexity and very good flavour depth.

Vintage	04	03	02	01	00
WR	5	4	5	5	5
Drink	04-08	04-06	04-06	04-06	04-05

DRY $20 AV

TW Gisborne Chardonnay   ★★★★

'TW' stands for Tietjen and Witters, long-experienced Gisborne grape-growers. The excellent 2002 vintage (★★★★) was fermented and matured for 10 months in one and two-year-old French oak casks, with partial malolactic fermentation. It's a refined wine with very sweet, ripe-fruit characters, good weight, mealy, oaky touches and strong, fresh flavours of grapefruit, pears and butterscotch. Delicious already, the 2003 (★★★★) shows good body, richness and roundness, with strong, peachy, slightly toasty flavours and a creamy-smooth finish.

Vintage	03	02	01	00
WR	5	6	5	6
Drink	04-08	04-06	04-05	P

DRY $27 AV

Twin Islands Marlborough Chardonnay   ★★★

Produced by the wine distributor, Negociants, this is a lightly wooded, drink-young style. The 2003 vintage (★★★) was mostly tank-fermented, with some oak-aging, malolactic fermentation and lees-aging. It's a lemony, appley wine, uncomplicated, fresh and lively, with a crisp, dry finish.

Vintage	03	02	01	00
WR	7	7	7	6
Drink	04-05	P	P	P

DRY $17 AV

Vavasour Awatere Valley Chardonnay ★★★★

A powerful wine with deep, citrusy, appley, creamy flavours. Instantly appealing, the 2003 vintage (★★★★☆) was estate-grown, hand-picked, fermented with indigenous yeasts and lees-aged for nine months in French oak casks (20 per cent new). Light lemon/green, it is fragrant, fleshy and rounded, with sweet, ripe-fruit characters, a creamy texture and concentrated grapefruit and butterscotch flavours. Delicious drinking now onwards.

Vintage	03	02	01	00	99
WR	6	6	6	6	6
Drink	04-08	04-07	04-06	04	P

DRY $26 AV

Vic Williams Selection Marlborough Chardonnay (★★★☆)

Sold by mail-order wine clubs, the 2003 vintage (★★★☆) is a fresh, flavoursome wine, citrusy and toasty, with some complexity and aging potential.

DRY $25 -V

Vidal Estate Hawke's Bay Chardonnay ★★★

This is typically a fruit-driven style with plenty of crisp, peachy, citrusy flavour. The 2002 vintage (★★★) was 40 per cent fermented and lees-aged for six months in oak casks; the rest was handled in stainless steel tanks. It's a very easy-drinking style, moderately complex, with good weight (14 per cent alcohol), ripe peachy flavours to the fore, a hint of honey, subtle oak and a smooth, rounded finish. (The 2003, from a frost-affected, very low-cropping season, was fully barrel-fermented and oak-aged for six months.)

Vintage	03	02	01	00	99	98
WR	6	6	7	6	6	6
Drink	04-06	04-05	P	P	P	P

DRY $18 AV

Vidal Estate Reserve Chardonnay ★★★★★

Clearly one of Hawke's Bay's finest Chardonnays, with a string of top wines stretching back to the mid-1980s. The exceptional 2002 vintage (★★★★★) was hand-picked in three vineyards, whole-bunch pressed, and fermented and lees-aged for 11 months in French oak barriques (40 per cent new), with a small percentage of malolactic fermentation. It has a voluminous, complex bouquet of toast and butterscotch. Seamless and soft, but not flabby, with substantial body and very ripe peach/grapefruit flavours shining through, it is very refined and creamy, and should reward cellaring to at least 2005. There is no 2003.

Vintage	03	02	01	00	99	98	97	96
WR	NM	7	NM	6	6	6	6	6
Drink	NM	04-06	NM	P	P	P	P	P

DRY $32 V+

Villa Maria Cellar Selection Hawke's Bay Chardonnay ★★★★

Good value. The substantial, rich 2002 vintage (★★★★) was fermented and matured for nine months in French oak barriques, 60 per cent new, giving it a much stronger new oak influence than its Marlborough stablemate (below). Toasty oak aromas lead into a full-bodied wine with ripe tropical-fruit flavours, well seasoned with oak, a hint of butterscotch and gentle acidity. It's a high-flavoured style, deliciously ripe and rounded, and builds to a powerful finish.

Vintage	02	01	00	99
WR	7	4	7	6
Drink	04-07	P	P	P

DRY $20 V+

Villa Maria Cellar Selection Marlborough Chardonnay ★★★★

A consistently elegant, good-value wine. The 2003 vintage (★★★★) was grown in vineyards in the Wairau and Awatere valleys, and 45 per cent of the blend was fermented and matured for nine months in French oak barriques (30 per cent new); the rest was handled in stainless steel tanks. It's a highly attractive wine, with excellent body and depth of ripe citrus and tropical-fruit flavours, a seasoning of toasty oak and a crisp, lively finish.

Vintage	03	02	01	00
WR	6	6	6	6
Drink	04-07	04-06	04-05	P

DRY $20 V+

Villa Maria Private Bin East Coast Chardonnay ★★★

At its best, this is an excellent wine and never less than enjoyable. It's a drink-young, fruit-driven style rather than a complex style for cellaring. The 2003 vintage (★★★☆) was made mostly from Hawke's Bay and Gisborne grapes, but includes some Marlborough fruit. It's a fresh, lively wine with crisp acidity, ripe citrus and tropical-fruit flavours, a touch of toasty oak and a slightly creamy finish.

Vintage	03	02	01	00	99	98
WR	5	6	5	6	6	7
Drink	04-05	P	P	P	P	P

DRY $16 AV

Villa Maria Private Bin Marlborough Chardonnay (★★★★)

The 2003 vintage (★★★★) is only of limited availability. A pity, because it's great value. Grown in the Awatere and Wairau valleys, and made with some oak and lees-aging and malolactic fermentation, it's full-bodied and citrusy, with fresh, vibrant fruit characters showing good intensity, a touch of oak and good acid spine.

Vintage	03
WR	6
Drink	04-05

DRY $16 V+

Villa Maria Reserve Gisborne Chardonnay (★★★★★)

Launched from the 2002 vintage (★★★★★), this superb wine effectively replaces the lush, multiple award-winning Villa Maria Barrique Fermented Chardonnay, last produced in 2000 and usually (but not always) made from Gisborne grapes. Fermented and matured for 10 months in French oak barriques (70 per cent new), it's a highly fragrant wine with beautifully fresh and vibrant, concentrated tropical-fruit flavours and a seductively smooth finish. Mealy and finely oaked, with a tight, complex palate showing very good delicacy and length, it should offer great drinking during 2005. There is no 2003.

Vintage	03	02
WR	NM	6
Drink	NM	04-09

DRY $33 V+

Villa Maria Reserve Hawke's Bay Chardonnay ★★★★☆

The 2002 vintage (★★★★★) was fermented and lees-aged for 10 months in French oak barriques, with a notably high (90 per cent) new oak influence. It's a strapping wine (14.5 per cent alcohol), yet very soft and delicate, with rich tropical-fruit flavours that have effortlessly soaked up the new oak. Deliciously creamy and smooth, with some butterscotch showing, it's a good cellaring prospect.

Vintage	02	01	00	99	98
WR	7	NM	7	6	7
Drink	04-10	NM	04-08	P	04-07

DRY $33 AV

Villa Maria Reserve Marlborough Chardonnay   ★★★★★

With its rich, slightly mealy, citrusy flavours, this is a distinguished wine, very concentrated and finely structured. A marriage of intense, ripe Marlborough fruit with premium French oak, it is one of the region's greatest Chardonnays. Over the years, the Waldron and Fletcher vineyards in the Wairau Valley have been the major sources of fruit, now supplemented by grapes from Seddon Vineyards in the Awatere Valley. It is fully barrel-fermented, typically in 60 per cent new oak. The 2002 (★★★★☆) is a high-alcohol style (14.5 per cent), still youthful, with rich grapefruit flavours, mealy, biscuity characters and impressive complexity. The 2003 vintage (★★★★★) has a beautifully fragrant, nutty, complex bouquet. Rich and creamy, tight-knit and slightly minerally, with good acid spine, it's an intense and highly refined wine that should blossom with cellaring.

Vintage	03	02	01	00	99	98	97	96	DRY $33 V+
WR	6	7	7	7	7	6	7	6	
Drink	04-10	04-10	04-09	04-08	04-05	P	P	P	

Villa Maria Single Vineyard Fletcher Chardonnay   ★★★★

Hand-picked in the Fletchers' Rocenvin vineyard in Old Renwick Road, Marlborough, and given 'the works' in the winery, the 2002 vintage (★★★★) was fermented and matured for 10 months in French oak barriques (80 per cent new). Ripe and smooth, with grapefruit and pear flavours, good fruit/oak balance and mealy, biscuity complexities, it's a more elegant but slightly less intense wine than the 2000 (★★★★☆).

Vintage	02	DRY $35 -V
WR	6	
Drink	04-08	

Villa Maria Single Vineyard Keltern Chardonnay   ★★★★☆

Grown at the Keltern vineyard, on State Highway 50, in Hawke's Bay, the 2002 vintage (★★★★☆) was fermented and matured for 10 months in French oak barriques (40 per cent new), and given a full, softening malolactic fermentation. Toasty oak aromas lead into a big, soft, very generous wine with rich, ripe-grapefruit and peach flavours and some mealy complexity. It's a very harmonious wine, for drinking now or cellaring. The 2003, tasted just prior to bottling (and so not rated), is a generous, substantial, rounded wine with peachy, mealy, biscuity flavours showing good complexity.

Vintage	03	02	DRY $35 -V
WR	6	7	
Drink	05-08	04-10	

Villa Maria Single Vineyard Taylors Pass Chardonnay   (★★★★)

The fleshy, creamy 2002 vintage (★★★★) was grown in Marlborough's Awatere Valley and fermented and aged for 10 months in French oak barriques (60 per cent new), with 60 per cent malolactic fermentation. Showing a distinct 'malo'-derived butterscotch character, it's a weighty, complex wine with rich melon and biscuit flavours, promising to mature well.

Vintage	02	DRY $35 -V
WR	7	
Drink	04-08	

Villa Maria Single Vineyard Waikahu Chardonnay   ★★★★★

Grown at Maraekakaho, in Hawke's Bay, the 2002 (★★★★★) is my pick of the five Single Vineyard wines from that vintage. Fermented with indigenous yeasts and matured for 10 months in French oak barriques (75 per cent new), with lots of 'batonnage' (lees-stirring), it's a fleshy and highly complex wine, already lovely, with rich, ripe-grapefruit, pear and fig flavours, mealy, biscuity characters and a creamy, sustained finish.

DRY $35 AV

Villa Maria Single Vineyard Waldron Chardonnay   (★★★★☆)

Grown at Rapaura, in Marlborough, fermented with indigenous yeasts and matured on its yeast lees in all-new French oak barriques, with 50 per cent malolactic fermentation, the 2002 vintage (★★★★☆) is a powerful, weighty wine with peach, melon and butterscotch flavours, showing lovely depth and harmony. It's a robust wine, likely to be at its best in 2005. The 2003, tasted just before bottling (and so not rated), is again powerful and tight, with fresh acidity woven through its rich, ripe flavours, strongly seasoned with toasty oak.

Vintage	03	02	
WR	6	7	**DRY $35 -V**
Drink	05-09	04-10	

Villa Maria Vintage Selection Chardonnay/Chenin Blanc   ★★★

It seems odd to brand a wine as 'Vintage Selection' and then not put the vintage on the label, but this is still a good buy. The wine on the market in late 2004 (★★★) is a blend of New Zealand and Australian wines. Light yellow, it's a characterful, full-bodied, peachy, citrusy wine with plenty of flavour, some development showing and a slightly sweet (6 grams/litre of residual sugar) finish. Ready.   **MED/DRY $11 V+**

Vin Alto Chardonnay La Riserva   (★★★★)

Grown on the Clevedon hills in South Auckland, the debut 2002 vintage (★★★★) was barrel-fermented and oak-aged for six months, with some malolactic fermentation. It shows impressive depth and complexity, with sweet, ripe, peachy, slightly biscuity flavours and well-balanced acidity. Drinking well now, it's the best white wine yet from Vin Alto.

Vintage	02	
WR	6	**DRY $25 AV**
Drink	05-06	

Voss Estate Reserve Chardonnay   ★★★★

Typically a powerful, richly flavoured Martinborough wine. Fermented and lees-aged for 10 months in French oak barriques, the 2003 vintage (★★★★) is a stylish, fragrant, mouthfilling wine with ripe-grapefruit flavours, a subtle seasoning of oak, hints of nuts and butterscotch and a creamy, rounded finish.

Vintage	03	02	01	00	99	98	
WR	6	7	6	6	6	6	**DRY $26 AV**
Drink	04-05	P	P	P	P	P	

Waimarie Gimblett Road/Ormond Chardonnay   ★★★☆

From Nicholas and Stephen Nobilo (third-generation members of the famous wine family), the 2002 vintage (★★★☆) was grown in Hawke's Bay and Gisborne, hand-picked, and fermented with indigenous yeasts in French oak barriques (new and one-year-old). Light yellow, it's a tightly structured wine with good body and depth of crisp, citrusy flavour.

Vintage	02	01	
WR	7	6	**DRY $22 AV**
Drink	04-07	04-06	

Waimarie Marlborough Chardonnay   (★★★)

Released at two years old, the 2001 vintage (★★★) was hand-picked at 24 brix and fermented and matured for 10 months in new (50 per cent) and one-year-old French oak casks, with weekly lees-stirring. Light yellow, it's a full-bodied, citrusy, toasty wine, full-flavoured, with a strong oak influence and a crisp, off-dry finish.

Vintage	01	
WR	6	**MED/DRY $19 AV**
Drink	04-05	

Waimea Estates Bolitho Reserve Nelson Chardonnay ★★★★☆

Named after proprietors Trevor and Robyn Bolitho, the 2002 vintage (★★★★☆) was hand-picked in four Nelson vineyards at an average of 25 brix, fermented with indigenous yeasts and lees-aged for 10 months in French oak barriques (half new). Light-medium yellow/green, with a complex bouquet, it is a powerful yet elegant wine, big, concentrated and multi-faceted, with deep grapefruit and nut flavours, still fresh and vibrant, and a tight, focused finish. It's still developing; open 2005–06.

Vintage	02	01	00
WR	7	6	5
Drink	05-06	04-05	P

DRY $30 AV

Waimea Estates Nelson Chardonnay ★★★☆

The 2002 vintage (★★★★) is a full, creamy wine with good weight, strong, ripe-peach and grapefruit flavours and finely balanced acidity. A harmonious wine with subtle oak and malolactic fermentation influences, it was half tank, half barrel-fermented.

Vintage	02	01	00	99	98
WR	7	6	5	7	4
Drink	04-06	04-05	P	P	P

DRY $20 AV

Waipara Downs Barrel Fermented Chardonnay ★★★

This is generally the most successful wine grown at Keith and Ruth Berry's farm at Waipara. The 2001 vintage (★★★☆), harvested at over 24 brix, shows fresh, appley fruit characters and creamy, nutty touches. The 2002 (★★☆), harvested at 22 brix, is leaner and crisper, with a Chablis-like steeliness.

DRY $19 AV

Waipara Hills Barrel Fermented Canterbury Chardonnay ★★☆

Light gold, with a developed colour and honeyed nose showing some botrytis influence, the 2002 vintage (★★) was lees-aged in French oak casks for six months, and 40 per cent went through a softening malolactic fermentation. Peachy and honeyed on the palate, but also slightly dull, it's unlikely to be long-lived. The pale, youthful 2003 (★★☆) is a fresh, simple wine with lemony, appley flavours.

Vintage	02
WR	5
Drink	04-07

DRY $20 -V

Waipara Hills Marlborough Unoaked Chardonnay ★★★

The enjoyable 2003 vintage (★★★) was partly matured on its yeast lees and half of the blend went through a softening malolactic fermentation. Freshly scented, it's a good example of the style, with satisfying depth of citrus and stone-fruit flavours, very clean and vibrant, with a fully dry finish.

Vintage	03	02
WR	5	5
Drink	04-05	04-05

DRY $18 AV

Waipara Hills Wickham Vineyards
Marlborough Chardonnay (★★★☆)

Showing good potential, the youthful 2002 vintage (★★★☆) was grown in the Wickham vineyard at Grovetown and fermented and matured for a year in new French oak casks. Fresh and crisp, with grapefruit and nut flavours showing good concentration, it's a restrained, tightly structured wine.

Vintage	02
WR	7
Drink	04-10

DRY $37 -V

Waipara Springs Barrique Chardonnay ★★★☆

A full-flavoured North Canterbury wine with lots of character. Based on 22-year-old vines, the 2003 vintage (★★★☆) was fermented and lees-aged for nine months in French oak barriques (20 per cent new). Bright, light yellow, it's an overtly oaky wine, but full and rich, with grapefruit and toast flavours and a crisp, tight finish.

Vintage	03	02	01	00	99
WR	7	7	6	6	6
Drink	04-07	04-06	04-06	04-05	P

DRY $25 -V

Waipara Springs Lightly Oaked Chardonnay ★★★

A fruit-driven style, grown at Waipara, the 2003 vintage (★★★) is full-bodied, with citrus and tropical-fruit flavours offering fresh, easy drinking.

Vintage	04	03	02	01	00
WR	7	6	7	7	5
Drink	05-07	04-06	04-05	P	P

DRY $19 AV

Waipara West Waipara Chardonnay ★★★★

This label shows consistently good form. The 2001 vintage (★★★★) was harvested from ultra low-cropping vines (2.7 to 4.7 tonnes/hectare), whole-bunch pressed and fermented and lees-aged for 10 months in French oak barriques (25 per cent new), with 45 per cent malolactic fermentation. It's a richly fragrant wine, weighty, with deep citrusy flavours, butterscotch and mineral characters adding complexity and fresh acid spine. The 2003 (★★★★) is light lemon/green, with a creamy, nutty bouquet. A weighty, citrusy, slightly limey wine with good concentration, fresh underlying acidity and buttery 'malo' characters, it's quite forward in its appeal; drink 2005 onwards.

Vintage	03	02	01	00
WR	6	6	6	6
Drink	04-06	04-06	04-05	P

DRY $25 AV

Wairau River Marlborough Chardonnay ★★★☆

This is a consistently attractive, tight, understated wine with the ability to age well. Still on the market in 2004, the 2000 vintage (★★★☆), matured for nine months in French oak casks (new and older), is an elegant, subtle style with gentle oak, crisp, citrusy flavours and some toasty complexity. Ready; no rush.

Vintage	01	00	99	98	97
WR	7	6	6	6	6
Drink	04-06	04-06	04-05	P	P

DRY $22 AV

Wairau River Reserve Marlborough Chardonnay ★★★★

Released in early 2004, the 2000 vintage (★★★★) was hand-picked, whole-bunch pressed and French oak-aged for 14 months. An elegant, tightly structured wine with lemony, minerally flavours and finely integrated oak, it's likely to be long-lived.

DRY $28 AV

Waitiri Creek Chardonnay ★★★

The 2003 vintage (★★★☆) of this Central Otago wine was hand-harvested at Gibbston and 30 per cent of the blend was French oak-matured; the rest was handled in tanks. It's a fresh, tight, elegant wine with subtle oak enriching its crisp, lemony fruit flavours, which show good depth. Slightly minerally, with a touch of complexity, it shows some aging potential.

Vintage	03
WR	4
Drink	05

DRY $23 -V

West Brook Barrique Fermented Chardonnay   ★★★☆

The 2002 vintage (★★★★) is a 3:1 blend of Marlborough and Gisborne grapes, fermented and lees-aged for 16 months in French oak barriques (30 per cent new). Yellow/green, with toasty wood aromas, it is mouthfilling, ripe and rich, with grapefruit, peach and nut flavours showing good concentration and harmony.

Vintage	02	01	00
WR	7	5	7
Drink	04-06	04-05	P

DRY $20 AV

West Brook Blue Ridge Marlborough Chardonnay   ★★★★

West Brook Chardonnays are consistently distinguished. The 2002 vintage (★★★★) is bright yellow, with a fragrant, citrusy, toasty bouquet. It's a high-alcohol style (14.5 per cent) with smooth, rich grapefruit flavours, sweet oak characters, a touch of butterscotch and good harmony.

Vintage	02	01	00	99	98
WR	6	7	7	7	7
Drink	04-07	04-07	04-06	04-05	04-05

DRY $25 AV

White Cloud Chardonnay   ★★☆

Nobilo's easy-drinking, non-vintage wine is blended from grapes grown in Gisborne and Hawke's Bay. Fermented in tanks and not oak-aged, it is typically a slightly sweet (6 grams per litre of sugar), lemony, simple wine, clean and fresh. The wine I tasted in 2003 (★★★) was an unexpectedly good, upfront style with ripe, peachy flavours and a buttery, off-dry finish.

MED/DRY $9 V+

Whitehaven Marlborough Chardonnay   ★★★☆

Matured in French and American oak casks, the 2003 vintage (★★★★) is a softly mouthfilling wine with good harmony and length. Weighty and rounded, with some toasty complexity on the nose, it has ripe, citrusy, slightly limey flavours showing very good depth.

Vintage	03	02
WR	6	6
Drink	04-06	04-05

DRY $21 AV

Whitehaven Reserve Marlborough Chardonnay   ★★★☆

Made in a highly user-friendly style, the 2002 vintage (★★★☆) was fermented and matured for a year, with frequent lees-stirring, in French and American oak barriques (50 per cent new). The fragrant, sweetly oaked bouquet leads into a rich palate with strong, ripe-peach, grapefruit and toasty oak flavours and a smooth finish. Delicious in its youth.

Vintage	03	02	01
WR	6	6	6
Drink	04-05	04-07	04-05

DRY $26 -V

William Hill Chardonnay   ★★★

This is typically a good Central Otago wine. Fermented and matured for six months in French oak casks, the light yellow 2002 vintage (★★★☆) is fleshy, with citrusy fruit characters, some leesy complexity and a soft, creamy texture.

Vintage	02	01	00
WR	5	5	4
Drink	04-07	04-05	P

DRY $23 -V

William Hill Reserve Chardonnay (★★★☆)

Made from the 'best fruit' from the 'best blocks', the 2002 vintage (★★★☆) of this Central Otago wine was harvested at 24 brix and fermented and lees-aged for 11 months in new French oak barriques. Light yellow, it is very oaky on the nose, with some mealy complexity and ripe, rounded fruit characters showing considerable richness.

Vintage 02
WR 6
Drink 04-08

`DRY $36 -V`

Winslow White Rock Barrique Fermented Chardonnay ★★☆

The single-vineyard 2002 vintage (★★☆) was harvested from low-cropping (3.5 tonnes/hectare) vines at Martinborough and matured for nine months in new French oak barriques, with 100 per cent malolactic fermentation. Yellow hued, it's a fleshy, very toasty wine, peachy and weighty, but (at least in its youth) oak-dominated.

`DRY $28 -V`

Wishart Barrique Fermented Chardonnay ★★★

The 2003 vintage (★★☆) was grown on the coast at Bay View, in Hawke's Bay, and fermented and matured on its yeast lees for three months in three and four-year-old barrels. Fresh, citrusy and appley, with a sliver of sweetness (4.5 grams/litre of residual sugar) balanced by crisp acidity, it's a vibrant but fairly simple wine that shows less complexity than most wines labelled 'Barrique Fermented'.

`DRY $22 -V`

Wishart Late Harvest Chardonnay (★★★)

Ensconced in a half bottle, the 2003 vintage (★★★) was harvested at Bay View, in Hawke's Bay, two weeks after the first pick at 27 brix, and stop-fermented with 39 grams per litre of residual sugar, making it a medium/sweet style. Light lemon/green, with light, citrusy aromas, it's a ripe, rounded wine with gentle flavours of pears and lemons, fresh and pure.

`MED $21 (375ML) -V`

Wishart Reserve Chardonnay ★★★★

Grown at Bay View, in Hawke's Bay, and fermented and lees-aged for 10 months in French and American oak casks (50 per cent new), with no malolactic fermentation, the 2002 vintage (★★★★) is ripe and rounded, with fullness of body, good depth of peach and grapefruit flavours and a slightly sweet oak influence.

`DRY $27 AV`

Wither Hills Marlborough Chardonnay ★★★★★

This is a classy wine with a formidable track record in shows. Powerful, with a mealy, biscuity complexity from fermentation and lees-aging in French oak casks (typically 60 per cent new), it offers the intense flavours of Marlborough fruit, with a long, creamy finish. The seductively full-bodied and rich 2002 vintage (★★★★☆) has strong toast and butterscotch aromas. A high-alcohol style (14.5 per cent) with a bold presence in the mouth, it offers deliciously lush grapefruit and peach-fruit characters, well-seasoned with toasty oak. The 2003 (★★★★☆) has rich toast and butterscotch aromas leading into a smooth, peachy, mealy, rounded palate, impressively concentrated, in a bold, upfront style.

Vintage	03	02	01	00	99	98
WR	7	7	7	7	6	7
Drink	05-09	04-07	04-06	04-05	P	P

`DRY $28 V+`

Woollaston Estates Nelson Chardonnay   (★★★)

Enjoyable in its youth, the 2002 vintage (★★★) is lemony, appley and moderately oaked, with fullness of body and slightly creamy, biscuity characters adding a touch of complexity.

DRY $18 AV

Yarrum Vineyard Marlborough Chardonnay   (★★★☆)

Sold by mail-order wine clubs, the 2003 vintage (★★★☆) is a crisp, elegant wine with citrusy, gently oaked flavours showing good freshness and depth. It should mature well.

DRY $20 AV

Yelas Marlborough Chardonnay   (★★☆)

The 2003 vintage (★★☆) is a fresh, vibrantly fruity wine with crisp, lemony flavours showing only moderate complexity.

DRY $22 -V

Chenin Blanc

Today's Chenin Blancs are far riper, rounder and more enjoyable to drink than the typically thin, sharply acidic and austere wines of a decade ago. Yet this great grape of Vouvray, in the Loire Valley, is still struggling for an identity in New Zealand. Over the last few years, several labels have been discontinued – not for lack of quality or value, but lack of buyer interest.

A good New Zealand Chenin Blanc is fresh and buoyantly fruity, with melon and pineapple-evoking flavours and a crisp finish. In the cooler parts of the country, the variety's naturally high acidity (an asset in the warmer viticultural regions of South Africa, the United States and Australia) can be a distinct handicap. But when the grapes achieve full ripeness here, this classic grape yields sturdy wines that are satisfying in their youth yet can mature for many years, gradually unfolding a delicious honeyed richness.

Only three wineries have consistently made impressive Chenin Blancs over the past decade: Millton (whose Te Arai Vineyard Chenin Blanc 2002 was judged best Chenin Blanc at the San Francisco International Wine Competition 2004), Collards and Esk Valley. Many growers, put off by the variety's late-ripening nature and the susceptibility of its tight bunches to botrytis rot, have uprooted their vines. Plantings have plummeted from 372 hectares in 1983 to an estimated 104 hectares of bearing vines in 2005.

Chenin Blanc is the country's fifteenth most widely planted variety, with plantings concentrated in Hawke's Bay and Gisborne. In the future, winemakers who plant Chenin Blanc in warm, sunny vineyard sites with devigorating soils, where the variety's vigorous growth can be controlled and yields reduced, can be expected to produce the ripest, most concentrated wines. New Zealand winemakers are still getting to grips with Chenin Blanc; the finest wines are yet to come.

Collards Hawke's Bay Chenin Blanc ★★★☆

Given a delicate touch of wood, at its best this is a rich, vibrantly fruity wine that can offer great value. Grown in the Gimblett Gravels district, the flinty 2003 vintage (★★★☆) is youthful, with lemony, pineappley flavours, crisp and dry. A strongly varietal wine, very fresh and lively, it's worth cellaring and – as usual – bargain-priced.

Vintage	04	03	02	01	00	99	98	DRY $13 V+
WR	7	7	7	6	6	6	7	
Drink	05-07	04-06	04-05	P	P	P	P	

Collards Summerfields Chenin/Chardonnay ★★☆

This is the all-purpose dry white (or dryish white – there's a sliver of sweetness) in the Collards range. Blended from Hawke's Bay and Auckland fruit, it's typically an easy-drinking wine with plenty of fresh, crisp, citrusy, green-edged flavour. At below $10, a good buy.

Vintage	04	03	02	01	00	DRY $9 V+
WR	6	6	7	6	6	
Drink	04-05	P	P	P	P	

Esk Valley Hawke's Bay Chenin Blanc ★★★★

This is one of New Zealand's best (and few really convincing) Chenin Blancs, with the ability to mature well for several years. In the past, it was partly fermented in seasoned oak casks, but since 2001 has been handled entirely in stainless steel tanks. Richly scented, the 2002 vintage (★★★★) is an intensely varietal wine with fresh, finely balanced acidity and strong, tropical-fruit aromas and flavours, pure and vibrant. There is no 2003. The 2004 (★★★☆), a single-vineyard wine grown at Moteo Pa, is richly scented and ripely flavoured, with gentle acidity giving it drink-young appeal.

Vintage	04	03	02	01	00	99	98
WR	7	NM	6	6	NM	6	6
Drink	04-10	NM	04-08	04-05	NM	P	P

DRY $19 AV

Forrest Vineyard Selection Chenin Blanc ★★★★

Chenin Blanc is a rare beast in Marlborough, but the 2001 vintage (★★★★), handled in old oak barrels, is an unexpectedly good wine. Made in a medium style (28 grams/litre of sugar), it's smooth, peachy and mouthfilling, with good sugar/acid balance and faintly honeyed, concentrated, sweetly seductive flavours, now starting to unfold bottle-aged complexity.

Vintage	02	01
WR	5	6
Drink	04-10	04-05

MED $25 -V

Margrain Chenin Blanc Late Harvest ★★★

When this Martinborough producer purchased the neighbouring Chifney property in 2001, they acquired Chenin Blanc vines now well over 20 years old. The 2002 vintage (★★☆), the first to be labelled as Late Harvest, is a weighty (14 per cent alcohol), distinctly medium style (24 grams/litre of sugar) with crisp, tight, lemony, appley flavours. In its youth, it lacked the richness of the 2000 and 2001 vintages, but may open out with time. A medium-sweet style, the 2003 (★★★) is austere in its youth, with crisp, appley, high-acid flavours, showing some minerally intensity, and should be long-lived.

Vintage	02	01	00
WR	6	5	6
Drink	04-08	04-06	04-05

MED $24 -V

Millton Te Arai Vineyard Chenin Blanc ★★★★★

This Gisborne wine is New Zealand's greatest Chenin Blanc. It's a richly varietal wine with concentrated, fresh, vibrant fruit flavours to the fore in some vintages (2002, 2003); nectareous scents and flavours in others (1997, 1999). The grapes are grown organically and hand-picked at different stages of ripening, culminating in some years ('It's in the lap of the gods,' says James Millton) in a final harvest of botrytis-affected fruit. About half of the final blend is fermented in large, 620-litre French oak casks, used in the Loire for Chenin Blanc, but all of the wine is barrel-aged. The 2003 vintage (★★★☆) has fresh, pineappley aromas and a crisp, tight, youthful palate, showing no sign of noble rot. Dryish (6.8 grams/litre of residual sugar), flinty and minerally, it lacks the richness of a top year, but should be long-lived and could surprise with cellaring.

Vintage	04	03	02	01	00	99	98	97	96
WR	7	5	7	5	7	6	5	5	5
Drink	04-08	04-05	04-12	04-05	04-06	P	P	P	P

MED/DRY $22 AV

Gewürztraminer

Only a trickle of New Zealand Gewürztraminer is exported (8247 cases in 2004, just 0.2 per cent of total wine shipments), and most local bottlings lack the power and richness of the great Alsace model. Yet this classic grape is starting to get the respect it deserves from grape-growers and winemakers here, and Spy Valley Marlborough Gewürztraminer 2003 was judged best Gewürztraminer at the 2004 San Francisco International Wine Competition.

For most of the 1990s, Gewürztraminer's popularity was on the wane. Between 1983 and 1996, New Zealand's plantings of Gewürztraminer dropped by almost two-thirds. A key problem is that Gewürztraminer is a temperamental performer in the vineyard, being particularly vulnerable to adverse weather at flowering, which can decimate grape yields. Now there is proof of a strong renewal of interest: the area of bearing vines has surged from 85 hectares in 1998 to 265 hectares in 2005. Most of the plantings are in Marlborough and Hawke's Bay, with other significant pockets in Gisborne and Central Otago.

Slight sweetness and skin contact have been commonly used in the past to boost the flavour of Gewürztraminer, at the cost of flavour delicacy and longevity. Such outstanding wines as Dry River have revealed the far richer, softer flavours and greater aging potential that can be gained by reducing crops, leaf-plucking to promote fruit ripeness and avoiding skin contact.

Gewürztraminer is a high-impact wine, brimming with scents and flavours. 'Spicy' is the most common adjective used to pinpoint its distinctive, heady aromas and flavours; tasters also find nuances of gingerbread, freshly ground black pepper, cinnamon, cloves, mint, lychees and mangoes. Once you've tasted one or two Gewürztraminers, you won't have any trouble recognising it in a 'blind' tasting – it's one of the most forthright, distinctive grape varieties of all.

Allan Scott Marlborough Gewürztraminer (★★★☆)

The floral 2003 vintage (★★★☆) is full-bodied, with very good depth of citrusy, slightly spicy flavours that show a slight lack of delicacy and softness. However, it's strongly varietal and exotically perfumed.

MED/DRY $25 -V

Amor-Bendall Gisborne Gewürztraminer ★★★☆

The 2002 vintage (★★★☆) has a fresh, rich, musky perfume. It's a mouthfilling wine with strong pear, lychees and spice flavours and a crisp, slightly sweet finish. The 2003 (★★★☆) is highly aromatic, with fullness of body (13.4 per cent alcohol) and good depth of fresh, slightly sweet, spicy, peachy flavour.

MED/DRY $23 -V

Artisan Sunvale Estate Gewürztraminer ★★★

The 2003 vintage (★★★) is a Gisborne wine, based on 'very old' vines at Tolaga Bay. Gingery on the nose, it's a dryish, crisp wine with reasonable flavour depth, but lacks real richness, softness and charm.

MED/DRY $18 AV

Askerne Gewürztraminer   ★★★☆

This small Hawke's Bay winery has a good track record with Gewürztraminer. The 2003 (★★★☆) has a perfumed, spicy, musky bouquet, but is less lush and rich than the 2002 (★★★★). The 2004 vintage (★★★★) has scented, very ripe lychees and spice aromas. Weighty and well-spiced, with flavours of pears, lychees and ginger and a slightly oily mouthfeel, in its youth it looked highly promising.

Vintage	04	03	02	01	00	
WR	7	5	6	5	6	MED/DRY $22 -V
Drink	05-07	04-05	04-05	P	P	

Babich Winemakers Reserve Gewürztraminer   ★★★★

This consistently stylish Gewürztraminer is from a small (1.2-hectare) plot in the company's Gimblett Road vineyard, in Hawke's Bay. It's typically a sturdy wine, designed for cellaring, with deep yet delicate lemon/spice flavours. The 2003 vintage (★★★★), from an ultra low-cropping season, is beautifully perfumed, with good body, delicacy and depth of soft lychees and spice flavours. It's an intensely varietal wine, weighty, with gentle acidity and a slightly sweet finish.

Vintage	03	02	01	00	99	98
WR	5	6	7	7	7	7
Drink	04-08	04-08	04-08	04-07	04-06	P

MED/DRY $28 -V

Black Ridge Gewürztraminer   ★★★

The Gewürztraminer style at this Alexandra vineyard has varied over the years, but the wines are always interesting, with a cool-climate, appley edge. It is typically flavoursome, with good weight, firm acidity and a fractionally sweet, gently spicy finish.

DRY $19 -V

Black Ridge Late Harvest Gewürztraminer   (★★☆)

Stop-fermented in a medium-sweet style, the 2003 vintage (★★☆) of this Alexandra, Central Otago wine was harvested at 27 brix and fermented in a mix of tanks and old barrels. It shows some earthy, spicy complexity, but lacks the beguiling fragrance of fine Gewürztraminer.

MED $15 (375ML) -V

Bladen Marlborough Gewürztraminer   ★★★☆

Hand-picked in the Tilly vineyard, the soft, easy-drinking 2004 vintage (★★★☆) is a perfumed, medium-bodied wine (12.5 per cent alcohol) with fresh, ripe lychees, pears and spice flavours, showing good delicacy and depth, and a slightly sweet (14 grams/litre of residual sugar) finish.

MED/DRY $24 -V

Brookfields Ohiti Estate Gewürztraminer   ★★★★

Grown in stony soils in Ohiti Road, inland from Fernhill, this is typically a weighty Hawke's Bay wine with deep, lingering flavours. The 2004 vintage (★★★★), harvested at over 23 brix, shows good body (14 per cent alcohol) and richness, with strong, ripe, well-spiced flavours and a slightly oily texture. It's a big wine, worth cellaring to mid-2005 onwards.

Vintage	04
WR	7
Drink	08-09

MED/DRY $18 V+

Chard Farm Central Otago Gewürztraminer   ★★★☆

The full, fresh 2002 vintage (★★★★) is a blend of grapes grown in the Chard Farm home block at Gibbston and at Cromwell. A medium-dry style, it is still youthful, with rich pear and spice flavours showing intense varietal character. Mouthfilling, with a soft, well-rounded finish, it offers delicious drinking now onwards.

Vintage	02	01
WR	6	5
Drink	04-06	P

MED/DRY $24 -V

Classic Regional Selection Gisborne Gewürztraminer (★★★)

Sold by mail-order wine clubs, the 2003 vintage (★★★) has gingery aromas leading into a crisp, spicy wine, fresh and clean, with clearcut varietal character. Ready.

MED/DRY $18 AV

Clearview Estate Gewürztraminer ★★★☆

The powerful, robust 2003 vintage (★★★☆), grown at Te Awanga, on the Hawke's Bay coastline, has a well-spiced, slightly gingery bouquet and strong lychees and spice flavours, finishing slightly sweet and crisp. Tasted prior to bottling (and so not rated), the 2004 is from an ultra low-cropping season (1.25 tonnes/hectare). It looked good – perfumed and mouthfilling, with intensely varietal, ripe, spicy flavours.

Vintage	03
WR	6
Drink	04-07

MED/DRY $25 -V

Cloudy Bay Marlborough Gewürztraminer ★★★★★

To experience the Cloudy Bay magic at its most spellbinding, try the rare, less-fashionable wines, made in small volumes. The 2002 vintage (★★★★☆), grown at Rapaura and in the Brancott Valley, was harvested at an average of 25.5 brix and fermented with indigenous yeasts and lees-aged in old French oak barrels. Light and youthful in colour, it is richly perfumed, big-bodied (14.4 per cent alcohol) and rounded, with concentrated pear, spice and lychee flavours, plus the almost earthy complexity typical of the label. It's less opulent than the gorgeous 2001 (★★★★★), but offers the substantial body weight and deliciously soft texture found in the classic Gewürztraminers of Alsace.

Vintage	02	01	00	99	98	97
WR	6	6	6	4	NM	5
Drink	04-06	04-06	P	P	NM	P

MED/DRY $29 V+

Collards Hawke's Bay Gewürztraminer (★★★☆)

The smartly priced 2002 vintage (★★★☆) is the first Gewürztraminer for many years from a firm that once pioneered the variety in New Zealand. Perfumed and mouthfilling, it offers very good depth of ripe lychees, ginger and spice flavours, with a soft, basically dry finish. There is no 2003 or 2004.

Vintage	03	02	01
WR	NM	7	NM
Drink	NM	P	NM

DRY $15 V+

Coopers Creek Gisborne Gewürztraminer ★★★☆

A single-vineyard wine, fermented close to dryness (5 grams/litre of residual sugar), the 2004 vintage (★★★☆) is attractively perfumed, with fresh, strong lychees and spice flavours, good texture and weight.

Vintage	04	03
WR	6	5
Drink	04-06	04-05

MED/DRY $17 V+

Crab Farm Gewürztraminer ★★★

The 2001 vintage (★★★) of this Hawke's Bay wine is from an ultra low-yielding season (less than 1 tonne/hectare). Light gold, it's full-bodied and dry, but lacks a bit of freshness and softness. Maturing gracefully, the 2002 (★★★☆) has bright, youthful colour, good weight and plenty of ripe, citrusy, spicy flavour, gingery and earthy. It's a strongly varietal wine, for drinking now onwards.

DRY $15 AV

Crossroads Destination Series Gewürztraminer ★★★

The 2003 vintage (★★), grown in Gisborne, is far less attractive than the scented, ripely flavoured 2002 (★★★☆), from Hawke's Bay. The 2003 is slightly dull, with firm acidity, and lacks freshness, ripeness and roundness.

MED/DRY $19 -V

Dry River Gewürztraminer   ★★★★★

This intensely perfumed and flavoured Martinborough Gewürztraminer is the country's finest, in terms of its gorgeous quality from one vintage to the next. Medium-dry or medium in most years, in top vintages it shows a power and richness comparable to Alsace's *vendange tardive* (late-harvest) wines. Always rich in alcohol and exceptionally full-flavoured, it is also very delicate, with a tight, concentrated, highly refined palate that is typically at its most seductive at two to four years old (although in a recent vertical tasting of the 1992–2003 vintages, the 1996 and younger wines were all drinking well). The 2003 (★★★★) is very expressive in its youth – pale gold, sturdy and intensely varietal, with ripe ginger and spice flavours showing excellent intensity, a hint of honey, good weight and a long, rich finish. The 2004 (★★★★☆), grown in the Lovat Vineyard, is yellow-hued, with a rich, gingery fragrance. A hedonistic wine, robust (14 per cent alcohol), with soft, gently sweet, slightly honeyed flavours, notably rich and rounded, it's already delicious.

Vintage	03	02	01	00	99	98	97	96	MED $37 AV
WR	6	7	7	7	7	6	7	6	
Drink	05-08	04-08	04-07	P	P	P	P	P	🍇 🍇 🍇

Eskdale Winegrowers Gewürztraminer   ★★★☆

Kim Salonius prefers a low profile, but his Hawke's Bay wine (usually several years old) is worth searching for. Typically made from very ripe, late-harvested fruit grown in the Esk Valley, it bursts with character. Most vintages display mouthfilling body and a pungent spiciness; in some years botrytis adds a honeyish intensity.

DRY $20 AV

Forrest Marlborough Gewürztraminer   ★★★★

The exotically perfumed, softly textured 2003 vintage (★★★★) is a weighty and intensely varietal wine with a long, slightly sweet, well-spiced finish. The 2004 (★★★★) is highly promising in its youth. Pale lemon/green, with fresh, pure aromas of lychees, pears and spice, it is mouthfilling (14 per cent alcohol), vibrant, ripe and rounded, with a splash of sweetness (11.5 grams/litre of residual sugar) and loads of varietal character.

Vintage	04	03	02	01	MED/DRY $25 -V
WR	5	6	5	5	
Drink	04-08	04-07	P	P	

Framingham Marlborough Gewürztraminer   ★★★★

This label has shown rising form in recent vintages and the 2003 (★★★★) is already drinking well. Estate-grown at Renwick, it is musky and smooth, with ripe, delicate, slightly sweet flavours of lychees and spice, showing excellent richness. It's a high-alcohol style (14 per cent), weighty and soft.

Vintage	03	02	01	00	99	MED/DRY $27 -V
WR	5	6	7	6	5	
Drink	04-06	04-05	04-05	P	P	

Francis-Cole Marlborough Gewürztraminer   (★★★)

The fresh, smooth 2003 vintage (★★★) was made from first-crop vines in the Omaka Valley and fermented dry. It's a full-bodied, softly structured wine with moderately ripe, citrusy, appley, spicy flavours showing good depth.

Vintage	03	DRY $21 -V
WR	6	
Drink	04-07	

Fromm La Strada Gewürztraminer   (★★★★)

'A pet variety on the sideline' is winemaker Hatsch Kalberer's description of Gewürztraminer, which occupies a tiny, 0.1-hectare plot in the estate vineyard. The bone-dry 2003 vintage (★★★★) is a rare beast

– only 32 cases were produced. Impressively weighty and well-rounded, with deep lychees and spice flavours, it is rich and long, although the total absence of sweetness does expose a bit of Gewürztraminer's characteristic phenolic hardness.

Vintage	04	03	02	01
WR		6	6	5	6
Drink	04-08	04-07	04-06	04-06

DRY $34 -V

Glenmark Waipara Gewürztraminer ★★☆

The dry, lemony 2001 vintage (★★☆) is less attractive and clearly varietal than the 2002 (★★★), a crisp, fresh and lively wine with good depth of citrusy, gently spiced flavour.

DRY $24 -V

Grove Mill Winemakers Reserve Gewürztraminer (★★☆)

The 2001 vintage (★★☆) is a single-vineyard Marlborough wine, grown in the Waihopai Valley and stop-fermented with a distinct splash (22 grams/litre) of residual sugar. It's a solid, lemony, appley wine, but lacks the exotic aromas and flavours of this variety at its best.

MED $20 -V

Huia Marlborough Gewürztraminer ★★★★

This is a consistently characterful wine. The excellent 2003 vintage (★★★★) was hand-harvested at two Wairau Valley sites, fermented with indigenous yeasts, and a small portion was briefly matured in seasoned French oak casks. Rich and soft, with a perfumed, musky bouquet, it shows very good ripeness, delicacy and concentration, with a slightly oily texture and strong drink-young appeal.

Vintage	03	02	01
WR	6	6	7
Drink	04-07	04-05	04-05

DRY $23 AV

Huntaway Reserve Gisborne/Marlborough Gewürztraminer (★★★☆)

Verging on four-star quality, the 2002 vintage (★★★☆) is a ripely aromatic wine from Allied Domecq, full-bodied and slightly sweet, with good palate weight, varietal character and depth of lychees, spice and ginger flavours. Lush and exotically perfumed, it has strong upfront appeal.

Vintage	02
WR	7
Drink	04-10

MED/DRY $20 AV

Hunter's Marlborough Gewürztraminer ★★★★

Hunter's produces an excellent Gewürztraminer, with good weight and clearly defined varietal character. The 2004 vintage (★★★☆) has a full-bloomed, musky bouquet leading into a slightly sweet, mouthfilling (14 per cent alcohol) wine with lots of ripe, lychees and spice flavours and balanced acidity, but also a slightly hard finish.

Vintage	03	02	01	00	99	98
WR	6	5	6	6	5	5
Drink	06	05	04-05	P	P	P

MED/DRY $19 V+

Johanneshof Marlborough Gewürztraminer ★★★★☆

The hard-to-resist 2003 vintage (★★★★★) was harvested at up to 25 brix from first-crop vines in the lower Wairau Valley and handled entirely in tanks, with some lees-aging. An unabashedly medium style (24 grams/litre of residual sugar), it is exotically perfumed, with a heady bouquet of ginger and spice. Rich, lush and soft, it shows lovely harmony, concentration and length.

MED $27 AV

Kahurangi Estate Nelson Gewürztraminer ★★★☆

This Upper Moutere winery produces a consistently enjoyable Gewürztraminer. The 2003 vintage (★★★☆), grown in the Moutere hills and on the Waimea Plains, is a mouthfilling, medium style (15 grams/litre of residual sugar) with a slightly oily texture and good depth of ripe pear, ginger and spice flavours. Drink now onwards.

Vintage	03
WR	5
Drink	04-07

MED $19 AV

Kaikoura Marlborough Gewürztraminer ★★★☆

The 2002 vintage (★★★☆), grown on the south side of the Wairau Valley, is a slightly sweet style, richly perfumed, with substantial body and very good depth of citrusy, spicy flavour.

MED/DRY $19 AV

Kaimira Estate Brightwater Gewürztraminer (★★★)

Tasted shortly after bottling, the full-bodied 2004 vintage (★★★) is a slightly sweet Nelson wine, based on first-crop vines in the estate vineyard. It offers fresh flavours of lemons and lychees and a gently spiced, smooth finish.

Vintage	04
WR	5
Drink	05-06

MED/DRY $22 -V

Kathy Lynskey Single Vineyard Gewürztraminer (★★★)

Grown in Marlborough, the 2003 vintage (★★★) is a full-bodied, slightly sweet wine with fresh, citrusy, gently spicy flavours.

MED/DRY $25 -V

Kemblefield The Distinction Gewürztraminer ★★★

Blended from estate-grown and other Hawke's Bay grapes, and bottled after extended aging on its yeast lees, the 2002 vintage (★★★) is citrusy, spicy and gingery, with a slightly off-dry finish. The 2003 (★★★), grown in Gisborne, offers decent depth of pear and spice flavours, with a slightly sweet, soft finish.

MED/DRY $19 -V

Landmark Estate Gisborne Gewürztraminer (★★☆)

Golden, quite developed in colour, the 2002 vintage (★★☆) is a characterful wine, citrusy and very gingery, with plenty of flavour, but also shows a slight lack of freshness. Drink now.

MED/DRY $19 -V

Lawson's Dry Hills Marlborough Gewürztraminer ★★★★★

This is consistently one of the country's most impressive Gewürztraminers. Grown near the winery in the Lawson and adjacent Woodward vineyards, at the foot of the Wither Hills, the 2003 (★★★★☆) is a forward vintage, delicious from the start. Harvested at over 24 brix, it was mostly cool-fermented in stainless steel tanks, but 7 per cent was given 'the full treatment', with a high-solids, indigenous yeast ferment in seasoned French oak barriques, malolactic fermentation and lees-stirring. Light yellow/green, it is intensely varietal, mouthfilling and concentrated, with lovely freshness and delicacy of lychees, pear and spice flavours, fresh acidity, impressive harmony and a dryish (7.8 grams/litre of sugar) finish.

Vintage	04	03	02	01	00	99	98
WR	7	7	7	6	6	6	5
Drink	04-09	04-07	04-06	04-05	P	P	P

MED/DRY $22 V+

Lincoln Heritage Gisborne Gewürztraminer   (★★★★)

The richly perfumed 2004 vintage (★★★★) is a fully dry wine (unusual for Gewürztraminer), tank-fermented and matured for six months on its yeast lees, with weekly lees-stirring. Weighty (13.5 per cent alcohol) and spicy, with rich, peppery, gingery aromas and flavours, fresh and crisp, it carries the dry style well. Drink 2005–06.

DRY $19 V+

Longridge Vineyards Gewürztraminer   ★★★☆

From one vintage to the next, this is a bargain. As a long-popular Corbans brand, it was always a Hawke's Bay wine, but the 2002 vintage (★★★☆) from Allied Domecq is blended from Hawke's Bay (46 per cent), Gisborne (38 per cent) and Marlborough (16 per cent) grapes. It's an aromatic, characterful wine, weighty, with strong spicy, peachy flavours and a slightly sweet, rounded finish. There is no 2003 or 2004, but the label has not been phased out.

Vintage	04	03	02	01
WR	NM	NM	6	NM
Drink	NM	NM	04-07	NM

MED/DRY $15 V+

Longview Gewürztraminer   (★★)

Grown in Northland, just south of Whangarei, the 2002 vintage (★★) lacks the perfume typical of Gewürztraminer. It's a crisp, slightly sweet wine with some varietal spiciness, but the flavour is also restrained.

Vintage	02
WR	5
Drink	04-05

DRY $21 -V

Margrain Martinborough Gewürztraminer   ★★★★

Sturdy and impressively concentrated, the 2002 vintage (★★★★) is a late-harvest style, picked at 26.5 brix and stop-fermented with 33 grams per litre of residual sugar. It's a medium-sweet style with noticeably high alcohol (14.5 per cent), an aromatic, intensely varietal bouquet, strong lychees and spice flavours, gentle acidity and a soft finish. The 2003 (★★★☆) is again a medium style, with a spicy, full-bloomed bouquet, light body (11.5 per cent alcohol) and fresh, crisp flavours of lychees and spices showing good delicacy and length.

Vintage	03	02	01	00
WR	7	7	7	6
Drink	04-07	04-06	04-05	P

MED $30 -V

Matawhero Reserve Gewürztraminer   ★★★★

An acclaimed Gisborne wine in the late 1970s and early 1980s, when it was arrestingly perfumed and concentrated, since then its style has been slightly less pungent, with a soft finish. The use of indigenous yeasts and malolactic fermentation has toned down the varietal character, but the wine is impressively weighty, with strong gingery, slightly honeyed and toasty flavours.

DRY $28 -V

Matua Valley Judd Estate Gewürztraminer   (★★★★)

The ripely perfumed 2004 vintage (★★★★) was grown at the Judd Estate vineyard in Gisborne. It's a substantial wine (14 per cent alcohol) with excellent varietal definition and depth of lychees and spice flavours, finishing smooth and just off-dry.

Vintage	04
WR	5
Drink	04-06

MED/DRY $25 -V

Melness Late Harvest Gewürztraminer   (★★★☆)

Estate-grown in Canterbury, harvested at a very ripe 27.5 brix and stop-fermented in a distinctly medium style (28 grams/litre of residual sugar), the 2003 vintage (★★★☆) is a softly seductive wine with elegant lychees and spice aromas. Fresh and lively, it shows good body and depth, with very pure varietal flavours and some lushness.

Vintage	03
WR	7
Drink	04-10

MED $19 (375ML) -V

Mills Reef Gewürztraminer   (★★★☆)

Already drinking well, the 2004 vintage (★★★☆) is a Hawke's Bay wine with well-spiced aromas and good weight and texture. Its ripe lychees and spice flavours show plenty of depth, with a slightly sweet finish.

MED/DRY $17 V+

Mills Reef Reserve Gewürztraminer   ★★★☆

Grown in Hawke's Bay, the 2004 vintage (★★★☆) is a medium to full-bodied wine (12.5 per cent alcohol) with a punchy, spicy bouquet. Tightly structured, with fresh acidity and good depth of citrus fruit, lychee and spice flavours, it's a dryish wine, likely to be at its best from mid-2005 onwards.

Vintage	04
WR	7
Drink	05-06

MED/DRY $22 -V

Millton The Growers Series Gisborne Gewürztraminer   ★★★☆

Grown in the McIldowie vineyard, which is not managed organically, the 2004 vintage (★★★★) is the best yet. Fermented in a mix of tanks (90 per cent) and large barrels (10 per cent), it has loads of character, with rich, full-spiced flavours, fresh, ripe and vibrant, balanced acidity and a slightly sweet (7 grams/litre of residual sugar) finish. Still youthful, it's worth keeping to mid-2005+.

Vintage	04
WR	5
Drink	04-08

MED/DRY $19 AV

Mission Church Road Gewürztraminer   ★★★

Typically an easy-drinking style, fruity, fresh and flavoursome. The 2003 vintage (★★★), estate-grown at Greenmeadows, Taradale, in Hawke's Bay, has a slightly musky perfume, with ripe, citrusy, moderately spicy flavours and a gingery, off-dry, rounded finish.

MED/DRY $15 AV

Montana Patutahi Estate Gewürztraminer   ★★★★☆

Full of character, at its best this is a mouthfilling wine with a musky perfume and intense pepper and lychees-like flavours, delicate and lush. Grown hard against the hills inland from the city of Gisborne, it is harvested very ripe, with some botrytis-affected, nobly rotten grapes, picked at a super-ripe 28 to 30 brix, imparting an apricot-like lusciousness to the final blend. The 2003 vintage (★★★★) was made from low-cropped vines (less than 5 tonnes/hectare), harvested (60 per cent by hand) at 22.5 brix and stop-fermented in a medium-dry style (14.7 grams/litre of residual sugar). It's a richly perfumed wine, with strong yet delicate flavours of lychees, pears and spice and crisper acidity than usual, balanced by a distinct splash of sweetness. It's a refined, firmly structured wine, less lush than from a top season, but still rewarding.

Vintage	03	02	01	00	99	98
WR	6	7	NM	6	NM	6
Drink	04-06	04-06	NM	P	NM	P

MED/DRY $24 V+

Montana Reserve Gewürztraminer (★★★★)

The debut 2004 vintage (★★★★) is a highly attractive blend of Gisborne (77 per cent) and Marlborough grapes, made in a medium-dry style (10 grams/litre of residual sugar). Mouthfilling and smooth, it has strong, ripe lychee and spice flavours, good weight, texture and harmony and a lingering, well-spiced finish. Drink now onwards.

MED/DRY $20 V+

Ohinemuri Estate Gisborne Gewürztraminer ★★★

Grown at Ormond, the 2002 (★★★) is an obviously sweet wine (15 grams/litre of sugar), crisp and flavoursome, with lychees and spice characters showing some richness.

Vintage	02	01
WR	6	6
Drink	04-06	04-05

MED $20 -V

Olssen's Central Otago Gewürztraminer ★★★☆

The 2003 vintage (★★☆) was estate-grown at Bannockburn, picked at 23.4 brix and mostly tank-fermented, but 15 per cent of the blend was fermented and lees-aged for three months in old French oak barriques. It's a dry style (only 3.4 grams/litre of residual sugar), mouthfilling (14 per cent alcohol), with green-edged, gently spiced flavours that lack the intensity of earlier vintages.

Vintage	03
WR	6
Drink	04-13

DRY $24 -V

Paradox Marlborough Gewürztraminer (★★☆)

Sold by mail-order wine clubs, the 2003 vintage (★★☆) is a solid but plain wine with lemony, appley, gently spiced flavours, slightly sweet and crisp.

MED/DRY $20 -V

Peregrine Central Otago Gewürztraminer ★★★☆

The 2003 vintage (★★★) was grown in two vineyards at Lowburn Inlet (in the Cromwell Basin). It's a pale, medium-bodied wine with crisp flavours of lemons, apples and spices and a slightly sweet finish.

DRY $23 -V

Pleasant Valley Marlborough Gewürztraminer ★★★

Drinking well now, the 2002 vintage (★★★) is a soft, full-bodied wine (13.5 per cent alcohol) with good depth of lychees and spice flavours and a slightly sweet (7 grams/litre of residual sugar), rounded finish.

MED/DRY $16 AV

Revington Vineyard Gisborne Gewürztraminer ★★★★

The Revington vineyard in Gisborne's Ormond Valley yields a rare wine that has ranked among the country's finest Gewürztraminers. The 2004 vintage (★★★★☆), low-cropped (below 5 tonnes/hectare) and harvested at over 26 brix, is already delicious. Light yellow, with a rich, ripe, well-spiced bouquet, it's a weighty, medium style (18 grams/litre of residual sugar) with lychees, ginger and spice flavours showing lovely ripeness, depth and roundness, a slightly oily texture and rich finish.

Vintage	04
WR	7
Drink	05+

MED $26 -V

Rockburn Central Otago Gewürztraminer   (★★★)

Restrained in its youth, the 2003 vintage (★★★) was made from first-crop vines at Lowburn, in the Cromwell Basin. Tank-fermented and lees-aged for seven months, it's a pale, full-bodied wine with fresh apple, pear and spice aromas and flavours, showing good delicacy, and a dry (4 grams/litre of residual sugar), rounded finish. Worth cellaring for a year or two.

DRY $25 -V

Rossendale Canterbury Gewürztraminer   ★★☆

The 2002 vintage (★★), tasted in 2004, looked tired and past its best.

MED $18 -V

St Jerome Gisborne Gewürztraminer   (★★)

The 2002 vintage (★★) is a slightly rustic, soft wine with a distinct splash of sweetness. It lacks the richness and enticing perfume of fine-quality Gewürztraminer.

MED $19 -V

Saints Gisborne Gewürztraminer   ★★★☆

Grown at Patutahi, Allied Domecq's wine is typically rich and flavour-packed, with loads of varietal character. The 2003 (★★☆) is less lush than past vintages, with crisp, gingery, dryish flavours that lack real delicacy and depth, but the excellent 2004 (★★★★) brings a return to form. Light yellow, with a lifted, spicy, perfumed bouquet, it's a smooth, generous wine with soft, rich lychees and spice flavours, already delicious, and a slightly sweet (12 grams/litre of residual sugar) finish.

Vintage	04	03	02	01	00
WR	6	6	6	NM	7
Drink	04-08	04-08	04-07	NM	P

MED/DRY $17 V+

Seifried Nelson Gewürztraminer   ★★★★

Gewürztraminer is represented in the Seifried range in two styles: medium-dry and the sweet Ice Wine. This is typically a floral, well-spiced, crisp wine, very easy-drinking, and recent vintages have been of excellent quality. The 2003 (★★★★) is a strongly varietal wine with a spicy, musky bouquet, good weight, a rich, oily texture and gently sweet (14 grams/litre of residual sugar), gingery flavours showing excellent depth. The 2004 (★★★☆) has a fresh, well-spiced bouquet leading into a medium to full-bodied palate with finely balanced, ripe flavours of lychees and spice, showing good depth, and a sweetish (20 grams/litre of residual sugar) finish.

Vintage	04	03	02	01	00	99	98
WR	6	7	7	6	6	6	6
Drink	04-07	04-07	04-06	04-05	04-05	P	P

MED $18 V+

Seifried Winemaker's Collection Nelson Gewürztraminer ★★★★

This is typically a rich wine with loads of character. Based on the oldest vines in the company's Redwood Valley vineyard, the 2003 vintage (★★★★) has a pungent, gingery bouquet, good weight and strong, well-spiced flavours with a slightly sweet (13 grams/litre of residual sugar), lasting finish. The 2004 (★★★★) is light yellow, with a rich, gingery bouquet. Already drinking well, it has concentrated flavours of lychees, ginger and spice, with a slightly sweet (10 grams/litre of residual sugar), rich finish.

Vintage	04	03	02	01	00	99
WR	6	7	7	6	6	6
Drink	04-07	04-09	04-08	04-07	04-06	P

MED/DRY $23 AV

Soljans Gisborne Gewürztraminer ★★★

Drinking well from the start, the 2002 vintage (★★★) is ripely scented, fruity and vibrant, with mouthfilling body, lychees and spice flavours and a slightly sweet, smooth finish. An earthy character gives it a slightly European feel.

MED/DRY $16 AV

Spy Valley Marlborough Gewürztraminer ★★★★

The 2003 vintage (★★★★☆) was estate-grown in the Waihopai Valley, picked at a ripe 23.5 to 24 brix and stop-fermented with a splash (7.5 grams/litre) of residual sugar. Headily perfumed, it's a powerful, weighty wine (14 per cent alcohol), very ripe and spicy, with gentle acidity and excellent intensity and mouthfeel. It's a highly expressive wine, delicious in its youth.

Vintage	04	03
WR	6	6
Drink	04-07	04-06

MED/DRY $20 V+

Stonecroft Gewürztraminer ★★★★★

Based on 20-year-old vines, the Gewürztraminers from this tiny Hawke's Bay winery are striking and among the finest in the country. Fermented and matured for three months in French oak casks, the 2003 vintage (★★★☆) is a bone-dry wine from an ultra low-yielding season (less than 1 tonne/hectare). It carries the dry style well, with ripe, citrusy, spicy flavours, but is less powerful and lush than the wines of top years. (The rich, oily 1994 vintage, opened in 2004, was amazingly youthful.)

Vintage	03	02	01	00	99
WR	5	6	6	6	6
Drink	06+	04-10	04-06	04-10	04-06

DRY $25 V+

Te Whare Ra Marlborough Gewürztraminer ★★★★★

Arrestingly powerful and rich, this hedonistic wine (in the past labelled as Duke of Marlborough) usually crams more sheer flavour into the glass than most other Gewürztraminers from the region – or anywhere else. Made from 25-year-old vines at Renwick, the 2004 vintage (★★★★☆) is more restrained in its youth than some past releases, but built to last. Harvested at 24.3 brix and stop-fermented in a medium-dry style (13 grams/litre of residual sugar), it possesses lovely depth of delicate pear, lychees and spice flavours, very fresh and vibrant, with a seductively soft texture. Open mid-2005+.

MED/DRY $28 V+

Torlesse Waipara Gewürztraminer (★★☆)

Made in a fully dry style, the 2002 vintage (★★☆) is crisp, with lemony, slightly spicy and gingery, green-edged flavours. It's a moderately varietal wine that lacks a bit of richness and softness.

Vintage	02
WR	7
Drink	04-05

DRY $17 -V

Villa Maria Cellar Selection East Coast Gewürztraminer (NR)

Exotically perfumed, with richly spiced flavours, the 2004 vintage (tasted before bottling, and so not rated) looked highly promising. It's an almost bone-dry style (3 grams/litre of residual sugar).

DRY $20 V?

Villa Maria Private Bin East Coast Gewürztraminer   ★★★☆

This long-popular wine is fruity and well-spiced, with a sliver of sweetness. A regional blend of Marlborough, Hawke's Bay and Gisborne fruit, the 2003 vintage (★★★★) shows good weight and texture, with strong, ripe-citrus and spice flavours, fresh acidity and a richly perfumed, spicy, gingery bouquet. Tasted just after bottling, the 2004 (★★★★) looked equally good, with gentle acidity, mouthfilling body, concentrated varietal spiciness and a full-bloomed fragrance.

Vintage	04	03	02	01	00	99	98
WR	6	5	6	6	6	5	7
Drink	04-06	04-05	P	P	P	P	P

MED/DRY $18 V+

Vinoptima Ormond Gewürztraminer   (★★★★☆)

From Nick Nobilo, for many years head of Nobilo Vintners, the debut 2003 vintage (★★★★☆) is from a young vineyard at Ormond, in Gisborne, devoted solely to Gewürztraminer. Harvested at an average of 24.5 brix and fermented in tanks and large German oak casks, it's an exotically perfumed, distinctly medium style (16 grams/litre of residual sugar), mouthfilling, with rich, ripe flavours of lychees and spices. From a challenging season, it lacks the seductive softness of great Gewürztraminer, but shows excellent weight, structure and depth.

MED $48 -V

Waipara Hills Marlborough Gewürztraminer   ★★★★☆

The 2003 vintage (★★★★★) is rewarding. A fleshy, soft, single-vineyard wine, made in a medium style, it has a gently musky, perfumed bouquet, good weight, strong, ripe flavours of pears, lychees and spice, and lovely varietal character and texture. The 2004 (★★★★) is similar, with a musky bouquet, soft, punchy flavours of lychees, ginger and spice and plentiful sweetness (15 grams/litre of residual sugar).

Vintage	03
WR	7
Drink	04-13

MED $22 V+

Wairau River Marlborough Gewürztraminer   ★★★☆

The easy-drinking 2003 vintage (★★★☆) has a sliver of sweetness (7.9 grams/litre of residual sugar) amidst its ripe, citrusy, spicy flavours, with a soft finish. The 2004 (★★★★) has great upfront appeal, with a richly perfumed bouquet, mouthfilling body (14 per cent alcohol) and loads of lychee, spice and stone-fruit flavours, ripe and smooth.

Vintage	03	02
WR	7	7
Drink	04-06	04-06

MED/DRY $20 AV

Whitehaven Single Vineyard Reserve Gewürztraminer   ★★★★

The 2003 vintage (★★★) is less memorable than the lush, softly seductive wines of the past. The bouquet is restrained; the palate is slightly sweet, lemony and gingery, with good but not great intensity.

MED/DRY $20 V+

William Hill Gewürztraminer   ★★★☆

Gewürztraminer is a minor variety in Central Otago, but the William Hill winery at Alexandra has long crusaded on its behalf. Estate-grown, the 2002 (★★★★) is a perfumed and weighty wine (although only 12.5 per cent alcohol), with gentle acidity and a delicious delicacy and depth of ripe lychees and spice flavours. The 2003 vintage (★★★), harvested at 23 brix and stop-fermented in an off-dry style (5.8 grams/litre of residual sugar), is a full-bodied wine with decent depth of pear and spice flavours, but it lacks real intensity.

Vintage	03	02	01
WR	5	5	6
Drink	04-06	04-05	P

MED/DRY $23 -V

Müller-Thurgau

Every country has had its 'vin ordinaire' grape varieties: the south of France its endless tracts of red Carignan and white Ugni Blanc; Australia its ubiquitous Sultana and Trebbiano (Ugni Blanc); New Zealand its highly prolific Müller-Thurgau.

Professor Hermann Müller, a native of the Swiss canton of Thurgau, who worked at the Geisenheim viticultural station in Germany, wrote in 1882 of the benefits of 'combining the superb characteristics of the Riesling grape with the reliable early maturing qualities of the Sylvaner'. The variety Müller created (most likely a crossing of Riesling and Sylvaner, as he intended, but possibly of two different Rieslings) became extremely popular in Germany after the Second World War. Müller-Thurgau was prized by German growers not for the Riesling-like quality of its wine (it is far blander) but for its ability to ripen early with bumper crops.

In New Zealand, where plantings started to snowball in the early 1970s, by 1975 the same qualities had made it our most widely planted variety. Today, Müller-Thurgau is only number 10 in terms of its area of bearing vines, and between 2000 and 2006 its plantings are projected to contract from 430 hectares to 227 hectares.

The grape's dramatic decline reflects New Zealand's success with far more prestigious white-wine varieties like Sauvignon Blanc and Chardonnay. Allied Domecq also now finds it much cheaper to import the bulk wine it needs to fill its highly price-sensitive casks. The remaining Müller-Thurgau vines are concentrated in three regions: Gisborne (with almost half of all plantings), Hawke's Bay and Marlborough.

Müller-Thurgau should be drunk young, at six to 18 months old, when its garden-fresh aromas are in full flower. To attract those who are new to wine, it is typically made slightly sweet. Its fruity, citrusy flavours are typically mild and soft, lacking the intensity and crisp acid structure of Riesling.

Corbans White Label Müller-Thurgau ★★☆

This cheap wine is typically smooth and lemon-scented, with moderate sweetness balanced by crisp acidity in a light-bodied style with mild, appley flavours.

`MED/DRY $9 AV`

Jackman Ridge Müller-Thurgau ★★☆

Produced by Allied Domecq, this regional blend offers pleasant lemony, appley flavours and a distinct splash of sweetness (it is markedly sweeter than its stablemate, the Corbans White Label, above). Not vintage-dated, it is typically medium-bodied, with a soft finish.

`MED $8 AV`

Opihi Vineyard Müller-Thurgau ★★★

Müller-Thurgau is out of fashion in New Zealand, but of those still around this is one of the best. Grown at Pleasant Point in South Canterbury, it is typically fresh and floral, light and easy, with soft, ripe, lemony fruit characters. A good lunch wine.

`MED/DRY $11 AV`

Reminisce Müller-Thurgau   (★★★★)

From veteran winemaker Nick Nobilo (whose Nobilo Müller-Thurgau enjoyed runaway popularity in the 1960s and 1970s), the debut 2003 vintage (★★★★) is a highly enjoyable trip down memory lane. A Gisborne wine, freeze-concentrated to intensify its flavours, it is light (10.5 per cent alcohol) and lively, with fresh, lemony, limey (Riesling-like) flavours showing much greater depth and zestiness than most Müller-Thurgaus and a slightly sweet (12 grams/litre of residual sugar), crisp finish.

 MED/DRY $14 AV

Villa Maria Private Bin Müller-Thurgau   ★★★

In its youth, this wine is scented and lively – as Müller-Thurgau must be to have any appeal. A medium style, grown on the east coast of the North Island, it's typically fresh and smooth, with delicate, ripe, lemony flavours, refreshing and floral.

 MED $9 V+

Wohnsiedler Müller-Thurgau   ★★

Wohnsiedler won a gold medal or two for Montana decades ago, when Müller-Thurgau ruled the roost in New Zealand. Now a non-vintage regional blend, it's typically light, fruity, lemony and soft. Made in a medium style, it is fractionally sweeter than its Jackman Ridge stablemate (above).

MED $8 AV

Osteiner

This crossing of Riesling and Sylvaner is a rarity not only in New Zealand (with less than two hectares planted) but also in its native Germany. Only Rippon, at Lake Wanaka, has shown long-term interest in this obscure variety.

Rippon Osteiner   ★★☆

This fragile Lake Wanaka wine tastes like a restrained Riesling. It is typically pale and tangy, with light body and lemon, apple and lime flavours cut with fresh acidity.

DRY $17 -V

Pinot Blanc

If you love Chardonnay, try Pinot Blanc. A white mutation of Pinot Noir, Pinot Blanc is highly regarded in Italy and California for its generous extract and moderate acidity, although in Alsace and Germany, the more aromatic Pinot Gris finds greater favour.

With its fullness of weight and restrained, appley aroma, Pinot Blanc can easily be mistaken for Chardonnay in a blind tasting. The variety is still rare in New Zealand, but between 2003 and 2006, the area of bearing vines will expand from 6 to 9 hectares, mostly in Canterbury and Central Otago.

Escarpment Pinot Blanc/Chardonnay   (★★★★)

Grown in the Escarpment Vineyard at Martinborough, the 2003 vintage (★★★★) is a fleshy, slightly creamy dry wine with subtle flavours of citrus fruits, peaches and apples. It shows good mouthfeel and texture, with moderate acidity, a hint of oak and some complexity.

DRY $29 -V

Gibbston Valley Central Otago Pinot Blanc   ★★★☆

Arguably the finest Pinot Blanc yet made in New Zealand, the 2002 vintage (★★★★☆) is fat and rich, with a strong surge of flavour, impressive weight (14.5 per cent alcohol) and a dry finish. The 2003 (★★★) was matured for 11 months in old, neutral casks, with frequent lees-stirring and full malolactic fermentation. Full-bodied, citrusy and spicy, with slightly candied aromas, it's less powerful and lush than the 2002, but still has good mouthfeel and presence.

Vintage   03
WR   5
Drink   04-09

DRY $28 -V

Pinot Gris

Pinot Gris has soared in popularity in recent years, making this one of the fastest-growing sections of the *Buyer's Guide*. It will account for only 2.3 per cent of the total producing vineyard area in 2005, but the vine is spreading swiftly – from 130 hectares of bearing vines in 2000 to 462 hectares in 2005. Pinot Gris is now the country's fourth most widely planted white-wine variety, behind only Sauvignon Blanc, Chardonnay and Riesling.

A mutation of Pinot Noir, Pinot Gris has skin colours ranging from blue-grey to reddish-pink, sturdy extract and a fairly subtle, spicy aroma. It is not a difficult variety to cultivate, adapting well to most soils, and ripens with fairly low acidity to high sugar levels. In Alsace, the best Pinot Gris are matured in large casks, but the wood is old, so as not to interfere with the grape's subtle flavour.

What does Pinot Gris taste like? Imagine a wine that couples the satisfying weight in the mouth of Chardonnay with some of the rich spiciness of Gewürztraminer. If you like substantial, refined dry whites that enhance food and can flourish long term in the cellar (the Germans recommend drinking the wine when it has 'grey hairs'), Pinot Gris is well worth getting to know.

In terms of style and quality, New Zealand Pinot Gris vary widely. Many of the wines lack the mouthfilling body, flavour richness and softness of the benchmark wines from Alsace. These lesser wines, probably made from heavily cropped vines, are lean and crisp – more in the tradition of cheap Italian Pinot Grigio.

Popular in Germany, Alsace and Italy, Pinot Gris is now playing an important role here too. Over half of all plantings are concentrated in Marlborough and Otago, but there are also significant pockets of Pinot Gris in Gisborne, Hawke's Bay, Martinborough and Canterbury.

Akarua Pinot Gris   ★★★☆

Grown at Bannockburn, in Central Otago, and 15 per cent barrel-fermented, the 2003 vintage (★★★☆) is faintly pink, with pear, lemon and spice flavours in a crisp, distinctly cool-climate style. It's a full-bodied, fresh and flavoursome wine, slightly sweet (7 grams/litre of residual sugar), with some complexity and length.

Vintage	03	02	01
WR	6	6	5
Drink	04-08	04-07	04-05

MED/DRY $25 -V

Alan McCorkindale Waipara Valley Pinot Gris   ★★★★☆

A label to watch. The 2002 vintage (★★★★☆) is distinctly Alsace-like, and so is the rich, opulent 2003 (★★★★★). Harvested at a very high sugar level (over 26 brix) in the Kimball vineyard at Waipara, it has lovely depth of peach, pear and spice flavours in a high-alcohol, medium-dry style (12.5 grams/litre of residual sugar) with a deliciously soft texture and excellent weight, ripeness and richness.

MED/DRY $28 AV

Allan Scott Marlborough Pinot Gris   (★★★)

An easy-drinking style, the 2004 vintage (★★★) is faintly pink, with fresh lychee and spice scents. A medium-bodied wine with clearly varietal flavours and a slightly sweet finish, it should open out during 2005–06.

MED/DRY $25 -V

Amisfield Central Otago Pinot Gris   (★★★★)

The faintly pink, debut 2002 vintage (★★★★) was grown at Amisfield Vineyard, in the Cromwell Basin, and 20 per cent of the blend was fermented and lees-aged for five months in large (600-litre) French oak casks. Spice and stone-fruit aromas lead into a fresh, full-bodied (13.9 per cent alcohol), slightly oily and rounded wine with peach, lemon and distinctly spicy flavours, subtle oak and lees-aging characters and a fractionally sweet finish.

Vintage	04
WR	4
Drink	04-06

MED/DRY $30 -V

Amor-Bendall Gisborne Pinot Gris   ★★★☆

A dry style, the 2004 vintage (★★★☆) has fresh, strong, pear-like aromas leading into a tight, youthful palate with gently spicy, citrus and pear flavours showing good depth. Worth cellaring to 2006.

DRY $22 AV

Ascension Matakana Pinot Gris   (★★★★)

The 2002 vintage (★★★★) is a richly varietal wine, grown north of Auckland, harvested ripe (at 25 brix) and fermented and lees-aged in seasoned French oak barriques. It's full and rounded, with excellent depth of clearly delineated stone-fruit, pear and spice flavours, subtle oak adding complexity and a well-rounded, lingering finish.

DRY $25 AV

Ata Rangi Lismore Pinot Gris   ★★★★☆

Harvested at 26 brix in Ro and Lyle Griffiths' Lismore vineyard in Martinborough, 'just a stone's throw from the Ata Rangi home block', the 2004 vintage (★★★★☆) is a weighty (13.5 per cent alcohol) wine with fresh pear and spice aromas. A slightly sweet style (13 grams/litre of residual sugar), it's a finely balanced, intensely varietal wine with gentle acidity and lovely texture. It's already delicious.

Vintage	04	03	02	01	00
WR	7	7	7	6	6
Drink	04-07	04-05	P	P	P

MED/DRY $28 AV

Babich Marlborough Pinot Gris   ★★★☆

Grown in the Pigou vineyard, on the Rapaura (north) side of the Wairau Valley, the 2003 vintage (★★★★) was 50 per cent fermented in seasoned French oak casks; the rest was handled in tanks. It shows good fragrance, ripeness and texture. Fresh and weighty, it offers strong peach, pear and spice flavours, with a fractionally sweet finish. The 2004 (★★★) is a clearly varietal, slightly sweet wine with fresh pear and spice aromas and flavours, but in its infancy looked less powerful and concentrated than the 2003.

Vintage	03	02	01	00	99	98
WR	7	7	7	7	7	7
Drink	04-06	04-05	04-05	P	P	P

MED/DRY $20 AV

Bald Hills Pigeon Rocks Pinot Gris   (★★★☆)

From the Hunt family's tiny (1-hectare) vineyard at Bannockburn, in Central Otago, the debut 2003 vintage (★★★☆) is a dry style, fresh and lively, with soaring alcohol (14.5 per cent), very good depth of lychees and apple flavours and a well-spiced finish.

Vintage	04	03
WR	5	6
Drink	04-10	04-09

DRY $24 -V

Bilancia Pinot Grigio ★★★★

Bilancia is based in Hawke's Bay, but this wine is often made from Marlborough grapes; the 2004 vintage (★★★★☆) is the first since 1999 to be grown in Hawke's Bay. Instantly appealing, with a light lemon/green hue and fresh, forthcoming pear and spice aromas, it's a weighty, ripely flavoured, softly textured wine with substantial body, a sliver of sweetness (6 grams/litre of residual sugar) and lovely richness and harmony.

Vintage	04	03	02	01
WR	7	6	7	6
Drink	04-07	04-06	04-06	P

MED/DRY $30 -V

Bilancia Reserve Pinot Grigio ★★★★

Grown in Hawke's Bay, the 2003 vintage (★★★★) was fermented and lees-aged for six months in old barrels, with full malolactic fermentation. The bouquet is fresh and vibrantly fruity; the palate youthful, with excellent depth of ripe grapefruit and pear flavours, subtle oak and a dryish, spicy finish. It's a harmonious wine, built to last; open 2005+.

Vintage	03	02
WR	6	6
Drink	04-07	04-06

MED/DRY $33 -V

Blackenbrook Vineyard Nelson Pinot Gris (★★★)

Fresh and lively, the 2004 vintage (★★★) is a medium-dry style (11 grams/litre of residual sugar). It's a pale wine with decent depth of fresh, citrusy, peachy, spicy flavours and mouthfilling body.

Vintage	04
WR	6
Drink	04-07

MED/DRY $26 -V

Bladen Marlborough Pinot Gris ★★★

The 2004 vintage (★★★★) looked highly attractive in its infancy. Showing good richness and harmony, it's a slightly sweet style (7 grams/litre of residual sugar), satisfyingly full-bodied, with strong, well-ripened flavours of peaches, lychees and spices and a deliciously soft texture.

MED/DRY $27 -V

Brick Bay Matakana Pinot Gris ★★★★

At its best this is one of the country's finest Pinot Gris, rich and rounded. Hand-picked and mostly cool-fermented in tanks, with a small proportion briefly oak-aged, the 2003 vintage (★★★) is a slightly sweet style with crisp, citrusy, slightly spicy and pear-like aromas and flavours. It lacks the weight, lushness and softness of a top vintage, but shows good varietal character.

Vintage	03	02	01	00	99	98
WR	6	7	6	7	6	7
Drink	04-07	04-07	04-06	04-05	P	P

MED/DRY $27 -V

Brookfields Ohiti Estate Pinot Gris ★★★★

Peter Robertson's Hawke's Bay wine is typically sturdy, with plenty of peachy, slightly earthy and spicy flavour. Grown at Ohiti Estate, near Fernhill, the 2004 vintage (★★★★) is fresh and vibrant, with mouthfilling body and ripe flavours of pears, lychees and spice that build to a well-rounded, lasting finish. Looks good for 2005–06.

Vintage	04
WR	7
Drink	08-09

MED/DRY $18 V+

Cairnbrae Marlborough Pinot Gris (★★★☆)

Launched from the 2004 vintage (★★★☆), this is a finely balanced, easy-drinking wine with well-defined varietal characters. The bouquet is fresh and spicy; the flavours are smooth and lingering, with ripe pear and spice notes and gentle acidity giving an appealingly soft texture.

`MED/DRY $17 V+`

Canadoro Pinot Gris (★★★☆)

Grown in Martinborough, the 2003 vintage (★★★☆) is a slightly honeyed, medium style with soft, clearly varietal pear and spice flavours showing good richness.

`MED $27 -V`

Canterbury House Waipara Pinot Gris ★★★★

This is an irresistibly well-priced North Canterbury wine, in style reminding me more of a fine-quality Pinot Grigio from northern Italy than the more robust, softer wines of Alsace. The excellent 2003 vintage (★★★★☆) was mostly handled in tanks, but a small proportion was barrel-fermented and all of the final blend was matured on its yeast lees. Weighty, with rich lemon, spice and pear flavours, it's a very charming, slightly sweet wine with excellent varietal character, harmony and length. The 2004 (★★★★) is again mouthfilling and richly varietal, with strong pear, spice and apple flavours cut with fresh acidity.

`MED/DRY $17 V+`

Carrick Central Otago Pinot Gris ★★★

The 2003 vintage (★★★) was grown at Cairnmuir, in the Cromwell Basin, and 20 per cent barrel-fermented; the rest was handled in tanks. It's a clearly varietal wine in a slightly off-dry style (6 grams/litre of residual sugar) with citrusy, appley, spicy flavours showing cool-climate crispness and vigour.

Vintage	04	`MED/DRY $24 -V`
WR	6	
Drink	04-08	

Chard Farm Central Otago Pinot Gris ★★★☆

Matured on its yeast lees but not oak-aged, the 2003 vintage (★★★☆) is a basically dry style (4 grams/litre of sugar) with a youthful, pale lemon/green hue and attractive, peachy, spicy fragrance. It shows good body, depth and roundness, with a slightly oily texture, ripe flavours and a smooth finish.

Vintage	03	02	01	`DRY $24 -V`
WR	5	6	6	
Drink	04-06	04-06	P	

Coopers Creek Huapai Pinot Gris ★★☆

A good debut, the 2003 vintage (★★★) was estate-grown in West Auckland and handled entirely in tanks, with brief lees-aging. Fresh and lively, it has ripe pear and spice aromas and flavours, with a slight earthy character, and an off-dry (5 grams/litre of sugar), soft finish. In its infancy, the pale, slightly sweet 2004 (★★☆) showed delicate flavours of lychees and spice, but lacked depth.

Vintage	04	03	`MED/DRY $16 AV`
WR	6	5	
Drink	04-05	04-05	

Corbans Pinot Gris ★★★

Consistently good value. A slightly sweet Gisborne style with citrus fruit, pear and spice flavours offering good depth, the 2002 vintage (★★★) is a sharply priced wine from Allied Domecq. The 2003 (★★★) is very similar, with a medium-bodied, smooth palate offering slightly sweet peach, pear and spice flavours, showing good varietal character.

Vintage	03	02	`MED/DRY $14 V+`
WR	6	6	
Drink	04-05	P	

Cracroft Chase Canterbury Pinot Gris   (★★★☆)

A single-vineyard wine grown in the Port Hills at Christchurch, the 2003 vintage (★★★☆) is a pale, lively, cool-climate style with good body and depth of citrus and stone-fruit flavours and a slightly oily texture. Youthful and immaculate, it should reward cellaring; open 2005 onwards.

DRY $24 -V

Craggy Range Otago Station Vineyard Pinot Gris   (★★★☆)

The pale lemon/green 2004 vintage (★★★☆) was grown in the Waitaki Valley of North Otago. It's a clearly varietal wine with vibrant pear and spice flavours cut with fresh acidity in a cool-climate style with very good intensity.

MED/DRY $30 -V

Drylands Marlborough Pinot Gris   ★★★

The straw/pink 2003 vintage (★★★☆) shows good body and roundness, with smooth, peachy, gently sweet flavours (7.4 grams/litre of residual sugar) and a slightly creamy texture.

Vintage	03	02	01	00
WR	7	7	7	7
Drink	04-07	04-06	P	P

MED/DRY $20 -V

Dry River Pinot Gris   ★★★★★

Since its first vintage in 1986, Dry River has towered over other New Zealand Pinot Gris, by virtue of its exceptional body, flavour richness and longevity. It's a satisfyingly sturdy Martinborough wine with peachy, spicy characters that can develop great subtlety and richness with maturity (at around five years old for top vintages, which also hold well for a decade). To avoid any loss of varietal flavour, it is not oak-aged. Pale yellow/green, the 2003 vintage (★★★★★) is from an ultra low-yielding season. Already delicious, with great harmony and richness, it is full, soft and honeyed, with deep, very fresh and pure lemon, pear and spice flavours, a splash of sweetness and a slightly oily texture. Winemaker Neil McCallum sees it as his 'best yet'.

Vintage	03	02	01	00	99	98	97	96
WR	7	7	NM	6	7	6	7	NM
Drink	07-13	04-10	NM	04-07	04-07	04-06	04-05	NM

MED/DRY $39 AV

Escarpment Martinborough Pinot Gris   ★★★★★

The 2003 vintage (★★★★★) from Larry McKenna is the finest yet. Fermented and matured in seasoned French oak barriques (new oak is deliberately avoided), it shows a fullness of body, richness and roundness that is highly Alsace-like. Light yellow, with ripe stone-fruit aromas, it is sturdy and smooth, with a subtle oak influence, lovely concentration and harmony and a slightly honeyed richness.

Vintage	03	02	01
WR	7	6	6
Drink	05-06	04-05	P

DRY $29 V+

Esk Valley Hawke's Bay Pinot Gris   ★★★★

A blend of Esk Valley and Te Awanga grapes, hand-picked, whole-bunch pressed and 25 per cent fermented in old oak casks, the 2004 vintage (★★★★) is a stylish, finely balanced wine with a sliver of sweetness amid its citrus fruit, pear and spice flavours, which show good freshness, delicacy and roundness. Well worth cellaring.

Vintage	04	03	02	01
WR	6	7	6	5
Drink	04-07	04-07	04-06	04-05

MED/DRY $23 AV

Fairhall Downs Marlborough Pinot Gris ★★★★

This Brancott Valley vineyard produces a weighty style with an appealing, floral bouquet and deep stone-fruit, pear and spice flavours, typically threaded with crisp Marlborough acidity. Notably rich, ripe and rounded, with strikingly deep flavours and a slightly sweet finish, the 2002 (★★★★★) is a finely balanced wine with highly impressive weight, richness and harmony. The 2003 (★★★) is less memorable, with crisp, appley, slightly sweet and spicy flavours that lack the richness and roundness of a top vintage.

Vintage	03	02	01
WR	7	7	7
Drink	04-07	04-05	P

MED/DRY $27 -V

Forrest Estate Marlborough Pinot Gris (★★★☆)

This wine came about by accident – due to a planting mix-up, 10 per cent of the Pinot Noir vines supplied for the company's Northbank vineyard, on the north side of the Wairau Valley, turned out to be Pinot Gris. Made from first-crop vines, the debut 2003 vintage (★★★☆) was hand-picked and whole-bunch pressed. It's a smooth, full-bodied wine, less alcoholic (12.5 per cent) than many Pinot Gris, with citrus, pear, apple and spice flavours showing good depth and a slightly sweet (7 grams/litre of residual sugar), lingering finish.

MED/DRY $30 -V

Framingham Marlborough Pinot Gris ★★★★

Launched in 1999, this has been a consistently impressive wine. Made from 'very ripe grapes with a reasonable amount of shrivel', handled in tanks and stop-fermented with 14 grams per litre of residual sugar, the 2003 vintage (★★★★☆) is lush, concentrated and strongly varietal, with a heady aroma and rich, ripe pear and spice flavours. It's a distinctly medium style with an oily texture, great structure and well-rounded finish.

Vintage	03	02	01	00	99
WR	6	6	6	5	6
Drink	04-06	04-05	04-06	04-05	P

MED/DRY $27 -V

Francis-Cole Marlborough Pinot Gris (★★★☆)

The fresh, floral 2003 vintage (★★★☆) was grown in the Schoolhouse Vineyard, in the Omaka Valley. Medium to full-bodied, with a slightly oily texture, it offers good depth of pear, lemon and spice flavours, with a hint of sweetness and a finely balanced finish.

Vintage	03
WR	6
Drink	04-08

MED/DRY $24 -V

Gibbston Valley Central Otago Pinot Gris ★★★☆

This wine is typically full of personality. The 2003 vintage (★★★) is aromatic and slightly nettley, with crisp, citrusy flavours showing good length. From a difficult season, the 2004 (★★☆) is fresh, crisp and vibrant, with high acidity for Pinot Gris, and its green apple and lime notes suggest a slight lack of ripeness. Frisky and slightly sweet (10 grams/litre of residual sugar), it could almost be mistaken for a Riesling, or even a Sauvignon Blanc.

Vintage	04	03	02	01	00	99	98
WR	3	5	6	6	6	6	6
Drink	04-06	04-09	04-10	04-10	04-08	04-06	P

MED/DRY $27 -V

Gladstone Pinot Gris   ★★★

The easy-drinking 2002 vintage (★★★) of this Wairarapa wine is a slightly sweet style (7 grams/litre of sugar), blended from estate-grown grapes and fruit from the McGovern vineyard at Opaki, north of Masterton. Matured on its yeast lees for four months, it has a gently spicy bouquet, fullness of body, decent depth of lemon, pear and spice flavours, gentle acidity and a soft finish. The rare 2003 (★★★), from a frost-decimated vintage, is a full-bodied wine with crisp acids woven through its pear and spice flavours, which show some richness.

MED/DRY $25 -V

Grove Mill Marlborough Pinot Gris   ★★★★

Grove Mill is a key pioneer of Pinot Gris in Marlborough, since 1994 producing a richly flavoured style with abundant sweetness. The fleshy 2002 vintage (★★★★☆) was grown principally in the Omaka Valley, stop-fermented in a distinctly medium style (with 17 grams/litre of sugar), and given a full malolactic fermentation. Deliciously mouthfilling, rich and rounded, it has good mouthfeel and texture, and a strong surge of peach, lemon and spice flavours.

Vintage	02	01	00	99	98
WR	7	6	7	7	NM
Drink	04-06	04-05	04-05	P	NM

MED $25 AV

Hawkesbridge Marlborough Pinot Gris   (★★☆)

Sold by mail-order wine clubs, the 2003 vintage (★★☆) is slightly pink-hued, with crisp, spicy flavours that lack real ripeness and richness.

MED/DRY $23 -V

Herzog Marlborough Pinot Gris   ★★★★☆

Grown alongside the Wairau River and harvested at an ultra-ripe 26 brix, the powerful 2004 vintage (★★★★☆) is a sturdy (14.5 per cent alcohol) Marlborough wine, partly fermented and lees-aged in new French oak casks. Unlike almost all other New Zealand Pinot Gris, it's a bone-dry style, subdued on the nose by the wood handling but rich and rounded on the palate, with sweet fruit delights, gentle acids and stone-fruit, pear and spice flavours, showing an almost honeyed richness.

Vintage	02	01
WR	6	6
Drink	04-06	P

DRY $39 -V

Huia Marlborough Pinot Gris   ★★★☆

The 2004 vintage (★★★☆) was harvested in the Anderson vineyard in the upper Brancott Valley, whole-bunch pressed and fermented with indigenous and inoculated yeasts in tanks (70 per cent) and seasoned French oak casks. A dry style (4 grams/litre of residual sugar), it's very full-bodied (14.5 per cent alcohol), with fresh lychee, pear and spice flavours showing a cool-climate freshness and crispness and good mouthfeel and depth. It should age well; open mid-2005+.

Vintage	04
WR	7
Drink	04-08

DRY $25 -V

Huntaway Reserve Marlborough/Gisborne Pinot Gris   ★★★☆

The easy-drinking 2004 vintage (★★★☆) from Allied Domecq is a 2:1 blend of Awatere Valley (Marlborough) and Manutuke (Gisborne) grapes. Lees-aged for two months, with a small percentage fermented in old casks, it is full-bodied and fresh, with stone-fruit, pear and spice flavours and a slightly sweet (8.2 grams/litre of residual sugar), well-rounded finish.

Vintage	03
WR	5
Drink	04-06

MED/DRY $20 AV

Hyperion Phoebe Pinot Gris   ★★☆

Estate-grown at Matakana, north of Auckland, the easy-drinking 2002 vintage (★★☆) is a medium-bodied, slightly sweet style, clean and fresh, with moderate depth of citrusy, gently spicy flavour and a crisp finish. From a challenging season, the 2003 (★★☆), 10 per cent barrel-fermented, is clean and lively, with fresh, citrusy, appley, limey flavours that lack real ripeness and richness.

Vintage	03	02	
WR	3	5	MED/DRY $22 -V
Drink	04-05	04-05	

Isabel Marlborough Pinot Gris   ★★★★

The sturdy, rich 2002 vintage (★★★★☆) was harvested at 22 to 24 brix and most of the wine was handled in tanks, but a minority was barrel-fermented and given a softening malolactic fermentation. Pale, with delicate, spicy aromas, it's a weighty wine with excellent intensity of pear, lychees and spice flavours in a dryish style (5 grams/litre of sugar) with a slightly oily texture and excellent varietal character. There is no 2003. Released early (in October 2004), the 2004 vintage (★★★☆) is pale, with a slightly oily texture and fresh, crisp, clearly varietal pear and spice flavours, showing good but not great depth.

Vintage	04	03	
WR	6	NM	MED/DRY $25 AV
Drink	05-06	NM	

Johanneshof Marlborough Pinot Gris   ★★★☆

The 2003 vintage (★★★★) is one of the best. Pale straw, with a full-bloomed fragrance, it is full-bodied and smooth, with peachy, distinctly spicy, slightly honeyed flavours, gentle acidity and a slightly sweet finish. Showing good depth and harmony, it's already delicious.

MED/DRY $25 -V

Kaituna Valley Marlborough Pinot Gris   (★★★★)

Based on first-crop vines in the Awatere Valley, the 2004 vintage (★★★★) was harvested at 24 brix and fermented to a medium-dry (9 grams/litre of residual sugar) style. Mouthfilling, fresh and crisp, it shows very good depth of pear and spice flavours, cool-climate delicacy and substantial body (14.5 per cent alcohol). Still youthful, with clearly defined varietal characters, it should be at its best from mid-2005 onwards.

Vintage	04	
WR	5	MED/DRY $23 AV
Drink	04-06	

Kaituna Valley Canterbury Pinot Gris   (★★★★★)

The stunning 2004 vintage (★★★★★) is a late-harvest style, hand-harvested at 27 brix (with no botrytis but a large amount of shrivelling) from very young vines in the Summerhill vineyard at Tai Tapu, on Banks Peninsula. Seductively rich, ripe and rounded, it's a medium style (30 grams/litre of residual sugar), with a striking intensity of peach, pear, lychee and spice flavours, soft and lush. A deeply scented wine with great mouthfeel (14 per cent alcohol) and texture, it's one of New Zealand's finest Pinot Gris to date.

Vintage	04	
WR	7	MED $30 AV
Drink	04-08	

Kathy Lynskey Marlborough Pinot Gris   (★★☆)

The faintly pink 2003 vintage (★★☆) is a single-vineyard wine, harvested at 25.4 brix and fermented in tanks (principally) and seasoned French oak casks. It's a full-bodied wine with ripe stone-fruit flavours, but lacks softness and charm.

MED/DRY $30 -V

Kevern Walker Pinot Gris   (★★★☆)

From the Hawke's Bay winery originally called Huthlee Estate, the 2004 vintage (★★★☆) is an estate-grown wine, full-bodied (14 per cent alcohol), fresh and smooth. A dry style (4 grams/litre of residual sugar), handled entirely in tanks, it has ripe pear and spice flavours, with slightly leesy characters adding interest. It should mature well.

DRY $19 AV

Kim Crawford Boyszone Vineyard
Marlborough Pinot Gris   ★★★

The 2002 vintage (★★★) includes 10 per cent Gewürztraminer and 3 per cent Chardonnay. A single-vineyard wine, it was partly (15 per cent) fermented in one-year-old American oak casks, with some malolactic fermentation. A dryish style (5 grams/litre of sugar), it is freshly aromatic and vibrantly fruity in an easy-drinking style with lemony, appley, slightly spicy flavours and a smooth finish.

Vintage	04	03	02	01
WR	5	6	7	6
Drink	05-07	04-05	04-05	P

MED/DRY $25 -V

Kim Crawford Marlborough Pinot Gris   (★★★☆)

A fruit-driven style with clearcut varietal characters, the 2004 vintage (★★★☆) was mostly handled in tanks, but 10 per cent was fermented in seasoned oak barrels and 20 per cent went through a softening malolactic fermentation. Fresh and smooth, it offers vibrant lychees and pear flavours, with a slightly sweet (6 grams/litre of residual sugar), spicy finish.

Vintage	04
WR	3
Drink	05-06

MED/DRY $20 AV

Koura Bay Shark's Tooth Marlborough Pinot Gris   ★★★

The skilfully crafted, very easy-drinking 2002 vintage (★★★☆) was estate-grown in the Awatere Valley and lees-aged in tanks, with no oak handling. It's a medium-dry style with good body and depth of ripe pear and lychees flavours, a hint of honey, gentle acidity and a well-rounded finish.

Vintage	02
WR	6
Drink	04-05

MED/DRY $20 -V

Kumeu River Pinot Gris   ★★★★

This is a consistently attractive wine. Grown at Kumeu, in West Auckland, matured on its yeast lees but not oak-matured (future releases will be fermented in large, 600-litre oak casks), the 2003 vintage (★★★★) is weighty, with a floral bouquet, peach and pear flavours showing excellent richness, a slightly oily texture and a long, crisp finish. The 2004 (★★★★) has fresh, vibrant stone-fruit, pear and spice flavours showing lovely ripeness and length. A crisp, slightly sweet style (10 grams/litre of residual sugar), it should unfold extremely well during 2005–06.

Vintage	04	03	02	01	00
WR	7	6	6	6	6
Drink	04-07	04-06	04-06	04-06	P

MED/DRY $25 AV

Lawson's Dry Hills Marlborough Pinot Gris ★★★☆

The 2003 vintage (★★★★☆) is clearly the best yet. Grown in the Hutchison vineyard, in the heart of the Wairau Valley, it was mostly handled in tanks, but 10 per cent of the blend was fermented with indigenous ('wild') yeasts in seasoned French oak barriques. Deliciously ripe and soft, it's a slightly sweet style (11 grams/litre of residual sugar) with highly scented aromas of pears and spice, good weight, gentle acidity, and excellent texture and richness.

Vintage	03	02	
WR	7	6	
Drink	04-07	04-05	**MED/DRY $23 -V**

Loopline Vineyard Wairarapa Pinot Gris (★★★)

Faintly pink-hued, the 2002 vintage (★★★) is a dry style, full-bodied and crisp, with strongly spicy, gingery, citrusy flavours that could almost be mistaken for Gewürztraminer.

Vintage	02	
WR	6	
Drink	04-06	**DRY $25 -V**

Lucknow Estate Quarry Bridge Vineyard Pinot Gris ★★☆

Grown in Hawke's Bay and fermented and matured, with weekly lees-stirring, in two and three-year-old French oak casks, the 2003 vintage (★★☆) is a crisp, lemony wine that slightly lacks freshness and vibrancy.

Vintage	03	
WR	6	
Drink	08	**DRY $28 -V**

Margrain Martinborough Pinot Gris ★★★☆

Lees-aged but not matured in oak barrels, the 2002 vintage (★★★☆) is a robust (14.5 per cent alcohol) wine, lemon-scented, with strong citrusy, spicy, slightly minerally flavours and a tight, dry finish. From an ultra low-cropping season (below 2.5 tonnes of grapes/hectare), the 2003 (★★★) is a slightly austere, bone-dry wine with firm acidity and fresh, vibrant, citrusy flavours.

Vintage	03	02	01	00	99	98	
WR	7	7	6	6	7	7	
Drink	04-08	04-07	04-06	04-06	04-05	P	**DRY $28 -V**

Marsden Bay of Islands Pinot Gris ★★★

One of the country's most northerly Pinot Gris, the golden 2003 vintage (★★★) is peachy and honeyed, with a clear botrytis influence showing. Full-bodied, with a splash of sweetness (11 grams/litre of residual sugar) and fresh acidity, it shows good flavour depth, but is probably not a long-term cellaring proposition.

Vintage	03	02	
WR	5	5	
Drink	05	04-05	**MED/DRY $23 -V**

Martinborough Vineyard Pinot Gris ★★★★★

Since its launch from 1996, this powerful, concentrated wine has emerged as one of the finest Pinot Gris in the country. It is fermented with a high percentage of indigenous yeasts, and lees-aged, partly in seasoned oak casks, in a bid to produce a 'Burgundian style with complexity, texture and weight' (small pockets of Pinot Gris can be found in Burgundy). The 2002 vintage (★★★★☆) was grown in the McCreanor vineyard at Martinborough and the St Francis vineyard, in central Wairarapa. Showing good weight and complexity, with strong peachy, nutty flavours, a deliciously creamy texture and a slightly buttery, bone-dry finish, it could probably be mistaken in a blind tasting for Chardonnay, but the pear and spice characters of Pinot Gris are also in evidence.

DRY $35 AV

Matakana Estate Pinot Gris   ★★★☆

Estate-grown north of Auckland, the fleshy, slightly sweet 2002 vintage (★★★★) is ripely scented, with good weight and plenty of well-rounded, citrusy, peachy flavour. The 2003 (★★☆) was mostly handled in tanks, but 25 per cent was fermented and matured for five months in seasoned oak casks. From a difficult season, it's a substantial wine with stone-fruit flavours, but shows a slight lack of freshness and fragrance.

MED/DRY $29 -V

Matua Valley Innovator Pinot Gris   (★★★★)

Grown in the company's Shingle Peak vineyard in Marlborough, the 2004 vintage (★★★★) was hand-picked, whole-bunch pressed and fermented with indigenous and cultured yeasts in a mix of tanks and old oak barriques. It's a mouthfilling, concentrated wine with a slightly oily texture, fresh, pure flavours of pears and spice, showing good richness, and an almost fully dry (4 grams/litre of residual sugar) finish.

Vintage	04
WR	6
Drink	04-07

DRY $29 -V

Mission Hawke's Bay Pinot Gris   ★★★☆

The Mission has long been a standard-bearer for Pinot Gris. The 2002 vintage (★★★) was grown in three vineyards at Greenmeadows, Havelock North and Patangata (Central Hawke's Bay). Lees-aged, with some malolactic fermentation but no oak handling, it's a ripe, lemony and spicy wine with fresh acidity, vibrant fruit characters, a slightly oily texture and a rounded finish.

Vintage	02	01	00	99	98
WR	6	5	6	7	6
Drink	04-08	P	P	04-06	04-05

MED/DRY $16 V+

Morton Estate White Label Hawke's Bay Pinot Gris   ★★★☆

Grown in the elevated, inland Riverview and Colefield vineyards at Mangatahi, the 2002 vintage (★★★☆) was fermented and lees-aged in old French oak barrels. It's a weighty wine with peach, lemon and spice flavours, slightly nutty and honeyed, and a crisp finish. Good value.

Vintage	04
WR	7
Drink	04-06

DRY $16 V+

Mt Rosa Pinot Gris   (★★★★☆)

The seductively soft and rich 2003 vintage (★★★★☆) was grown at Gibbston, in Central Otago. Slightly honeyed and richly spicy on the nose, it has the mouthfeel and texture of classic Alsace Pinot Gris, with plentiful sweetness and gentle acidity giving it a delicious, easy-drinking appeal. Citrusy and peachy, it's a very harmonious and characterful wine, one of the region's finest Pinot Gris yet.

MED $25 AV

Murdoch James Martinborough Pinot Gris   (★★★★)

An auspicious debut, the 2003 vintage (★★★★) was harvested at 23 brix in the Blue Rock vineyard, south of Martinborough, and fermented dry. Weighty (14 per cent alcohol) and soft, it's a strongly varietal wine with ripe pear, lychees and spice flavours showing excellent depth and a well-rounded finish. It should mature well.

Vintage	03
WR	6
Drink	04-05

DRY $29 (500ML) -V

Nautilus Marlborough Pinot Gris   ★★★☆

The skilfully crafted 2003 vintage (★★★☆) was grown in the Awatere Valley (on 12-year-old vines, originally Cabernet Sauvignon, top-grafted to Pinot Gris), and a small portion of the blend was barrel-fermented. It shows balanced acidity and fresh, strong pear and spice flavours in a dryish (6 grams/litre of residual sugar) style, still unfolding.

Vintage	04	03	02	01	00
WR	6	6	7	6	5
Drink	04-07	04-06	04-05	P	P

MED/DRY $25 -V

Neudorf Moutere Pinot Gris   ★★★★☆

The floral, softly textured 2002 vintage (★★★★☆) was harvested at 24 brix from ultra low-cropping vines (below 4 tonnes/hectare) in the Home Vineyard at Upper Moutere, fermented with indigenous yeasts in old French oak barrels and stop-fermented with 16 grams per litre of residual sugar (making it a medium style). It's a highly scented, beautifully rounded wine, weighty, fresh and vibrant, with rich peach, pear and spice flavours.

Vintage	04
WR	6
Drink	04-09

MED $31 -V

Neudorf Nelson Pinot Gris   (★★★★)

The finely balanced 2003 vintage (★★★★) is a blend of grapes from the home vineyard at Upper Moutere and first-crop vines at Brightwater. Handled entirely in stainless steel tanks and made in a dryish (5 grams/litre of residual sugar) style, it's a weighty wine (14 per cent alcohol), very fresh and vibrant, with good varietal character and excellent depth of pear, lychees and spice flavours.

Vintage	03
WR	5
Drink	04-07

MED/DRY $25 AV

Nevis Bluff Pinot Gris   ★★★★☆

This Central Otago wine is always full of character. The richly flavoured 2002 vintage (★★★★) was grown at Nevis Bluff Estate and the neighbouring Pociecha vineyard at Gibbston. Fermented and lees-aged for nine months in tanks, it is fleshy and ripe, with concentrated stone-fruit flavours, hints of honey and spice and a deliciously soft, smooth finish.

Vintage	03	02
WR	6	6
Drink	04-08	04-07

DRY $30 AV

Odyssey Marlborough Pinot Gris   (★★★)

Grown in the Odyssey vineyard, in the Brancott Valley, the 2003 vintage (★★★) was whole-bunch pressed and fully French oak-fermented. Light yellow, it's a full-bodied wine with ripe flavours of peach, melon and pineapple, showing some complexity and good depth, but its toasty oak flavours slightly overwhelm the fruit. Crisp and dry, it's a tightly structured wine, worth cellaring.

Vintage	04
WR	5
Drink	05-09

DRY $27 -V

Omaka Springs Marlborough Pinot Gris   ★★★

Grown in the Omaka Valley, the easy-drinking 2003 vintage (★★★☆) is a mouthfilling wine (14 per cent alcohol), with strong, ripe, peachy, slightly honeyed flavours, a slightly oily texture, fresh acidity and a sliver of sweetness. Good value.

MED/DRY $18 AV

Opihi Pinot Gris   ★★★☆

Grown on a north-facing slope inland from Timaru, in South Canterbury, this is typically a highly attractive wine, hand-picked and made with some use of indigenous yeasts and lees-stirring. The 2003 vintage (★★★★), harvested at 23.7 brix and tank-fermented, is an aromatic, fleshy wine with ripe, peachy, spicy flavours showing excellent varietal definition and a slightly sweet, rounded finish.

MED/DRY $25 -V

Packspur Central Otago Pinot Gris   (★★★)

Grown at Alexandra, the 2003 vintage (★★★) was mostly handled in tanks, but a third of the blend was fermented and matured for four months in old French oak casks. It's a pale, dry wine with fresh, crisp, citrusy, appley flavours in a delicate, distinctly cool-climate style.

DRY $19 AV ·

Palliser Estate Martinborough Pinot Gris   ★★★★

The 2002 vintage (★★★★) was whole-bunch pressed, cool-fermented and lees-aged for four months in tanks, and stop-fermented with 7 grams per litre of residual sugar. Full-bodied, it has good mid-palate weight and richness, fresh pear and spice characters and a dryish, lingering finish. The 2003 (★★★★) is a floral, clearly varietal wine with pear, spice and slight honey flavours showing excellent depth and an off-dry finish.

MED/DRY $26 -V

Peregrine Central Otago Pinot Gris   ★★★★

Grown at Gibbston and matured on its yeast lees, although not oak-aged, this is one of the region's top Pinot Gris. The 2002 vintage (★★★☆) is a dry style with strong stone-fruit and spice flavours and substantial body. There's a touch of phenolic hardness on the finish, but that's unlikely to bother most drinkers.

Vintage	02
WR	6
Drink	04-06

DRY $23 AV

Peregrine Saddleback Pinot Gris   (★★★☆)

The 2003 vintage (★★★☆) of this Central Otago wine, grown at Gibbston, is fragrant and mouthfilling, with ripe stone-fruit flavours that show a slight lack of delicacy, but also good concentration.

MED/DRY $18 V+

Porters Martinborough Pinot Gris   ★★★☆

The 2002 vintage (★★★☆) was harvested from ultra low-cropping vines (2.5 tonnes/hectare) and lees-aged in tanks. The bouquet is spicy and slightly earthy; the palate is strongly spiced and nutty, with good weight, a slightly oily texture and a dryish finish. The 2003 was barrel-aged (for the first time) because none of Porters' tanks were small enough to hold the season's tiny production.

Vintage	03	02	01	00	99	98
WR	6	7	6	7	6	7
Drink	04-10	04-06	04-07	04-06	04-05	P

MED/DRY $30 -V

Putiki Bay Waiheke Island Pinot Gris   (★★☆)

Fermented in tanks and then matured for five months in seasoned French oak casks, the 2003 vintage (★★☆) is a light yellow, slightly creamy wine, showing considerable development in its youth and lacking real fruit intensity.

DRY $29 -V

Quartz Reef Central Otago Pinot Gris ★★★★

The tightly structured 2003 vintage (★★★☆) was hand-picked in the Bendigo Estate and Parkburn Terrace vineyards, whole-bunch pressed, fermented dry and lees-stirred for six months in tanks. It's a pale, fresh wine, sturdy (14 per cent alcohol), with lemon, pear and spice flavours that show good depth and a slightly nutty complexity, but lack the richness and lushness of a top year. A crisp, youthful wine, it's worth cellaring to mid-2005+.

Vintage	03	02	01	00
WR	6	6	6	6
Drink	04-05	04-05	P	P

DRY $28 -V

Rabbit Ranch Central Otago Pinot Gris (★★☆)

The debut 2003 vintage (★★☆) lacks the class and obviously good value of its Pinot Noir stablemate. Pale, with lemony, appley aromas, it's a crisp, simple wine, slightly spicy and peachy, with cool-climate lightness and freshness, but lacks real ripeness and richness.

Vintage	03
WR	5
Drink	04-05

DRY $20 -V

Ransom Clos De Valerie Pinot Gris ★★★

Estate-grown at Mahurangi, near Warkworth, north of Auckland, this wine is named after the road on which the vineyard lies – Valerie Close. The fully dry 2002 vintage (★★☆) is crisp and lemony, with slightly high acidity for the variety. Medium-bodied, with a slight lack of lushness and fruit sweetness, it's much more in the mould of northern Italian Pinot Grigio than Alsace Pinot Gris.

Vintage	02	01	00	99
WR	6	5	6	5
Drink	04-08	04-06	P	P

DRY $23 -V

Rimu Grove Nelson Pinot Gris ★★★

The 2003 vintage (★★☆) is a crisp wine, mostly lees-aged in tanks, but 15 per cent of the blend was aged 'sur lie' for four months in old French oak barrels. It offers solid depth of pear, apple and spice flavours, but lacks real richness. The 2004 (★★★☆), estate-grown and harvested at 23.2 brix, is mouthfilling, leesy and slightly nutty, with ripe, stone-fruit flavours and a slightly sweet (10 grams/litre of residual sugar) finish. It's still very youthful but shows very good depth; open mid-2005+.

MED/DRY $26 -V

Rockburn Central Otago Pinot Gris ★★★☆

The pale 2003 vintage (★★★☆) is a blend of grapes grown at Lowburn, in the Cromwell Basin (84 per cent) and Gibbston. Tank-fermented and lees-aged for seven months, it's a full-bodied wine with moderate acidity, good intensity of pear, apple and lemon flavours, tight and youthful, slightly nutty, yeasty characters adding interest and a dry but not austere finish. Best drinking mid-2005+.

DRY $27 -V

St Francis Marlborough Pinot Gris – see Francis-Cole
Marlborough Pinot Gris

St Helena Canterbury Pinot Gris ★★★

Estate-grown on the northern outskirts of Christchurch, the 2003 vintage (★★★) is a tank-fermented wine with distinctly spicy, almost Gewürztraminer-like aromas and flavours. Fresh, crisp and lively, it's well-balanced for early drinking, with gentle sweetness (13 grams/litre of residual sugar), pear and lychee characters and good body.

MED/DRY $17 AV

St Helena Reserve Pinot Gris ★★★☆

Estate-grown at Belfast, the 2003 vintage (★★★★) of this Canterbury wine was mostly tank-fermented, but the recipe included some barrel fermentation and 20 per cent malolactic fermentation. Ripely scented, it's a slightly drier wine (8 grams/litre of residual sugar) than the non-reserve (above), fresh and vibrantly fruity, with excellent depth of peachy, spicy flavour and a well-rounded finish. Drink now onwards.

DRY $25 -V

Sacred Hill Marlborough Vineyards Pinot Gris   (★★★)

The 2002 vintage (★★★) was grown in the company's Jacksons Road vineyard and partly French oak-fermented. Fragrant, pear/spice aromas lead into a full-bodied wine with strong pear, herb and spice flavours, restrained oak and a crisp, dryish, green-edged finish.

MED/DRY $23 -V

Sacred Hill Whitecliff Estate Pinot Gris   (★★☆)

A blend of New Zealand and Italian wine, the 2002 vintage (★★☆) is a pale, restrained wine that lacks richness.

MED/DRY $16 -V

Saint Clair Godfrey's Creek Reserve Pinot Gris   (★★★☆)

Mostly grown in the Walsh vineyard, at the head of the Brancott Valley, in Marlborough, the debut 2003 vintage (★★★☆) was mainly handled in tanks, but 10 per cent was fermented in seasoned oak casks and all of the blend went through a softening malolactic fermentation. It has good mouthfeel, with fresh citrus fruit, pear and spice flavours, a touch of complexity and a slightly sweet (7 grams/litre of residual sugar), crisp finish. The 2004 (★★★☆), 20 per cent oak-aged for three months, is fresh, full-bodied and vibrant, with slightly sweet pear, grapefruit and spice flavours showing good harmony, texture and depth.

Vintage	04	MED/DRY $25 -V
WR	6	
Drink	04-06	

Sanctuary Limited Release Marlborough Pinot Gris   (★★☆)

Sold by mail-order wine clubs, the 2003 vintage (★★☆) is a fresh, lemony but simple wine with green-edged flavours and flinty acidity.

MED/DRY $23 -V

Sanctuary Marlborough Pinot Gris   (★★★)

From Grove Mill, the debut 2004 vintage (★★★) offers fine value. It's a medium to full-bodied wine (13 per cent alcohol), clearly varietal and slightly sweet (7.5 grams/litre of residual sugar), with fresh, vibrant pear and spice aromas and flavours showing good balance and depth.

MED/DRY $17 V+

Seifried Nelson Pinot Gris ★★★

The apple and lime-flavoured 2003 vintage (★★☆) was made from young (first-crop) vines in the company's Cornfield Vineyard at Appleby. It's a crisp, lively but green-edged wine in a refreshing, lighter style. Faintly pink-hued, the 2004 (★★★☆) is full-bodied and smooth, with slightly sweet (11 grams/litre of residual sugar) flavours of peaches and spice, generous and richly varietal.

Vintage	04	MED/DRY $20 -V
WR	6	
Drink	04-07	

Seresin Pinot Gris ★★★★☆

One of Marlborough's top Pinot Gris. The 2003 vintage (★★★★) was hand-picked at 23.8 brix and began its ferment in tanks, 'to retain the subtle fruit characters'. It was then transferred to old French oak barriques, 'to add complexity and texture', where it completed its fermentation and aged on its yeast lees, with weekly lees-stirring. Still youthful, it's a robust wine (14 per cent alcohol), tightly structured, with pear, lemon and spice flavours, slightly nutty and minerally characters adding complexity and a crisp, dry, lingering finish.

Vintage	03	02	01	00	99	98
WR	6	6	6	6	7	6
Drink	04-09	04-08	04-07	04-06	04-05	P

DRY $28 AV

Shingle Peak Marlborough Pinot Gris ★★★

The 2004 vintage (★★★) from Matua Valley is a full-bodied (14 per cent alcohol), dryish wine (6 grams/litre of residual sugar), handled entirely in tanks. In its youth, it showed clearcut varietal character, with good depth of pear and spice flavours.

Vintage	04
WR	5
Drink	04-07

MED/DRY $19 AV

Spy Valley Marlborough Pinot Gris ★★★★

The powerful 2003 vintage (★★★★) was estate-grown in the Waihopai Valley, picked at 24 to 25 brix, tank-fermented and lees-aged for four months. Richly scented, it's a slightly sweet style (7.5 grams/litre of residual sugar) with substantial body (14.5 per cent alcohol) and strong, peachy, spicy, slightly honeyed flavours. The richly scented 2004 (★★★☆) is slightly lighter in body (13.5 per cent alcohol), with generous, peachy, slightly sweet flavours and a soft finish.

Vintage	04	03	02	01
WR	5	7	7	6
Drink	04-07	04-06	04-07	04-06

MED/DRY $20 V+

Staete Landt Marlborough Pinot Gris ★★★★☆

A rare, single-vineyard wine, well worth tracking down. The 2002 vintage (★★★★☆) was hand-picked at 24.9 brix, whole-bunch pressed, and fermented and matured on its light yeast lees for four months in six-year-old French oak puncheons. A dry style (3 grams/litre of residual sugar), it is weighty and concentrated, with sweet fruit delights, citrus and stone-fruit flavours, a slightly nutty complexity and a long, tight finish. It should really blossom with cellaring; open 2005+.

Vintage	02
WR	6
Drink	04-05

DRY $34 -V

Stonecutter Martinborough Pinot Gris ★★★

The 2004 vintage (★★★☆) is a sturdy (14 per cent alcohol) dry wine with good varietal character and depth of ripe, peachy, spicy, slightly nutty flavours. Still settling down when tasted in September 2004, it shows definite potential; open mid-2005+.

DRY $23 -V

Stoneleigh Rapaura Series Marlborough Pinot Gris   (★★★★★)

The sensuous, beautifully fragrant and concentrated 2003 vintage (★★★★★) was harvested at 24.8 brix, tank-fermented and 20 per cent of the blend was lees-aged for three months. Showing the fullness, richness and roundness of fine Pinot Gris, it's a generous wine with slight sweetness (10.4 grams/litre of residual sugar), lush, deep flavours of pear, spice and melon and a creamy-soft texture.

Vintage 03
WR   7   MED/DRY $23 V+
Drink   04-05

Tasman Bay Vintage Special Selection Pinot Gris   (★★★)

Balanced for easy drinking, the 2004 vintage (★★★) is a blend of Nelson and Marlborough grapes, 20 per cent French oak-aged. Pale and fresh-scented, it's a slightly sweet wine (8.5 grams/litre of residual sugar) with good depth of pear and spice flavours, crisp and vibrant.

Vintage 04
WR   5   MED/DRY $18 AV
Drink   04-06

Te Kairanga Martinborough Pinot Gris   (★★★★)

The concentrated, harmonious 2003 vintage (★★★★) was harvested at 23.5 brix and French oak-aged for eight months. Showing good weight and texture, it has rich, ripe flavours of peach, pear and spice, with subtle oak adding a touch of complexity and gentle acidity giving a soft, rounded finish.

Vintage 03
WR   6   DRY $25 AV
Drink   04-06

Terrace Heights Estate Marlborough Pinot Gris   (★★★☆)

Showing strong drink-young appeal, the 2004 vintage (★★★☆) was harvested at 22.2 to 25.8 brix and handled entirely in tanks. It's a fresh, vibrant, distinctly medium style (18 grams/litre of residual sugar) with clearcut varietal character and very good depth of pear and spice flavours, ripe and rounded.

Vintage 04
WR   6   MED $22 AV
Drink   04-06

Thornbury Marlborough Pinot Gris   (★★★☆)

Attractive in its youth, the 2004 vintage (★★★☆) has fresh, spicy varietal aromas leading into a full-bodied, flavoursome wine with a slightly oily texture, citrusy, peachy, spicy characters and a dry, crisp finish. It's a good debut, and worth cellaring to mid-2005 onwards.

Vintage 04
WR   6   DRY $20 AV
Drink   05-07

Torlesse Pinot Gris   ★★★

The 2004 vintage (★★★) is a blend of Waipara and other Canterbury grapes, partly barrel-fermented. Tasted in its infancy, it's a citrusy, slightly spicy and appley wine, fresh and crisp, but needs time; open 2005+.

DRY $19 AV

Trinity Hill Gimblett Gravels Pinot Gris   ★★★★

The 2003 vintage (★★★★) was hand-picked in Hawke's Bay and fermented and matured for five months in seasoned French oak barrels. A medium-dry style, it is mouthfilling, with strong pear and spice characters, a hint of honey, very subtle oak and loads of character.

Vintage	04	03	02
WR	5	4	5
Drink	04-07	04-05	04-05

MED/DRY $30 -V

Vavasour Awatere Valley Marlborough Pinot Gris   (★★★)

A good but not great debut, the 2002 vintage (★★★) is a distinctly cool-climate style, full and fresh, with pear, spice and apple flavours and a crisp finish. There is no 2003, but the label returns from 2004.

Vintage	04
WR	7
Drink	04-07

MED/DRY $20 -V

Villa Maria Cellar Selection Pinot Gris   (★★★★)

Grown in Marlborough's Awatere Valley, the 2003 vintage (★★★★) is an Alsace-style wine with fresh pear and spice aromas, showing good intensity. Weighty and finely textured, it has well-rounded peach and pear flavours that build across the palate to a slightly sweet, lasting finish. The 2004 (tasted prior to bottling, and so not rated), has mouthfilling body, clearcut lychee, pear and spice varietal characters, and a slightly sweet (8 grams/litre of residual sugar), rounded, lingering finish.

MED/DRY $24 AV

Villa Maria Single Vineyard Seddon Vineyard
Pinot Gris   (★★★★★)

One of Marlborough's most convincing Pinot Gris yet, the gorgeous 2003 vintage (★★★★★) was grown in the Awatere Valley and handled entirely in tanks, with three months' lees-aging. Bright, light/medium yellow, it's a powerful (14.5 per cent alcohol) wine, lush and highly concentrated, with striking depth of pear, spice and honey flavours and a soft, slightly sweet (8 grams/litre of residual sugar) finish.

MED/DRY $30 AV

Villa Maria Single Vineyard Taylors Pass Vineyard
Pinot Gris   (NR)

The 2004 vintage (tasted prior to bottling, and so not rated), looked extremely promising. Grown in Marlborough, it's a powerful, very weighty wine (14.5 per cent alcohol) with crisp acidity woven through its rich lychee and spice flavours.

MED/DRY $30 V?

Vin Alto Pinot Grigio/Chardonnay   ★★★

Grown in the Clevedon hills, in South Auckland, the 2002 vintage (★★★) is a blend of 70 per cent Pinot Grigio (the Italian name for Pinot Gris), handled in tanks, and 30 per cent oak-aged Chardonnay. Lemony and savoury, crisp and slightly spicy, it's a distinctive wine with plenty of flavour, made in a more 'oxidative', less fruity style than is the custom in New Zealand.

Vintage	02
WR	5
Drink	05-06

DRY $20 -V

Waimea Estates Nelson Pinot Gris   (★★★★)

The fine-value 2003 vintage (★★★★) was hand-picked in Nelson at 23.4 brix, whole-bunch pressed and mostly handled in tanks; 10 per cent was fermented with indigenous yeasts in old French oak casks. Fragrant and sturdy (14 per cent alcohol), it's a very harmonious wine with good texture and intensity of peach, pear and spice flavours, showing some lushness, and a crisp, off-dry (5 grams/litre of residual sugar) finish.

Vintage	03	MED/DRY $20 V+
WR	5	
Drink	05-08	

Waipara Hills Marlborough Pinot Gris   (★★☆)

The 2003 vintage (★★☆) is fresh, crisp and green-edged, with a dry (3.5 grams/litre of residual sugar) finish. It's clean and lively, but lacks real ripeness and richness.

DRY $22 -V

Wairau River Marlborough Pinot Gris   ★★★☆

Estate-grown, the 2004 (★★★☆) is a distinctly medium style. Weighty and rounded, it's a finely balanced wine with very good depth of fresh lychee, pear and spice flavours, plentiful sweetness and strong drink-young appeal.

Vintage	02	MED $20 AV
WR	7	
Drink	04-06	

William Hill Central Otago Pinot Gris   (★★★)

Lees-aged in tanks, the 2003 vintage (★★★) is a slightly pink-hued, finely balanced wine with a sliver of sweetness (6 grams/litre of residual sugar) amid its ripe-pear and spice flavours, which linger well.

Vintage	03	MED/DRY $23 -V
WR	6	
Drink	04-06	

Riesling

Riesling isn't yet one of New Zealand's major international wine successes – the 70,879 cases shipped in the year to June 2004 accounted for just 2 per cent of our total wine exports. Yet overseas acclaim is starting to flow. Spy Valley Marlborough Riesling 2003 won a gold medal and the German Wine Institute Trophy for Best Riesling at the 2004 International Wine and Spirit Competition in London.

Captivated by Chardonnay and Sauvignon Blanc, Kiwi wine lovers until a few years ago ignored this country's equally delightful Rieslings. At last, Riesling is slowly growing in popularity and starting to achieve the profile it richly deserves.

Scentedness and intense lemon/lime flavours enlivened by fresh, appetising acidity are the hallmarks of the top New Zealand Rieslings. Around the world, Riesling has traditionally been regarded as Chardonnay's great rival in the white-wine quality stakes, well ahead of Sauvignon Blanc. So what took New Zealand wine lovers so long to appreciate Riesling's lofty stature?

Several factors tethered Riesling's popularity. A long-lived confusion over names (with 'Riesling-Sylvaner' used as an alternative to Müller-Thurgau and 'Rhine Riesling' as a synonym for the true Riesling) hardly helped Riesling build a distinctive identity. Riesling is typically made in a slightly sweet style to balance the grape's natural high acidity, but this gentle sweetness runs counter to the fashion for bone-dry wines. And fine Riesling demands time to unfold its full potential; drunk in its infancy, as it often is, it lacks the toasty, minerally, honeyed richness that is the real glory of Riesling.

Riesling ranks as New Zealand's third most extensively planted white-wine variety. Between 2000 and 2006, the total area of bearing vines is expanding from 503 to 725 hectares. The great grape of Germany, Riesling is a classic cool-climate variety, particularly well suited to the cooler growing temperatures and lower humidity of the South Island. Its stronghold is Marlborough, where half of the vines are clustered, but the grape is also extensively planted in Nelson, Canterbury and Central Otago.

Riesling styles vary markedly around the world. Most Marlborough wines are medium to full-bodied (12.5 to 13.5 per cent alcohol), with just a touch of sweetness. However, a new breed of Riesling has recently emerged – lighter (only 8 to 10 per cent alcohol) and markedly sweeter. These refreshingly light, sweet Rieslings offer a more vivid contrast in style to New Zealand's other major white wines, and are much closer in style to the classic German model.

Alana Estate Martinborough Riesling ★★★☆

Harvested at 21–23 brix, the 2003 vintage (★★★☆) is a slightly sweet style (7 grams/litre of residual sugar) with bright, youthful colour and a crisp, still youthful palate. It offers strong lemon, lime and passionfruit flavours, with lively acidity and good cellaring potential.

Vintage	03	02	01
WR	6	6	6
Drink	04-08	04-06	04-05

MED/DRY $21 -V

Alan McCorkindale Waipara Valley Dry Riesling ★★★★☆

The 2003 vintage (★★★★) is a classy wine, made from 'low-crop, unirrigated vines' in the Lough Group vineyard. Delicious now, it's a fleshy, ripely flavoured wine with good intensity and a slightly sweet (7 grams/litre of residual sugar), honeyed finish.

MED/DRY $25 -V

Alexandra Wine Company Crag An Oir Riesling   ★★★

The 2002 vintage (★★★☆) of this Central Otago wine is a zesty, medium style (16 grams/litre of sugar).
It offers fresh, crisp lemon/lime flavours showing good balance and intensity.

Vintage	02	01	00	99
WR	5	5	5	6
Drink	04-06	04-05	04-05	P

MED $18 AV

Alexia Nelson Riesling   ★★★☆

The 2003 vintage (★★★☆) from winemaker Jane Cooper is fresh, vibrant and tangy, with ripe-lemon/lime
aromas and flavours showing very good depth.

Vintage	02
WR	6
Drink	04-07

MED/DRY $17 V+

Allan Scott Marlborough Riesling   ★★★★☆

Top vintages of this wine are highly impressive. Made from vines approaching 25 years old, the 2003
vintage (★★★★★) was a 'steal'. Fleshy and slightly sweet (9 grams/litre of residual sugar), it possesses
lifted apple, ginger and spice aromas that open out to a generous, well-structured palate with lovely
richness. The 2004 (★★★★☆) is again very elegant and rich, with deep, citrusy, slightly minerally flavours
cut with fresh acidity and good weight. A finely balanced wine with good structure, it's well worth cellaring
and bargain-priced.

MED/DRY $17 V+

Allan Scott Vineyard Select Riesling   (★★★☆)

There's no region of origin on the label, but the 2003 vintage (★★★☆) is a South Island wine. Light
lemon/green, it is ripely scented and mouthfilling, with strong lemon, lime and passionfruit flavours, slightly
sweet and tangy.

MED/DRY $17 V+

Amisfield Rocky Knoll Riesling – see Sweet White Wines

Amor-Bendall Gisborne Riesling   (★★★☆)

The fresh-scented 2003 vintage (★★★☆) shows good varietal character, with vibrant, pure lemon/apple
flavours, firm acidity and a slightly sweet (5 grams/litre of residual sugar) finish. It's a scented, slightly
honeyed wine, maturing well.

MED/DRY $22 -V

Ascension Marlborough Riesling   ★★★☆

The attractively floral 2003 vintage (★★★☆) is a medium style (18 grams/litre of residual sugar) with good
depth of crisp, citrusy flavour, showing good delicacy and freshness.

MED $20 AV

Awanui Marlborough Riesling   (★★☆)

Sold by mail-order wine clubs, the 2003 vintage (★★☆) is a solid but not intense wine with fresh, crisp,
lemony flavours and a slightly sweet (7.5 grams/litre of residual sugar) finish. Verging on three-star quality.

MED/DRY $20 -V

Babich Marlborough Riesling ★★★★

This is typically a beautifully crafted, ripe, flavour-packed wine with great drinkability. A medium-dry style, grown in the Pigou vineyard at Rapaura, in the Wairau Valley, the 2003 vintage (★★★★) is scented, lively and immaculate, with fresh, strong lemon/lime flavours, a hint of honey and good sugar/acid balance (7.5 grams/litre of residual sugar).

Vintage	03	02	01	00	99	98
WR	7	7	7	7	7	7
Drink	04-09	04-09	04-08	04-06	04-05	P

MED/DRY $20 AV

Black Ridge Riesling ★★☆

Grown in rocky terrain in one of the world's southernmost vineyards, at Alexandra in Central Otago, this is typically a green-appley wine with a crisp, fresh, Mosel-like delicacy. The 2003 vintage (★★☆) is green-edged, with a splash of sweetness (11 grams/litre of residual sugar), but it lacks real freshness and vibrancy.

MED/DRY $18 -V

Bladen Marlborough Riesling ★★★

The 2004 vintage (★★★★) is one of the best yet, with ripe, floral and citrus aromas leading into a distinctly medium style (24 grams/litre of residual sugar) with very good weight and depth of crisp, lemony, slightly honeyed flavour. Forward in its appeal, it shows good freshness and intensity.

MED $20 -V

Borthwick Wairarapa Riesling ★★★

Grown near Masterton, the 2003 vintage (★★★) has a musky perfume and spicy flavours that are distinctly reminiscent of Gewürztraminer. It's a crisp, citrusy wine, medium-bodied, with a just off-dry (4.8 grams/litre of residual sugar) finish.

DRY $19 -V

Brightwater Vineyards Nelson Riesling ★★★☆

Estate-grown on the Waimea Plains, this wine is always full of personality. The 2003 vintage (★★★☆) is a dry style (only 4.6 grams/litre of residual sugar), with good depth of lemon, lime and passionfruit flavours and firm acid spine. It's a youthful wine, worth cellaring.

Vintage	03	02	01	00
WR	6	6	6	7
Drink	04-07	04-07	04-05	P

DRY $18 AV

Brookfields Ohiti Estate Riesling ★★★☆

Peter Robertson's Hawke's Bay wines are full of interest. Grown on the Ohiti Estate, inland from Fernhill, the 2004 vintage (★★★☆) is ripely scented, with grapefruit and lemon flavours showing good depth, a slight minerally streak and a dryish, rounded finish.

Vintage	04
WR	7
Drink	08-09

MED/DRY $18 AV

Burnt Spur Martinborough Riesling (★★★)

The 2002 vintage (★★★) is a ripely scented, slightly honeyed wine with citrusy, limey flavours of good depth, fresh acidity and a bone-dry finish.

Vintage	02
WR	6
Drink	04-10

DRY $21 -V

Burnt Spur Martinborough Riesling – see Sweet White Wines

Cairnbrae Old River Marlborough Riesling ★★★☆

Attractive in its youth, the 2003 vintage (★★★☆) has fresh, ripe-lemon/lime aromas and flavours, showing good delicacy and depth. A medium-dry style (8 grams/litre of residual sugar) with a hint of passionfruit, it's crisp and lively and should mature well.

Vintage	03		MED/DRY $17 V+
WR	6		
Drink	04-06		

Canterbury House Waipara Riesling ★★★☆

Estate-grown in North Canterbury, the 2003 vintage (★★★☆) was matured for six months on its light yeast lees. It's a highly scented wine with lush pear and slight honey flavours, showing some botrytis influence, and a high level of sweetness (40 grams/litre of residual sugar).

MED $17 V+

Carrick Central Otago Riesling ★★★☆

The punchy, richly varietal 2003 vintage (★★★★) has fresh, lifted lemon/lime aromas. A gently sweet style, it has tight, minerally notes and impressive delicacy, structure and length. From the frost-stricken 2004 season (★★★☆), 90 cases were made, compared to the expected 1000 cases. Harvested at 21.8 brix in Bannockburn, it's a tense, high-acid wine, with good sugar/acid balance (13 grams/litre of residual sugar) and intensity of citrusy, limey, slightly minerally flavours.

Vintage	03	02	MED/DRY $19 AV
WR	6	6	
Drink	04-10	04+	

Catchfire Marlborough Riesling ★★★☆

Sold by mail-order wine clubs, this wine has been a great buy in such vintages as 1998 and 2000. However, the 2003 (★★☆) is less exciting, with crisp, green-edged, nettley flavours that lack real ripeness and a medium-dry (7.5 grams/litre of residual sugar) finish.

MED/DRY $18 AV

Chard Farm Central Otago Riesling ★★★☆

The standard of this Central Otago wine varies, reflecting the marginal growing climate, but is typically high. The 2002 vintage (★★★★), grown in the Cromwell Basin, is a tangy, slightly sweet wine (7.5 grams/litre of residual sugar) with strong lemon/lime flavours, punchy, vibrant and long. Now moderately developed, with toasty, bottle-aged characters, it shows good richness and charm.

Vintage	02	01	00	99	MED/DRY $21 -V
WR	6	6	5	6	
Drink	04-07	04-05	P	P	

Charles Wiffen Marlborough Riesling ★★★☆

The 2004 vintage (★★★★) is full of promise, with strong citrusy flavours, very fresh and vibrant. A slightly sweet wine (9 grams/litre of residual sugar), threaded with appetising acidity, it shows excellent poise and depth.

MED/DRY $17 V+

Classic Regional Selection Nelson Riesling ★★★

Fleshy and ripe, the 2003 vintage (★★★☆) is citrusy and finely balanced, with plenty of slightly sweet (7.5 grams/litre of residual sugar) flavour. Sold by mail-order wine clubs.

MED/DRY $19 -V

Clearwater Vineyards Waipara Riesling (★★★)

From Sherwood Estate, the 2003 vintage (★★★) is a zesty wine with a sliver of sweetness (7 grams/litre of residual sugar) and green-edged flavours, fresh and lively.

Vintage	03
WR	6
Drink	04-06

DRY $22 -V

Clifford Bay Marlborough Riesling ★★★☆

This single-vineyard Awatere Valley wine matures well. Still youthful, the 2003 vintage (★★★☆) is fresh, tight and vibrant, with lemon, apple and lime flavours showing good depth and a slightly sweet (6.8 grams/litre of residual sugar), finely balanced finish.

Vintage	03	02	01	00	99
WR	6	6	6	6	6
Drink	04-09	04-08	04-07	04-05	P

MED/DRY $18 AV

Coney Ragtime Riesling ★★★★

This is a consistently excellent Martinborough wine, fragrant, fleshy and forward. The 2003 vintage (★★★★) is a floral, slightly honeyed, medium-dry style (13 grams/litre of residual sugar) with rich, citrusy flavours, gentle acidity and a sustained finish. The 2004 (★★★★) is full-bodied (13.5 per cent alcohol), with good richness of lemony, limey, slightly honeyed flavours, a splash of sweetness and lively acidity.

Vintage	03	02
WR	5	4
Drink	04-05	04-05

MED/DRY $19 V+

Coney Rallentando Riesling ★★★★

Made in a much drier style than its stablemate (above), the 2003 vintage (★★★★) of this Martinborough wine is attractively scented, with good delicacy, balance and intensity of citrusy, almost fully dry (3.3 grams/litre of residual sugar) flavour. The pale lemon/green 2004 (★★★★) is weighty (13.5 per cent alcohol) and finely balanced, with smooth, ripe, citrusy, limey flavours showing good harmony and intensity. It's a satisfyingly full-bodied, ripe and rounded wine, well worth cellaring.

Vintage	03	02
WR	6	5
Drink	04-06	04-05

DRY $19 V+

Coopers Creek Marlborough Riesling ★★★

The 2003 vintage (★★☆) is a solid but plain wine, with green-apple aromas and flavours, now showing some toasty, minerally development. The far more attractive 2004 (★★★★) has floral, lemony scents and slightly sweet lemon/lime flavours showing good delicacy, freshness and purity. 'It's the best Riesling I've made at Coopers Creek,' says winemaker Simon Nunns.

Vintage	04	03	02
WR	6	5	5
Drink	04-08	04-07	04-06

MED/DRY $16 AV

Corbans Marlborough Riesling ★★★☆

Both the surprisingly rich 2001 (★★★☆) and 2003 (★★★★) vintages from Allied Domecq have offered outstanding value. The 2003 is light (11 per cent alcohol) and vivacious, with attractive floral scents and gently sweet (12 grams/litre of residual sugar), citrusy, appley flavours, showing excellent depth and harmony. As a low-priced Riesling for everyday drinking, this is hard to beat.

Vintage	04	03	02	01
WR	5	5	6	6
Drink	04-06	04-06	04+	P

MED/DRY $14 V+

Corbans Private Bin Amberley Riesling   (★★★★)

The tangy, limey, minerally 2002 vintage (★★★★) is the first vintage of this once-famous label since 1996. Grown at Waipara (rather than Amberley) in North Canterbury, it is light and lively, with good flavour intensity, a splash of sweetness (8 grams/litre of residual sugar), and a tight, slightly flinty finish. It is now developing a toasty, bottle-aged complexity.

Vintage 02
WR   5   MED/DRY $22 AV
Drink   04-10

Craggy Range Fletcher Family Vineyard Riesling   (★★★★☆)

The tight, intensely flavoured 2004 vintage (★★★★☆) was grown on the Rocenvin Estate, in Marlborough's Wairau Valley. Made from two hand-picked parcels of fruit, the first 'superbly ripe', the second infected with noble rot, it's a pale lemon/green, citrusy, limey, slightly minerally wine, finely scented, with a hint of marmalade and racy acidity. In its infancy, it looks excellent and a classic candidate for cellaring.

MED/DRY $24 AV

Craggy Range Te Muna Road Vineyard Riesling   ★★★☆

Launched from the 2003 vintage (★★★★), this Martinborough wine was hand-picked at 21 brix, whole-bunch pressed and matured on its yeast lees in tanks. Pale and floral, it offers fresh, delicate, pure flavours of lemons and apples, showing excellent balance of acidity and slight sweetness, and a finely textured, lingering finish. The 2004 (★★★☆) is pale and crisp, with good intensity of tight, lemony, appley, limey flavours and a slightly sweet, racy finish. It needs time; open mid-2005+.

MED/DRY $22 -V

Crosse Vineyard Marlborough Riesling   (★★☆)

Sold by mail-order wine clubs, the 2003 vintage (★★☆) is lemony, appley and gently sweet (7.5 grams/litre of residual sugar), but shows a slight lack of fresh, vibrant fruit characters.

MED/DRY $19 -V

Crossroads Destination Series Riesling   ★★★

Full-bodied, with lemon/lime flavours, the 2002 vintage (★★★) of this Hawke's Bay wine offers some richness, with a hint of honey and dryish, crisp finish. The 2003 (★★★) is a distinctly medium style (15 grams/litre of residual sugar), with fresh, limey flavours, balanced for easy drinking.

Vintage 03   02
WR   5   6   MED $19 -V
Drink   04-06 04-06

Culley Marlborough Riesling   (★★★)

Sold by mail-order wine clubs, the 2003 vintage (★★★) is full-bodied and fresh, with good depth of ripe, citrusy, limey flavours and a slightly sweet (7.5 grams/litre of residual sugar), crisp finish.

MED/DRY $19 -V

Delta Marlborough Riesling   (★★☆)

Quite developed for its age, the light yellow 2003 vintage (★★☆) is a medium-dry style (7.5 grams/litre of residual sugar) with firm acidity, honeyed aromas and flavours and a slightly hard finish. Sold by mail-order wine clubs.

MED/DRY $18 -V

Drylands Marlborough Dry Riesling ★★★☆

The pale yellow 2002 vintage (★★★☆) is a weighty, citrusy wine with developed, bottle-age characters emerging. Still youthful, the 2003 (★★★☆) is slightly off-dry (4 grams/litre of residual sugar), with strong lemony, limey flavours showing good delicacy, fresh acidity and a lingering finish. A finely balanced wine, it should mature well.

Vintage	03	02	01	00
WR	7	7	7	7
Drink	04-07	04-05	P	P

DRY $20 AV

Dry River Craighall Riesling ★★★★★

Winemaker Neil McCallum believes that, in quality terms, Riesling is at least the equal of Pinot Noir in Martinborough. His Craighall Riesling, one of the finest in the country, is a wine of exceptional purity, delicacy and depth, with a proven ability to flourish in the cellar for many years: 'It's not smart to drink them at less than five years old,' says McCallum. The grapes are grown in a part of the Craighall vineyard now owned by Dry River, with yields limited to an average of 6 tonnes per hectare. The 2003 vintage (★★★★☆) is finely scented, with very impressive delicacy and harmony of citrusy, slightly sweet flavours. It needs years to unfold: McCallum's suggestion is to 'drink from about three years and evaluate'.

Vintage	03	02	01	00	99	98	97	96
WR	7	6	7	7	6	7	7	7
Drink	06-10	04-07	05-11	04-10	04-10	P	04-06	P

MED/DRY $33 AV

Esk Valley Hawke's Bay Riesling ★★★☆

This label ranks among the finest Rieslings in the Bay. Tasting the tightly structured 2004 vintage (★★★☆) is like biting a crunchy Granny Smith apple. Blended from grapes grown at a cool, inland site in Central Hawke's Bay and warmer sites on the Heretaunga Plains, it is light and lively, crisp, appley and lemony, with good delicacy and a crisp, slightly minerally finish. It should blossom with cellaring.

Vintage	04	03	02	01	00
WR	6	7	6	6	6
Drink	05-10	04-08	04-07	04-07	04-06

MED $19 AV

Felton Road Block 1 Riesling – see Sweet White Wines

Felton Road Dry Riesling ★★★★

Based on low-yielding vines in schisty soils at Bannockburn, in Central Otago, this is typically a classy wine, but the 2003 vintage (★★☆) was disappointing in 2004. Hand-picked, whole-bunch pressed and fermented with indigenous yeasts, it's a pale wine with a funky, slightly grubby bouquet that winemaker Blair Walter describes as 'wet stone, wet wool characters'. Medium-bodied (11 per cent alcohol), with tense, youthful, slightly austere flavours and a slightly sweet (9 grams/litre of residual sugar) finish, it may look better with time.

Vintage	03	02	01
WR	6	7	6
Drink	04-13	04-12	04-10

MED/DRY $23 -V

Felton Road Riesling ★★★★★

Estate-grown at Bannockburn, in Central Otago, this is typically a gently sweet wine with deep flavours cut with fresh acidity. It offers more drink-young appeal than its Dry Riesling stablemate, but invites long-term cellaring. The 2003 vintage (★★★★★) was stop-fermented with an alcohol level of 9.5 per cent and 38 grams per litre of residual sugar, making it a truly medium style. Very light lemon/green, it is deliciously light and zingy, with pure, intense lemon/lime flavours, lovely sugar/acid balance and a crisp, racy finish. A great aperitif.

Vintage	03	02	01	00	99	98
WR	7	7	6	6	6	7
Drink	04-16	04-15	04-12	04-11	04-12	04-09

MED $23 V+

Fiddler's Green Dry Riesling   (★★★★)

Grown at Waipara, the 2003 vintage (★★★★) is an impressive wine with good intensity of ripe, lemony flavours, a sliver of sweetness (5 grams/litre of residual sugar) and a finely balanced, persistent finish.

MED/DRY $21 AV

Fiddler's Green Waipara Riesling   ★★★★

A consistently rewarding North Canterbury wine. The 2004 vintage (★★★★) is tight, crisp and slightly minerally, with strong, citrusy, slightly limey flavours and fine sugar/acid balance (13 grams/litre of residual sugar). An elegant wine, it shows obvious aging potential.

Vintage	04	03	02	01	00	99	98
WR	6	6	6	6	6	6	5
Drink	04-07	04-08	04-06	04-05	04-05	P	P

MED/DRY $20 AV

Firstland Marlborough Riesling   ★★★☆

A single-vineyard wine, grown at Conders Bend, near Renwick, the 2002 vintage (★★★★) has lovely toasty, bottle-aged aromas. Light in body, with lemony, slightly minerally characters unfolding, it's a medium-dry style (10 grams/litre of residual sugar), still fresh and vibrant, with excellent delicacy and depth.

MED/DRY $15 V+

Floating Mountain Waipara Riesling   (★★☆)

The 2003 vintage (★★☆) was picked early, in the search for 'a Mosel-style wine with lower alcohol, residual sweetness and good natural acidity'. It's a high-acid style with lemony, appley flavours and a distinct splash of sweetness (20 grams/litre of residual sugar), but lacks real fragrance and freshness.

MED $19 -V

Forrest Estate Dry Riesling   ★★★★☆

This is proprietor John Forrest's 'personal favourite', at its best dry but not austere, with intense, limey flavours and slatey, minerally characters adding complexity. The 2003 vintage (★★★★) was hand-picked in the Wairau and Brancott valleys and fermented to a slightly off-dry style (5.2 grams/litre of residual sugar). Pale lemon/green, it's an elegant, tightly structured wine with strong lemony, appley flavours, moderate acidity and good harmony. Drink now or cellar.

Vintage	03	02
WR	5	6
Drink	04-10	05-10

MED/DRY $25 -V

Forrest Marlborough Riesling   ★★★☆

John Forrest believes Riesling will one day be Marlborough's greatest wine, and his own wine is helping the cause. Grown at three sites, the ripely scented 2004 vintage (★★★★) is fresh and vibrant, with plenty of citrusy, appley, limey flavour in a medium-dry style (14 grams/litre of residual sugar) with crisp, racy acids and a rich finish. Delicious from the start.

Vintage	04	03	02	01	00
WR	6	4	4	5	5
Drink	04-08	04-05	P	P	P

MED/DRY $17 V+

Fossil Ridge Nelson Riesling   ★★★☆

Grown in the Richmond foothills, the 2003 vintage (★★★☆) is fresh and youthful, with citrusy, appley, slightly sweet (8 grams/litre of residual sugar) flavours, showing good delicacy and depth, and a slightly minerally, lingering finish.

MED/DRY $18 AV

Framingham Classic Riesling ★★★★

Estate-grown at Renwick, top vintages of this Marlborough wine are deliciously aromatic, richly flavoured and zesty. The 2003 vintage (★★★★) is a gently sweet style (18 grams/litre of residual sugar), with punchy lemon, apple and lime flavours, a hint of honey and a crisp, racy finish. Best drinking mid-2005+.

Vintage	03	02	01	00	99	98	97
WR	6	6	7	6	6	7	5
Drink	04-07	04-06	04-05	P	P	P	P

MED $20 AV

Framingham Dry Riesling ★★★★☆

This is the Marlborough winery's flagship. Estate-grown at Conders Bend, Renwick, the pale lemon/green 2003 vintage (★★★★☆) is tight and youthful in a just off-dry style (5.5 grams/litre of residual sugar). Placing its accent on complexity and a minerally element, rather than vibrant fruit characters, it's one of the region's most individual Rieslings, intense, light and lingering.

Vintage	03	02	01	00	99
WR	7	6	7	7	7
Drink	04-10	04-08	04-10	04-08	04-06

MED/DRY $28 -V

Francis-Cole Marlborough Riesling (★★★)

Estate-grown in the Omaka Valley, the 2003 vintage (★★★) is fresh and lively, with a sliver of sweetness (5 grams/litre of residual sugar) amid its youthful, citrusy, slightly minerally flavours. Worth cellaring.

Vintage	03
WR	6
Drink	04-08

MED/DRY $19 -V

Fromm La Strada Dry Riesling ★★★★☆

Typically a beautifully poised, delicate Marlborough wine with citrusy, minerally flavours and a zingy, lasting finish. The 2003 vintage (★★★★) is still very youthful, with obvious cellaring potential. It's an intense, medium-dry wine (10 grams/litre of residual sugar) with strong lemony, appley flavours, a minerally streak and racy acidity. It needs time; open 2006+.

Vintage	04	03	02	01	00
WR	6	6	6	6	6
Drink	04-14	04-13	04-12	04-11	04-10

DRY $27 -V

Fromm La Strada Riesling – see Sweet White Wines

Gibbston Valley Central Otago Riesling ★★★☆

At its best, this is a deliciously zingy wine, awash with lemon and lime flavours, showing an almost Germanic lightness and vivacity. Grown at four sites, the 2003 vintage (★★★★) is a distinctly cool-climate style, scented and racy, with plentiful sweetness (24 grams/litre of residual sugar) balanced with fresh, zingy acids. The palate is finely textured, with strong, vibrant, citrusy flavours showing good delicacy and balance.

Vintage	04	03	02	01
WR	4	6	6	6
Drink	05-08	04-09	04-08	04-06

MED/DRY $24 -V

Giesen Marlborough/Canterbury Riesling ★★★☆

From one vintage to the next, this is one of the best-value Rieslings around. Early releases were based solely on Canterbury grapes, but the 2003 vintage (★★★☆) is a blend of fruit from Marlborough and Canterbury. A distinctly medium style (20 grams/litre of sugar), with 'a hint of noble rot', it has a slightly honeyed bouquet. Tangy and full-flavoured, it has pungent lemon/lime characters and more obvious sweetness than most New Zealand Rieslings, balanced by lively acidity.

Vintage	04	03		MED $15 V+
WR	7	7		
Drink	05-08	04-10		

Gladstone Wairarapa Riesling   ★★★

The slightly honeyed 2003 vintage (★★★) was grown in two vineyards, at Gladstone and Waipipi. Light yellow, it's a dry style (3.6 grams/litre of residual sugar), full-bodied (13.3 per cent alcohol), with a hint of botrytis amid its ripe-lemon/lime flavours and a rounded finish.

DRY $18 AV

Glenmark Proprietors Reserve Waipara Riesling   ★★★

Labelled in different vintages as 'Dry' or 'Medium', this North Canterbury wine is always full of interest. The slowly evolving 1999 Dry (★★★) has firm, steely acidity and kerosene and toast characters emerging. The 2000 Medium (★★★☆), the pick of recent releases, is drinking well now, with a good balance of sweetness and acidity and strong lemony, slightly minerally flavours. Offering more drink-young appeal than the 1999, the 2002 Dry is citrusy, limey, fresh and flavourful, with a dry but not austere finish.

DRY-MED $21 -V

Glover's Dry Riesling   (★★☆)

The 2002 vintage (★★☆) of this Nelson wine is lean and austere, with green-apple flavours and high acidity.

Vintage	02	01		DRY $17 -V
WR	7	6		
Drink	04-08	04-07		

Goldridge Marlborough Riesling   (★★★)

The tightly structured 2003 vintage (★★★) is a slightly austere but flavoursome wine with lemony, appley characters and a splash of sweetness (12 grams/litre of residual sugar) to balance its firm acidity.

MED/DRY $16 AV

Greenhough Hope Vineyard Riesling   (★★★★☆)

The debut 2004 vintage (★★★★☆) is an intensely flavoured Nelson wine, made from 25-year-old vines. Hand-harvested with 'a small botrytis component', whole-bunch pressed and stop-fermented with 25 grams per litre of residual sugar, it's a light lemon/green, distinctly medium style, light (11.5 per cent alcohol), lively and bursting with lemony, citrusy, spicy flavours, ripe, delicate and mouth-wateringly crisp. Open mid-2005+.

Vintage	04			MED $23 AV
WR	6			
Drink	05-10			

Greenhough Nelson Vineyards Dry Riesling   ★★★★

Andrew Greenhough produces a classy Riesling, at its best strikingly perfumed, incisively flavoured and zesty. Hand-picked and whole-bunch pressed, the 2004 vintage (★★★☆) is a crisp, citrusy, limey, slightly minerally wine, not fully dry (7 grams/litre of residual sugar), with very good depth and balance and a tight finish. It needs time; open mid-2005+.

Vintage	04	03	02	01	00	99	98	MED/DRY $19 V+
WR	5	6	6	5	6	6	5	
Drink	04-07	04-07	04-06	04-05	P	P	P	

Grove Mill Innovator Riesling   (★★★☆)

The 2002 vintage (★★★☆) from this Marlborough winery is a Canterbury wine, harvested on 22 May and stop-fermented with 5.8 grams per litre of residual sugar. Light yellow/green, it is quite Germanic on the nose, minerally, earthy and slightly honeyed, with a light (11 per cent alcohol), lemony palate, quite developed for its age, a sliver of sweetness and firm acid spine. Drink now.

DRY $20 AV

Grove Mill Marlborough Riesling ★★★★☆

At its best highly perfumed, with intense lemon/lime flavours, this is a classy wine. It typically harbours 15 to 20 grams per litre of residual sugar, but that plentiful sweetness is finely balanced with lush, concentrated fruit characters and appetising acidity. Some botrytis has been present in most vintages and, unusually for New Zealand, winemaker Dave Pearce puts about half the final blend through malolactic fermentation, 'not to modify acidity but to enhance the wine's texture'. The 2004 vintage (★★★★☆) is highly impressive in its youth. Light lemon/green, it is intense and tangy, with concentrated lemon/lime flavours, passionfruit and ginger touches, and lovely sugar/acid balance. Showing strong personality, it is delicious in its youth.

Vintage	03	02	01	00	99	98	97	96
WR	6	6	6	7	6	6	7	7
Drink	04-10	04-06	04-06	04-05	04-06	P	P	P

MED/DRY $18 V+

Hanmer Junction, The, Waipara Valley Riesling ★★★

From Alpine Pacific, which also markets wine under the Mount Cass label, the 2002 vintage (★★★) is a full-bodied, slightly sweet style (14 grams/litre of residual sugar) with ripe lemony, slightly honeyed flavours.

Vintage	02	01
WR	5	6
Drink	P	P

MED/DRY $17 AV

Highfield Marlborough Riesling ★★★☆

The light lemon/green 2002 vintage (★★★☆) was stop-fermented in an off-dry style (6.7 grams/litre of residual sugar). The bouquet is lemony and minerally; the palate is crisp and tight, with strong citrusy flavours cut with fresh acidity.

Vintage	02
WR	6
Drink	04-07

MED/DRY $24 -V

Huia Marlborough Riesling ★★★☆

Already enjoyable, the 2004 vintage (★★★☆) was grown in the Two Ponds and Fairhall vineyards and fermented to an off-dry (5.7 grams/litre of residual sugar) style. It's a fleshy and harmonious wine with ripe, citrusy, appley flavours showing very good depth and a crisp, finely balanced finish.

Vintage	03	02	01
WR	6	7	6
Drink	04-08	04-08	04-06

DRY $23 -V

Hunter's Flax Mill Marlborough Riesling (★★☆)

Sold by mail-order wine clubs, the 2003 vintage (★★☆) is a pale wine with tight, appley, green-edged flavours and a slightly sweet (7.5 grams/litre of residual sugar) finish.

MED/DRY $20 -V

Hunter's Marlborough Riesling ★★★★

This wine is consistently good and in top vintages beautifully poised, with lovely depth of citrusy flavours, some riper tropical-fruit characters and a dryish finish. The 2004 vintage (★★★★), harvested at 22 to 23 brix, is a typically immaculate wine, full-bodied, youthful, tight and crisp, with good intensity of lemony, limey, slightly flinty flavour. It should mature well; open mid-2005+.

Vintage	03	02	01	00
WR	6	6	5	4
Drink	06-08	05-06	04-05	P

MED/DRY $17 V+

Hunter's Stoneburn Marlborough Riesling ★★★

Sold by mail-order wine clubs, the 2003 vintage (★★★) is a solid wine, crisp and lively, with lemony, appley, moderately ripe flavours and a slightly sweet (7.5 grams/litre of residual sugar) finish.

MED/DRY $19 -V

Hurunui River Riesling (★★★☆)

Light and lively, the 2002 vintage (★★★☆) was grown at Hawarden, north-west of Waipara in North Canterbury, and stop-fermented with plentiful (20 grams/litre) residual sugar. It's a light-bodied wine (11 per cent alcohol) with zingy, vibrant lemon/lime flavours showing well-defined, cool-climate varietal characters, fresh acidity and good vigour.

MED $18 AV

Isabel Marlborough Dry Riesling ★★★★☆

Top vintages of this wine are minerally and taut, with citrusy, appley flavours, crisp and intense. The 2003 vintage (★★★★☆) is limey, with notable vigour and depth. Tightly structured, with racy acidity, locked-in power and a lasting, slightly off-dry finish, it should be at its best from 2005 onwards.

Vintage	03	02	01	00	99
WR	6	6	6	6	5
Drink	04-11	04-10	04-09	04-08	04-05

DRY $20 V+

Jackson Estate Homestead Block Riesling ★★★★

Proprietor John Stichbury took some convincing that Riesling is fashionable, so until a few years ago this wine was labelled Marlborough Dry, with the name of the variety in small print. Estate-grown in the middle of the Wairau Valley, the 2002 vintage (★★★★) is a full-bodied, ripely flavoured wine with lively acidity, excellent intensity of dryish, citrusy characters, and hints of lime and pineapple.

Vintage	02	01	00	99	98
WR	5	5	6	6	5
Drink	04-07	04-05	04-05	P	P

DRY $17 V+

Jules Taylor Marlborough Riesling ★★★★☆

Grown on the Ellin Estate, in Dog Point Road, the 2002 vintage (★★★★☆) was hand-picked, whole-bunch pressed and stop-fermented with 8 grams per litre of sugar, making it a medium-dry style. More forward than the very refined and pure 2001 (★★★★★), it's a highly characterful, full-bodied wine (13 per cent alcohol), with excellent intensity of citrusy, minerally flavour.

MED/DRY $23 AV

Julicher Martinborough Riesling (★★★☆)

Grown on the Te Muna Terraces, just south of Martinborough township, the 2003 vintage (★★★☆) was made by Chris Buring, scion of the famous Australian winemaking family. Full-bodied (13.5 per cent alcohol), citrusy and slightly pineappley, it's a ripe, fully dry style (below 3 grams/litre of residual sugar), not highly scented but generously flavoured, with cellaring potential.

Vintage	03
WR	5
Drink	04+

DRY $20 AV

Kahurangi Estate Heaphy Series Moutere Riesling (★★☆)

Sold by mail-order wine clubs, the 2003 vintage (★★☆) is full-bodied, with crisp, appley, lemony flavours and a slightly sweet (7.5 grams/litre of residual sugar) finish. It's a solid wine, but lacks flair.

MED/DRY $19 -V

Kahurangi Estate Moutere Riesling ★★★☆

Produced 'from the South Island's oldest Riesling vines' (planted by the Seifrieds in the 1970s), the 2003 vintage (★★★★) is a very fresh and lively Nelson wine with pristine fruit characters and excellent depth of lemon/lime flavours. An elegant, medium-dry style (10 grams/litre of residual sugar), it shows good balance and structure.

Vintage 03
WR 6
Drink 04-07

MED/DRY $18 AV

Kahurangi Estate Reserve Nelson Riesling (★★★★)

The floral, charming 2003 vintage (★★★★) is a generous, finely balanced wine, hand-picked and whole-bunch pressed. It's a full-bodied style (13.5 per cent alcohol), with excellent depth of crisp, slightly sweet (8.8 grams/litre of residual sugar), citrusy flavours.

Vintage 03
WR 6
Drink 04-07

MED/DRY $20 AV

Kaikoura Canterbury Riesling (★★☆)

Verging on three-star quality, the 2002 vintage (★★☆) is a gently sweet (15.5 grams/litre of residual sugar), medium-bodied wine, lemony and slightly honeyed, with firm acidity. It lacks fragrance, but is maturing solidly.

MED $16 -V

Kaimira Estate Brightwater Riesling ★★★

Estate-grown at Brightwater, in Nelson, the 2003 vintage (★★★☆) is tight and zesty, with very good depth of lemony, appley flavour, refreshing acidity and plenty of cellaring potential. The 2004 (not rated, because it was still bottle-shocked when I tasted it in August) is a medium-dry style (9 grams/litre of residual sugar), with strong citrusy flavours woven with fresh acidity.

MED/DRY $17 AV

Kim Crawford Marlborough Dry Riesling ★★★★

The 2004 vintage (★★★☆) was grown at three sites and fermented to full dryness, but prior to bottling some late-harvest wine was blended to give a hint of sweetness (7 grams/litre of residual sugar). Fresh and racy, with youthful lemon, apple and lime flavours showing good delicacy, it should mature well; open 2006+.

Vintage	04	03	02	01	00	99	98
WR	7	4	6	7	5	7	5
Drink	05-10	06	04-10	04-06	04-06	04-05	P

MED/DRY $20 AV

Koura Bay Barney's Rock Awatere Valley Riesling ★★☆

The 2002 vintage (★★☆) lacks a bit of scentedness and charm and seems past its best. Balanced for easy drinking, the 2003 (★★☆) is crisp, citrusy and slightly sweet (7.2 grams/litre of residual sugar), but restrained and lacking real depth.

Vintage 03 02
WR 7 6
Drink 06-08 06-08

MED/DRY $17 -V

Lake Chalice Marlborough Riesling ★★★★

The 2004 vintage (★★★★) was grown at two Rapaura sites (the estate's stony Falcon Vineyard and a grower's vineyard on heavier soils), harvested at an average of 21.5 brix and fermented to a medium-dry

style (7 grams/litre of residual sugar). Full-bodied and rich, with punchy, citrusy, limey flavours and hints
of passionfruit, fresh acidity and a finely balanced finish, it should unfold really well during 2005–06.

Vintage	04	03
WR	6	6
Drink	04-09	04-08

MED/DRY $19 V+

Lawson's Dry Hills Marlborough Riesling   ★★★☆

Offering loads of flavour in its infancy, the 2004 vintage (★★★★) was grown in the Wairau and Waihopai
valleys, harvested at 20.3 to 22 brix and stop-fermented in a medium-dry style (7 grams/litre of residual
sugar). Bright, light lemon/green, it's a full-bodied wine (13 per cent alcohol), ripe and concentrated, with
fresh, strong lemon/lime flavours, finely judged sugar/acid balance and a tight finish.

Vintage	04	03	02	01	00	99	98
WR	6	6	6	5	5	6	6
Drink	05-08	04-07	04-06	04-06	04-05	P	P

MED/DRY $19 AV

Leaning Rock Central Otago Riesling   ★★★

Estate-grown at Alexandra, the 2003 vintage (★★★) is light (11.4 per cent alcohol) and racy. Showing
youthful, green-tinged colour, it's a slightly sweet style (16 grams/litre of residual sugar) with citrusy, limey
flavours and a fresh, mouth-wateringly crisp finish. Worth cellaring.

Vintage	03
WR	6
Drink	04-06

MED $19 -V

Loopline Riesling Medium Dry   (★★★)

Grown at Opaki, north of Masterton in the Wairarapa, the 2003 vintage (★★★) is a slightly honeyed wine
with limey, pineappley flavours. It shows good ripeness and depth, with a splash of sweetness (12
grams/litre of residual sugar) and an appetisingly crisp finish. Drink 2004–05.

MED/DRY $20 -V

Main Divide Riesling   ★★★

Grown in three sub-regions of Canterbury (Waipara, Swannanoa and Burnham), the 2003 vintage (★★★)
is a youthful, light-bodied wine with strong lemon/lime flavours. Green-edged, with plentiful sweetness (19
grams/litre of residual sugar) and steely acidity, it's an enjoyable aperitif. The 2004 (★★★), grown in the
same districts, is a light wine (8 per cent alcohol), crisp and gently sweet, with lemon and green apple
flavours showing good delicacy and racy acidity.

Vintage	04	03
WR	5	6
Drink	04-06	04-06

MED/DRY $17 AV

Margrain Proprietors Selection Riesling   ★★★☆

The 2003 vintage (★★★★), grown in Martinborough, is a medium-dry style (12 grams/litre of residual
sugar). Already drinking well, it is light-bodied, crisp, lemony and minerally, with good intensity and
harmony.

Vintage	03	02
WR	6	6
Drink	04-10	04-08

MED/DRY $22 -V

Marlborough Wines Limited Riesling   (★★☆)

The 2003 vintage (★★☆) is a solid wine, lemony, appley, crisp and slightly sweet, but plain. Priced right.

MED/DRY $15 AV

Martinborough Vineyard Jackson Block Riesling   ★★★★☆

This is one of the jewels of the Martinborough Vineyard range. Full of promise, the 2003 vintage (★★★★☆) is based on 13-year-old vines in Bernie and Jane Jackson's vineyard, just 'around the corner' from the winery. Tight and youthful, dryish but not austere, it shows good weight and intensity of delicate grapefruit and lime flavours, with fresh acidity and a long finish. A top candidate for cellaring. (Opened in early 2004, the 2001 vintage is starting to develop toasty, bottle-aged characters, but is still unfolding, with youthful freshness and zing.)

Vintage	03	02	01	00	99	98	97	96	
WR	7	6	7	7	5	7	6	6	MED/DRY $23 AV
Drink	04-10	04-09	04-08	04-07	04-05	04-05	P	P	

Martinborough Vineyard Manu Riesling   (★★★★☆)

Delicious from the start, the 2003 vintage (★★★★☆) was hand-picked from 13-year-old vines in the Jackson Block, left to develop 'a touch' of noble rot. A medium-sweet style (harbouring 28 grams/litre of residual sugar), it has fresh, vibrant passionfruit and lime flavours, crisp, intense and lingering. Drink now or cellar.

MED $28 -V

McCashin's Waipara Riesling   ★★★

The 2002 vintage (★★★) is steely, with high acidity and green-edged flavours showing good persistence. It's a dryish style (6.5 grams/litre of sugar) with lots of character.

MED/DRY $17 AV

Melness Riesling   ★★★★

This Canterbury wine is always full of personality. The 2003 vintage (★★★★), made from 'super-ripe' fruit with some noble rot, is fresh, tangy and vivacious, with ample sweetness (28 grams/litre of residual sugar) and strong, vibrant flavours of lemons, apples and limes. Richly scented, it's a light-bodied wine (9 per cent alcohol), but there's no shortage of flavour.

Vintage	03	02	01	
WR	7	7	6	MED $22 AV
Drink	04-09	04-07	04-06	

Mills Reef Hawke's Bay Riesling   ★★★

This is a slightly sweeter style than its stablemate (below), produced in an easy-drinking style. The 2002 vintage (★★☆), grown at Meeanee and lees-aged for three months, is a medium-bodied style. It's not intense, but fresh, crisp and lively, with drink-young appeal. (The 2003 vintage is a Marlborough wine.)

Vintage	04	03	02	01	00	
WR	7	7	7	7	6	MED $16 AV
Drink	04-08	04-06	04-05	P	P	

Mills Reef Reserve Riesling   ★★★☆

The 2002 vintage (★★★☆) was grown in Hawke's Bay and matured on its gross lees for four months. It's a punchy, tangy wine with tight lemon/lime flavours and a persistent, dryish finish. There is no 2003.

Vintage	03	02	01	00	99	98	97	96	
WR	NM	6	NM	6	NM	6	NM	5	MED/DRY $19 AV
Drink	NM	04-05	NM	P	NM	P	NM	P	

Millton Opou Vineyard Riesling   ★★★★☆

Typically finely scented, with rich, lemony, often honeyed flavours, this is the country's northernmost fine-quality Riesling. Grown in Gisborne (some of the vines are 23 years old), it is gently sweet, in a softer, typically less racy style than the classic Marlborough wines. The grapes, grown organically in the Opou vineyard at Manutuke, are hand-harvested over a month at three stages of ripening, usually culminating in a final pick of botrytis-affected fruit. The finely scented 2004 vintage (★★★★☆) is slender (9.6 per cent alcohol), light and lovely, with a strong surge of lemon/lime flavours, no sign of botrytis, lively acidity and great immediacy of appeal. A distinctly medium style (30 grams/litre of residual sugar), it's a great drink-now or cellaring proposition.

Vintage	04	03	02	01	00	99	98	97	96	MED $22 AV
WR	7	5	7	NM	7	5	7	5	6	
Drink	04-08	P	04-15	NM	04-12	04-05	04-10	P	P	

Millton Riesling Special Bunch Selection   (★★★)

The 2002 vintage (★★★) is a fleshy Gisborne wine with overt sweetness (28 grams/litre of residual sugar), gentle acidity and slightly honeyed flavours.

MED $28 -V

Mission Riesling   ★★★☆

Mission's Rieslings are typically more lively than most from Hawke's Bay. From a frost-affected vintage, the 2003 (★★★☆) is a medium-dry wine blended from Canterbury (55 per cent) and Nelson grapes. It's an upfront style, with lemon/lime aromas and flavours showing good freshness and intensity.

Vintage	03	02	01	00	MED/DRY $15 V+
WR	6	6	5	7	
Drink	04-06	04-06	P	04-05	

Montana Marlborough Riesling   ★★★☆

One of New Zealand's best wine buys, this old favourite can mature well for a decade or longer. It is typically full-bodied and slightly sweet, with strong lemon and lime flavours hinting of tropical fruits. The 2003 vintage (★★★☆) is a well-ripened blend of Wairau Valley and Awatere Valley grapes, with generous lemon and pear flavours and a splash of sweetness (10 grams/litre of residual sugar) adding an easy-drinking appeal. Tasted prior to bottling (and so not rated), the 2004 looked very similar – ripely scented, with strong lemon/lime flavours, slightly sweet and crisp.

Vintage	04	03	02	MED/DRY $15 V+
WR	6	5	6	
Drink	04-08	04-07	04+	

Montana Reserve Marlborough Riesling   ★★★★

Released after a couple of years in the bottle, this is a slightly drier style than its cheaper stablemate (above). Harvested at 22 to 24 brix in the Brancott Estate vineyard, the highly scented 2002 vintage (★★★★) possesses ripe citrus and tropical-fruit flavours, with a sliver of sweetness (7 grams/litre of sugar) and good intensity. Yellow-hued, with toasty, bottle-aged characters emerging, it's drinking well now.

Vintage	02	01	00	99	98	MED/DRY $20 AV
WR	5	7	7	7	6	
Drink	04-09	04+	04+	P	P	

Morton Estate Stone Creek Marlborough Riesling   ★★★

The 2003 vintage (★★★), a single-vineyard wine, is a full-bodied (13.5 per cent alcohol) style, fresh and youthful, with good depth of lemon and apple flavours, slightly sweet, crisp and tightly structured. It should unfold well during 2005.

Vintage	03	02	MED/DRY $18 AV
WR	5	7	
Drink	04-09	04-10	

Morworth Estate Vineyard Selection Canterbury Riesling ★★★☆

The 2002 vintage (★★★☆) has a floral bouquet, with a touch of honey. It's a medium-dry style (14 grams/litre of residual sugar) with limey, gently honeyed flavours showing good richness and a steely, long finish. Harvested at 20 brix and matured on its yeast lees, the 2003 (★★★☆) is a drier style (7 grams/litre of residual sugar), slightly honeyed, with lemony, tight flavours woven with firm acidity. Floral, with good delicacy, depth and sugar/acid balance, it should mature well.

`MED/DRY $19 AV`

Mount Edward Central Otago Riesling ★★★☆

Alan Brady's wine is a poised, lively medium-dry style with lemony, crisp flavours, zesty and lingering. A single-vineyard Gibbston wine, the 2003 vintage (★★★☆) has fresh, citrusy, appley aromas leading into a slightly more full-bodied wine than usual (12 per cent alcohol, compared to the customary 10.5 per cent), with strong flavours, ample sweetness (12 grams/litre of residual sugar) and tense acidity.

Vintage	03	02	01	00	99	98
WR	6	6	6	6	5	6
Drink	05-08	04-07	04-06	04-05	P	P

`MED/DRY $20 AV`

Mount Edward The Late Edward Late Harvest Riesling (★★★★)

Grown on the shores of Lake Hayes, near Queenstown, the 2002 vintage (★★★★) was made from a small block of Riesling grapes, left to hang on the vines until long after the main harvest. Bright lemon/green in hue, it has fresh, strong lemon and Granny Smith apple flavours, showing lovely balance of plentiful sweetness (40 grams/litre of residual sugar) and tangy acidity. It's a deliciously light and lively wine, with obvious cellaring potential.

Vintage	02
WR	5
Drink	05-09

`MED $28 -V`

Mount Riley Marlborough Riesling ★★★

A blend of Marlborough and Nelson grapes, the 2003 vintage (★★★☆) is a juicy, medium style with ripe lemon, lime and passionfruit flavours showing good depth and an upfront, punchy appeal. Sourced entirely from the Wairau Valley, the 2004 is also a medium style (15 grams/litre of residual sugar). Pale and light-bodied (11 per cent alcohol), with lemony, appley flavours, it's an easy-drinking style, but was still bottle-shocked when tasted in August, so it has not been rated.

Vintage	04
WR	5
Drink	05-08

`MED $17 AV`

Moutere Hills Dry Riesling ★★★

The 2002 vintage (★★★) is a slightly rustic but honest and characterful Nelson wine. It's a powerful wine with apple, mineral and slight 'kerosene' notes on the nose, good weight, flavour depth and ripeness, and a firm, dryish finish.

`MED/DRY $20 -V`

Mt Difficulty Dry Riesling ★★★☆

Grown at Bannockburn, in Central Otago, this is a wine for purists – steely and austere in its youth, but rewarding (almost demanding) time. The 2003 vintage (★★★☆) is finely scented, tight and elegant, with youthful green apple and lime flavours and searching acidity. Open 2006.

`MED/DRY $21 -V`

Mt Difficulty Target Gully Riesling ★★★☆

Grown in the Target Gully vineyard at Bannockburn, in Central Otago, the 2003 vintage (★★★★) is a richly flavoured wine with vibrant lemon/lime characters and a long finish. A medium style (with over 20 grams/litre of residual sugar), it's already delicious, but shows obvious potential.

MED $21 -V

Mudbrick Vineyard Nelson Riesling ★★★☆

The 2003 vintage (★★★☆) from this Waiheke Island winery is scented and incisively flavoured, with a gentle splash of sweetness (9 grams/litre of residual sugar) and steely acidity.

MED/DRY $18 AV

Muddy Water James Hardwick Waipara Riesling ★★★★

Showing lovely lightness and freshness, the 2002 vintage (★★★★) was stop-fermented in a medium style (15 grams/litre sugar). A pale, green-tinged wine, it is finely balanced, with strong lemon/apple flavours, crisp and vivacious. (Note: the Riesling Dry was not produced in 2002 or 2003.)

Vintage	03	02	01	00	99
WR	NM	7	7	7	7
Drink	NM	04-13	04-12	04-10	04-06

MED $22 AV

Muddy Water Riesling Unplugged ★★★★

Grown at Waipara, the 2003 vintage (★★★★) was late-harvested at 25 to 27 brix and stop-fermented in a medium-sweet style (36 grams/litre of residual sugar). From a wet autumn, in which much of Muddy Water's Riesling was infected by botrytis, this is the only Riesling made. Light lemon/green, it is intensely flavoured, sweet and zingy, with mouthfilling body (13.4 per cent alcohol) and rich botrytis-derived, marmalade and honey characters. It should mature well, but is already delicious.

Vintage	03	02
WR	6	6
Drink	04-08	04-07

MED $22 AV

Mud House Marlborough Riesling ★★★★

Bargain-priced, the 2003 vintage (★★★★) is lemon-scented, with pure, citrusy, limey flavours showing lovely delicacy and a slight minerally character. Fresh, tightly structured and youthful, it has well-balanced acidity and a long life ahead.

MED/DRY $18 V+

Murdoch James Martinborough Riesling ★★★☆

The 2003 vintage (★★★), harvested at 20 brix, is a slender wine (only 9 per cent alcohol) with abundant sweetness (over 20 grams/litre of residual sugar) and appetising acidity. Offering fresh, strong green-apple flavours, it is light and lively, with good sugar/acid balance, but needs time; open 2005.

Vintage	03
WR	5
Drink	04-05

MED $19 AV

Neudorf Brightwater Riesling ★★★★

Grown at Brightwater, on Nelson's Waimea Plains, this is a consistently rewarding wine, intense and finely poised. The 2004 vintage (★★★★) was harvested at 20.4 to 21.3 brix, partly (18 per cent) fermented with indigenous yeasts and lees-aged. Showing good vigour and varietal character, it is a tangy, tightly structured wine with citrusy, slightly minerally characters and lots of passionfruit and fine sugar/acid balance. Open mid-2005+.

Vintage	04	03	02
WR	5	5	6
Drink	04-10	04-08	04-08

MED/DRY $22 AV

Neudorf Moutere Riesling   ★★★★★

This is a copybook cool-climate style, with exciting flavour intensity. The 2003 vintage (★★★★★) was picked at 22.2 brix in the Home Vineyard with some botrytis infection and stop-fermented with 10.5 per cent alcohol and 37 grams per litre of residual sugar. Light lemon/green, with a scented, floral bouquet, it offers intense, vibrant flavours of lemons, apples and pears, ripe and slightly honeyed. Very refined, delicate and racy, it's hard to resist now, but still youthful.

Vintage	04	03	02	01	00	99	98
WR	5	6	5	6	5	6	7
Drink	04-10	04-12	04-09	04-08	04-06	04-05	04-09

MED $30 AV

Nga Waka Martinborough Riesling   ★★★★

A consistently powerful wine, with mouthfilling body and deep, bone-dry flavour. The 2002 vintage (★★★★), harvested at 22.4 brix, is a typically rich, sturdy wine (13.3 per cent alcohol), carrying the dry style well. Light lemon/green, it possesses strong citrus and tropical-fruit flavours, slightly minerally and toasty, but not austere, with loads of personality.

Vintage	02	01	00	99	98
WR	6	6	7	6	7
Drink	05+	05+	05+	05+	05-08

DRY $20 AV

Ohinemuri Estate Patutahi Riesling   ★★☆

German winemaker Horst Hillerich makes a characterful Riesling, but the 2003 vintage (★★), grown in Gisborne, is not one of the best. From a difficult season, it was partly barrel-fermented, but lacks fragrance, delicacy and charm.

MED $21 -V

Olssen's Riesling   ★★★

The 2003 vintage (★★☆) was estate-grown at Bannockburn, in Central Otago, harvested at 20.6 to 21.3 brix, and fermented to an almost dry style (5.8 grams/litre of sugar). Pale lemon/green, with freshly acidic, appley flavours, it's a solid but green-edged wine that lacks real ripeness and intensity.

Vintage	03
WR	6
Drink	04-08

MED/DRY $20 -V

Omaka Springs Marlborough Riesling   ★★★

The 2003 vintage (★★☆) is fresh and lively, with appley, green-edged flavours of decent depth. The 2004 (★★★) is a medium to full-bodied wine with strong, citrusy flavours, slight sweetness (9 grams/litre of residual sugar) and fresh, appetising acidity.

MED/DRY $18 -V

Opihi Riesling   ★★★☆

The youthful, green-tinged 2002 vintage (★★★☆) was grown near Pleasant Point, 30 km inland from Timaru in South Canterbury. Scented, with a sliver of sweetness amid its crisp, lively lemon/lime flavours, it's a distinctly cool-climate style, with good delicacy and depth.

Vintage	02	01
WR	6	5
Drink	04-06	04-06

MED/DRY $19 AV

Packspur Central Otago Riesling   ★★★

Harvested in mid-May, stop-fermented in a medium style (16 grams/litre of residual sugar) and matured on its yeast lees, the 2003 vintage (★★★) is a fresh, cool-climate style, light-bodied, with appley, limey aromas and flavours, showing decent depth and an appetisingly crisp finish.

MED $17 AV

Palliser Estate Autumn Riesling   (★★★★☆)

The 2004 vintage (★★★★☆) was harvested in Martinborough 'late in the autumn with a significant level of botrytis'. A distinctly medium style (24 grams/litre of residual sugar), it is fleshy (12.5 per cent alcohol) faintly honeyed, with rich peach, lemon and pear flavours woven with fresh, balanced acidity and lovely sugar/acid balance. It's a deliciously harmonious wine, likely to be at its best 2006+.

MED $26 -V

Palliser Estate Martinborough Riesling   ★★★★★

Allan Johnson's Rieslings are typically beautifully scented, with intense, slightly sweet flavour and a racy finish. Top vintages mature well, for up to a decade. The 2003 vintage (★★★★), harvested with some botrytis and stop-fermented with 7 grams per litre of residual sugar, has a fragrant, slightly honeyed bouquet. Weighty (13.5 per cent alcohol) and rounded, with rich, ripe flavours of lemons, limes and passionfruit, it's a forward vintage, already drinking well, but should also be worth cellaring. In its infancy, the 2004 (★★★) was less beguiling, with a restrained bouquet, good weight and crisp flavours of citrus fruits, limes and passionfruit. Solid, rather than exciting.

MED/DRY $19 V+

Pegasus Bay Aria (Late Harvest Riesling) – see Sweet White Wines

Pegasus Bay Riesling   ★★★★★

This is very classy stuff. Estate-grown at Waipara, in North Canterbury, at its best it is richly fragrant and thrillingly intense, with concentrated flavours of citrus fruits and honey, complex and luscious. The 1995, 1998, 2000, 2001 and 2002 vintages are all memorable. The 2003 (★★★★★) was hand-picked, whole-bunch-pressed, cool-fermented with cultured yeasts in stainless steel tanks and bottled early. Gorgeously perfumed and intense, it's a fleshy, distinctly medium wine (19 grams/litre of residual sugar) with zingy acidity, a powerful surge of lemon, apple and apricot flavours and a slightly honeyed richness. A lovely aperitif.

Vintage	03	02	01	00	99	98	97	96	95
WR	7	7	6	7	6	6	5	4	6
Drink	04-13	04-12	04-11	04-10	04-09	04-07	P	P	P

MED $23 V+

Peregrine Central Otago Riesling   ★★★☆

Likely to age well, the 2003 vintage (★★★☆) was hand-picked in three vineyards around Lake Dunstan, in the Cromwell Basin, and cool-fermented to a dry style (4 grams/litre of residual sugar). It's an attractive wine, fresh and well-balanced, with good depth of citrusy, limey flavour and an appetisingly crisp, lingering finish.

Vintage	03	02
WR	6	6
Drink	04-07	04-06

DRY $20 AV

Peregrine Rastasburn Riesling   (★★☆)

Harvested near Lake Dunstan, in Central Otago, with 10 per cent botrytis infection of the berries, the 2003 vintage (★★☆) is a medium style (19 grams/litre of residual sugar) that shows a slight lack of delicacy and freshness.

MED $20 -V

Phoenix Canterbury Dry Riesling   (★★★)

Slightly Germanic in style, the 2002 vintage (★★★) is light (11.5 per cent alcohol) and crisp, with honeyed characters on the nose and palate and a fractionally sweet (5 grams/litre of residual sugar), freshly acidic finish.

Vintage	02			
WR	6			
Drink	P			

MED/DRY $15 AV

Phoenix Marlborough Riesling   ★★★☆

The Pacific winery's 2002 vintage (★★★☆) is a great buy. A single-vineyard wine grown in the Rapaura district, it was made in a distinctly medium style (17 grams/litre of sugar). Crisp, with good vigour and length, it offers appealing, bottle-aged, toast and honey characters.

Vintage	02	01	00	99
WR	6	6	5	6
Drink	P	P	P	P

MED $14 V+

Pleasant Valley Yelas Marlborough Riesling   (★★★☆)

The well-crafted 2003 vintage (★★★☆) is fresh and tightly structured, with slightly sweet (9 grams/litre of residual sugar) flavours of lemons and apples. Pale lemon/green, crisp and lively, with good depth, it's drinking well now but should also reward cellaring.

MED/DRY $18 AV

Pond Paddock Riesling   (★★☆)

The tangy 2003 vintage (★★☆), grown in Martinborough, is a moderately ripe-tasting, slightly sweet wine (7 grams/litre of residual sugar), with citrusy, green-edged flavours and firm acid spine.

Vintage	03
WR	6
Drink	04-06

MED/DRY $17 -V

Pukeora Estate San Hill Riesling   (★★☆)

Pukeora Estate is near Waipukurau, an hour's drive south of Napier, but the grapes for the 2002 vintage (★★☆) were grown near Hastings. It's a light wine (10.5 per cent alcohol) with lemon/apple aromas and a crisp, dry palate showing good balance and moderate flavour depth.

DRY $14 AV

Rippon Riesling   ★★★☆

In its youth, this Lake Wanaka wine is typically restrained, with invigorating acidity, but it can flourish with bottle-age. The 2002 vintage (★★★) is tautly structured, crisp and appley, with a dry, steely finish. Austere in its youth, it needs time; open 2005+.

DRY $21 -V

Riverby Estate Marlborough Riesling   ★★★

Grown in Jacksons Road, in the heart of the Wairau Valley, the 2002 vintage (★★★★) is a highly characterful wine – lemon-scented, crisp and tightly structured, with slightly minerally, toasty, bottle-aged characters emerging and a dryish finish.

MED/DRY $18 AV

Rockburn Central Otago Riesling   (★★☆)

The 2003 vintage (★★☆) was grown at Lowburn, in the Cromwell Basin. Harvested on 12 May from low-cropping (5 tonnes/hectare) vines, it's a light-bodied wine (11.5 per cent alcohol) with fresh, green-apple aromas and flavours, crisp acidity and a dry (4 grams/litre of residual sugar) finish. Open 2005+.

DRY $27 -V

Rossendale Canterbury Riesling ★★★

Some past vintages have been highly attractive, but the crisp, appley 2002 (★★) lacks real freshness and vibrancy. It's a medium style (15 grams/litre of residual sugar).

MED $15 AV

Rossendale Marlborough Riesling ★★☆

A slightly sweet style, the 2002 vintage (★★☆) has lemony, appley aromas and flavours, with a crisp, slightly hard finish. It's a reasonably flavoursome wine, but lacks real delicacy and finesse.

MED $17 -V

St Helena Riesling ★★★

In top vintages, St Helena produces a Mosel-like wine, fresh, vibrant and racy. The 2002 (★★☆) doesn't identify a region of origin on the label, except for 'South Island', but the winery says it was grown in Canterbury. A lemony, appley wine with firm acidity, a splash of sweetness and decent depth, it's verging on three-star quality.

Vintage	02
WR	5
Drink	04-06

MED $16 AV

Sacred Hill Marlborough Vineyards Riesling (★★★)

The 2002 vintage (★★★) is a single-vineyard (Jacksons Road) wine. Tangy, with very good depth of lemon/lime flavours, it is fresh and tight, with a dryish (5.7 grams/litre of residual sugar) finish and biting acidity. It demands time; open 2005+.

MED/DRY $22 -V

Saint Clair Marlborough Riesling ★★★★

This is typically a delicious wine, priced right. The elegant 2003 vintage (★★★★) is ripely scented and harmonious, with mouthfilling body and fresh, strong, slightly sweet (10 grams/litre of residual sugar) flavours. In its infancy, the 2004 (★★★★) also looks excellent, with fine sugar/acid balance and good intensity of ripe lemon, lime and passionfruit flavours, very fresh and vibrant.

Vintage	03	02	01	00	99	98
WR	6	6	6	6	6	6
Drink	04-08	04-07	04-05	04-05	P	P

MED/DRY $20 AV

Saint Clair Vicar's Choice Marlborough Riesling (★★★)

Priced right, the 2003 vintage (★★★) is a slightly sweet style (9 grams/litre of residual sugar) with fresh, crisp and lively flavours of lemons and apples, showing decent depth.

Vintage	03
WR	5
Drink	04-06

MED/DRY $17 AV

Sanctuary Marlborough Riesling ★★★☆

From Grove Mill, the 2003 (★★★☆) is fragrant, light (11 per cent alcohol) and lively, in a distinctly medium style with lemony, appley flavours showing good delicacy and sugar/acid balance. The 2004 vintage (★★★☆) has a floral, citrusy bouquet and crisp, tight, slightly sweet flavours (14 grams/litre of residual sugar). It's a frisky young wine, very fresh and clean, with lemony, limey flavours, instantly attractive.

Vintage	03	02	01	00	99	98
WR	6	6	6	6	6	6
Drink	04-05	P	P	P	P	P

MED/DRY $17 V+

Seifried Nelson Riesling ★★★★

The scented, concentrated 2003 vintage (★★★★) was made from 15-year-old vines grown in heavy clays in the Moutere hills. It offers strong, vibrant lemon and lime flavours with a distinct splash of sweetness, crisp acidity and a lingering finish. Drinking well from the start, the 2004 (★★★★) is an elegant and harmonious wine with strong yet delicate, citrusy, faintly honeyed flavours and ample sweetness (16 grams/litre of residual sugar) to balance its appetising acidity.

Vintage	04	03	02	01
WR	6	7	7	7
Drink	04-08	04-07	04-06	04-05

MED $17 V+

Seifried Riesling Dry ★★★☆

The 2003 vintage (★★★) was grown in heavy clay soils in the Moutere hills. It's a crisp, appley, limey wine with a dry finish, but lacks the harmony and charm of its sweeter stablemate (above).

MED/DRY $19 AV

Seifried Winemakers Collection Nelson Riesling ★★★★

Showing real power through the palate, the opulent 2003 vintage (★★★★☆) was made from young vines at Brightwater. Weighty and ripe, with concentrated citrus and tropical-fruit flavours and a slightly honeyed richness, it's a medium-sweet style (49 grams/litre of residual sugar) with excellent varietal definition and purity.

MED/DRY $25 -V

Selaks Premium Selection Marlborough Riesling ★★★

The Selaks brand (now part of the Nobilo stable) is best known for Sauvignon Blanc, but the Rieslings are also typically good. The 2003 vintage (★★★★) is a slightly sweet wine (11 grams/litre of residual sugar). Showing impressive intensity in a strongly varietal, cool-climate style, it's a great buy, with fresh, tight, lemony flavours, lively acidity and considerable elegance.

Vintage	03	02	01	00
WR	7	7	7	7
Drink	04-06	04-05	P	P

MED/DRY $15 AV

Seresin Riesling ★★★★☆

Estate-grown at Renwick, in Marlborough, the 2003 vintage (★★★★☆) was made without any botrytis influence ('We sort the grapes hard,' says winemaker Brian Bicknell), whole-bunch pressed and fermented to dryness. It's a classic dry Riesling with mouthfilling body and intense flavours, bone-dry, lemony and long. Still tight and youthful, with minerally, flinty characters and crisp, balanced acidity, it's a very harmonious wine that should flourish with cellaring.

Vintage	03	02	01
WR	6	5	6
Drink	04-10	04-08	04-10

DRY $22 AV

Sherwood Estate Stratum Riesling (★★★)

Pale, with lemony, appley flavours, the 2003 vintage (★★★) is a Marlborough wine, light and slightly sweet. It's fragrant and refreshing, although not concentrated.

MED/DRY $15 AV

Sherwood Estate Waipara Riesling (★★★)

Offering strong lemony flavours, the 2003 vintage (★★★☆) is a medium style (15 grams/litre of residual sugar) with firm, crisp acidity. It's a citrusy, cool-climate style, fresh and lively.

MED $16 AV

Shingle Peak Marlborough Riesling ★★★☆

Matua Valley's Riesling is consistently attractive and priced sharply. Still unfolding, the 2003 vintage (★★★☆), grown in three vineyards in the Wairau and Brancott valleys, is a tight-knit wine with fresh, strong, lemony, limey flavours and a crisp, dryish (7 grams/litre of residual sugar) finish. Good drinking during the summer of 2004–05.

Vintage	03	02	01
WR	5	6	6
Drink	04-05	04-06	04-06

MED/DRY $16 V+

Soljans Marlborough Riesling ★★☆

The 2002 (★★☆) is medium-bodied, with lemony, appley flavours, a sliver of sweetness and a slightly short finish. The 2003 vintage (★★☆) is crisp and lemony, with plentiful sweetness (20 grams/litre of residual sugar) but only moderate depth.

MED $17 -V

Solstone Classic Riesling (★★★☆)

The floral, slightly honeyed 2001 vintage (★★★☆) from this Wairarapa-based winery was made from Canterbury grapes. It's a medium-bodied, slightly sweet wine, attractively balanced, with fresh acidity and citrusy, slightly honeyed flavours of good depth.

Vintage	01
WR	6
Drink	P

MED $18 AV

Solstone Wairarapa Riesling (★★☆)

Grown at Paulownia Estate, Masterton, the 2003 vintage (★★☆) is a slightly austere dry wine with steely acidity and lemon and green-apple flavours showing moderate depth. Light in body (11.4 per cent alcohol), it lacks a bit of easy-drinking charm.

Vintage	03
WR	4
Drink	05-07

DRY $16 -V

Spy Valley Marlborough Dry Riesling (★★★★)

The 2003 vintage (★★★★) is a light yellow, forward, welcoming wine with a voluminous bouquet. Rich and ripe in flavour, it's a fractionally sweet style (6 grams/litre of residual sugar) with an attractively soft texture and rich finish.

Vintage	04
WR	6
Drink	04-08

MED/DRY $20 AV

Spy Valley Marlborough Riesling ★★★☆

The 2003 vintage (★★★☆) of this Waihopai Valley wine was harvested at 21 to 23 brix and fermented to a medium-dry style (11 grams/litre of residual sugar). It has good upfront appeal, with a scented, slightly honeyed bouquet and plenty of peachy, limey flavour, fresh and tangy.

Vintage	04	03	02	01
WR	6	6	6	5
Drink	04-07	04-06	04-07	04-06

MED/DRY $17 V+

Stafford Lane Nelson Riesling   ★★★

Hand-picked on the Waimea Plains, the 2004 vintage (★★★) is a crisp, youthful, medium-bodied wine with citrusy, appley, green-edged flavours, a sliver of sweetness and racy acidity. Open mid-2005+.

Vintage	04
WR	4
Drink	04-09

MED/DRY $18 AV

Stoneleigh Marlborough Riesling   ★★★★

Deliciously fragrant in its youth, this is typically a refined wine from Allied Domecq with good body, excellent depth of lemon/lime flavour and a crisp, impressively long finish. The wine's style is evolving towards more sheer varietal character, less sweetness and less botrytis than in the past. Harvested at 22.7 brix and fermented to a medium-dry style (9 grams/litre of residual sugar), the 2003 vintage (★★★★) has punchy, lifted lemon/lime aromas leading into a stylish wine, full-bodied (12.6 per cent alcohol), fresh and full-flavoured.

Vintage	03	02	01	00	99	98
WR	6	6	6	6	5	7
Drink	04-12	04-11	04-10	04-09	04-06	04-08

MED/DRY $19 V+

Stratford Riesling   ★★★☆

Stratford is the personal label of Strat Canning, winemaker at Margrain Vineyard in Martinborough. The 2003 vintage (★★★☆) is crisp and dryish (7 grams/litre of residual sugar), with strong lemony flavours, crisp and youthful. It's a tightly structured wine that needs time; open 2006+.

Vintage	02	01	00
WR	7	5	7
Drink	04-10	04-07	04-06

MED/DRY $20 AV

Te Kairanga Martinborough Riesling   ★★★☆

Harvested at 21.8 brix and fermented to almost full dryness (4.2 grams/litre of residual sugar), the 2003 vintage (★★☆) has a restrained bouquet, with strong lemony, minerally flavours that show a slight lack of freshness and charm.

Vintage	03	02	01
WR	6	5	5
Drink	04-06	04-05	P

DRY $20 AV

Te Mania Nelson Riesling   ★★★☆

Offering fine value, the 2003 vintage (★★★★) is a floral, finely balanced wine in a dryish style (6 grams/litre of residual sugar). It's a crisp wine with good weight and pure, incisive lemon/lime flavours, fresh and lingering.

Vintage	03
WR	7
Drink	04-07

MED/DRY $17 V+

Terrace Heights Estate Marlborough Riesling   (★★★)

Balanced for easy drinking, the 2004 vintage (★★★) was harvested at 21 brix from 10-year-old vines. Stop-fermented in a medium-dry style (11 grams/litre of residual sugar), it is fresh and lively, with crisp, lemony, appley flavours showing decent depth.

Vintage	04
WR	5
Drink	05-07

MED/DRY $17 AV

Terrace Road Marlborough Riesling   (★★☆)

Grown at Renwick, the 2003 vintage (★★☆) from Cellier Le Brun is a pale, medium-bodied wine with crisp, appley, minerally flavours. It's a slightly austere wine, clearly varietal, with a sliver of sweetness (8 grams/litre of residual sugar), but lacks a bit of delicacy and charm.

`MED/DRY $19 -V`

Te Whare Ra Marlborough Riesling   ★★★★

The latest vintages of this wine are the best. The scented, highly refined 2004 (★★★★☆) was 80 per cent estate-grown at Renwick, where the grapes were harvested at 23.4 brix; the rest was picked at 20 brix in the Awatere Valley. A medium-dry style (6.5 grams/litre of residual sugar), it is tight and slightly minerally, with excellent weight and texture and concentrated lemon/lime flavours, fresh, ripe, finely balanced and lingering. Open mid-2005+.

`MED/DRY $19 V+`

Three Sisters Riesling   ★★★

Grown at Takapau, in Central Hawke's Bay, the 2001 vintage (★★★) is a dry style (4 grams/litre of sugar), clean and steely, with firm acidity woven through its lemon and green-apple flavours and a slightly tart finish. Attractively scented, with fresh, lemony aromas, the 2002 (★★★) is a crisp, clearly varietal wine, slightly honeyed, with lively lemon/lime flavours and racy acidity.

Vintage	02	01
WR	6	5
Drink	04-06	04-05

`DRY $16 AV`

Timara Riesling   ★★☆

The 2003 vintage (★★☆), blended by Allied Domecq from Australian and New Zealand wines, is a smooth, medium style with a light, floral bouquet and moderate depth of citrus and tropical-fruit flavours, clean and fresh.

`MED $10 V+`

Torlesse Canterbury Riesling   ★★★

The 2003 vintage (★★★) is a medium style (20 grams/litre of residual sugar) with crisp, ripe citrus and tropical-fruit flavours, showing good depth. The 2004 (★★☆) is fruity, lemony and appley, with moderate flavour depth, a distinct splash of sweetness and firm acid spine. Fresh and lively, it's priced right.

`MED $15 AV`

Torlesse Waipara Riesling   ★★★☆

Fleshy and slightly creamy in texture, the 2002 vintage (★★★☆) is a ripe style with citrus and tropical-fruit flavours. The 2003 (★★★) is fresh, lively and well-balanced, with good depth of ripe, slightly honeyed, lemon/lime flavours and a slightly sweet (9.3 grams/litre of residual sugar), crisp finish.

Vintage	03	02	01
WR	5	7	6
Drink	04-06	04-06	04-05

`MED/DRY $17 V+`

Trinity Hill Wairarapa Riesling   ✎   ★★★☆

Trinity Hill is a Hawke's Bay-based winery, but this wine is grown at the Petrie vineyard, near Masterton. The 2003 vintage (★★★☆) is tight and youthful, with good intensity of lemon, lime and passionfruit flavours and a slightly sweet, finely balanced finish. It's a light-bodied wine (11.5 per cent alcohol) with good potential; open mid-2005+.

Vintage	04	03	02	01	00	99	98	97
WR	5	4	5	5	4	5	6	4
Drink	04-10	04-08	04-10	04-10	04-05	04-08	04-06	04-05

`MED/DRY $20 AV`

Vavasour Awatere Valley Riesling   ★★★☆

Delicious now, the 2002 vintage (★★★★) is a single-vineyard Marlborough wine, harvested at 23 brix and fermented (partly with indigenous yeasts) to a medium-dry style (8 grams/litre of residual sugar). Light yellow/green, it's a ripe-tasting wine with very good intensity of lemon, lime and passionfruit flavours and toasty, bottle-aged characters emerging.

MED/DRY $20 AV

Vidal Estate Marlborough Riesling   ★★★☆

Showing good intensity, with a mineral component, the 2003 (★★★★) is still fresh and youthful, with lemon/apple flavours showing good delicacy and a crisp, medium-dry, slightly flinty finish. The 2004 vintage (tasted prior to bottling, and so not rated) was grown in the Awatere Valley and lees-aged over winter. It's a citrusy, slightly limey wine, tightly structured, vibrant and incisively flavoured, with a slightly sweet (6 grams/litre of residual sugar), crisp finish.

Vintage	04	03	02	01	00	99
WR	7	6	6	5	6	6
Drink	05-07	04-07	04-06	P	P	P

MED/DRY $18 AV

Villa Maria Cellar Selection Marlborough Riesling   ★★★☆

Grown in the Wairau and Awatere valleys, the 2003 vintage (★★★☆) is more austere in its youth than its Private Bin stablemate, but also more delicate and may mature better over the long haul. Youthful lemon/green, it is tightly structured, with strong lemon and green-apple flavours cut with fresh acidity and a slightly sweet (8.4 grams/litre of residual sugar), persistent finish. Tasted prior to bottling (and so not rated), the 2004 was richly scented and zingy, with ripe, limey flavours, crisp and punchy.

Vintage	04	03	02	01
WR	7	6	6	5
Drink	05-10	04-09	04-08	04-08

MED/DRY $20 AV

Villa Maria Private Bin Marlborough Riesling   ★★★★

A consistently enjoyable wine, priced very sharply. The 2003 vintage (★★★★) is a refined, elegant wine with a scented, floral bouquet showing a hint of honey, intense flavours of stone-fruits, lemons and limes, lively acidity and a gently sweet finish. Grown in the Wairau and Awatere valleys, the 2004 (★★★★) is fresh-scented, with good intensity of vibrant passionfruit and lime flavours, a sliver of sweetness (11.3 grams/litre of residual sugar) and lively acidity.

Vintage	04	03	02	01	00
WR	7	6	5	6	7
Drink	04-09	04-07	04-06	04-05	P

MED/DRY $16 V+

Villa Maria Reserve Marlborough Riesling   ★★★★★

This label is an emerging classic. The 2001 vintage (★★★★☆) was grown in the Fletcher vineyard, in the Wairau Valley, and fermented to near dryness (5 grams/litre of residual sugar). It's a tightly structured wine, slightly minerally, with good intensity and a long, freshly acidic finish. There is no 2002 or 2003. The 2004 (tasted prior to bottling, and so not rated) is a more Germanic style than previously, lighter and sweeter. Light-bodied (11.5 per cent alcohol), with abundant sweetness (17 grams/litre of residual sugar), it is richly perfumed, with citrusy, limey flavours, intense and zesty.

Vintage	04	03	02	01	00	99	98	97	96
WR	7	NM	NM	6	6	7	6	7	7
Drink	05-10	NM	NM	04-10	04-08	04-07	04-06	04-05	P

MED $25 AV

Voss Riesling   ★★★☆

This Martinborough wine is usually full of character. The 2004 vintage (★★★☆), made with a small percentage of botrytised fruit, has lifted, limey aromas and a tight, slightly minerally palate with gentle sweetness (7 grams/litre of residual sugar) and a finely balanced finish.

Vintage	04	03	02	01	00	
WR	6	6	6	5	6	MED/DRY $18 AV
Drink	05-08	04-08	05-08	04-07	04-09	

Vynfields Martinborough Dry Riesling   (★★☆)

Light gold, with a slightly honeyed bouquet, the 2003 vintage (★★☆) shows considerable development for its age. It's a crisp, flavoursome wine, but lacks real delicacy and finesse.   DRY $20 -V

Waimea Estates Classic Riesling   ★★★★

Balanced for easy drinking, this Nelson wine is consistently good and delivers fine value. Harvested at 22.6 brix, the 2003 vintage (★★★☆) is fresh, lively and tangy, with plentiful sweetness (15 grams/litre of residual sugar) amid its ripe citrus and pineapple flavours. Zesty and harmonious, it's a delicious aperitif.

Vintage	03	02	01	00	
WR	7	7	7	6	MED $18 V+
Drink	04-10	04-06	04-06	04-06	

Waipara Hills Canterbury/Marlborough Riesling   ★★★☆

The 2003 vintage (★★★), a medium style grown in eight vineyards, shows good varietal character, with plenty of crisp, ripe, lemony, limey flavour. The 2004 (★★★☆) is a very harmonious wine with strong lemony, faintly honeyed flavour, abundant sweetness (17 grams/litre of residual sugar) and lively acidity. Finely balanced, with more body than its alcohol (11.5 per cent) suggests, it is quite forward in its appeal.

Vintage	03	
WR	6	MED $19 AV
Drink	04-13	

Waipara Hills Riesling   ★★★

More forward in its appeal than its stablemate (above), the 2002 vintage (★★★) is a blend of Canterbury and Marlborough grapes, made in a distinctly medium style (16 grams/litre of sugar). It's a fresh, crisp wine, lemony and limey, with good sugar/acid balance and plenty of flavour. The 2003 (★★★), blended from grapes grown in eight vineyards in Canterbury and Marlborough, is again a medium style, with good depth of appley flavours, fresh, slightly sweet and crisp.   MED/DRY $20 AV

Waipara Springs Riesling   ★★★☆

The slightly austere 2003 vintage (★★☆) is perfumed and slightly minerally, with firm acidity and a dryish (5 grams/litre of residual sugar), flinty finish.

Vintage	03	02	
WR	6	7	MED/DRY $18 AV
Drink	04-10	04-10	

Waipara West Riesling   ★★★☆

This North Canterbury wine is typically flinty and punchy. The fleshy, slightly honeyed 2003 (★★★) is rounder and softer than usual, with a splash of sweetness (7.5 grams/litre of residual sugar). The 2004 vintage (★★★☆) is a more austere style, built to last. Tight and minerally, with youthful, green-apple and lime flavours showing good intensity and a steely, long finish, it's worth cellaring to 2006+.

Vintage	04	
WR	6	MED/DRY $20 AV
Drink	04-07	

Waipipi Wairarapa Riesling (★★★)

Grown at Opaki, north of Masterton, the 2002 vintage (★★★) is aging well, with youthful colour. It's a tangy, medium-bodied wine, crisp and minerally, in a slightly austere but clearly varietal style.

MED/DRY $19 -V

Wairau River Marlborough Riesling ★★★☆

The 2004 vintage (★★★☆) is a slightly sweet wine with lemony, minerally characters and hints of honey and passionfruit giving it drink-young appeal.

Vintage	02	01
WR	7	7
Drink	04-06	04-06

MED/DRY $20 AV

Warrior Cove Marlborough Riesling (★★☆)

Sold by mail-order wine clubs, the 2003 vintage (★★☆) is a crisp, green-edged wine. A medium-dry style (7.5 grams/litre of residual sugar), it lacks really fresh, vibrant fruit characters.

MED/DRY $17 -V

West Brook Marlborough Riesling ★★★★

The delicious 2003 vintage (★★★★) is an attractively scented wine with rich flavour and a crisp, slightly sweet (8 grams/litre of residual sugar), persistent finish. It's a very harmonious wine with a lovely texture.

Vintage	03	02	01	00
WR	7	7	5	6
Drink	04-07	04-06	04-05	04-05

MED/DRY $18 V+

Whitehaven Marlborough Riesling ★★★

This is typically a lively and flavourful wine, slightly sweet and zesty. The 2003 vintage (★★☆) is not one of the best – green-edged, with lemony, appley flavours and a slightly tart finish.

Vintage	03	02	01	00
WR	5	6	6	6
Drink	04-06	04-07	04-06	P

MED/DRY $18 AV

William Hill Riesling ★★★

Grown at Alexandra, in Central Otago, and made in a medium-dry style (8.5 grams/litre of residual sugar), the 2003 vintage (★★☆) is a pale, citrusy, appley wine, fresh and well-balanced, but it lacks flavour intensity.

Vintage	03	02	01	00	99	98
WR	5	5	4	4	4	3
Drink	04-06	04-07	P	P	P	P

MED/DRY $19 -V

Woollaston Estates Nelson Riesling ★★★★

Grown on the Waimea Plains and made in a distinctly medium style, the 2002 vintage (★★★★) is impressive. Pale, tangy, slightly minerally and flinty, it shows excellent freshness and vigour, with citrusy, slightly sweet flavours, crisp and penetrating.

MED $18 V+

Yarrum Vineyard Marlborough Riesling ★★★

Sold by mail-order wine clubs, the 2003 vintage (★★☆) is a solid wine, crisp, lemony and appley, with firm acid spine and decent depth.

MED/DRY $20 -V

Roussanne

Roussanne is a traditional ingredient in the white wines of France's northern Rhône Valley, where typically it is blended with the more widely grown Marsanne. Known for its fine acidity and 'haunting aroma', likened by some tasters to herb tea, it is also found in the south of France, Italy and Australia, but this late-ripening variety is extremely scarce in New Zealand.

Trinity Hill Gimblett Gravels Roussanne   (★★★★)

The 2002 vintage (★★★★) was grown in Hawke's Bay, fermented in seasoned oak barrels and given a full, softening malolactic fermentation. Full-flavoured and fleshy, it's a finely balanced wine with citrusy fruit characters and firm underlying acidity.

DRY $30 AV

Sauvignon Blanc

Sauvignon Blanc is New Zealand's key calling card in the wine markets of the world. At the 2004 International Wine and Spirit Competition, judged in London, the Silverado Trophy for the champion Sauvignon Blanc was awarded (yet again) to a New Zealand wine – Villa Maria Cellar Selection Marlborough Sauvignon Blanc 2003. At the 2004 International Wine Challenge, also staged in London, Saint Clair Wairau Reserve Sauvignon Blanc 2003 scooped the trophy for top Sauvignon Blanc, and Whitehaven Marlborough Sauvignon Blanc 2003 was judged best Sauvignon Blanc at the San Francisco International Wine Competition 2004.

Yet Kiwi Sauvignon Blanc has also attracted criticism during the past couple of years, for too often lacking the intensity of aroma and flavour for which it is famous. With the international demand exceeding the supply, some of those leaping on the Marlborough Sauvignon Blanc bandwagon appear more interested in quantity, rather than quality, wine production. Those fears have been intensified by the heavy-cropping 2004 vintage, which has yielded many ordinary wines. The good news is that the major players on the world stage – Allied Domecq (previously Montana), Villa Maria, Nobilo, Cloudy Bay and others – have released 2004 wines right up to their usual standard.

The rise to international stardom of New Zealand Sauvignon Blanc was swift. The variety was first introduced to the country in the early 1970s; Matua Valley marketed the first varietal Sauvignon Blanc in 1974. Montana then planted sweeping vineyards in Marlborough, allowing Sauvignon Blanc to get into a full commercial swing in the early 1980s. In the year to June 2004, 64.7 per cent by volume of all New Zealand's wine exports were based on Sauvignon Blanc.

Sauvignon Blanc is New Zealand's most extensively planted variety, in 2003 (the latest figures available) comprising 33.7 per cent of the national vineyard. Over 85 per cent of all vines are concentrated in Marlborough, with Hawke's Bay the other significant stronghold. Plantings are expanding like wildfire: between 2000 and 2006, the area of bearing Sauvignon Blanc vines is projected to increase from 2485 hectares to 7026 hectares.

The flavour of New Zealand Sauvignon Blanc varies according to fruit ripeness. At the herbaceous, under-ripe end of the spectrum, vegetal and fresh-cut grass aromas hold sway; riper wines show capsicum, gooseberry and melon-like characters; very ripe fruit displays tropical-fruit flavours.

Intensely herbaceous Sauvignon Blancs are not hard to make in the viticulturally cool climate of the South Island and the lower North Island (Wairarapa). 'The challenge faced by New Zealand winemakers is to keep those herbaceous characters in check,' says Kevin Judd, chief winemaker at Cloudy Bay. 'It would be foolish to suggest that these herbaceous notes detract from the wines; in fact I am sure that this fresh edge and intense varietal aroma are the reason for its recent international popularity. The better of these wines have these herbaceous characters in context and in balance with the more tropical-fruit characters associated with riper fruit.'

There are two key styles of Sauvignon Blanc produced in New Zealand. Wines handled entirely in stainless steel tanks (by far the most common) place their accent squarely on their fruit flavours and are usually labelled as 'Sauvignon Blanc'. Wood-fermented and/or wood-matured styles are often called 'Sauvignon Blanc Oak Aged' or 'Reserve Sauvignon Blanc'.

Another major style difference is regionally based: the crisp, incisively flavoured wines of Marlborough contrast with the softer, less pungently herbaceous Hawke's Bay style. These are wines to drink young (within 18 months of the vintage) while they are irresistibly fresh, aromatic and tangy, although the more complex, oak-aged Hawke's Bay wines (currently an endangered species, despite their quality), can mature well for several years.

Alana Estate Martinborough Sauvignon Blanc ★★★★

This wine is consistently attractive. The 2003 vintage (★★★★) was picked in two batches, at 21 brix (for 'lively fruit flavours') and 23.5 brix (for 'complexity and palate weight'), and lees-aged for three months. It's a mouthfilling, very fresh and youthful wine, ripely scented, with crisp, finely balanced melon/lime flavours, offering good drinking through the summer of 2004–05.

DRY $22 AV

Alan McCorkindale Marlborough Sauvignon Blanc ★★★☆

The 2004 vintage (★★★★) is a rich, finely balanced wine with fresh, ripe melon, capsicum and passionfruit flavours showing excellent depth.

DRY $20 AV

Allan Scott Marlborough Sauvignon Blanc ★★★★

The Scotts aim for a 'ripe, tropical-fruit' Sauvignon – a style typical of the Rapaura area of the Wairau Valley, where the company's vineyards are clustered. The crisp, dry 2004 vintage (★★★★) has the slight 'armpit' aromas of ripe fruit, with a frisky, tangy palate showing very good vigour and depth of grapefruit, melon and lime flavours.

DRY $19 V+

Allan Scott Prestige Marlborough Sauvignon Blanc (★★★★☆)

The rich and zingy 2003 vintage (★★★★☆) is a single-vineyard wine, barrel-fermented and briefly oak-aged. It's a full-bodied wine with fresh, ripe, incisive melon/lime flavours, a subtle seasoning of wood and a long finish.

DRY $30 -V

Alpha Domus Hawke's Bay Sauvignon Blanc ★★★☆

The fully dry 2004 vintage (★★★) is attractive in its youth. Estate-grown at Maraekakaho, cool-fermented and lees-aged in tanks, it is fresh and flavoursome, with passionfruit, melon and lime characters and lively acidity. It's at the less herbaceous end of the ripeness spectrum, but shows no shortage of flavour or vigour.

DRY $17 V+

Amisfield Central Otago Sauvignon Blanc (★★★★☆)

One of the region's finest Sauvignon Blancs yet, the debut 2003 vintage (★★★★☆) was picked at over 23 brix from the estate vineyard in the Cromwell Basin. It was mostly fermented in tanks, but a small part of the crop, retained on the vines for an extra 10 days, was fermented with indigenous yeasts and lees-aged in old French oak barriques. The bouquet is lovely – fresh, lifted and intensely varietal. Dry but not austere, it's an immaculate wine with concentrated, well-ripened gooseberry and lime flavours, a touch of complexity and a notably persistent finish.

Vintage 04
WR 4
Drink 04-05

DRY $23 AV

Amor-Bendall Limited Edition
Gisborne Sauvignon Blanc   (★★★★★)
The debut 2004 vintage (★★★★★) is the best Gisborne Sauvignon Blanc to date. A single-vineyard wine, grown south and inland from Manutuke, it was cultivated on very high trellises (over 5 metres), which shaded the canopy and limited the grapes' exposure to sunshine. Already delicious, it is richly scented, with ripe, tropical-fruit aromas. The palate shows lovely weight, richness and roundness, with pure flavours of gooseberry and lime and sweet fruit delights.

DRY $23 V+

Ashwell Sauvignon Blanc   (★★★☆)
The 2004 vintage (★★★☆) of this Martinborough wine is ripely scented, full-bodied and crisp, with melon/capsicum flavours showing good balance and depth.

DRY $20 AV

Askerne Hawke's Bay Sauvignon Blanc   ★★★☆
This small Havelock North winery makes a good, often excellent Sauvignon. The 2004 vintage (★★★★) is weighty (14 per cent alcohol) and well-ripened, with tropical-fruit flavours showing impressive power and richness, a touch of complexity and a bone-dry, well-rounded finish.

DRY $18 AV

Astrolabe Marlborough Sauvignon Blanc   ★★★★
The 2003 vintage (★★★) is a mouthfilling, ripe wine with melon/lime flavours showing good but not great depth. The 2004 (★★★★☆) is freshly herbaceous, very intense and tangy.

Vintage	04
WR	6
Drink	04-05

DRY $19 AV

Ata Rangi Sauvignon Blanc   ★★★★
A consistently attractive Martinborough wine, with ripe, tropical-fruit rather than grassy, herbaceous flavours. The 2004 vintage (★★★★) was mostly handled in tanks, but 15 per cent of the blend was fermented and lees-aged in seasoned oak barrels. Full-bodied, fresh and smooth, with ripe flavours of melons and limes, it has good weight, depth and roundness, with very subtle oak adding richness.

Vintage	04	03
WR	6	6
Drink	04-05	P

DRY $20 AV

Auntsfield Long Cow Sauvignon Blanc   ★★★
The 2004 vintage (★★★☆) was grown in the Long Cow paddock at the Auntsfield property, on the south side of the Wairau Valley, where Marlborough's first wines were made in the 1870s. It's a fleshy, weighty wine (14 per cent alcohol), not highly scented, but offering good intensity of ripe melon/capsicum flavours, with zingy acids and a lingering, lively finish.

DRY $20 -V

Awarua Terraces Goldstones Sauvignon Blanc   ★★★★
The impressive 2003 vintage (★★★★) was grown in the elevated, inland Mangatahi district of Hawke's Bay, hand-picked, whole-bunch pressed and matured on its yeast lees in tanks before bottling. Rich, ripe-fruit aromas lead into a fresh, zingy, vibrantly fruity wine with passionfruit, melon and lime flavours showing good concentration and vivacity. Racy and intense, it builds to a strong finish.

DRY $22 AV

Babich Marlborough Sauvignon Blanc   ★★★★

The 2004 vintage (★★★★) reflects the rising input of grapes from the company's Cowslip Valley vineyard in the Waihopai Valley, described by Babich as giving 'riper, less herbaceous' fruit characters than its Awatere Valley and Wairau Valley vineyards. Scented, with vibrant, punchy melon/lime flavours, it's an immaculate, finely balanced wine with excellent delicacy and depth.

DRY $20 AV

Babich Winemakers Reserve Sauvignon Blanc   ★★★★☆

A top example of gently wooded Marlborough Sauvignon Blanc, with ripely herbaceous flavours and lovely poise and intensity. The 2003 vintage (★★★★☆), grown in the Waihopai and Awatere valleys, was mostly handled in tanks, but 10 per cent of the blend was fermented and lees-aged in French oak barriques. Fragrant, with a freshly herbaceous, slightly grassy bouquet, it's an elegant and expressive wine with good body and vibrant, finely balanced melon/capsicum flavours, dry, well-rounded and lingering.

Vintage	03	02
WR	7	7
Drink	04-05	04-05

DRY $23 AV

Black Barn Hawke's Bay Sauvignon Blanc   ★★★★

An excellent example of the regional style, the 2004 vintage (★★★) was estate-grown at Havelock North and mostly handled in stainless steel tanks, but 5 per cent of the blend was matured in seasoned French oak casks. Fresh, crisp, vibrantly fruity and dry, with strong, ripe melon/lime flavours, it's a skilfully made wine with good delicacy, varietal character and length, and great drinkability.

DRY $19 AV

Blackenbrook Vineyard Nelson Sauvignon Blanc   (★★★☆)

Harvested at 22.6 brix in the Tasman district and handled entirely in stainless steel tanks, the 2004 vintage (★★★☆) is a scented, full-bodied wine with good varietal character and depth of melon and capsicum flavours, crisp and lively.

Vintage	04
WR	6
Drink	04-05

MED/DRY $18 AV

Bladen Marlborough Sauvignon Blanc   ★★★☆

The 2004 vintage (★★★☆) of this single-vineyard wine is full-bodied, ripe and rounded, with very good depth of tropical-fruit flavours and moderate acidity giving an appealing softness of texture.

DRY $20 AV

Brightwater Vineyards Nelson Sauvignon Blanc   ★★★☆

Grown on the Waimea Plains, this is a consistently enjoyable wine, ripely flavoured and fully dry. The 2003 vintage (★★★☆) is fleshy and generous, with a touch of complexity and zingy finish. The 2004 (★★★☆) offers ripe tropical-fruit flavours, fresh and lively, with very good depth.

Vintage	03	02	01
WR	5	6	6
Drink	04-05	P	P

DRY $19 AV

Burnt Spur Martinborough Sauvignon Blanc   ★★★★

A wine of strong individuality, the weighty, rounded 2003 vintage (★★★★☆) is a partly barrel-aged wine (20 per cent of the blend was matured for four months in mostly old French oak casks). Based on a 'very low' crop of 'absolutely clean and very ripe' grapes, it's a successful attempt at a rich, complex style of Sauvignon Blanc, with flavours well into the tropical-fruit end of the ripeness spectrum. It carries the bone-dry style easily, with a lovely softness of texture.

DRY $20 AV

Cable Bay Marlborough Sauvignon Blanc ★★★★

Waiheke Island-based winemaker Neill Culley aims for a Sauvignon Blanc with 'restraint and textural interest, to enjoy with food'. In its youth, the 2004 vintage (★★★★), grown in the Rapaura and Brancott districts, is freshly herbaceous, with an aromatic bouquet, good weight and intensity. It's an intensely varietal wine with punchy melon and green-capsicum flavours and zingy acids.

Vintage	04	03	02
WR	7	6	6
Drink	04-07	04-06	P

DRY $22 AV

Cairnbrae The Stones Marlborough Sauvignon Blanc ★★★★

A consistently excellent wine, now part of the Sacred Hill stable. The 2004 vintage (★★★★) is ripely scented, with fresh, pure, vibrant flavours of melons, limes and capsicums, showing impressive delicacy and depth, and a sliver of sweetness (4 grams/litre of residual sugar), balanced by mouth-watering acidity.

DRY $19 V+

Canterbury House Waipara Sauvignon Blanc ★★★★☆

Estate-grown, this is one of Canterbury House's major successes – Sauvignon Blanc suits the company's cool grape-growing climate and warm, shingly soils. In most years it is fresh and pungently aromatic, with excellent depth of lively, crisply herbaceous flavour. The 2003 vintage (★★★★☆) is an intensely varietal wine with nettley aromas and crisp, punchy flavours of passionfruit and lime, notably fresh and zingy. The 2004 (★★★★) is also very aromatic, intense and nettley.

DRY $18 V+

Cape Campbell Marlborough Sauvignon Blanc ★★★

The 2004 vintage (★★★) from Murray Brown (who formerly owned the Cairnbrae winery) is fresh, vibrant and lively, with green-edged, apple and lime flavours and appetising acidity.

DRY $18 -V

Carrick Sauvignon Blanc ★★★

Grown at Bannockburn, in Central Otago, this is a distinctly cool-climate style, fresh and strongly herbaceous. The 2004 vintage (★★☆) was mostly handled in tanks, but 18 per cent was fermented in old barrels. It's a crisp, fresh wine with green-apple and fresh-cut grass flavours and bracing acidity balanced by slight sweetness (6 grams/litre of residual sugar), but lacks real ripeness and richness.

Vintage	04
WR	4
Drink	04-06

MED/DRY $18 -V

Cat's Pee on a Gooseberry Bush Sauvignon Blanc ★★☆

From 'Purr Productions' (a division of Coopers Creek), the 2002 vintage (★★★) is an easy-drinking blend of Marlborough, Waikato and Gisborne grapes. Fresh and light, it's a clearly varietal wine with strong melon/capsicum flavours and a fractionally sweet (6 grams/litre of sugar), crisp finish.

Vintage	04	03	02
WR	6	6	5
Drink	04-06	04-05	04-05

MED/DRY $13 AV

Charles Wiffen Marlborough Sauvignon Blanc ★★★☆

The 2004 vintage (★★★) is a weighty, faintly honeyed wine with tropical-fruit and herbal flavours showing good depth and a dry, crisp finish.

DRY $19 AV

Church Road Sauvignon Blanc

★★★★☆

Aiming for a wine that is 'more refined and softer than a typical New Zealand Sauvignon Blanc, with restrained varietal characters', in 2003 (★★★★) Montana blended Marlborough and Hawke's Bay fruit and fermented and lees-aged 40 per cent of the blend in mostly seasoned French oak barriques. Only free-run juice was used (with minimal skin contact), giving the wine delicacy and the potential for greater longevity. It's a ripe, rounded wine with sweet fruit delights, the freshness and varietal definition of Marlborough fruit, subtle oak, gentle acidity and a lingering finish.

Vintage	03	02
WR	5	7
Drink	04-06	P

DRY $22 V+

C.J. Pask Roys Hill Sauvignon Blanc

★★☆

Winemaker Kate Radburnd aims for 'an easy-drinking style with its emphasis on tropical-fruit flavours and a tangy lift'. The 2004 vintage (★★☆), grown in the Gimblett Gravels and Crownthorpe districts of Hawke's Bay, is a crisp, medium-bodied dry wine, citrusy, appley and limey, with reasonable depth. It lacks real ripeness and intensity, but is priced right.

DRY $15 AV

Clearview Reserve Sauvignon Blanc

★★★☆

Grown in the Wilkins vineyard, close to the sea at Te Awanga, the 2002 vintage (★★★☆) of this Hawke's Bay wine was barrel-fermented and oak-aged for eight months. Toasty and oaky on the nose, it's a powerful wine, robust, rich and rounded, with strong, ripe, guava-like flavours, but would have been even better with a more restrained wood influence.

DRY $22 -V

Clearwater Vineyards Marlborough Sauvignon Blanc

(★★☆)

Made by Sherwood Estate, the 2003 vintage (★★☆) is a green-edged, crisp dry wine, solid but lacking real ripeness and richness.

DRY $20 -V

Clifford Bay Estate Marlborough Sauvignon Blanc

★★★★

A consistently impressive single-vineyard wine, grown in the Awatere Valley. The 2003 vintage (★★★★) is vibrantly fruity and freshly herbaceous, with good intensity. Intensely varietal, it's balanced for easy drinking, with lively acidity, a sliver of sweetness (4.2 grams/litre) and a lingering finish. The 2004 (★★★★) is also scented and lively, with pungent melon, capsicum and lime flavours, finely balanced and long.

Vintage	04	03	02
WR	6	7	6
Drink	04-07	04-06	P

DRY $18 V+

Clos Henri Marlborough Sauvignon Blanc

(★★★★★)

The Clos Henri vineyard near Renwick is owned by Henri Bourgeois, a highly rated, family-owned producer in the Loire Valley. The debut 2003 vintage (★★★★★) is bone-dry (unusual for Marlborough Sauvignon Blanc) and richly scented, in a flinty, minerally rather than herbaceous style. A highly satisfying wine with intense, ripe, non-aggressive, almost subtle flavours, it's a significant style departure from the regional norm of grassy, off-dry wines, and displays very impressive delicacy, tightness and length.

DRY $27 AV

Clos Marguerite Marlborough Sauvignon Blanc   (★★★★☆)

Grown in the Awatere Valley, hand-picked, whole-bunch pressed and briefly lees-aged, the 2003 vintage (★★★★☆) has a lifted, freshly herbaceous bouquet and weighty palate, punchy and intensely varietal. Rich, with tropical-fruit flavours but also a distinctly nettley thread, it's a well-rounded, dry wine with a touch of minerality and loads of personality.

DRY $20 V+

Cloudy Bay Sauvignon Blanc   ★★★★★

New Zealand's most internationally acclaimed wine is highly sought after from Sydney to New York and London. Its irresistibly aromatic and zesty style and rapier-like flavours stem, chief winemaker Kevin Judd is convinced, from 'the fruit characters that are in the grapes when they arrive at the winery'. It is sourced from eight company-owned and contract growers' vineyards in the Rapaura, Fairhall, Renwick and Brancott districts of the Wairau Valley. The juice is cool-fermented in stainless steel tanks; the wine does not have any significant oak maturation, but is briefly aged on its yeast lees before bottling. The 2004 vintage (★★★★★) is already an outstanding mouthful, with great mouthfeel and texture. Showing real weight and richness across the palate, it is mouthfilling (13.5 per cent alcohol), tight and punchy, with an array of intense fruit flavours, appetising acidity giving it a slight minerally character and a dry, lasting finish. Its retail price of $29.95 arouses high expectations, but the wine delivers.

Vintage	04	03	02	01	00
WR	6	6	6	6	6
Drink	05	P	P	P	P

DRY $30 AV

Cloudy Bay Te Koko – see Branded and Other White Wines

Collards Rothesay Sauvignon Blanc   ★★★☆

Who says you can't make good Sauvignon Blanc in Auckland? Grown in the company's Rothesay Vineyard at Waimauku, in West Auckland, at its best it shows the weight and ripe tropical-fruit flavours of North Island grapes, with good acidity keeping things fresh and lively. The 2003 vintage (★★★☆) was hand-picked and partly barrel-fermented, and 20 per cent of the blend went through a softening malolactic fermentation. It's a full-bodied wine with distinctly grassy aromas, gently herbaceous, slightly nutty and leesy flavours showing good depth and a rounded finish.

Vintage	04	03	02	01	00
WR	6	6	6	6	7
Drink	05-07	04-06	04-05	P	P

DRY $16 V+

Coopers Creek Marlborough Sauvignon Blanc   ★★★★

A consistently good wine, bargain-priced. The 2003 vintage (★★★★) is ripely scented and punchy, with zingy melon, passionfruit and lime flavours showing excellent balance and intensity. The freshly aromatic, richly varietal 2004 (★★★★) is vibrantly fruity, with good intensity of melon, nectarine and capsicum flavours.

Vintage	04	03	02	01	00
WR	6	6	6	6	6
Drink	04-05	04-05	P	P	P

DRY $16 V+

Coopers Creek Reserve Marlborough Sauvignon Blanc   ★★★★

The 2003 vintage (★★★★) is very fragrant and appealing, with strong melon/lime flavours and a slightly creamy texture. There is no 2004.

Vintage	04	03	02	01	00	99
WR	NM	7	NM	7	NM	7
Drink	NM	04-05	NM	P	NM	P

DRY $20 AV

Corbans Cottage Block Marlborough Sauvignon Blanc ★★★★☆

The 2002 vintage (★★★★☆) was mostly handled in tanks, but 8 per cent was fermented and matured in French oak barriques. Weighty, ripe and rounded, it's very much a style wine, with rich tropical-fruit flavours, subtle oak adding complexity and a deliciously soft, fully dry finish.

Vintage	02
WR	6
Drink	04-08

DRY $30 -V

Corbans Private Bin Marlborough Sauvignon Blanc   ★★★★

The 2002 vintage (★★★★) is the first since 1999. Partly (6 per cent) French oak-aged, it's an intensely aromatic, strongly varietal wine with rich tropical-fruit and herbaceous flavours and a fresh, rounded finish.

Vintage	02
WR	6
Drink	04-06

DRY $22 AV

Corbans Sauvignon Blanc   ★★☆

The 2003 vintage (★★☆), a blend of 54 per cent Chilean and 46 per cent Hawke's Bay wine, is crisp and lively, with tropical-fruit/lime flavours showing decent depth. The 2004 (★★★), based solely on Hawke's Bay grapes, is full-bodied, smooth and ripe, with melon/lime flavours showing good depth and a fractionally off-dry (4 grams/litre of residual sugar) finish. It's an attractive wine, offering fresh, easy drinking.

Vintage	04	03	02	01
WR	6	5	6	6
Drink	04-06	P	P	P

DRY $14 AV

Corbans White Label Sauvignon Blanc   ★★☆

This quaffer from Allied Domecq Wines (NZ) is an easy-drinking style with moderate depth of melon and cut-grass flavours, slightly sweet and smooth. The 2004 vintage (★★☆) claims on the front label to be a 'Wine of New Zealand', but the information sheet sent to wine writers describes the 'region' as 'Chile and New Zealand'.

MED/DRY $9 V+

Crab Farm Reserve Sauvignon Blanc   (★★★★)

Hand-picked in Hawke's Bay 'at peak ripeness', the 2004 vintage (★★★★) is a robust (14.5 per cent alcohol) wine with ripe, sweet fruit characters of melons, gooseberries and limes, fresh, crisp and lively. Weighty and rich, it should offer excellent drinking during 2005.

DRY $19 V+

Crab Farm Sauvignon Blanc   ★★★

The attractive 2004 vintage (★★★☆) of this Hawke's Bay wine is crisp and lively, with fresh, citrusy, appley, limey aromas and flavours showing good punch and vivacity.

DRY $17 AV

Craggy Range Avery Vineyard
Marlborough Sauvignon Blanc   ★★★☆

Grown in Richard and Linda Avery's vineyard, a slightly cooler site in the Wairau Valley than the Old Renwick Vineyard (below), the 2004 vintage (★★☆) is full-bodied, fresh and vibrant, with moderate depth of melon, lime and green-apple flavours, a sliver of sweetness and crisp acidity.

Vintage	04	03	02
WR	6	7	5
Drink	04-06	04-05	P

 MED/DRY $22 -V

Craggy Range Old Renwick Vineyard Sauvignon Blanc ★★★★☆

Based on mature, 16-year-old vines in the heart of the Wairau Valley, the 2004 vintage (★★★★☆) shows good intensity of melon and lime flavours, with a slightly minerally character adding interest. Aromatic, punchy, crisp and zesty, with a lasting finish, it's worth cellaring to mid-2005+.

Vintage	03	02	01	00	99	DRY $22 V+
WR	6	6	6	6	6	
Drink	04-05	04	P	P	P	

Craggy Range Te Muna Road Vineyard Martinborough Sauvignon Blanc ★★★★

Grown a few kilometres south of Martinborough township, this wine is revealing a strong personality, based (as the winery puts it) on its 'unique, dry grainy texture on the palate'. It is mostly fermented and lees-aged in tanks, but a minor portion is barrel-fermented with indigenous yeasts. The refined 2004 vintage (★★★☆) is pale, with fresh aromas and flavours of melons and limes, finely balanced acidity and a smooth, dry, lingering finish.

Vintage	03	02	DRY $19 AV
WR	6	6	
Drink	04-05	04	

Crossings, The, Catherine's Run Reserve Sauvignon Blanc (★★★☆)

Grown in the Medway vineyard, at 200 metres above sea level in the Awatere Valley of Marlborough, and 20 per cent fermented in old barrels, the 2002 vintage (★★★☆) is crisp and lively, with fullness of body, a hint of oak and very good length of melon/lime, slightly chalky, minerally flavours. There is no 2003.

Vintage	03	02	DRY $22 -V
WR	NM	7	
Drink	NM	04-07	

Crossings, The, Marlborough Sauvignon Blanc ★★★☆

The punchy 2002 vintage (★★★☆), grown in the Awatere Valley and lees-aged for three months, is a fully dry wine with gooseberry, passionfruit and lime flavours and a tight, minerally finish. Drinking well now, the 2003 (★★★☆) has good weight and depth of ripe, tropical-fruit flavours, with a dry, rounded finish.

Vintage	03	DRY $19 AV
WR	7	
Drink	04-06	

Crossroads Destination Series Sauvignon Blanc ★★★☆

Hawke's Bay Sauvignon at its best, the weighty, zingy 2002 vintage (★★★★) was based principally on grassy Dartmoor Valley grapes, blended with riper fruit from the coastal Te Awanga district. It's a satisfyingly full-bodied wine with a strong surge of pineappley, limey flavours and a crisp, sustained finish. The 2004 (★★★☆) is a Marlborough wine with good weight and depth of crisp, vibrant melon/capsicum flavours.

DRY $20 AV

Dashwood Marlborough Sauvignon Blanc ★★★☆

The Vavasour winery's drink-young, unwooded Sauvignon Blanc is typically great value. The 2004 vintage (★★★☆) is a blend of Awatere Valley (54 per cent) and Wairau Valley grapes. It's a scented, ripe, vibrantly fruity, melon and lime-flavoured wine with good depth and harmony and a dryish (4.9 grams/litre of sugar) finish.

Vintage	04	03	02	01	00	DRY $17 V+
WR	7	6	7	6	7	
Drink	04-05	P	P	P	P	

Delegat's Marlborough Sauvignon Blanc   ★★★

Winemaker Michael Ivicevich is aiming for 'a tropical fruit-flavoured style, a bit broader and softer than some'. The 2004 vintage (★★★) is an attractive, easy-drinking wine with good depth of melon and lime flavours, woven with fresh acidity. It's not intense, but offers good value.

Vintage	04	03	02		DRY $15 V+
WR	7	7	6		
Drink	04-05	P	P		

Domaine Georges Michel Golden Mile Sauvignon Blanc   ★★☆

Grown in the Rapaura ('golden mile') district of the Wairau Valley, this wine has been of uneven quality since it was launched in 1998. The 2003 vintage (★★) is a full-bodied dry wine, but offers no real flavour delights, lacking the intense aromas and fresh, vibrant fruit characters of good Marlborough Sauvignon Blanc.

DRY $17 -V

Drylands Marlborough Sauvignon Blanc   ★★★★

This is typically an upfront style from Nobilo with strong, crisply herbaceous flavours. The 2003 (★★★☆) was cool-fermented and lees-aged for three months in tanks. Freshly herbaceous, it has lively, green-capsicum and slightly grassy flavours showing good depth and a smooth finish. The 2004 vintage seemed bottle-shocked when I tasted it in August and September 2004 (and so is not rated), but showed ripe-fruit aromas (with a hint of 'armpit'), and crisp, punchy melon/capsicum flavours.

Vintage	04	03	02	01	00	DRY $20 AV
WR	7	7	7	7	7	
Drink	04-05	04-05	P	P	P	

Dry River Sauvignon Blanc   ★★★★

Estate-grown in Martinborough, this is typically a sturdy, notably ripe-tasting wine, but it is not a star of the Dry River range. Winemaker Neil McCallum aims to 'minimise herbaceous and vegetal flavours and provide a wine with attractive aging qualities'. Bright, light lemon/green, the 2004 vintage (★★★☆) is a restrained but quietly satisfying wine with fresh gooseberry, lime and green-apple flavours, balanced acidity and a dry finish.

Vintage	03	02	01	00	99	98	97	96	DRY $24 -V
WR	7	6	6	7	6	6	7	7	
Drink	06-12	04-13	04-12	04-10	04-05	P	P	P	

Esk River Hawke's Bay Sauvignon Blanc   (★★☆)

From the winery until recently called Linden Estate, the 2004 vintage (★★☆) is a dry, medium to full-bodied wine with ripe pineapple, melon and lime flavours, fresh and crisp.

DRY $15 AV

Esk River Reserve Sauvignon Blanc   (★★☆)

The crisp, dry 2003 vintage (★★☆) is a Hawke's Bay wine, 50 per cent French oak-aged for three months (the rest was handled in tanks). It's a tight, flinty, limey wine, but slightly austere, lacking a bit of fruit sweetness and roundness.

DRY $22 -V

Esk Valley Hawke's Bay Sauvignon Blanc   ★★★★

In warm vintages this is a robust wine with rich, ripe, tropical-fruit flavours; cooler years produce a less powerful but zesty wine. The 2004 vintage (tasted prior to bottling, and so not rated) was mostly handled in tanks, and 7.5 per cent of the blend was fermented in seasoned oak barrels. Viewed by winemaker Gordon Russell as 'the best for many years', it's a ripe, tropical fruit-flavoured wine with very good depth, fresh, balanced acidity, a touch of complexity and substantial body.

Vintage	04	03	02	DRY $19 AV
WR	6	6	5	
Drink	04-06	04-05	04-05	

Esk Valley Limited Release
Heretaunga Plains Sauvignon Blanc (★★★)

Sold by mail-order wine clubs, the 2003 vintage (★★★) is a smooth, moderately ripe, citrusy, appley wine, fresh and flavoursome.

DRY $20 -V

Fairhall Downs Marlborough Sauvignon Blanc ★★★★

Estate-grown at the head of the Brancott Valley, this is a consistently classy wine. The 2003 vintage (★★★★) is full and fresh, with rich, ripe-passionfruit and lime flavours, pure and zesty, lively acidity and an easy-drinking balance. The 2004 (★★★☆) is full-bodied (13.5 per cent alcohol), with fresh, ripe, passionfruit-like flavours and a fractionally off-dry, crisp finish.

Vintage	04	03
WR	7	7
Drink	04-08	04-07

DRY $18 V+

Fairmont Estate Sauvignon Blanc ★★★☆

This Wairarapa wine is grown at Gladstone, between Masterton and Martinborough. The 2003 vintage (★★★☆) is a slightly sweet wine with crisp, green-edged flavours showing some intensity and length.

MED/DRY $18 AV

Fiddler's Green Waipara Sauvignon Blanc ★★★☆

A distinctly cool-climate style, typically with good vigour and intensity. Estate-grown, hand-picked and tank-fermented, the 2004 vintage (★★★★) is very fresh and lively, with mouthfilling body and vibrant melon, lime and apple flavours, crisp and slightly minerally. A finely balanced wine, it should age well.

Vintage	04
WR	6
Drink	05-06

DRY $20 AV

Floating Mountain Mark Rattray Vineyard
Sauvignon Blanc (★★☆)

Grown at Waipara, the 2004 vintage (★★☆) is a pale wine with citrusy, appley flavours, fresh and vibrant, but only showing moderate depth.

DRY $18 -V

Forrest Marlborough Sauvignon Blanc ★★★★

John Forrest's wine is fresh, fragrant and full-flavoured in a smooth, very easy-drinking style that offers good value. The 2004 vintage (★★★★) is one of the best yet. Fractionally off-dry (4.5 grams/litre of sugar) in style, it has a punchy bouquet of melons, capsicums and limes, leading into a mouthfilling (14 per cent alcohol), vibrantly fruity palate with excellent weight and intensity. It's a clearly herbaceous, tangy wine with a rounded, lasting finish.

Vintage	04	03	02	01	00
WR	7	7	5	6	7
Drink	04-06	04-05	P	P	P

DRY $19 V+

Foxes Island Marlborough Sauvignon Blanc (★★★★☆)

The characterful 2003 vintage (★★★★☆) was mostly handled in tanks, but 10 per cent of the blend was oak-aged. Finely scented, it's a full-bodied, finely textured wine with strong, ripe-melon, gooseberry and capsicum flavours, a touch of complexity and a well-rounded finish. A wine of individuality, it's delicious now.

Vintage	03
WR	6
Drink	04-05

DRY $25 AV

Framingham Marlborough Sauvignon Blanc ★★★★★

This label has emerged recently as one of the most finely crafted Sauvignon Blancs in the region. Andrew Hedley makes a dry style with no use of oak: 'Complexity comes from different sites and levels of fruit maturity.' The 2003 vintage (★★★★★) is very delicate, with a hint of 'sweaty armpit' on the nose and a lovely spread of flavours, pure and intense. Ripe, with sweet fruit characters and fresh, finely balanced acidity, it's a sophisticated wine that carries the dry style superbly, with a very long finish. In its infancy, the 2004 (★★★★☆) is rich and rounded, with lovely texture and strong melon/lime flavours, zingy and long.

Vintage	03	02	01	00	DRY $20 AV
WR	6	7	6	5	
Drink	04-06	P	P	P	

Francis-Cole Marlborough Sauvignon Blanc (★★★)

'Best consumed within the next five minutes', the 2003 vintage (★★★) is a full-bodied, freshly herbaceous wine with decent depth of melon and green-capsicum flavours and a crisp, dry finish.

Vintage	03	DRY $21 -V
WR	5	
Drink	04-05	

Gibbston Valley Marlborough Sauvignon Blanc (★★★☆)

The 2004 vintage (★★★☆) is punchy and tangy, with fresh, clearly herbaceous aromas and incisive melon/capsicum flavours, showing good vivacity and length.

Vintage	04	DRY $20 AV
WR	5	
Drink	04-07	

Giesen Marlborough Sauvignon Blanc ★★★

This is by far the largest-volume wine from the Canterbury-based Giesen brothers. The 2004 vintage (★★★) is fresh and crisp, with good depth of ripe melon, apple and lime flavours in a clean, vibrant style with plenty of youthful impact.

Vintage	04	03	02	01	00	DRY $15 V+
WR	7	7	7	7	7	
Drink	04-07	04-06	P	P	P	

Giesen Single Vineyard Selection Marlborough Sauvignon Blanc (★★★★☆)

Made from 'the vineyard producing the best quality Sauvignon Blanc', the 2003 vintage (★★★★☆) is a highly scented wine with lovely delicacy and purity of fruit characters. Concentrated, with strong personality, it shows good body and roundness, with ripe tropical-fruit flavours, a slight minerally streak and fresh acidity. Delicious current drinking.

DRY $22 V+

Gifford Road Marlborough Sauvignon Blanc (★★☆)

The 2003 vintage (★★☆) is a solid but plain wine with citrusy, appley, limey flavours and firm acid spine.

DRY $17 -V

Gladstone Vineyard Wairarapa Sauvignon Blanc ★★★★

Grown in the home block at Gladstone and the Dakins Road district, closer to Masterton, the 2004 vintage (★★★☆) was harvested at 21.5 to 23 brix, tank-fermented and lees-aged for a month. It's a bone-dry wine with fresh, herbaceous aromas and strongly varietal flavours, grassy, nettley and punchy, with a crisp, dry finish.

DRY $20 AV

Glover's Moutere Sauvignon Blanc ★★

Estate-grown at Upper Moutere, this is a bone-dry style with flinty, nettley flavours and biting acidity. The 2001 vintage (★★) is an austere wine, lacking fresh fruit characters, liveliness and charm.

DRY $17 -V

Goldridge Estate Premium Reserve Marlborough Sauvignon Blanc ★★☆

The 2004 vintage (★★☆) is a solid but plain wine, crisp, citrusy, appley and limey, but restrained.

DRY $19 -V

Goldwater New Dog Marlborough Sauvignon Blanc ★★★★

Bold and weighty, with a striking intensity of pineapple and passionfruit-like flavours in top vintages, in the past this wine was grown mainly in the Dog Point vineyard in the Brancott Valley, but in 2003 the grapes were drawn principally from a vineyard in St Leonard's Road, in the heart of the Wairau Valley (hence the label change from 'Dog Point' to 'New Dog'). The wine is fermented almost to full dryness (the 2004 vintage has 3.4 grams/litre of residual sugar) and lees-aged for three months, with frequent stirring, in stainless steel tanks; a small percentage is barrel-fermented. The 2003 vintage (★★★★) has good weight, a freshly herbaceous bouquet and strong, tangy gooseberry/lime flavours, woven with lively acidity. The 2004 (★★★☆) is ripely scented and flavoured, with good body and depth of tropical-fruit flavours, tangy and dry.

Vintage	04	03	02
WR	7	7	7
Drink	04-06	04-05	P

DRY $20 AV

Gravitas Sauvignon Blanc ★★★★☆

The arresting 2002 vintage (★★★★★) was produced by St Arnaud's Vineyards, which owns 30 hectares of vineyards near Renwick, in Marlborough. One of the most powerful and intense Sauvignon Blancs I've tasted from the region, it's a robust wine (14.5 per cent alcohol), richly fragrant, with bold, highly concentrated gooseberry/lime flavours, fine acidity and a resounding, fully dry finish. The 2003 (★★★★) has slight 'armpit' aromas and a weighty, dry palate with ripe melon and lime flavours, a touch of complexity and good acid spine.

DRY $22 V+

Greenhough Nelson Vineyards Sauvignon Blanc ★★★★☆

Andrew Greenhough aims for a 'rich Sauvignon Blanc style with ripe, creamy mouthfeel' – and hits the target with ease. The 2003 vintage (★★★★★) is outstanding. The 2004 (★★★★) was harvested from the Avery and Barnicoat vineyards at Hope, at three different levels of ripeness. Most of the blend was handled in tanks, but 5 per cent was fermented in new American oak. Bone-dry, it's a strongly varietal wine, punchy and aromatic, with crisp melon/capsicum flavours showing excellent vigour and intensity.

Vintage	04	03	02
WR	5	6	6
Drink	04-06	04-05	P

DRY $18 V+

Grove Mill Marlborough Sauvignon Blanc ★★★★★

With a shower of awards around the world a few years ago, this label established itself as a regional classic. At its best, it's a powerful Sauvignon Blanc, opulent and weighty, with huge drinkability. The grapes are drawn from vineyards (both company-owned and growers') scattered across the Wairau Valley. In most years, the blend includes minor portions of Sémillon and (unusually) Chardonnay, and around 20 per cent goes through malolactic fermentation to 'improve the wine's complexity and texture'. Light lemon/green, the 2004 vintage (★★★★☆) is fresh and tight, with strong, ripely herbaceous flavours threaded with mouth-watering acidity and a dry, slightly flinty and minerally finish. Drink 2005–06.

Vintage	03	02	01	00	99
WR	6	5	7	7	6
Drink	04-05	P	P	P	P

DRY $22 V+

Gunn Estate Sauvignon Blanc   ★★★☆

From Sacred Hill (which now owns the Gunn Estate brand), the 2004 vintage (★★★☆) is a Hawke's Bay wine, fresh, crisp and well balanced, with good intensity of melon/lime flavours.

DRY $16 V+

Hawkesbridge Marlborough Sauvignon Blanc   (★★☆)

Sold by mail-order wine clubs, the 2003 vintage (★★☆) is a fractionally sweet, appley wine with crisp acidity and moderate flavour depth.

DRY $20 -V

Highfield Marlborough Sauvignon Blanc   ★★★★☆

Typically a very classy wine – freshly scented and finely balanced, with rich, limey fruit characters and excellent vigour and depth. The 2004 vintage (★★★★☆) was grown in three parts of the Wairau Valley, fermented 'predominantly' in stainless steel tanks, and matured on its yeast lees for four months before bottling. Mouthfilling and smooth, with lovely texture, it has ripe, delicate melon and capsicum flavours, finely balanced and harmonious, and a slightly minerally, lasting finish.

Vintage	03	02	01	00
WR	7	7	7	7
Drink	04-05	04-05	P	P

DRY $24 AV

Himmelsfeld Moutere Sauvignon Blanc   ★★★☆

From a small vineyard in the Upper Moutere hills, the 2003 vintage (★★★★) is scented and full-bodied, with good intensity of ripely herbaceous, gooseberry/lime flavours, fresh, vibrant and punchy.

DRY $18 AV

Holmes Organic Marlborough Sauvignon Blanc   (★★☆)

The light, tangy 2003 vintage (★★☆) is crisp and appley, but lacks flavour depth and richness.

DRY $19 -V

Huia Marlborough Sauvignon Blanc   ★★★★

This is a substantial, satisfying wine. Grown in eight vineyards spread around the Wairau Valley and 20 per cent fermented with indigenous yeasts, the finely balanced 2004 vintage (★★★★) is richly scented and vibrant, with strong melon, gooseberry and green-capsicum flavours, crisp acidity and a rich finish.

Vintage	04	03	02	01	00	99
WR	6	6	7	6	7	6
Drink	04-07	04-05	04-05	04-05	P	P

DRY $21 AV

Hunter's Marlborough Sauvignon Blanc   ★★★★★

Hunter's fame rests on the consistent excellence of this wine, which exhibits the intense aromas of ripe, cool-climate grapes, uncluttered by any oak handling. The style goal is 'a strong expression of Marlborough fruit – a bell-clear wine with a mix of tropical and searing gooseberry characters'. The grapes are sourced from vineyards in the Wairau Valley, and to retain their fresh, vibrant characters, they are processed quickly, with protective anaerobic techniques and minimal handling. The wine usually takes a year to break into full stride. The typically classy 2004 vintage (★★★★☆) is weighty and soft (in the sense of great delicacy through the palate, rather than any lack of acidity). A dry style (2.0 grams/litre of sugar), it offers good intensity of melon/capsicum flavours, with a long, lively finish.

Vintage	04	03	02	01	00
WR	6	6	5	6	5
Drink	05-07	04-06	04-05	P	P

DRY $18 V+

Hunter's Single Vineyard Sauvignon Blanc   ★★★★☆

Grown 'predominantly' in the Spelsbury Vineyard, in the Wairau Valley of Marlborough, the 2002 vintage (★★★★☆) shows impressive delicacy and finesse. It is fragrant, with ripe-melon and passionfruit flavours, a touch of minerality, gentle herbaceous characters and a fully dry, rounded finish. It's the sort of Sauvignon Blanc that keeps drawing you back for another glass.

Vintage	03	02
WR	6	5
Drink	05	P

DRY $22 V+

Hunter's Stoneburn Marlborough Sauvignon Blanc   (★★★☆)

Sold by mail-order wine clubs, the 2003 vintage (★★★☆) is a fresh-scented, middleweight wine with tangy melon, lime and green-capsicum flavours showing good depth and vigour.

DRY $19 AV

Hunter's Winemaker's Selection Sauvignon Blanc   ★★★★★

This regional classic is based on Hunter's ripest, least-herbaceous Marlborough grapes, grown usually in the early-ripening estate vineyard in Rapaura Road, adjacent to the winery. Part of the blend is handled entirely in stainless steel tanks; another portion is barrel-fermented; another is tank-fermented but barrel-aged. It typically offers pure, deep, incisive fruit flavours, plenty of body and acidity, and well-judged, subtle wood handling. The 2002 vintage (★★★★) has toasty oak aromas leading into a robust, creamy palate with ripely herbaceous flavours, a stronger than usual seasoning of wood and a well-rounded finish.

Vintage	03	02	01	00	99	98
WR	5	6	5	5	5	4
Drink	05-06	04-05	P	P	P	P

DRY $22 V+   🍇🍇🍇

Isabel Estate Marlborough Sauvignon Blanc   ★★★★★

Grown in the Isabel Estate vineyard near Renwick, in the heart of the Wairau Valley, and (since 2003) in the company-owned Clansman vineyard in the Awatere Valley, this is a typically stunning wine. It is harvested at a range of ripeness levels and a small portion of the blend (10 per cent) is fermented with indigenous yeasts in French oak barriques; the rest is tank-fermented and lees-aged. It is typically finely scented, fresh, crisp and punchy, but not one-dimensional, with lovely passionfruit, lychee and pineapple flavours, tight and long, and the barest hint of oak. The 2004 vintage (★★★★☆) shows good intensity of limey, slightly minerally flavours, with racy acidity balanced by slight sweetness. It's a tightly structured wine, with strong personality.

Vintage	04	03	02	01	00	99
WR	5	6	6	6	7	6
Drink	04-05	04-06	P	P	P	P

DRY $25 AV   🍇🍇

Jackman Ridge Sauvignon Blanc   (★★)

The non-vintage wine (★★) released by Montana (now Allied Domecq) in mid-late 2003 is a blend of Chilean and New Zealand wines. The bouquet is subdued; the flavours ripe, citrusy and vaguely herbaceous, with fresh acidity. It's a solid but plain wine with limited varietal character.

MED/DRY $9 AV

Jackson Estate Sauvignon Blanc   ★★★★☆

Grown in John Stichbury's vineyards in the heart of the Wairau Valley, this is typically a lush, ripe and rounded, fully dry wine with good concentration and huge drinkability. The 2004 vintage (★★★★★) is the finest for several years. Deliciously weighty, lively and rich, with slight 'armpit' aromas, it has concentrated, sweet fruit characters and fresh, vibrant melon, passionfruit and lime flavours showing lovely depth.

Vintage	04	03	02
WR	6	6	7
Drink	04-07	04-05	P

DRY $20 V+

Johanneshof Marlborough Sauvignon Blanc   ★★★☆
The 2003 vintage (★★★) from this small Koromiko producer is vibrantly fruity, with fresh, ripely herbaceous flavours and a soft, slightly sweet finish. The 2004 (★★★☆) is similar – fleshy and ripe, with gently herbaceous flavours and a very smooth finish.

MED/DRY $19 AV

Jules Taylor Marlborough Sauvignon Blanc   (★★★★)
The debut 2004 vintage (★★★★) was grown in the Wairau and Awatere valleys. It's a crisp, tightly structured wine with pure, nettley aromas and flavours, showing good freshness and richness.

DRY $19 V+

Kahurangi Estate Moutere Sauvignon Blanc   ★★★
Grown at Upper Moutere, in Nelson, the 2003 vintage (★★★☆) is scented and crisp, with lively acidity and plenty of grassy, freshly herbaceous flavour.

Vintage	03
WR	5
Drink	04-05

DRY $18 AV

Kaikoura Marlborough Sauvignon Blanc   ★★★☆
From a small winery overlooking the ocean at Kaikoura, this is typically a fragrant wine with good depth of passionfruit and green-capsicum flavours and slight sweetness adding an easy-drinking appeal. The 2003 vintage (★★★☆) is fresh, flavoursome and ripe, with tropical-fruit and herbaceous characters, crisp and lively, and a dryish (5 grams/litre of residual sugar) finish.

MED/DRY $18 AV

Kaimira Estate Nelson Sauvignon Blanc   ★★★☆
A freshly herbaceous wine, typically crisp, full-flavoured and zesty. The 2004 vintage (★★★☆) was grown on the plains and in the hill country, and 10 per cent of the blend was handled in old oak barrels. The bouquet is aromatic and nettley; the palate punchy and vibrant, with appetisingly crisp, melon and green-capsicum flavours showing good freshness and intensity.

DRY $17 AV

Kaituna Valley Marlborough Sauvignon Blanc   ★★★★
Grown in the company's closely planted vineyard in the Awatere Valley, the 2004 vintage (★★★☆) was harvested at 22.8 to 24.5 brix and lees-aged before bottling. It's a scented, mouthfilling wine (14 per cent alcohol) with strong passionfruit/lime flavours, fresh acidity and a slightly sweet (9 grams/litre of residual sugar) finish.

Vintage	04	03	02	01
WR	6	7	7	6
Drink	04-07	04-06	04-05	P

MED/DRY $20 AV

Kaituna Valley Marlborough Sauvignon Blanc Reserve   (★★★★)
The debut 2004 vintage (★★★★) was more lightly cropped than the 'standard' wine (above) and harvested at 23.8 to 24.5 brix. It is punchy, vibrant and intense, with substantial body (14.5 per cent alcohol) and a distinct splash of sweetness (9 grams/litre of residual sugar) amid its crisp, deep capsicum and passionfruit flavours.

Vintage	04
WR	7
Drink	04-07

MED/DRY $21 AV

Kathy Lynskey Vineyard Select Marlborough Sauvignon Blanc (★★☆)

The 2004 vintage (★★☆) is a medium-bodied style with moderate depth of crisp melon and green-capsicum flavours, fresh and lively.

DRY $19 -V

Kawarau Estate Sauvignon Blanc ★★☆

The flinty 2003 vintage (★★☆) is a dry Central Otago wine. Medium-bodied (11.5 per cent alcohol), with a restrained bouquet, it's crisp, appley and lemony, offering solid but not exciting drinking.

DRY $19 -V

Kemblefield The Distinction Sauvignon Blanc ★★★☆

Fragrant, slightly minerally and oaky on the nose, the 2002 vintage (★★★☆) was estate-grown in the relatively cool, elevated Mangatahi district of Hawke's Bay. A blend of Sauvignon Blanc (80 per cent) and Sémillon, it was fermented and lees-aged in stainless steel tanks and French oak barrels. Offering greater complexity than most Sauvignon Blancs, it is buoyant and penetrating, with tropical-fruit characters, a subtle seasoning of oak and crisp acidity keeping things lively.

DRY $20 AV

Kemblefield Winemakers Signature Sauvignon Blanc ★★★

The 2004 vintage (★★★) of this unoaked wine, estate-grown at Mangatahi, is full-bodied and dry, with fresh, lively, tropical-fruit flavours in the Hawke's Bay regional style.

DRY $16 AV

Kennedy Point Marlborough Sauvignon Blanc ★★★☆

The 2004 vintage (★★★★) from this Waiheke Island-based producer, grown in the Wairau Valley, is a refined wine with mouthfilling body, fresh, delicate melon/lime flavours showing good intensity and a dry, softly textured finish.

DRY $18 V+

Kerr Farm Kumeu Sauvignon Blanc ★★☆

Estate-grown in West Auckland, in some years this wine is appley and tart, but favourable seasons yield a full-bodied, ripe-tasting wine with tropical-fruit characters, balanced acidity and a dry finish.

DRY $16 -V

Kevern Walker Sauvignon Blanc (★★☆)

Not punchy, but offering good drinkability, the 2004 vintage (★★☆) is from the Hawke's Bay winery previously called Huthlee Estate. Estate-grown in the Ngatarawa district, it is weighty and fleshy, with a slightly creamy texture and melon, pear and lime flavours, ripe and rounded.

DRY $16 -V

Kim Crawford Flowers Marlborough Sauvignon Blanc ★★★★☆

The company's flagship Marlborough Sauvignon Blanc. The 2004 vintage (★★★★☆) has lush, very ripe and pure fruit aromas and a softly structured palate with rich, yet very delicate, passionfruit and lime flavours. Full, vibrant, intense and smooth, it's a deliciously easy-drinking wine.

Vintage 04
WR 6
Drink 05-06

DRY $25 AV

Kim Crawford Marlborough Sauvignon Blanc ★★★★

At its best, this is a punchy style with deliciously strong, fresh, tropical-fruit and capsicum flavours. The 2003 vintage (★★★★☆) is scented, ripe and tangy, with melon/lime flavours showing excellent intensity and a long finish. 'Ideal as a zesty pick-me-up', the 2004 (★★★☆) is finely balanced for easy drinking, with good depth of melon/lime flavours, fresh and crisp.

Vintage	04	03	02	01	00	DRY $20 AV
WR	5	5	6	6	6	
Drink	05-06	04-05	P	P	P	

Kim Crawford Sauvignon Blanc ★★★

The 2004 vintage (★★★), with no region of origin stated on the front label, is a blend of 'predominantly' Hawke's Bay and Nelson grapes. Flavoursome and ripe, it's a gently herbaceous wine with melon and lime flavours, cut with fresh acidity.

Vintage	04	DRY $16 AV
WR	4	
Drink	05-06	

Konrad Marlborough Sauvignon Blanc ★★★★

Delicious from the start, the 2004 vintage (★★★★☆) is a very finely balanced wine, grown in the Wairau and Waihopai valleys. It is weighty and rounded, fleshy and harmonious, with deep yet delicate melon and capsicum flavours, showing excellent richness.

Vintage	04	03	02	01	00	DRY $20 AV
WR	6	6	6	6	6	
Drink	04-06	04-05	P	P	P	

Koura Bay Whalesback Marlborough Sauvignon Blanc ★★★★

This single-vineyard wine is grown in the Awatere Valley. The 2004 vintage (★★★★) is one of the best – vibrant and punchy, with good intensity of gooseberry and capsicum flavours enlivened by mouth-watering acidity. It's a strongly varietal, freshly herbaceous wine, slightly minerally and long.

Vintage	04	03	DRY $19 V+
WR	7	7	
Drink	04-05	04-05	

Kumeu River Sauvignon Blanc (★★★★)

The debut 2004 vintage (★★★★) is a distinctive wine, well worth trying. Grown in a single Wairau Valley vineyard, partly fermented with indigenous yeasts and given extended lees contact, it is not pungently herbaceous, but shows good weight and presence in the mouth. Fresh, crisp, citrusy, minerally and zingy, it's a very satisfying alternative to mainstream styles, with an attractively rounded texture and dry finish.

DRY $20 V+

Lake Chalice First Release
Marlborough Sauvignon Blanc (★★★☆)

Bottled on 19 May and released the next day (making it the first new season's wine on the market), the well-crafted 2004 vintage (★★★☆) was harvested at 23 brix on 26 March in the company's Falcon vineyard at Rapaura. 'Especially made for consumption in 2004', it has fresh, lifted, limey aromas and smooth, melon/lime flavours, instantly appealing, with good depth.

DRY $19 AV

Lake Chalice Marlborough Sauvignon Blanc ★★★★

The 2004 vintage (★★★★) was grown in four vineyards in the Wairau and Awatere valleys, including the stony Falcon Vineyard at Rapaura. Harvested at an average of 21.5 brix, it has very fresh, punchy, limey aromas leading into a crisp, vibrantly fruity palate with good intensity of immaculate, passionfruit/lime flavours, racy, slightly minerally and long.

Vintage	04	03	02	01	00	DRY $19 V+
WR	6	7	6	7	7	
Drink	04-05	P	P	P	P	

Lake Chalice The Raptor Sauvignon Blanc (★★★★)

The 2002 vintage (★★★★) is a single-vineyard Marlborough wine, grown in the Awatere Valley and fermented and lees-aged for seven months in French oak barriques, with full malolactic fermentation. Fragrant, with nutty oak aromas, it is weighty, with strong, ripe, passionfruit and herb fruit flavours, gentle acidity, a deliciously creamy texture and a slightly buttery finish. There is no 2003. The 2004 vintage was not oak-aged.

Vintage	03	02	DRY $29 -V
WR	NM	7	
Drink	NM	04-07	

Lake Hayes Sauvignon Blanc ★★★☆

The 2004 vintage (★★★☆) is a blend of grapes grown in three Marlborough vineyards and the Amisfield vineyard, at Lowburn, in Central Otago. Aromatic, dry and punchy, it is fresh and intensely herbaceous, with slightly minerally, melon, capsicum and lime flavours and firm acid spine.

Vintage	04	DRY $20 AV
WR	5	
Drink	04-05	

Lawson's Dry Hills Marlborough Sauvignon Blanc ★★★★★

Consistently among the region's finest Sauvignon Blancs, this is a powerful and stylish wine, vibrantly fruity, intense and structured. The 2004 vintage (★★★★☆), picked between 27 March and 4 May at 21.2 to 23.9 brix, was grown at 11 sites in the Wairau, Waihopai, Omaka and Brancott valleys, and given a partial, softening malolactic fermentation. To add a subtle extra dimension, 6.7 per cent of the blend was fermented in seasoned French oak casks. Weighty and intense, with a hint of 'sweaty armpit' on the nose, it's a powerful wine with excellent mouthfeel, a rich array of fruit flavours and a crisp, long finish.

Vintage	04	03	02	01	00	DRY $21 V+
WR	6	6	6	6	7	
Drink	04-06	04-05	04	P	P	🍇 🍇

Lincoln Heritage Hawke's Bay Sauvignon Blanc (★★☆)

Grown in two vineyards, in the Dartmoor Valley and at Te Mata, near Havelock North, the 2004 vintage (★★☆) is a fresh, very easy-drinking, clearly varietal wine with crisp, limey, lively flavours. Verging on three stars.

Vintage	04	DRY $15 AV
WR	6	
Drink	04-06	

Longridge Vineyards Sauvignon Blanc ★★★

Under Corbans' direction, this traditionally Hawke's Bay wine was a lightly oaked style, typically full-bodied, with fresh, limey, tangy flavours. Now, as an Allied Domecq brand, the wood influence has been dropped. The 2003 vintage (★★★), a blend of Chilean (54 per cent) and Hawke's Bay wine, is full-bodied, with good depth of tropical-fruit flavours and a touch of lees-aging complexity. The 2004 (★★★) is full-bodied and freshly herbaceous, with melon/lime flavours showing good depth and a smooth, dry finish.

DRY $16 AV

Mahi Byrne Vineyard Sauvignon Blanc ★★★★

Mahi ('your work, your craft') is the personal brand of Brian Bicknell, chief winemaker at Seresin Estate. The 2003 vintage (★★★★☆), grown in the Byrne vineyard at Conders Bend, near Renwick, in Marlborough, was whole-bunch pressed and mostly tank-fermented and lees-aged for five months, but 12 per cent of the blend was French oak-fermented with indigenous yeasts. The bouquet is complex, with the slightly earthy, rustic character conferred by indigenous yeasts; the palate is rich, ripe and weighty, tightly structured, minerally and complex, with sweet fruit delights, lovely texture, and strong personality.

Vintage	03	02	01
WR	6	6	6
Drink	04-06	04-07	04-08

DRY $23 AV

Main Divide Sauvignon Blanc ★★★☆

From Pegasus Bay, the 2003 vintage (★★★) is a blend of Marlborough and Canterbury grapes, handled in stainless steel tanks, with a small percentage of barrel-aged Sémillon. Fleshy, with tropical-fruit and herbaceous characters, it's a full-bodied, faintly honeyed wine, crisp and flavoursome, with an off-dry finish.

Vintage	04	03	02
WR	7	5	6
Drink	04-07	04-06	P

MED/DRY $18 AV

Marlborough Wines Sauvignon Blanc (★★☆)

The 2003 vintage (★★☆) is a solid, ripe-tasting but slightly hard, phenolic wine, lacking delicacy and finesse, but priced right.

DRY $13 AV

Martinborough Vineyard Sauvignon Blanc ★★★★

The 2003 vintage (★★★★) was grown in the Pirinoa Block, at Martinborough, and a small portion (5 per cent) was fermented in old French oak barriques. Fresh and lively, with ripe melon, lime and capsicum flavours and a slightly flinty finish, it shows good delicacy, complexity and length. The 2004 (★★★☆) is smoothly mouthfilling, with ripe-fruit flavours showing very good length.

DRY $20 AV

Matahiwi Estate Nelson Sauvignon Blanc (★★★☆)

Launched from the 2004 vintage (★★★☆), this skilfully crafted, nettley wine was grown in three vineyards on the Waimea Plains and mostly handled in tanks, but 10 per cent was fermented in seasoned oak barrels and lees-stirred for two months. It's a fresh, clearly herbaceous wine with smooth, vibrant melon and capsicum flavours, showing a touch of complexity, and very good delicacy and depth.

Vintage	04
WR	6
Drink	04-05

DRY $17 V+

Matahiwi Estate Wairarapa Sauvignon Blanc (★★★☆)

The debut 2004 vintage (★★★☆) was mostly (86 per cent) estate-grown at Opaki, north of Masterton. Grassy aromas lead into a fresh, smooth palate with good body and strongly herbaceous flavours, smooth and lively.

Vintage	04
WR	5
Drink	04-05

DRY $17 V+

Matariki Hawke's Bay Sauvignon Blanc ★★★☆

Grown in the Gimblett Gravels district, the 2003 vintage (★★☆) was handled entirely in stainless steel tanks and lees-aged for three months. Still youthful in colour, it is citrusy and limey, in a restrained style that lacks real ripeness and richness, with an off-dry, crisp finish.

Vintage	04	03	02	01	MED/DRY $20 AV
WR	7	6	6	5	
Drink	04-08	04-06	04-06	P	

Matariki Reserve Sauvignon Blanc ★★★☆

This is generally among Hawke's Bay's richest, most satisfying Sauvignon Blancs. The 2003 vintage (★★★☆) was grown in Gimblett Road and mostly handled in tanks, but 40 per cent of the blend was fermented and lees-aged in new French oak barriques. Fragrant, with tropical-fruit aromas, it is fresh, full-bodied and vibrant, with tightly structured, ripe-fruit characters, subtle oak adding complexity and firm acid spine.

Vintage	03	02	01	00	99	98	DRY $25 -V
WR	6	6	5	7	6	7	
Drink	04-08	04-07	04-05	P	P	P	

Matua Valley Hawke's Bay Sauvignon Blanc ★★★

This isn't a pungent, 'leap-out-of-the-glass style', but it delivers easy, moderately priced drinking. The 2004 vintage (★★★), released on 19 May, was grown at Bay View, on the coast, and inland at Puketapu. It has a lifted, limey, appley bouquet, and a sliver of sweetness (5 grams/litre of residual sugar) in balance with tangy acids. It's a fresh, flavoursome wine with good immediacy.

Vintage	04	MED/DRY $16 AV
WR	5	
Drink	04-06	

Matua Valley Matheson Sauvignon Blanc ★★★★

Since the first 1986 vintage, this wine has ranked among the country's finest oak-aged Sauvignons. In the past, it was usually estate-grown at Waimauku in West Auckland, but since 1998 the fruit supply has switched to the Maraekakaho district in Hawke's Bay. It is typically a beautifully harmonious and subtle wine, with good body and excellent depth of fresh, ripe passionfruit and melon-like flavours, lightly seasoned with oak. The 2002 vintage (★★★★) is a blend of 90 per cent Sauvignon Blanc and 10 per cent Sémillon, matured for eight months in one and two-year-old French and American oak casks. Maturing well, it's a full-bodied wine with rich pear, gooseberry and grapefruit flavours, firm acidity, a gentle oak influence and smooth finish. The 2003 (★★★) is currently quite oaky, with tropical-fruit and herbaceous flavours and a slightly creamy texture. It needs time; open mid-2005+.

Vintage	03	02	01	00	99	98	DRY $18 V+
WR	6	6	NM	6	6	7	
Drink	04-08	04-06	NM	04-05	P	P	

Matua Valley Paretai Marlborough Sauvignon Blanc ★★★★☆

This is the winery's flagship Sauvignon Blanc. The 2003 vintage (★★★★), grown at seven sites in the Wairau and Awatere valleys (to achieve 'layers of flavour'), is pungently scented, with good weight and depth of ripe-passionfruit, lime and capsicum flavours and a crisp, long finish. The 2004 (★★★★★) shows outstanding intensity of ripe, tropical-fruit flavours, deliciously rich, fresh, vibrant and rounded.

Vintage	04	DRY $25 AV
WR	6	
Drink	04-07	

McCashin's Marlborough Sauvignon Blanc   ★★★★

Enticingly scented, the 2004 vintage (★★★★) is fresh and lively, with strong passionfruit and lime flavours. It's youthful, crisp and vibrantly fruity, offering excellent drinking over the summer of 2004–05.

DRY $19 V+

McCashin's Nelson Sauvignon Blanc   ★★★☆

Estate-grown at Hope, the 2004 vintage (★★★☆) is mouthfilling, with ripe melon/capsicum flavours, punchy and smooth.

DRY $19 AV

Melness Marlborough/Canterbury Sauvignon Blanc   ★★★☆

The 2002 vintage (★★★★) is a weighty, deeply flavoured regional blend, principally cool-fermented in tanks but with a small portion of barrel-fermented Sémillon. It's a fleshy wine with ripe gooseberry and crisp herbal flavours showing excellent depth and subtle oak and lees-aging characters adding complexity. The 2003 (★★★) is fleshy and smooth, with a hint of oak and soft, rounded finish.

MED/DRY $22 -V

Mills Reef Hawke's Bay Sauvignon Blanc   ★★★

The lower-tier Sauvignon Blanc from Mills Reef is grown in Hawke's Bay and made in an off-dry, easy-drinking style. The 2004 vintage (★★☆), grown in three, relatively cool coastal vineyards and harvested at 23 brix, is fresh and smooth, with a splash of sweetness, medium body and crisp lemon, apple and lime flavours.

Vintage	04	03	02
WR	6	6	7
Drink	04-06	P	P

MED/DRY $16 AV

Mills Reef Reserve Sauvignon Blanc   ★★★☆

The 2004 vintage (★★★☆) of this Hawke's Bay wine was partly fermented in French oak barriques. Pale lemon/green, with fresh, ripely herbaceous aromas, it shows very good depth of melon and capsicum flavours, with a twist of oak and dry, slightly minerally finish. It's a tightly structured wine with good potential.

Vintage	04	03	02	01	00
WR	6	7	7	7	6
Drink	04-06	04-05	P	P	P

DRY $19 AV

Mission Sauvignon Blanc   ★★★

The 2004 vintage was still bottle-shocked when tasted in mid-2004 (so is not star-rated). A blend of Marlborough (80 per cent) and Hawke's Bay grapes, it's a light lemon/green, full-bodied dry wine with tropical-fruit flavours, ripe and rounded.

DRY $15 V+

Moana Park Pascoe Series Sauvignon Blanc   ★★☆

The 2004 vintage (★★★) is the best yet. A ripely scented, fresh and crisp Hawke's Bay wine, it shows good body and roundness, with ripe, gently herbaceous, citrus fruit and melon flavours. It's not a dramatic wine, but enjoyable.

DRY $14 AV

Montana Brancott Estate Sauvignon Blanc ★★★★★

Promoted as a 'complex style of Sauvignon Blanc', this wine lives up to its billing. It is grown in the company's sweeping Brancott Estate vineyard in Marlborough and a small portion of the final blend is fermented and lees-aged in French oak barriques (half new). The 2003 vintage (★★★★★) is a powerful, vibrant, ripe-tasting wine with intense tropical-fruit flavours, creamy, nutty complexities and great personality. Delicious now, it should also mature well.

Vintage	03	02	01	00	99	98	DRY $24 V+
WR	6	7	6	7	7	6	
Drink	04-06	04-05	P	P	P	P	

Montana Marlborough Sauvignon Blanc ★★★☆

This famous, bargain-priced label rests its case on the flavour explosion of slow-ripened Marlborough fruit – a breathtaking style of Sauvignon Blanc which this wine, more than any other, has introduced to wine lovers in key markets around the world. Recent vintages are less lush, more pungently herbaceous than some other Marlborough labels; 'this is the style we can sell locally and the UK wants,' reports Allied Domecq. It lives forever – the 1984 vintage, opened in September 2003, was golden, toasty, herbal and honeyed. The 2004 vintage (★★★) is aromatic, with good freshness, depth and zing. Enjoyable in its youth, it's a medium-bodied, very lively wine, intensely varietal, with strong melon/lime flavours and crisp, zingy acids.

Vintage	04	03	02	01	00	DRY $16 V+
WR	7	7	7	7	7	
Drink	04-06	04-05	P	P	P	

Montana Reserve Marlborough Sauvignon Blanc ★★★★☆

This is a richer, riper, less pungently herbaceous style of Marlborough Sauvignon Blanc than its stablemate (above). The grapes are grown mainly at Brancott Estate, on the south side of the Wairau Valley, blended with fruit from Squire Estate, at Rapaura. The 2004 vintage (★★★☆) has lifted, ripely herbaceous aromas and strong passionfruit, melon and capsicum flavours showing good purity, roundness and length.

Vintage	04	03	02	01	00	DRY $20 V+
WR	6	6	7	7	7	
Drink	04-05	P	P	P	P	

Morton Estate Stone Creek Marlborough Sauvignon Blanc ★★★☆

The 2004 vintage (★★★☆) is a tightly structured, mouthfilling wine (14 per cent alcohol) with ripe, gently herbaceous flavours showing very good depth.

Vintage	04	MED/DRY $18 AV
WR	7	
Drink	04-06	

Morton Estate White Label Hawke's Bay Sauvignon Blanc ★★★

Morton's Hawke's Bay wine is more restrained than the classic Marlborough model, but crisp and lively, with satisfying flavour depth. The 2004 vintage (★★★) is typical – fresh and lively, with plenty of tangy, citrusy, appley, limey flavour.

Vintage	04	03	02	01	00	99	DRY $15 V+
WR	6	6	7	6	6	5	
Drink	04-06	04-05	04-05	P	P	P	

Morton Estate White Label
Marlborough Sauvignon Blanc   ★★★

The 2003 vintage (★★★) shows good varietal character, freshness and depth, with ripely herbaceous flavours, crisp and punchy.

Vintage	04	03	02	01	DRY $17 AV
WR	6	6	7	6	
Drink	04-06	04-05	04-05	P	

Morworth Estate Vineyard Selection
Marlborough Sauvignon Blanc   ★★★☆

The 2003 vintage (★★★☆) was harvested at 20.8 brix and mostly handled in stainless steel tanks, but a small portion of the blend was barrel-fermented. Scented, herbaceous aromas, fresh and lifted, lead into a crisp, citrusy, limey wine, vibrantly fruity and lingering.

DRY $20 AV

Mount Nelson Marlborough Sauvignon Blanc   ★★★★★

Mount Nelson is owned by Lodovico Antinori, of the famous Tuscan winemaking family, who with his brother, Piero, is establishing vineyards in Marlborough and Waipara and a winery that will focus exclusively on Sauvignon Blanc. Since the first 1998 vintage, the wine has been based on high-quality batches purchased from other companies, blended by Antinori and Waipara-based winemaker Danny Schuster, and sold mainly in Italy. Fermented to full dryness and matured on its yeast lees for up to 15 months, with no exposure to oak, it is typically a rich yet subtle, tautly structured wine with excellent mouthfeel and slightly flinty, minerally characters adding complexity. The 2002 vintage (★★★★☆) shows good weight, strong, ripe flavours, finely balanced acidity and a long, tight, bone-dry finish. It should mature gracefully. (From the 2004 vintage onwards, this wine will be re-branded as Daniel Schuster Marlborough Selection Sauvignon Blanc.)

Vintage	03	DRY $30 AV
WR	7	
Drink	06-07	

Mount Riley Marlborough Sauvignon Blanc   ★★★☆

The 2004 vintage (★★★★) is one of the best yet – highly scented, very fresh and vibrant, with strong, zesty passionfruit, melon and lime flavours and a long, rich finish. Fine value.

Vintage	04	DRY $17 V+
WR	6	
Drink	04-06	

Mount Riley Seventeen Valley Sauvignon Blanc   ★★★★☆

The 2003 vintage (★★★★) is an excellent example of oak-aged Marlborough Sauvignon Blanc, although overshadowed by the outstanding 2002 (★★★★★). Grown in the Wairau Valley, fermented with indigenous yeasts and matured for six months in seasoned oak casks, it's a dry wine with strong, ripely herbaceous flavours, creamy, nutty complexities and good body and richness.

Vintage	03	DRY $22 V+
WR	6	
Drink	05-08	

Mount Riley Winemakers Selection Sauvignon Blanc   (★★★★)

An easy-drinking Marlborough wine with class, the debut 2004 vintage (★★★★) was hand-picked and made in an off-dry (5 grams/litre of residual sugar) style. Pale lemon/green, it is full-bodied and harmonious, with smooth melon/capsicum flavours showing excellent delicacy and richness.

Vintage	04	MED/DRY $19 V+
WR	6	
Drink	04-06	

Moutere Hills Nelson Sauvignon Blanc ★★☆

Made for easy drinking, the 2003 vintage (★★☆) was mostly handled in tanks, but a third of the blend was fermented in seasoned French oak barrels and the wine harbours a splash of sweetness (8 grams/litre of residual sugar). It's a crisp, medium-bodied wine with gently herbaceous, fresh and lively flavours.

MED/DRY $19 -V

Mud House Marlborough Sauvignon Blanc ★★★☆

Grown in the Wairau Valley, the ripely scented 2003 (★★★☆) has strong tropical-fruit and gently herbaceous flavours, showing good freshness and length. The 2004 vintage (★★★★) is balanced for easy drinking, with smooth, lively melon, lime and capsicum flavours that linger well.

Vintage	03	02	01
WR	6	6	7
Drink	04-05	P	P

DRY $19 AV

Mud House White Swan Reserve
Marlborough Sauvignon Blanc (★★★★★)

Grown at Conders Bend, near Renwick, and in the Awatere Valley, the 2004 vintage (★★★★★) is richly scented, mouthfilling and ripe, with striking intensity of gooseberry and capsicum flavours.

DRY $25 AV

Murdoch James Martinborough Sauvignon Blanc ★★★★

This is Murdoch James' best white wine – so incisive and zingy, it could easily pass for a Marlborough wine. The 2003 vintage (★★★★) offers pungent flavours of passionfruit and limes, very fresh, vibrant and tangy.

DRY $24 -V

Murdoch James River Run Sauvignon Blanc (★★★★)

Made from bought-in Martinborough grapes, not grown organically – unlike the above, estate-grown wine – the debut 2004 vintage (★★★★) is full of character. Richly aromatic, it is fresh, ripe and punchy, with tropical-fruit and capsicum flavours threaded with racy acidity.

DRY $20 AV

Murray Ridge Sauvignon Blanc (★★☆)

Restrained on the nose, the 2003 vintage (★★☆) from Allied Domecq is a blend of Chilean and New Zealand wine. It's a slightly sweet, rounded wine with ripe, tropical-fruit flavours, gentle acidity and a soft finish. An easy-drinking quaffer, it tastes more of Chile than New Zealand, lacking the pungency typical of local Sauvignon Blanc.

MED/DRY $9 V+

Mystery Creek Marlborough Sauvignon Blanc (★★★)

The 2004 vintage (★★★) from this small Waikato winery is fresh, vibrant and crisp, with ripe melon/capsicum flavours, balanced for easy drinking.

DRY $17 AV

Nautilus Marlborough Sauvignon Blanc ★★★★

Typically a richly fragrant wine with mouthfilling body and a surge of ripe, passionfruit and lime-like flavours, enlivened by fresh acidity. Oak plays no part in the wine, but it is briefly matured on its yeast lees. Grown in three company-owned and five growers' vineyards in the Wairau and Awatere valleys, the 2004 vintage (★★★★) shows good weight and freshness. Full-bodied, with an array of ripe-grapefruit, melon, lime and capsicum flavours, it's a crisp, finely balanced wine with a dry, lingering finish.

Vintage	04	03	02	01	00
WR	7	6	7	7	7
Drink	04-05	P	P	P	P

DRY $22 AV

Neudorf Nelson Sauvignon Blanc   ★★★★☆

An immaculate, intensely flavoured wine, aromatic and zippy. The 2004 vintage (★★★★) was grown in two vineyards, at Brightwater and Motueka, and 10 per cent of the blend was matured in old oak casks. It's a weighty, finely balanced wine with crisp melon and green-capsicum flavours, fresh and punchy.

Vintage	04	03	02	01	00	DRY $21 V+
WR	6	5	6	6	6	
Drink	04-07	04-05	P	P	P	

Ngatarawa Glazebrook Hawke's Bay Sauvignon Blanc (★★★☆)

Not oak-matured, the 2003 vintage (★★★☆) offers very good depth of ripe-melon and pineapple flavours, with 7 grams per litre of residual sugar giving a smooth finish. It's still very fresh and lively.

Vintage	03	MED/DRY $22 -V
WR	6	
Drink	04-05	

Ngatarawa Glazebrook Marlborough Sauvignon Blanc   ★★★☆

In the past, this was an export-only label, but the 2003 vintage (★★★☆) was released in New Zealand. Grown in three vineyards in the Wairau and Awatere valleys, it has a punchy, ripe bouquet and fresh, incisive flavours of melons and green capsicums. A splash of sweetness (7 grams/litre of residual sugar) is balanced by appetising acidity, and the wine shows good intensity and vigour.

Vintage	03	MED/DRY $22 -V
WR	6	
Drink	04-05	

Ngatarawa Stables Sauvignon Blanc   ★★★

The 2003 vintage (★★☆) is a medium-dry style, grown in Hawke's Bay (principally) and Marlborough. It's a fresh, crisp wine with lively acidity, unobtrusive sweetness and decent depth of appley, limey flavours.

Vintage	03	02	01	00	99	98	MED/DRY $16 AV
WR	6	6	NM	6	6	5	
Drink	04-05	P	NM	P	P	P	

Nga Waka Martinborough Sauvignon Blanc   ★★★★★

Substantial in body, with concentrated, ripe, bone-dry flavours, this is a cool-climate style of Sauvignon Blanc, highly aromatic and zingy, with the ability to mature gracefully for several years. Bright, light lemon/green, the 2003 vintage (★★★★☆) is full-bodied and fresh, with ripe flavours of pineapple, passionfruit and guava, a hint of honey, lively acidity and a dry but not austere, long finish.

Vintage	03	02	01	DRY $25 AV
WR	6	7	6	
Drink	04+	04-05	04-05	🍇🍇

Nikau Point Hawke's Bay Sauvignon Blanc   ★★★☆

From One Tree Hill Vineyards (owned by Morton Estate), the 2003 vintage (★★★) is a full-bodied wine with good depth of fresh, ripely herbaceous flavours and a smooth (4.5 grams/litre of residual sugar) finish. The bargain-priced 2002 (★★★★) was notably intense and zingy.

Vintage	04	DRY $16 V+
WR	6	
Drink	04-05	

Nikau Point Marlborough Reserve Sauvignon Blanc (★★★☆)

Based on first-crop vines in the Waihopai Valley, this is Morton Estate's 'most minerally, acidic and grassy' Sauvignon Blanc. The debut 2003 vintage (★★★☆) is a distinctly herbaceous wine, very fresh, tangy and lively, with punchy green-apple and capsicum flavours and a hint of passionfruit.

Vintage	04	
WR	6	DRY $19 AV
Drink	04-05	

Nobilo Fall Harvest Sauvignon Blanc – no longer a New Zealand wine (the 2002 vintage was grown in the south of France)

Nobilo Fernleaf Sauvignon Blanc ★★☆

Grown 'predominantly' in Hawke's Bay, the 2004 vintage (★★☆) is a solid quaffer with ripe, slightly honeyed flavours and a smooth, fractionally sweet (5 grams/litre of residual sugar) finish. Priced right.

Vintage	03	
WR	5	MED/DRY $13 AV
Drink	04-05	

Nobilo Grand Reserve Marlborough Sauvignon Blanc (★★★★)

Made from young vines in the Wairau and Awatere valleys, the 2003 vintage (★★★★) has fresh, pure, delicate flavours at the riper end of the spectrum, showing good richness. It has excellent body and persistence, building across the palate to a tight, crisp finish.

Vintage	04	03	
WR	6	6	DRY $28 -V
Drink	04-06	04-05	

Nobilo Icon Marlborough Sauvignon Blanc ★★★★☆

A consistently delightful wine. The 2003 vintage (★★★★☆), lees-aged for four to six weeks, shows lovely fullness and intensity of very ripe, passionfruit/lime aromas and flavours. The 2004 (★★★★☆) is similar – fleshy, with sweet fruit characters and excellent depth of tropical-fruit flavours, rounded and rich.

Vintage	04	03	02	01	
WR	7	7	7	7	DRY $24 AV
Drink	04-07	04-06	04-05	P	

Nobilo Regional Collection Marlborough Sauvignon Blanc ★★★

The 2004 vintage (★★★) is a ripe yet still clearly herbaceous style with nettley aromas and flavours coupled with fresh, vibrant passionfruit/lime characters, balanced for easy drinking.

Vintage	04	03	02	01	00	
WR	6	7	7	7	7	DRY $16 AV
Drink	04-05	04-05	P	P	P	

Northrow Marlborough Sauvignon Blanc ★★★★

From Villa Maria, this wine is aimed at the restaurant trade. The 2004 vintage (★★★★) is a classy wine, vibrant and tangy, with impressive intensity of melon, capsicum and slight passionfruit flavours. Finely balanced and immaculate, mouthfilling and punchy, it shows strong personality.

DRY $20 AV

Odyssey Marlborough Sauvignon Blanc   ★★★★

The 2003 vintage (★★★★) was grown in the Odyssey vineyard in the Brancott Valley and 14 per cent of the blend was matured in seasoned oak casks. Ripe, with a very non-herbaceous bouquet, it is fresh and mouthfilling, with tight, youthful tropical-fruit flavours and a dry, slightly minerally, flinty finish.

DRY $22 -V

Okahu Estate Shipwreck Bay Sauvignon Blanc   ★★☆

Grown at Te Kauwhata, in the Waikato, and fermented in stainless steel tanks, the 2004 vintage (★★☆) is pale and light, with fresh, citrusy, slightly limey, moderately varietal flavours and an off-dry (5 grams/litre of residual sugar) crisp finish.

MED/DRY $17 -V

Old Coach Road Nelson Sauvignon Blanc   ★★☆

Seifried Estate's lower-tier Sauvignon. The 2004 vintage (★★☆) is a solid wine with decent depth of crisp, appley, limey flavours and appetising acidity.

Vintage	04
WR	6
Drink	04-05

DRY $16 -V

Olssen's Central Otago Sauvignon Blanc   ★★☆

The 2003 (★★☆) is a solid wine, but less vibrant and punchy than top vintages. Grown at Bannockburn and handled entirely in tanks, it has restrained, green-apple aromas and flavours, slightly austere, crisp and dry. The 2004 (★★☆) is pale, light and green-edged.

Vintage	03
WR	5
Drink	04-06

DRY $19 -V

Omaka Springs Marlborough Sauvignon Blanc   ★★★☆

This wine, which includes 10 per cent Sémillon, typically has fresh, direct, grassy aromas in a traditional style of Marlborough Sauvignon Blanc with zesty, strongly herbaceous flavours. The 2004 vintage (★★★) is fresh, limey and crisp, with a slightly sweet (5.3 grams/litre of residual sugar), tangy finish.

MED/DRY $16 V+

One Tree Wairarapa Sauvignon Blanc   ★★★☆

Made by Capricorn, a division of Craggy Range, for sale exclusively in restaurants and Foodstuffs supermarkets, the classy, characterful 2003 vintage (★★★★) has a fresh, rich, clearly herbaceous bouquet. It shows good weight and intensity, with tropical-fruit and fresh-cut grass flavours, vibrant, crisp and punchy. The 2004 (★★★) is well-rounded, with herbaceous and passionfruit flavours.

DRY $17 V+

Oyster Bay Marlborough Sauvignon Blanc   ★★★★

Oyster Bay is a Delegat's brand, reserved for Marlborough wines. Handled entirely in stainless steel tanks, the wine is typically zesty and flavour-packed, with strong melon and capsicum characters. It is grown at dozens of vineyards around the Wairau Valley, from the coast to the Oyster Bay vineyard in the west (the furthest inland), and from the Omaka Valley in the south to the banks of the Wairau River at Rapaura. The 2004 vintage (★★★★) has fresh, lifted, gently herbaceous aromas. Coming together swiftly, it's a finely balanced dry wine (3 grams/litre of residual sugar) with ripe-fruit characters and melon/lime flavours showing good delicacy and length.

Vintage	04	03	02	01	00
WR	7	7	7	7	7
Drink	04-05	P	P	P	P

DRY $20 AV

Palliser Estate Martinborough Sauvignon Blanc ★★★★★

This wholly seductive wine is one of the greatest Sauvignon Blancs in the country. A distinctly cool-climate style, it offers an exquisite harmony of crisp acidity, mouthfilling body and fresh, penetrating fruit characters. The grapes give the intensity of flavour – there's no blending with Sémillon, no barrel fermentation, no oak-aging. The 2003 vintage (★★★★★) is weighty, ripe and rounded, with concentrated tropical-fruit flavours showing the extra edge of intensity so typical of the label, and great texture and drinkability.

DRY $20 V+

Pegasus Bay Sauvignon/Sémillon ★★★★☆

At its best, this North Canterbury wine is strikingly lush and concentrated, with loads of personality. The 2003 vintage (★★★★☆) is a blend of Sauvignon Blanc (70 per cent) and Sémillon (30 per cent). Fermented with indigenous yeasts, it was matured on its yeast lees for nine months (the Sémillon component in old oak barriques) and underwent a full, softening malolactic fermentation. It's a full-bodied, tight, dry wine with good intensity of grapefruit, lime and passionfruit flavours, subtle oak and a slightly minerally and flinty, rich finish. Drink 2005+.

Vintage	03	02	01	00	99	98	97
WR	6	7	7	6	7	7	7
Drink	04-12	04-09	04-08	04-07	04-06	04-05	P

DRY $24 AV

Pencarrow Martinborough Sauvignon Blanc ★★★☆

Pencarrow is the second-tier label of Palliser Estate, but this is typically a satisfying wine in its own right. The 2004 vintage (★★★) is fleshy and rounded, with good depth of ripe-melon/lime flavours, but in its infancy was less scented and penetrating than the 2003 (★★★☆).

DRY $18 AV

Peregrine Marlborough Sauvignon Blanc (★★★☆)

Past releases were from Central Otago, but from the frost-afflicted 2004 vintage (★★★☆), Peregrine produced this Marlborough wine. It is full-bodied and punchy, with fresh, ripely herbaceous flavours showing good acid spine and intensity.

DRY $19 AV

Pleasant Valley Yelas Marlborough Sauvignon Blanc (★★★★)

Delicious in its infancy, the skilfully crafted 2004 vintage (★★★★) is finely scented, fresh and lively, with mouthfilling body, excellent delicacy and depth of melon/lime flavours and a rich, off-dry (5 grams/litre of residual sugar) finish.

MED/DRY $19 V+

Ponder Estate Marlborough Sauvignon Blanc (★★★)

Sold by mail-order wine clubs, the 2003 vintage (★★★) is a distinctly cool-climate style with appley, limey aromas and flavours and a crisp, slightly flinty finish.

DRY $20 -V

Ra Nui Marlborough Wairau Valley Sauvignon Blanc ★★★☆

The 2004 vintage (★★★☆) was hand-picked in the Roughan-Lee vineyard, near Renwick, whole-bunch pressed, tank-fermented and lees-aged for two months. It's a full-bodied wine with very good depth of fresh melon, lime and capsicum flavours and a lingering, crisp finish.

DRY $20 AV

Richmond Plains Nelson Sauvignon Blanc   ★★★

The Holmes Brothers vineyard at Richmond in Nelson is one of the few in New Zealand to enjoy full Bio-Gro (certified organic) status. The 2004 vintage (★★★) is lively and nettley, with plenty of freshly herbaceous flavour and a smooth finish.

DRY $19 AV

Rippon Sauvignon Blanc   ★★★

This estate-grown, partly barrel-fermented wine from Lake Wanaka, in Central Otago, is typically a grassy style with some complexity, crisp, herbaceous flavours gently seasoned with oak and a freshly acidic finish.

DRY $22 -V

Riverby Estate Marlborough Sauvignon Blanc   ★★★

A single-vineyard wine, grown in Jacksons Road in the heart of the Wairau Valley, the 2003 vintage (★★★) is a crisp, citrusy, gently herbaceous wine. The 2004 (★★☆) is full-bodied, with decent depth of fresh, lively melon/lime flavours.

DRY $18 -V

Riverside Dartmoor Sauvignon Blanc   ★★☆

Grown in the Dartmoor Valley, this is typically a solid Hawke's Bay wine with moderate depth of smooth, citrusy, green-edged flavours in an easy-drinking style. The 2004 (★★★) is a top vintage, with plenty of fresh and lively, ripely herbaceous flavour and drink-young appeal.

Vintage	04	03	02
WR	6	6	6
Drink	04-05	P	P

DRY $15 AV

Rockburn Central Otago Sauvignon Blanc   (★★★☆)

Showing good depth, the 2003 vintage (★★★☆) is a single-vineyard wine from Gibbston, ultra low-cropped (2.5 tonnes/hectare) and fermented almost to full dryness (3 grams/litre of residual sugar). It is fresh and vibrant, with racy melon and green-capsicum flavours.

DRY $25 -V

Ruben Hall Sauvignon Blanc   ★★☆

Ruben Hall is a Villa Maria brand. The 2003 vintage (★★☆) on the market in late 2004 is a fractionally sweet style (5 grams/litre of residual sugar) with crisp, lemony, grassy, slightly honeyed flavours.

MED/DRY $10 V+

Rymer's Change Hawke's Bay Sauvignon Blanc   (★★★)

From Te Mata Estate, the 2004 vintage (★★★) is a dry, tank-fermented wine, fresh and full-bodied, with melon/apple flavours, ripe and rounded, offering very easy drinking.

Vintage	04
WR	7
Drink	04-05

DRY $15 V+

St Helena Marlborough Sauvignon Blanc   ★★☆

Launched from the 1999 vintage, this has typically been a reasonably flavoursome wine with firm acidity and clearly herbaceous flavours, lacking the fragrance and richness to rate more highly.

Vintage	04
WR	5
Drink	04-05

MED/DRY $16 -V

St Jerome Te Kauwhata Sauvignon Blanc (★★)

The 2003 vintage (★★) is a solid but plain wine with appley aromas and moderate depth of green-edged flavours.

`DRY $17 -V`

Sacred Hill Barrel Fermented Sauvignon Blanc ★★★☆

At its best, this Hawke's Bay wine is deliciously rich, with strong, ripe, non-herbaceous fruit flavours and complexity from partial fermentation and lees-aging in French oak barriques. The ripely scented 2002 vintage (★★★★) is full-bodied, with finely balanced acidity, a twist of oak and strong melon/lime flavours.

Vintage	03	02	01	00
WR	6	7	NM	7
Drink	04-05	04-05	NM	P

`DRY $20 AV`

Sacred Hill Marlborough Vineyards Sauvignon Blanc ★★★★

The very harmonious 2004 vintage (★★★★☆) offers intense melon, capsicum and lime flavours, with 6 grams per litre of residual sugar adding richness rather than obvious sweetness, due to its lively acidity. Mouthfilling, fresh and vibrant, it's a highly scented, freshly herbaceous and punchy wine.

`MED/DRY $20 AV`

Sacred Hill Sauvage ★★★★☆

One of the country's most expensive and complex Sauvignon Blancs. The 2002 vintage (★★★★★) is an absorbing example of the widely underrated, barrel-matured Hawke's Bay Sauvignon Blanc style. Fermented with indigenous ('wild') yeasts in one-year-old French oak barriques, followed by a year's lees-aging in wood, it has mouthfilling body (14 per cent alcohol). Complex and creamy, with rich grapefruit and guava characters, mealy, nutty notes adding complexity and layers of flavour, it offers outstanding drinking from 2004 onwards.

Vintage	02
WR	7
Drink	04-08

`DRY $30 -V`

Sacred Hill Whitecliff Sauvignon Blanc ★★★☆

This is the junior partner in the winery's numerous Sauvignons, but it offers great value. The vibrantly fruity 2004 vintage (★★★☆), a blend of Marlborough and Hawke's Bay grapes, is a fresh, limey wine, green-edged and zingy, with good length.

`DRY 17 V+`

Saint Clair Marlborough Sauvignon Blanc ★★★★☆

This label has shown great form lately. The richly scented 2004 vintage (★★★★☆) was blended from grapes grown in the Wairau and Awatere valleys. It shows lovely weight, richness and roundness, with gooseberry, lime and passionfruit flavours and fresh acidity in a lush, instantly appealing style that builds to a rich, dry (3.9 grams/litre of residual sugar) finish.

Vintage	04
WR	7
Drink	04-05

`DRY $20 V+`

Saint Clair Vicar's Choice Marlborough Sauvignon Blanc ★★★☆

The 2003 (★★★★) is a fresh, aromatic wine with good balance and depth of lively, green-capsicum flavours, pure and punchy. The 2004 (★★★☆) is vibrant and smooth, with fresh acidity and strong melon/capsicum flavours. Good value.

Vintage	04	03
WR	6	6
Drink	04-05	04-05

`DRY $17 V+`

Saint Clair Wairau Reserve Sauvignon Blanc ★★★★★

The 2001 and subsequent vintages have generally been exceptional, in a deliciously ripe and concentrated style, lush and rounded, that has enjoyed glowing success on the show circuit. Made from two parcels of grapes from the lower Wairau Valley, the 2004 (★★★★☆) is richly scented, weighty and concentrated, with citrus, passionfruit and lime flavours, fresh, underlying acidity and a long finish. Lush, vibrant and fruit-packed, it's a very user-friendly style, bound to unfold well during 2005.

Vintage	04	03	02
WR	7	7	7
Drink	04-06	P	P

DRY $26 AV

Saints Marlborough Sauvignon Blanc ★★★★☆

The 2004 vintage (★★★★☆) was made from Allied Domecq's young vines in the Awatere Valley. It's a subliminally oaked style – 12 per cent of the blend was matured in 10,000-litre French cuves and 225-litre French oak barriques, and a very small proportion was barrel-fermented. Fresh and incisive, with a lovely spread of passionfruit, grapefruit and capsicum flavours, a touch of complexity and crisp, lingering finish, it's a great buy (like the earlier vintages).

Vintage	04	03	02
WR	5	5	7
Drink	04-06	04-05	P

DRY $17 V+

Sanctuary Marlborough Sauvignon Blanc ★★★☆

Grove Mill's lower-tier label consistently offers good value. The 2004 vintage (★★★☆) is an instantly appealing, finely balanced wine, full-flavoured and rounded, with strong gooseberry/lime flavours, fresh acids and a rich finish.

Vintage	03	02	01	00
WR	7	6	6	6
Drink	04	P	P	P

DRY $17 V+

Seifried Nelson Sauvignon Blanc ★★★☆

Pale, with fresh, punchy aromas, the 2004 vintage (★★★☆) is a medium-bodied wine with melon and green-capsicum flavours, crisp and lively, with good depth.

Vintage	04	03	02	01	00
WR	6	6	7	6	5
Drink	04-05	P	P	P	P

DRY $18 AV

Seifried Winemakers Collection Sauvignon Blanc ★★★☆

The 2003 vintage (★★★☆) was made from the 'very best fruit' and matured on its yeast lees before bottling. It's a strongly flavoured, herbaceous Nelson wine with some riper, melon and pineapple characters in a crisp, lively, cool-climate style. The 2004 (★★★★) is very fresh and pure, with substantial body, lively acidity and vibrant melon and lime flavours, ripe and smooth.

DRY $22 -V

Selaks Drylands Sauvignon Blanc – see Drylands Sauvignon Blanc

Selaks Founders Reserve Oak Aged Sauvignon Blanc ★★★★

One of the flagship Sauvignons from the Nobilo Group (which owns Selaks). The 2003 vintage (★★★★), grown in the Awatere and Wairau valleys, finished its ferment in French oak barriques and was wood-aged for three months, with weekly lees-stirring. It's a weighty, well-rounded wine with ripe tropical-fruit flavours seasoned with toasty oak and an attractively creamy texture.

Vintage	03	02	01
WR	6	6	6
Drink	04-06	04-05	P

DRY $27 -V

Selaks Premium Selection Marlborough Sauvignon Blanc ★★★☆

This is Selaks' lower-tier Sauvignon Blanc, fermented in stainless steel tanks and bottled early. Designed as an 'intensely herbaceous' style, in contrast to its riper, rounder stablemate under the Nobilo brand, from one vintage to the next, it offers top value. Full of character and drink-young appeal, the 2004 vintage (★★★☆) is fresh and lively, with melon and green-capsicum flavours showing good vigour and depth.

Vintage	04	03	02	01	00	
WR	6	7	7	7	6	MED/DRY $15 V+
Drink	04-05	04-05	P	P	P	

Seresin Marama Sauvignon Blanc ★★★★☆

The 2002 vintage (★★★★☆) was grown on the relatively cool upper terraces in the estate vineyard at Renwick, in Marlborough, whole-bunch pressed, fermented with indigenous yeasts in seasoned French oak barrels and wood-matured for 14 months. Light yellow, with a nettley, nutty bouquet, it's a clearly herbaceous wine, rich, dry and complex, with excellent intensity and a slightly minerally, tight, long finish.

DRY $29 -V

Seresin Marlborough Sauvignon Blanc ★★★★★

One of the region's most sophisticated, subtle and satisfying Sauvignons. It's a complex style; the 2003 vintage (★★★★★), fermented with indigenous and cultured yeasts, includes a small proportion of Sémillon, and 10 per cent of the blend was fermented and lees-aged in seasoned French oak casks. Slightly funky on the nose (reflecting the indigenous yeasts), it is crisp and incisive, nutty and dry, with flinty melon/capsicum flavours showing excellent intensity and a finely textured, dry, long finish. A Sauvignon Blanc to ponder over, it offers loads of individuality and interest.

DRY $23 V+

Shepherds Ridge Marlborough Sauvignon Blanc (★★★★)

From Wither Hills, the 2003 vintage (★★★★) is a well-structured wine with strong, pure melon/lime flavours, a flinty element that flows through the palate and a dry, sustained finish. (Compared to its stablemate, Wither Hills Sauvignon Blanc, it's a slightly drier, more austere style, but not necessarily a lesser wine, as its identical price suggests.)

Vintage	04	
WR	7	DRY $20 AV
Drink	04-06	

Shingle Peak Marlborough Sauvignon Blanc ★★★☆

The Shingle Peak label is reserved by Matua Valley for its Marlborough wines. For the excellent 2004 vintage (★★★★), 'the majority' of the grapes were grown in the company's vineyard on the north bank of the Wairau River. Showing good weight (13.5 per cent alcohol), depth and roundness, it's an instantly attractive, dry wine (3.6 grams/litre of residual sugar), with an array of tropical-fruit and herbaceous flavours, fresh, vibrant and strong.

Vintage	04	03	02	01	00	
WR	6	7	6	6	5	DRY $17 V+
Drink	04-06	04-05	P	P	P	

Sileni Cellar Selection Marlborough Sauvignon Blanc (★★★★)

Delicious from the start, the 2004 vintage (★★★★) is a freshly herbaceous, generous wine with rich, gooseberryish flavours, crisp, punchy and lively.

DRY $20 AV

Springvale Sauvignon Blanc   (★★☆)

Grown at Alexandra, in Central Otago, the 2003 vintage (★★☆) is an easy-drinking, medium-bodied wine with pleasant melon/lime flavours showing moderate varietal character.

`DRY $20 -V`

Spy Valley Marlborough Sauvignon Blanc   ★★★★

Estate-grown in the Waihopai Valley, on the south side of the Wairau Valley, the 2004 vintage (★★★★) was harvested at 21 to 25 brix and lees-aged in tanks before bottling. Tangy and ripely herbaceous, it is fresh and full-bodied, with generous gooseberry, melon and capsicum flavours, good acid spine and a smooth (5 grams/litre of residual sugar) finish.

Vintage	04	03
WR	6	6
Drink	04-06	04-05

`MED/DRY $17 V+`

Squawking Magpie Reserve
Marlborough Sauvignon Blanc   ★★★☆

The 2004 vintage (★★★) from this Hawke's Bay-based winery is drinking well now. Fleshy and ripe, with tropical-fruit flavours, it offers good depth, with fresh acid enlivening the finish.

`DRY $20 AV`

Staete Landt Marlborough Sauvignon Blanc   ★★★★☆

Ripely scented, rich and zingy, this single-vineyard wine is grown at Rapaura and mostly handled in tanks, with some fermentation in seasoned (at least six-year-old) French oak casks. The 2004 vintage (★★★★) is fleshy and concentrated with crisp, tropical-fruit flavours and scents.

Vintage	03
WR	7
Drink	04-05

`DRY $23 AV`

Stafford Lane Estate Nelson Sauvignon Blanc   (★★★)

Based on 14-year-old vines at Appleby, on the Waimea Plains, the 2003 vintage (★★★) has fresh, grassy aromas leading into a flinty, herbaceous wine, punchy and racy. The 2004 was tasted soon after bottling, while still clearly 'bottle-shocked', and so is not rated. Grown in three vineyards on the plains, it is citrusy, grassy and flinty.

Vintage	04
WR	6
Drink	04-07

`DRY $19 -V`

Stonecroft Sauvignon Blanc   ★★★☆

This Hawke's Bay winery uprooted its own Sauvignon Blanc vines after the 2001 vintage, but due to the tiny size of its total 2003 crop, purchased grapes from a vineyard near the coast. A 'oncer', the 2003 vintage (★★★☆) is a fully dry wine with fresh, strong, sweet fruit flavours showing good richness.

`DRY $19 AV`

Stoneleigh Marlborough Sauvignon Blanc   ★★★★

Once an internationally acclaimed Corbans wine, now part of the Allied Domecq stable, this consistently impressive wine is grown in the shingly Rapaura district of the Wairau Valley, which produces a relatively ripe style, yet retains good acidity and vigour. Harvested at 23–24 brix, the excellent 2004 vintage (★★★★☆) is scented, weighty, ripe and smooth (4 grams/litre of residual sugar), with refined melon, lime and capsicum flavours showing good delicacy through the palate and great drinkability.

Vintage	04	03	02	01	00
WR	6	6	6	7	6
Drink	04-06	04-05	P	P	P

`DRY $18 V+`

Stoneleigh Vineyards Rapaura Series Marlborough Sauvignon Blanc ★★★★☆

A richly flavoured wine, seasoning ripe, tropical-fruit flavours with a touch of oak. Most of the 2003 vintage (★★★★☆) was handled in tanks, but 7 per cent was fermented and lees-aged for three months in new and one-year-old French oak barriques. Still youthful, it's a sophisticated wine, finely scented, with rich, concentrated, ripe-fruit flavours in a gently herbaceous style with racy acidity and lovely intensity. Drink now to 2005.

Vintage	03	02	01	00
WR	6	6	7	6
Drink	04-06	04-05	P	P

DRY $23 AV

Tasman Bay Vintage Special Selection Sauvignon Blanc (★★★)

Past vintages have produced separate Marlborough and Nelson wines, but the 2004 (★★★), released in June, is a blend of the two regions. Partly French oak-aged, it's a full-bodied wine with a freshly herbaceous, nettley bouquet and smooth palate offering crisp, passionfruit and lime flavours, showing good but not great depth.

Vintage	04
WR	5
Drink	04-07

DRY $18 -V

Te Awa Sauvignon Blanc ★★★☆

Up to and including the 2002 vintage labelled as Frontier Sauvignon Blanc, this is a worthy attempt at a rich, complex style of Hawke's Bay Sauvignon. The powerful 2003 (★★★★) was 80 per cent fermented and lees-aged for seven months in French oak casks (25 per cent new); 20 per cent was handled in tanks. Youthful, tight and dry, it's a robust wine (14 per cent alcohol) with generous, ripe, tropical-fruit flavours strongly seasoned with oak, in a very non-herbaceous style with good mouthfeel and texture. Drink 2006.

Vintage	03	02	01	00	99
WR	6	7	6	6	6
Drink	04-07	04-07	04-06	04-05	04-05

DRY $22 -V

Te Kairanga Martinborough Sauvignon Blanc ★★★

Up to and including the 2001 vintage, this was a slightly sweet, oak-aged style. The 2002 was handled solely in tanks and fermented almost to dryness; the 2003 was 60 per cent barrel-fermented. The 2004 (★★★) is a vibrant, fruit-driven style with searching acidity, fresh gooseberry and green-apple flavours and a dry (3.5 grams/litre of residual sugar), tangy finish.

Vintage	03	02	01
WR	6	5	5
Drink	04-05	P	P

DRY $22 -V

Te Mania Nelson Sauvignon Blanc ★★★☆

Typically a fresh, crisply herbaceous style of Sauvignon from the Waimea Plains. The 2004 vintage (★★★★) is an intensely varietal wine with punchy, ripe-melon/capsicum flavours and a crisp, long finish.

Vintage	04	03	02	01	00
WR	6	6	6	6	6
Drink	04-06	04-05	04-05	P	P

DRY $17 V+

Te Mata Estate Cape Crest Sauvignon Blanc ★★★★☆

This Hawke's Bay label is impressive for its ripely herbal, complex, sustained flavours. The grapes are grown in the company's Woodthorpe Terraces vineyard in the Dartmoor Valley and at Havelock North, with fermentation and maturation in French oak barriques (30 per cent new in 2003) adding depth and clearly differentiating the wine from its stablemate under the Woodthorpe label. The notably concentrated 2003 vintage (★★★★★) has rich, sweet fruit flavours, excellent body and mouthfeel. A multi-faceted wine with tropical-fruit characters, oak and lees-aging richness, a hint of butterscotch and layers of flavour, it should be at its best around 2006.

Vintage	03	02	01	00	99	98	97	96
WR	7	7	7	7	7	7	7	6
Drink	05-07	04-06	04-06	04-05	P	P	P	P

DRY $25 AV

Te Mata Estate Woodthorpe Sauvignon Blanc   ★★★☆

Grown at the company's inland Woodthorpe Terraces vineyard, in the Dartmoor Valley of Hawke's Bay, the 2004 vintage (★★★☆) was handled entirely in tanks and fermented to dryness. Ripely scented, with good body and depth of passionfruit/lime flavours, it's an appetisingly crisp wine, very fresh and lively.

Vintage	04	03
WR	7	7
Drink	04-06	P

DRY $19 AV

Terrace Heights Estate Marlborough Sauvignon Blanc   ★★★☆

Scented and lively, the 2004 vintage (★★★☆) is fresh and smooth, with passionfruit, lime and melon flavours and a sliver of sweetness (5 grams/litre of residual sugar) adding an easy-drinking appeal.

Vintage	04
WR	6
Drink	04-05

MED/DRY $17 AV

Terrace Road Marlborough Sauvignon Blanc   ★★★★

The latest vintages of Cellier Le Brun's wine are the best. The 2003 vintage (★★★★) is impressive – ripely scented, weighty and fleshy, with excellent depth of pineapple, passionfruit and lime flavours, fresh, delicate and rounded. Fine value.

DRY $17 V+

Te Whare Ra Marlborough Sauvignon Blanc   (★★★★☆)

The debut 2004 vintage (★★★★☆) is very classy. Grown in the Flowerday vineyard in the Awatere Valley, it shows lovely purity of melon/capsicum flavours. Freshly aromatic and crisply herbaceous, it is weighty and finely balanced, with racy, slightly minerally acidity and excellent intensity.

DRY $20 V+

Thornbury Marlborough Sauvignon Blanc   ★★★★

Made by Steve Bird, for many years winemaker at Morton Estate, this wine has enjoyed high critical acclaim in the United States. Grown mostly in the shingly, relatively early-ripening Rapaura district of the Wairau Valley, it places its accent on palate weight and texture, rather than pungent herbaceous characters. Top vintages are weighty and concentrated, with deep tropical-fruit flavours and a deliciously well-rounded finish. The 2004 (★★★★) is mouthfilling and dry, with ripe-fruit characters, crisp acidity, a hint of 'sweaty armpit' and good concentration.

Vintage	04	03	02
WR	6	6	5
Drink	05-07	04-05	P

DRY $18 V+

Timara Sauvignon Blanc   (★★☆)

The fresh, crisp 2003 vintage (★★☆) from Allied Domecq is a blend of Chilean and New Zealand wines. A restrained style of Sauvignon Blanc, citrusy and appley, rather than strongly herbaceous, it tastes more of Chile than New Zealand.

DRY $11 AV

Tohu Marlborough Sauvignon Blanc ★★★★

Tohu is a joint venture between three Maori land incorporations. This is a consistently good wine and the 2004 vintage (★★★★☆) is the best yet. Made in huge volumes (52,200 cases), it's an immaculate wine, very rich and vibrant, with melon, grapefruit and lime flavours, punchy and racy. Delicious from the start, it's a great buy.

DRY $17 V+

Torlesse Waipara Sauvignon Blanc ★★★

Woven with fresh acidity, the 2004 vintage (★★★) was grown at two sites in Waipara. Fresh, grassy, nettley aromas lead into a strongly varietal, distinctly cool-climate North Canterbury wine with green-capsicum flavours, good acid spine and length.

Vintage	02
WR	7
Drink	04

DRY $18 AV

Trinity Hill Shepherd's Croft Sauvignon Blanc ★★★

Grown in the Shepherd's Croft vineyard in the Ngatarawa district of Hawke's Bay, the 2004 vintage (★★★) is a fresh, smooth wine with lively, ripe, tropical-fruit and gently herbaceous flavours.

DRY $20 -V

Tuatara Bay Marlborough Sauvignon Blanc ★★☆

Made by Saint Clair Estate, in its infancy the 2004 vintage (★★☆) showed moderate depth of crisp, limey, green-edged flavours.

Vintage	04
WR	5
Drink	04-05

DRY $17 -V

Twin Islands Marlborough Sauvignon Blanc ★★★

Negociants' wine is finely balanced for easy drinking and priced right. The 2004 vintage (★★★) is a freshly herbaceous wine with melon, apple and capsicum flavours, crisp and lively.

Vintage	04	03	02	01	00
WR	7	6	6	6	6
Drink	04-05	P	P	P	P

DRY $17 AV

Vavasour Awatere Valley Marlborough Sauvignon Blanc ★★★★☆

A consistently classy, high-impact wine, with flinty acidity underpinning its penetrating tropical-fruit and green-edged flavours, which always show impressive delicacy and length. Sourced entirely from Awatere Valley vineyards, the 2004 vintage (★★★★☆) is weighty and penetratingly flavoured, with good texture, slightly minerally, flinty characters and a lasting finish.

Vintage	04	03	02
WR	7	6	7
Drink	04-05	04-05	P

DRY $25 AV

Vavasour Single Vineyard
Awatere Valley Sauvignon Blanc   ★★★★★

The outstanding 2002 vintage (★★★★★) is the first time Vavasour's premier Sauvignon Blanc has
appeared since 1999. Grown at the Vavasour vineyard in the Awatere Valley, it was hand-picked and
fermented and matured for nine months, with weekly lees-stirring, in seasoned French oak barriques. The
bouquet is complex, mingling ripe-fruit aromas with subtle oak; the palate is mouthfilling and rounded,
with sweet fruit delights, ripe tropical-fruit flavours, lovely weight and texture and a fully dry, rounded
finish.

`DRY $30 AV`

Vic Williams Selection Marlborough Sauvignon Blanc   ★★★☆

Sold by mail-order wine clubs, the 2003 vintage (★★★★) is full-bodied and finely balanced, with tropical-
fruit and herbaceous flavours, fresh acidity and excellent depth.

`DRY $22 -V`

Vidal Estate Marlborough Sauvignon Blanc   (NR)

Tasted before bottling (and so not rated), the 2004 vintage was grown in the Awatere and Wairau valleys
and lees-aged. It looked promising – punchy and ripe, with crisp melon/capsicum flavours showing good
intensity.

Vintage	04	03
WR	6	6
Drink	04-06	04-05

`DRY $18 V?`

Villa Maria Cellar Selection
Marlborough Sauvignon Blanc   ★★★★☆

An intense, fruit-driven style, this is typically of a very high standard. Grown in the Wairau and Awatere
valleys, the 2003 vintage (★★★★☆) shows good body and punch, with lovely depth of melon,
passionfruit and lime flavours building across the palate to a rich, zingy finish. The 2004 (tasted before
bottling, and so not rated), was almost entirely handled in tanks, but 1.5 per cent of the blend was French
oak-aged. It's a ripe, tropical fruit-flavoured, gently herbaceous wine cut with fresh acidity.

Vintage	04	03	02	01	00
WR	6	7	6	6	7
Drink	04-06	04-05	P	P	P

`DRY $20 V+`

Villa Maria Private Bin Marlborough Sauvignon Blanc   ★★★★

Villa Maria's third-tier label offers impressive quality and top value. The excellent 2004 vintage (★★★★)
was grown in the Wairau and Awatere valleys. Richly scented, it's a full-bodied, impressively concentrated
wine with tropical-fruit and herbaceous characters and a sliver of sweetness (4.5 grams/litre of residual
sugar) finely balanced by racy acids. Showing excellent weight and harmony, it's a delicious wine in its
youth and a great buy.

Vintage	04	03	02	01	00
WR	6	6	6	6	7
Drink	04-05	P	P	P	P

`DRY $16 V+`

Villa Maria Reserve Clifford Bay Sauvignon Blanc ★★★★★

Grown in the Awatere Valley (although the label refers only to 'Clifford Bay', into which the Awatere River empties), this is an exceptional Marlborough wine. Most of the fruit comes from Seddon Vineyards, a large block of vines in the Awatere Valley not owned but managed by Villa Maria. Handled entirely in stainless steel tanks, it typically exhibits the leap-out-of-the-glass fragrance and zingy, explosive flavour of Marlborough Sauvignon Blanc at its inimitable best. The 2003 vintage (★★★★★) is intense, limey and zingy, with the flinty character typical of the Awatere Valley and lovely concentration and freshness. Tasted prior to bottling (and so not rated), the 2004 looked slightly riper, less pungently herbaceous than usual, with good weight and intense, dry melon/capsicum flavours, showing lovely delicacy and purity.

Vintage	04	03	02	01	00	99	98	DRY $25 AV
WR	6	7	6	7	6	6	5	
Drink	05-06	04-05	P	P	P	P	P	

Villa Maria Reserve Wairau Valley Sauvignon Blanc ★★★★★

An authoritative wine with tremendous depth and drive, it is typically ripe and zingy, with marvellous weight and length of flavour, and tends to be fuller in body, less herbaceous and rounder than its Clifford Bay stablemate (above). In the past, a small proportion of the final blend (up to 10 per cent) was oak-aged, but the 2001 to 2003 vintages were handled entirely in tanks. The 2004 was handled in tanks (97 per cent) and French oak barriques (3 per cent). Tasted prior to bottling (and so not rated), it looked excellent – fleshy and rich, with impressively concentrated, crisp and lively melon/capsicum flavours, tightly structured, fully dry and lasting.

Vintage	04	03	02	01	00	99	98	DRY $25 AV
WR	6	7	7	7	6	5	5	
Drink	05-06	04-05	P	P	P	P	P	

Villa Maria Single Vineyard Jackson Sauvignon Blanc (NR)

The 2004 vintage (tasted prior to bottling, and so not rated) was grown in the heart of the Wairau Valley, near Cloudy Bay, and 10 per cent of the blend was fermented in French oak barriques. It's a powerful, delicious wine with fresh acidity, slightly nettley aromas and penetrating tropical-fruit and herbaceous flavours.

DRY $25 V?

Villa Maria Single Vineyard Seddon Sauvignon Blanc (★★★★☆)

Showing an extra edge of intensity, the 2003 vintage (★★★★☆) was grown high on the south bank of the Awatere River and lees-aged before bottling. It's a rich, weighty Marlborough wine with fresh, ripe-melon/capsicum flavours, vibrant and tangy.

DRY $25 AV

Villa Maria Single Vineyard Taylors Pass Sauvignon Blanc (★★★★★)

The rich, pungently varietal 2003 vintage (★★★★★) was grown in Marlborough's Awatere Valley, only half a kilometre from the Seddon Vineyard wine (above). A powerful (14.5 per cent alcohol), bone-dry wine, it is tangy and herbaceous, with an explosion of melon and fresh-cut grass flavours, lively and long. The 2004 (tasted prior to bottling, and so not rated) is again robust (14.5 per cent alcohol), with ripe, limey, slightly minerally, lasting flavours.

Vintage	04	DRY $25 AV
WR	6	
Drink	04-06	

Voss Estate Sauvignon Blanc   ★★★☆

The 2004 vintage (★★★☆) is a crisp, minerally, ripely herbaceous Martinborough wine with fresh, vibrant fruit characters, very good flavour depth and appetising acidity.

DRY $18 AV

Waimea Estates Bolitho Reserve Sauvignon Blanc   ★★★★

The 2003 vintage (★★★★) was harvested in the company's Annabrook Vineyard in Nelson at 23 brix (compared to 21.7 brix for the standard wine) and mostly fermented and lees-aged in tanks, but 20 per cent of the blend was fermented with indigenous yeasts in seasoned French oak casks. It's a fleshy, full-bodied wine (14 per cent alcohol) with sweet fruit delights, ripe, gently oaked, tropical-fruit flavours and slightly minerally touches adding complexity.

Vintage	03	02	01
WR	6	7	5
Drink	04-06	04-05	P

DRY $22 AV

Waimea Estates Nelson Sauvignon Blanc   ★★★

The 2003 vintage (★★☆) lacked real richness and charm. Harvested at 21.8 brix, the 2004 (★★★) is a fresher, more appealing wine with melon, lime and green-capsicum flavours, punchy and crisp.

Vintage	03	02	01	00
WR	5	6	6	5
Drink	04-05	P	P	P

DRY $18 AV

Waipara Hills Marlborough Sauvignon Blanc   ★★★★

Typically a herbaceous style with strong, nettley flavours, a hint of passionfruit and crisp acidity. The 2004 vintage (★★★☆), grown in the Elley and Wickham vineyards, is fresh and zingy, with punchy melon and fresh-cut grass flavours. In its infancy, it looked slightly less intense than the beautifully rich and zingy 2003 (★★★★☆).

DRY $19 V+

Waipara Springs Sauvignon Blanc   ★★★★

This North Canterbury wine is a very lightly oaked style of consistently high quality and good value. The 2003 (★★★★) is ripely scented, fresh, pure and zingy, with good intensity of melon, passionfruit and lime flavours and a rich, long finish. The 2004 vintage (★★★★) was mostly handled in tanks, but 3 per cent was barrel-fermented. It shows good weight and mouthfeel, with ripely herbaceous flavours, fresh and sustained.

Vintage	04	03	02	01	00
WR	7	6	7	7	6
Drink	04-06	04-05	04-05	P	P

DRY $19 V+

Waipara West Sauvignon Blanc   ★★★★

An intensely flavoured North Canterbury wine with racy acidity. The 2004 vintage (★★★★) is a dry style, fresh and full-bodied, with ripely herbaceous, slightly flinty flavours, minerally, finely balanced and long. It's a distinctly cool-climate style, full of personality.

Vintage	04
WR	6
Drink	04-06

DRY $21 AV

Waipipi Wairarapa Sauvignon Blanc   (★★☆)

The 2004 vintage (★★☆) was grown at Opaki, north of Masterton. It's a pale, smooth, appley wine with good body, but no real flavour delights.

DRY $19 -V

Wairau River Marlborough Sauvignon Blanc ★★★☆

Phil and Chris Rose produce a substantial style of Sauvignon Blanc, at its best offering a tantalising interplay of rich, lush, tropical-fruit flavours and pungent, zingy, herbaceous characters. The grapes are grown in the Roses' Giffords Road vineyard alongside the Wairau River, on the north side of the valley. The 2003 vintage (★★★) is a citrusy, green-edged wine, mouthfilling, crisp and dry. The 2004 (★★★☆) is tightly structured and slightly minerally, with gooseberry and lime flavours, fresh, crisp and punchy.

Vintage	03	02	01	00	99	98	DRY $20 AV
WR	7	7	7	7	7	7	
Drink	04-06	04-05	P	P	P	P	

Wairau River Reserve Sauvignon Blanc ★★★★

The Marlborough winery's top wine is based on low-cropping vines and fermented and matured for nine months in seasoned French oak casks. The 2002 vintage (★★★★) is a tight and immaculate wine with good weight, fresh, strong gooseberry and capsicum flavours, a hint of nutty oak adding complexity and a well-rounded finish.

Vintage	03	02	01	DRY $25 -V
WR	7	7	7	
Drink	04-07	04-06	04-05	

Walnut Ridge Marlborough Sauvignon Blanc (★★★)

A second label of the Ata Rangi winery, in Martinborough. The 2004 vintage (★★★), blended from Marlborough and Martinborough grapes, is a full-bodied, rounded wine, not highly aromatic, but offering good weight and depth of ripe, smooth flavour.

Vintage	04	DRY $20 -V
WR	6	
Drink	04-05	

Warrior Cove Marlborough Sauvignon Blanc ★★★

Sold by mail-order wine clubs, the 2003 vintage (★★★) is a crisp, appley, limey wine, not highly concentrated but fresh and finely balanced.

DRY $18 AV

West Brook Marlborough Sauvignon Blanc ★★★★

The 2004 vintage (★★★★☆) looked very impressive in its infancy, with scented, ripe-fruit aromas, including a touch of 'sweaty armpit'. It's a fleshy, full-bodied wine with pure, intense, tropical-fruit flavours and a lasting finish.

DRY $19 V+

Whitehaven Marlborough Sauvignon Blanc ★★★★★

Whitehaven adopts a low profile, but this is a consistently impressive wine. Grown in the Wairau and Awatere valleys, the 2003 vintage (★★★★☆) is excellent, with fresh, strong melon/lime flavours, delicate, smooth and long. The 2004 (★★★★) also shows good freshness and harmony, with strong, ripe-melon/capsicum flavours and a dry, well-rounded finish.

DRY $19 V+

White Rock Wairarapa Sauvignon Blanc   ★★☆

From Capricorn Wine Estates, a division of Craggy Range, the 2003 vintage (★★★) is an easy-drinking, fresh, citrusy and limey wine with clear varietal character, decent depth and a slightly sweet, crisp finish. The 2004 (★★☆) is limey, appley, slightly sweet and smooth, with moderate depth.

MED/DRY $17 ·V

Wishart Estate Sauvignon Blanc   ★★★

Grown on the coast at Bay View and harvested at 22.8 brix, the 2003 vintage (★★★) is an enjoyable example of the Hawke's Bay regional style. Lees-aged in tanks for two months, it is fresh and vibrant, with ripe-passionfruit characters, crisp acidity and a smooth, off-dry (6 grams/litre of residual sugar) finish. The 2004 (★★★) is ripe and rounded, with good depth and a splash of sweetness to smooth the finish.

MED/DRY $19 ·V

Wither Hills Marlborough Sauvignon Blanc   ★★★★★

This is typically a striking wine, with a voluminous fragrance, mouthfilling body and very rich, sweet-tasting fruit flavours. Winemaker Brent Marris says he's not after 'a high-acid, steely wine; I want a fleshy, ripe, weighty style with charm and elegance'. There's a subliminal oak influence (3 per cent of the 2004 vintage was barrel-fermented), but maturation on yeast lees (and regular lees-stirring) play a much more significant role in the wine's style, 'adding to the layers of complexity, without interfering with the fruit'. Harvested at 22 to 24 brix, the 2004 vintage (★★★★☆) has a richly scented bouquet and a lovely array of fruit flavours. A full-bodied, harmonious wine with impressive intensity and a fractionally off-dry (4 grams/litre of residual sugar), crisp finish, in its youth it's a delicious mouthful.

Vintage	04	03	02	01	00	99	98
WR	7	6	7	7	7	6	5
Drink	04-06	04-05	P	P	P	P	P

DRY $22 V+

Woollaston Estates Nelson Sauvignon Blanc   ★★★

The 2003 vintage (★★★) is a briskly herbaceous wine, grown in the company's Wai-iti River and other vineyards. It has crisp, racy acidity woven through its melon and fresh-cut grass flavours, which show good depth.

DRY $17 AV

Scheurebe

Highly regarded in Germany, Scheurebe is a Sylvaner-Riesling cross that ripens easily, while retaining good acid spine. It is also prone to noble rot, yielding luscious sweet wines. A rare variety in New Zealand, it is not listed separately in the latest national vineyard survey.

Floating Mountain Scheurebe (★★★☆)

Grown in the Mark Rattray vineyard at Waipara, the 2004 vintage (★★★☆) is attractive in its youth, with good depth of ripe, citrusy flavours, a distinct splash of sweetness and fresh acidity enlivening the finish. A medium-bodied wine (12.5 per cent alcohol), it offers very easy drinking.

MED $18 AV

Sémillon

You'd never guess it from the small selection of labels on the market, but Sémillon is New Zealand's sixth most widely planted white-wine variety. The few New Zealand winemakers who a decade ago played around with Sémillon could hardly give it away, so aggressively stemmy and spiky was its flavour. Now, there is a new breed of riper, richer, rounder Sémillons emerging – and they are 10 times more enjoyable to drink.

The Sémillon variety is beset by a similar problem to Chenin Blanc. Despite being the foundation of outstanding white wines in Bordeaux and Australia, Sémillon is out of fashion in the rest of the world, and in New Zealand its potential is still largely untapped.

Sémillon is highly prized in Bordeaux, where as one of the two key varieties both in dry wines, most notably white Graves, and the inimitable sweet Sauternes, its high levels of alcohol and extract are perfect foils for Sauvignon Blanc's verdant aroma and tartness. With its propensity to rot 'nobly', Sémillon forms about 80 per cent of a classic Sauternes.

Cooler climates like those of New Zealand, Tasmania and Washington state, however, bring out a grassy-green character in Sémillon which, coupled with its higher acidity in these regions, can give the variety strikingly Sauvignon-like characteristics. Sémillon's plantings in New Zealand are expanding slowly.

Grown principally in Gisborne, Marlborough and Hawke's Bay, Sémillon is commonly used in New Zealand as a minor (and anonymous) partner in wines labelled Sauvignon Blanc, contributing complexity and aging potential. By curbing the variety's natural tendency to grow vigorously and crop bountifully, winemakers are now overcoming the aggressive cut-grass characters that in the past plagued the majority of New Zealand's unblended Sémillons. The relatively recent arrival of clones capable of giving riper fruit characters (notably BVRC-14 from the Barossa Valley) is also contributing to quality advances. You'll hear more about this grape in the future.

Alpha Domus AD Sémillon   ★★★★

One of the country's few high-quality Sémillons, this wine is estate-grown at Maraekakaho, in Hawke's Bay. The 2002 vintage (★★★★) was fermented (30 per cent with indigenous yeasts) and matured for 10 months on its yeast lees in French oak barriques (half new). The bouquet is nutty and slightly grassy; the palate mouthfilling, citrusy and slightly herbaceous, with barrel-aging complexity and balanced acidity. Still fairly youthful, it's a dry, complex wine, worth cellaring.

Vintage	02	01	00	99
WR	7	NM	7	NM
Drink	04-10	NM	04-05+	NM

DRY $30 -V

Alpha Domus Sémillon   ★★★

The 2002 vintage (★★★☆) is a fruit-driven style; most of the wine was handled in tanks, but 15 per cent was barrel-fermented. Fresh and lively, with grassy aromas, it's a fairly herbaceous style with punchy flavours, a bare hint of oak and a bone-dry, crisp finish. It should age well. The pale, youthful 2003 (★★☆) is a more austere wine, minerally, slightly nutty and flinty, with searching acidity and a dry finish.

Vintage	02	01	00	99	98
WR	7	4	7	6	6
Drink	04-08	04-05	04-05	P	P

DRY $17 AV

Askerne Sémillon   ★★★☆

Showing good complexity, the 2002 vintage (★★★☆) of this Hawke's Bay wine has fresh, lemony, grassy aromas. Estate-grown near Havelock North and 40 per cent French oak-aged, it's a medium-bodied style (11.5 per cent alcohol), crisp and tight, with a touch of nutty oak and good varietal character and intensity.

Vintage	03	02	01	
WR	NM	6	5	DRY $18 AV
Drink	NM	04-07	04-07	

Awarua Terraces Goldstones Sémillon   (★★★☆)

Still youthful in colour, the 2002 vintage (★★★☆) is a tightly structured wine, grown at Mangatahi, in Hawke's Bay, and fermented and lees-aged in new French oak barriques. It shows good concentration of lemon, melon and fresh-cut grass flavours, strongly seasoned with oak, and lively acidity.

DRY $27 -V

Babich East Coast Sémillon/Chardonnay   ★★☆

A decent, everyday-drinking white, the 2003 vintage (★★☆) is a blend of Gisborne and Henderson grapes. Slightly grassy, it is fresh, clean and lemony, with a dry finish. (Past vintages were labelled as Fumé Vert.)

DRY $13 AV

Clearview Sémillon   (★★★★)

The richly flavoured 2002 vintage (★★★★) was grown at Te Awanga, on the Hawke's Bay coast, blended with 20 per cent Sauvignon Blanc and handled without oak. It's a fresh, weighty wine, intensely varietal, with strong, lemony, grassy aromas and flavours and a slightly buttery, long finish. 'It'll be unbelievable at four years old,' says winemaker Tim Turvey.

DRY $20 AV

Kerr Farm Kumeu Sémillon   ★★☆

Estate-grown in West Auckland, the 2000 vintage (★★☆) was fermented and matured in seasoned French and American oak casks. Light straw in colour, it is crisp and dry, with restrained fruit characters and nutty, minerally flavours in a slightly austere style, now slightly past its best.

Vintage	00	
WR	7	DRY $17 -V
Drink	04-06	

Matakana Estate Sémillon   ★★★

Sémillon is a variety 'we have a real passion for,' say the proprietors. The 2002 vintage (★★★) shows good potential, with well-ripened fruit characters and powerful, toasty oak aromas and flavours. The 2003 (★★★) is a moderately ripe-tasting wine but shows good depth of citrusy, gently herbaceous flavour, with well-integrated oak.

DRY $24 -V

Montana Gisborne Sémillon   ★★★☆

The launch of the easy-drinking 2000 vintage helped to introduce Sémillon to a wider audience in New Zealand. The 2002 (★★★☆) was mostly handled in tanks, but 15 per cent of the blend was barrel-fermented. Maturing well, it's a generous, full-bodied wine with ripe, tropical-fruit flavours, showing good depth, and a fractionally off-dry, creamy-smooth finish.

Vintage	02	01	00	
WR	6	6	6	DRY $14 V+
Drink	P	P	P	

Sileni Estate Selection The Circle Sémillon   ★★★☆

The 2003 vintage (★★★☆) of this Hawke's Bay wine was mostly fermented and lees-aged in tanks, but
20 per cent of the blend finished its fermentation in barrels. Full-bodied and dry, it's a youthful, weighty
wine with good varietal characters of melons and fresh-cut grass, maturing well.

Vintage	03	02	01	00
WR	5	6	5	5
Drink	04-07	04-06	04-05	04-05

MED/DRY $25 -V

Verdelho

Verdelho, a Portuguese variety traditionally grown on the island of Madeira, preserves its
acidity well in hot regions, yielding enjoyably full-bodied, lively, lemony table wines in
Australia. Although still extremely rare in New Zealand, from 2003 to 2006 the area of
bearing Verdelho vines will rise from 5 to 9 hectares.

Esk Valley Hawke's Bay Verdelho   ★★★☆

Described as an 'early-ripening' variety with 'built-in resistance to botrytis', the 2003 vintage (★★★☆) was
grown in the Gimblett Gravels district, hand-picked, whole-bunch pressed and handled entirely in tanks.
It's an aromatic wine with good vigour and intensity of citrusy, slightly pineappley and spicy flavours, fresh
and crisp. The full-bodied (14.5 per cent alcohol) 2004 (★★★★) is pale, with subtle pear and spice
aromas. Still very youthful and lively, with citrus and pear-like flavours, it could easily be mistaken in a
blind tasting for Pinot Gris.

Vintage	04	03
WR	6	5
Drink	04-07	04-06

DRY $19 AV

Viognier

Viognier is a classic grape of the northern Rhône, where it is renowned for its exotically perfumed, substantial, peach and apricot-flavoured dry whites. A delicious alternative to Chardonnay, Viognier (pronounced vee-yon-yay) is an internationally modish variety, now starting to pop up in shops and restaurants here.

Viognier accounts for only 0.2 per cent of the national vineyard, but the area of bearing vines is expanding swiftly, from 15 hectares in 2002 to 39 hectares in 2005. As in the Rhône, Viognier's flowering and fruit 'set' have been highly variable here. The deeply coloured grapes go through bud-burst, flowering and 'veraison' (the start of the final stage of ripening) slightly behind Chardonnay and are harvested about the same time as Pinot Noir.

The wine is generally fermented in seasoned oak barrels, yielding scented, substantial, richly alcoholic wines with gentle acidity and subtle flavours. If you enjoy mouthfilling, softly textured dry or dryish white wines, but feel like a change from Chardonnay and Pinot Gris, try Viognier. You won't be disappointed.

Ascension Matakana Viognier ★★★☆

Top vintages, such as 2002 (★★★★) offer deep yet delicate pear and lychees flavours, with leesy characters adding complexity and a well-rounded finish. The 2003 (★★★) is less ripe-tasting wine, but still shows good weight and texture, with moderate acidity and a dry finish.

DRY $25 -V

Babich Winemakers Reserve Viognier ★★★☆

Sold only at the winery in Henderson, the 2002 vintage (★★★★) is a bone-dry Hawke's Bay wine, grown at Fernhill and fermented and matured in a mix of old French oak barriques (60 per cent) and tanks. It's a very weighty wine (14 per cent alcohol) with an oily texture and strong peach, pear and fig flavours, with a slightly honeyed richness.

Vintage	02	01
WR	7	7
Drink	P	P

DRY $24 AV

Collards Rothesay Viognier ★★★☆

The 2002 vintage (★★★☆) was grown at the Rothesay Vineyard in Waimauku, West Auckland and matured on its yeast lees in old oak barriques. It's a subtle wine, lightly floral, full-bodied and soft, with gentle peach, pear and spice flavours showing great delicacy and a lingering finish. There is no 2003.

Vintage	04	03	02	01	00
WR	6	NM	6	NM	6
Drink	05-06	NM	04-05	NM	P

DRY $25 -V

Coopers Creek Gisborne Viognier ★★★

Handled entirely in tanks, the 2004 vintage (★★★☆) is based on second-crop vines in the Bell vineyard at Hexton. A robust wine (14.5 per cent alcohol), fermented to near dryness (4.5 grams/litre of residual sugar), it is still youthful, but shows attractively ripe pear and spice flavours, with a slightly creamy texture. Good drinking through the summer of 2004–05 – and great value.

Vintage	04	03
WR	6	5
Drink	04-06	04-05

DRY $20 AV

Herzog Marlborough Viognier ★★★★

The 2002 vintage (★★★★☆) was picked at a ripe 25 brix and fermented and lees-aged for a year in a single, 500-litre French oak cask. Floral, with good freshness and varietal character, it's a full-bodied wine (14 per cent alcohol) with delicate peach, pear and spice flavours, good fruit/oak balance and a lingering, rounded finish.

Vintage	02	01		DRY $39 -V
WR	6	7		
Drink	04-08	04-05		

Millton Growers Series Briants Vineyard Viognier (★★★★)

Fermented in old barrels with indigenous yeasts, but not grown organically, the 2003 vintage (★★★★) is a powerful Gisborne wine with clearcut varietal character. Light lemon/green in hue, with a floral bouquet, it has pure peach, pear and spice flavours showing good intensity, substantial body and a smooth finish (13 grams/litre of residual sugar). The 2004 is a markedly drier style (4.8 grams/litre of residual sugar).

Vintage	03		MED/DRY $28 AV
WR	6		
Drink	04-08		

Te Mata Woodthorpe Viognier ★★★★☆

This single-vineyard wine is grown at Te Mata's Woodthorpe Terraces property, on the south side of the Dartmoor Valley in Hawke's Bay, hand-picked, whole-bunch pressed and fermented and lees-aged for six months in seasoned French oak barriques. From a very low-cropping season, the 2003 vintage (★★★★) has a floral, strongly spicy bouquet. The palate is weighty, with finely balanced acidity and fresh, lush peach and pear flavours. It's already delicious.

Vintage	03	02	01	00	99	98	DRY $32 AV
WR	6	7	6	6	6	5	
Drink	04-07	04-05	P	P	P	P	

Trinity Hill New Wave Viognier (★★★★★)

Launched from the 2004 vintage (★★★★★), this is a powerful, lush wine, grown in the Gimblett Gravels district of Hawke's Bay and matured for four months in seasoned French oak barriques. Robust, fleshy and concentrated, with rich, slightly honeyed, stone-fruit flavours, it's already delicious and a memorable mouthful.

DRY $30 V+

TW Reserve Viognier (★★★★)

The 2004 vintage (★★★★) was hand-picked in Gisborne and fermented and matured for four months in old oak casks. Mouthfilling and creamy, it's a rich, rounded wine with a subtle oak influence and good concentration of pear, lychees and spice flavours.

Vintage	04		DRY $27 AV
WR	5		
Drink	05-09		

TW Viognier ★★★☆

Already drinking well, the 2004 vintage (★★★☆) is a Gisborne wine, hand-harvested and fermented and matured for four months in seasoned oak barrels. Weighty and fresh, it's a crisp, vibrantly fruity wine with pear, grapefruit and spice flavours showing very good depth.

Vintage	04		DRY $19 V+
WR	5		
Drink	05-08		

Sweet White Wines

Sweet white wines (often called dessert wines) account for just 0.1 per cent of the total volume of wine sold in supermarkets. Yet around the country, winemakers work hard to produce some ravishingly beautiful, honey-sweet white wines that are well worth discovering.

New Zealand's most luscious, concentrated and honeyish sweet whites are made from grapes which have been shrivelled and dehydrated on the vines by 'noble rot', the dry form of the *Botrytis cinerea* mould. Misty mornings, followed by clear, fine days with light winds and low humidity, are ideal conditions for the spread of noble rot, but in New Zealand this favourable interplay of weather factors occurs irregularly.

Some enjoyable but never exciting dessert wines (often labelled Ice Wine) are made by the freeze-concentration method, whereby a proportion of the natural water content in the grape juice is frozen out, leaving a sweet, concentrated juice to be fermented.

Marlborough has so far yielded a majority of the finest sweet whites. Most of the other wine regions, however – except Auckland (too wet) and Central Otago (too dry and cool) – can also point to the successful production of botrytised sweet whites in favourable vintages.

Riesling has been the foundation of the majority of New Zealand's most opulent sweet whites, but Sauvignon Blanc, Sémillon, Gewürztraminer, Pinot Gris, Müller-Thurgau, Chenin Blanc and Chardonnay have all yielded fine dessert styles. With their high levels of extract and firm acidity, most of these wines repay cellaring.

Alan McCorkindale Waipara Valley Noble Riesling (★★★☆)

Light green/gold in hue, the 2002 vintage (★★★☆) is a hand-picked selection of 100 per cent botrytis-infected berries, grown in the Lough Group vineyard. It has a minerally, rather than floral, bouquet leading into a citrusy, honeyed palate with good sugar/acid balance and rich flavour. Drink now onwards.

SW $25 (375ML) AV

Alpha Domus Leonarda Late Harvest Sémillon ★★★☆

The 2002 vintage (★★★☆) of this Hawke's Bay wine is a gently oaked style (20 per cent barrel-fermented). Green/gold, it's a sweet but not super-sweet wine (120 grams/litre of residual sugar) with good body and concentration of ripe, honeyed flavour and a well-rounded finish. The 2004 (★★★☆) is light gold and honeyed, with some richness and good drink-young appeal.

Vintage	03	02	01	00	99	98
WR	NM	7	NM	7	5	5
Drink	NM	04-08	NM	04-06	P	04-05

SW $19 (375ML) V+

Alpha Domus Noble Selection Sémillon ★★★★★

Estate-grown at Maraekakaho, in Hawke's Bay, and fully barrel-fermented, the 2000 vintage (★★★★★) is gold/amber, with a strongly honeyed fragrance. It's a classy, weighty wine with abundant sweetness (220 grams/litre of residual sugar), a deliciously oily texture and rich, ripe, honeyed, complex flavours.

Vintage	00
WR	7
Drink	04-14

SW $30 (375ML) V+

Amisfield Central Otago Noble Riesling   (★★★★)

The floral, very elegant 2003 vintage (★★★★) was harvested on 7 June at 38.2 brix. Light (8.4 per cent alcohol) and sweet (205 grams/litre of residual sugar), it has crisp, lemony, appley, gently honeyed aromas and flavours, very fresh and tangy. (From 2004 flows an oak-aged Noble Sauvignon Blanc.)

SW $40 (375ML) -V

Amisfield Rocky Knoll Riesling   (★★☆)

The 2003 vintage (★★☆) was estate-grown in the Cromwell Basin, harvested at 20.2 brix and made in a low-alcohol (8.5 per cent), gently sweet (55 grams/litre of residual sugar) style. It shows strong, green-apple aromas and flavours, but lacks real fragrance and delicacy.

SW $29 (750ML) -V

Askerne Botrytis Chardonnay   (★★★)

Made from fully botrytised bunches, estate-grown in Hawke's Bay, the 2003 vintage (★★★) is golden, with honey and tea aromas. It's a rich, powerful, almost heavy wine (15 per cent alcohol), with some complexity and crisp, sweet, apricot flavours.

SW $25 (375ML) -V

Askerne Botrytised Sémillon   ★★★☆

The 2002 vintage (★★★★☆) is by far the best yet. Grown in Hawke's Bay, harvested at 45 brix and fermented and matured for nine months in old French oak barriques, it's a golden, Sauternes-style wine with a rich, honeyed, complex bouquet. Oily and sweet (180 grams/litre of residual sugar), it's very lush and concentrated, with substantial body (despite being only 10 per cent alcohol), good sugar/acid balance and a powerful botrytis influence. Classy stuff.

Vintage	03	02	01	00
WR	7	7	NM	6
Drink	05-09	04-08	04-05	04-05

SW $30 (375ML) -V

Ata Rangi Kahu Botrytis Riesling   ★★★★☆

Grown in the Kahu (Australasian harrier) vineyard, neighbouring the Ata Rangi winery in Martinborough, the 2004 vintage (★★★★☆) is a pale gold, rich and honeyed wine with pear and honey aromas. Already lovely, it's an opulent, lush wine with concentrated stone-fruit flavours, soft and succulent.

Vintage	04	03
WR	7	6
Drink	04-07	04-05

SW $28 (375ML) V+

Babich Mara Estate Botrytised Sauvignon Blanc   (★★☆)

Still on sale in 2004, the 1996 vintage (★★☆) of this Hawke's Bay wine is golden, with sweet tea and honey flavours, now tasting a bit tired.

SW $16 (375ML) -V

Babich Winemakers Reserve Late Harvest Riesling   (★★☆)

The 1999 vintage (★★☆), grown in the Pigou vineyard in Marlborough, was still on sale in 2004. Deep gold, with citrusy, honeyed flavours, firm acid spine and minerally, toasty, bottle-aged characters, it was highly attractive in its youth, but is now past its best.

SW $24 (375ML) -V

Briar Vale Ice Wine   ★★★

True ice wine (the Germans call it 'eiswein') is exceptionally rare in New Zealand, but the 2002 vintage (★★★) was made from frozen Riesling grapes, harvested near Alexandra, in Central Otago, from 16 to 19 June. Pale lemon/green, it's a light (8.5 per cent alcohol), gently sweet wine with fresh, ripe, late-harvest fruit flavours. It's not intense, but attractive and still youthful.

SW $25 (375ML) -V

Brightwater Vineyards Riesling Ice Wine   (★★☆)

Grown at Nelson, picked at 23.5 brix and freeze-concentrated, the 2003 vintage (★★☆) is a pale lemon/green wine with crisp, delicate, green-apple aromas and flavours. It's a moderately sweet wine (95 grams/litre of residual sugar), still youthful, but lacks the ripeness and richness to rate more highly.

Vintage 03
WR 6
Drink 04-06

SW $23 (375ML) -V

Burnt Spur Martinborough Riesling   (★★★☆)

Sold as an 'aperitif style', the 2003 vintage (★★★☆) is a light-bodied wine (8.7 per cent alcohol), with a bright, light yellow/green hue and a gently honeyed bouquet. Already enjoyable, it has crisp, appley, lemony, slightly honeyed flavours, tense and youthful, suggesting good cellaring potential.

SW $23 (375ML) AV

Canterbury House Late Harvest Pinot Gris   ★★★★

Smooth and sweet, the 2002 (★★★☆) is an elegant Waipara wine with ripe aromas and flavours of citrus fruits, pears and spice. It shows good weight, delicacy, length and roundness, with slight honey characters adding richness. Soft and rich, the more heavily botrytised 2003 vintage (★★★★★) was barrel-fermented and stop-fermented at only 8.5 per cent alcohol. Lush and opulent, with concentrated stone-fruit and pear flavours, it has gentle acidity and lovely smoothness, delicacy and richness. A great buy.

SW $23 (375 ML) V+

Charles Wiffen Dessert Riesling   ★★★☆

Packaged in a 500 ml bottle, the 2002 vintage (★★★★) is a freeze-concentrated, partly oak-aged Marlborough wine. Now at its peak, it is deep gold, oily and concentrated, with good acid spine and sweet (220 grams/litre of residual sugar) apricot and honey flavours, long and rich.

SW $30 (500ML) AV

Church Road Reserve Noble Sémillon   ★★★★

This Sauternes-style wine appears only in years when Montana Virtu Noble Sémillon is not produced (and vice versa). The 1999 vintage (★★★☆) was made from individually selected, botrytised berries harvested at 31 to 55 brix in five 'passes' through the Korokipo vineyard in Hawke's Bay, from late May to mid-June. Fermented and matured for 14 months in all-new French oak barriques, it is amber-hued, with a honeyed bouquet. Weighty and sweet (140 grams/litre of residual sugar), it's a powerful Sauternes style with an oily texture and concentrated apricot and honey flavours, but the botrytis character is almost overwhelming, and the wine shows a slight lack of freshness. Ready.

Vintage 99
WR 6
Drink 04-06

SW $33 (375ML) -V

Clearview Estate Late Harvest Chardonnay   (★★★★)

The robust (14.5 per cent alcohol), gently honeyed 2002 vintage (★★★★) was grown at Te Awanga, in Hawke's Bay, hand-picked at 36 brix, and fermented and matured for 11 months in oak casks (50 per cent new). Golden, it offers rich, well-ripened grapefruit and peach flavours, seasoned with toasty oak, and a sweet, crisp finish.

Vintage	02
WR	6
Drink	04-07

SW $30 (375ML) AV

Clearview Estate Noble Harvest   (★★★★)

Already enjoyable, the 2003 vintage (★★★★) is a 2:1 blend of fully botrytised Chardonnay and Riesling, grown in Hawke's Bay and fermented and matured for 11 months in new French oak barriques. It's a golden wine with fresh, lively acidity and a strong surge of honey-sweet flavour.

SW $65 (375ML) -V

Cloudy Bay Late Harvest Riesling   ★★★★★

Cloudy Bay only makes this Marlborough dessert wine about every second year, on average, but it's usually well worth waiting for. The light gold 2000 (★★★★★) has a gorgeous balance of rich, citrusy fruit flavours, botrytis-derived honey characters, sweetness and acidity. The more restrained 2002 vintage (★★★☆) was harvested in early May in the Ashmore vineyard at Fairhall, when the grape sugar levels had reached an average of 30.1 brix and over half of the berries were botrytis-affected. Fermented in a mix of tanks and barrels, then matured on its yeast lees in old French oak casks for 18 months, it's a light yellow, youthful wine, citrusy and slightly honeyed, with a gentle botrytis influence. A low-alcohol style (10 per cent), with plentiful sweetness (141 grams/litre of residual sugar) balanced by fresh acidity, it should unfold well for several years.

Vintage	02	01	00	99	98	97	96
WR	6	NM	6	6	NM	NM	6
Drink	04-07	NM	P	P	NM	NM	P

SW $29 (375ML) V+

Collards Botrytis Riesling   (★★★)

Still on sale in 2004, the amber-hued 1999 vintage (★★★) is a sweet (92 grams/litre of sugar) but not super-sweet Marlborough wine with good depth of lemony, honeyed flavours cut with firm acidity and toasty, bottle-aged characters. Ready.

Vintage	99
WR	7
Drink	P

SW $19 (375ML) AV

Coopers Creek Late Harvest Riesling   ★★★

Light yellow, the 2002 (★★★☆) is an elegant late-harvest style. Harvested in the Wairau Valley at 30 brix, with a 'moderate' level of botrytis, and stop-fermented with 150 grams per litre of residual sugar, it's a light-bodied wine (9 per cent alcohol), with lemony, gently honeyed aromas and flavours, fresh, sweet and lively. There is no 2003. Tasted prior to bottling (and so not rated), the 2004 looked excellent. Picked at 30 brix and stop-fermented with 8.5 per cent alcohol and 150 grams per litre of residual sugar, it has scented, pear and honey aromas and flavours, vibrant, pure and rich.

Vintage	04	03	02	01	00
WR	5	NM	6	NM	6
Drink	04-06	NM	04-05	NM	P

SW $20 (375ML) AV

Corbans Cottage Block Marlborough Noble Riesling ★★★★★

The very refined 2002 vintage (★★★★★) was hand-picked at 38 brix and fermented in tanks to 13 per cent alcohol, leaving 156 grams per litre of residual sugar. Lemon-scented, with fresh, crisp flavours of citrus fruits, pears and apricots, it has a gentle, honeyed botrytis influence that enriches but doesn't dominate the pure, beautifully ripe fruit flavours. Very elegant and harmonious.

Vintage	02	
WR	7	SW $30 (375ML) V+
Drink	04-10	

Craggy Range Noble Riesling (★★★★☆)

Showing lovely freshness, vigour and length, the 2003 vintage (★★★★☆) is a classy, finely scented Marlborough wine, lush and oily, with intense flavours of lemons and pears enriched by botrytis-derived honey.

SW $45 (375ML) -V

Dry River Late Harvest Craighall Riesling ★★★★★

Dry River produces breathtakingly beautiful botrytised sweet wines in Martinborough – sometimes light and fragile, sometimes high in alcohol and very powerful – from a range of varieties. For winemaker Neil McCallum, Riesling is the queen of dessert wines, and his wines are made for cellaring, rather than drink-young appeal. The 2002 vintage (★★★★★) was hand-picked in mid-May, after most of the leaves had fallen, 'with a sprinkling of botrytis and berry shrivel'. It's a light lemon/green, beautifully harmonious wine, finely scented and rich, with intense, ripe, faintly honeyed flavours of lemons and apples, showing great delicacy and length. Likened by McCallum to a Mosel spatlese, 'for its clarity of expression, but with greater weight and concentration overall', it's already hugely drinkable, but best cellared to 2005+. (The Super Classic designation applies to Dry River's range of sweet whites from different varieties.)

Vintage	02	
WR	7	SW $41 (750ML) AV
Drink	04-08	🍇🍇🍇

Felton Road Block 1 Riesling ★★★★☆

Grown on a 'steeper slope' which yields 'riper fruit' without noble rot, this Bannockburn, Central Otago wine is made in a style 'similar to a late-harvest, Mosel spatlese', says winemaker Blair Walter. The youthful 2003 vintage (★★★☆) was still coming together in mid-2004. Light lemon/green, it's a light-bodied (9 per cent alcohol), sweet wine (60 grams/litre of residual sugar) with strong flavours of lemons, apples and limes and appetising acidity. It needs time but shows good intensity; open mid-2005+.

Vintage	03	02
WR	7	6
Drink	04-16	04-15

SW $28 (375ML) V+

Forrest Botrytised Chenin Blanc ★★★☆

Soft and rich, the 2003 vintage (★★★★) is a Marlborough wine, harvested with 50 per cent botrytis infection of the berries and stop-fermented in a light-bodied style with 9.5 per cent alcohol and plentiful sweetness (150 grams/litre of residual sugar). Delicious in its youth, it's very harmonious, with ripe-peach and pear flavours, balanced acidity and a seductively sweet, well-rounded finish.

Vintage	03	
WR	4	SW $20 (375ML) AV
Drink	04-08	

Forrest Estate Botrytised Riesling   ★★★★★

Since 2001, this Marlborough beauty has been consistently outstanding. The light (10 per cent alcohol) and lovely 2003 vintage (★★★★★) is golden, very elegant and rich, with intense, ripe-fruit flavours of lemons and pears woven with botrytis-derived honey characters. A very harmonious sweet wine (220 grams/litre of residual sugar) with good acid spine, it's delicious now, but a good candidate for cellaring.

Vintage	03	02	SW $35 (375ML) AV
WR	7	6	
Drink	04-10	04-05	

Forrest Estate Late Harvest Riesling   ★★★☆

The 2003 vintage (★★★☆), grown in Marlborough, is a true late-harvest style, fresh and ripe, with pear and slight honey aromas and flavours and good sugar/acid balance (90 grams/litre of residual sugar).

Vintage	03	SW $25 (375ML) AV
WR	5	
Drink	04-14	

Framingham Noble Selection   ★★★★

The very elegant 2003 vintage (★★★★☆) is a Marlborough Riesling, hand-picked on 9 May and 9 June with a 'heavy' botrytis influence and fermented, but not aged, in old barrels. It's a pale, beautifully scented wine with crisp, concentrated flavours, tight, citrusy, honeyed and persistent.

Vintage	03	02	SW $28 (375ML) AV
WR	7	5	
Drink	04-08	P	

Framingham Select Riesling   (★★★★)

Designed for long-term cellaring, the 2003 vintage (★★★★) was estate-grown and late-harvested in Marlborough with no botrytis; the bunches were selected on the basis of their 'green/gold colour, as in Germany'. Pale lemon/green, with fresh, appley scents, it is light and juicy, with sweet (60 grams/litre of residual sugar) lemon and apple flavours and cleansing acidity. Showing impressive freshness, intensity and vivacity, it needs time to unveil its full potential; open 2006+.

Vintage	03	SW $35 (750ML) AV
WR	6	
Drink	04-10	

Fromm La Strada Riesling   ★★★★☆

The light and vivacious 2003 vintage (★★★★☆) is 'basically our late-harvest style,' says Marlborough winemaker Hatsch Kalberer. Light-bodied (only 8 per cent alcohol) with intense lemon, apple and lime flavours showing lovely delicacy and freshness, it's a moderately sweet style (71 grams/litre of residual sugar) with appetising acidity and no sign of botrytis. 'Drink it on a Sunday afternoon, with a slight breeze from the sea,' suggests Kalberer.

Vintage	04	03	02	01	SW $27 (750ML) AV
WR	7	5	6	6	
Drink	04-14	04-13	04-10	04-13	

Fromm La Strada Riesling Auslese   ★★★★

The 2003 vintage (★★★☆) is recommended by the winery for 10–15 years' cellaring. Still a baby, it's a light Marlborough wine (7.5 per cent alcohol) with ample sweetness (100 grams/litre of residual sugar) and no botrytis influence: 'Just clean varietal purity and elegance.' Pale, very fresh and vibrant, it has lemony, appley flavours, sweet and crisp, with a lasting finish, but is crying out for more time; open 2006+.

Vintage	03	02	01	00	99	98	SW $22 (750ML) V+
WR	6	7	7	6	5	7	
Drink	04-13	04-14	04-13	04-12	04-09	04-13	

Gibbston Valley Late Harvest Riesling ★★★

The 2003 vintage (★★★) was picked in Central Otago with a 'good' botrytis infection. Pale lemon/green, it's a true late-harvest style, slightly honeyed and gently sweet (135 grams/litre of residual sugar), with ripe-fruit characters of lemons and apples and crisp, steely acidity.

Vintage 03
WR 6
Drink 04-12

SW $29 (375ML) -V

Giesen Late Harvest Riesling Reserve Selection ★★★☆

The golden 2002 vintage (★★★★) is a bargain. Grown in Canterbury, it's a strongly botrytised style with a honeyed bouquet and a rich, sweet palate (harbouring 95 grams/litre of sugar), with grapefruit, lime and honey flavours and refreshing acidity. Delicious now, it should be long-lived, and at $20 for a full (750 ml) bottle, it offers irresistible value. (Still on the market in 2004, the 1999 vintage (★★☆) is bright gold, with some richness, but slightly tired and past its best.)

Vintage 02
WR 7
Drink 04-15

SW $22 (750ML) AV

Glover's Late Harvest Riesling (★★★)

Grown in Nelson, the 2002 vintage (★★★) is pale, light and crisp, with youthful, sweet-apple flavours. It's still very youthful; open 2005+.

Vintage 02 01
WR 6 5
Drink 04-10 04-07

SW $21 (750ML) AV

Hunter's Late Harvest Sauvignon Blanc (★★★★)

The rich, gently honeyed 2002 vintage (★★★★) was picked at 36.8 brix in Marlborough in early June. Bright, light lemon/green, it is citrusy, sweet (143 grams/litre of residual sugar) and slightly honeyed in a fresh and lively style with lovely depth, ripeness and roundness. Drink now onwards.

SW $27 (375ML) AV

Isabel Noble Sauvage ★★★★☆

The 2002 vintage (★★★★☆) is a botrytised Marlborough Sauvignon Blanc, oak-matured for 14 months. Golden, with an inviting, honeyed fragrance, it is rich, nectareous and rounded, with ripe, very non-herbaceous fruit characters and balanced acidity. Lush and lovely, it's lighter than a classic Sauternes, but out of the same mould.

SW $35 (375ML) AV

Kahurangi Estate Nelson Late Harvest Riesling ★★★

Grown at Upper Moutere, the 2003 vintage (★★★☆) is a slightly honeyed wine with good intensity of lemony, appley flavour, fresh and sweet (120 grams/litre of residual sugar).

Vintage 03
WR 4
Drink 04-10

SW $25 (375ML) -V

Kaikoura Noble Riesling (★★★★☆)

The luscious, light-gold 2003 vintage (★★★★☆) was hand-picked in Marlborough over a fortnight and fermented to 10.5 per cent alcohol, with 184 grams per litre of residual sugar. The bouquet is richly honeyed; the palate is opulent, with excellent intensity, firm acid spine and a strong, overt botrytis influence contributing apricot and marmalade characters. Sharply priced.

SW $24 (375ML) V+

Kim Crawford Reka   ★★★★

The region and variety for Kim Crawford's sweet white (Reka means 'sweet') may vary with the vintage, but the 2002 (★★★★) is a Marlborough Riesling. Light yellow, with a fresh, lemony bouquet, it's a very elegant late-harvest style with well-ripened, citrusy flavours and a gentle botrytis influence.

SW $35 (500ML) V+

Konrad Sigrun Noble Riesling   ★★★★☆

A consistent high-flier. The 2003 vintage (★★★★☆) was grown in the Waihopai Valley of Marlborough, hand-picked over four weeks, French oak-fermented and stop-fermented with 10.5 per cent alcohol and 184 grams per litre of residual sugar. Elegant and intense, it's a golden, rich wine with well-spined, pear and honey flavours, showing a strong botrytis influence in harmony with sweet, late-harvested fruit characters. Well worth cellaring.

Vintage	03	02	01
WR	7	6	7
Drink	04-15	04-10	04-10

SW $33 (500ML) V+

Lake Chalice Botrytised Riesling   ★★★★☆

The 2002 vintage (★★★★) was made from individually selected, late-harvested bunches of botrytis-affected grapes in the Falcon vineyard. Yellow/green, it is full-bodied (13 per cent alcohol), fresh and youthful, with strong lemon, lime and honey characters and a slightly oily richness. There is no 2003 or 2004.

SW $25 (375ML) V+

Lincoln Ice Wine   ★★☆

The 2002 vintage (★★☆) is a freeze-concentrated wine, made from Chardonnay (55 per cent) and Chenin Blanc grapes grown at Te Kauwhata. It's a light-bodied wine (10 per cent alcohol) with lemony, slightly appley flavours, sweet (105 grams/litre of sugar), simple, fresh, crisp and lively. Tasted prior to bottling (and so not rated), the 2004 is a Gisborne Sémillon, harvested at 25 to 26 brix with some botrytis infection. Showing well-ripened pear and honey flavours, it looked highly promising.

Vintage	03	02
WR	5	6
Drink	04-06	04-06

SW $18 (500ML) AV

Margrain Botrytis Selection Chenin Blanc   ★★★★

Harvested in Martinborough at the end of May from 25-year-old vines, the 2003 vintage (★★★★☆) is light gold, with excellent harmony and depth. Full-bodied, it is ripely flavoured and honeyed, with finely balanced sweetness and acidity and pure, clean botrytis adding an apricot-like richness.

Vintage	02
WR	6
Drink	04-07

SW $27 (375ML) AV

Martinborough Vineyard Late Harvest Riesling   ★★★★☆

The 2003 vintage (★★★★) was harvested at over 36 brix from 13-year-old vines in the Jackson Block and stop-fermented with 170 grams per litre of residual sugar. It's a golden, strongly botrytised wine with a rich, oily texture and crisp, concentrated, lingering flavours of honey and apricots.

SW $35 (375ML) AV

Matariki Late Harvest Riesling ★★★☆

The slightly honeyed 2002 vintage (★★★☆) has strong citrusy flavours in a late-harvest style with ripe-fruit characters, gentle sweetness (100 grams/litre of residual sugar) and lively acidity. Toasty, bottle-aged characters are now adding complexity.

Vintage	02	01	00	99
WR	7	6	6	7
Drink	04-06	04-06	P	P

SW $33 (375ML) -V

Matua Valley Late Harvest Muscat ★★★

The heady perfume is a highlight of this low-priced dessert wine. Grown in Gisborne and freeze-concentrated, it is typically fruity, sweet and smooth, with clearcut citrus/orange varietal characters in an enjoyable although not luscious or complex style. The 2004 vintage (★★★☆) is one of the best. Scented, it's a full-bodied wine (13 per cent alcohol) with pure, delicate flavours of lemons and pears, abundant sweetness (70 grams/litre of residual sugar) and a finely balanced, rounded finish.

Vintage	04
WR	5
Drink	04-06

SW $12 (375ML) V+

Millton Essencia Chardonnay
Individual Berry Selection (★★★★)

Probably at its peak, the lush, concentrated 2002 vintage (★★★★) is a deep-gold Gisborne wine with a powerful palate, peachy, oily, sweet and honeyed.

SW $36 (375ML) -V

Mission Ice Wine ★★★

The 2002 vintage (★★☆) is pale gold, with a restrained bouquet. It's a simple wine with lemony, appley flavours, plentiful sweetness (90 grams/litre of sugar) and firm acidity cutting in on the finish.

SW $15 (375ML) AV

Montana Late Harvest Selection (★★★☆)

Made from 'botrytised Marlborough grapes' (Müller-Thurgau and Riesling), the yellow-hued 2002 vintage (★★★☆) is a ripely scented wine with lemony, gently honeyed flavours and plentiful sweetness (140 grams/litre of residual sugar). An elegant late-harvest style, it's drinking well now and priced sharply.

Vintage	02
WR	5
Drink	04-08

SW $15 (375ML) V+

Montana Virtu Noble Sémillon – see Virtu Noble Sémillon

Mount Cass Vineyards Waipara Valley
Late Harvest Selection (★★★★)

Honey-sweet, golden, oily and rich, the 2002 vintage (★★★★) is a good buy. A blend of Chardonnay (83 per cent) and the German variety Optima (17 per cent), it was harvested in July at 42 brix and slow-fermented in seasoned French oak barrels. It's a weighty wine with abundant sweetness (174 grams/litre of sugar), good acidity and concentrated, apricot-like flavours.

Vintage	02
WR	6
Drink	04-05

SW $22 (375ML) V+

Neudorf Riesling Botrytis Selection   (★★★★)

Still very tight and youthful, the 2003 vintage (★★★★) was harvested at 29.3 brix in the Home vineyard at Upper Moutere, with a 'high proportion of botrytis shrivel', and stop-fermented with 11.5 per cent alcohol and 103 grams per litre of residual sugar. Light yellow/green, with a scented, honeyish bouquet, it is crisp and citrusy, with lovely delicacy and intensity and a lasting finish. It needs time; open 2006+.

SW $28 (375ML) AV

Ngatarawa Alwyn Reserve Noble Harvest Riesling   ★★★★★

'Botrytis plays a huge part in this wine,' says Hawke's Bay winemaker Alwyn Corban. The estate-grown 2002 vintage (★★★★☆), made from bunches that had more than 80 per cent of their berries raisined by botrytis, was hand-harvested at 43.5 brix and fermented and matured for eight months in seasoned French oak barriques. Amber-green, with rich honey and apricot aromas, to which the oak adds complexity, it's an abundantly sweet wine (189 grams/litre of sugar), full-bodied and very concentrated, with high acidity giving a slightly tart finish.

Vintage	02	01	00	99	98	97	96	95	94
WR	7	NM	7	NM	NM	NM	NM	NM	7
Drink	04-10	NM	04-10	NM	NM	NM	NM	NM	P

SW $60 (375ML) ·V

Ngatarawa Glazebrook Noble Harvest Riesling   ★★★★★

Typically a richly botrytised, honey-sweet wine, concentrated and treacly. The grapes are estate-grown at the Ngatarawa winery in Hawke's Bay, in a block in front of the winery specially dedicated to the production of nobly rotten grapes. The deep-gold 2002 vintage (★★★★) was late-harvested at 41.5 brix, but unlike its Alwyn stablemate (above), not cask-aged. It's a full-on, rampantly botrytised style with 155 grams per litre of residual sugar, richly honeyed aromas and flavours and firm acid spine.

Vintage	02	01	00	99	98	97	96	95	94
WR	7	NM	6	NM	NM	6	7	NM	6
Drink	04-10	NM	04-07	NM	NM	04-06	04-07	NM	04-05

SW $32 (375ML) V+   🍷🍷

Ngatarawa Stables Late Harvest Vintage Selection   ★★★

This Hawke's Bay wine is called 'a fruit style' by winemaker Alwyn Corban, meaning it doesn't possess the qualities of a fully botrytised wine. The current release (★★★☆), the first to be labelled 'Vintage Selection', is a blend of wines from the 2003 (76 per cent), 2002 (4 per cent) and 2001 (20 per cent) vintages. Made from Chardonnay (two-thirds) and Riesling, it's a light-gold, attractively scented wine with stone-fruit and lime flavours, gentle sweetness (90 grams/litre of residual sugar) and a hint of honey.

SW $17 (375ML) AV

Nga Waka Late Harvest Riesling   ★★★★

A celebration of ripe, late-harvest fruit characters, the 2003 vintage (★★★★★) is a captivating wine. Based on ultra low-yielding Martinborough vines (2.5 tonnes/hectare), it was harvested at 36 brix and fermented to 12 per cent alcohol and 160 grams per litre of residual sugar. Light yellow, with a scented, slightly honeyed bouquet, it shows deliciously ripe fruit flavours of lemons and pears, with a gentle botrytis influence. Luscious and oily, with a well-rounded, resounding finish, it shows great harmony and is already hard to resist.

Vintage	03	02	01
WR	7	NM	6
Drink	04+	NM	04+

SW $30 (375ML) AV

Okahu Estate Chenin Blanc Ice Wine   (★★★)

The light-gold 2003 vintage (★★★) was grown at Te Kauwhata, in the Waikato. Already showing considerable development, it has honey and tea flavours showing some richness, a slightly oily texture and a sweet (150 grams/litre of residual sugar) finish. Drink 2004–05.

SW $19 (375ML) AV

Olssen's Autumn Gold Late Harvest Chardonnay   ★★★

Estate-grown at Bannockburn, in Central Otago, the 2003 vintage (★★★) was picked at 36 brix and stop-fermented with 175 grams/litre of residual sugar. Light lemon/green, with fresh, ripe fruit aromas, it's a light-bodied wine, sweet, lemony and appley, with pure, vibrant fruit characters in an elegant, late-harvest style.

Vintage	03
WR	6
Drink	05-13

SW $35 (375ML) -V

Olssen's Desert Gold Late Harvest Riesling   ★★★★

Delightful in its youth, the pale yellow/green 2003 vintage (★★★★) is a highly refined late-harvest style from Bannockburn, in Central Otago. Floral, with a lemony, faintly honeyed bouquet, it is light-bodied, with pure, delicate flavours of lemons and pears, a trace of honey and a finely balanced, sweet (114 grams/litre of residual sugar), refreshingly crisp finish.

Vintage	03
WR	6
Drink	05-13

SW $35 (375ML) -V

Pegasus Bay Aria   ★★★★☆

After 'the most perfect, lingering autumn', the 2002 vintage (★★★★★) was harvested in late June at Waipara in multiple stages, each time selecting only Riesling berries that were 'fully ripened, shrivelled and in perfect condition'. Bright yellow/green, it's beautifully fresh, poised and concentrated, with lively acidity and intense, ripe, lemony, honeyed flavours, sweet but not super-sweet (160 grams/litre of residual sugar). A ravishingly beautiful wine, it shows great harmony and richness, and at $30 for a full-size bottle delivers fine value.

Vintage	02	01	00	99	98	97	96	95
WR	7	6	6	7	6	NM	5	4
Drink	04-12	04-11	04-10	04-10	04-05	NM	P	P

SW $30 (750ML) V+

Pegasus Bay Finale   ★★★★

The golden 2000 vintage (★★★☆) was made from botrytised Chardonnay grown at Waipara and fermented and aged in seasoned French oak barriques for two years. It's a medium to full-bodied, rich and rounded wine with peach, apricot and honey flavours, now tasting quite mature. Ready; no rush.

SW $35 (375ML) -V

Peregrine Late Harvest Pinot Gris   (★★★)

Light and refreshing, the 2003 vintage (★★★) was picked at Gibbston, in Central Otago, at 31 brix, with no botrytis showing. It's a fragrant, light-bodied wine (11 per cent alcohol), with lemon and pear flavours showing some richness, crisp acidity and a sweet (110 grams/litre of residual sugar) finish.

SW $25 (375ML) -V

Peregrine Late Harvest Riesling   (★★★)

Grown in Central Otago, the 2003 vintage (★★★) is a gently sweet wine with citrusy fruit characters to the fore, simple but fresh and lively.

SW $25 (375ML) -V

Ransom Grand Mere Noble Chardonnay   (★★★)

The Matakana winery's first dessert wine flowed from the 2003 vintage (★★★). Light-gold, it has citrus and stone-fruit flavours, sweet (68 grams/litre of residual sugar) and rounded.

SW $21 (375ML) -V

Rongopai Reserve Special Late Harvest   (★★★)

The gently botrytised 2002 vintage (★★★) is a blend of Riesling and Chardonnay, grown in the company's vineyards at Te Kauwhata, in the Waikato. Pale gold, it shows good depth of pear and honey flavours, with some complexity and moderate sweetness (72 grams/litre of residual sugar) balanced by crisp acidity.

SW $20 (375ML) AV

Rongopai Ultimo Noble Late   (★★★★)

The richly botrytised 2002 vintage (★★★★) was harvested at Te Kauwhata, in the Waikato, and oak-aged for 15 months. A 2:1 blend of Chardonnay and Gewürztraminer, it is golden and weighty (12.5 per cent alcohol), with concentrated peach and honey flavours, an oily, raisined richness and firm acid spine. Well worth cellaring.

SW $75 (375ML) -V

Sacred Hill Halo Botrytis Sémillon   ★★★★

The green-gold 2002 vintage (★★★★) was harvested in Hawke's Bay at 52 brix and fermented and matured for a year in new French oak barriques. A very sweet wine (220 grams/litre of residual sugar) with a relatively low alcohol content (10 per cent), it is smooth, rich and oily, with concentrated, honeyish flavours and firm acidity cutting in on the finish. Delicious drinking now onwards.

Vintage 02
WR 7
Drink 04-08

SW $40 (375ML) -V

Sacred Hill XS Noble Selection   ★★★★

A strongly botrytised Riesling, harvested at 32 brix in George Gunn's vineyard in the Ohiti Valley of Hawke's Bay, the 2000 vintage (★★★★) is golden, with concentrated apricot and honey flavours and a slightly limey, sweet, crisp finish. The 2003 (★★★★) is a Marlborough wine, made from nobly rotten grapes hand-picked at 35 brix. It possesses pure, well-defined, citrusy Riesling flavours, with abundant sweetness (124 grams/litre of residual sugar), apricot and honey characters adding richness and mouth-watering acidity.

Vintage 03
WR 6
Drink 05-06

SW $25 (375ML) AV

Saint Clair Doctor's Creek Noble Riesling   ★★★☆

The gently floral 2003 vintage (★★★☆) was grown in Marlborough and fermented in old oak casks. Light gold, it is full-bodied (13 per cent alcohol), sweet and honeyed, with well-balanced acidity and strong, ripe pear, peach and honey flavours, showing considerable lushness. It's quite forward; drink now onwards.

SW $25 (375ML) AV

Saints Gisborne Noble Sémillon   ★★★☆

The great value 2002 vintage (★★★★) is a light-gold, 'Sauternes-style' wine from Allied Domecq, harvested at Patutahi, in Gisborne, at over 32 brix and fermented and matured in French oak barriques. Lush, with a honeyed fragrance and powerful surge of sweet apricot and honey flavours, beautifully fresh, rich and rounded, it's a pleasure to drink from now onwards. A 'steal'.

Vintage 03   02
WR 5   6
Drink 04-10   04-10

SW $17 (375ML) V+

Seifried Riesling Late Harvest   (★★☆)

Still on the market in 2004, the 2001 vintage (★★☆) was harvested in Nelson's Redwood Valley on 25 May at 32 brix, with 'minimal' botrytis. Medium gold, with apple and tea flavours and plentiful sweetness (142 grams/litre of residual sugar), it's a solid wine, but now shows a slight lack of freshness.

SW $35 (375ML) -V

Seifried Winemakers Collection Riesling Ice Wine   ★★★☆

The 2003 vintage (★★★☆) was made from slightly shrivelled grapes, late-picked in the company's vineyard at Redwood Valley, in Nelson. Freeze-concentrated and briefly oak-aged, it's a light-yellow/green, crisp, light wine (11 per cent alcohol) with good intensity of limey, lemony, slightly honeyed aromas and flavours and abundant sweetness (148 grams/litre of residual sugar), balanced by racy acidity.

SW $19 (375ML) V+

Selaks Founders Reserve Noble Riesling   (★★★★★)

The luscious 2001 vintage (★★★★★) was grown in the Matador Vineyard in Marlborough, where in three sweeps through the vineyard, shrivelled, nobly rotten grapes were hand-harvested at 42 to 43 brix. Pale gold, with a voluminous fragrance of citrus fruits and marmalade, it is lush, sweet (200 grams/litre of residual sugar) and highly concentrated, with a rich, oily, botrytis influence and great harmony. A classic sweet Riesling.

Vintage	01
WR	7
Drink	04-08

SW $29 (375ML) V+

Selaks Premium Selection Ice Wine   ★★★☆

This low-priced Marlborough wine is popular in supermarkets – and it's easy to see why. Made from Riesling (60 per cent) and Gewürztraminer, the freeze-concentrated 2003 vintage (★★★) has a spicy, 'Gewürz' bouquet and crisp, lemony flavours, simple, but deliciously fresh and lively.

Vintage	03	02	01	00	99	98
WR	7	7	7	7	7	7
Drink	04-07	04-06	04-05	P	P	P

SW $15 (375ML) V+

Shingle Peak Botrytis Riesling   (★★★★☆)

The golden, honey-sweet 2003 vintage (★★★★☆) was hand-picked in Marlborough over a two-week period at an average of 42 brix, with a powerful botrytis influence. It tastes like liquid honey, with sweet (230 grams/litre of residual sugar), concentrated, treacly flavours, impressive weight and an oily richness.

Vintage	03
WR	7
Drink	04-10

SW $29 (375ML) V+

Sileni Estate Selection Late Harvest Sémillon   ★★★☆

The 2003 vintage (★★★) was harvested in Hawke's Bay with 20 per cent botrytis infection and stop-fermented in tanks with 85 grams per litre of residual sugar. The bouquet is faintly honeyed; the palate is fresh and vibrant, citrusy and grassy, with moderate acidity and a rounded finish. It's not super-ripe or lush, but should age solidly.

Vintage	03	02
WR	6	5
Drink	04-06	04-06

SW $22 (375ML) AV

Sileni Pourriture Noble   ★★★★

The 2001 vintage (★★★★) was made from 100 per cent botrytis-affected Hawke's Bay Sémillon. Not oak-aged, it's a golden, sturdy (14 per cent alcohol) wine with smooth, concentrated peach, apricot and honey flavours in a sweet (95 grams/litre of residual sugar) but not super-sweet style.

Vintage	01
WR	5
Drink	04-05

SW $32 (375ML) -V

Soljans Dessert Gewürztraminer   (★★★)

The enjoyable 2003 vintage (★★★) was grown at Tolaga Bay, north of Gisborne. Bright yellow, with a citrusy, gently spicy bouquet, it has fresh, sweet flavours of lemons and spices, with good sugar/acid balance and a soft finish.

SW $17 (375ML) AV

Solstone Noble Riesling   (★★★★)

Light gold, with a honeyed bouquet, the 2003 vintage (★★★★) was picked near Masterton, in the Wairarapa, at 41 brix, and stop-fermented with 11 per cent alcohol and 190 grams per litre of residual sugar. It shows excellent intensity, with crisp, citrusy, strongly honeyed flavours, a powerful botrytis influence, plentiful sweetness and tense acidity keeping things lively. It should be long-lived.

Vintage	03
WR	6
Drink	05-09

SW $38 (375ML) -V

Spy Valley Marlborough Noble Riesling   (★★★)

A late-harvest style, the 2003 vintage (★★★) is fresh and lively, with pure, delicate, lemony aromas and flavours and a gentle sweetness (75 grams/litre of residual sugar). Ensconced in a 500 ml bottle, it offers good value.

Vintage	03
WR	5
Drink	04-08

SW $20 (500 ML) V+

Stratford Noble Riesling   ★★★★

Picked in late May at 48.5 brix, with a high level of botrytis shrivel, the 2002 (★★★★☆) is golden, with a full-bloomed, honeyed fragrance. It's a deliciously concentrated Martinborough wine with apricot and honey flavours, rich, very sweet (280 grams/litre of residual sugar) and lingering. Light gold, the 2003 vintage (★★★★) is a finely poised wine with a citrusy, honeyed bouquet and beautifully ripe, sweet (180 grams/litre of residual sugar), lemony, botrytis-enriched flavours.

Vintage	03	02
WR	7	7
Drink	04-08	04-07

SW $20 (375ML) V+

Te Kairanga Reserve Noble Riesling   (★★★)

The distinctive 2003 vintage (★★★) was hand-picked in Martinborough at 36.4 brix, with 80 per cent botrytis infection of the berries, and fermented in barrels until it reached 13.5 per cent alcohol, leaving 140 grams per litre of residual sugar. Light lemon/green, it has gentle pear and honey aromas and a soft, weighty and rich palate. The wood influence adds complexity, but also subdues the fruit flavours. It's a different style, worth cellaring.

Vintage	03
WR	7
Drink	04-09

SW $35 (375ML) -V

Te Mania Late Harvest Botrytis Riesling   ★★★★

The sharply priced 2003 vintage (★★★★) is concentrated, vibrant and tangy, with good sugar/acid balance (135 grams/litre of residual sugar) and fresh, strong, citrusy, slightly honeyed flavours.

Vintage	03
WR	7
Drink	04-08

SW $22 (375ML) V+

Te Whare Ra Noble Sémillon   (★★★)

Still on the market in 2004, the 1999 vintage (★★★) is a substantial Marlborough wine (14.5 per cent alcohol), not oak-aged. Light gold, with a slightly honeyed bouquet, it shows ripe lemon, lime and grapefruit characters and a gentle botrytis influence, but is now slightly past its best.

SW $24 (375ML) -V

Torlesse Waipara Late Harvest Riesling   (★★★)

Weighty, with a high alcohol level for the variety (14 per cent), the 2001 vintage (★★★) was harvested at over 30 brix and matured in old oak barrels. The bouquet is restrained but the palate is substantial, with citrusy, lemony, late-harvest characters holding sway – rather than botrytis-derived honey flavours – and a moderate degree of sweetness (90 grams/litre of residual sugar).

SW $17 (375ML) AV

TW Botrytis Chardonnay   (★★☆)

The 2003 vintage (★★☆) is a lemon-hued, briefly oak-aged Gisborne wine with gentle pear, apple and honey flavours, a hint of botrytis, plentiful sweetness (180 grams/litre of residual sugar) and crisp acidity.

Vintage 03
WR 6   **SW $27 (375ML) -V**
Drink 04-09

TW Botrytis Sémillon   (★★★☆)

Late-harvested at Gisborne in May at 48 brix, the light-gold 2003 vintage (★★★☆) is full of character. Matured for four months in old oak casks, it's rich and creamy, with very sweet (180 grams/litre of residual sugar) pear and apricot flavours, honeyed, concentrated and soft.

Vintage 03
WR 5   **SW $27 (375ML) -V**
Drink 04-07

Villa Maria Cellar Selection
Late Harvest Gewürztraminer   (★★★★)

Delicious now, the 2003 vintage (★★★★) is a single-vineyard Hawke's Bay wine, picked in May. Light gold, with a gingery bouquet, it's a sturdy wine (13.5 per cent alcohol) with rich ginger, spice and honey flavours, a clear botrytis influence and a moderately sweet (95 grams/litre of residual sugar), rounded finish.

SW $20 (375ML) V+

Villa Maria Cellar Selection Late Harvest Riesling   ★★★★

The floral, elegant 2003 vintage (★★★★) was made from late-picked but not botrytised Marlborough grapes, harvested over two weeks in May. It's a gently sweet wine (119 grams/litre of residual sugar), richly scented, with ripe pear, lemon and lime flavours showing excellent delicacy, purity and depth.

SW $20 (375ML) V+

Villa Maria Reserve Noble Riesling   ★★★★★

New Zealand's top sweet wine on the show circuit. It is typically stunningly perfumed, weighty and oily, with intense, very sweet honey/citrus flavours and a lush, long finish. The grapes are grown mainly in the Fletcher vineyard, in the centre of Marlborough's Wairau Plains, where sprinklers along the vines' fruit zone create ideal conditions for the spread of noble rot. The 2001 vintage (★★★★★) is outstanding. Golden, with a richly botrytised fragrance, it's a classic sweet Riesling, with a lovely intensity and purity of fruit and botrytis adding a honeyed, marmalade-like lusciousness. I have never tasted the 2002, but the winery's own rating of the vintage (see below) is not high. Tasted prior to bottling (and so not rated), the 2003 is light gold and laden with sweetness and flavour. Light (9.7 per cent alcohol), rich and oily, with succulent pear and honey flavours, it looked gorgeous.

Vintage	03	02	01	00	99	98	97	96
WR	5	4	5	7	7	7	NM	7
Drink	06-10	05-09	04-08	04-10	04-08	04-08	NM	04-05

SW $50 (375ML) AV

Virtu Noble Sémillon ★★★★★

The 2000 vintage (★★★★★) from Allied Domecq is a very classy Sauternes-style, harvested at 38 to 40 brix in Hawke's Bay and fermented and matured in all-new French oak barriques. Golden, with a beguiling array of peach, honey and oak aromas, it is highly concentrated, with toasty, minerally characters developing in a powerful, complex style with layers of flavour.

Vintage	02	01	00
WR	7	NM	7
Drink	04-08	NM	04-10+

SW $40 (375ML) AV

Voss Late Harvest Riesling (★★★☆)

A true late-harvest style, the 2002 vintage (★★★☆) is a gently sweet Martinborough wine. Freshly scented, it is ripe-tasting, citrusy and limey, with good balance, freshness and aging potential, but also lots of drink-young charm.

SW $19 (375ML) V+

Waimea Estates Reserve Bolitho Noble Chardonnay (★★★★★)

The 2003 vintage (★★★★★) is a cracker. Light gold, with a gently honeyed bouquet, it was made from fully botrytised grapes, hand-harvested at 45 brix in Nelson in early winter (11 June) and fermented in French oak casks (one year old). It's a beautifully fresh and luscious wine with abundant sweetness (220 grams/litre of residual sugar), rich pear and honey flavours, an oily texture and lovely depth and poise.

Vintage	03
WR	7
Drink	05-08

SW $40 (375ML) AV

Waipara Hills Marlborough Botrytis Riesling (★★★★★)

A forward style, already delicious, the 2003 vintage (★★★★★) was harvested at 36 brix and lees-aged in tanks for 10 months. Golden, oily and rich, it has lovely sugar/acid balance (177 grams/litre of residual sugar) and citrusy fruit flavours showing excellent ripeness and concentration. Fine value.

Vintage	03
WR	7
Drink	04-13

SW $26 (375ML) V+

Wairau River Botrytised Riesling Reserve ★★★★☆

Still on the market in 2004, the 1999 vintage (★★★★☆) of this Marlborough wine is maturing gracefully. Made from hand-selected, nobly rotten berries, it was matured for 20 months in French oak casks and then bottle-aged prior to release. Light gold, it is crisp and sweet, with a rich, honeyed botrytis influence and impressive depth and harmony.

Vintage	99
WR	7
Drink	04-10

SW $40 (375ML) -V

Sparkling Wines

Fizz, bubbly, méthode traditionnelle, sparkling – whatever name you call it by (the word Champagne is reserved for the wines of that most famous of all wine regions), wine with bubbles in it is universally adored.

How good are Kiwi bubblies? Good enough for the local industry to ship 212,322 cases of bubbly in the year to June 2004 – mostly Lindauer to the UK (although the Americans are starting to show interest too). In the past year, sparkling wine accounted for 6.1 per cent of New Zealand's wine exports.

Yet the range of New Zealand sparklings is not expanding swiftly. Most small wineries view the production of fine, bottle-fermented sparkling wine as too time-consuming and costly, and the domestic demand for premium bubbly is limited. Although 16 per cent of the wine we drink is sparkling, the vast majority of purchases are under $15.

New Zealand's sparkling wines can be divided into two key classes. The bottom end of the market is dominated by extremely sweet, simple wines that acquire their bubbles by simply having carbon dioxide pumped into them. Upon pouring, the bubbles race out of the glass.

At the middle and top end of the market are the much drier, bottle-fermented, 'méthode traditionnelle' (formerly 'méthode Champenoise', until the French got upset) labels, in which the wine undergoes its secondary, bubble-creating fermentation not in a tank but in the bottle, as in Champagne itself. Ultimately, the quality of any fine sparkling wine is a reflection both of the standard of its base wine, and of its later period of maturation in the bottle in contact with its yeast lees. Only bottle-fermented sparkling wines possess the additional flavour richness and complexity derived from extended lees-aging.

Pinot Noir and Chardonnay, both varieties of key importance in Champagne, are also the foundation of New Zealand's top sparkling wines (Pinot Meunier, the least prestigious but most extensively planted grape in Champagne, is still rare here). Marlborough, with its cool nights preserving the grapes' fresh natural acidity, has emerged as the country's premier region for bottle-fermented sparkling wines.

The vast majority of sparkling wines are ready to drink when marketed, and need no extra maturation. A short spell in the cellar, however, can benefit the very best bottle-fermented sparklings.

Alan McCorkindale Blanc de Blancs (★★★)

Grown at Waipara, the 2002 vintage (★★★) is based entirely on Chardonnay. It's a fresh, crisp, lemony, appley wine with gentle yeast autolysis characters adding a touch of complexity. **MED/DRY $23 -V**

Allan Scott Méthode Traditionnelle Blanc de Blancs NV ★★★☆

Based entirely on Chardonnay, this non-vintage Marlborough wine is typically fresh and harmonious. Its quality and style have varied slightly between batches, but at its best it shows refined fruit characters and well-developed yeastiness. The wine on the market during 2004 (★★★★) was excellent, with bready aromas and toasty, citrusy flavours showing a powerful yeast autolysis influence. **MED/DRY $26 -V**

Aquila   ★★☆

This Asti-style bubbly is just what you'd expect – fresh, fruity and flavoursome, with a sweetish, soft finish. Within Allied Domecq's range of bubblies, in terms of sweetness Aquila (which has 50 grams/litre of sugar) sits between the medium Lindauer Sec and the unabashedly sweet Bernadino Spumante. The wine I tasted in mid to late 2004 was fresh, smooth and light (10.5 per cent alcohol), with crisp, lemony, appley flavours, sweet and slightly frothy.

SW $9 AV

Arcadia Brut NV   ★★★☆

This bottle-fermented bubbly is produced by Amisfield Vineyards in Central Otago. The non-vintage wine on the market in 2004 (★★★☆) is pale straw, crisp and refined, with moderately yeasty, lemony, appley flavours showing good vigour and harmony.

MED/DRY $25 AV

Arcadia Lake Hayes Central Otago
Cuvée Brut Vintage   ★★★☆

The 1999 vintage (★★★) from Amisfield is a 2:1 blend of Pinot Noir and Chardonnay, disgorged after three years on its yeast lees. Drier than its non-vintage stablemate (above), it's light yellow/green, fresh and crisp, with lively, lemony flavours showing some elegance, but only moderately complex.

Vintage	99	98
WR	5	6
Drink	06-07	P

MED/DRY $30 -V

Bernadino Spumante   ★★★

What great value! Allied Domecq's popular Asti-style wine is an uncomplicated bubbly based on Muscat grapes. It is sometimes a blend of New Zealand and Australian wines, but the bottle I tasted in mid to late 2004 (★★★) was made from Gisborne fruit. It's a higher alcohol style (10 per cent) than most true Asti Spumantes (which average around 7.5 per cent) and less ravishingly perfumed, but it's still delicious, with a light, grapey, well-balanced palate, fresh, distinctly sweet (75 grams/litre of residual sugar), vibrantly fruity and smooth.

SW $8 V+

Coopers Creek First Edition   ★★★☆

The current release is a non-vintage wine (★★★★), based entirely on Pinot Noir grown in Marlborough. Fermented and aged for a year on its gross lees in old hogsheads, then bottled and matured 'en tirage' for a further three years, it's light yellow, refined and lively, with crisp, lemony, yeasty flavours showing good vigour and yeast-derived complexity. The best wine yet under this label.

MED/DRY $24 AV

Corbans Verde – see Verde

Cuvée No. 1   ★★★☆

This is a non-vintage blanc de blancs style, based entirely on Marlborough Chardonnay. Made by Daniel Le Brun (in his family company) and matured for two years on its yeast lees, it sometimes appears a bit simple in blind tastings, but on other occasions looks crisp, refined and lively, with good yeastiness and intensity.

MED/DRY $36 -V

Cuvée No. 8 ★★★★

This 'easy-drinking aperitif style' (from Daniel Le Brun's family company), is a blend of Pinot Noir (60 per cent) and Chardonnay, grown in Marlborough and disgorged after three years on its yeast lees. At its best, it is rich and full of personality, but the wine I tasted in 2004 (★★★) was fresh, crisp and lively, with gently yeasty, lemony, appley flavours showing moderate complexity.

MED/DRY $30 AV

Cuvée Virginie ★★★☆

Named as a tribute to Daniel and Adele Le Brun's daughter, Virginie, this vintage-dated wine is a 50/50 blend of Marlborough Pinot Noir and Chardonnay, disgorged after three years on its yeast lees. The 1999 (★★★), on the market in 2004, exhibits delicate fruit flavours, almost overwhelmed by pungent yeast autolysis characters.

MED/DRY $49 -V

Daniel Le Brun Blanc de Blancs ★★★★

Some early vintages of this Chardonnay-based Marlborough wine were outstanding. The 1997 (★★★★), based on low-cropping vines and disgorged after five years on its yeast lees, is light gold, with plenty of crisp, citrusy flavour and good yeast autolysis characters. It's a complex wine, smooth and lingering.

Vintage	97	96	95	94	93	92	91	MED/DRY $38 -V
WR	6	7	5	NM	NM	5	7	
Drink	04-07	04-05	P	NM	NM	P	P	

Daniel Le Brun Brut NV ★★★★

The latest release (★★★☆) is a Pinot Noir-predominant blend (60 per cent), with smaller portions of Chardonnay (30 per cent) and Pinot Meunier (10 per cent). Light straw, it's a high-flavoured Marlborough style, toasty, nutty and yeasty, with considerable complexity and a dryish finish.

MED/DRY $28 AV

Daniel Le Brun Brut Taché ★★★☆

This non-vintage sparkling rosé from Marlborough is taché (stained) with the colour of red grapes. The latest release (★★★☆), blended from Pinot Noir, Chardonnay and Pinot Meunier, is pink, dry and fresh, with good balance of strawberryish, gently yeasty flavours and a crisp, lively finish.

MED/DRY $28 -V

Daniel Le Brun Vintage Brut ★★★★☆

Over the years, this has been the most distinguished Le Brun bubbly. A 50/50 blend of Pinot Noir and Chardonnay, matured for up to five years on its yeast lees, it is a high-flavoured style with loads of character. From 'the New World's premier wine region, Marlborough', the 1997 vintage (★★★★☆) shows good fragrance, intensity and vigour, with rich, yeasty, toasty, complex flavours and a notably (for sparkling wine) dry finish (only 4 grams/litre of sugar). Retasted in 2004, it's maturing extremely well.

Vintage	97	96	95	94	93	92	91	DRY $38 -V
WR	7	7	6	NM	NM	4	7	
Drink	04-08	04-06	P	NM	NM	P	P	

Deutz Marlborough Cuvée   ★★★★★

The marriage of Allied Domecq's fruit at Marlborough with the Champagne house of Deutz's 150 years of experience created an instant winner. Bottled-fermented and matured on its yeast lees for at least two years, this non-vintage wine has evolved over the past five years into a less overtly fruity, more delicate and flinty style. The Pinot Noir and Chardonnay grapes are drawn from the company's own vineyards throughout the Wairau Valley, and before being bottled, the base wine is lees-aged for up to three months and given a full malolactic fermentation. Ten per cent of the final blend is reserve wine, a year or two older than the rest. The latest release (★★★★☆) is finely balanced and harmonious, with a steady 'bead' and crisp, lemony, appley, yeasty flavours showing attractive freshness and vivacity. It's a lean, complex style with a dryish, flinty finish.

MED/DRY $30 V+

Deutz Marlborough Cuvée Blanc de Blancs   ★★★★☆

Matured for several years on its yeast lees, this Chardonnay-dominated blend is typically an elegant cool-climate style with delicate, piercing, lemon/apple flavours, well-integrated yeastiness and a slightly creamy finish. The vivacious 1999 vintage (★★★★★) is fragrant, tightly structured and complex, its lemony, appley fruit flavours enriched with strong, bready yeast characters. Intensely flavoured, with a long, yeasty, creamy-smooth finish, it's the finest wine yet under this label.

Vintage	99
WR	7
Drink	04-07

MED/DRY $35 AV

Diamonds and Pearls   (★★★)

The non-vintage wine on the market in 2004 (★★★) is a Gisborne-grown bubbly from Twilight Vineyards, based in South Auckland. Fresh, lifted Muscat aromas lead into a crisp, sweet wine with good vigour, although it lacks intensity.

SW $13 AV

Elstree Cuvée Brut   ★★★★★

This is a distinguished wine from Highfield, guided since 1993 by Michel Drappier, from Champagne, and typically one of the most Champagne-like New Zealand sparklings, intense and tight-knit. The 1998 vintage (★★★★) is a 50/50 blend of Marlborough Chardonnay and Pinot Noir, given its primary alcoholic fermentation in a mix of old barrels (50 per cent) and tanks and disgorged after three years' maturation on its yeast lees. Broader, less flinty than usual, it is light gold, fragrant, rich and smooth, with citrusy, toasty, yeasty aromas and flavours showing very good complexity.

Vintage	98	97	96
WR	6	6	6
Drink	04-05	P	P

MED/DRY $29 V+

Equinox Méthode Traditionnelle   (★★☆)

Grown in Hawke's Bay, the 2002 vintage (★★☆) is a blend of Chardonnay (50 per cent), Pinot Noir (35 per cent) and Pinot Meunier (15 per cent). Straw-hued, it's a high-flavoured wine, lemony, toasty and yeasty, but slightly heavy, lacking real finesse.

MED/DRY $25 -V

Fierte Méthode Champenoise Cuvée Number Five   ★★★★

Sold by mail-order wine clubs, this is a non-vintage Marlborough bubbly (each successive batch bears a different cuvée number), with an excellent-quality track record. Light straw, with a rich, yeasty bouquet, Cuvée Number Five (★★★★) is a powerful wine with smooth, very yeasty flavours and a lasting finish.

MED/DRY $35 -V

Fusion Sparkling Muscat ★★★☆

Soljans produces this delicious bubbly from Muscat grapes. The latest batch (★★★★) is the best yet – fresh and vivacious, perfumed and sweetly seductive, with low alcohol (9 per cent), a steady stream of bubbles and rich, lemony, appley flavours, ripe and smooth. An excellent Asti Spumante copy, it's full of easy-drinking charm and bargain-priced.

SW $13 V+

Hawkesbridge Marlborough Méthode Champenoise   (★★★★)

Sold by mail-order wine clubs, the 2000 vintage (★★★★) is a vivacious blend of Chardonnay, Pinot Noir and Pinot Meunier. Pale straw, with yeasty aromas, it has rich, citrusy, yeasty flavours, showing good freshness, vigour and complexity.

MED/DRY $35 -V

Huia Marlborough Brut ★★★☆

The 2000 vintage (★★★★) is a marriage of Chardonnay and Pinot Noir with 23 per cent Pinot Meunier – an unusually high proportion by New Zealand standards of a variety grown widely in Champagne, but little used here. The base wine was fermented and matured for nine months in old French oak casks and the wine spent 42 months on its yeast lees before it was disgorged. One of the best wines yet under this label, it's pale straw, crisp and refined, with a slightly nutty fragrance, lively, yeasty, citrusy, toasty flavours showing good complexity and a tightly structured, dryish finish (only six grams/litre of residual sugar).

Vintage	00	99	98	97
WR	6	7	6	6
Drink	04-07	04-05	P	04-05

MED/DRY $35 -V

Hunter's Brut ★★★★

Full and vigorous, with loads of citrusy, yeasty, nutty flavour and a creamy, long finish, this has long been one of Marlborough's finest sparklings. The typical blend in recent years has been 55 per cent Pinot Noir, 35 per cent Chardonnay and 10 per cent Pinot Meunier, and the wine is matured on its yeast lees for an average of three and a half years. The 2000 vintage (★★★★) has gently yeasty aromas and crisp, elegant flavours, citrusy, yeasty, intense and lingering.

Vintage	00	99	98	97	96	95	94
WR	5	6	5	6	6	6	6
Drink	04-07	04-06	04-05	P	P	P	P

MED/DRY $29 AV

Hunter's Miru Miru ★★★★

'Miru Miru' means bubbles. The fresh, elegant and lively 2001 vintage (★★★★) is a Marlborough blend of Chardonnay (54 per cent), Pinot Noir (38 per cent) and Pinot Meunier (8 per cent). It's a moderately complex but deliciously easy-drinking style with good balance of lemony, limey fruit flavours, gentle yeast characters and lovely delicacy and lightness.

Vintage	01
WR	6
Drink	05-06

MED/DRY $30 AV

Jackson Vintage Brut ★★★☆

Bargain-priced, the 1996 vintage (★★★☆) is a Marlborough blend of Pinot Noir (60 per cent) and Chardonnay (40 per cent), disgorged after six years on its yeast lees. Youthful in colour, it's a slightly austere wine but crisp, lively and moderately complex, with lemony, slightly nutty and toasty flavours. At just under $20, it's worth buying.

Vintage	96
WR	6
Drink	04-05

MED/DRY $20 V+

Kaikoura Méthode Champenoise   ★★★☆

The non-vintage bubbly on the market in 2004 (★★★) is a 50/50 blend of Pinot Noir and Chardonnay, made in 1999. Straw-hued, it is crisp and flavoursome, with considerable complexity, but its pungent yeast characters almost overwhelm the citrusy fruit characters.

MED/DRY $25 AV

Kim Crawford Rory Brut   ★★★☆

Faintly pink, the 2002 vintage (★★★☆) is a Marlborough blend of equal portions of Chardonnay and Pinot Meunier. It's a softly structured wine with moderately yeasty, strawberryish flavours in a smooth, fruity style that slides down very easily.

Vintage	02
WR	6
Drink	05-07

MED/DRY $30 -V

Lindauer Brut   ★★★

Given its good quality, low price and huge volumes, this non-vintage bubbly is one of the miracles of modern winemaking. The recipe is Pinot Noir (50 per cent), Chardonnay (30 per cent) and Chenin Blanc (20 per cent), grown in Marlborough, Hawke's Bay and Gisborne, and 15 months' maturation on yeast lees. It's a fractionally sweet style (12 grams/litre of sugar) with good vigour and flavour depth in a refined style, crisp and finely balanced. The wine I tasted in mid to late 2004 (★★★) was faintly pink and moderately complex, with crisp, strawberryish, slightly nutty and yeasty flavours. At $12 or less (often under $10 and even down to $7.95), it offers unbeatable value.

MED/DRY $12 V+

Lindauer Fraise   (★★☆)

Launched in 2002 and now a blend of New Zealand and Australian wines, 'strawberry Lindauer' is 'aimed at the RTD [ready-mixed drinks] market', according to one major wine retailer. Made 'with an added touch of natural strawberry', it has a pink/onion skin colour and a fruity, rather than yeasty, bouquet. The flavours are crisp and – well – strawberryish, in a fresh, light and lively, fairly simple style with gentle yeast characters and quite high acidity, balanced by ample sweetness (at 24 grams/litre of sugar, twice as sweet as Lindauer Brut). It's unlikely to appeal to regular wine drinkers, but we are obviously not the target market.

MED $14 AV

Lindauer Grandeur   ★★★★★

The vivacious, Rolls-Royce version of Lindauer is a blend of Pinot Noir (70 per cent) and Chardonnay, grown in Marlborough (90 per cent) and Hawke's Bay. Blended across vintages, including old reserve stocks, it spends an average period of four years maturing on its yeast lees. Pale straw, with an eruption of small bubbles, the stylish wine on the market in 2004 (★★★★★) is tight-knit, complex, yeasty and smooth, with impressive delicacy and a lasting finish. Classy stuff.

MED/DRY $36 AV

Lindauer Rosé   ★★★

Allied Domecq's bottle-fermented rosé is blended from Pinot Noir, Chardonnay, Chenin Blanc and Pinotage, grown in Marlborough, Gisborne and Hawke's Bay. The non-vintage wine (★★★☆) I tasted in mid to late 2004 was pink, with strawberryish, yeasty aromas and flavours, fresh and lively, and a smooth, dryish finish. A great buy.

MED/DRY 12 V+

Lindauer Sec ★★★

The medium version of Allied Domecq's best-seller is exactly twice as sweet (24 grams/litre of sugar) as its Brut stablemate (which has 12 grams/litre). A bottle-fermented blend of Pinot Noir (40 per cent), Chardonnay (40 per cent) and Chenin Blanc (20 per cent), the wine I tasted in mid to late 2004 (★★★) was straw-hued, fresh and vivacious, with moderately yeasty flavours and a crisp, gently sweet finish. Top value.

MED $12 V+

Lindauer Special Reserve ★★★☆

Allied Domecq's vivacious, immensely drinkable bubbly is a non-vintage blend of Pinot Noir (70 per cent) and Chardonnay (30 per cent), grown in Hawke's Bay and Marlborough, given a full malolactic fermentation and matured *en tirage* (on its yeast lees) for two years. Retasted in mid to late 2004 (★★★☆), it is pink and lively, with gently yeasty, strawberryish flavours and a dryish, smooth finish.

MED/DRY $16 V+

Matariki Blanc de Blancs ★★★★

The stylish 2001 vintage (★★★★) is a blend of Marlborough (73 per cent) and Hawke's Bay grapes. The base wines were fermented in tanks and seasoned oak barriques, and the blend was disgorged after 20 months on its yeast lees. It's a complex, lean and lively wine, tight, minerally and flinty, with good yeast autolysis characters and a crisp, lasting finish.

Vintage 01	
WR 6	MED/DRY $36 -V
Drink 04-08	

Morton Black Label Méthode Champenoise ★★★★

Light gold, with a mature, toasty bouquet, the 1997 vintage (★★★☆) is a Pinot Noir-dominant blend, with smaller portions of Chardonnay and Pinot Meunier, grown in Hawke's Bay, Marlborough and the Bay of Plenty. Disgorged after five years on its yeast lees, it has toasty, biscuity, nutty, yeasty flavours and a crisp, dryish finish. It's a complex wine that shows considerable development, but would have been better slightly fresher.

Vintage 97	
WR 6	MED/DRY $33 -V
Drink P	

Morton Blanc de Blancs ★★★★

Launched in late 2004, the 1999 vintage (★★★★) is based entirely on Marlborough Chardonnay, given a full, softening malolactic fermentation and disgorged after five years on its yeast lees. Pale straw, with a fine 'bead', it's an attractively scented wine, crisp and refined, with citrusy, slightly limey, strongly yeasty flavours showing excellent vigour, intensity, complexity and harmony.

Vintage 99	
WR 7	MED/DRY $28 AV
Drink P	

Morton Premium Brut ★★★★

This has long been a deliciously easy-drinking, creamy-smooth, bottle-fermented bubbly. Blended from Pinot Noir and Chardonnay, grown in Marlborough and Hawke's Bay, and given a full, softening malolactic fermentation, it is disgorged on demand after a minimum of 18 months on its yeast lees. The wine on the market in mid to late 2004 (★★★☆) shows some elegance, with crisp, citrusy, appley flavours and gentle yeast autolysis characters.

MED/DRY $19 V+

Nautilus Cuvée Marlborough   ★★★★★

The latest releases of this non-vintage, bottle-fermented sparkling reveal an intensity and refinement that positions the label among the finest in the country. A blend of Pinot Noir (75 per cent) and Chardonnay (25 per cent), it is blended with older, reserve stocks held in old oak barriques and disgorged after five years aging on its yeast lees. Lean and crisp, piercing and long, it is a beautifully tight, vivacious and refined wine, its Marlborough fruit characters subjugated by intense, bready aromas and flavours. The blend on the market in mid to late 2004 (★★★★☆) is distinctly Pinot Noir-ish, rich, yeasty, biscuity and high-flavoured, with excellent harmony and length.

MED/DRY $35 AV

Omaka Springs Jaime   (★★★☆)

The aromatic, lively 1999 vintage (★★★☆) is a 50/50 blend of Marlborough Chardonnay and Pinot Noir, matured on its yeast lees for three and a half years. It's a crisp, yeasty, moderately rich wine, citrusy and nutty, with good vigour and length.

MED/DRY $35 -V

Palliser Estate Martinborough Méthode Champenoise   ★★★★

This is Martinborough's finest sparkling (although few have been produced). The 1998 vintage (★★★★) has an attractive lightness, vivacity and complexity, with citrusy, yeasty, lingering flavours. The 2000 (★★★) is a blend of Pinot Noir (58 per cent) and Chardonnay (42 per cent). When tasted in mid to late 2004, it was fresh and lively, but lacked the richness and complexity of past vintages.

MED/DRY $32 -V

Paradox Pinot Noir/Chardonnay
Méthode Traditionnelle NV   (★★★★☆)

Sold by mail-order wine clubs, the blend on the market in mid to late 2004 (★★★★☆) is pale straw, with an invitingly fragrant, strongly yeasty bouquet. Crisp and vivacious, it's an incisively flavoured Marlborough wine with pronounced yeast autolysis characters, adding a biscuity, bready complexity, and a sustained finish.

MED/DRY $35 AV

Pelorus   ★★★★★

Cloudy Bay's bottle-fermented sparkling is typically a very powerful wine, creamy, nutty and superbly full-flavoured. A blend of Pinot Noir and Chardonnay – with always a higher proportion of Pinot Noir – it is given its primary alcoholic fermentation (partly with indigenous yeasts) in a mixture of stainless steel tanks, large oak vats and French oak barrels, followed by malolactic fermentation and lengthy lees-aging of the base wines prior to blending, and once bottled it is matured for at least three years on its yeast lees before it is disgorged. The 1999 (★★★★☆) is straw/pink, very soft and creamy, with complex, strawberryish, yeasty, nutty flavours, hard to resist. From a cooler growing season, the 2000 vintage (★★★★★) is a more Champagne-like wine. Slightly pink-hued, it is very fresh, crisp, lively and punchy, with strawberryish, yeasty aromas and flavours, tight-knit, dry and racy.

Vintage	00	99	98	97	96	95	94
WR		6	5	5	NM	6	5	4
Drink	04-07	P	P	NM	P	P	P

MED/DRY $42 AV

Pelorus NV ★★★★

Cloudy Bay's non-vintage Marlborough bubbly is a Chardonnay-dominant style, with 20 per cent Pinot Noir, matured for at least two years on its yeast lees (a year less than for the vintage). It is deliberately made in a more fruit-driven style than the vintage, and so less complex, but still very refined and refreshing. The blend on the market in mid to late 2004 (★★★★) is an elegant wine, very crisp, lively and yeasty, with attractive, bready aromas and flavours showing good richness, complexity and length.

MED/DRY $34 -V

Quartz Reef Chauvet NV ★★★★

This consistently impressive non-vintage bubbly is from a small Central Otago company involving Rudi Bauer and Clotilde Chauvet (whose family owns the Champagne house of Marc Chauvet). The latest release (★★★★) is a blend of Chardonnay (58 per cent) and Pinot Noir (42 per cent), grown in Central Otago. Bottle-fermented and disgorged after 26 months aging on its yeast lees, it's pale straw, with a tight-knit, feathery-light palate with rich, citrusy, appley, slightly nutty flavours, showing excellent vivacity, harmony and length.

MED/DRY $28 AV

St Aubyns Black Label Dry Sparkling Wine ★★☆

Made by Villa Maria for the cheap and cheerful market, this is a simple, fruity blend of New Zealand and Australian wines. The wine on the market in mid to late 2004 (★★☆) is fresh, crisp and appley, with a slightly sweet (16 grams/litre of residual sugar) finish.

MED/DRY $8 AV

St Aubyns Gold Label Medium Sparkling Wine ★★☆

Marketed by Maison Vin, a Villa Maria subsidiary used for bottom-tier wines, this simple bubbly is a blend of New Zealand and Australian wines, made in an unabashedly sweet style (50 grams/litre of residual sugar). The wine on the market in mid to late 2004 (★★☆) has lemony, apple flavours, fresh, crisp and lively. No complaints about the price.

SW $8 AV

Seifried Johanna (★★☆)

Grown in Nelson and based entirely on Chardonnay, the 2003 vintage (★★☆) is a simple style with lemon and green-apple flavours, showing a touch of sweetness.

MED $20 -V

Terrace Road Classic Brut NV ★★★☆

From Cellier Le Brun, this bargain-priced bubbly is based on grapes from young vines, bottle-fermented and lees-aged for up to two and a half years before it is disgorged. The non-vintage wine (★★★☆) on the market in mid to late 2004 is a typically good buy. A Pinot Noir-dominant style, with smaller amounts of Chardonnay and Pinot Meunier, it has crisp, moderately yeasty, citrusy, appley flavours, showing good delicacy and length.

MED/DRY $19 V+

The Sounds Marlborough Méthode Champenoise NV ★★★☆

Sold by mail-order wine clubs, the non-vintage wine on the market in mid to late 2004 (★★★☆) is a blend of Pinot Noir, Chardonnay and Pinot Meunier. It's an attractive wine with very good depth of citrusy, moderately complex, slightly biscuity flavours.

MED/DRY $35 -V

Three Hands   (★★★)

Marketed by Caro's, the Auckland wine retailer, the 2001 vintage (★★★) is an attractive, finely balanced Marlborough wine with fresh, crisp, slightly sweet flavours, citrusy and gently yeasty.

MED/DRY $22 -V

Verde NV   ★★★☆

A good aperitif, this is a fresh, elegant Marlborough bubbly from Allied Domecq, based on Chardonnay (60 per cent) and Pinot Noir (to provide a style contrast to the Pinot Noir-dominant Lindauer Special Reserve). Matured on its yeast lees for 18 months, the wine I tasted in mid to late 2004 (★★★☆) was full-flavoured and smooth, with yeasty, slightly toasty flavours and a crisp, dryish (10 grams/litre of residual sugar) finish.

MED/DRY $18 V+

Vic Williams Selection
Pinot Noir/Chardonnay/Pinot Meunier   ★★★☆

Sold by mail-order wine clubs, the 2000 vintage (★★★★☆) is an impressively complex Marlborough wine, rich and harmonious, with a lifted, yeasty fragrance leading into a crisp palate with creamy, toasty flavours, dry and long.

MED/DRY $35 -V

Voyage Special Cuvée Brut   ★★★☆

Giesen's non-vintage, bottle-fermented sparkling is made from Pinot Noir (70 per cent) and Chardonnay (30 per cent), grown in Canterbury and Marlborough. Matured on its yeast lees for two years, the wine on the market in mid to late 2004 (★★★) is an attractive commercial style with gently yeasty, moderately complex flavours.

MED/DRY $22 AV

Waipipi Brut Méthode Traditionnelle   (★★★)

Disgorged from its yeast lees in early 2004, the 2001 vintage (★★★) was made from Chenin Blanc grapes, grown at Opaki, north of Masterton, in the Wairarapa. Light/medium yellow, with a floral, slightly honeyed bouquet, it's a characterful, moderately complex, dryish wine with crisp, honeyed flavours, gently yeasty and lively.

MED/DRY $35 -V

White Cloud (Sparkling)   ★★☆

From Nobilo, this blend of Müller-Thurgau and Muscat, grown in Gisborne, is just what you'd expect – totally undemanding, with fruity, medium-sweet flavours (34 grams/litre of sugar), lemony, simple, fresh, lively and crisp.

MED $9 AV

Rosé Wines

Pink wines until recently attracted negligible attention in New Zealand, from winemakers, wine judges or wine lovers. At the 2001, 2002 and 2003 Air New Zealand Wine Awards, the judges chose not to award the trophy for champion rosé – which was no surprise, given the near-total absence of gold or silver medal winners. During the past couple of years, however, the number of labels on the market has exploded, as consumers discover that rosé is not an inherently inferior lolly water, but a worthwhile and delicious wine style in its own right.

In Europe many pink or copper-coloured wines, such as the rosés of Provence, Anjou and Tavel, are produced from red-wine varieties. (Dark-skinned grapes are even used to make white wines: Champagne, heavily based on Pinot Meunier and Pinot Noir, is a classic case.) To make a rosé, after the grapes are crushed, the time the juice spends in contact with its skins is crucial; the longer the contact, the greater the diffusion of colour, tannin and flavour from the skins into the juice.

Pinot Noir and Merlot are the grape varieties most commonly used in New Zealand to produce rosé wines. These are typically charming, 'now-or-never' wines, peaking in their first six to 18 months with seductive strawberry/raspberry-like fruit flavours and crisp, appetising acidity. Freshness is the essence of the wines' appeal.

Amisfield Saignee Rosé   (★★★☆)

Estate-grown in Central Otago, the 2003 vintage (★★★☆) is based entirely on Pinot Noir, harvested at 23.8 to 26.2 brix. Tank-fermented, it's a bright pink/red, full-bodied wine with fresh, strong, raspberry and cherry flavours and a whisker of sweetness (4.5 grams/litre of residual sugar) balanced by crisp acidity.

Vintage	04
WR	5
Drink	04-05

DRY $23 -V

Ata Rangi Summer Rosé   ★★★☆

The 2003 vintage (★★★) is a blend of Cabernet Sauvignon and Merlot grapes, grown in Hawke's Bay (75 per cent) and Martinborough. Cool-fermented in tanks and bottled with a sliver of sweetness (7 grams/litre of sugar), it's a pink/light red, buoyantly fruity wine, fresh and lively, with slightly grassy aromas and flavours, light, berryish and smooth. The 2004 (★★★☆) is a blend of Martinborough Merlot and Pinot Meunier (75 per cent), with Hawke's Bay Cabernet Sauvignon (25 per cent). Bright pink, with strawberryish aromas, it's a crisp, slightly earthy wine with raspberry and spice flavours, fresh and lively.

Vintage	04	03
WR	6	6
Drink	04-05	P

MED/DRY $18 AV

Christensen Estate Feather White   (★★★☆)

A satisfying food wine, flavoursome and dry, the 2003 vintage (★★★☆) is a blend of Merlot, Cabernet Sauvignon and Cabernet Franc, grown in the Awaawaroa Valley, on Waiheke Island. Matured in five-year-old French oak barriques, it is copper/pink, fresh, crisp and lively, with berryish, slightly earthy and spicy characters, gentle tannins and good depth.

DRY $21 -V

Clearview Blush   ★★★

The 2004 vintage (tasted prior to bottling, and so not rated), is a full-flavoured Hawke's Bay wine. Chambourcin (a deeply coloured French hybrid) accounts for 60 per cent of the blend, with smaller portions of Merlot, Malbec, Cabernet Sauvignon and Cabernet Franc. Two days' skin contact has imparted strong, berryish, plummy flavours and a degree of red-wine character, with an off-dry finish.

MED/DRY $17 AV

Coopers Creek Hawke's Bay Rosé   (★★★)

Launched from 2004 (★★★), this is a blend of Merlot and Cabernet Franc. Light pink/red, with fresh, raspberryish aromas, it's a slightly sweet style (10 grams/litre of residual sugar) with good body and vibrant, plummy, berryish flavours, finely balanced and charming.

MED/DRY $16 AV

Corazon The Collective Rosé   (★★)

Briefly oak-matured, the 2003 vintage (★★) was made from Merlot grapes grown in Craig Miller's vineyard on the Awhitu Peninsula, in South Auckland. Light red, with a hint of development, it's a light-bodied rosé (11 per cent alcohol) with gentle tannins on the finish and slightly rustic, berry and herb flavours that lack real freshness and vibrancy.

MED/DRY $17 -V

Cottle Hill Sailor's Sky   ★★☆

The non-vintage wine (★★☆) on the market in mid to late 2004 is soft and mellow, with a mature, pink/orange colour, medium body (11 per cent alcohol) and slightly sweet and spicy, strawberryish flavours showing decent depth.

MED $16 -V

Crossroads Homeblock Rosé   (★★★)

The smartly packaged, salmon pink 2003 vintage (★★★) shows good balance and depth of berryish, slightly earthy flavours, with gentle tannins and a smooth, dry finish. Estate-grown in Hawke's Bay, it was blended from Merlot, Syrah, Cabernet Sauvignon and 'other' varieties.

DRY $15 AV

Domaine Georges Michel Summer Folly Rosé   (NR)

Tasted as a pre-bottling sample (and so not rated), the debut 2004 vintage was made from Marlborough Pinot Noir. It has an inviting, delicate pink hue, with floral, strawberryish aromas and flavours, fresh, light and crisp.

DRY $15 V?

Esk Valley Merlot/Malbec Rosé   ★★★★☆

This is New Zealand's best widely available rosé. The outstanding 2004 vintage (★★★★★), blended from Merlot and Malbec, grown in Hawke's Bay, is a slightly sweet (8 grams/litre of residual sugar), weighty wine (14 per cent alcohol), pink/red, with lovely mouthfeel, excellent depth of ripe, plum and cherry flavours, gentle tannins and acids and a well-rounded finish. This is as good as New Zealand rosé gets – don't miss it.

Vintage	04	03	02	01	00	99	98
WR		6	6	7	NM	7	6	6
Drink	04-05	P	P	NM	P	P	P

MED/DRY $19 V+

Forrest Estate Marlborough Rosé ★★★☆

At its best, this is an enticingly fragrant Marlborough rosé, fresh and charming. 'I aim it to be perfect on New Year's Day [after the vintage],' says John Forrest. The 2003 (★★★☆), blended from Cabernet Sauvignon (40 per cent), Pinot Noir (30 per cent), Merlot (20 per cent) and Syrah (10 per cent), has raspberryish, strawberryish, slightly spicy flavours, showing good delicacy and depth. The 2004 vintage (★★★) is bright pink/red, with fresh, floral aromas and raspberry/plum flavours, slightly sweet (6 grams/litre of residual sugar), smooth and lively.

Vintage	04	03	02	01
WR	6	5	6	6
Drink	04-06	P	P	P

MED/DRY $16 V+

Gibbston Valley Blanc de Pinot Noir ★★★

Sporting an inviting, bright pink hue, the 2004 vintage (★★★☆) of this Central Otago wine has fresh, lifted, berryish aromas leading into a buoyantly fruity palate with berry, plum and spice flavours showing good intensity and a slightly sweet (15 grams/litre of residual sugar), crisp and lively finish.

Vintage	04
WR	6
Drink	04-05

MED $25 -V

Gladstone Rosé (★★★)

Launched from the 2003 vintage (★★★), this is a Cabernet Sauvignon-based wine, with 10 per cent Malbec, grown in the Wairarapa. Bright pink/light red, it is fresh and smooth, with slightly sweet (6.5 grams/litre of residual sugar) raspberry and plum flavours delivering easy, summer drinking.

MED/DRY $18 -V

Hunter's Marlborough Rosé (★★☆)

The 2003 vintage (★★☆) is a Pinot Noir-dominant style (86 per cent), with Merlot (10 per cent) and Malbec (4 per cent). Light pink, it's a slightly sweet style (6 grams/litre of residual sugar) with straightforward, raspberryish flavours and a crisp finish.

MED/DRY $15 -V

Kevern Walker Rosé (★★☆)

Full-bodied and dryish (5 grams/litre of residual sugar), the 2004 vintage (★★☆) was made from 'old' Cabernet Franc vines in Hawke's Bay and 10 per cent oak-aged. Bright pink/light red, it has strong, raspberryish, slightly earthy flavours, but lacks a bit of delicacy, softness and charm.

MED/DRY $15 -V

Kim Crawford Pansy Rosé (★★★★)

Full of drink-young charm, the 2003 vintage (★★★★) is a vivacious, bright pink/red Nelson wine with inviting, raspberryish aromas and a buoyantly fruity palate with strong red-berry and plum flavours, fresh and lively.

MED/DRY $20 AV

Kirkpatrick Estate Merlot Wild Rosé (NR)

Grown in Gisborne and fermented mostly with indigenous ('wild') yeasts, the promising 2004 vintage was tasted prior to bottling, and so not rated. It's a pink/red, full-bodied, dryish wine (7 grams/litre of residual sugar), with strong, plummy flavours, ripe and smooth.

MED/DRY $16 V?

Kumeu River Village Kumeu Rosé   (★★★)

Now at its peak, the 2003 vintage (★★★) is a blend of Merlot (65 per cent) and Pinot Noir (35 per cent), pink-hued and dry, with plenty of berryish, spicy, slightly earthy, crisp flavour.

DRY $17 AV

Lake Chalice Black Label Rosé   (★★☆)

Designed for 'fun brunches, leisurely lunches or barbecues', the simple, pleasant 2003 vintage (★★☆) is a blend of Merlot, Pinot Noir and Cabernet Franc, grown in Hawke's Bay and Marlborough. Light pink/red, it is lively and berryish, with moderate flavour depth and a freshly acidic finish.

Vintage	03
WR	4
Drink	P

DRY $19 -V

Lawson's Dry Hills Pinot Rosé   ★★★

Bright pink/light red, the 2004 vintage (★★★) of this Marlborough wine was given a day's skin contact. Fresh, lively and slightly sweet (5.9 grams/litre of residual sugar), it's a pretty wine with raspberry/plum flavours, crisp and refreshing.

MED/DRY $18 AV

Lincoln Heritage Rosé   ★★★

The 2003 (★★☆), grown in Gisborne, offers fresh, simple, raspberryish flavours, slightly sweet and smooth. The 2004 vintage (★★★☆) was blended mostly from Cabernet Franc and Malbec, sourced from Hawke's Bay and Gisborne. Bright pink/red, with lifted, ripe, berryish aromas, it's vibrantly fruity, with fresh plum and red-berry flavours and a slightly sweet (7.5 grams/litre of residual sugar) finish.

Vintage	04
WR	6
Drink	04-06

MED/DRY $15 AV

Martinborough Vineyard Rosé   ★★★★

This ranks among the country's finest rosés. Ensconced in a 500 ml bottle ('designed for two'), the pink/light red 2003 vintage (★★★★☆) was made from Pinot Noir grapes grown in Martinborough, fermented in tanks and drained from its skins after 24 hours' contact. Smooth, with strong raspberry, cherry and spice flavours woven with fresh acidity, it shows good body and richness.

MED/DRY $16 (500ML) AV

Matahiwi Estate Wairarapa Rosé   ★★★★

The delicious 2004 vintage (★★★★) is a blend of estate-grown Pinot Noir (82 per cent) and 18 per cent bought-in Merlot. Harvested at an average of 23.4 brix, it is bright pink/red, full-bodied, fresh, vibrant and smooth, with loads of plummy, berryish, dryish (7 grams/litre of residual sugar) flavour and strong drink-young appeal.

Vintage	04
WR	6
Drink	05-08

MED/DRY $17 V+

Matua Valley Innovator Rosé   (★★★☆)

The weighty, ripely flavoured 2004 vintage (★★★☆) was blended from Grenache (70 per cent) and Syrah (30 per cent), grown in the Bullrush vineyard, in Hawke's Bay. Handled entirely in tanks, with some indigenous yeast fermentation, it is bright pink/red, with good body (13.5 per cent alcohol), plenty of raspberryish, plummy flavour, rounded acidity and a dryish (6 grams/litre of residual sugar) finish.

Vintage	04
WR	6
Drink	04-06

MED/DRY $19 AV

Millton Merlot Rosé   ★★★

Enjoyed during summer in 'bars, cafés and back gardens all around the country', this very easy-drinking wine is grown organically in the company's Te Arai Vineyard at Gisborne. Stop-fermented in a fractionally sweet style (5 grams/litre of sugar), the invitingly pink-hued 2004 vintage (★★★☆) is crisp, with very good depth and balance of raspberryish, spicy flavour.

Vintage	04
WR	6
Drink	04-05

MED/DRY $20 -V

Moana Park Pascoe Series Rosé   (★★★)

Bright pink/red, with fresh, attractive, berryish aromas, the 2004 vintage (★★★) was grown in the Dartmoor Valley of Hawke's Bay. Looking good for the summer of 2004–05, it's a simple but lively wine with plenty of raspberryish, plummy flavour, fresh and crisp.

MED/DRY $15 AV

Moutere Hills Nelson Rosé   ★★☆

The easy-drinking 2003 vintage (★★☆) is a blend of Chardonnay (70 per cent) and Pinot Noir (30 per cent), light pink, with crisp, slightly sweet (10 grams/litre of residual sugar) flavours of strawberries and peaches.

MED/DRY $18 -V

Neudorf Kina Merlot Rosé   (★★★★)

Delightful in its youth, the 2003 vintage (★★★★) was grown near the coast at Kina Beach, in Nelson. An attractive pink/light red, it is berryish and plummy, fresh and smooth, with loads of flavour and a long, dry finish.

Vintage	04	03
WR	6	6
Drink	04-08	04-07

DRY $22 AV

Odyssey Hawke's Bay Rosé   (★★★☆)

Still drinking well, the 2003 vintage (★★★☆) was made from Cabernet Franc. Bright pink/red, it has good body and depth of raspberry and plum flavours, finely balanced, slightly spicy and vivacious.

DRY $19 AV

Okahu Estate Shipwreck Bay Rosé   ★★☆

The easy-drinking 2004 vintage (★★★), grown in the Hawke's Bay and Waikato regions, is bright pink, with berryish aromas and flavours and a slightly sweet (6 grams/litre of residual sugar), refreshingly crisp finish.

MED/DRY $17 -V

One Tree Merlot Rosé   (★★☆)

The 2003 vintage (★★☆) is a Hawke's Bay wine, light red in colour, with raspberryish, strawberryish flavours, fresh and smooth, with moderate depth.

MED/DRY $17 -V

Peregrine Rosé   (★★★☆)

The instantly appealing 2004 vintage (★★★☆), made from Central Otago Pinot Noir, is a vibrantly fruity wine with plummy, slightly sweet flavours, fresh, crisp and full of drink-young charm.

MED/SW $23 -V

Redmetal Vineyards Rosé   ★★★★☆

This distinguished Hawke's Bay wine is designed 'more in the style of a Mediterranean light red wine than a typical rosé'. A serious style of rosé, it is barrel-fermented, dry and mouthfilling, with a strong surge of berry-fruit flavours, crisp and lively, and oak adding complexity and nuttiness. The 2003 (★★★★), light red in colour, offers strong berry and plum characters, subtle oak and balanced acidity. It has a lot more flavour interest than most rosés, with a fully dry finish.

Vintage	04	03	02	01
WR	6	6	6	5
Drink	04-06	04-05	P	P

DRY $20 V+

Richmond Plains Escapade Rosé   (★★★☆)

The fresh, smooth 2003 vintage (★★★☆) is a Nelson blend of several red-wine varieties, principally Merlot, Malbec and Cabernet Franc. Grown organically, it's a finely balanced wine with raspberryish, plummy aromas and flavours, good depth and a slightly sweet finish.

MED/DRY $17 V+

Rymer's Change Hawke's Bay Rosé   ★★★

Designed as 'a verandah wine for alfresco dining', this Hawke's Bay rosé was previously called Te Mata Rosé. Blended from Merlot and Cabernet Sauvignon, the 2004 vintage (★★★) is bright pink/light red, with fresh, vibrant, strawberryish flavours and a well-rounded, dry finish.

Vintage	04	03	02
WR	7	7	7
Drink	04-05	P	P

DRY $15 AV

Sacred Hill White Cabernet   (★★★☆)

Made from Cabernet Sauvignon grapes grown in Hawke's Bay, the debut 2004 vintage (★★★☆) is pale pink, with a scented bouquet. It has good weight (13.5 per cent alcohol), freshness and smoothness, with satisfying depth of strawberry and spice flavours (non-herbaceous, but less berryish than most Merlot-based rosés) and light tannins on the finish.

MED/DRY $20 AV

Sacred Hill Whitecliff Rosé   (★★★★)

Fresh, light and lively, the 2004 vintage (★★★★) was made from Hawke's Bay Merlot. Bright pink/light red, it's a gently sweet style (9 grams/litre of residual sugar), raspberryish and refreshingly crisp, with lovely harmony and length. A top buy.

MED/DRY $15 V+

Saint Clair Marlborough Rosé   (★★☆)

The fresh, crisp 2003 vintage (★★☆) is a blend of Pinot Noir and Merlot, tank-fermented and finally blended with Riesling 'to enhance the sweet, floral, citrus aromas and flavours'. It's a slightly sweet style (8 grams/litre of residual sugar) with simple, berryish flavours, light and undemanding.

Vintage 03
WR   5   ┃ MED/DRY $18 -V ┃
Drink   04-05

Sileni Cellar Selection Saignée Rosé   ★★★★

The 2003 vintage (★★★★), labelled Saignée (the French term for bleeding unfermented juice off red-wine ferments), was grown in Hawke's Bay, barrel-fermented and oak-aged for three months. Light pink/red, with berryish, slightly earthy aromas, it is raspberryish and slightly nutty, with a dryish (6 grams/litre of residual sugar), well-rounded finish.

Vintage 04   03   02
WR   6   6   6   ┃ MED/DRY $20 AV ┃
Drink   04-06 04-05 P

Soljans Vineyard Selection Rosé   (★★☆)

A single-vineyard Gisborne wine, made entirely from Pinotage, the 2003 vintage (★★☆) is light ruby, smooth and fruity, with red-berry flavours and a fractionally sweet, crisp finish.

┃ MED/DRY $16 -V ┃

Te Kairanga Castlepoint Rosé   ★★☆

The 2003 vintage (★★) is a dry Gisborne wine. Light red/orange, with some development showing, it is crisp and berryish, but mellow and past its best.

Vintage 03   02
WR   5   5   ┃ DRY $14 AV ┃
Drink   04-05 P

Terrace Heights Estate Pinot Rosé   (★★★☆)

Based on first-crop Pinot Noir vines in Marlborough, the 2004 vintage (★★★☆) is bright pink, very fresh and vibrant, with attractive, plummy, strawberryish, slightly spicy flavours and a dryish (6 grams/litre of residual sugar), crisp and lively finish.

Vintage 04
WR   5   ┃ MED/DRY $17 V+ ┃
Drink   04-05

Terrace Road Rosé   (★★★)

Maturing solidly, the 2002 vintage (★★★) is a pink/orange Marlborough wine from Cellier Le Brun with good depth of strawberry, raspberry and spice flavours, slightly sweet and smooth. Ready.

┃ MED/DRY $18 -V ┃

Trinity Hill Shepherd's Croft Rosé   ★★★

Easy summer sipping, the light-bodied 2003 vintage (★★★) is light pink/red, with pleasant flavours of raspberries and strawberries, smooth and refreshing. The 2004 (★★★) is bright pink, with fresh, raspberryish aromas and flavours, a hint of herbs and a gentle touch of tannin on the finish.

┃ MED/DRY $19 -V ┃

Villa Maria Private Bin Rosé   (★★★★)

Delicious from the start, the debut 2004 vintage (★★★★) is a Hawke's Bay blend of Merlot (80 per cent) and Malbec (20 per cent), grown in the Gimblett Gravels and Dartmoor Valley sub-regions. Five per cent of the final blend spent one month in seasoned French oak casks. Almost a light red in style, it is full-bodied (14 per cent alcohol) but very fresh and lively, with strong raspberry/plum flavours, slightly sweet (7 grams/litre of residual sugar) and seductively smooth.

MED/DRY $16 V+

Waimea Estates Nelson Rosé   (★★★☆)

The 2003 vintage (★★★☆), made from Pinot Noir, was mostly handled in tanks, but 25 per cent was fermented in new American oak casks. Pink/orange in hue, it is mouthfilling (14 per cent alcohol) and well-rounded, with strawberry and spice flavours showing good depth, a touch of complexity and a slightly sweet (9 grams/litre of residual sugar) finish. It's maturing well.

Vintage	03
WR	7
Drink	P

MED/DRY $18 AV

Waipara Hills Pinot Rosé   ★★★

The 2004 vintage (★★★) was made entirely from Pinot Noir, grown in Canterbury and Marlborough. A slightly sweet style (12 grams/litre of residual sugar), it has a beautiful, bright pink hue and smooth-flowing palate, plummy, vibrant, light and lively.

MED/DRY $15 AV

Wairau River Pinot Noir Blush   (★★)

Made from Marlborough Pinot Noir, the 2003 vintage (★★) is pink/orange, with simple, green-edged flavours that now lack freshness.

MED/DRY $17 -V

Weeping Sands Waiheke Island Rosé   (★★★★)

From the Obsidian vineyard at Onetangi, the debut 2004 vintage (★★★★) is a dry (4 grams/litre of residual sugar), Merlot-based wine with an enticing, bright pink hue. The bouquet is fresh and floral; the palate is lively, with delicious depth of smooth, strawberry/plum flavours.

DRY $19 V+

Wishart Hawke's Bay Merlot Rosé   (★★★☆)

Still drinking well, the 2003 vintage (★★★☆) was grown at Bay View, tank-fermented and matured on its yeast lees before bottling. Bright pink/red, with ripe, berryish aromas, it is charmingly fresh and lively, with raspberry and plum flavours showing good depth, balanced acidity and a smooth, dry (4 grams/litre of residual sugar) finish.

DRY $20 AV

Red Wines

Branded and Other Reds

The vast majority of New Zealand red wines carry a varietal label, such as Pinot Noir, Merlot or Cabernet Sauvignon (or blends of the last two). Those not labelled prominently by their principal grape varieties – often prestigious wines such as Tom, Esk Valley The Terraces, Mills Reef Elspeth One or Unison Selection – can be found here.

Although not varietally labelled, these wines are mostly of high quality and sometimes outstanding.

Alpha Domus AD The Aviator ★★★★★

The 2000 vintage (★★★★★) is a triumph for Hawke's Bay claret-style reds. A blend of Cabernet Sauvignon (predominantly), Merlot, Malbec and Cabernet Franc, it was matured for 22 months in French oak barriques (80 per cent new). Still on sale in mid-2004, it shows striking all-round intensity, with bold, youthful colour and bottomless depth of brambly, nutty, minty, spicy, slightly gamey flavours. Even an Aussie red-wine lover would be forced to sit up and pay attention. There is no 2001.

Vintage	01	00	99
WR	NM	7	6
Drink	NM	04-10	04-08

DRY $60 AV

Alpha Domus The Navigator ★★★★

From a year in which the top label (above) was not produced, the 2001 (★★★☆) is a full-coloured and sturdy blend of Merlot (58 per cent), Cabernet Sauvignon (26 per cent), Cabernet Franc (12 per cent) and Malbec (4 per cent). Matured for 18 months in French and American oak casks (55 per cent new), it's a concentrated Hawke's Bay red with deep blackcurrant, spice, herb and nut flavours, firm tannins and obvious cellaring potential, but also a slight lack of warmth and softness.

Vintage	01	00	99	98
WR	6	7	6	7
Drink	04-10	04-08	04-06	04-06

DRY $30 AV

Artisan Fantail Island Dominic ★★☆

Grown in Rex Sunde's vineyard at Oratia, in West Auckland, the 2003 vintage (★★☆) is a blend of Gamay Noir and Pinot Noir, matured in seasoned French oak casks. A pleasant, light, easy-drinking red, it is ruby-hued, with spicy, plummy aromas and flavours showing decent depth and gentle tannins. Verging on three stars.

DRY $19 -V

Ascension Epiphany Matakana Pressings (★★★☆)

Designed as the winery's 'very best Bordeaux-style red wine', the 2002 vintage (★★★☆) was grown in the warmest part of the hillside vineyard and matured for 18 months in all-new French oak casks. The exact blend is a secret, but the key variety is Merlot. Boldly coloured, it is berryish, gamey and concentrated, with substantial body and moderate tannins, but there's a herbal streak running through and the wine shows a slight lack of ripeness and softness.

DRY $60 -V

Ata Rangi Célèbre   ★★★★

Pronounced *say-lebr*, this distinctive Martinborough red blends Merlot and Syrah (principally) with
Cabernet Sauvignon and Cabernet Franc. Robust and vibrantly fruity, it's typically tinged with the leafy
character that cool-climate conditions accentuate in Merlot and Cabernet-based reds, but also displays
impressive weight and depth of plummy, minty, spicy flavour in a complex style that matures well. The
2002 (★★★☆) is a blend of 40 per cent Merlot, 40 per cent Syrah and 20 per cent 'Cabernets' (Sauvignon
and Franc). Matured for 18 months in French oak barriques (25 per cent new), it is full but not dense in
colour, with a slightly herbaceous bouquet. Fruity and supple, with good but not great depth of plummy,
cherryish flavours, slightly spicy, leafy and nutty, it's already drinking well.

Vintage	02	01	00	99	98
WR	6	6	6	7	7
Drink	04-06	04-05	P	P	P

DRY $32 -V

Babich Gimblett Gravels Quartet   (★★★★)

The bargain-priced 2002 vintage (★★★★) is a Hawke's Bay blend of Merlot (principally), Cabernet
Sauvignon and Malbec, with 'a good dollop' of Syrah. Matured in American and French oak casks (mostly
seasoned), it has inky, purple-flushed colour and strong blackcurrant, plum, herb and distinctly spicy
flavours. It's a weighty, firmly structured wine, in a style that nods both at Bordeaux and the Rhône.

Vintage	02
WR	7
Drink	04-08

DRY $20 V+

Babich The Patriarch   ★★★★★

This is Babich's best red, regardless of the variety or vineyard, and only produced in top vintages. All
vintages up to and including the 2000 (★★★★★) were unblended Cabernet Sauvignons grown in the
company's shingly vineyards in Gimblett Road, Hawke's Bay. Dark and lush, with the aromas of
blackcurrants and spicy oak, The Patriarch is typically a seductively warm, ripe and complex red,
deliciously rich. Early releases were American oak-aged, to give a more upfront style than Irongate
Cabernet/Merlot, but the wine is now matured in French oak barriques (25 to 30 per cent new). Built for
long-term cellaring, the 2002 vintage (★★★★★) is a blend of Cabernet Sauvignon (60 per cent), Merlot
(20 per cent) and Malbec (20 per cent). Dense and youthful in colour, it's a powerful, fruit-crammed wine
with vibrant blackcurrant, plum and spice flavours, highly concentrated and firm. There is no 2001 or
2003.

Vintage	02	01	00	99	98	97	96	95	94
WR	7	NM	7	NM	7	NM	7	7	7
Drink	04-12	NM	04-10	NM	04-07	NM	04-05	04-05	P

DRY $45 AV

Benfield & Delamare   ★★★★★

Bill Benfield and Sue Delamare specialise in claret-style reds of exceptional quality and impressive longevity
at their tiny Martinborough winery. Benfield & Delamare is typically slightly leaner than the leading
Hawke's Bay reds, yet very elegant, intensely flavoured and complex. The 2002 vintage (★★★★★) is a
blend of Merlot (50 per cent), Cabernet Sauvignon (43 per cent) and Cabernet Franc (7 per cent), matured
in French oak barriques (70 per cent new). Stylish and concentrated, with sweet fruit delights and rich
cassis, plum, herb and spice flavours, it shows excellent complexity, with a firm tannin backbone. Fleshy,
generous and well-structured, it's a wine of real class and individuality.

Vintage	01	00	99	98	97	96	95
WR	6	5	6	6	5	6	6
Drink	04-11	04-10	04-09	04-08	04+	04+	04+

DRY $52 AV

Benfield & Delamare A Song For Osiris ★★★☆

Dedicated to Osiris, an ancient patron of the grape and wine, this Martinborough red is designed as a 'lively, fruit-driven style, suitable for early drinking'. Made from barrels excluded from the premium blend (above), it is typically vibrantly fruity, with strong, fresh, plummy, spicy flavours, gently oaked and smooth. Blended from Merlot, Cabernet Sauvignon and Cabernet Franc, the 2003 vintage (★★★☆) has promisingly deep, bright colour, and red-berry and pencil shaving aromas. It's a fruity, buoyant wine with gentle tannins and blackcurrant, herb and raspberry flavours showing very good depth.

DRY $25 AV

Bilancia (★★★★☆)

Simply labelled 'Bilancia', the generous 2001 vintage (★★★★☆) is a Merlot-based blend, with smaller portions of Malbec, Cabernet Franc and Cabernet Sauvignon. Grown in Gimblett Road, Hawke's Bay, and matured for two years in predominantly French oak barriques (40 per cent new), it is deeply coloured, with impressively concentrated cassis, spice and mint chocolate flavours, warm and complex. Still fresh and vibrant, it shows good cellaring potential; open 2005+.

Vintage	01	
WR	6	DRY $39 AV
Drink	04-08	

Brick Bay Pharos ★★★

Brick Bay's top red is named after the famous lighthouse off the coast of Alexandria. A blend of Cabernet Sauvignon (40 per cent), Cabernet Franc (22 per cent), Merlot (20 per cent) and Malbec (18 per cent), the 2002 vintage (★★★) was grown at Sandspit, near Matakana, and matured for 18 months in predominantly French oak barriques. It's a full-coloured wine with a nutty, leafy, spicy bouquet, satisfying body and green-edged but generous flavours.

Vintage	02	01	00
WR	7	NM	7
Drink	04-09	NM	04-08

DRY $29 -V

C.J. Pask Reserve Declaration ★★★★☆

The 1999 (★★★★☆) is a powerful Hawke's Bay blend, perfumed, concentrated, firm and complex, although arguably over-oaked. The 2002 vintage (★★★★★), made from 21-year-old Cabernet Sauvignon, Malbec and Merlot vines in Gimblett Road, spent 20 months in new American and French oak barriques. It's a power-packed wine, dark, robust (13.8 per cent alcohol) and intense, with warm, spicy, savoury, earthy flavours showing great concentration and complexity and a very long finish.

Vintage	02	01	00	99
WR	7	NM	NM	7
Drink	04-09	NM	NM	04-05

DRY $50 -V

Clearview Enigma ★★★★

The deeply coloured 2002 vintage (★★★★) is a Merlot-predominant red (57 per cent), with equal portions of Malbec, Cabernet Franc and Cabernet Sauvignon. Grown at Te Awanga, in Hawke's Bay, and matured in French oak barriques (mostly new), it has firmly structured plum, herb, chocolate and spice flavours showing excellent complexity and density.

Vintage	01	
WR	6	DRY $40 -V
Drink	04-10	

Clearview Old Olive Block   ★★★★

This Hawke's Bay red is grown in the estate vineyard at Te Awanga, which has an old olive tree in the centre. Past vintages were Cabernet Sauvignon-centred, but the 2002 (★★★★) is a blend of Cabernet Franc (50 per cent), Cabernet Sauvignon (27 per cent), Merlot (17 per cent) and Malbec (6 per cent), matured for 15 months in new French oak barriques. It's a full-coloured wine with good intensity of fresh blackcurrant, herb and spice flavours, toasty oak and firm tannins. The 2003 (★★★☆) is the only reserve red from the vintage. Merlot holds centre stage (57 per cent), with smaller portions of Malbec (17 per cent), Cabernet Sauvignon (17 per cent) and Cabernet Franc (9 per cent). It's a tightly structured wine, still very youthful, with firm, plummy, berryish, slightly gamey flavours showing good depth.

DRY $30 AV

Craggy Range Le Sol   ★★★★★

Made from Syrah, the super-charged 2002 vintage (★★★★★) pushes the boundaries in terms of its enormous scale – and succeeds brilliantly. Grown in the Gimblett Gravels district of Hawke's Bay, it was harvested at 24 to 25 brix, fermented with indigenous yeasts, matured for 18 months in French oak barriques (55 per cent new) and bottled without fining or filtering. It's a statuesque wine (15 per cent alcohol), incredibly concentrated, yet still fresh and intensely varietal, with layers of ripe blackcurrant, plum and black pepper flavours and noble tannins. It should blossom for a decade – or longer.

Vintage	02
WR	7
Drink	04-12+

DRY $70 AV

Craggy Range Sophia   ★★★★☆

The bold, densely coloured 2002 vintage (★★★★☆) is a Gimblett Gravels, Hawke's Bay blend of Merlot (63 per cent), Cabernet Franc (27 per cent), Malbec (5 per cent) and Cabernet Sauvignon (5 per cent), harvested at 23.5 to 24.8 brix, matured for a year in French oak barriques (100 per cent new), then for a further eight months in older barrels, and bottled unfiltered. It's a notably power-packed wine with a tidal wave of cassis, plum, coffee and spice flavours, very youthful and tannic.

Vintage	02	01
WR	7	6
Drink	04-12+	06-11

DRY $40 AV

Craggy Range The Quarry   ★★★★☆

The inky-black 2001 (★★★★★) is a notably concentrated, brambly, spicy and nutty Hawke's Bay wine with huge potential. The 2002 vintage (★★★☆) is Cabernet Sauvignon-based (80 per cent), with Merlot (15 per cent) and Cabernet Franc (5 per cent). Grown in the stoniest part of the company's Gimblett Gravels vineyard and harvested at 23.5 to 24.8 brix, it was matured for a year in all-new French oak barriques, then for a further eight months in older barrels, and bottled unfiltered. Densely coloured and packed with blackcurrant, spice and nut flavours, it's a splendidly intense and tannic wine, built to last, but let down by a distinct whiff of acetic acid (a vinegary character which bothers some tasters, but not others).

Vintage	02	01
WR	6	6
Drink	04-12+	06-13

DRY $60 -V

Crossroads Talisman ★★★★☆

A blend of six red grapes whose identities the winery delights in concealing (I see Malbec as a prime suspect), Talisman was formerly grown in the estate vineyard at Fernhill in Hawke's Bay, but in future will be sourced from Mere Road, in the Gimblett Gravels district. The 2000 vintage (★★★★☆), grown at Fernhill, was matured for two years in French and American oak barriques (60 per cent new). Full and still youthful in colour, it's a highly fragrant, instantly likeable wine, ripe and supple, with brambly, plummy flavours and earthy, savoury, leathery notes adding complexity. Moderate in alcohol (12.5 per cent), it's an elegant rather than powerful red, still developing.

Vintage	00	99	98	97	96	95	94
WR	6	6	7	6	6	6	7
Drink	04-08	04-06	04-07	04-05	04-05	P	04-06

DRY $38 AV

Dog Rock (★★☆)

Labelled as 'a fun, full-bodied red', the 2001 vintage (★★☆) is a Marlborough blend of Gamay Noir (70 per cent), Merlot (15 per cent) and Pinot Noir (15 per cent), from the Omaka Springs winery. It's a fruit-driven style with youthful, purple-flushed colour and crisp, plummy, berryish, slightly spicy flavours that lack real warmth and roundness.

DRY $17 -V

Esk Valley The Terraces ★★★★★

Grown on the steep terraced hillside flanking the winery at Bay View, Hawke's Bay, this is a strikingly bold, dark wine with bottomless depth of blackcurrant, plum and strongly spicy flavour. Malbec and Merlot are typically the major ingredients, supplemented by Cabernet Franc; the Malbec gives 'perfume, spice, tannin and brilliant colour'. The vines' yields are very low, averaging only 5 tonnes per hectare, and the wine is matured for 15 to 18 months in all-new French oak barriques. The 2002 vintage (★★★★★) is super-charged, with inky, opaque colour and a rich, spicy fragrance. Densely packed with cassis, plum and dark chocolate flavours, braced by firm tannins, it's a robust (14.7 per cent alcohol), hugely concentrated, gamey, richly spicy wine, built for the long haul. There is no 2001 or 2003.

Vintage	03	02	01	00	99	98	97	96	95
WR	NM	7	NM	7	NM	7	NM	NM	7
Drink	NM	04-12	NM	04-10	NM	04-10	NM	NM	04-08

DRY $95 AV

Glenmark Waipara Red ★★☆

This North Canterbury red is typically crisp, berryish and leafy. The 2001 vintage (★★☆) is a blend of Cabernet Sauvignon (70 per cent), Merlot, Cabernet Franc and Pinot Noir. Fullish in colour, it's fruity, plummy and smooth, with distinctly herbaceous aromas and flavours. You could call it an 'old style New Zealand red', but it has a certain gutsy, flavoursome appeal.

DRY $18 -V

Glover's Lionheart (★★★☆)

Deeply coloured, the 2001 vintage (★★★☆) of this Nelson red is youthful, with strong, plummy, peppery flavours, a hint of dark chocolate and a firm tannin grip. It shows a slight lack of warmth and softness, but also good depth and complexity and should develop well. (Dave Glover recommends it for cellaring to 2010 and beyond.)

DRY $40 -V

Hamish Jardine Pukera Terraces (★★★★)

The richly coloured 2002 vintage (★★★★) is a Hawke's Bay blend of Malbec and Merlot, grown on a terraced hill site ('pukera' means 'sunny hill') and matured for 15 months in new French oak casks. Fragrant, berry and spice aromas lead into a generous wine with loads of ripe, plummy, berryish, spicy flavour, seasoned with quality oak, a slightly gamey character and firm, balanced tannins. Drink now or cellar.

DRY $29 AV

Harrier Rise Uppercase   ★★★

A characterful West Auckland red, previously based on Merlot. The 2001 vintage (★★☆) clearly reflects the challenging season. Made principally from Cabernet Franc (60 per cent), blended with Merlot (32 per cent) and Cabernet Sauvignon (8 per cent), it was matured for 10 months in new and seasoned French oak barriques. Lightish in colour, it lacks real fruit sweetness and concentration, but shows some coffee and spice complexity, with a firm finish. Ready.

`DRY $18 AV`

Hatton Estate Gimblett Road Tahi   ★★★★

Tahi (Maori for 'number one') is a Bordeaux-style red, grown in Gimblett Road, Hawke's Bay. The 2000 vintage (★★★★) is a blend of Merlot (33 per cent) and Cabernet Franc (17 per cent) with 50 per cent Cabernet Sauvignon, harvested at 21 to 22 brix and matured for 18 months in French and American oak casks. It's an oaky, plummy, spicy wine with good intensity and slightly chewy tannins.

Vintage	00	99	98
WR	7	NM	6
Drink	04-10	NM	04-08

`DRY $70 -V`

Kim Crawford Tane   ★★★★

This Hawke's Bay blend of Merlot and Cabernet Franc is typically dark and bold, with a perfumed bouquet and lush, concentrated flavours seasoned with sweet, toasty oak. It's an upfront, delicious style. The 2000 vintage (★★★★), a blend of Merlot (69 per cent) and Cabernet Franc (31 per cent), was matured for 14 months in all-new American oak barriques. The colour is dense and the palate is substantial, soft and rich, with lashings of oak but impressive warmth and concentration.

Vintage	02	01	00
WR	6	NM	6
Drink	07-09	NM	06-08

`DRY $40 -V`

Kumeu River Melba   ★★★★

Kumeu River's top claret-style red is named in honour of the company matriarch, Melba Brajkovich. The 2000 vintage (★★★★☆), blended from Merlot (70 per cent) and Malbec (30 per cent)) and matured for 20 months in French oak barriques (25 per cent new), is a richly coloured, beautifully fragrant wine with concentrated spice, leather and chocolate characters and warm, ripe tannins. The 2001 (★★★★) is a worthy successor. From 'an incredibly low-yielding season', it shows good colour depth, ripe-fruit characters and strong berry/plum flavours, with a firm foundation of tannin. There is no 2002 or 2003.

Vintage	04	03	02	01	00
WR	6	NM	NM	5	7
Drink	08-14	NM	NM	04-07	04-12

`DRY $25 AV`

Lucknow Estate Halterman   (★★☆)

Designed as a 'soft, easy' red, the 2003 vintage (★★☆) is a light-bodied (11.5 per cent alcohol) blend of Merlot, Malbec and Cabernet Franc, grown in Hawke's Bay. It's a fruit-driven style with moderate depth of colour and pleasant, berryish, plummy, earthy flavours, with a slightly high-acid finish.

Vintage	03
WR	5
Drink	04-05

`DRY $16 -V`

Lucknow Estate Saignée   (★★★)

Made by running off juice from crushed but not fermented Merlot grapes in Hawke's Bay, the 2003 vintage (★★★) is not labelled as a rosé, although that's the intended style. It looks and tastes more like a light red than a rosé, with smooth, vibrant berry/plum flavours, gentle tannins and good drink-young appeal.

Vintage	03
WR	5
Drink	04-05

`DRY $16 AV`

Mad Red ★★☆

From the Margrain winery at Martinborough, the 2003 vintage (★★☆) is blended from an unidentified variety, plus Cabernet Sauvignon and Merlot. Full-coloured, it's a slightly rustic wine with strong, plummy, spicy flavours and a high-acid finish.

Vintage	02
WR	5
Drink	P

DRY $22 -V

Matariki Quintology ★★★★☆

This Gimblett Road, Hawke's Bay red is a complex blend of Cabernet Sauvignon, Merlot, Cabernet Franc, Malbec and Syrah. Matured in French and American oak casks (45 per cent new), the 2002 vintage (★★★★☆) has youthful, full, although not dense colour and a fragrant, sweetly oaked, spicy bouquet. It's a satisfyingly mouthfilling and flavoursome wine, warm, nutty, plummy and spicy, with good, savoury complexity and moderately firm tannins. It shows excellent drinkability and is well worth cellaring.

Vintage	02	01	00	99	98	97
WR	7	6	7	6	7	6
Drink	04-10	04-08	04-12	04-05	P	P

DRY $36 AV

Matua Valley Settler Series Tin Shed Red (★★☆)

Named after 'the tin shed where Bill and Ross Spence started Matua', the 2002 vintage (★★☆) is a blend of Pinotage, Cabernet Sauvignon and Malbec, grown in Gisborne and Hawke's Bay. It's a solid quaffer, full-coloured, with a leafy bouquet and plenty of fruity, spicy flavour, fresh and crisp.

DRY $12 AV

Miller's Serious One ★★★☆

The debut 2000 vintage (★★★★) was grown by Craig Miller (of Miller's Coffee) at his tiny Garden of Dreams vineyard on the Awhitu Peninsula, overlooking Auckland's Manukau Harbour. A blend of Merlot (principally) and Cabernet Franc, matured in one-year-old French oak barriques, it's a concentrated, mouthfilling red with strong blackcurrant, spice and dark chocolate flavours and a smooth finish. The 2001 was sold as Miller's Merlot (see the Merlot section). Drinking well now, the 2002 vintage (★★★☆) is a 3:1 blend of Merlot and Cabernet Franc. Full and slightly developed in colour, it's an attractive, full-bodied wine, fleshy and firm, with cassis, plum and spice flavours, oak complexity and firm tannins, but tastes quite forward and is probably not a long-term cellaring proposition.

Vintage	00
WR	6
Drink	04-07

DRY $60 -V

Mills Reef Elspeth One ★★★★★

Named after Elspeth Preston (mother of winemaker Paddy Preston), who died at the age of 94, two days after the launch of the debut 2000 vintage, this is a distinguished Hawke's Bay red. A complex marriage of Merlot (40 per cent), Cabernet Franc, Malbec, Syrah and Cabernet Sauvignon, the sturdy 2000 (★★★★★) is an extremely classy wine, deep and still youthful in colour, with densely packed blackcurrant and spice flavours to which the Syrah adds a distinctive twist of black pepper. The 2002 (★★★★★) is fragrant, dark and dense, with hugely concentrated cassis, spice and coffee flavours and bold tannins. It's a classic cellaring style; open 2006+.

Vintage	02	01	00
WR	7	NM	7
Drink	04-10	NM	04-08

DRY $50 AV

Moana Park Symphony ★★★

Grown in the Dartmoor Valley of Hawke's Bay, the 2002 vintage (★★★) is a blend of Cabernet Franc, Syrah and Malbec. Richly coloured, it has herbal aromas and green-edged flavours, with some concentration and toasty oak adding complexity, but also a slight lack of softness on the finish.

Vintage	02		DRY $35 -V
WR	6		
Drink	07-08		

Morton Estate The Regent of Morton (★★★★☆)

Named after James Douglas, a sixteenth-century Regent of Morton, the debut 2002 vintage (★★★★☆) is a Merlot-based red (61 per cent), with 21 per cent Cabernet Sauvignon and 18 per cent Cabernet Franc. Matured in all-new French and American oak casks, it's a fragrant, strongly oaked, mouthfilling Hawke's Bay wine with fresh, vibrant blackcurrant, plum, herb and coffee flavours, tightly structured and youthful. Open 2006+.

Vintage	02		DRY $55 -V
WR	7		
Drink	04-10		

Morton Estate White Label The Mercure ★★★

The 2002 vintage (★★★) is a blend of Merlot, Cabernet Sauvignon and Cabernet Franc, grown in Hawke's Bay and matured for a year in American and French oak barriques. Full-coloured, with an earthy bouquet, it is warm and slightly rustic, with mouthfilling body, spicy, leathery characters, a hint of sweet oak and firm tannins.

DRY $18 AV

Nobilo Fernleaf Vintage Red ★☆

The 2002 vintage (★★), not oak-aged, is a North Island blend of Pinotage (principally) and Cabernet Sauvignon, made in a 'soft, accessible, fruity style'. It's a ruby-hued wine, fruity and simple, with plummy, berryish flavours and a very smooth finish.

Vintage	02	01	DRY $11 -V
WR	5	6	
Drink	04-05	P	

Obsidian ★★★★☆

The Obsidian vineyard at Onetangi produces one of the most stylish claret-style reds on Waiheke Island. Matured in new French (45 per cent), one-year-old French (22 per cent) and new American (33 per cent) oak barriques, the 2002 (★★★★☆) is the first Merlot-predominant vintage (45 per cent), with 36 per cent Cabernet Sauvignon, 11 per cent Malbec and 8 per cent Cabernet Franc. Deep and youthful in colour, it is generous, lush and silky, with lovely depth of cassis, plum, herb and spice flavours and ripe, supple tannins. It's drinking well now, but should be at its best from 2006 onwards.

Vintage	02	01	00	99	98	97	DRY $49 -V
WR	7	NM	7	6	6	5	
Drink	04-08	NM	04-10	04-08	04-06	P	

Passage Rock Forté ★★★★

The 2002 vintage (★★★) is a Waiheke Island blend of Merlot (40 per cent), Cabernet Sauvignon (30 per cent), Cabernet Franc (20 per cent) and Malbec (10 per cent), matured for 15 months in French and American oak casks (30 per cent new). Boldly coloured, it is robust, plummy and spicy, with a firm tannin grip, but leafy, herbaceous characters are emerging with age. Open 2005+.

DRY $35 -V

Passage Rock Sisters ★★★

Labelled as 'our earlier drinking style of Bordeaux wine', the 2002 vintage (★★★) is a gutsy Waiheke Island blend of Cabernet Sauvignon (predominantly), Cabernet Franc, Merlot and Malbec, matured for a year in oak casks (35 per cent new). It's a slightly herbaceous wine, full-coloured, with mouthfilling body, oak complexity and firm blackcurrant, plum and green-leaf flavours.

Vintage	01	
WR	5	DRY $27 -V
Drink	04-09	

Pegasus Bay Maestro ★★★★☆

Past vintages rank as the finest claret-style reds yet from Canterbury. Grown at Waipara and matured for 18 months in French oak barriques (40 per cent new), the 2001 (★★★★) is a blend of Merlot (75 per cent), Malbec (15 per cent), Cabernet Sauvignon (5 per cent) and Cabernet Franc (5 per cent). The colour is bold and bright; the palate is fleshy, with deep, warm plum, herb and spice flavours that build across the palate to a firm, resounding finish.

Vintage	01	
WR	7	DRY $42 -V
Drink	04-06	

Pleiades Vineyard Maia ★★★★☆

Grown in the Waihopai Valley of Marlborough, this is a consistently impressive red. The 2002 vintage (★★★★☆), blended from Malbec and Merlot, was matured in half new, half one-year-old French oak casks. Deep and purple-flushed in colour, with a spicy, slightly gamey bouquet, it is firm and concentrated, with loads of blackcurrant, plum and pepper flavour, a hint of licorice, oak complexity, fine-grained tannins and impressive warmth and complexity. If you like full-on reds, this is for you.

Vintage	02	01	00	99	98	
WR	6	7	7	6	5	DRY $31 AV
Drink	05-10	04-10	04-10	04-08	04-06	

Providence ★★★★★

This is New Zealand's most expensive wine, sold in a dozen overseas markets but rarely seen here. The 2.5-hectare vineyard at Matakana is close-planted in Merlot (principally), Cabernet Franc and Malbec, and the wine is matured for up to two years in all-new French oak barriques. With its beguiling fragrance, lush fruitiness and sweet, silky, sustained finish, the 1993 stood up well against the other (and cheaper) top Auckland reds of the vintage, but did not overshadow them. The 1998 vintage (★★★★★) was a perfumed and graceful red that impresses not with sheer power, but with its harmony, complexity and silky elegance. If you're a Bordeaux fan, you'll love it.

DRY $185 -V

Puriri Hills ★★★☆

Worth discovering, the 2002 vintage (★★★★) is a Clevedon (South Auckland) blend of Merlot (66 per cent), Cabernet Franc (18 per cent), Cabernet Sauvignon (13 per cent) and Malbec (3 per cent). Full-coloured, it is fragrant and generous, with plummy, spicy, slightly earthy flavours showing good harmony, warmth and roundness, and a strong, toasty oak influence (from 21 months in mostly new French oak barriques). Drink now or cellar.

DRY $33 -V

Puriri Hills Reserve   (★★★★☆)

Grown at Clevedon, in South Auckland, the very stylish 2002 vintage (★★★★☆) is a blend of Merlot (50 per cent), Cabernet Franc (42 per cent) and Malbec (8 per cent), matured for 21 months in French oak barriques (75 per cent new). Densely coloured and highly fragrant, it has lovely mouthfeel and texture, with an array of plum, spice, herb, leather and chocolate flavours, good supporting tannins and excellent harmony. It's a sensuous red, savoury and silky. Drink now to 2008.

DRY $50 -V

Red Rock Gravel Pit Red   ★★★★

From Capricorn Wine Estates, a division of Craggy Range, the 2002 vintage (★★★★) is a flavour-packed Hawke's Bay blend of Merlot (65 per cent) and Malbec (35 per cent). Harvested at 24.5 brix and matured for 16 months in French oak barriques (40 per cent new), it is richly coloured, sturdy and crammed with plummy, strongly spiced flavour. Warm, concentrated and firmly structured, it offers exceptional quality for a sub-$20 New Zealand red.

DRY $20 V+

Robert The Bruce A Bannockburn Red   ★★★☆

Made by Olssen's, the mouthfilling (14 per cent alcohol) 2002 vintage (★★★☆) is a Central Otago blend of Pinotage, Cabernet Sauvignon and Syrah, matured for 14 months in French and American oak casks (20 per cent new) and bottled unfiltered. Purple-flushed, with red-berry and sweet oak aromas, it is fresh, vibrant and smooth, with berryish, spicy, slightly gamey flavours, coconutty oak and a slightly crisp finish.

Vintage	02
WR	6
Drink	04-09

DRY $28 -V

Seifried Sylvia   ★★★☆

Named after Agnes Seifried's late mother, this Nelson red is made from an Austrian variety, Zweigelt, which the Seifrieds are pioneering in New Zealand. Grown at Brightwater and matured for a year in French oak barriques (new and three years old), the 2003 vintage (★★★) is deep ruby, fresh and lively, with plenty of plummy, spicy, slightly nutty and earthy flavour and a crisp finish. It's a very good quaffer, priced right.

Vintage	03
WR	6
Drink	04-08

DRY $19 V+

Stonecroft Crofters   ★★★

The Hawke's Bay winery's lower-priced red is made from fruit off young vines, together with wine which, at blending, winemaker Alan Limmer prefers to omit from his top Ruhanui label. Each release is numbered rather than vintage-dated. Crofters VI (★★★) is a blend of Cabernet Sauvignon (58 per cent), Merlot (28 per cent) and Syrah (14 per cent), mostly from the 2002 vintage, matured for 18 months in French oak barriques. It's a full-coloured wine with spice and herb aromas and plenty of firm, peppery, nutty flavour.

DRY $19 AV

Stonecroft Ruhanui   ★★★★

Ruhanui is a mix of Bordeaux varieties and Syrah, grown in the Gimblett Gravels district of Hawke's Bay. French oak-aged for 18 months, the 2002 vintage (★★★★) is a blend of Cabernet Sauvignon (41 per cent), Merlot (39 per cent) and Syrah (20 per cent). Deeply coloured, with a slightly leafy bouquet, it is fleshy and generous, with rich blackcurrant, herb, spice and dark chocolate flavours and a firm finish. (The 1990 vintage, opened in early 2004, is maturing well – concentrated and complex, with deep cassis, plum and coffee flavours.)

Vintage	02	01	00	99	98	97
WR	6	6	5	6	6	NM
Drink	06+	04-10	04-10	04-10	04-10	NM

DRY $30 AV

Te Awa Boundary   ★★★★★

This is typically a Hawke's Bay red of rare breed. Grown near Gimblett Road, it is made by Jenny Dobson, who was once maitre d'chais at a well-respected Haut-Médoc cru bourgeois, Château Senejac. Subtle, multi-faceted and beautifully harmonious, it is more complex and savoury than most New Zealand reds. The 2001 (★★★★) is a blend of Merlot (82 per cent), Cabernet Sauvignon (15 per cent) and Cabernet Franc (3 per cent), matured for 15 months in French oak barriques (20 per cent new). Fullish in colour, with a hint of development, it is nutty, spicy, leathery and complex, with good warmth and supple tannins. Drink now onwards.

Vintage	01	00	99	98	97	96	95	
WR	6	7	6	7	6	6	6	DRY $40 AV
Drink	04-08	04-08	04-06	04-05	P	P	P	

Te Mania Three Brothers   ★★★

The richly coloured 2002 vintage (★★★) is a blend of Merlot, Malbec and Cabernet Sauvignon, grown in Nelson, Marlborough and Hawke's Bay. French and American oak-aged for 10 months, it has blackcurrant, herb and plum flavours, with subtle oak and a cool-climate freshness. Smooth and flavoursome, it's a moderately complex style.

Vintage	03	02	01	
WR	7	6	6	DRY $20 AV
Drink	04-07	04-07	04-06	

Te Whare Ra Sarah Jennings   ★★★

For the first time in 2002 (★★★), the principal variety in this Marlborough red is Cabernet Franc (38 per cent), with smaller amounts of Malbec (28 per cent), Merlot (26 per cent) and Cabernet Sauvignon (8 per cent). Estate-grown at Renwick, it's a deeply coloured, purple-flushed wine with berry and spice aromas and a vibrantly fruity palate with cool-climate freshness, moderately ripe flavours and gentle tannins.

Vintage	03	02	01	00	
WR	NM	6	6	5	DRY $22 -V
Drink	NM	06-10	05-12	05-10	

Te Whau The Point   ★★★★★

This very classy Waiheke Island red flows from the steeply sloping Te Whau vineyard at Putiki Bay. The highly characterful 2002 (★★★★★) is a Merlot-dominant blend (50 per cent), with Cabernet Sauvignon (25 per cent), Cabernet Franc (15 per cent) and Malbec (10 per cent). Matured for 15 months in French oak barriques (30 per cent new), it's distinctly Merlot-ish – plummy, spicy, earthy and savoury, with sweet, ripe-fruit characters, ripe tannins and notable complexity. A distinctly Bordeaux-like wine, it scores with silky elegance rather than sheer power. Tasted just prior to bottling (and so not rated), the 2003 vintage is a typically complex and savoury wine with plummy, earthy, herbal, chocolatey, spicy flavours.

Vintage	03	02	01	00	99	
WR	7	7	NM	7	7	DRY $40 AV
Drink	05-10	04-08	NM	04-12	04-06	

Tom   ★★★★★

Allied Domecq's Hawke's Bay claret-style red, promoted as 'the New Zealand equivalent of Grange', honours pioneer winemaker Tom McDonald, the driving force behind New Zealand's first prestige red, McWilliam's Cabernet Sauvignon. The savoury, earthy and complex 1995 (★★★★★) and firm, densely packed 1998 vintages (★★★★★) are outstanding, but the 1996 was green-edged and there was no Tom from the 1997, 1999 and 2001 vintages. The very classy 2000 (★★★★★) was blended from Merlot (55 per cent), Cabernet Sauvignon (40 per cent) and Malbec (5 per cent), matured for 18 months in French oak barriques (73 per cent new) and bottle-aged for more than two years prior to its release. Rich and youthful in colour, with a welcoming, spicy bouquet, it displays intense blackcurrant and spice flavours, complex and refined, ripe tannins and a velvet-smooth texture. Already drinking well, it should flourish for a decade.

Vintage	02	01	00	99	98	DRY $130 -V
WR	7	NM	7	NM	7	
Drink	04-15	NM	04-15	NM	04+	

TW 55/45 Red   (★★☆)

An oak-matured Gisborne blend of Merlot and Malbec, the 2003 vintage (★★☆) is ruby-hued, fresh, vibrant and berryish, but it lacks complexity, warmth and softness, with a slightly high-acid finish.

Vintage	03	DRY $15 AV
WR	4	
Drink	05-08	

TW Makauri   (★★★★)

The vibrantly fruity 2002 vintage (★★★★) is a blend of Malbec (two-thirds) and Merlot, named after the Makauri district in Gisborne. Purple-flushed, with a sweet oak perfume, it's a ripe-tasting wine with rich berry, plum and dark chocolate flavours, firm tannins and substantial body.

DRY $27 AV

Unison   ★★★★★

Husband and wife team, Bruce and Anna-Barbara Helliwell, own a block of densely planted vines in an old river bed near Hastings. A blend of Merlot, Cabernet Sauvignon and Syrah, matured for a year in large, 3000-litre Italian oak casks and 225-litre oak barriques, it is typically dark and highly concentrated, with rich flavours of cassis, plum and spice and a long, firm finish. The 2002 (★★★★★) is described by the Helliwells as 'the most exciting and rewarding vintage we have ever had'. Boldly coloured, it has the distinctive bouquet of cassis, black pepper and slight earthiness, so typical of the label. The palate is weighty, warm and multi-faceted, with deep plum, spice and dark chocolate flavours and noble tannins. Already delicious, it's a great cellaring prospect. There is no 2003 (see Fencepost Merlot/Cabernet).

Vintage	02	01	00	99	98	97	96	DRY $28 V+
WR	7	6	7	6	6	6	6	
Drink	04-12	04-09	04-08	04-08	04-08	04-06	04-06	

Unison Selection   ★★★★★

Designed for cellaring and oak-matured longer than the above wine, this is a consistently outstanding Hawke's Bay red. The 2002 vintage (★★★★★) is a vineyard (rather than barrel) selection of Merlot, Cabernet Sauvignon and Syrah, matured initially for a year in French and American oak barriques (half new), then (for 'harmonising') for a further 15 months in large Italian casks of French and Slavonian oak. It has dense, noble, youthful colour and a beautifully warm and spicy fragrance. A wine of great class, it is sturdy (14 per cent alcohol) and firm, with layers of blackcurrant, plum, spice and liquorice flavours. Powerful and exceptionally concentrated, it's the finest Unison Selection yet.

Vintage	02	01	00	99	98	97	DRY $44 AV
WR	7	6	7	6	6	6	
Drink	04-15	04-13	04-13	04-10	04-10	04-07	

Vin Alto Celaio   (★★★★)

Only produced in top vintages, this Clevedon, South Auckland red is a reserve version of Di Sotto (see below). The 1998 vintage (★★★★) is a blend of Sangiovese, Cabernet Franc, Merlot and Montepulciano, oak-aged for two years. Fullish in colour, it has a savoury, spicy, fragrant bouquet. Full-bodied, spicy, nutty and leathery, it's a mellow, complex wine with strong personality, maturing gracefully and drinking well now. There is no 1999 or 2001; the next release is from the 2000 vintage.

Vintage	98	DRY $38 -V
WR	6	
Drink	09	

Vin Alto Di Sotto ★★★☆

This Clevedon, South Auckland red was previously labelled as Ordinario. The 1998 vintage (★★★) is a blend of Cabernet Franc, Cabernet Sauvignon, Merlot, Sangiovese and a touch of Nebbiolo. Oak-aged for a year, it is fullish and mature in colour, with a leathery, spicy bouquet. Mellow and flavoursome, spicy and slightly herbal, it's a characterful wine with a firm, slightly chewy finish. Ready.

Vintage	98
WR	5
Drink	07

DRY $29 -V

Vin Alto Retico ★★★★

In hill country at Clevedon, in South Auckland, Enzo Bettio has set out 'to make traditional Italian-style wines in New Zealand'. His most prized wine, Retico, based on air-dried, highly concentrated grapes, is Clevedon's equivalent of the prized amarones of Verona. Based on Italian and French grape varieties (Cabernet Franc, Merlot and Montepulciano), and oak-aged for two years, the 1999 vintage (★★★★) is strapping (15 per cent alcohol), with deep, maturing colour. Nutty, spicy, leathery and raisiny, with an impression of sweetness (but fully dry), it's a muscular and complex wine, best served at the end of a meal, 'with cheese, in front of the fire'.

Vintage	99
WR	7
Drink	05-10

DRY $94 -V

Vin Alto Ritorno ★★★★

Created in the Veronese ripasso tradition, the 1999 vintage (★★★★) was grown at Clevedon in South Auckland. A blend of French and Italian varieties (Cabernet Franc, Merlot and Montepulciano), it was fermented on the skins of the air-dried Retico grapes (above) and oak-matured for two years. Dry (although it gives the impression of slight sweetness), it has substantial body and firm, savoury, complex flavours, spicy, herbal, leathery and raisiny.

Vintage	99
WR	7
Drink	05-10

DRY $68 -V

Waimarie Testament ★★★

The 2001 vintage (★★★) is a Hawke's Bay red, matured for 19 months in new and one-year-old French oak casks. A Dartmoor Valley blend of Merlot (65 per cent) and Malbec, it's a smooth, middleweight wine with plum, raspberry and spice flavours and gentle tannins.

Vintage	01
WR	5
Drink	04-09

DRY $26 -V

Waipipi Red (★★)

Dominated by green, leafy characters, the 2001 vintage (★★) was grown at Opaki, north of Masterton, in the Wairarapa. A French oak-aged blend of Cabernet Sauvignon (44 per cent), Cabernet Franc (29 per cent) and Merlot (27 per cent), it's a full-coloured, honest, flavoursome red, but too herbaceous to rate more highly.

DRY $19 -V

Cabernet Franc

New Zealand's fifth most common red-wine variety, wedged behind Syrah but ahead of Malbec, Cabernet Franc is probably a mutation of Cabernet Sauvignon, the much higher-profile variety with which it is so often blended. Jancis Robinson's phrase, 'a sort of claret Beaujolais', aptly sums up the nature of this versatile and underrated red-wine grape.

As a minority ingredient in the recipe of many of New Zealand's top reds, Cabernet Franc lends a delicious softness and concentrated fruitiness to its blends with Cabernet Sauvignon and Merlot. However, admirers of Château Cheval Blanc, in the illustrious St Émilion district (which is two-thirds planted in Cabernet Franc) have long appreciated that Cabernet Franc need not always be Cabernet Sauvignon's bridesmaid, but can yield fine red wines in its own right. The supple, fruity wines of Chinon and Bourgueil, in the Loire Valley, have also proved Cabernet Franc's ability to produce highly attractive, soft light reds.

The latest national vineyard survey predicted the bearing area of Cabernet Franc will rise from 121 to 210 hectares between 2000 and 2006. Over 70 per cent of the vines are in Hawke's Bay. As a varietal red, Cabernet Franc is lower in tannin and acid than Cabernet Sauvignon; or as Michael Brajkovich of Kumeu River puts it: 'more approachable and easy'.

Black Barn Cabernet Franc   (★★★)

Grown in Hawke's Bay, the 2002 vintage (★★★) has good colour and depth of firm, nutty flavour, but its minty, herbal characters show a slight lack of ripeness and roundness.

DRY $48 -V

Inverness Estate Cabernet Franc   ★★★

Grown at Clevedon, in South Auckland, the 2001 vintage (★★☆) is lightish in colour, with some development showing. A middleweight red, it lacks real ripeness and stuffing, reflecting the difficult season, but has some mellow, earthy appeal, with slightly chewy tannins.

DRY $27 -V

Judge Valley Limited Edition
Cabernet Franc/Merlot/Malbec   ★★★☆

This rare wine is grown at Puahue, midway between Cambridge and Te Awamutu, in central Waikato. The 2003 vintage (★★★) is a full-coloured, floral, green-edged blend of Cabernet Franc (66 per cent), Malbec (24 per cent) and Merlot (10 per cent), matured for a year in French, American and East European casks. Less ripe-tasting and concentrated than the dark, exuberantly fruity, brambly and gamey 2002 (★★★★), labelled 'Cottage Block', it has strong, fresh, berryish, herbal flavours, well-seasoned with oak, and a slightly high-acid finish.

DRY $54 -V

Kim Crawford Hawke's Bay Cabernet Franc   (−)

Grown in two vineyards and matured for a year in American oak casks, the 2002 vintage (−) is deeply coloured and gutsy (14 per cent alcohol), but my bottle had a distinct whiff of acetic acid, giving it a slight vinegary character.

Vintage	02
WR	3
Drink	05-06

DRY $20 -V

Lucknow Estate Cabernets/Merlot   (★★☆)

The 2002 vintage (★★☆) is a full-coloured blend of Cabernet Franc (60 per cent), Merlot (30 per cent) and Cabernet Sauvignon (10 per cent), grown in Hawke's Bay and matured for five months in seasoned oak casks. It's a vibrantly fruity wine with raspberry and plum flavours and a fresh, crisp finish.

DRY $16 -V

Mills Reef Elspeth Cabernet Franc   ★★★★

A single-vineyard wine, grown in Mere Road, on the edge of the Gimblett Gravels district in Hawke's Bay, and French oak-matured for 18 months, the 2002 vintage (★★★★) is dark and concentrated, with cassis, spice, herb, coffee and nut flavours and a firm foundation of tannin. Still very youthful, it's a cellaring style; open mid-2005+.

Vintage	02	01	00
WR	7	NM	7
Drink	04-14	NM	04-05

DRY $38 -V

Mission Reserve Cabernet Franc   ★★★★

The 2002 vintage (★★★☆), estate-grown at Greenmeadows, in Hawke's Bay, and French oak-aged for 14 months, shows spicy, earthy, slightly herbal, Bordeaux-like characters and good complexity. It's a flavoursome, supple wine, drinking well now.

Vintage	02	01	00	99	98
WR	6	NM	5	6	6
Drink	04-08	NM	04-05	04-05	P

DRY $25 AV

Moana Park Vineyard Tribute Cabernet Franc   (★★★)

Maturing solidly, the 2002 vintage (★★★) was grown in the Dartmoor Valley of Hawke's Bay. Deep and youthful in colour, with strong, herbaceous characters on the nose and palate, it shows good concentration of blackcurrant and plum flavours, seasoned with toasty oak, and a smooth finish. It's too leafy to rate higher, but offers considerable complexity and richness.

Vintage	02
WR	6
Drink	06-07

DRY $25 -V

Murdoch James Blue Rock Cabernet Franc   ★★★☆

The 2002 vintage (★★★) of this Martinborough red was matured in French oak barriques (30 per cent new). Deeply coloured, it offers good intensity of blackcurrant, herb and mint flavours, but lacks real ripeness, with a slightly high-acid finish. The 2003 (★★★★) is purple/black, with a spicy, leafy bouquet. It's a weighty, notably intense wine with loads of blackcurrant, plum and spice flavour, slightly minty and leafy, braced by firm tannins. There's a slight lack of softness and warmth, but there's no denying the concentration.

Vintage	02	01	00
WR	7	6	6
Drink	05-08	04-08	04-07

DRY $30 -V

Murdoch James Fraser Cabernet Franc   ★★★

The 2002 vintage (★★★) of this Martinborough red was picked at over 23 brix and matured in French oak barriques (30 per cent new). Deeply coloured, with green-leaf aromas, it offers good intensity of blackcurrant, herb and mint flavours, but lacks real ripeness, with a slightly high-acid finish.

Vintage	02	01	00
WR	7	6	6
Drink	05-08	04-08	04-07

DRY $30 -V

Ohinemuri Estate Hawke's Bay Cabernet Franc (★★★)

The characterful 2002 vintage (★★★) was grown in the Ngatarawa Triangle, blended with 13 per cent Cabernet Sauvignon, and French oak-aged for nine months. Full-coloured, it's a savoury, earthy wine, spicy and nutty, with good flavour depth.

DRY $24 -V

Okahu Estate Shipwreck Bay Cabernet Franc (★★☆)

American oak-matured, the 2002 vintage (★★☆) is a Gisborne red, fullish in colour, with plummy, spicy flavours that lack real warmth and softness. It's a green-edged, high-acid wine, but offers some attractive berry/plum characters.

DRY $17 -V

Seifried Cabernet Franc/Merlot (★★☆)

The 2003 vintage (★★☆) of this Nelson red is a blend of Cabernet Franc (70 per cent), grown in the Redwood Valley, and Merlot (30 per cent), grown at Brightwater. Matured in two to three-year-old French oak casks, it is fullish in colour, with leafy, green-edged flavours and a slightly high-acid finish.

DRY $18 -V

Solstone Cabernet Franc Reserve ★★★☆

The 2001 vintage (★★★☆) of this Wairarapa red was matured for almost two years in French oak barriques. It's a fairly concentrated wine, fullish in colour, with brambly, nutty, spicy, plummy flavours, a savoury, earthy complexity and firm foundation of tannin.

Vintage	01	00
WR	6	6
Drink	05-11	04-07

DRY $42 -V

Solstone Wairarapa Cabernet Franc (★★☆)

Verging on three-star quality, the 2002 vintage (★★☆) is a single-vineyard wine, blended with 10 per cent Merlot and matured for 20 months in French oak casks (70 per cent new). Fullish in colour, with a green-edged bouquet, it is flavoursome, spicy, berryish and herbal, with firm tannins and some complexity, but shows a slight lack of fruit sweetness and richness.

Vintage	02
WR	5
Drink	05-10

DRY $25 -V

West Brook Cabernet Franc/Merlot/Shiraz ★★★

The 2001 vintage (★★★), grown 'predominantly' in Auckland, is fullish in colour, with a distinctly spicy, peppery bouquet. It offers decent depth of moderately ripe plum/pepper flavours, to which the Shiraz makes a clear contribution, with a firm tannin grip.

DRY $19 AV

Wishart Basket Press Cabernet Franc/Merlot (★★★★)

The excellent 2002 vintage (★★★★) is a Hawke's Bay red, blended from Cabernet Franc (75 per cent), Merlot (20 per cent) and Malbec (5 per cent). Matured for 10 months in French and American oak barriques, it has generous, youthful colour and substantial body (14 per cent alcohol). Brambly, spicy, slightly earthy and savoury, it's a concentrated and complex, silky-smooth red that builds to a rich finish. Drinking well now, it should also reward cellaring.

DRY $25 AV

Cabernet Sauvignon and Cabernet-predominant Blends

Cabernet Sauvignon has proved a tough nut to crack in New Zealand. Mid-priced New Zealand Cabernet Sauvignon is typically of lower quality than a comparable offering from Australia, where the relative warmth suits the late-ripening Cabernet Sauvignon variety. Yet a top New Zealand Cabernet-based red from a favourable vintage can hold its own in all but the most illustrious company.

Vidal Joseph Soler Cabernet Sauvignon 1998 was judged top wine in a 2004 'State of Origin' tasting of Cabernet Sauvignons organised by the Australian magazine *Divine Food and Wine*. In second place, ahead of many high-profile Australian Cabernet Sauvignons, came Villa Maria Reserve Cabernet Sauvignon/Merlot 2002.

Cabernet Sauvignon was first planted here in the nineteenth century. By the 1890s, this most famous variety of red Bordeaux was well-respected throughout the colony. The modern resurgence of interest in Cabernet Sauvignon's potential was led by Tom McDonald, the legendary Hawke's Bay winemaker, whose string of elegant (though, by today's standards, light) Cabernet Sauvignons under the McWilliam's label, from the much-acclaimed 1965 vintage to the gold-medal winning 1975, proved beyond all doubt that fine-quality red wines could be produced in New Zealand. With the growing selection of fine claret-style reds that has emerged from the region in the past 20 years, Hawke's Bay has established itself as the country's major source of Cabernet-based reds.

A decade ago, Cabernet Sauvignon ruled the red-wine roost in New Zealand. Since then, it has been pushed slightly out of the limelight by Pinot Noir and Merlot. Winemakers are searching for red-wine varieties that will ripen more fully and consistently than Cabernet Sauvignon in our cool growing environment. Between 2000 and 2006, the country's total area of bearing Cabernet Sauvignon vines will grow from 671 to 733 hectares. During the same period, Pinot Noir plantings will skyrocket from 1126 to 3754 hectares and Merlot plantings will surge from 674 to 1590 hectares.

Over 70 per cent of the country's Cabernet Sauvignon vines are clustered in Hawke's Bay. In Marlborough, where most of the Cabernet-based reds have lacked warmth and richness, during the past decade Cabernet Sauvignon plantings have nose-dived. This magnificent, late-ripening variety's future in New Zealand clearly lies in the warmer vineyard sites of the north.

What is the flavour of Cabernet Sauvignon? When newly fermented a herbal character is common, intertwined with blackcurrant-like fruit aromas. New oak flavours, firm acidity and taut tannins are other hallmarks of young, fine Cabernet Sauvignon. With maturity the flavour loses its aggression and the wine develops roundness and complexity, with assorted cigar-box, minty and floral scents emerging. It is infanticide to broach a Cabernet Sauvignon-based red with any pretensions to quality at less than three years old; at about five years old the rewards of cellaring really start to flow.

Alexander Barrel Selection Cabernet/Merlot   (★★★☆)

The concentrated 2002 vintage (★★★☆) is a sturdy Martinborough wine (14.6 per cent alcohol), blended from Cabernet Sauvignon (56 per cent), Cabernet Franc (26.5 per cent) and Merlot (17.5 per cent). Maturation was in French (90 per cent) and American oak barriques (25 per cent new). It shows good structure and density, with deep colour and strong blackcurrant, plum and herb flavours, seasoned with spicy oak.

`DRY $25 AV`

Ashwell Cabernet/Merlot Reserve   ★★★

The 2002 vintage (★★★), a blend of Cabernet Sauvignon, Cabernet Franc and Merlot, was French oak-aged for 18 months. Fullish in colour, it's a flavoursome Martinborough red, spicy and nutty, with a distinctly cool-climate, herbal character running through.

Vintage	02
WR	6
Drink	08-10

`DRY $39 -V`

Askerne Cabernet/Merlot/Franc Young Vines   ★★★☆

The 2003 vintage (★★★☆), French oak-matured, is a deeply coloured Hawke's Bay red. Mouthfilling, with lots of character, it shows slightly high acidity, but is gamey and earthy, with generous, brambly flavours seasoned with toasty oak and considerable complexity.

Vintage	03	02	01
WR	6	5	4
Drink	05-09	04-08	04-06

`DRY $20 AV`

Awarua Terraces Foundation
Cabernet Sauvignon/Merlot/Franc   ★★★★☆

The beautiful 2000 vintage (★★★★★) is one of the best reds yet from the inland Mangatahi district, in Hawke's Bay. Grown on a river terrace with red metal soils, the 2002 (★★★★) is a blend of Cabernet Sauvignon (45 per cent), Merlot (30 per cent), Cabernet Franc (21 per cent) and Malbec (4 per cent), matured for 15 months in French and American oak casks (new and old). Deep and youthful in colour, with herbal, Cabernet Sauvignon aromas to the fore, it shows impressive density of blackcurrant, herb and plum flavours, seasoned with quality oak, and firm but supple tannins. A complex wine with sweet fruit characters, it's worth cellaring.

Vintage	03	02	01	00
WR	NM	7	NM	7
Drink	NM	05-10	NM	04-08

`DRY $36 AV`

Babich Hawke's Bay Cabernet/Merlot   ★★☆

Typically a decent quaffer, matured for six months in seasoned American and French oak casks. The 2002 vintage (★★☆), grown at Fernhill, is a green-edged, middleweight wine, fruity and berryish, with a slightly spicy, smooth finish. The 2003 (★★☆), blended from Cabernet Sauvignon (64 per cent) and Merlot (36 per cent), is a fruit-driven style, lightly oaked, with medium body and fresh, plummy, berryish flavours.

Vintage	03	02	01	00
WR	5	6	6	7
Drink	04-07	04-07	04-05	04-05

`DRY $15 AV`

Babich Irongate Cabernet/Merlot/Franc ★★★★☆

Grown in the Irongate vineyard in Gimblett Road, Hawke's Bay and matured in French oak barriques (new and seasoned), this is typically a deeply flavoured, complex, firmly structured red, designed for cellaring. The 2001 vintage (★★★★) is a blend of Cabernet Sauvignon (63 per cent), Merlot (33 per cent) and Cabernet Franc (4 per cent). Elegant, rather than a blockbuster, it is full-coloured, fresh and vibrant, with sweet fruit flavours, savoury, spicy characters adding complexity and ripe, supple tannins. It's a relatively forward vintage; drink now onwards.

Vintage	03	02	01	00	99	98	97	96	95	DRY $33 AV
WR	NM	7	6	7	7	7	6	6	7	
Drink	NM	04-10	04-07	04-07	04-05	04-07	04-06	P	P	

Babich The Patriarch Cabernet Sauvignon –
see Babich The Patriarch in the Branded and Other Reds section

Barrier Oasis Cabernet Sauvignon/Merlot (★★☆)

Grown on Great Barrier Island, the 2001 vintage (★★☆) is a 2:1 blend of Cabernet Sauvignon and Merlot. It's a slightly rustic wine with developed colour and firm, green-edged flavours.

DRY $40 -V

Black Ridge Cabernet Sauvignon (★★☆)

Grown on 'steep, bony, north-facing slopes' at Alexandra, in Central Otago, the 2003 vintage (★★☆) includes 5 per cent Merlot and was oak-aged for nine months. Full ruby, it is fresh, with plenty of plummy, spicy flavour, but lacks ripeness and warmth.

DRY $25 -V

Brick Bay Matakana Cabernets ★★★

From a challenging season, the 2001 vintage (★★★) was blended from Cabernet Sauvignon (60 per cent), Cabernet Franc (30 per cent) and Malbec (10 per cent), and matured for a year in French oak casks. Fullish in colour, with a hint of development, it is fruity and smooth, with spicy, slightly herbaceous flavours showing some savoury complexity. It's an honest, characterful red, for current drinking.

Vintage	01	DRY $22 -V
WR	6	
Drink	04-07	

Brookfields Ohiti Estate Cabernet Sauvignon ★★★

Hawke's Bay winemaker Peter Robertson believes that Ohiti Estate produces 'sound Cabernet Sauvignon year after year – which is a major challenge to any vineyard'. The 2003 vintage (★★★), matured for a year in French oak casks, is a clearly varietal wine with some substance. Already enjoyable, it is full-coloured, with good depth of red-berry, plum and herb flavours, well-integrated oak and a smooth finish.

Vintage	03	02	01	00	99	98	DRY $18 AV
WR	7	7	6	7	6	7	
Drink	04-09	05-08	04-06	04-05	04-05	04-05	

Brookfields Reserve Vintage Cabernet/Merlot ★★★★★

Brookfields' 'gold label' Cabernet/Merlot is one of the most powerful and long-lived reds in Hawke's Bay. At its best, as in 2000 (★★★★★), it is a thrilling wine – robust, tannin-laden and overflowing with very rich cassis, plum and mint flavours. The grapes are cultivated in an old riverbed in Ohiti Road, behind Roys Hill, and the wine is matured for 18 months in French oak barriques (mostly new). The 2002 (★★★★☆) is based on Cabernet Sauvignon (85 per cent), Merlot (10 per cent) and Malbec (5 per cent). Deep and youthful in colour, with a fragrant, nutty, complex bouquet, it is firm, savoury and concentrated, with cassis, herb and nut flavours. It's more approachable in its youth than some past vintages, but still youthful; open 2006+.

Vintage	02	01	00	99	98	97	96	95
WR	7	NM	7	NM	7	7	NM	7
Drink	04-10	NM	05-12	NM	04-08+	04-07	NM	04-05

DRY $55 AV

Canadoro Cabernet Sauvignon ★★★

Typically a gutsy, full-flavoured Martinborough red. The 2002 vintage (★★★), matured in new and seasoned French oak barriques, is an enjoyable, harmonious wine with plenty of spicy, slightly leafy flavour.

Vintage	02	01	00	99	98	97	96	95
WR	6	6	6	NM	7	6	5	5
Drink	04-09	04-08	04-08	NM	04-10	P	P	P

DRY $32 -V

Church Road Cabernet/Merlot – see Church Road Merlot/Cabernet

C.J. Pask Gimblett Road Cabernet/Merlot ★★★★

Made from vines mostly over 15 years old, the 2002 vintage (★★★★) of this Hawke's Bay red is a Cabernet Sauvignon-predominant blend, matured for 14 months in French and American oak casks. Full-coloured, with a spicy, nutty, plummy fragrance, it is firmly structured and concentrated, with good cellaring potential.

Vintage	02	01	00	99	98
WR	7	NM	7	6	7
Drink	04-09	NM	04-06	P	P

DRY $25 AV

C.J. Pask Roys Hill Cabernet/Merlot ★★☆

A 'fruity, soft, easy-drinking' style is the goal for this mid-priced red. The 2003 vintage (★★☆), labelled as of 'New Zealand' rather than Hawke's Bay origin, was partly oak-aged (half of the blend was matured in seasoned French and American oak barriques). Ruby-hued, with berryish aromas, it is medium-bodied, fresh and fruity, but lacks real warmth and richness. Priced right.

Vintage	03	02
WR	5	5
Drink	04-07	04-06

DRY $15 AV

Clearview Cape Kidnappers Cabernet/Merlot ★★★☆

Grown at Te Awanga, on the Hawke's Bay coast, and matured for 15 months in new and one-year-old French and American oak casks, this is typically a sturdy red with sweet fruit characters and plenty of savoury, spicy flavour. Blended from Cabernet Sauvignon (62 per cent) and Merlot (38 per cent), the 2002 vintage (★★★☆) is deeply coloured, weighty and generous, with blackcurrant, plum and spice flavours, savoury, earthy characters and a sweet oak influence. It's an instantly likeable wine, drinking well now.

Vintage	02
WR	6
Drink	04-06

DRY $20 AV

Collards Cabernet/Merlot   ★★☆

An unpretentious, smooth, fruity, gently oaked quaffer. Grown in Auckland, the Waikato and Hawke's Bay, it's typically a berryish, supple red. The 2002 vintage (★★☆) is a medium-bodied, slightly herbaceous wine with plummy, spicy flavours and gentle tannins. Priced right.

Vintage	02	01	00	99	98	DRY $13 AV
WR	6	5	6	6	7	
Drink	04-05	P	P	P	P	

Collards Rothesay Cabernet Sauvignon   ★★★

Collards' vineyard at Waimauku in West Auckland yields a characterful wine with strong blackcurrant/spice flavours in good years, but in other vintages it is distinctly herbaceous. The 2001 vintage (★★★), oak-aged for a year, is like a minor Bordeaux. Fullish in colour, with some maturity showing, it is leafy, berryish and spicy, with decent flavour depth, some leathery, savoury complexity, good balance and gentle tannins. Drink now.

Vintage	02	01	00	99	98	97	DRY $19 AV
WR	7	7	6	6	7	6	
Drink	05-06	04-05	04-05	P	P	P	

Coopers Creek Hawke's Bay Cabernet Sauvignon/Franc   ★★☆

The 2002 vintage (★★☆), blended from Cabernet Sauvignon (principally) and Cabernet Franc, is a full-coloured, moderately ripe-tasting red with plummy, leafy, green-edged flavours.

Vintage	02	01	00	99	98	97	DRY $16 -V
WR	5	5	6	5	7	NM	
Drink	04-06	04-05	P	P	P	NM	

Coopers Creek Reserve Hawke's Bay Cabernet/Merlot   (★★★)

The full-flavoured 2002 vintage (★★★) is a blend of Cabernet Sauvignon (60 per cent) and Merlot (40 per cent) grown in the Ohiti Valley and on State Highway 50, and French oak-aged. Deeply coloured, it's a slightly herbaceous wine with good depth of berry, plum, spice and nut flavours and some savoury complexity.

DRY $33 -V

Corbans Cabernet Sauvignon/Merlot   (★★☆)

A decent quaffer, the 2002 vintage (★★☆) from Allied Domecq is a vibrantly fruity Hawke's Bay red with fresh red-berry and green-leaf flavours. It's a lightly oaked style, flavoursome and smooth.

DRY $14 AV

Corbans White Label Cabernet Sauvignon   (★★☆)

The smooth, berryish and plummy 2003 vintage (★★☆) from Allied Domecq is a blend of Australian and New Zealand wines. Wood-aged (predominantly with American oak), it's ruby-hued, vibrantly fruity and smooth, in a medium-bodied, no-fuss style, balanced for easy drinking.

DRY $9 V+

Cornerstone Cabernet/Merlot/Malbec –
see Newton/Forrest Cornerstone Cabernet/Merlot/Malbec

Cottle Hill Cabernet/Merlot (★★☆)

Ready for drinking, the 2000 vintage (★★☆) is a Hawke's Bay red, matured for 18 months in French and American oak casks. Medium-full in colour, with sweet oak aromas, it offers mature, plummy, nutty, leafy flavours, not intense but smooth.

Vintage	00
WR	6
Drink	04-08

DRY $20 -V

Crab Farm Cabernet/Merlot (★★☆)

Described on the label as possessing 'a soft, young, ripe body', the 2001 vintage (★★☆) is a 60/40 blend, grown in Hawke's Bay and oak-aged for 15 months. It's a full-coloured wine, buoyantly fruity, with berryish, plummy flavours, but lacks real warmth, with a slightly high-acid finish.

Vintage	01
WR	4
Drink	P

DRY $17 -V

Crab Farm Cabernets (★★★★)

The dark, firm, deeply flavoured 2002 vintage (★★★★) is a Hawke's Bay blend of Cabernet Sauvignon (45 per cent), Cabernet Franc (35 per cent), Merlot (10 per cent) and Malbec (10 per cent), matured for 18 months in French oak casks (30 per cent new). The bouquet is spicy and complex; the palate is generous, with ripe, berryish flavours, coffee, leather, earth and black pepper characters adding complexity and firm underlying tannins. Fine value.

DRY $22 V+

Delegat's Gimblett Gravels
Cabernet Sauvignon/Merlot (★★★★★)

The densely coloured 2000 vintage (★★★★★) is a 3:1 blend, matured for two years in oak barriques, new and one-year-old. Plump, with sweet fruit characters, it is still youthful, with beautifully ripe, blackcurrant, plum and spice flavours, good complexity and long, firm tannins.

DRY $35 V+

Delegat's Hawke's Bay Cabernet/Merlot ★★☆

The richly coloured 2003 vintage (★★★) is a 50/50 blend of Cabernet Sauvignon and Merlot. Still youthful, it offers plenty of vibrant, blackcurrant and plum flavour, gently oaked and smooth.

DRY $15 AV

Delegat's Hawke's Bay/Marlborough Cabernet/Merlot ★★★

The supple, full-flavoured 2002 vintage (★★★) is a blend of Cabernet Sauvignon (50 per cent) and Merlot (50 per cent), mostly grown in Hawke's Bay, but 15 per cent was sourced from Marlborough. Dark, with blackcurrant and herb flavours, it shows strong Cabernet Sauvignon varietal characters, with a leafy bouquet and good depth on the palate.

DRY $15 AV

Delegat's Reserve Cabernet Sauvignon/Merlot ★★★★

This Hawke's Bay red typically offers good value (up to and including the 2000 vintage, it was a straight Cabernet Sauvignon). The 2002 vintage (★★★★) is dark, with a bouquet of blackcurrants and mint, showing considerable complexity. Fresh, vibrant and supple, it is concentrated, ripe and powerful. Drink now onwards.

Vintage	03	02	01	00	99	98	97
WR	NM	6	6	6	6	7	6
Drink	NM	04-05	P	P	P	P	P

DRY $20 V+

Doubtless Bay Cabernet Sauvignon (★★☆)

Grown at Doubtless Bay, in Northland, the 2002 vintage (★★☆) is a middleweight red with fullish colour and a slightly leafy bouquet. It shows some Bordeaux-like touches, with blackcurrant, red-berry and spice flavours, but lacks a bit of fruit sweetness and warmth on the finish. Tasted as a barrel sample (and so not rated), the 2003 looked superior: boldly coloured, with fullness of body and generous blackcurrant and plum flavours, braced by riper tannins.

DRY $25 -V

Dunleavy Cabernet/Merlot ★★★☆

The second-tier red from Waiheke Vineyards, best known for Te Motu Cabernet/Merlot. It is typically like a minor Bordeaux – savoury and leafy, with plummy, spicy flavours, balanced for early consumption.

DRY $35 -V

Fenton Cabernet Sauvignon/Merlot/Franc/Malbec ★★★★

This little-known Waiheke Island red is grown at Barry Fenton's Twin Bays vineyard at Oneroa, where Cabernet Sauvignon is the principal variety, supplemented by Merlot and Cabernet Franc. The fragrant 2002 vintage (★★★★) was made principally from Cabernet Sauvignon (77 per cent) and matured in French and American oak casks. A dense, warm wine with bold colour and concentrated blackcurrant, nut and mint flavours, it opens out well across the palate, with charm, generosity and impressive length.

Vintage	02	01	00	99	98	97	96
WR	6	NM	5	NM	7	6	7
Drink	04-08	NM	04-08	NM	P	P	P

DRY $40 -V

Fenton Matt Cabernet Sauvignon/Merlot/Franc (★★★★☆)

The dark, sturdy, densely packed 2002 vintage (★★★★☆) is a Waiheke Island blend of Cabernet Sauvignon (41 per cent), Merlot (41 per cent) and Cabernet Franc (18 per cent), matured in American and French oak barrels (mostly new) and minimally filtered. It's a complex style with highly concentrated blackcurrant, red-berry, spice and coffee flavours, firm tannins and power through the palate.

Vintage	02
WR	6
Drink	04-15

DRY $80 -V

Ferryman Cabernet Sauvignon/Merlot ★★★

Grown on Waiheke Island, and matured in French oak casks, the 2001 vintage (★★☆) is a full-coloured, slightly rustic wine with a high-acid finish. Over-priced.

DRY $40 -V

Firstland Hawke's Bay Cabernet/Merlot (★★★)

The 2002 vintage (★★★) is a blend of 75 per cent Cabernet Sauvignon and 25 per cent Merlot, grown in the Gimblett Gravels district and American oak-aged. Full and bright in colour, it has concentrated blackcurrant, plum and green-leaf flavours, braced by firm, tight tannins.

DRY $24 -V

Firstland Reserve Hawke's Bay Cabernet/Merlot (★★★)

The full-coloured 2001 vintage (★★★) is a blend of Cabernet Sauvignon (70 per cent) and Merlot (30 per cent). It's a spicy, leafy wine with very good flavour depth, but an assertive oak influence and tight, dry tannins.

DRY $50 -V

Foreman's Vineyard Cabernet Sauvignon/Merlot   ★★★

Grown at Onetangi, on Waiheke Island, the 2000 vintage (★★★) is a richly coloured wine with strong berry/plum flavours braced by firm tannins. It's fresh and vibrant, with good concentration, but the finish shows a slight lack of warmth and softness.

DRY $30 -V

Gladstone Cabernet Sauvignon/Merlot/Cabernet Franc   ★★★

The easy-drinking 2002 vintage (★★☆) is a blend of Cabernet Sauvignon (60 per cent), Merlot (30 per cent) and Cabernet Franc (10 per cent), estate-grown at Gladstone, in the Wairarapa, and matured for a year in French oak casks (70 per cent new). Lightish in colour, it lacks real ripeness and intensity, but is leafy, earthy and spicy, with a smooth finish.

DRY $22 -V

Glover's Moutere Cabernet Sauvignon   ★★★☆

Dave Glover's Nelson red is typically sturdy, with strong cassis/plum flavours laden with tannin. It demands time. Power, rather than finesse, is the key attribute, but if you're prepared to wait, it can be rewarding.

Vintage	01	00	99	98	97	96	95	94
WR	7	5	7	7	7	NM	NM	7
Drink	04-10+	04-07	04-10	04-10	04-07	NM	NM	P

DRY $40 -V

Goldwater Cabernet Sauvignon & Merlot   ★★★★★

Kim and Jeanette Goldwater's Waiheke Island wine is one of New Zealand's greatest claret-style reds. 'To begin with, we were preoccupied with enormity,' recalls Kim Goldwater after 23 vintages. 'Now we aim for elegance.' The vines are cultivated in sandy clay soils on the hillside overlooking Putiki Bay and vinification is based on classic Bordeaux techniques, including maturation for 12 to 21 months in Nevers oak barriques (typically half new). The lighter wines drink well at six or seven years old, and top vintages reward cellaring for at least a decade. The 2002 (★★★★☆) is a full-coloured, generous, supple wine with sweet fruit characters and blackcurrant, spice and plum flavours showing excellent warmth, complexity and length.

Vintage	02	01	00	99	98	97	96	95	94
WR	7	NM	7	7	7	7	7	6	7
Drink	04-12	NM	04-10	04-11	04-08	04-10	04-05	04-05	04-08

DRY $69 -V   🍇 🍇 🍇

Goldwater Wood's Hill Cabernet/Merlot   (★★★☆)

Showing good concentration and complexity, the 2002 vintage (★★★☆) was made from grapes off young vines and others not selected for the top label (above). Estate-grown on Waiheke Island and matured for a year in French and American oak casks (50 per cent new), it's a blend of Cabernet Sauvignon (69 per cent) and Merlot (31 per cent). Full-coloured, with cassis, green-leaf and spice aromas, it's a full-bodied wine with strong blackcurrant-like flavours, nutty oak and firm tannins. Best drinking 2004–06.

Vintage	02
WR	6
Drink	04-09

DRY $29 -V

Himmelsfeld Moutere Cabernet Sauvignon   ★★★☆

Grown on a north-facing clay slope, this Upper Moutere, Nelson red is typically a sturdy, characterful, full-coloured wine with a slightly leafy bouquet, good body and depth of blackcurrant, plum and spice flavours and a firm tannin grip.

DRY $28 -V

Hyperion Kronos Cabernet/Merlot/Malbec ★★★☆

Grown at Matakana, north of Auckland, the 2002 vintage (★★★) is a blend of Cabernet Sauvignon (60 per cent), Merlot (30 per cent) and Malbec (10 per cent), matured for over a year in American and 'European' oak casks. Full-coloured, with a spicy bouquet, it's a flavoursome wine with blackcurrant and red-berry flavours, leafy, earthy touches and considerable complexity.

Vintage	02	01	00	99	98
WR	6	NM	6	6	7
Drink	06-10	NM	04-08	P	P

DRY $32 -V

Hyperion The Titan Cabernet Sauvignon (★★★★)

It's not as gigantic as 'Titan' suggests, but the debut 2002 vintage (★★★★) of this Matakana red is deeply coloured and fragrant, with strong, well-ripened blackcurrant and spice flavours, free of undue herbaceousness. Brambly, with sweet fruit characters, it's a strongly varietal wine, already a pleasure to drink.

Vintage	02
WR	7
Drink	04-10

DRY $42 -V

Isola Estate Cabernet Sauvignon/Merlot (★★☆)

Grown on Waiheke Island, the 2002 vintage (★★☆) is full-coloured, with a spicy, slightly leafy bouquet. It's a plummy, reasonably flavoursome wine but also shows a slight lack of warmth, with a crisp, minty finish.

DRY $30 -V

John Mellars Great Barrier Cabernet (★ − ★★★★)

At its best, John Mellars' Great Barrier Island red is fragrant and full-bodied, with very good depth of blackcurrant, spice and plum flavours, oak richness and firm, balanced tannins. However, some vintages have been slightly flawed. The 2000 vintage was still on sale in 2004, but there is no 2001 or 2002. The next release will be from 2003.

DRY $25 -V

Kemblefield The Reserve Cabernet Sauvignon (★★★☆)

The debut 2000 vintage (★★★☆) was estate-grown at Mangatahi, in Hawke's Bay, and matured for 15 months in French oak casks. Full but not dense in colour, with the slightly leafy aromas of cool-climate Cabernet Sauvignon, it's a full-bodied, mellow, well-rounded wine with strong blackcurrant and plum flavours, some green, herbal notes and savoury, spicy complexities.

DRY $36 -V

Kemblefield Winemakers Signature Cabernet Sauvignon/Merlot ★★☆

The 2002 vintage (★★) was estate-grown at Mangatahi, in Hawke's Bay, and French oak-aged. A blend of Cabernet Sauvignon (50 per cent), Merlot (35 per cent) and Cabernet Franc (15 per cent), it shows lightish colour, with slightly leafy aromas. It's a medium-bodied, slightly rustic wine with moderate depth of red-berry and herb flavours and a crisp finish.

DRY $17 -V

Kennedy Point Vineyard
Cabernet Sauvignon/Merlot/Cabernet Franc/Malbec ★★★★

The 2002 vintage (★★★★) is an excellent Waiheke Island red. Cabernet Sauvignon-based (75 per cent), with 17 per cent Merlot and splashes of Cabernet Franc and Malbec, it is richly coloured, with fresh, youthful blackcurrant, spice and nut flavours, showing good concentration, some savoury, gamey complexity and a firm foundation of tannin. It should mature well.

Vintage	00	99		
WR	6	6		
Drink	04-10	04-10		

DRY $39 -V

Kerr Farm Kumeu Cabernet Sauvignon ★★★

This is typically a solid West Auckland red with berryish, spicy, slightly leafy flavours. The 2001 vintage (★★★) was matured for a year in French and American oak casks (30 per cent new). Deeply coloured, with slightly leafy aromas and some cedary oak adding complexity, it has berry and plum flavours showing some richness, but finishes with green-edged tannins.

Vintage	01	00
WR	7	7
Drink	04-07	04-05

DRY $22 -V

Kingsley Estate Gimblett Gravels Cabernet/Malbec ★★★★☆

The firm, concentrated 2002 vintage (★★★★☆) is a blend of Cabernet Sauvignon (71 per cent), Malbec (15 per cent) and Merlot (14 per cent), grown in three vineyards in the Gimblett Gravels district of Hawke's Bay and matured in French oak barriques. Boldly coloured, it is smooth, rich and complex, with lovely depth of blackcurrant, plum, herb and spice flavours, hints of coffee and nuts, and firm underlying tannins. It's already approachable but built to last; open 2006 onwards.

Vintage	02	01
WR	6	6
Drink	04-10	04-08

DRY $40 AV

Linden Estate Dam Block Cabernet/Malbec/Merlot ★★★★

A single-vineyard Hawke's Bay wine, grown in the Esk Valley, the 2000 vintage (★★★★) is a blend of Cabernet Sauvignon (70 per cent), Malbec (20 per cent) and Merlot (10 per cent), matured in French oak barriques (30 per cent new). Richly coloured, with a perfumed bouquet, it's a generous, supple and harmonious wine with strong, plummy, slightly gamey, sweetly oaked flavours, good complexity and a lingering finish. It's drinking well now.

Vintage	00
WR	6
Drink	04-06

DRY $30 AV

Longlands Cabernet/Merlot ★★★☆

From the Te Awa winery in Hawke's Bay, the 2002 vintage (★★★★) was matured for 15 months in French oak barriques (20 per cent new). Deep and youthful in colour, it shows good warmth and richness, with strong blackcurrant, spice, herb and nut flavours, savoury, earthy touches and a firm underlay of tannin. Great value.

Vintage	02	01	00	99	98
WR	6	5	6	5	6
Drink	04-08	04-06	04-05	04-05	04-05

DRY $20 AV

Loopline Vineyard Wairarapa Cabernet ★★☆

The 2003 vintage (★★☆) is a blend of Cabernet Sauvignon (77 per cent), Cabernet Franc (14 per cent) and Malbec (9 per cent), grown at Opaki, near Masterton in the Wairarapa. It's a medium-bodied red, vibrant, berryish and plummy, but only moderately ripe-tasting, and lacks warmth and roundness on the finish.

Vintage	02		DRY $23 -V
WR	6		
Drink	04-09		

Lucknow Estate Cabernets/Merlot ★★★

The 2002 vintage (★★★) of this Hawke's Bay red is a blend of Cabernet Franc, Merlot and Cabernet Sauvignon. Full-coloured, with berry, plum and herb flavours and a touch of spicy oak, it's a fresh and vibrant, fruit-driven style with moderate tannins and very decent depth.

DRY $19 AV

Margrain Martinborough Merlot ★★★☆

Harvested at 24 brix, the 2002 vintage (★★★☆) is deeply coloured, with a slightly leafy bouquet. It's a full-bodied, generous wine with strong blackcurrant, red-berry and herb flavours, fresh and vibrantly fruity, with well-integrated oak and the potential to age well. The 2003 (★★★☆) is also attractive. French oak-matured for 10 months, it is deep ruby, youthful and vibrant, with very good depth of plum, berry, spice and nut flavours, ripe and firm. It's an elegant rather than blockbuster style, showing good harmony.

Vintage	03	02	01	00	99	98	DRY $32 -V
WR	5	7	7	6	6	7	
Drink	05-08	04-08	04-06	04-06	04-05	04-06	

Matariki Reserve Hawke's Bay Cabernet Sauvignon ★★★★

The 2000 vintage (★★★★☆), an unblended Cabernet Sauvignon, was grown in Gimblett Road, matured for a year in seasoned oak casks and then aged for a further eight months in new French oak barriques. Dark, it's a highly concentrated wine with blackcurrant, plum and mint flavours, cedary, nutty oak adding complexity and a firm tannin grip. A worthy effort from a difficult year, the 2001 (★★★☆) is deeply coloured, with a fragrant bouquet of herbs and nuts. It's a weighty wine, slightly high in acidity, with very good depth of blackcurrant, plum and spice flavours, quality oak and tight tannins. Open 2005+.

Vintage	01	00	DRY $40 -V
WR	6	7	
Drink	04-09	04-12	

Matua Valley Ararimu Cabernet Sauvignon/Merlot (★★★☆)

Most recent vintages of Matua's flagship red have been Merlot-predominant, but the 2001 (★★★☆) was blended from Cabernet Sauvignon (55 per cent), Merlot (38 per cent) and Malbec (7 per cent). Matured for over a year in all-new French (80 per cent) and American oak barriques, it's a full-coloured Hawke's Bay red with strong blackcurrant and plum flavours and some leathery, savoury complexity. However, it lacks the notable power and concentration of this label at its best and is probably only for short-term cellaring.

DRY $40 -V

Matua Valley Hawke's Bay Cabernet Sauvignon/Merlot ★★☆

The ruby-hued 2003 vintage (★★☆) is a blend of Cabernet Sauvignon (60 per cent) and Merlot (40 per cent), matured in seasoned French and American oak casks. It's a fruity, lightly wooded, smooth wine with berry and plum flavours that lack any real intensity, but offer pleasant, easy drinking.

Vintage	03		DRY $17 -V
WR	4		
Drink	04-06		

Matua Valley Matheson Cabernet/Merlot ★★★☆

Grown in the Ngatarawa district of Hawke's Bay and matured in French and American oak casks (half new), the 2002 vintage (★★★) is a richly coloured, distinctly herbal blend of Cabernet Sauvignon (80 per cent) and Merlot. Balanced for easy drinking, it possesses strong, vibrantly fruity blackcurrant and spice flavours, leafy, minty characters and a very smooth finish. (The 2003 is a Merlot/Cabernet blend.)

Vintage	02	01
WR	6	6
Drink	04-05	P

DRY $20 AV

Mills Reef Elspeth Cabernet/Merlot ★★★★★

Grown in the company's stony, close-planted Mere Road vineyard, near Hastings, this is a consistently impressive Hawke's Bay red, dark, highly concentrated and built to last. The 2002 vintage (★★★★☆) is densely coloured, with rich blackcurrant, plum, herb and spice flavours seasoned with quality French oak and a firm tannin grip. It needs time; open 2006+.

Vintage	02	01	00	99	98
WR	7	6	7	6	7
Drink	04-10	04-06	04-05	P	P

DRY $40 AV

Mills Reef Elspeth Cabernet Sauvignon ★★★★★

Grown in the company's shingly vineyard at Mere Road, near Hastings, the 2000 vintage (★★★★☆) is based entirely on Cabernet Sauvignon. Densely coloured, it's a natural candidate for cellaring, with substantial body (14 per cent alcohol), good fruit sweetness, a seasoning of fine-quality French oak and bold, concentrated flavours, spicy, nutty and tannic. The 2001, tasted just prior to bottling (and so not rated), was deeply coloured, with spicy French oak aromas. It's a relatively forward vintage, supple and not hugely concentrated, but still showing rich blackcurrant, plum and herb flavours, nutty and complex. There is no 2002.

Vintage	02	01	00	99	98	97
WR	NM	6	7	6	7	7
Drink	NM	04-06	04-05	P	P	P

DRY $40 AV

Mills Reef Reserve Cabernet/Merlot ★★★☆

The 2002 vintage (★★★★) of this French oak-matured Hawke's Bay red is substantial and tightly structured. Dark and youthful in colour, it is fragrant and spicy, warm and complex, with excellent depth of blackcurrant and plum flavours, hints of coffee and spice, and the potential to mature well.

Vintage	02	01
WR	7	7
Drink	04-07	04-06

DRY $25 AV

Mission Hawke's Bay Cabernet/Merlot ★★☆

The 2003 vintage (★★☆) is an oak-aged blend of Cabernet Sauvignon, Cabernet Franc and Merlot, with a small percentage of Syrah and Malbec. Ruby-hued, with moderate depth, it is fresh, berryish, spicy and slightly leafy, with gentle tannins giving a smooth finish. Easy, no-fuss drinking.

DRY $15 AV

Mission Hawke's Bay Cabernet Sauvignon ★★☆

In favourable vintages, this reasonably priced Hawke's Bay red can offer very appealing value; in lesser years it is light and leafy. The oak-aged 2003 vintage (★★☆) is a youthful, green-edged wine that lacks real ripeness and depth.

DRY $15 AV

Mission Reserve Cabernet Sauvignon ★★★

Grown in Gimblett Road, Hawke's Bay, and matured for 16 months in French oak casks (50 per cent new), the 2002 vintage (★★★☆) includes 9 per cent Cabernet Franc and 3 per cent Merlot. Bold and youthful in colour, it's a robust wine (14.5 per cent alcohol), with tight, concentrated cassis, plum and herb flavours, oak complexity and a firm tannin grip. It should be long-lived; open 2006+.

Vintage	02	01	00	99	DRY $22 -V
WR	5	5	5	7	
Drink	04-12	P	04-08	04-10	

Montana Fairhall Estate Cabernet Sauvignon/Merlot ★★★★

The richly coloured 2001 vintage (★★★★) from Allied Domecq is a classy claret-style red from Marlborough. Its blackcurrant, plum and herb flavours are fresh and strong, with good warmth and complexity and ripe tannins. Drink 2005 onwards.

DRY $29 AV

Moutere Hills Nelson Cabernet/Merlot ★★☆

Estate-grown at Upper Moutere, this is typically a berryish, slightly herbal, middleweight red. The 2002 vintage (★★☆), matured for 10 months in French and American oak casks, has a youthful, ruby hue and leafy bouquet. Plummy, fresh, fruity and soft, it's a light (11.5 per cent alcohol), pleasant summer red.

Vintage	02	01	00	99	98	97	DRY $24 -V
WR	5	5	5	5	4	5	
Drink	06-08	P	04-05	P	P	P	

Mudbrick Vineyard Cabernet/Malbec/Syrah (★★★☆)

Brambly, spicy and gamey on the nose, the 2002 vintage (★★★☆) is a Waiheke Island blend of Cabernet Sauvignon (76 per cent), Malbec (12 per cent) and Syrah (12 per cent), matured for a year in French and American oak barriques (30 per cent new). Richly coloured, with a strong, sweet oak influence, it's forward in its appeal, with loads of berryish, spicy flavour, the rustic character of Malbec, and slightly chewy tannins.

DRY $25 AV

Mudbrick Vineyard Reserve Cabernet/Merlot (★★★)

Grown on Waiheke Island, the 2002 vintage (★★☆) is a blend of Cabernet Sauvignon (72 per cent) and Merlot (28 per cent). Matured for a year in French oak barriques (30 per cent new), it's a boldly coloured wine with raspberry and pencil shavings aromas and flavours that show a slight lack of warmth and softness.

DRY $38 -V

Murdoch James Kathleen Mary Cabernet Sauvignon (★★★)

Only sold at the Martinborough cellar door, the 2002 vintage (★★★) is densely coloured, with blackcurrant, plum and green-leaf flavours that are impressively concentrated, but too crisply herbaceous to rate more highly.

DRY $60 -V

Nautilus Marlborough Cabernet Sauvignon/Merlot   ★★★★

Cabernet Sauvignon has struggled to succeed in Marlborough, but Nautilus is keeping the flag flying. Deeply coloured, the 2001 vintage (★★★★) is a blend of Cabernet Sauvignon (60 per cent) and Merlot (40 per cent), matured in French oak casks (30 per cent new). It's a generous wine with vibrant plum, blackcurrant and spice flavours, fresh, ripe and finely balanced.

Vintage	01		
WR	6		
Drink	04-07		

DRY $30 AV

Newton/Forrest Cornerstone Cabernet/Merlot/Malbec   ★★★★★

Grown in the Cornerstone Vineyard, on the junction of Gimblett Road and State Highway 50, in Hawke's Bay, this is a consistently distinguished wine. The robust (14.5 per cent alcohol) 2002 vintage (★★★★★) is a blend of Cabernet Sauvignon (35 per cent), Merlot (34 per cent) and Malbec (31 per cent), matured in French (principally) and American oak barriques. Dark, fragrant and very fleshy, with genuinely sweet, ripe-fruit characters, a spicy Malbec influence and complex, highly concentrated flavours, it's still very young, but firmly structured and should mature well. There is no 2003.

Vintage	03	02	01	00	99	98
WR	NM	6	4	7	6	7
Drink	NM	04-10	04-05	05-10	04-05	04-10

DRY $40 AV

Newton Forrest Cornerstone Cabernet Sauvignon   ★★★★★

The 2002 vintage (★★★★★) is a straight Cabernet Sauvignon, grown in Gimblett Road, Hawke's Bay. Rich and full, with dense, youthful colour, it has a slightly earthy, spicy nose seasoned with sweet oak. The palate is bold, with firm but supple tannins, sweet, ripe-fruit characters and generous blackcurrant, plum, spice and mint flavours. Still youthful, it's worth cellaring long term.

Vintage	02
WR	6
Drink	04-10

DRY $40 AV

Ngaruroro Estate Rockhill Cabernet/Merlot   ★★★☆

Grown at two Hawke's Bay sites, the 2002 vintage (★★★☆) is a 50/50 blend of Cabernet Sauvignon and Merlot, American oak-aged for a year. Full and bright in colour, it is fresh and smooth, with blackcurrant, spice and green-leaf flavours showing good concentration.

DRY $25 AV

Ngatarawa Stables Cabernet/Merlot   ★★★

Typically a sturdy Hawke's Bay red with drink-young appeal. The 2002 vintage (★★★), a blend of Cabernet Sauvignon (47 per cent), Merlot (44 per cent) and Malbec (9 per cent), is an attractive red with sweetly oaked red-berry, spice and herb flavours showing good length.

Vintage	02	01	00	99	98
WR	6	6	6	5	7
Drink	04-05	04-05	P	P	P

DRY $16 AV

Nobilo Icon Cabernet/Merlot   (★★★)

The fresh, vibrant 2001 vintage (★★★) is a Marlborough blend of equal parts of Cabernet Sauvignon and Merlot, matured for a year in French and American oak casks (new and seasoned). It's a boldly coloured wine with herbal characters, plenty of blackcurrant, plum and spice flavour, some oak complexity and a slightly green, high-acid finish.

DRY $23 -V

Odyssey Kumeu Cabernet Sauvignon   ★★☆

The 2004 vintage (★★☆), matured briefly in seasoned oak casks, is a straight Cabernet Sauvignon, grown at the Heralds Cove vineyard. Ruby-hued, with berry and herb aromas, it is fresh and smooth, although not rich, in a medium-bodied style with raspberry and plum flavours and gentle tannins.

DRY $19 -V

Okahu Estate Ninety Mile
Cabernet Sauvignon/Cabernet Franc/Merlot   ★★★☆

At its best this is an excellent red, fleshy, with lots of savoury, spicy flavour. The 2000 vintage (★★★☆) marries Cabernet Sauvignon, Cabernet Franc and Merlot, grown in the estate vineyard at Kaitaia, Northland, with Cabernet Franc from Clevedon, in South Auckland, and Merlot from Hawke's Bay. Matured in French and American oak casks (20 per cent new), it has a fragrant, berryish bouquet, with integrated oak. The palate is fresh and supple, with blackcurrant and plum flavours, slightly savoury and earthy touches and gentle tannins. It's not a blockbuster, but quietly satisfying.

Vintage	00	99	98	97	96
WR	6	5	6	6	5
Drink	04-08	04-08	04-06	04-05	P

DRY $24 AV

Onetangi Road Cabernet/Merlot   (★★★)

Grown on Waiheke Island, the 2002 vintage (★★★) is deeply coloured and sturdy, with strong, brambly, spicy flavours, tight and firm.

DRY $29 -V

Peacock Ridge
Cabernet Sauvignon/Malbec/Merlot/Cabernet Franc   ★★★

Grown at Onetangi, on Waiheke Island, the 2003 vintage (★★★) is based principally on Cabernet Sauvignon (75 per cent), with 15 per cent Cabernet Franc and minor portions of Malbec and Merlot. Matured for a year in French and American oak casks, it is full-coloured, with a slightly herbaceous bouquet. It lacks a bit of warmth and softness, but offers plenty of blackcurrant and herb flavour, seasoned with toasty oak.

Vintage	02
WR	6
Drink	04-07

DRY $35 -V

Peninsula Estate Hauraki
Cabernet Sauvignon/Merlot/Cabernet Franc/Malbec   ★★★☆

This Waiheke Island red is typically robust, complex and firmly structured, but less opulent and sweet-fruited than the island's most famous wines. The 1999 vintage (★★★), French oak-aged for 18 months, was blended from Cabernet Sauvignon (67 per cent), Merlot (20 per cent), Cabernet Franc (10 per cent) and Malbec (3 per cent). A substantial, brambly, herbal, spicy red with some complexity and concentration, it tastes fully developed. Drink now.

Vintage	99	98	97
WR	6	7	5
Drink	04-09	04-08	04-10

DRY $45 -V

Peninsula Estate Oneroa Bay Cabernet/Syrah/Merlot   ★★★☆

This sturdy Waiheke red is Peninsula Estate's second-tier, claret-style red. The 2000 vintage (★★★) is a blend of Cabernet Sauvignon (64 per cent), Syrah (25 per cent) and Merlot (11 per cent), French oak-aged for a year. It's a gutsy, rustic, characterful wine with fullish, slightly developed colour, firm tannins and good depth of spicy, brambly flavour.

DRY $25 AV

Pleasant Valley Yelas Hawke's Bay Cabernet/Merlot   (★★☆)

The 2002 vintage (★★☆), matured for a year in new and used French oak barriques, is a strongly herbaceous wine, fullish in colour, with blackcurrant and green-leaf aromas and flavours. It lacks ripeness, but shows reasonable depth.

DRY $20 -V

Ransom Dark Summit Cabernet Sauvignon   ★★★☆

Grown at Mahurangi, north of Auckland, and oak-aged for 21 months, the 2000 vintage (★★★★) is the best yet. It's a dark, weighty wine with concentrated cassis, plum, herbal and spice flavours, quality oak, leathery, savoury touches adding complexity and a firm tannin grip. Drink now or cellar.

Vintage	00	99	98	DRY $26 -V
WR	6	NM	5	
Drink	04-06	NM	P	

Riverside Dartmoor Cabernet/Merlot   ★★☆

Grown in the Dartmoor Valley, Hawke's Bay, and matured for a year in French and American oak casks, this is typically a light, green-edged red, made in an easy-drinking style and priced fairly. The 2002 vintage (★★☆) is full-coloured, with a leafy, spicy bouquet. Verging on three-star quality, it has decent depth of blackcurrant, herb and spice flavours, with some oak-derived complexity.

Vintage	02	01	DRY $15 AV
WR	6	5	
Drink	04-06	04-05	

Rymer's Change Hawke's Bay Cabernet/Merlot   (★★★)

Te Mata Estate's fourth-tier claret-style red is matured for over a year in French and American oak casks. Fullish in colour, the 2003 vintage (★★★) is fruity and vibrant, with plummy, spicy flavours showing a touch of complexity and moderately firm tannins. It's not rich or concentrated, but a decent red, priced right.

Vintage	03	DRY $15 AV
WR	6	
Drink	04-06	

St Jerome Kara Creek Cabernet/Merlot   (★★☆)

On sale in 2004, the 1999 vintage (★★☆) is a ruby-hued, moderately flavoursome but leafy red that lacks ripeness and richness.

DRY $16 -V

Sacred Hill Basket Press Cabernet/Merlot (★★★)

The firmly structured 2003 vintage (★★★) is a Hawke's Bay blend of Cabernet Sauvignon (65 per cent), Merlot (27 per cent), Syrah (5 per cent) and Malbec (3 per cent), oak-aged for a year. Full ruby, it's a slightly rustic but characterful wine with blackcurrant, spice and earth flavours showing some warmth and density and grippy tannins.

Vintage	03
WR	7
Drink	04-06

DRY $20 AV

Sacred Hill Helmsman Cabernet/Merlot ★★★★☆

The powerful 2002 vintage (★★★★☆) is a Hawke's Bay blend of Cabernet Sauvignon (49 per cent), Merlot (36 per cent), Malbec (11 per cent) and Cabernet Franc (4 per cent), matured for 20 months in French oak barriques. Grown entirely in the Gimblett Gravels district (for the first time), it's a powerful (14 per cent alcohol), densely coloured wine with concentrated cassis, plum, spice and coffee flavours and powerful tannins. It should be long-lived, but is slightly less distinguished than the company's Brokenstone Merlot of the same vintage (see that entry).

Vintage	02	01	00	99	98
WR	7	NM	6	NM	5
Drink	05-10	NM	04-08	NM	04-05

DRY $40 AV

Saints Cabernet Sauvignon/Merlot ★★★☆

The 2002 vintage (★★★☆), blended by Allied Domecq from Hawke's Bay and South Australian wine, is deeply coloured, with spicy, minty flavours seasoned with toasty oak. It's a smooth, finely balanced wine with very good depth and sharply priced.

DRY $18 V+

Schubert Hawke's Bay Cabernet Sauvignon ★★★★

The 2002 vintage (★★★☆) is a Gimblett Road red, matured for over two years in French oak casks (75 per cent new). It's a boldly coloured and sturdy wine (14.5 per cent alcohol). It's green-edged, with a slight lack of warmth and softness, yet also shows impressive power through the palate, with rich blackcurrant, plum, spice and herb flavours and considerable complexity.

Vintage	02	01	00	99
WR	6	6	7	6
Drink	04-12	04-10	04-10	04-09

DRY $45 -V

Schubert Wairarapa Cabernet Sauvignon/Merlot ★★★

From a winery with a reputation for quality reds, the 2002 vintage (★★) is disappointing. Fullish in colour, it is lean and green, with minty, leafy flavours that lack ripeness and richness.

Vintage	01	00
WR	6	6
Drink	04-11	04-10

DRY $38 -V

Seifried Nelson Cabernet Sauvignon ★★☆

Grown at Appleby and matured for nine months in seasoned French oak casks, the 2002 vintage (★★☆) is berryish and spicy, with a leafy streak. It's a gently oaked wine, full-bodied and flavoursome, with a firm finish. Verging on three stars.

DRY $19 -V

Selaks Premium Selection Cabernet Sauvignon   ★★

Typically a plain, green-edged wine. Grown in Marlborough and Hawke's Bay, the 2002 vintage (★★☆) is full-coloured, with a leafy bouquet. A fruity wine with very little oak showing, it offers reasonable depth of blackcurrant, red-berry and herb flavours and a slightly high-acid finish.

Vintage	02		
WR	6		
Drink	04-05		

MED/DRY $15 -V

Solstone Wairarapa Cabernet/Merlot   (★★☆)

The green-edged 2002 vintage (★★☆), grown at Masterton, is a 2:1 blend of Cabernet Sauvignon and Merlot, matured for 20 months in French (90 per cent) and American oak casks (half new). Full and moderately youthful in colour, with a herbaceous bouquet, it's a medium-bodied red (12.7 per cent alcohol) with plummy, spicy, leafy flavours that lack real warmth and softness.

Vintage	02		
WR	4		
Drink	05-08+		

DRY $25 -V

Solstone Wairarapa Cabernet Sauvignon   (★★☆)

Estate-grown at Masterton, the 2002 vintage (★★☆) is a decent but green-edged blend of Cabernet Sauvignon (85 per cent), Merlot (9 per cent) and Cabernet Franc (6 per cent), matured for 20 months in French (80 per cent) and American oak casks (half new). With its herbaceous flavours and slightly high-acid finish, it doesn't make a convincing case for Cabernet Sauvignon in the Wairarapa, but shows good body and flavour depth.

Vintage	02		
WR	4		
Drink	05-08+		

DRY $25 -V

Solstone Wairarapa Valley Cabernet/Merlot Reserve   ★★★☆

Made from 20-year-old vines at Masterton and matured for nearly two years in French oak casks, the 2001 vintage (★★★☆) is deeply coloured, with strong blackcurrant, spice, herb and nut flavours. It's a slightly leafy but characterful, Bordeaux-style wine with good concentration and complexity, and firm tannins.

Vintage	01	00	
WR	5	6	
Drink	05-11+	05-10	

DRY $40 -V

Squawking Magpie Cabernet Sauvignon/Merlot   ★★★★☆

The 2002 vintage (★★★★☆) is a single-vineyard wine, grown in Gimblett Road, Hawke's Bay. A blend of Cabernet Sauvignon (80 per cent) and Merlot (20 per cent), matured in French oak barriques, it's a fragrant, tight, very well-structured red with concentrated, well-ripened flavours of plums and spice, showing good complexity and harmony. It needs more time, but should develop for years; open 2006+.

DRY $35 AV

Squawking Magpie The Cabernets   (★★★★★)

The beautifully ripe and intense 2002 vintage (★★★★★) is a blend of Cabernet Sauvignon (70 per cent), Merlot (20 per cent) and Cabernet Franc (10 per cent), grown in Gimblett Road, Hawke's Bay. A single-vineyard red, it is densely coloured and warm, with highly concentrated blackcurrant, spice and nut flavours, complex and long. It's a firmly structured wine, built to last, yet already accessible and full of personality.

DRY $37 V+

Squawking Magpie The Chatterer
Cabernet Sauvignon/Cabernet Franc/Merlot   (★★☆)

'Balanced to drink young', the 2003 vintage (★★☆) is a Hawke's Bay blend of Cabernet Sauvignon (50 per cent), Cabernet Franc (40 per cent) and Merlot (10 per cent), French oak-aged. Spicy and leafy on the nose, it is fresh, vibrant and youthful, with berry, plum and spice flavours that lack real ripeness and richness.

DRY $22 -V

Station Road Cabernet/Pinotage/Merlot   (★★☆)

A solid quaffer from Nobilo, the 2003 vintage (★★☆) is a North Island blend, full-coloured, with berry, plum and green-leaf flavours and a slightly high-acid finish. Priced right.

Vintage	03
WR	5
Drink	04-07

DRY $13 AV

Stonyridge Larose Cabernets   ★★★★★

Typically a stunning Waiheke wine. Dark and seductively perfumed, with smashing fruit flavours, at its best it is a magnificently concentrated red that matures superbly for a decade or longer, acquiring great complexity. The vines, grown in poor clay soils threaded with rotten rock, a kilometre from the sea at Onetangi, are extremely low-yielding. The wine is matured for a year in French (80 per cent) and American oak barriques; in a top year, 80 per cent of the casks are new or freshly shaved. The wine is sold largely on an 'en primeur' basis, whereby the customers, in return for paying for their wine about nine months in advance of its delivery, secure a substantial price reduction. The 2002 (★★★★) is a blend of Cabernet Sauvignon (51 per cent), Malbec (27 per cent), Petit Verdot (11 per cent), Merlot (8 per cent) and Cabernet Franc (4 per cent). That these figures total 101 per cent is understandable, given that the wine is Larose! It's a densely coloured, purple-black wine with a fragrant bouquet of spice, blackcurrants, eucalypt and berries and rich, ripe, concentrated flavours. It's a fruit bomb (as Robert Parker would put it), but (perhaps due to the high Malbec content), does not show the breed – the sheer class – of past Laroses.

Vintage	02	01	00	99	98	97	96	95	94	93
WR	7	6	7	7	6	7	7	6	7	5
Drink	05-15	04-10	04-13	04-11	04-10	04-12	04-14	04-05	04-10	04-05

DRY $125 -V

Sunset Valley Vineyard Cabernet Sauvignon   ★★☆

Grown organically at Upper Moutere, in Nelson, the 2003 vintage (★★☆) is a ruby-hued wine, French oak-aged, with crisp, plummy, spicy flavours, slightly earthy and green-edged.

DRY $24 -V

Te Awa Zone 10 Cabernet Sauvignon   ★★★★★

Straight (unblended) Cabernet Sauvignon is out of fashion in New Zealand, but this wine works brilliantly. Grown in the Gimblett Gravels of Hawke's Bay, it comes from part of the vineyard that 'ripens behind other zones', giving grapes 'with more generosity and less austerity than other Cabernet Sauvignon plantings'. The 2002 vintage (★★★★★) was matured for 18 months in French oak barriques (half new). Dense and youthful in colour, it's still a baby, with highly concentrated cassis, spice and mint flavours, cedary oak adding complexity and a firm backbone of tannin. It's a tightly structured, very rich, complete wine, worth tucking away for several years.

Vintage	02	01	00	99	98
WR	7	NM	6	NM	6
Drink	04-10	NM	04-08	NM	04-05

DRY $65 -V

Te Kairanga Castlepoint Cabernet Sauvignon/Merlot ★★

The 2002 vintage (★★) is a blend of Cabernet Sauvignon (75 per cent) and Merlot, grown in the Hawke's Bay (principally), Wairarapa and Gisborne regions, and matured for six months in French oak. It's a light, simple, under-ripe wine, herbaceous and high in acidity.

Vintage	02
WR	5
Drink	04-05

DRY $14 -V

Te Mata Awatea Cabernet/Merlot ★★★★★

Positioned slightly below its Coleraine stablemate in the Te Mata red-wine hierarchy, Awatea was once a top single-vineyard Hawke's Bay red, but since the 1989 vintage has been a blend of wines from several of Te Mata's original vineyards in the Havelock North hills, combined with more recent plantings in the 'Ngatarawa triangle'. Compared to Coleraine, in its youth Awatea is more seductive, more perfumed, and tastes more of sweet, ripe fruit, but is more forward and slightly less concentrated. The wine can mature gracefully for many years, but is also delicious at two years old. The 2002 vintage (★★★★) is a blend of Cabernet Sauvignon (37 per cent), Merlot (36 per cent), Cabernet Franc (17 per cent) and Petit Verdot (10 per cent), matured for 18 months in new and seasoned French oak barriques. Full-coloured, with spice, green-leaf and French oak aromas, it offers well-ripened flavours of plums, spices and herbs, with excellent depth and complexity.

Vintage	02	01	00	99	98	97	96	95	94
WR	7	6	7	6	7	5	6	7	6
Drink	05-10	05-08	04-10	04-06	04-12	04-05	P	04-07	P

DRY $32 V+

Te Mata Coleraine Cabernet/Merlot ★★★★★

Breed, rather than brute power, is the hallmark of Coleraine, which since its first vintage in 1982 has carved out a reputation second to none among New Zealand's claret-style reds, although it does show marked vintage variation. At its best (as in 1991, 1998 and 2000) it is a magical wine, with an intensity, complexity and subtlety on the level of a top-class Bordeaux. A single-vineyard Hawke's Bay red from 1982 to 1988, since 1989 Coleraine has been blended from several sites (including the original Coleraine vineyard) at Havelock North. Compared with its Awatea stablemate (above), Coleraine is more strongly influenced by new oak, more concentrated and more slowly evolving. The wine is matured for 18 to 20 months in French oak barriques, typically 70 per cent new. The 2002 vintage (★★★★★), from a season in which the Cabernet Sauvignon variety shone brightest, has an unusually low percentage of Cabernet Sauvignon (25 per cent), blended with Cabernet Franc (36 per cent) and Merlot (39 per cent). It's a richly coloured, highly fragrant, very complex and structured wine, with excellent concentration of plum, spice and coffee flavours and firm tannins. A generous wine with great depth, it should flourish for many years.

Vintage	02	01	00	99	98	97	96	95	94
WR	7	6	7	6	7	6	6	7	6
Drink	06-15	07-13	05-15	06-09	04-20	04-10	04-08	04-10	04-06

DRY $60 AV

Te Mata Estate Woodthorpe Cabernet/Merlot ★★★☆

Up to and including the 2000 vintage, this Hawke's Bay red was called Te Mata Cabernet/Merlot (the name change reflects its origin in the company's Woodthorpe Terraces vineyard in the Dartmoor Valley). Not to be confused with its Coleraine and Awatea big brothers, it can still be an impressive mouthful. Matured in new and seasoned oak barrels, the 2003 vintage (★★★☆) is a blend of Cabernet Sauvignon (28 per cent), Merlot (32 per cent), Cabernet Franc (24 per cent) and Petit Verdot (16 per cent). It's a vibrantly fruity, full-bodied wine with berryish, spicy flavours, some savoury complexity, good depth and a smooth finish.

Vintage	03	02	01	00
WR	7	7	7	6
Drink	05-08	05-07	04-06	04-05

DRY $22 AV

Te Motu Cabernet/Merlot ★★★★☆

The Dunleavy family's flagship Waiheke Island red is grown at Onetangi (over the fence from Stonyridge) and matured in French and American oak barriques. The 1994 vintage (★★★★★) is the star to date – dark, intense and chewy – followed by the elegant, scented and savoury 1996 (★★★★☆), but the wine is not consistently brilliant, and so struggles to justify its super-high price. The 1999 vintage (★★★★☆) is one of the best – generous, mouthfilling and complex, with strong blackcurrant, plum and spice flavours, warm, leathery and savoury. Deeply coloured, with a fragrant, welcoming bouquet, it's a wine of style and complexity rather than brute power. Highly attractive in its youth, the 2000 (★★★★) is ripely flavoured and savoury, with good density and complexity and smooth tannins.

Vintage	00	99	98	97	96	95	94	93
WR	7	7	7	6	7	6	7	5
Drink	04-08	04-06	P	P	04-05	P	P	P

DRY $80 -V ·

Terravin J Cabernet/Merlot/Malbec ★★★★

One of the finest claret-style reds from Marlborough, it is grown in the Omaka Valley by Mike and Jo Eaton (hence the 'J'). The 2002 vintage (★★★★) is boldly coloured, with leafy aromas and an impressively concentrated palate offering blackcurrant, herb and spice flavours. Showing good complexity and tannin structure, it's slightly less distinguished than the 2001 (★★★★☆), but well worth cellaring.

DRY $39 -V

Te Whare Ra Henrietta Cabernet Sauvignon/Merlot ★★★

Estate-grown at Renwick, in Marlborough, the 2003 vintage (★★★) is a fresh, lively, minty blend of Cabernet Sauvignon (54 per cent) and Merlot (17 per cent), with minor portions of Cabernet Franc, Malbec and Pinot Noir. Bright and full in colour, it's slightly leafy and high in acidity, but offers loads of blackcurrant, spice and plum flavour. A good quaffer.

Vintage	02	01
WR	5	6
Drink	04-09	04-08

DRY $18 AV

Torlesse Cabernet/Merlot ★★★

The 2002 vintage (★★☆) is a blend of Waipara and Marlborough grapes. Fresh and vibrantly fruity, it has fullish colour, berryish, slightly leafy flavours and a slightly high-acid finish.

Vintage	02
WR	7
Drink	04-06

DRY $18 AV

Trinity Hill Gimblett Road Cabernet Sauvignon/Merlot ★★★★

In top years, this is a finely balanced, concentrated Hawke's Bay wine in the classic claret style. It is matured for up to 20 months in French oak barriques, typically 30 per cent new. Generous, with true varietal characters, spicy new oak adding complexity and a firm tannin backbone, the 2002 vintage (★★★★) is an intense wine with deep colour and rich cassis, plum and spice flavours.

Vintage	02	01	00	99	98	97
WR	6	5	5	5	7	5
Drink	05-12	04-08	04-10	04-07	04-08	04-06

DRY $30 AV

Vidal Joseph Soler Cabernet Sauvignon   (★★★★★)

Still youthful, the 1998 (★★★★★) is a powerful Hawke's Bay red that reflects the quality of the exceptionally hot, dry vintage. Launched in late 2002, it's a densely coloured, single-vineyard wine, grown in the Gimblett Gravels district and matured for 21 months in French and American oak barriques. It shows great depth and structure, with strikingly concentrated blackcurrant and nut, slightly chocolatey flavours and a firm tannin grip. It needs more time to unfold its full potential; open 2005 onwards. (There are no subsequent vintages.)

Vintage	98
WR	7
Drink	04-10

DRY $89 -V

Vidal Reserve Cabernet Sauvignon   ★★★★★

This Hawke's Bay label has a distinguished show track record, stretching back over more than a decade to the gloriously deep-scented, flavour-packed and complex 1990. The stylish and tight-knit 2000 vintage (★★★★★) was matured for the unusually long period of 20 months in French and American oak barriques. Still unfolding, it's an extremely elegant, classic claret style with rich, vibrant plum and spice flavours, slightly chewy tannins and a long finish. The 2002 (★★★★★), grown in the Gimblett Gravels, is dark, mouthfilling and concentrated, with beautifully ripe blackcurrant and dark chocolate flavours, great texture and ripe, supple tannins.

Vintage	02	01	00	99	98	97	96	95	94
WR	6	NM	7	NM	NM	6	NM	6	6
Drink	05-12	NM	05-10	NM	NM	P	NM	P	P

DRY $44 AV

Villa Maria Private Bin Cabernet Sauvignon/Merlot   ★★★

The 2003 vintage (★★★) is a Hawke's Bay red, matured for 14 months in French and American oak barriques (40 per cent new). It's a full-flavoured wine, vibrant, plummy, spicy and firm, with a leafy edge and a slight lack of softness, but considerable complexity and good structure.

Vintage	03
WR	6
Drink	05-07

DRY $17 AV

Villa Maria Reserve Cabernet Sauvignon/Merlot   ★★★★★

Past vintages have been outstanding. Grown in the company's Ngakirikiri vineyard in the Gimblett Gravels district of Hawke's Bay and matured for 18 months in French and American oak barriques, the 2002 vintage (★★★★★) is a powerful red (14.5 per cent alcohol), densely coloured, with highly concentrated blackcurrant, plum, mint and spice flavours, impressive complexity and a lasting finish.

Vintage	02	01
WR	7	7
Drink	05-11	05-10

DRY $40 AV

Villa Maria Vintage Selection
Cabernet Sauvignon/Merlot/Shiraz   (★★☆)

The non-vintage blend (★★☆) on sale in late 2004 was assembled from New Zealand, Australian and Chilean wines. It's a plummy, peppery, green-edged wine with a firm, slightly high-acid finish.

DRY $11 AV

Waimea Estates Nelson Cabernet/Merlot ★★☆

The 2003 vintage (★★☆), blended from Cabernet Sauvignon (58 per cent), Merlot (35 per cent) and Cabernet Franc (7 per cent), is a medium-bodied, slightly high-acid red with berry, plum and green-leaf flavours that lack real ripeness and richness.

Vintage	02	
WR	5	
Drink	04-05	

DRY $20 -V

Waimea Estates The Hill
Cabernet Sauvignon/Cabernet Franc (★★★★)

The well-ripened 2001 vintage (★★★★) was made from 10-year-old low-cropping vines on a north-facing slope in Nelson and matured in French and American oak. Offering strong berry, spice and mint flavours, with nutty oak and some savoury complexity, it shows good weight, roundness and sheer drinkability.

DRY $34 -V

Waipara Springs Cabernet Sauvignon (★★★)

A middleweight style, based on mature vines at Waipara and French oak-aged, this tends to be a supple, vibrant red with satisfying although not great depth of berryish, plummy, spicy flavours and a smooth finish.

Vintage	03	02
WR	5	5
Drink	04-05	04-05

DRY $20 AV

Weeping Sands Waiheke Cabernet/Merlot ★★★☆

This is the second label of Obsidian, grown at Onetangi ('weeping sands'). The skilfully crafted 2003 vintage (★★★☆) is a blend of Cabernet Sauvignon (53 per cent), Merlot (40 per cent) and Malbec (7 per cent), matured for a year in French oak barriques (50 per cent new). Full but not dense in colour, with perfumed, sweet oak aromas, it is fresh, vibrant and mouthfilling (13.5 per cent alcohol), with good depth of cassis/plum flavours and gentle tannins. Drink during 2005.

Vintage	03	02	01	00
WR	4	7	4	6
Drink	04-07	04-06	04-05	04-05

DRY $24 AV

Winslow Petra Cabernet ★★★☆

Winslow's 100 per cent Cabernet Sauvignon is a less 'complete' Martinborough wine than its blended stablemate, but in top vintages is a delicious mouthful. The dark 2001 vintage (★★★★) is a powerful, mouthfilling wine (14 per cent alcohol), with a streak of mint running through its highly concentrated cassis, plum and spice flavours, which are braced by firm tannins. The 2002 (★★★) was matured for 18 months in French (90 per cent) and American oak casks. Fullish in colour, it has strong, minty, herbal characters, mingled with blackcurrant and plums, and a slightly high-acid finish. (I have also tasted a strongly herbaceous Winslow Art Series Cabernet Sauvignon/Merlot 2002, which lacked ripeness and richness.)

Vintage	01	00	99	98	97	96	95	94
WR	7	6	NM	NM	4	7	5	6
Drink	04-11	04-10	NM	NM	P	04-05	P	P

DRY $32 -V

Chambourcin

Chambourcin is one of the more highly rated French hybrids, well known in Muscadet for its good disease resistance and bold, crimson hue. Rare in New Zealand (with 5 hectares of bearing vines), it is principally used as a blending variety, to add colour.

Marsden Estate Chambourcin   ★★★☆

The 2002 vintage (★★★☆) is a dark Bay of Islands, Northland red, matured for 16 months in seasoned oak barrels. It shows the slightly rustic character typical of Chambourcin, but also good body (13.5 per cent alcohol) and plenty of berryish, plummy, sweetly oaked flavour. Gutsy and firm, it's a good example of the variety, enjoyable now.

Vintage	02	01	00
WR	5	4	6
Drink	04-07	04-06	04-06

DRY $24 -V

Gamay Noir

Gamay Noir is single-handedly responsible for the seductively scented and soft red wines of Beaujolais. The grape is still rare in New Zealand, although the area of bearing vines will rise between 2003 and 2006 from 7 to 9 hectares. In the Omaka Springs vineyard in Marlborough, Gamay ripens later than Cabernet Sauvignon (itself an end-of-season ripener), with higher levels of acidity than in Beaujolais, but at Te Mata's Woodthorpe Terraces vineyard in Hawke's Bay, the crop is harvested as early as mid-March.

Lucknow Estate QBV Gamay Noir ★★★

The 2002 vintage (★★★) is a Hawke's Bay red 'that takes fun seriously'. Grown in the Quarry Bridge vineyard at Maraekakaho and not oak-aged, it's a ruby-hued, vibrantly fruity wine with lots of fresh, red-berry and plum flavour and a slightly spicy, refreshingly crisp finish.

Vintage	04	
WR	5	**DRY $20 AV**
Drink	04-05	

Te Mata Estate Woodthorpe Gamay Noir ★★★☆

This single-vineyard Hawke's Bay red is whole-bunch fermented (in the traditional Beaujolais manner) and matured for four months in old French oak casks. The 2003 vintage (★★★★) was delicious in its youth – bright ruby, with an enticingly floral bouquet, sweet fruit characters, fresh, strong raspberry and spice flavours and gentle tannins. The light ruby-hued 2004 (★★★☆) is smooth and supple, with fresh, strong cherry, plum and raspberry flavours.

Vintage	04	
WR	7	**DRY $21 AV**
Drink	04-06	

Grenache

Grenache, the world's second most extensively planted grape variety, thrives in the hot, dry vineyards of Spain and southern France. It is starting to yield some exciting wines in Australia, especially from old, unirrigated, bush-pruned vines, but is exceedingly rare in New Zealand, with a total producing area in 2003 of less than 2 hectares.

Matua Valley Innovator Grenache   ★★★★

Grown in the Ngatarawa district of Hawke's Bay, the 2002 vintage (★★★★) was made from the ripest grapes the winery has seen since the outstanding, sturdy, sweet-fruited 1998. Matured for 10 months in French oak barriques (40 per cent new), it's a fresh, vibrantly fruity wine with acids under control and strong, plummy, spicy flavours.

DRY $26 AV

Malbec

With a leap from 25 hectares of bearing vines in 1998 to 176 hectares in 2004, this old Bordeaux variety is starting to make its presence felt in New Zealand, where over two-thirds of all plantings are clustered in Hawke's Bay. It is typically used as a blending variety, adding brilliant colour and rich, sweet fruit flavours to its blends with Merlot, Cabernet Sauvignon and Cabernet Franc. A sprinkling of unblended Malbecs have also been released recently, possessing loads of flavour and often the slight rusticity typical of the variety.

Arahura Malbec   ★★★★☆

Grown at Clevedon in South Auckland, the 2002 vintage (★★★★☆) was matured in French and American oak barriques. It's a densely coloured wine, rich, vibrant and supple, with lovely depth of plum and spice flavours, oak complexity and loads of character.

Vintage 02
WR   6
Drink   04-05

DRY $30 AV

Church Road Cuve Series Malbec   (★★★★)

The densely coloured 2002 vintage (★★★★) from Allied Domecq was grown in Hawke's Bay and matured in French oak barriques (70 per cent new). It's a bold, robust wine with rich, ripe, plummy, spicy aromas and flavours, the earthy character typical of Malbec and a tight, firm finish. Worth cellaring to mid-2005+.

Vintage 02
WR   6
Drink   04-08

DRY $35 -V

Collards Shanty Block Malbec   ★★★★

The 2002 vintage (★★★★) was made from second-crop vines in the estate vineyard at Henderson and oak-aged. One of the country's most enjoyable Malbecs, it's richly coloured, with a fragrant bouquet of raspberry, plum and spice. Warm and supple, slightly earthy and chocolatey, with sweet fruit characters and gentle tannins, it shows good ripeness, complexity and depth.

DRY $25 AV

Crab Farm Hamish Jardine
Pukera Terraces Malbec/Merlot   (★★★☆)

Grown on a north-facing, terraced site at Puketapu, the 2002 vintage (★★★☆) is a blend of Malbec (60 per cent) and Merlot (40 per cent), matured for 20 months in French oak casks (60 per cent new). Dense and youthful in colour, it's a fruit-crammed wine, berryish and plummy, with a seasoning of quality oak and finely balanced tannins. Verging on four stars.

DRY $30 -V

Delegat's Gimblett Gravels Malbec   (★★★★☆)

Still youthful, the 2000 vintage (★★★★☆) was grown in Hawke's Bay and matured for two years in French oak barriques (new and one-year-old). It's a boldly coloured wine with sweet, ripe-fruit characters and rich flavours of plums and spice, seasoned with fine-quality oak. One of the classiest Malbecs on the market.

DRY $35 AV

Fromm La Strada Malbec Reserve   ★★★★

Grown in Marlborough (which gives the wine a slightly fresher, crisper feel than Hawke's Bay Malbec) and matured for 14 months in French oak casks (20 per cent new), the 2002 vintage (★★★★) is a robust (14 per cent alcohol), boldly coloured wine with intensely spicy aromas. Vibrantly fruity, it has plummy, peppery flavours showing excellent concentration and firm tannins. Winemaker Hatsch Kalberer suggests drinking it with 'a large piece of wild venison'.

Vintage	03	02	01	00	99	98
WR	NM	6	7	5	6	7
Drink	NM	05-12	04-11	04-08	04-09	04-10

DRY $44 -V

Kemblefield Reserve Malbec/Merlot   (★★★☆)

Drinking well now, the 2002 vintage (★★★☆) is a Hawke's Bay blend of estate-grown Malbec (55 per cent) and Merlot (45 per cent), French oak-matured for 18 months. Deeply coloured and full-bodied (14 per cent alcohol), with strong plum and red-berry flavours, it is spicy and slightly herbal, with finely integrated oak and supple tannins.

DRY $35 -V

Mahurangi Estate Malbec/Cabernet/Merlot   (★★☆)

Estate-grown near Warkworth, north of Auckland, the 2002 vintage (★★☆) is a blend of Malbec (50 per cent), Cabernet Sauvignon (30 per cent) and Merlot (20 per cent). It's a full-coloured, gutsy but green-edged red, berryish, leafy and firm.

DRY $18 -V

Mills Reef Elspeth Malbec   ★★★★★

The densely coloured and flavoured 2002 vintage (★★★★★) was grown in Mere Road, in the Gimblett Gravels district of Hawke's Bay, and French oak-aged for 18 months. Very youthful, it has spicy, plummy aromas leading into a blockbuster palate with gobs of plum, spice and raspberry fruit, quality oak and grippy tannins. It's a powerful brute, opaque, hugely concentrated and tautly structured, likely to be at its best from 2005 onwards.

Vintage	02	01	00
WR	7	7	7
Drink	04-14	04-06	04-05

DRY $40 AV

Mills Reef Reserve Malbec/Merlot   (★★★☆)

The dark, purple-flushed 2003 vintage (★★★☆) is a Hawke's Bay blend with floral, spice and toasty oak aromas. It's a gutsy, firm wine with oak complexity and blackcurrant, plum and spice flavours showing a slight lack of warmth but good intensity.

DRY $25 AV

Millton Te Arai Vineyard Gisborne Malbec   (★★★☆)

The fruit-packed, organically grown 2002 vintage (★★★☆) was hand-picked, fermented with indigenous yeasts (including 25 per cent whole-berry fermentation) and matured for a year in two-year-old French oak barrels. Bottled unfiltered, it's a deeply coloured wine with ripe plum and spice fruit aromas and flavours holding centre stage, a subtle oak influence, and firm but not grippy tannins. It's still unfolding; open mid-2005+.

Vintage	02
WR	6
Drink	04-09

DRY $22 AV

Moana Park Vineyard Tribute Malbec (★★★)

Grown in the Dartmoor Valley, Hawke's Bay, the 2002 vintage (★★★) is full but not densely coloured. It possesses fresh, fairly strong red-berry, plum and spice flavours, with the earthiness typical of Malbec, well-integrated oak and firm tannins. Drink now onwards.

Vintage	02	01
WR	6	5
Drink	05-06	P

DRY $25 -V

Okahu Estate Shipwreck Bay Malbec/Chambourcin/Pinotage (★★)

This is the Kaitaia-based winery's 'red wine for non red-wine drinkers', says proprietor Monty Knight. Grown in the Waikato, Northland and Hawke's Bay, and matured in seasoned French and American oak casks, the 2002 vintage (★★) is a deeply coloured but rustic wine with crisp, herbaceous flavours that lack ripeness and roundness.

Vintage	02
WR	7
Drink	04-07

DRY $17 -V

Putiki Bay Malbec ★★★

Grown on Waiheke Island, the 2002 vintage (★★★☆) is full and youthful in colour, with ripe, plummy flavours showing some depth and elegance.

DRY $37 -V

Rongopai Reserve Malbec (★★★☆)

Grown at Te Kauwhata, in the Waikato, and oak-aged for a year, the 2002 vintage (★★★☆) is a buoyantly fruity red with deep, purple-flushed colour and fresh, plum and black pepper aromas. It shows good ripeness and depth, with strong raspberry, plum and spice flavours, subtle oak and a slightly chewy finish. A great buy.

DRY $19 V+

Villa Maria Single Vineyard Omahu Gravels Malbec (★★★★☆)

The super-charged 2002 vintage (★★★★☆) is a Hawke's Bay red, matured for 18 months in French oak barriques. It's a robust wine, densely coloured, with perfumed, toasty oak aromas, firm tannins and an array of blackcurrant, plum, spice, chocolate and nut flavours, ripe, well-balanced and rich.

Vintage	02
WR	7
Drink	05-11

DRY $55 -V

West Brook Estate Range Malbec (★★★)

The debut 2002 vintage (★★★) was picked from first-crop vines in the estate vineyard at Waimauku, in West Auckland. Matured for 14 months in a 50/50 split of American and French oak barriques, it's a deeply coloured, purple-flushed wine with a highly scented, floral rather than gamey bouquet. Gutsy, with sweet fruit characters and plenty of spicy, slightly pruney and herbal flavour, it has firm tannins and lots of character.

DRY $33 -V

Merlot

Pinot Noir is New Zealand's high-profile red on the world stage, but our top Merlots are also starting to attract attention. At the Tri Nations Wine Challenge, held in Sydney in November 2003 to evaluate the best of Australia, South Africa and New Zealand, the champion Merlot was Villa Maria Reserve Hawke's Bay Merlot 2001, with Matariki Reserve Hawke's Bay Merlot 2000 as runner-up.

Excitement is especially high in Hawke's Bay about this most extensively cultivated red-wine grape in Bordeaux. Everywhere in Bordeaux – the world's greatest red-wine region – except in the Médoc and Graves districts, the internationally much higher-profile Cabernet Sauvignon variety plays second fiddle to Merlot. The elegant, fleshy wines of Pomerol and St Émilion bear delicious testimony to Merlot's capacity to produce great, yet relatively early-maturing, reds.

In New Zealand, after decades of preoccupation with the more austere and slowly evolving Cabernet Sauvignon, the rich, persistent flavours and (more practically) earlier-ripening ability of Merlot are now fully appreciated. Poor set can be a major drawback with the older clones, reducing yields, but Merlot ripens ahead of Cabernet Sauvignon, a major asset in cooler wine regions, especially in vineyards with colder clay soils. Merlot grapes are typically lower in tannin and higher in sugar than Cabernet Sauvignon's; its wines are thus silkier and a shade stronger in alcohol.

Hawke's Bay has over 70 per cent of New Zealand's Merlot vines; the rest are clustered in Marlborough, Auckland and Gisborne. The country's fourth most extensively planted grape variety, Merlot now covers double the area of Cabernet Sauvignon. Between 2000 and 2006, the total area of bearing Merlot vines will soar by more than 135 per cent.

Merlot's key role in New Zealand was traditionally that of a minority blending variety, bringing a soft, mouthfilling richness and floral, plummy fruitiness to its marriages with the predominant Cabernet Sauvignon. With the fast-rising stream of straight Merlots and Merlot-predominant blends, this aristocratic grape is now fully recognised as a top-flight wine in its own right.

Alpha Domus Hawke's Bay Merlot   ★★★

The 2003 vintage (★★★) is a light, drink-young style of Hawke's Bay red, oak-aged for five months. Fresh, crisp and vibrantly fruity, with youthful, purple-flushed colour, berryish, slightly spicy aromas and flavours and gentle tannins, it should be at its best during the summer of 2004–05.

DRY $17 AV

Alpha Domus Merlot/Cabernet   ★★★☆

This Hawke's Bay red is designed for early drinking. The deeply coloured 2002 vintage (★★★☆) is a blend of Merlot, Cabernet Sauvignon, Cabernet Franc and Malbec, matured for a year in French and American oak casks (20 per cent new). Full-flavoured and supple, with fresh cassis, plum and green-leaf characters, a hint of sweet oak and some complexity, it offers good value.

Vintage	02	01	00	99	98
WR	6	6	6	5	7
Drink	04-09	04-07	04-06	04-05	P

DRY $19 V+

Arahura Merlot/Malbec   (★★★★)

The stylish 2000 vintage (★★★★) was grown at Clevedon, in South Auckland, and matured for a year in French and American oak casks. It's a fragrant, spicy, dark, youthful wine, with finely integrated oak and fresh, rich flavours of plums and spice.

Vintage	00	
WR	6	
Drink	04-06	**DRY $30 AV**

Artisan Riverstone Vineyard Merlot   ★★★

Grown in the Gimblett Gravels district of Hawke's Bay, the 2002 vintage (★★☆) has full, youthful colour. Matured in oak barriques (30 per cent new), it's slightly austere in its youth, with firm, tight tannins and only moderately sweet fruit characters, but offers plenty of berryish, plummy, spicy flavour, seasoned with toasty oak.

Vintage	02	
WR	4	
Drink	04-07	**DRY $19 AV**

Ascension Matakana Merlot   (★★☆)

The 2002 vintage (★★☆) is a solid wine, but too herbaceous to rate higher. Matured in French and American oak, it shows fresh, berryish, leafy characters and some earthy, spicy complexity. A drink-young style.

DRY $22 -V

Ascension The Ascent Merlot/Malbec/Cabernet Sauvignon ★★★

Estate-grown at Matakana, the 2002 vintage (★★★☆) is a blend of Merlot (68 per cent), Malbec (22 per cent) and Cabernet Sauvignon (10 per cent), matured for over a year in French and American oak casks (half new). It's an elegant, youthful wine with ripe, spicy fruit aromas and concentrated flavours showing slightly high acidity, but also good structure and length.

DRY $30 -V

Babich Winemakers Reserve Merlot   ★★★☆

Grown in Gimblett Road, Hawke's Bay, and matured in French oak casks (old and new), the moderately complex 2002 vintage (★★★☆) has bright, youthful colour of good depth. It offers fresh, vibrantly fruity berry and plum flavours, with a subtle oak influence and gentle tannins.

Vintage	03	02	01	00	
WR	6	7	6	7	
Drink	04-08	04-08	04-07	04-06	**DRY $25 AV**

Beach House The Track Vineyard Merlot/Cabernet   (★★☆)

The full-coloured, green-edged 2002 vintage (★★☆) is a Hawke's Bay red, blended from equal portions of Merlot and Cabernet Sauvignon and matured for a year in French oak casks. It's a plummy, spicy wine, offering decent depth, but slightly under-ripe and leafy.

DRY $24 -V

Black Barn Merlot/Cabernet Sauvignon/Cabernet Franc   ★★★

Hill-grown at Havelock North, the 2002 vintage (★★★) is a Merlot-based red (53 per cent), blended with Cabernet Sauvignon (28 per cent), Cabernet Franc (12 per cent) and Malbec (7 per cent), matured in French (mostly) and American oak casks (25 per cent new). It's a slightly herbaceous wine but shows very good complexity of plum, spice and green-leaf flavours, braced by firm tannins.

Vintage	02	
WR	4	
Drink	04-06	**DRY $24 -V**

Black Barn Reserve Hawke's Bay Merlot   ★★★★

Grown on a north-facing slope at Havelock North, the 2002 vintage (★★★★) was matured in French oak barriques (60 per cent new). It's a vibrantly fruity Hawke's Bay red, deeply coloured, with rich flavours of spices, coffee, nuts and herbs and a firm finish. The pick of the winery's reds, it shows good density, complexity and harmony.

Vintage	02	
WR	6	
Drink	06-08	

DRY $38 ·V

Brajkovich Merlot – see Kumeu River Village Merlot

Brightwater Vineyards Nelson Merlot   ★★★

French oak-aged for a year, this wine shows slightly high acidity in cooler seasons, but top vintages are deeply coloured, with brambly, plummy, spicy, impressively concentrated flavours.

Vintage	02	01	00	99
WR	5	7	5	4
Drink	04-07	04-07	P	P

DRY $28 ·V

Cable Bay Five Hills
Merlot/Malbec/Cabernet Sauvignon   (★★★☆)

Grown on five hillside sites on Waiheke Island and matured in French oak barriques, the debut 2002 vintage (★★★☆) is a full-coloured wine with plum and spice aromas. Fresh and youthful, with good ripeness and flavour depth, some savoury complexity and firm tannins, it should be at its best from 2005 onwards.

DRY $35 ·V

Charles Wiffen Marlborough Merlot   ★★☆

The 2003 vintage (★★☆), oak-matured for a year, has fullish colour and smooth, berryish, plummy, herbal flavours, lacking real richness. It's a sweetly oaked wine, medium-bodied, offering easy drinking.

DRY $25 ·V

Christensen Estate Merlot   (★★★)

Grown on Waiheke Island, blended with Cabernet Sauvignon and Cabernet Franc (a total of 10 per cent), and matured in all-new French oak barriques, the 2003 vintage (★★★) is fullish in colour, with the savoury, spicy, earthy characters of Merlot, although not highly concentrated. It's a Bordeaux-like wine, warm, with considerable complexity, although arguably over-oaked.

DRY $34 ·V

Church Road Merlot/Cabernet   (★★★★)

The 2002 vintage (★★★★) is the first of Allied Domecq's Church Road reds from Hawke's Bay (apart from the reserve) to be Merlot-predominant. Deeply coloured, with a slightly herbal bouquet, it's a blend of Merlot (61 per cent), Cabernet Sauvignon (26 per cent) and Malbec (12 per cent), matured for 14 months in French oak barriques (43 per cent new). It shows excellent body and flavour depth, with generous blackcurrant, herb and spice flavours, savoury, nutty, earthy complexities and a smooth finish. Retasted in mid-2004, it is maturing impressively.

Vintage	02	
WR	6	
Drink	04-08	

DRY $22 V+

Church Road Reserve Merlot/Cabernet ★★★★☆

The Bordeaux-like 2001 vintage (★★★★) from Allied Domecq is a blend of Merlot (54 per cent), Cabernet Sauvignon (30 per cent), Cabernet Franc (11 per cent) and Malbec (5 per cent), matured in French oak barriques (70 per cent new). Full-coloured, it's a stylish wine, intensely varietal, with rich, spicy, leathery, earthy, nutty flavours showing excellent complexity and depth.

Vintage	01
WR	6
Drink	04-10

DRY $35 AV

C.J. Pask Gimblett Road Merlot ★★★★

Matured for over a year in French and American oak casks, the 2002 vintage (★★★★) came from low-cropped (4.5 to 6 tonnes/hectare), three to 13-year-old vines grown in Gimblett Road, Hawke's Bay and harvested at 21 to over 25 brix. Full-coloured and mouthfilling (14 per cent alcohol), it has a spicy, savoury bouquet, sweet fruit characters of plums and spice, hints of herbs and dark chocolate, finely integrated oak and ripe, supple tannins. It's already delicious.

Vintage	02	01	00	99	98
WR	7	NM	7	6	7
Drink	04-08	NM	04-05	P	P

DRY $25 AV

C.J. Pask Reserve Merlot ★★★★★

Like its predecessors, the 2000 vintage (★★★★★) is one of the most distinguished Hawke's Bay Merlots. Based on the company's oldest, ungrafted vines in Gimblett Road (low-cropping at 6.5 tonnes/hectare), and matured for 16 months in all-new French and American oak barriques, it is dark and notably ripe, with layers of cassis, spice, nut and coffee flavours. A magical wine, built for the long haul, it proves the great complexity and concentration of which Merlot is capable. There is no 2001.

Vintage	02	01	00	99	98	97
WR	7	NM	7	6	7	6
Drink	04-09	NM	04-07	04-05	04-05	P

DRY $50 AV

🍇 🍇

C.J. Pask Roys Hill Merlot (★★★)

Designed for 'soft, easy drinking', the 2001 vintage (★★★) was grown in Gimblett Road, Hawke's Bay, and matured for 14 months in French and American oak barriques. Fullish in colour, with a sweet oak influence, it's a more serious style than the label suggests, nutty, leathery and spicy, with mouthfilling body (13.5 per cent alcohol) and firm tannins. There's a slight lack of fruit sweetness, but at $15, the wine offers fine value.

Vintage	01
WR	6
Drink	04-07

DRY $15 AV

Clearview Estate Cape Kidnappers Merlot ★★★

The 2002 vintage (★★★) is a full-coloured Hawke's Bay red, blended from Merlot (75 per cent), Cabernet Franc (17 per cent) and Cabernet Sauvignon (8 per cent), and matured for over a year in French and American oak casks (new and seasoned). Gutsy and chewy, it offers plenty of spicy, leathery, slightly leafy and nutty flavour, with some complexity and a firm tannin grip.

Vintage	02
WR	5
Drink	04-05

DRY $22 -V

Collards Hawke's Bay Merlot   ★★★

From the West Auckland winery that in 1980 made New Zealand's first straight Merlot, the 2001 vintage (★★★) was grown in the shingly Gimblett Road area of Hawke's Bay and oak-aged for a year. Fullish in colour, it's a middleweight style, fragrant, with ripe-berry, plum and spice flavours showing decent depth and moderately firm tannins.

Vintage	02	01	00	99	98	97
WR	7	7	6	6	7	6
Drink	05-07	04-06	04-05	P	P	P

DRY $19 AV

Coopers Creek Hawke's Bay Merlot   ★★★

This is Coopers Creek's most popular red. The ruby-hued 2002 vintage (★★★) is based mainly on Havelock North grapes and was matured for six months in American and French oak casks. Raspberry and spice aromas lead into a vibrantly fruity wine with good depth of berryish, spicy, slightly herbal flavours, a gentle oak influence and smooth finish. A drink-young style.

Vintage	03	02	01	00	99	98
WR	6	6	5	6	5	7
Drink	04-06	04-05	P	P	P	P

DRY $17 AV

Coopers Creek The Gardener Reserve Huapai Merlot   ★★★☆

The characterful 2002 vintage (★★★★) is a West Auckland red, estate-grown at Huapai. Full-coloured, it's a Bordeaux-like wine with rich, ripe flavours of plums and spice, a strong oak influence, savoury, earthy characters and good depth, complexity and structure. It's delicious now. There is no 2003.

Vintage	03	02	01	00
WR	NM	6	NM	6
Drink	NM	04-08	NM	04-06

DRY $30 -V

Corazon The Collective Merlot/Malbec   (★★★☆)

Fleshy and tightly structured, the debut 2002 vintage (★★★☆) is a single-vineyard red, grown at Waiohika Estate in Gisborne and matured for 10 months in French oak casks (one-third new). A blend of 60 per cent Merlot and 40 per cent Malbec, it has spicy, distinctly Malbec aromas and a youthful palate, showing good concentration and length. Full-coloured, gutsy and characterful, it's already drinking well but worth cellaring.

Vintage	02
WR	6
Drink	04-07

DRY $28 -V

Corbans Private Bin Hawke's Bay Merlot/Cabernet Sauvignon   ★★★★

The 2002 vintage (★★★★) from Allied Domecq was matured in French oak barriques (56 per cent new). Already drinking well, it's a deeply coloured red with a fragrant, berryish, spicy, toasty bouquet. Mouthfilling and concentrated, it offers excellent depth of plum and blackcurrant flavours, with earthy, savoury touches, good complexity and a rich, well-rounded finish.

Vintage	02	01	00	99
WR	6	NM	NM	5
Drink	04-06	NM	NM	P

DRY $22 V+

Cottle Hill Merlot (★★☆)

The mellow 2000 vintage (★★☆) is a Hawke's Bay red, matured for two years in French and American oak casks. Lightish in colour, with perfumed, sweet oak aromas, it's a mature wine with moderate depth of plummy, spicy flavour and some leathery, nutty complexity. Drink now.

Vintage	00
WR	7
Drink	04-08

DRY $30 -V

Crab Farm Reserve Merlot (★★★)

Hand-picked in Hawke's Bay and matured for 15 months in new French oak casks, the 2002 vintage (★★★) has deep, purple-flushed colour. Chewy and tannic, it has buckets of plummy, berryish fruit, but impresses more with its intensity than fragrance or finesse. Open 2005 onwards.

Vintage	02
WR	6
Drink	05-06

DRY $25 -V

Craggy Range Gimblett Gravels Vineyard Merlot ★★★★☆

A great buy, the 2002 vintage (★★★★☆) was blended with Malbec (9 per cent) and Cabernet Sauvignon (6 per cent), and matured for 16 months in French oak barriques (45 per cent new). It's a youthful Hawke's Bay red with huge, inky colour, rich, sweet fruit characters and highly concentrated, spicy, nutty, almost chocolatey flavours. Savoury, earthy, leathery complexities are emerging, but the wine has a tight tannin grip and is best cellared to 2006+.

Vintage	02	01
WR	6	6
Drink	04-08+	06-09

DRY $27 V+

Craggy Range Seven Poplars Vineyard Merlot ★★★★☆

In very limited supply, the 2002 vintage (★★★★★) was grown in stony soils at the Dolbel Estate vineyard in the lower Dartmoor Valley, matured for a year in French oak casks (80 per cent new), and then aged for another nine months in two-year-old barrels before bottling. It's a powerful, highly concentrated Hawke's Bay red with dense, purple-flushed colour, warm blackcurrant, plum and nutty oak flavours and bold tannins. Fleshy and firm, it shows obvious cellaring potential.

Vintage	02	01	00	99
WR	7	6	6	6
Drink	06-09	05-08	04-07	04-05

DRY $35 AV

Crossroads Destination Series
Merlot/Cabernet Sauvignon (★★★)

The 2001 vintage (★★★) is a moderately ripe Hawke's Bay red with plummy, spicy, slightly leafy flavours, a sweet oak influence and gentle tannins.

Vintage	01
WR	6
Drink	04-06

DRY $25 -V

Delegat's Gimblett Gravels Merlot (★★★★☆)

The 2000 vintage (★★★★☆) is a boldly coloured Hawke's Bay red, matured for two years in French oak barriques (new and one-year-old). It shows beautifully ripe, sweet fruit characters and highly concentrated blackcurrant, plum and spice flavours.

DRY $35 AV

Delegat's Reserve Merlot ★★★★

Typically a great buy. The 2003 (★★★☆) was grown in Hawke's Bay and matured in new and one-year-old French oak barriques for a year (compared to 15 to 18 months for past vintages). It's a full-coloured wine with gentle tannins and blackcurrant, plum and spice flavours showing very good depth, although slightly less intensity than such top vintages as the densely flavoured 2002 (★★★★).

Vintage	03	02	01	00	99	98	97	DRY $20 V+
WR	6	6	6	6	6	7	6	
Drink	04-05	04-05	04-05	04-05	P	P	P	

Drylands Marlborough Merlot ★★☆

The 2003 vintage (★★★) from Nobilo was matured in American and French oak barriques. It's a ruby-hued, moderately ripe-tasting, middleweight wine with slightly leafy aromas and raspberry and plum flavours, simple but pleasant.

Vintage	03	02	01	DRY $20 -V
WR	7	7	7	
Drink	04-07	04-06	P	

Equinox Hawke's Bay Merlot/Cabernet Sauvignon/Malbec ★★☆

The 2002 vintage (★★☆) is Merlot-based (52 per cent), with smaller portions of Cabernet Sauvignon and Cabernet Franc (23 per cent), Malbec (19 per cent) and Syrah (6 per cent). Matured for 18 months in French and American oak casks, it's a green-edged wine, lacking real ripeness and richness, although reasonably flavoursome.

DRY $16 -V

Esk River Reserve Merlot (★★★☆)

Showing good varietal character, the 2002 vintage (★★★☆) was grown in the Esk Valley, Hawke's Bay, and French oak-aged for a year. It's a full-bodied wine with ripe, plummy, spicy flavours, well seasoned with toasty oak, moderately firm tannins and satisfying depth.

DRY $26 -V

Esk River Reserve Merlot/Cabernet (★★★★)

The full-coloured, generously flavoured 2002 vintage (★★★★) was grown in the Esk Valley of Hawke's Bay, blended with 7 per cent Malbec, and matured for a year in French and American oak barriques. It's a vibrantly fruity wine with sweet fruit characters, excellent depth of plum, blackcurrant and spice flavours, earthy, nutty complexities and ripe, supple tannins.

DRY $28 AV

Esk Valley Hawke's Bay Merlot ★★★★☆

The 2002 vintage (★★★★) of this consistently excellent wine was grown in the Dartmoor Valley, Puketapu and Gimblett Road districts and matured for a year in French and American oak barriques. It's a muscular wine (14.5 per cent alcohol), densely coloured and very fragrant, with bold, vibrant fruit flavours of blackcurrants and plums, a hint of dark chocolate and firm tannins. Powerful, with a chewy finish, it should mature well for several years. There is no 2003.

Vintage	03	02	01	00	99	98	DRY $23 V+
WR	NM	7	NM	6	NM	7	
Drink	NM	04-08	NM	04-06	NM	04-05	

Esk Valley Merlot/Cabernet Sauvignon/Malbec ★★★★

This Hawke's Bay winery specialises in Merlot-based reds. The 2003 vintage (★★★☆) is a blend of Merlot (39 per cent), Cabernet Sauvignon (35 per cent) and Malbec (26 per cent), matured for a year in French and American oak casks (20 per cent new). Deeply coloured, with a distinctly Malbec-influenced, spicy, gamey bouquet, it's a vibrantly fruity wine with strong blackcurrant, plum and spice flavours and a sweet oak influence, but lacks the warmth and roundness of a top vintage.

Vintage	03	02	01	00
WR	5	7	6	6
Drink	04-07	04-10	04-06	04-06

DRY $23 V+

Esk Valley Reserve Merlot/Malbec/Cabernet Sauvignon ★★★★★

Dark, vibrantly fruity and bursting with ripe, sweet-tasting blackcurrant, plum and French oak flavours, this is one of the country's classiest reds. Its superb quality, even in cooler years, makes it an important signpost to the future of Hawke's Bay reds. Since 1995, the grapes have come largely 'off the stones' – the company-owned Ngakirikiri vineyard, near Gimblett Road, and a neighbouring site, both planted in the early 1990s. The wine is matured for a long period in French oak barriques (in 2002, 21 months in 75 per cent new barrels). The 2002 vintage (★★★★★) is a blend of Merlot (56 per cent), Malbec (24 per cent) and Cabernet Sauvignon (20 per cent). Dense and youthful in colour, it has a lovely fragrance of lush, ripe fruits, and is so crammed with plum, dark chocolate, spice, coffee and nut flavours that its bold alcohol (14.5 per cent) and firm tannins are barely noticeable. Showing great density and structure, it's clearly a top vintage, for drinking 2006 onwards.

Vintage	03	02	01	00	99	98	97	96	95
WR	NM	7	6	7	7	7	5	6	6
Drink	NM	04-12	04-07	04-08	04-08	04-08	04-06	04-06	04-05

DRY $50 AV 🍇🍇🍇

Fencepost Merlot/Cabernet (★★★☆)

From Unison Vineyard in Hawke's Bay, the 2003 vintage (★★★☆) is from a season in which the Merlot crop did not reach the standard required for the top (Unison) label. Made from estate-grown and other Gimblett Gravels grapes, it's a deeply coloured, generous, spicy, slightly herbal wine with very good flavour depth, some oak complexity and moderately firm tannins, but a slight lack of warmth and softness on the finish. It should develop through 2005–06 and is priced sharply.

DRY $15 V+

Forrest Gibsons Creek Marlborough Merlot/Malbec ★★★☆

The gutsy 2002 vintage (★★★☆) is an oak-aged blend of 60 per cent Merlot and 40 per cent Malbec. Full-coloured, with dark chocolate and spice aromas showing the earthy, rustic influence of Malbec, it is ripe, plummy, spicy and firm, with loads of flavour. Drink 2005.

Vintage	02
WR	4
Drink	04-06

DRY $25 AV

Framingham Marlborough Merlot/Malbec ★★★☆

The 2002 vintage (★★★) is a blend of 85 per cent Merlot and 15 per cent Malbec, matured in French (mostly) and American oak casks (30 per cent new). Deeply coloured, it's a slightly herbaceous wine, but offers plenty of fresh, gamey, moderately complex flavour.

Vintage	02
WR	5
Drink	04-07

DRY $24 AV

Fromm La Strada Marlborough Merlot/Malbec ★★★★

The 2001 vintage (★★★★) includes all the grapes from the Fromm Vineyard that in warmer seasons would have been reserved for the Merlot Reserve label. Matured in seasoned oak casks, it's a full-flavoured, sturdy wine, vibrant, plummy, spicy and firm, with good aging potential.

Vintage	02	01	00	99	DRY $28 AV
WR	6	6	5	5	
Drink	05-08	04-08	04-06	04-05	

Fromm La Strada Merlot Reserve ★★★★★

The robust 2002 vintage (★★★★★) is a massively concentrated Marlborough red, matured in French oak barriques (20 per cent new). Deeply coloured, it shows great density of blackcurrant, plum and spice flavours, warm and complex, with hints of dark chocolate, herbs, nuts and coffee and a powerful, firm but not grippy finish. Enjoy it over the next decade.

Vintage	02	01	00	99	98	97	96	DRY $44 AV
WR	6	NM	NM	7	6	6	6	
Drink	05-10	NM	NM	04-07	04-08	04-05	04-06	

Gibbston Valley Central Otago Merlot (★★★)

The 2003 vintage (★★★) has concentration and complexity, but also reflects the difficulty of fully ripening Merlot grapes in the deep south. Matured for 16 months in American and French oak barriques (30 per cent new), it has fullish but not deep colour, a leafy bouquet and smooth plum, herb and blackcurrant flavours, showing good depth.

Vintage	03	DRY $39 -V
WR	5	
Drink	06-12	

Gladstone Merlot/Cabernet Sauvignon (★★★)

The full-flavoured 2001 vintage (★★★) is a blend of estate-grown Merlot (50 per cent) and Cabernet Franc (5 per cent) with Cabernet Sauvignon (45 per cent) from another vineyard at Gladstone, in the Wairarapa. Matured for a year in French (two-thirds) and American oak casks, it is deeply coloured, with a leafy, spicy bouquet. Vibrantly fruity, with strong flavours of plums and herbs, it shows a slight lack of full ripeness, but good intensity and some savoury complexity.

DRY $29 -V

Gladstone Reserve Merlot ★★★

Grown at two sites in the Wairarapa (the home vineyard at Gladstone and at Opaki, north of Masterton), the 2001 vintage (★★☆) was matured for nine months in one to three-year-old French oak casks. Full-coloured, with a green-edged bouquet, it's a fresh wine with plenty of blackcurrant, plum and green-leaf flavours, but too herbaceous to rate more highly.

DRY $30 -V

Goldridge Estate Premium Reserve
Matakana Merlot/Cabernet (★★☆)

The 2002 vintage (★★☆) is a Merlot-predominant red, with Cabernet Sauvignon (16 per cent), Cabernet Franc (11 per cent) and Malbec (11 per cent). Light in colour, with sweet oak aromas and herbal, spicy flavours, it lacks ripeness and depth.

DRY $16 -V

Goldwater Esslin Merlot ★★★★☆

Grown in the Esslin Vineyard on Waiheke Island, the 2000 (★★★★☆), from a 'very good' season, was harvested at 24 brix and matured for 15 months in French oak barriques (80 per cent new). Full but not dense in colour, it is leathery, spicy and gamey, with impressive depth, warmth and complexity. Compared to Hawke's Bay Merlots, it is less vibrantly fruity, more earthy and savoury, and already highly enjoyable. Still youthful, the 2002 (★★★★) has a fragrant, spicy bouquet and complex array of blackcurrant, green-leaf, leather and coffee flavours, showing excellent depth. An impressive but not brilliant wine, it's priced too high.

Vintage	02	01	00	99	98	97	96
WR	6	NM	7	7	7	7	7
Drink	04-10	NM	04-10	04-10	04-07	04-05	04-05

DRY $90 -V

Gunn Estate Merlot/Cabernet (★★☆)

From the Sacred Hill winery, the 2002 vintage (★★☆) is a lightly oaked blend of Merlot (58 per cent), Cabernet Sauvignon (32 per cent) and Malbec (8 per cent), with minor portions of Pinot Noir and Cabernet Franc. A medium-bodied Hawke's Bay red, berryish, herbal and spicy, it's a drink-young style, only moderately ripe.

Vintage	02
WR	6
Drink	04-05

DRY $15 AV

Gunn Estate Woolshed Merlot/Cabernet/Malbec (★★★★)

The richly flavoured 2002 vintage (★★★★) is a Hawke's Bay blend of Merlot (66 per cent), Cabernet Sauvignon (17 per cent) and Malbec (17 per cent), French oak-aged for 18 months. Dark, with excellent depth of fresh plum, herb and spice flavours, strongly seasoned with oak, it's still youthful, with firm tannins and a lasting finish. Worth cellaring.

Vintage	02
WR	7
Drink	04-08

DRY $30 AV

Harrier Rise Uppercase Merlot –
see Harrier Rise Uppercase in the Branded and Other Reds section

Heron's Flight La Cerise Merlot/Sangiovese ★★★

This estate-grown, oak-aged Matakana blend is designed as 'a light style red, perfect for drinking with lunch or light evening meals'. It's typically a ruby-hued, medium-bodied wine with plenty of fresh, vibrant, plummy, cherryish flavour.

DRY $22 -V

Herzog Spirit of Marlborough Merlot/Cabernet Sauvignon ★★★★★

Grown on the banks of the Wairau River and matured for two years in new and one-year-old French oak barriques, the 2000 vintage (★★★★★) is a youthful, deeply coloured wine with a fragrant bouquet of plums, berries and spicy oak. A softly seductive red with substantial body (14.4 per cent alcohol), it possesses notably concentrated blackcurrant, plum, herb and spice flavours, with gentle tannins giving it great drink-young appeal. A blend of Merlot (60 per cent), Cabernet Sauvignon (15 per cent), Cabernet Franc (15 per cent) and Malbec (10 per cent), bottled without fining or filtration, it's a delicious mouthful, and the region's most successful claret-style red. The 2002 (★★★★★) is equally classy – dark, highly fragrant and awash with blackcurrant and spice flavours, ripe, tight-knit and long.

DRY $56 AV

Hinchco Family Matakana Merlot   (★☆)

The 2003 vintage (★☆) is a 'minimally' oaked wine with light, simple, very herbaceous aromas and flavours. Overpriced.

DRY $20 -V

Hinchco Family Reserve Matakana Merlot   (★★★)

The 2002 vintage (★★★) is richly coloured, with slightly herbaceous but concentrated flavours and firm tannins.

Vintage 02
WR   6
Drink   04-08

DRY $35 -V

Hinchco Family Vineyard Barrique Merlot   (★★☆)

The 2003 vintage (★★☆) was matured in one-year-old French (75 per cent) and American oak casks. Fullish in colour, it's a green-edged wine that lacks real warmth and roundness.

DRY $25 -V

Huapai Estate Merlot/Cabernet Franc   ★★☆

Grown in the Huapai vineyard once known as Bazzard Estate, the 2002 vintage (★★☆) is a solid debut. French oak-aged for 11 months, it's a full-coloured, medium-bodied wine with fresh, berryish flavours, the earthiness typical of Auckland reds and a slightly high-acid finish. The 2003 (★★☆), a 50/50 blend, is berryish and slightly herbal, and lacks real ripeness and warmth.

DRY $15 AV

Huntaway Reserve Merlot/Cabernet Sauvignon   ★★★

The 2000 vintage (★★★) from Allied Domecq is a middleweight, vibrantly fruity red from Hawke's Bay with plenty of plummy, spicy, slightly toasty flavour. The 2002 (★★★★) is a 'predominantly' Gisborne-grown wine, matured for nine months in French (70 per cent) and American oak casks (20 per cent new). Full and youthful in colour, with a fragrant, plummy, slightly earthy bouquet, it offers very satisfying depth of warm, ripe-blackcurrant and plum flavours, with nuances of dark chocolate and spices. Savoury and earthy, it's full of character; drink 2005.

Vintage 02   01   00
WR   6   NM   6
Drink   04-10 NM   P

DRY $20 AV

Hunter's Marlborough Merlot/Pinot/Cabernet   (★★☆)

The 2002 vintage (★★☆) is a blend of Merlot (47 per cent), Pinot Noir (40 per cent) and Cabernet Sauvignon (13 per cent). Ruby-hued, with fresh, berryish, herbal flavours, it's a middleweight style with decent depth, but a slightly high-acid finish.

DRY $17 -V

Hyperion Gaia Merlot   ★★★☆

Grown at Matakana, north of Auckland, the 2002 vintage (★★★☆) was oak-aged for 14 months. It's a full-coloured, plummy and berryish, sweetly oaked wine with savoury, earthy characters adding complexity, very good flavour depth and moderately firm tannins.

Vintage 02   01   00   99   98
WR   7   NM   7   NM   6
Drink   04-08 NM   04-08 NM   P

DRY $36 -V

Isola Estate Merlot (★★☆)

Grown on Waiheke Island, the 2002 vintage (★★☆) was aged for 14 months in French and American oak barriques (30 per cent new). Brightly coloured, with a perfumed, sweetly oaked bouquet, it's a fruity, spicy, plummy wine that lacks a bit of ripeness and warmth, with a slightly high-acid finish.

DRY $30 -V

Kahurangi Estate Wairarapa Merlot (★★★)

From a Nelson-based winery, the 2003 vintage (★★★) is ruby-hued, with plummy, berryish flavours, fresh and vibrant. It's a medium to full-bodied style with a touch of toasty oak and rounded tannins.

DRY $19 AV

Karikari Estate Merlot/Malbec/Cabernet (★★★)

From New Zealand's northernmost vineyard and winery, on the Karikari Peninsula, the debut 2003 vintage (★★★) is a blend of Merlot (53 per cent), Malbec (36 per cent) and Cabernet Sauvignon (11 per cent), matured for a year in new and seasoned French and American oak casks. Deep and youthful in colour, with blackcurrant and spice aromas, it's a tightly structured wine with a strong Malbec influence and concentrated, peppery flavours, firm and youthful. Open mid-2005+.

DRY $27 -V

Kathy Lynskey 15 Rows Reserve Marlborough Merlot (★★★★★)

The densely coloured 2002 vintage (★★★★★) was estate-grown, hand-picked and matured in French and American oak barriques, new and seasoned. Super-charged, with sweet oak and spice aromas, it has outstandingly intense blackcurrant, eucalypt, plum and liquorice flavours, braced by firm, ripe tannins. Worth cellaring to 2006 onwards.

DRY $55 AV

Kemblefield The Distinction Merlot ★★☆

This Hawke's Bay red is estate-grown at Mangatahi. The 2002 vintage (★★☆) includes 15 per cent Malbec and was matured for 18 months in French oak casks. Fullish in colour, it's a green-edged wine with berryish, plummy flavours and gentle tannins in an easy-drinking style.

DRY $21 -V

Kennedy Point Vineyard Merlot (★★★★)

The 2002 vintage (★★★★) of this Waiheke Island red is a full-coloured blend of Merlot (77 per cent), Cabernet Franc (18 per cent) and Malbec (5 per cent), French oak-aged for over a year. A generous, elegant wine with good warmth and concentration of plummy, leathery, spicy flavours, it's firmly structured and maturing gracefully.

Vintage	02
WR	6
Drink	06-08

DRY $35 -V

Kim Crawford Hawke's Bay Merlot (★★★☆)

Grown at two sites, coastal and inland, the 2002 vintage (★★★☆) was matured in new and older American oak casks. Deeply coloured, with lifted, sweet oak aromas, it's a mouthfilling wine (14 per cent alcohol) with strong, ripe, plummy, spicy flavours, seasoned with toasty oak, some complexity and firm, chewy tannins.

Vintage	02
WR	3
Drink	05-06

DRY $20 AV

Kim Crawford Merlot   (★★★)

The 2003 vintage (★★★) is a regional blend with full, purple-flushed colour and plenty of crisp, plummy, berryish flavour.

Vintage	03	DRY $16 AV
WR	4	
Drink	05-06	

Kim Crawford Te Awanga Merlot   ★★★

The 2002 vintage (★★★) of this Hawke's Bay red was matured for 10 months in American oak casks (half new). Full and bright in colour, it has strong blackcurrant, mint and plum flavours, with firm acidity and a slightly leafy streak.

Vintage	02	DRY $30 -V
WR	4	
Drink	07-09	

Kingsley Estate Gimblett Gravels Merlot/Malbec   (★★★★☆)

Grown in four vineyards in the Gimblett Gravels district of Hawke's Bay and matured in French oak barriques (45 per cent new), the 2002 vintage (★★★★☆) is a blend of Merlot (67 per cent), Malbec (19 per cent), Cabernet Franc (7 per cent) and Cabernet Sauvignon (7 per cent). Complex and rich, it's a densely coloured wine with ripe-fruit characters, concentrated, plummy, spicy, slightly gamey flavours seasoned with quality oak and a good tannin backbone. Drink 2005+.

Vintage	02	DRY $39 AV
WR	6	
Drink	04-07	

Kumeu River Village Merlot   ★★★

In the past sold under the Brajkovich brand, this West Auckland red is grown at Kumeu and matured for up to a year in old French oak barrels. It is typically spicy, berryish and firm. The 2001 vintage (★★☆) is lightish in colour, with some development showing. Spicy and earthy, it's a flavoursome, slightly lean and rustic wine with some leathery complexity and a firm finish. Priced right.

DRY $15 AV

Lake Chalice Black Label Vineyard Selection Merlot   ★★★

The 2003 vintage (★★★), grown in Marlborough (two-thirds) and on the East Coast, is a Merlot-based red (93 per cent) with 7 per cent Cabernet Sauvignon. Matured in tanks and (briefly) French oak casks, it's a skilfully balanced wine, vibrantly fruity, with fresh, plummy, spicy flavours showing good depth, gentle tannins and a smooth finish.

Vintage	03	02	DRY $19 AV
WR	6	6	
Drink	04-07	04-06	

Lake Chalice Platinum Merlot   ★★★★

Estate-grown in the Falcon Vineyard in Marlborough (where the vines were planted in the early 1990s), harvested at 24.2 brix and matured for a year in oak casks (half new), the 2002 vintage (★★★☆) is boldly coloured, with fresh plum and spice flavours showing very good depth, a seasoning of sweet oak and firm tannins.

Vintage	01	00	99	98	DRY $28 AV
WR	7	7	7	7	
Drink	04-07	04-06	04-05	P	

Lincoln Heritage Merlot (★★☆)

Grown in Gisborne and harvested at 20 brix, the 2003 (tasted prior to bottling, and so not rated), was matured for 14 months in seasoned French oak casks. The company's top red from the vintage, it's a tightly structured wine with plummy, berryish flavours, hints of herbs and chocolate, spicy oak and a firm finish.

Vintage	03	
WR	6	**DRY $17 -V**
Drink	04-08	

Lincoln Winemakers Series Gisborne Merlot ★★★

Past vintages have included some highly enjoyable, fruit-driven, Beaujolais-style reds. The 2003 (★★☆), the last of the label, is ruby-hued and tight, with firm, plum/spice flavours that lack the seductive fruitiness and softness of this wine at its best.

DRY $14 V+

Longlands Merlot ★★★☆

From the Te Awa winery in Hawke's Bay, the 2002 vintage (★★★☆) is highly appealing, with fresh, red-berry aromas and subtle oak. Full-coloured, it's mouthfilling and warm, with vibrant plum and spice flavours, some savoury, leathery characters and moderately firm tannins. A refined wine, it shows good density and structure.

Vintage	02	01	00	99	98
WR	7	5	6	6	6
Drink	04-08	04-06	04-05	P	P

DRY $20 AV

Longridge Hawke's Bay Merlot/Cabernet ★★★

Showing good colour depth, the 2002 vintage (★★☆) from Allied Domecq is a blend of Merlot (60 per cent), Cabernet Sauvignon (27 per cent) and Cabernet Franc (13 per cent), matured for nine months in a 3:1 mix of French and American oak casks (15 per cent new). It possesses plenty of blackcurrant, green-leaf and mint flavour, but slightly lacks warmth and roundness. Still, the price is right.

Vintage	02	01	00
WR	5	6	6
Drink	04-06	P	P

DRY $15 AV

Loopline Vineyard Wairarapa Merlot ★★☆

The 2002 vintage (★★☆), grown on the Opaki Plains, north of Masterton, is ruby-hued, with a leafy bouquet. It's a pleasantly fruity wine, with its accent on plum and red-berry flavours, but lacks real ripeness and stuffing. The 2003 (★★☆), matured for 10 months in French oak casks (mostly one-year-old), is fresh and simple, with plum, berry and herb flavours and a slightly high-acid finish.

DRY $27 -V

Lucknow Estate Quarry Bridge Vineyard Merlot ★★★

The 2002 vintage (★★★) is a Hawke's Bay red, full-coloured, with perfumed, sweet oak aromas, suggesting a strong American oak influence. It's a medium to full-bodied style with plummy, spicy flavours, some savoury complexity and decent depth. Ready; no rush.

Vintage	02	01
WR	6	7
Drink	05-06	05-06

DRY $22 -V

Main Divide Merlot/Cabernet ★★★

Drinking well now, the 2002 vintage (★★★) is a deeply coloured blend of Marlborough and Waipara grapes, matured in seasoned oak barrels. Leafy aromas lead into a smooth, slightly savoury red with generous blackcurrant, plum and herb flavours, gentle tannins and mouthfilling body.

Vintage	02	DRY $18 AV
WR	6	
Drink	04-08	

Margrain Martinborough Merlot ★★★☆

Harvested at 24 brix and French oak-matured for 10 months, the 2002 vintage (★★★☆) is deeply coloured, with a slightly leafy bouquet. It's a full-bodied, generous wine with strong blackcurrant, red-berry and herb flavours, fresh and vibrantly fruity, with well-integrated oak and the potential to age well.

Vintage	02	01	00	99	98	DRY $32 -V
WR	7	7	6	6	7	
Drink	04-08	04-06	04-06	04-05	04-06	

Matariki Aspire Merlot/Cabernet Sauvignon (★★★☆)

The stylish 2002 vintage (★★★☆) offers very good depth of blackcurrant, plum and spice flavour, with savoury, earthy, leafy touches and a subtle oak influence. A blend of 57 per cent Merlot and 43 per cent Cabernet Sauvignon, it was grown in the Gimblett Gravels district of Hawke's Bay and matured for 15 months in seasoned oak casks.

Vintage	02	DRY $20 AV
WR	6	
Drink	04-07	

Matua Valley Ararimu
Merlot/Syrah/Cabernet Sauvignon ★★★★★

Matua's flagship Hawke's Bay red from the 2002 vintage (★★★★☆) is a blend of Merlot (50 per cent), Syrah (25 per cent), Cabernet Sauvignon (20 per cent) and Malbec (5 per cent). Matured for a year entirely in French oak barriques (75 per cent new), it possesses noble colour and intense blackcurrant, plum and pepper flavours, although a herbaceous, leafy edge is emerging with bottle-age. It's a beautifully vibrant wine, crammed with fruit and showing savoury, gamey complexities.

Vintage	02	DRY $40 AV
WR	6	
Drink	04-10	

Matua Valley Bullrush Vineyard Merlot ★★★★

The 2002 vintage (★★★★) is a single-vineyard Hawke's Bay wine, grown in the Ngatarawa district and matured in French and American oak casks (70 per cent new). Fruity and full-flavoured, with raspberry, plum and spice characters showing excellent ripeness and warmth, it's a boldly coloured, seductively smooth wine with the depth and structure to mature well.

Vintage	03	02	01	DRY $29 AV
WR	5	7	7	
Drink	04-08	04-09	04-08	

Matua Valley Hawke's Bay Merlot   ★★★

The 2003 vintage (★★☆) was blended with 10 per cent Malbec and matured for seven months in seasoned oak casks. It's a ruby-hued, vibrant, moderately ripe-tasting wine with uncomplicated, berryish flavours.

Vintage	03	
WR	4	
Drink	04-06	

DRY $17 AV

Miller's Merlot   (★★★☆)

From a challenging season, the 2001 vintage (★★★☆) is on a slightly lower plane than the excellent 2000 (★★★★), which included Cabernet Franc and was labelled Miller's Serious One. Grown on the Awhitu Peninsula, in South Auckland, it has fullish colour, showing some development, generous, berryish, earthy, spicy flavours, seasoned with quality oak, slightly high acidity and moderate tannins. It shows lots of character, but is best drunk young.

DRY $45 -V

Mill Road Hawke's Bay Merlot/Cabernet   ★★☆

From Morton Estate, this is typically a fresh, uncomplicated style with moderate depth of red-berry/plum flavours, a hint of American oak and a smooth finish. The 2002 vintage (★★☆) is developed in colour, with spicy, green-edged flavours.

MED/DRY $13 AV

Mills Reef Elspeth Merlot   ★★★★☆

Grown in the company's Mere Road vineyard, near Hastings, the 2000 vintage (★★★★☆) is deeply coloured, with a fragrant bouquet of red berries, spices and cedary oak. A very elegant and approachable wine, it has concentrated plum and red-berry flavours, lovely fruit sweetness, a strong nutty oak influence and a powerful finish. Tasted just prior to bottling (and so not rated), the 2001 was full-coloured, with a spicy, leathery bouquet showing good complexity. Full-bodied, with fresh, plummy, spicy, savoury characters and firm tannins, it's a good but not great vintage, for drinking now onwards.

Vintage	02	01	00	99	98
WR	7	6	7	7	7
Drink	04-14	04-06	04-05	P	P

DRY $39 AV

Mills Reef Elspeth Merlot Block 3   (NR)

Tasted prior to bottling (and so not rated), the 2002 vintage was based on clone 6 Merlot vines, planted in the company's Mere Road vineyard, in the Gimblett Gravels district of Hawke's Bay, in 1993. Matured for 18 months in French oak barriques (half new), it has deep, youthful, purple-flushed colour and a highly fragrant bouquet of blackcurrants, plums, spice and new oak. Very powerful, with bold tannins and super-concentrated flavours, it's a complex, seriously structured wine for the long haul.

DRY $39 V?

Mills Reef Elspeth Merlot Block 4   (★★★★)

Made from 1997 plantings of newer clones at the company's Mere Road vineyard in the Gimblett Gravels, Hawke's Bay, the 2002 vintage (★★★★) is an inky-black, densely packed wine with sweet fruit characters, bold cassis, plum, spice and mint flavours and very chewy, almost tough tannins. It's crying out for cellaring.

DRY $39 -V

Mills Reef Elspeth Merlot/Cabernet   (★★★★)

The 2002 vintage (★★★★), grown in the Mere Road vineyard, in the Gimblett Gravels, is a blend of 60 per cent Merlot and 40 per cent Cabernet Sauvignon, French oak-aged for 16 months. It's still very youthful, with impressively dark colour, sweet fruit characters and powerful, spicy, nutty flavours, but needs time for its firm, almost aggressive tannins to mellow. Open 2006+.

DRY $39 ·V

Mills Reef Merlot/Cabernet   ★★★

The 2003 vintage (★★★) is a Merlot-predominant blend (71 per cent), grown in Hawke's Bay and French oak-aged for nine months. Full-coloured, with vibrant, plummy, spicy, herbal flavours, some toasty oak and gentle tannins, it's a moderately complex, easy-drinking wine.

Vintage	03	02	01	00
WR	7	7	6	6
Drink	04-06	04-06	04-05	P

DRY $18 AV

Mills Reef Reserve Merlot   ★★★★

The 2002 (★★★★☆) is a top vintage of this Hawke's Bay red, highly fragrant, with ripe, deliciously concentrated flavours. The 2003 (★★★☆), grown in the company's Mere Road vineyard, in the Gimblett Gravels district, was blended with 20 per cent Cabernet Franc. It's less intense than the 2002, but ripe and flavoursome, with savoury, earthy, nutty complexities and firm but supple tannins. Drink now onwards.

Vintage	03	02	01	00	99	98	97	96
WR	6	7	6	7	7	NM	7	5
Drink	04-08	04-07	04-06	P	P	NM	P	P

DRY $25 AV

Mills Reef Reserve Merlot/Cabernet   ★★★☆

The 2002 vintage (★★★), grown in Hawke's Bay, offers some savoury, earthy, spicy complexity, but is now showing considerable development and leafy, green-edged characters are emerging with bottle-age.

Vintage	02	01	00
WR	7	NM	6
Drink	04-07	NM	P

DRY $25 AV

Mills Reef Reserve Merlot/Cabernet/Syrah   (★★★★)

The 2001 vintage (★★★★) is a mouthfilling, complex Hawke's Bay red with earthy, spicy characters on the nose and good warmth and depth. It's a weighty wine with blackcurrant, coffee and nut flavours, silky tannins and plenty of personality.

DRY $24 V+

Mills Reef Reserve Merlot/Malbec   (★★★)

The full-coloured 2003 vintage (★★★) is a Hawke's Bay red, blended from Merlot (80 per cent) and Malbec (20 per cent). Berryish, spicy and slightly gamey, with firm tannins, it's a more fruity, less complex and supple wine than its Reserve Merlot stablemate from the same vintage (see above).

DRY $25 ·V

Millton Te Arai Vineyard Merlot   ★★★☆

The bold, purple-flushed 2002 vintage (★★★☆) was grown in Gisborne and matured for 20 months in new and seasoned oak casks. It's a concentrated wine with blackcurrant and plum flavours, firm tannins and a distinctly minty streak (attributed by Millton to the eucalyptus trees that surround the vineyard). It should be long-lived.

Vintage	02
WR	6
Drink	04-09

DRY $22 AV

Mission Hawke's Bay Merlot ★★☆

The 2003 vintage (★★), oak-aged, is medium-full in colour, with an earthy bouquet. It's a slightly rustic wine with crisp, plummy, berryish flavours that lack real freshness and charm.

DRY $15 AV

Mission Reserve Hawke's Bay Merlot (★★★)

Grown in Central Hawke's Bay and matured in French oak casks (40 per cent new), the 2002 vintage (★★★) has full colour, showing some development. Mouthfilling, with brambly, spicy, slightly herbal flavours showing good depth, it's ready for drinking.

DRY $25 -V

Mission Reserve Merlot (★★★)

Grown at Patutahi, in Gisborne, and French oak-aged, the 2002 vintage (★★★) has some earthy, savoury complexity, but its mature herb and spice flavours are only moderately ripe and concentrated.

DRY $25 -V

Moana Park Pascoe Series Merlot/Cabernet ★★☆

Designed as a 'fruit-driven' style, the 2003 vintage (★★☆) was grown in the Dartmoor Valley of Hawke's Bay. Full-coloured, with a herbaceous bouquet and fruity, gamey flavours, it's an honest, flavoursome red, with slightly high acidity.

DRY $16 -V

Montana Fairhall Estate Merlot/Cabernet Sauvignon ★★★☆

Montana's 1999 Marlborough red (★★★☆) was matured entirely in French oak barriques (58 per cent new). It shows good concentration of blackcurrant and nutty oak flavours, with green olive and fennel characters reflecting its cool-climate origin, good complexity and firm tannins. The 2001 (★★★☆) is again rich and complex, with full colour, the fresh acidity typical of Marlborough reds and lots of plummy, spicy, nutty flavour.

Vintage	01	00	99
WR	6	NM	6
Drink	04-07	NM	04-06

DRY $29 -V

Montana Reserve Barrique Matured Merlot ★★★☆

The 2002 vintage (★★★☆) is a blend of Marlborough and Hawke's Bay grapes, matured in American (55 per cent) and French (45 per cent) oak casks. Full-coloured, with a spicy bouquet, it has good depth of blackcurrant, plum, coffee, green-leaf and toast flavours, with a smooth, dry finish.

Vintage	02	01	00	99	98
WR	6	6	6	6	7
Drink	04-08	04-08	04-07	04-06	04-05

DRY $20 AV

Moteo Terroire Merlot Reserve (★★★☆)

Grown in Hawke's Bay, the 2002 vintage (★★★☆) was picked at 23.5 brix and matured in French oak casks (half new). Rich and youthful in colour, it has berryish, plummy, slightly herbal flavours, firm and rich.

DRY $18 V+

Mount Riley Marlborough Merlot/Malbec   (★★★☆)
The deeply coloured 2003 vintage (★★★☆) is a blend of Merlot (53 per cent) and Malbec (47 per cent), matured for a year in oak casks (30 per cent new). It's a smooth, sweetly oaked wine, fruit-packed, with moderate complexity but plenty of berry, spice and plum flavour, fresh and vibrant.

Vintage   03
WR   6   DRY $19 V+
Drink   05-08

Moutere Hills Nelson Merlot/Cabernet   ★★
A 2:1 blend of Merlot and Cabernet Sauvignon, the French and American oak-aged 2003 vintage (★★) is a ruby-hued, fresh, crisp, berryish red, but it lacks warmth, richness and roundness.

Vintage   02
WR   5   DRY $24 -V
Drink   06-08

Newton/Forrest Cornerstone Merlot   (★★★★★)
The dark and muscular (14.5 per cent alcohol) 2002 vintage (★★★★★) is a power-packed, single-vineyard Hawke's Bay red, grown in the Gimblett Gravels district. A firm, finely balanced wine that should be long-lived, it has rich blackcurrant, spice and coffee flavours showing excellent ripeness and concentration. Drink 2006+.

Vintage   02
WR   6   DRY $40 AV
Drink   04-08

Ngatarawa Alwyn Merlot/Cabernet   ★★★★☆
The dark, rich 2000 (★★★★★) is a real fruit bomb, bursting with blackcurrant, plum and mint characters, and developing real complexity with age. Still youthful, the 2002 vintage (★★★★) is a blend of 80 per cent Merlot and 20 per cent Cabernet Sauvignon, matured for 18 months in new French oak barriques. Deeply coloured, rich and smooth, it's a generous, spicy, plummy and slightly herbaceous wine with leathery, nutty complexities and a firm finish.

Vintage	02	01	00	99	98
WR	7	NM	7	NM	7
Drink	04-08	NM	04-10	NM	04-08

DRY $45 -V

Ngatarawa Glazebrook Merlot   ★★★★
The richly coloured 2002 vintage (★★★★) is a concentrated Hawke's Bay red, grown in the Ngatarawa Triangle (73 per cent) and Gimblett Gravels (27 per cent). Matured for a year in a 2:1 mix of American and French oak casks, it's rich and well-structured, with firm, spicy, nutty flavours showing good complexity and cellaring potential.

Vintage	02	01	00
WR	6	NM	6
Drink	04-07	NM	04-05

DRY $25 AV

Ngatarawa Glazebrook Merlot/Cabernet   ★★★★
The 2001 vintage (★★★☆) of this Hawke's Bay red is a blend of Merlot (55 per cent), Cabernet Sauvignon (37 per cent) and Malbec (8 per cent), matured in American (80 per cent) and French oak casks (25 per cent new). It's a deeply coloured, slightly herbaceous wine with rich blackcurrant, plum and spice flavours seasoned with sweet oak and moderate tannins.

Vintage	01	00	99	98
WR	6	6	6	7
Drink	04-09	04-07	04-06	04-08

DRY $25 AV

Ngatarawa Stables Merlot ★★★

A very decent quaffer, the 2003 vintage (★★★) was grown in Hawke's Bay and oak-aged. Gutsy and gamey, it's a full-coloured wine with blackcurrant, plum, spice and slightly toasty oak flavours, fresh and mouthfilling.

Vintage	03	
WR	6	DRY $16 AV
Drink	04-07	

Nikau Point Hawke's Bay Merlot/Cabernet (★★★)

Made for early drinking, the 2002 vintage (★★★) from One Tree Hill Vineyards (a division of Morton Estate) was matured for several months in American oak. It's a full-bodied wine, fresh and vibrant, with plummy fruit characters, hints of chocolate and mint and a smooth, off-dry finish.

Vintage	03	02	
WR	6	6	MED/DRY $16 AV
Drink	04-06	P	

Nobilo Merlot ★★★

The 2002 vintage (★★★) is a blend of Hawke's Bay, Gisborne and Marlborough grapes, French and American oak-matured. It's a slightly rustic and earthy, characterful wine with good colour depth, plenty of berry, plum and spice flavour and firm tannins.

Vintage	03	02	01	
WR	7	7	7	DRY $16 AV
Drink	04-07	04-06	P	

Odyssey Kumeu Merlot ★★★☆

The 2003 vintage (★★★) is a West Auckland red, grown in the Heralds Cove vineyard and matured in one-year-old French oak casks. Full but not dense in colour, with a slightly leafy bouquet, it is mouthfilling and smooth, with very good depth of plummy, spicy flavour, showing considerable complexity. The 2002 (★★★★) is blossoming with cellaring.

Vintage	03	02	
WR	5	6	DRY $24 AV
Drink	04-08	04-08	

Okahu Estate Ninety Mile Merlot (★★★)

The medium to full-bodied 2002 vintage (★★★) is a blend of Hawke's Bay (44 per cent), Gisborne (38 per cent) and Northland (18 per cent) grapes, American and French oak-aged. Fullish in colour, it is spicy, berryish and plummy, with some earthy, savoury characters, oak complexity and a firm finish. Drink 2005+.

Vintage	02	
WR	5	DRY $23 -V
Drink	04-06	

Omaka Springs Marlborough Merlot ★★☆

The 2002 vintage (★★), American oak-aged, is plummy and spicy but distinctly green-edged, lacking real ripeness and intensity.

DRY $16 -V

Onetangi Road Merlot (★★☆)

Grown on Waiheke Island, the 2002 vintage (★★☆) is full coloured, with green-edged flavours and a slightly high-acid finish.

DRY $49 -V

Onetangi Road Reserve
Merlot/Cabernet Sauvignon/Cabernet Franc/Malbec   (★★★)

The 2002 vintage (★★★) was grown on Waiheke Island. It's a characterful, full-coloured wine, spicy and flavoursome, but lacks real warmth and roundness.

DRY $49 -V

One Tree Hawke's Bay Merlot   (★★★☆)

Made by Capricorn Wine Estates (a division of Craggy Range) exclusively for Foodstuffs (New World, Pak 'N Save) supermarkets and restaurants, the 2003 vintage (★★★☆) was harvested at 23 brix in the Gimblett Gravels district, and 'a component' of the blend was oak-aged. Richly coloured and boldly fruity, it is fresh and vibrant, plummy and spicy, with a slightly chewy finish.

DRY $17 V+

Passage Rock Merlot   ★★★☆

The perfumed, concentrated 2002 vintage (★★★★) of this Waiheke Island red was grown at three sites and matured for 15 months in American and French oak barriques (40 per cent new). Youthful and deeply coloured, it's rich, brambly and spicy, with nutty oak adding complexity and a firm underlay of tannin. From a more difficult season, the 2003 (★★☆) is less impressive – full-coloured, but lacking in sweet, ripe-fruit characters, with a slightly hard, green-edged finish.

DRY $35 -V

Peacock Ridge Reserve Merlot   ★★★★

A highly impressive debut, the 2002 vintage (★★★★☆) was grown at Onetangi, Waiheke Island, and matured for a year in French and American oak casks. It's a dark, warm and concentrated wine with rich, brambly, spicy flavours, a hint of dark chocolate, good complexity and a firmly structured finish. The youthful 2003 (★★★☆) is full-coloured and smooth, but less intense than the 2002, with plummy, spicy, slightly earthy flavours showing good depth and some complexity.

Vintage	03	02
WR	6	7
Drink	04-07	04-06

DRY $37 -V

Pegasus Bay Merlot/Cabernet   (★★★☆)

Drinking well now, the 2002 vintage (★★★☆) is a blend of Merlot, Cabernet Sauvignon, Malbec and Cabernet Franc, grown at Waipara and matured in French and American oak barriques (30 per cent new). Full-coloured, with herbal notes on the nose, it's a smooth, fleshy wine with blackcurrant, plum and green-leaf flavours showing very good depth, oak complexity and gentle tannins.

Vintage	02
WR	5
Drink	04-09

DRY $28 -V

Prospect Vineyard Merlot   (★★★☆)

Full of character, the 2002 vintage (★★★☆) was grown in Maraekakaho Road, in Hawke's Bay, and French oak-aged for 15 months. Showing good body and depth, it is brambly, plummy, spicy and slightly earthy, with sweet fruit characters, balanced tannins and considerable complexity. Verging on four stars.

Vintage	02
WR	5
Drink	04-12

DRY $24 AV

Putiki Bay Merlot (★★☆)

The 2002 vintage (★★☆), grown on Waiheke Island, is a middleweight style, light in colour, with moderate depth of plummy, spicy flavour and a slightly green, high-acid finish.

DRY $45 -V

Rannach Merlot (★★★)

Like a minor Bordeaux, the 2002 vintage (★★★) was grown at Clevedon, in South Auckland, and matured for a year in French oak barriques. It's a clearly varietal wine, honest and characterful, with plummy, earthy, spicy flavours and moderate tannins.

Vintage	02
WR	4
Drink	04+

DRY $25 -V

Redmetal Basket Press Merlot/Franc ★★★★☆

At its best, this Maraekakaho, Hawke's Bay blend of Merlot and Cabernet Franc is a sophisticated, beautifully rich and supple wine, weighty and bursting with ripe blackcurrant/plum flavours. There have been no 2001 or 2003 vintages.

Vintage	03	02	01	00	99	98
WR	NM	6	NM	7	5	7
Drink	NM	04-10	NM	04-09	04-06	04-10

DRY $40 AV

Redmetal Merlot/Cabernet Franc ★★★★

This Hawke's Bay red is made for early drinking. A 2:1 blend, grown at Maraekakaho and matured for a year in French and American oak casks, the 2002 (★★★★) is the first vintage to exclude Cabernet Sauvignon. It's a skilfully crafted wine, fragrant, with very good depth of ripe-berry and plum flavours, a sweet, coconutty oak influence and strong drink-young appeal.

Vintage	03	02	01	00	99	98
WR	5	6	NM	6	5	6
Drink	05-07	04-06	NM	P	P	P

DRY $22 V+

Riverside Dartmoor Merlot ★★☆

This Dartmoor Valley, Hawke's Bay red is typically berryish and herbal, fresh and crisp. Matured in French and American oak, the 2003 vintage (★★☆) is bright and fullish in colour, with fresh, plummy, distinctly leafy, slightly high-acid flavours. It's a drink-young style, with gentle tannins.

Vintage	03	02
WR	5	5
Drink	04-06	04-05

DRY $15 AV

Rongopai Merlot/Malbec (★★★)

Made for early consumption, the 2002 vintage (★★★) has fullish, purple-flushed colour and the meaty, savoury, earthy aromas of Malbec. Fresh and supple, it's a very fruit-driven style with plum and red-berry flavours, gentle tannins and a smooth finish.

DRY $16 AV

Rongopai Reserve Merlot (★★★★)

Offering great value, the 2002 vintage (★★★★) is a gutsy, single-vineyard Gisborne red, oak-aged for a year. Boldly coloured, with a gamey, spicy bouquet, sweet fruit characters and lots of brambly, spicy, plummy, slightly chocolatey flavour, it's still youthful and well worth cellaring to 2005+.

DRY $19 V+

Rongopai Ultimo Merlot
(★★★★)

The powerful 2002 vintage (★★★★) was grown in Gisborne and matured for 18 months in new French oak casks. Deeply coloured, with buckets of ripe, sweet fruit and a strong, spicy oak influence, it's a fleshy, chocolatey wine with a silky richness on the front palate, building to a lasting, slightly chewy finish.

DRY $39 -V

Rossendale Hawke's Bay Merlot
(★★☆)

The light, berryish 2002 vintage (★★☆) is ruby-hued, with fresh, plummy, leafy flavours that lack real ripeness and depth.

DRY $20 -V

St Helena Marlborough Merlot
(★★☆)

Made in a 'fruit-driven' style with 'light oak', the 2002 vintage (★★☆) is medium-full in colour, with a herbaceous bouquet. Balanced for easy drinking, it offers plum, spice and green-leaf flavours, with gentle tannins giving a smooth finish.

Vintage	02
WR	5
Drink	04-05

DRY $22 -V

Sacred Hill Basket Press Merlot/Malbec
(★★★☆)

Densely coloured, the gutsy 2002 vintage (★★★☆) offers loads of spicy, plummy flavour. Grown in Hawke's Bay and oak-aged for a year, it's a blend of Merlot (57 per cent) and Malbec (28 per cent) principally, with smaller portions of Cabernet Sauvignon and Cabernet Franc. Vibrantly fruity and well-ripened, it has lots of drink-young charm.

Vintage	02
WR	7
Drink	04-08

DRY $25 AV

Sacred Hill Brokenstone Merlot
★★★★★

The brilliant 2002 vintage (★★★★★) is a blend of Merlot (92 per cent), Malbec (6 per cent) and Cabernet Franc (2 per cent), grown in the Gimblett Gravels district and matured for 20 months in French oak casks. A notably complete Hawke's Bay wine, it is dark and overflowing with lush, brambly, spicy, earthy flavours. Powerful, yet very elegant, silky and complex, it's already a delicious mouthful, but has the stuffing and structure to mature gracefully for many years. Don't miss it.

Vintage	02	01	00	99	98
WR	7	NM	6	NM	5
Drink	05-10	NM	04-07	NM	04-05

DRY $40 AV

Sacred Hill Whitecliff Estate Merlot
★★★☆

This Hawke's Bay red is typically delicious in its youth – fragrant and vibrantly fruity, with plenty of blackcurrant/plum flavour, fresh, ripe and smooth. The 2002 vintage (★★★) is attractive, with good colour depth, ripe-fruit flavours, hints of herbs and chocolate and moderate tannins.

DRY $16 V+

Saint Clair Marlborough Merlot
★★☆

Matured for five months in seasoned oak casks, the 2002 vintage (★★☆) is a fruit-driven, easy-drinking style, ruby-hued, with fresh, raspberryish, slightly leafy flavours and a very smooth finish.

Vintage	02	01	00
WR	6	6	6
Drink	04-05	P	P

DRY $18 -V

Saint Clair Rapaura Road Reserve Marlborough Merlot ★★★★

This is a more wood-influenced style than its stablemate (above), in warm years showing deep colour and powerful, ripe-fruit flavours. The 2002 vintage (★★★★), matured for 10 months in American oak casks, is fullish in colour, with toasty oak aromas and strong, plummy, sweetly oaked flavours. It's a moderately complex wine with an attractive silkiness of texture.

Vintage	02	01	00	99	98
WR	6	7	6	7	7
Drink	04-08	04-06	04-06	04-05	P

DRY $25 AV

Saint Clair Vicar's Choice Merlot (★★☆)

Grown in Marlborough and oak-aged for eight months, the 2002 vintage (★★☆) is a ruby-hued, green-edged wine with plummy, spicy, leafy flavours and a touch of savoury complexity.

Vintage	02
WR	5
Drink	04-05

DRY $17 -V

Selaks Founders Reserve
Hawke's Bay Merlot/Cabernet Franc ★★★★

The 2002 vintage (★★★★) was harvested in the Ngatarawa district at over 24 brix and matured for 14 months in new and one-year-old French oak casks. It's a highly attractive wine, very elegant, concentrated and supple, with impressive depth of blackcurrant, herb and plum flavours, good balance and complexity.

Vintage	02	01	00	99
WR	7	7	NM	6
Drink	04-07	P	NM	P

DRY $27 AV

Selaks Premium Selection Merlot (★★)

A solid, ruby-hued quaffing red, the 2003 vintage (★★) was grown in Hawke's Bay and Gisborne and 'a portion' was oak-aged. Fresh, fruity, crisp and berryish, it lacks real ripeness and stuffing, and would sit more easily at $10 than $15.

DRY $15 -V

Shepherds Point Merlot/Cabernet/Syrah (★★★★)

The powerful 2002 vintage (★★★★) was grown at Onetangi, on Waiheke Island, and matured for a year in French oak barriques (30 per cent new). Densely coloured, with buckets of fruit and intense blackcurrant, plum and pepper flavours, it's a complex, firmly structured wine, full of potential. Open 2005 onwards.

DRY $38 -V

Sherwood Estate Stratum Merlot/Pinot Noir/Pinotage (★★☆)

The full-coloured 2003 vintage (★★☆) has fresh, crisp, blackcurrant and green-leaf flavours, showing moderate depth.

DRY $18 -V

Sileni Cellar Selection Merlot ★★★

The unusually light 2003 vintage (★★☆) is a Hawke's Bay blend of Merlot (87 per cent), Malbec (2 per cent) and Cabernet Franc (11 per cent), matured for a year in old French and American oak casks. Ruby-hued, it offers smooth, red-berry and plum flavours, slightly earthy and spicy, but lacks depth.

Vintage	03	02	01	00
WR	5	5	NM	6
Drink	04-07	04-06	NM	04-06

DRY $22 -V

Sileni Estate Selection The Triangle Merlot   (★★★★)

The 2002 vintage (★★★★) of this Hawke's Bay red is medium to full-bodied, with elegance and complexity. Matured for a year in French and American oak casks (35 per cent new), it is full-coloured, with plum/red-berry flavours enriched with spicy oak, leathery, earthy, nutty characters and moderately firm tannins. It's drinking extremely well now, but also worth cellaring.

Vintage	02			DRY $35 -V
WR	6			
Drink	04-09			

Sileni EV Merlot   ★★★★★

'EV' stands for 'exceptional vintage'. The 2000 vintage (★★★★★), an unblended Merlot, was grown in Hawke's Bay and matured for a year in French and American oak casks (35 per cent new). Warm and rich, it's a sweet-fruited wine with deep plum, blackcurrant and coffee flavours, braced by supple yet firm tannins. It's built for the long haul, but already dangerously drinkable.

Vintage	00	99	98	DRY $95 -V
WR	5	NM	5	
Drink	04-12	NM	04-18	

Soljans Barrique Reserve Merlot   ★★★

Grown in Hawke's Bay, the 2002 vintage (★★★) has lots of drink-young charm. Fresh and supple, with full, bright colour, it's a buoyantly fruity wine with red-berry and plum flavours, some spicy oak and a gentle underlay of tannin.

DRY $20 AV

Soljans Tribute Merlot/Malbec   (★★★)

The debut 2002 vintage (★★★) is billed as 'without doubt the finest red ever produced by the estate', but I didn't find it that exciting. A Hawke's Bay blend of Merlot (61 per cent) and Malbec (39 per cent), barrel-aged for 18 months, mostly in new French oak, it offers strong, youthful, berryish flavours, moderate complexity and a slightly high-acid finish. Vibrant and supple, it's worth keeping to 2005–06.

DRY $35 -V

Solstone Reserve Wairarapa Merlot   (★★☆)

The green-edged 2001 vintage (★★☆) was grown at Masterton and French oak-aged for two years. Full and developed in colour, with a herbaceous bouquet and flavour, it shows some spicy, nutty complexity, but lacks real ripeness and richness.

Vintage	01		DRY $42 -V
WR	5		
Drink	05-11+		

Solstone Wairarapa Merlot   ★★☆

The 2002 vintage (★★★☆) was estate-grown at Masterton, blended with a splash (5 per cent) of Cabernet Sauvignon and matured for 20 months in seasoned French oak casks. It's a medium-bodied, herbaceous wine, fullish in colour, with leather, spice and green-leaf flavours that lack ripeness and roundness.

Vintage	02	01	DRY $23 -V
WR	6	6	
Drink	05-08	04-05	

Spy Valley Marlborough Merlot   (★★★☆)

The only vintage of this wine I have tasted is the deeply coloured 2001 (★★★☆), picked at 25 brix in the Waihopai Valley and matured in French oak casks. Fleshy and smooth (fractionally off-dry), it's crammed with berry, plum and mint flavours, with an almost Malbec-like richness.

Vintage	03	02	01	00
WR	6	5	6	5
Drink	04-07	04-06	04-06	04

DRY $20 AV

Squawking Magpie The Nest Merlot/Cabernet   (★★★★☆)

The elegant 2002 vintage (★★★★☆) was hand-picked from exceptionally low-cropping (1.2 tonnes/hectare), 20-year-old vines in the Gimblett Gravels district of Hawke's Bay. A blend of Merlot (52 per cent) and Cabernet Sauvignon (48 per cent), French oak-aged, it's a full-coloured wine with a slightly cedary bouquet. A Bordeaux-like red, it is well-structured, with warm, earthy, blackcurrant and nut flavours, showing good complexity, and a firm finish.

DRY $40 AV

Stonecutter Martinborough Merlot   ★★★

The ruby-hued 2002 vintage (★★★) is an attractive middleweight, fruity and smooth, with sweet fruit characters and plummy, spicy flavours.

DRY $28 -V

Stoneleigh Marlborough Merlot   (★★★☆)

The debut 2002 vintage (★★★☆) from Allied Domecq was blended with Malbec (9 per cent) and matured for nine months in French oak casks (34 per cent new). Maturing well, it's a richly coloured, vibrantly fruity wine with strong plum/spice flavours in a moderately complex style with firm tannins. Verging on four stars.

Vintage	02
WR	5
Drink	04-07

DRY $20 AV

Te Awa Farm Longlands Merlot – see Longlands Merlot

Te Kairanga Castlepoint Merlot   (★★)

A drink-young quaffer, the 2003 vintage (★★) was grown in Gisborne and French oak-aged for six months. It's a ruby-hued, medium-bodied wine with light, berryish, plummy, herbal flavours that lack real ripeness and depth.

Vintage	03
WR	5
Drink	04-06

DRY $14 -V

Te Kairanga Gisborne Merlot   ★★☆

French oak-aged for eight months, the 2003 vintage (★★☆) is a distinctly spicy wine, fullish in colour, with reasonable depth of plum and red-berry flavours and firm tannins. It's a solid wine, but lacks a bit of fruit sweetness and richness.

Vintage	03	02
WR	5	5
Drink	04-08	04-07

DRY $20 -V

Te Mania Three Brothers Merlot/Malbec/Cabernet ★★★

The boldly coloured 2003 vintage (★★★) is a Nelson blend of similar portions of Merlot, Malbec and Cabernet Franc, matured for 10 months in French and American oak casks. The bouquet is floral and raspberryish; the palate is vibrantly fruity, with plum and red-berry flavours showing good depth.

Vintage	03	DRY $20 AV
WR	7	
Drink	04-07	

Te Whau The Point
Merlot/Cabernet Sauvignon/Cabernet Franc/Malbec –
see Te Whau The Point in the Branded and Other Reds section

Te Whau Vineyard Single Barrel Merlot   (★★★★★)

From 'a great Merlot year on Waiheke Island', the 2002 vintage (★★★★★) is a selection of the best of 12 barrels, bottled without fining or filtering. Only 300 bottles were produced. Matured in French oak for 15 months, it's a very savoury, gamey, earthy and spicy wine, warm and complex, with a firm tannin backbone. Drink now or cellar. There is no 2003.

Vintage	03	02	DRY $43 AV
WR	NM	7	
Drink	NM	04-08	

Thyme Hill Vineyard Merlot   ★★★☆

One of the country's southernmost Merlots, grown at Alexandra, in Central Otago. The 2002 vintage (★★★☆) has deep, youthful colour and a leafy bouquet. It's a generous wine with loads of blackcurrant, herb and nut flavour, spicy, toasty and firm. The 2003 (★★★) is slightly less impressive, but still weighty, with some fruit sweetness and satisfying depth of berryish, plummy, distinctly herbal flavour. A worthy effort against the odds.

Vintage	02	DRY $28 -V
WR	5	
Drink	04-07	

Tom Cat Merlot   (★★☆)

From Coopers Creek, the 2003 vintage (★★☆) is a deep ruby blend of Hawke's Bay and Gisborne grapes. Designed as a drink-young style, it's plummy, berryish, leafy and smooth, with decent depth.

Vintage	03	DRY $15 AV
WR	5	
Drink	04-06	

Torlesse Waipara Merlot   (★★★☆)

One of the best claret-style reds from the region, the 2001 vintage (★★★☆) was grown in two sites at Waipara and French oak-aged for a year. Full but not dark in colour, with a fleshy mid-palate and firm finish, it has plum, spice and slight coffee flavours, seasoned with nutty oak, and very good depth, ripeness and complexity.

Vintage	01	DRY $30 -V
WR	7	
Drink	04-07	

Trinity Hill Gimblett Road Merlot ★★★★☆

The stylish 2002 vintage (★★★★) of this Hawke's Bay red was matured for 18 months in French oak barriques (partly new) and blended with 13 per cent Cabernet Franc 'to add an aromatic lift'. Deep and youthful in colour, it is warm and ripe, with excellent depth of fresh plum and spice flavours, toasty oak adding complexity and a firmly structured finish. A strong candidate for the cellar.

Vintage	03	02	01	00	99	98	97
WR	NM	6	5	5	5	6	5
Drink	NM	04-12	04-08	04-08	04-09	04-07	04-05

DRY $30 AV

Trinity Hill Shepherd's Croft Merlot/Cabernets/Syrah ★★★

The 2002 vintage (★★★) is a Hawke's Bay blend of Merlot, Cabernet Franc, Syrah and Cabernet Sauvignon. Grown in the Ngatarawa and Gimblett Gravels districts, it was matured for 16 months in seasoned oak casks. It's a vibrantly fruity, berryish, gently oaked wine, showing a slight lack of warmth and softness, but very fresh and flavoursome. Attractive drinking through 2004–05.

Vintage	03	02	01	00	99
WR	4	5	5	5	5
Drink	04-08	04-08	04-08	04-05	P

DRY $20 AV

Twin Islands Marlborough Merlot/Cabernet (★★☆)

The full-coloured 2002 vintage (★★☆), a 50/50 blend of Merlot and Cabernet Sauvignon, is a vibrantly fruity wine, plummy, leafy, fresh and crisp.

DRY $17 -V

Vidal Estate Merlot/Cabernet ★★★★

Offering superb value, the 2002 vintage (★★★★) is a dark Hawke's Bay red, blended from 70 per cent Merlot, 21 per cent Cabernet Sauvignon and 9 per cent Malbec, and matured for 16 months in French and American oak barriques. It's a robust, tight-knit wine with spice, coffee and nut flavours showing excellent depth and firm tannins. Tasted prior to bottling (and so not rated), the 2003 was full-coloured and fragrant, with vibrant plum, blackcurrant and spice flavours showing good depth, oak complexity and a firm finish.

Vintage	02	01	00
WR	7	6	NM
Drink	04-07	04-05	NM

DRY $19 V+

Vidal Reserve Merlot/Cabernet Sauvignon (★★★★★)

The serious yet beautiful 2000 vintage (★★★★★) is a single-vineyard red from the Gimblett Gravels district, matured for 20 months in French and American oak casks. A blend of Merlot (54 per cent), Cabernet Sauvignon (37 per cent) and Malbec (9 per cent), it is deeply coloured and fragrant, with firm, ripe tannins and concentrated cassis, plum and spice flavours in a classic claret style with lovely warmth, depth and structure. The 2002 (★★★★★) is a powerful red (14.5 per cent alcohol), densely coloured, with blackcurrant, spice and dark chocolate flavours, very deep, ripe and complex. It's approachable now, but should last a decade.

Vintage	02	01	00	99	98
WR	6	NM	7	7	NM
Drink	05-10	NM	04-08	04-07	NM

DRY $39 V+

Villa Maria Cellar Selection Merlot/Cabernet Sauvignon★★★★★

The 2000 vintage (★★★★★) offered sensational value and so does the 2002 (★★★★★), like its predecessor the Best Buy of the Year. A blend of Merlot (80 per cent), Cabernet Sauvignon (18 per cent) and Malbec (2 per cent), grown in the Gimblett Gravels district of Hawke's Bay, it was matured for 18 months in French and American oak barriques. A rich, concentrated wine with bold, inky colour and a fragrant, opulent bouquet, it shows lovely generosity on the palate, with beautifully ripe, plummy, spicy fruit characters and fine tannins. Buy a case. (For greater detail, see page 16.)

Vintage	02
WR	7
Drink	05-08

DRY $22 V+

Villa Maria Cellar Selection Two Vineyards Merlot   (★★★★)

The 2002 vintage (★★★★) is a densely packed, firmly structured Hawke's Bay red, matured for 18 months in new French oak barriques. It's a boldly coloured wine with an impressive, succulent palate offering rich flavours of spice and plums.

Vintage	02
WR	7
Drink	05-08

DRY $24 V+

Villa Maria Cellar Selection Two Vineyards Merlot/Cabernet Sauvignon   (★★★★)

Released at four years old, the 2000 vintage (★★★★) is a Hawke's Bay blend of Merlot (55 per cent), Cabernet Sauvignon (40 per cent) and Malbec (5 per cent), matured for 18 months in French and American oak casks. Showing only minor development for its age, it's a fragrant, brightly coloured wine with fresh, vibrant blackcurrant, spice and plum flavours showing excellent depth. Lots of life ahead.

DRY $25 AV

Villa Maria Private Bin East Coast Merlot/Cabernet Sauvignon   ★★★☆

The flavourful 2002 vintage (★★★☆) is a full-bodied wine with some complexity and very good depth of plum, blackcurrant and green-leaf flavours, seasoned with sweet, coconutty oak. The 2003 (★★★☆) is a blend of Merlot (85 per cent), Cabernet Sauvignon (10 per cent) and Cabernet Franc (5 per cent). Matured for over a year in French and American oak barriques (40 per cent new), it is full-coloured and firm, with plummy, spicy flavours showing good depth and complexity.

Vintage	03	02
WR	6	7
Drink	05-07	04-06

DRY $17 V+

Villa Maria Reserve Hawke's Bay Merlot   ★★★★★

Grown in three vineyards in the Gimblett Gravels district and matured for 18 months in French oak barriques, the 2002 vintage (★★★★☆) is a blend of Merlot (85 per cent), Malbec (10 per cent) and Cabernet Sauvignon (5 per cent). It's a densely coloured, sweet-fruited red with supple tannins and supercharged blackcurrant, plum, spice, coffee and herb flavours. The assertive, jammy Malbec reduces the wine's Merlot varietal character, explaining the lack of a five-star rating.

Vintage	02	01	00	99	98	97	96	95
WR	7	7	7	7	7	NM	6	7
Drink	05-12	04-12	04-10	04-05	04-06	NM	P	P

DRY $40 AV

Villa Maria Reserve Merlot/Cabernet Sauvignon   ★★★★★

Grown at the stony Ngakirikiri Vineyard, in the Gimblett Gravels district of Hawke's Bay, and matured in French (principally) and American oak casks, the very stylish 2000 vintage (★★★★★) is boldly coloured, warm and rounded, with sweet, concentrated fruit characters of cassis, plums and spice. A blend of Merlot (54 per cent), Cabernet Sauvignon (39 per cent) and Malbec (7 per cent), it is densely packed, fleshy and supple, with power right through the palate.

Vintage	00	99	98	97	96	95
WR	7	7	7	NM	NM	7
Drink	04-10	04-07	04-07	NM	NM	P

DRY $40 AV

West Brook Merlot/Cabernet Franc   (★★☆)

The green-edged 2002 vintage (★★☆) is a blend of Marlborough Merlot (60 per cent) and Auckland Cabernet Franc (40 per cent), oak-aged for 15 months. It's a smooth, plummy, spicy, leafy wine, with solid depth.

DRY $19 -V

Wishart Basket Press Merlot   ★★★★

Grown at Bay View, in Hawke's Bay, picked at over 25 brix and matured for 10 months in French and American oak casks, the rich, complex 2002 vintage (★★★★) is a good buy. Spicy and well-structured, with deep, youthful colour, it is plummy, ripe and muscular (14.5 per cent alcohol), with sweet fruit characters and supple tannins.

DRY $24 V+

Wishart Reserve Hawke's Bay Merlot   (★★★★☆)

The fruit-packed 2001 vintage (★★★★☆) was grown at Bay View and matured in French and American oak casks. Deeply coloured, it is warm and concentrated, with lovely depth of cassis, plum and spice flavours, the earthy richness of Malbec (10 per cent) and well-rounded tannins.

Vintage	01
WR	6
Drink	04-08

DRY $35 AV

Montepulciano

Montepulciano is widely planted across central Italy, yielding deeply coloured, ripe wines with good levels of alcohol, extract and flavour. In the Abruzzi, it is the foundation of the often superb value Montepulciano d'Abruzzo, and in the Marches it is the key ingredient in the noble Rosso Conero.

In New Zealand, Montepulciano is still a rarity and there has been confusion between the Montepulciano and Sangiovese varieties. Some wines may have been incorrectly labelled. According to the latest national vineyard survey, between 2003 and 2006 New Zealand's area of bearing Montepulciano vines will rise from 4 to 6 hectares.

Framingham Marlborough Montepulciano   ★★★☆

The 2002 vintage (★★★☆) was grown 'over the fence' from the estate vineyard at Renwick, and in the company's Kaituna vineyard, on the north side of the Wairau River. Harvested at 23 brix and matured for a year in new (30 per cent) and seasoned French and American oak casks, it is deeply coloured, with spicy oak aromas and strong, fresh, vibrant flavours of plums and berries, although the finish shows a slight lack of warmth and softness. It's drinking well now.

Vintage	02	DRY $24 AV
WR	5	
Drink	04-07	

Herzog Marlborough Montepulciano   ★★★★★

Typically a giant of a red, overflowing with sweet, ripe flavours of plum, liquorice and spice. The 2002 vintage (★★★★★) was harvested at 25 brix, matured for two years in French oak barriques (50 per cent new), and bottled unfined and unfiltered. Promoted as an 'exotic and kinky Marlborough-Italian', it's a dark, densely coloured wine with notable scale (14.4 per cent alcohol) and richness. Highly complex, with powerful blackcurrant, plum, coffee and spice flavours seasoned with quality oak and firm but balanced tannins, it looks set for a very long life.

DRY $59 AV

Trinity Hill Gimblett Road Montepulciano   (★★★★)

The debut 2002 vintage (★★★★) makes a powerful statement. Harvested in Hawke's Bay at 24.5 brix and matured for 16 months in a single American oak cask, it's a powerful, densely coloured red with high alcohol (14 per cent), sweet oak characters and fresh, rich flavours of blackcurrants and plums. Firm and concentrated, with a long finish, it should be at its best during 2005–06.

DRY $30 AV

Pinot Meunier

Pinot Meunier is one of the principal grape varieties of Champagne and was the mainstay of the early New Zealand wine industry, used to make white and red wines. Plantings later nose-dived, due to degenerative virus diseases, but are now gradually expanding, from 18 hectares of bearing vines in 2003 to 21 hectares by 2006.

Murdoch James Pinot Meunier (★★★)

The rare 2002 vintage (★★★) was grown at Martinborough and sold only at the cellar door. Full ruby, it has a spicy, earthy bouquet and slightly high acidity woven through its strong, plummy, earthy flavours.

DRY $45 -V

Pinotage

Pinotage lives in the shadow of more glamorous varieties in New Zealand, yet its plantings are expanding – from 75 hectares of bearing vines in 2000 to 101 hectares by 2006. After being passed during the past decade by Cabernet Franc, Syrah and Malbec, Pinotage currently ranks as the country's seventh most extensively planted red-wine variety.

Pinotage is a cross of the great Burgundian grape, Pinot Noir, and Cinsaut, a heavy-cropping variety popular in the south of France. Cinsaut's typically 'meaty, chunky sort of flavour' (in Jancis Robinson's words) is also characteristic of Pinotage. Valued for its reasonably early-ripening and disease-resistant qualities, and good yields, its plantings are predominantly in the North Island – especially Hawke's Bay, but also Gisborne and Auckland – with another significant pocket in Marlborough.

A well-made Pinotage displays a slightly gamey bouquet and a smooth, berryish, peppery palate that can be reminiscent of a southern Rhône. It matures swiftly and usually peaks within two or three years of the vintage.

Amor-Bendall Pinotage   (★★★★)

The 2002 vintage (★★★★) is a full-coloured, fleshy Gisborne red with rich, ripe plum/spice flavours and oak-derived complexity. It's a generous, full-bodied and rounded wine with slightly earthy, gamey varietal characters adding interest.

DRY $25 AV

Ascension Matakana Pinotage   ★★★

'Line it up against a $20 Pinot Noir and let the customer decide!' says winemaker Darryl Soljan, promoting his 2002 vintage (★★★☆). It's a full-coloured, oak-aged style with a gamey bouquet and strong, berryish, spicy, slightly earthy flavours, showing some complexity.

DRY $20 -V

Babich East Coast Pinotage/Cabernet   ★★★

Over more than three decades, this smooth, moderately priced red has built up a strong following. The 2003 vintage (★★★) is a blend of Pinotage (65 per cent) and Cabernet Franc, with 'a bit' of Cabernet Sauvignon, grown in Gisborne (mostly) and West Auckland. It's a fresh, gently oaked wine with a full, ruby hue and vibrant plum/berry flavours in a charming, supple, drink-young style.

DRY $13 V+

Babich Winemakers Reserve Pinotage   ★★★★☆

This is one of the country's finest Pinotages. Grown in Gimblett Road, Hawke's Bay, harvested at over 25 brix and matured for a year in new and seasoned American and French oak casks, the generous 2002 vintage (★★★★☆) is richly coloured and supple, with sweet fruit delights and strong, plummy, spicy, gamey flavours. It's a delightful red, for drinking now onwards.

Vintage	03	02	01	00	99
WR	6	7	7	6	7
Drink	04-07	04-08	04-07	04-05	P

DRY $25 V+

Kerr Farm Kumeu Pinotage ★★★☆

This is Kerr Farm's most consistently impressive wine. Made from 25-year-old vines in West Auckland and matured in seasoned French and American oak barriques, the 2002 vintage (★★★) is fruity and flavoursome, with full, bright colour, strong plum/spice characters and slightly rustic, earthy, gamey varietal notes. Drink now to 2005.

Vintage	02	01
WR	6	6
Drink	04-06	04-05

DRY $18 V+

Lincoln Heritage Pinotage (★★★)

Grown in Chris Parker's vineyard in Gisborne, the 2003 vintage (★★★) was matured for a year in seasoned French oak casks. It's a firmly structured wine with plum, spice and pepper flavours showing good depth.

Vintage	03
WR	6
Drink	04-08

DRY $16 AV

Muddy Water Waipara Pinotage ★★★★☆

'Not for the faint-hearted' (in the winery's words), the 2002 vintage (★★★★☆) was harvested at 25.5 to 26.5 brix (thus ending up with 14.8 per cent alcohol) and handled like Pinot Noir. Matured for 14 months in oak casks (10 per cent new), it's a muscular wine, generous in colour, body and flavour. It offers smooth, highly concentrated berry and plum flavours, with the gaminess typical of Pinotage, ripe tannins and good complexity.

Vintage	02	01	00
WR	6	NM	7
Drink	04-08	NM	04-06

DRY $28 AV

Pleasant Valley Yelas Auckland Pinotage ★★★☆

Hill-grown in the Henderson Valley of West Auckland, this is a highly characterful, smooth red made for early drinking, but it can also mature well. Matured for a year in new oak casks, the 2002 vintage (★★★☆) is ruby-hued, with perfumed oak aromas. Warm and supple, with good depth of berry and plum flavours seasoned with sweet oak and some savoury complexity, it's an ideal all-purpose red.

DRY $19 AV

Riverside Stirling Reserve Pinotage ★★★☆

Promisingly deep in colour, the 2002 vintage (★★★☆) was grown in the Dartmoor Valley of Hawke's Bay and oak-aged for over a year. Floral, slightly gamey and herbal aromas lead into a generous, concentrated wine, brambly, plummy, slightly leafy and smooth, offering lots of current-drinking pleasure.

Vintage	02	01	00
WR	6	6	5
Drink	04-06	04-05	P

DRY $22 -V

Saints Pinotage ★★★☆

If you haven't discovered the delights of Pinotage, try this sharply priced red. The 2002 vintage (★★★☆) is a Hawke's Bay wine, matured in American (55 per cent) and French oak casks. Grown in Allied Domecq's vineyard at Korokipo, it's full-coloured, with rich, brambly, spicy, slightly herbal flavours seasoned with toasty oak.

Vintage	02	01
WR	6	6
Drink	04-08	04+

DRY $17 V+

Sanctuary Marlborough Pinotage/Pinot Noir   ★★★

Made by Grove Mill, this is an attractive style for early drinking. French and American oak-aged, the ruby-hued 2002 vintage (★★★) has the berryish, gamey and earthy characters of Pinotage in a smooth, fruit-driven style with good depth.

Vintage	02	01	00
WR	7	7	6
Drink	04-05	P	P

DRY $17 AV

Soljans Vineyard Selection Pinotage   ★★★☆

The small West Auckland winery has a long-standing reputation for characterful Pinotages. Grown in Gisborne, the attractive 2003 vintage (★★★) is full-coloured, fresh and vibrantly fruity, although not complex, with good depth of plummy, spicy flavour.

DRY $18 V+

Te Awa Pinotage   (★★★★★)

The memorable 2002 vintage (★★★★) was grown in the Gimblett Gravels district of Hawke's Bay and matured for 15 months in French oak casks (15 per cent new). Handled like Pinot Noir in the winery, with minimal racking, it is mouthfilling, generous and supple, bursting with the delights of sweet, ripe fruit. Plummy and spicy, with the restrained oak influence letting its beautifully rich fruit flavours shine, and hints of liquorice and dark chocolate, it shows excellent concentration and structure and offers delicious drinking from now onwards. A star wine.

Vintage	02
WR	7
Drink	04-10

DRY $30 AV

Yelas Winemaker's Reserve Auckland Pinotage   ★★★★

Estate-grown at Henderson and oak-matured for nine months, the 2002 vintage (★★★☆) is a medium to full-bodied red with gamey, earthy touches, attractive berry and plum flavours and a firm tannin grip. A good food wine with the structure to age, it should be at its best during 2004–05.

Vintage	02
WR	7
Drink	04-06

DRY $22 AV

Pinot Noir

Accolades for New Zealand's rising tide of Pinot Noir continued to flow on the international show circuit during the past year. Amisfield Central Otago Pinot Noir 2002 was voted top Pinot Noir at the 2004 San Francisco International Wine Competition, and Wither Hills Marlborough Pinot Noir 2002 won the trophy for Best New World Red Wine at the 2004 Japan Wine Challenge. And at the 2003 Tri Nations Wine Challenge, a taste-off between Australia, New Zealand and South Africa, staged in Sydney late last year, the champion Pinot Noir was Felton Road Block 3 Pinot Noir 2002, with Villa Maria Reserve Marlborough Pinot Noir 2001 in second place.

The 2004 vintage yielded 20,145 tonnes of Pinot Noir grapes, far ahead of Merlot with 9330 tonnes and Cabernet Sauvignon with 4045 tonnes. The vine is spreading like wildfire. Between 2000 and 2006, New Zealand's area of bearing Pinot Noir vines will more than triple, from 1126 hectares to 3754 hectares.

Pinot Noir is the princely grape variety of red Burgundy. Cheaper wines typically display light, raspberry-evoking flavours that lack the velvety riches of classic Burgundy. Great red Burgundy has substance, suppleness and a gorgeous spread of flavours: cherries, fruit cake, spice and plums.

Pinot Noir over the past decade has become New Zealand's most internationally acclaimed red-wine style. The vine is our third most commonly planted variety overall, trailing only Sauvignon Blanc and Chardonnay. Almost 45 per cent of the country's total Pinot Noir plantings are in Marlborough (where 10 per cent of the vines are grown for bottle-fermented sparkling wine), and the variety is also well established in Central Otago, Canterbury, the Wairarapa, Hawke's Bay, Gisborne and Nelson.

Yet Pinot Noir is a frustrating variety to grow. Because it buds early, it is vulnerable to spring frosts; its compact bunches are also very prone to rot. One crucial advantage is that it ripens early, well ahead of Cabernet Sauvignon. Low cropping and the selection of superior clones are essential aspects of the production of fine wine.

The Wairarapa and Central Otago have been the capitals of New Zealand Pinot Noir during the past decade, but their supply of wine has been small. In the year to June 2004, New Zealand exported 183,545 cases of Pinot Noir (only 5.3 per cent of all wine exports). The Marlborough region's potential for the production of much larger volumes of Pinot Noir is now being tapped.

Akarua Central Otago Pinot Noir ★★★★☆

The 2003 vintage (★★★★), grown at Bannockburn, was matured for 10 months in French oak barriques. It's a graceful, ruby-hued, sweet-fruited wine with fresh plum, cherry, herb and spice flavours showing excellent depth, but less arresting than the robust, densely coloured, deliciously soft and concentrated 2002 (★★★★★). Still youthful, the 2003 is worth cellaring to mid-2005+.

Vintage	03	02	01	00	99
WR	7	7	6	6	5
Drink	04-11	04-10	04-07	04-07	P

DRY $40 AV

Akarua The Gullies Pinot Noir   ★★★☆

Grown at Bannockburn and matured for 10 months in French oak barriques, the charming 2003 vintage (★★★☆) is a youthful Central Otago red with fresh cherry, plum and spice flavours, gently oaked, ripe and lingering. With its silky tannins and very good depth, it's already highly enjoyable.

Vintage	03	02	01	00	DRY $33 -V
WR	7	7	6	5	
Drink	04-11	04-10	04-07	P	

Alana Estate Pinot Noir   ★★★★

This Martinborough red is typically full of charm – fragrant and supple, with strong, sweet cherry/plum flavours, integrated oak and easy tannins. Harvested at 24.5 brix and matured for a year in French oak barriques (25 per cent new), the ruby-hued 2002 vintage (★★★☆) has a fragrant bouquet, good but not great concentration of cherry, spice and nut flavours, considerable complexity and a fairly firm tannin grip. It shows some development; drink during 2005.

Vintage	02	01	00	99	98	DRY $44 -V
WR	6	7	6	7	6	
Drink	04-07	04-07	04-05	04-06	P	

Alana Estate Tuapapa Pinot Noir   (★★☆)

The Tuapapa ('Terraces') label was launched from 2002 (★★☆) as 'a selection of younger vines', conveying 'lightness and innocence'. Harvested at 23.5 brix and matured in French oak barriques (10 per cent new), it is light ruby, with considerable development showing. Green-edged, with nutty, spicy, herbal characters, it shows some complexity, but lacks real ripeness and richness.

DRY $25 -V

Alexander Dusty Road Pinot Noir   ★★★

The 2003 vintage (★★★☆) is superior to the 2002 (★★☆). Grown on the Te Muna Terraces, 4 kilometres from Martinborough, and matured for a year in French oak barriques (25 per cent new), the 2002 is light in colour, slightly under-ripe and herbal, lacking warmth and softness. The 2003 is fuller and brighter in colour, with very good depth of ripe, plummy, cherryish, spicy flavour and some nutty, savoury complexity.

DRY $29 -V

Alexander Martinborough Pinot Noir   ★★★☆

The 2002 (★★★), matured for a year in French oak barriques (25 per cent new), is not a top vintage, with plum, cherry and herb flavours showing moderate ripeness and depth. Much more powerful and meaty, the 2003 (★★★★) is deep ruby, with an earthy, spicy bouquet and substantial body. Firmly structured and ripe, with strong, plummy, spicy flavours and complex, savoury characters, it's worth cellaring to 2006+.

DRY $33 -V

Alexandra Wine Company Crag an Oir Pinot Noir   (★★★★)

The youthful, warm 2002 vintage (★★★★) is a single-vineyard Central Otago red, matured for 11 months in French oak casks (35 per cent new). It's a generous and fragrant wine with sweet, ripe-fruit flavours of plums, cherries and spice, good oak handling, gentle tannins and excellent depth and drinkability. Instantly likeable, with great texture, it's a drink-now or cellaring proposition.

Vintage	02	DRY $32 AV
WR	6	
Drink	04-06	

Alexandra Wine Company Davishon Pinot Noir ★★★★

Grown in the Davishon vineyard at Alexandra in Central Otago, the 2002 vintage (★★★★☆) is weighty and rich, with good complexity. Matured for 11 months in French oak barriques (35 per cent new), it is ruby-hued, warm, savoury and supple, with strong cherry, raspberry and spice flavours and good power through the palate. Slightly bolder than its Crag an Oir stablemate (above), it's maturing very gracefully.

Vintage	02	01	00	99	DRY $32 AV
WR	6	6	7	7	
Drink	04-06	04-05	P	P	

Allan Scott Marlborough Pinot Noir ★★★

The 2003 vintage (★★★☆) is richer than the middleweight, moderately complex 2002 (★★★). Grown in a single, company-owned vineyard (unlike its predecessor), the 2003 is a full-coloured, sweet-fruited and supple wine with fresh, ripe plum and raspberry flavours seasoned with toasty oak and good harmony.

DRY $25 -V

Alpha Domus Pinot Noir ★★★☆

The 2002 vintage (★★★) is a full-coloured Hawke's Bay red, oak-aged for a year. Youthful, it has strong cherry and plum flavours, showing some fruit sweetness, and a firm finish. Open mid-2004+.

Vintage	02	DRY $30 AV
WR	7	
Drink	04-08	

Amisfield Central Otago Pinot Noir ★★★★

Estate-grown at the foot of the Pisa Range, in the Cromwell Basin, and matured in French oak barriques (20 per cent new), the 2003 vintage (★★★☆) is less powerful and intense than the 2002 (★★★★☆), but still highly attractive. It's a mouthfilling wine (13.9 per cent alcohol), supple and sweet-fruited, with strong cherry and spice flavours and a floral bouquet. It's a softly textured, forward vintage, for drinking now onwards.

Vintage	03	DRY $40 AV
WR	5	
Drink	06-07	

Aravin Estate Pinot Noir (★★)

Harvested at 23.5 brix from second-crop vines in Central Otago, the 2003 vintage (★★) is light ruby in hue, with medium-full body, earthy flavours and a rustic bouquet.

DRY $25 -V

Ashwell Pinot Noir ★★★

The quality of this Martinborough red has been inconsistent. Retasted in mid-2004, the 2000 vintage (★★★) is slightly rustic, earthy and stalky, with some coffee and spice complexity and firm tannins. The 2002 (★★☆), French oak-aged for 18 months, shows light, slightly developed colour and raspberry, plum and herb flavours that lack real richness and roundness.

Vintage	02	01	00	DRY $39 -V
WR	5	5	7	
Drink	07-08	06-07	05-06	

Ata Rangi Pinot Noir ★★★★★

One of the greatest of all New Zealand wines, this stunning Martinborough red is powerfully built and concentrated, yet seductively fragrant and supple. 'Intense, opulent fruit with power beneath' is winemaker Clive Paton's goal. 'Complexity comes with time.' The grapes are drawn from numerous sites, including the estate vineyard, planted in 1980. The wine is fermented in small batches, with up to 15 per cent whole-bunch fermentation giving 'stalk-derived spiciness and tautness', and maturation is for a year in French oak barriques, typically 25 per cent new. At a vertical tasting held in mid-2003, the 1994 to 1996 vintages were mature, but the younger wines were still developing, demonstrating that Ata Rangi responds well to at least five years' cellaring; even more for the best vintages. The 2003 (★★★★★) is from an exceptionally low-yielding season (2.4 tonnes/hectare). Boldly coloured, it is very refined, warm and concentrated, with fresh, intense cherry, plum and spice flavours, savoury and complex, but needs another two years to fully unfold.

Vintage	03	02	01	00	99	98	97	96	95	94	DRY $60 AV
WR	7	6	7	7	7	6	7	7	6	7	
Drink	04-08	04-07	04-06	04-05	P	04-05	P	P	P	P	🍇🍇🍇

Auntsfield Hawk Hill Marlborough Pinot Noir   (★★★☆)

Built to last, the 2003 vintage (★★★★) is a youthful, spicy, tightly structured wine. Deep ruby, with very good depth of plum, cherry and spice flavours, seasoned with toasty oak, it is savoury, firm, and worth cellaring to 2006+.

DRY $40 -V

Aurum Central Otago Pinot Noir   (★★★☆)

A good debut, the 2003 vintage (★★★☆) was grown at Bannockburn and French oak-aged. It's an elegant, scented and supple wine, ruby-hued, with a silky elegance and lots of drink-young charm. Sweet-fruited, with plum, cherry and spicy oak flavours, it's a very harmonious, although not intense, wine, verging on four-star quality.

DRY $36 -V

Babich East Coast Pinot Noir   ★★☆

The 2002 vintage (★★) is a blend of Hawke's Bay and Henderson, West Auckland grapes, matured for six months in old French oak casks. It's a light wine with moderate depth of strawberryish, spicy flavours, crisp and leafy. (The 2003 is a blend of 60 per cent Marlborough and 40 per cent Henderson fruit.)

DRY $20 -V

Babich Winemakers Reserve Pinot Noir   ★★★☆

The 2002 vintage (★★★) was grown in the Wairau Valley and matured for nine months in French oak casks (new and seasoned). Ruby-hued, with a fragrant, cherryish, toasty bouquet, it is harmonious and supple, although not intense, with good balance and complexity. The 2003 (★★★☆), 45 per cent fermented with indigenous yeasts, has a gamey, spicy, complex bouquet. A ripe, sweet-fruited wine with good weight and depth of plummy, cherryish flavours and fairly firm tannins, it should mature well.

Vintage	03	02	01	00	DRY $30 AV
WR	7	7	7	6	
Drink	04-08	04-07	04-05	P	

Bald Hills Central Otago Pinot Noir ★★★☆

The 2003 vintage (★★★★) was grown in the Hunt family's vineyard at Bannockburn and matured for 11 months in French oak barriques (50 per cent new). Deep and youthful in colour, it is finely scented and elegant, with youthful cherry, plum and spice flavours showing excellent depth. A generous, tightly structured wine, it needs time; open mid-2005 onwards.

Vintage	03	02
WR	7	6
Drink	05-11	04-10

DRY $42 -V

Bannock Brae Barrel Selection Pinot Noir ★★★★☆

The notably lush and sensuous 2002 (★★★★★) was grown at Bannockburn, in Central Otago, picked at 24.5 brix and matured in French oak barriques (half new). Warm and generous, with beautifully ripe and intense aromas of cherries and spice, it has concentrated, very fresh and vibrant fruit characters showing great charm and ripeness, with savoury, mushroomy complexities emerging. The 2003 vintage (★★★★) is a mouthfilling, firm wine with deep ruby colour and strong cherry, plum and spice flavours. The 2002 is blossoming with cellaring, suggesting the 2003 should also be cellared.

Vintage	03	02	01
WR	6	6	5
Drink	05-08	04-08	04-06

DRY $44 AV

Bannock Brae Goldfields Pinot Noir ★★★★

The graceful, concentrated 2002 vintage (★★★★★) was grown at Bannockburn, in Central Otago, picked at 23.9 to 24.7 brix, and matured for a year in French oak barriques (one-third new). Maturing well, with full, youthful colour and a complex, highly attractive bouquet, it has rich, sweet fruit flavours of plums and spice, a lovely soft texture and long finish. Less striking in its youth, the 2003 (★★★☆) is a supple, raspberry, plum and herb-flavoured wine with some savoury, spicy complexity. Give it time; open mid-2005+.

Vintage	03	02	01
WR	6	6	5
Drink	05-08	04-08	04-06

DRY $29 V+

Bilancia Hawke's Bay Pinot Noir ★★★☆

The fresh, supple 2003 vintage (★★★☆) was grown at Glencoe Station, in the slightly cooler hill country south of the Heretaunga Plains, and matured for 11 months in French oak barriques (30 per cent new). Bright, medium ruby, it's a skilfully crafted wine with cherry, raspberry and plum flavours showing good depth, some spicy complexity and plenty of drink-young charm.

Vintage	03	02
WR	6	6
Drink	04-06	04-06

DRY $25 AV

Black Estate Waipara Pinot Noir ★★★★

This single-vineyard, North Canterbury label is consistently satisfying. The 2003 vintage (★★★★), matured for a year in French oak barriques (one-third new), has a distinctly spicy (almost Syrah-like) bouquet leading into a generous, warm palate with plummy, peppery, slightly earthy flavours, showing good concentration, and moderately firm tannins.

Vintage	03	02	01
WR	6	6	6
Drink	06+	05+	04-08

DRY $39 AV

Blackenbrook Nelson Pinot Noir   (★★★★)

The debut 2003 vintage (★★★★) is a single-vineyard wine, made from first-crop vines picked at 23.7 brix and matured in two-year-old French oak casks. Full-coloured, it's a generous, fleshy, sweet-fruited wine with good concentration of cherry, plum and spice flavours. Well worth cellaring.

Vintage 03	DRY $29 V+
WR 6	
Drink 04-06	

Black Ridge Pinot Noir   ★★★☆

This Alexandra, Central Otago red is typically sturdy, vibrantly fruity and supple. The 2003 vintage (★★★☆) is moderately complex and well-rounded, with floral and slightly earthy characters on the nose and strong, ripe, sweet fruit flavours of cherries, spice and plums.

DRY $38 -V

Burnt Spur Martinborough Pinot Noir   ★★★

The 2002 vintage (★★★) is ruby-hued, with cherryish, spicy, green-edged flavours and firm tannins. It's a middleweight style showing a slight lack of fruit sweetness, but also some savoury, earthy complexity.

Vintage 01	DRY $39 -V
WR 7	
Drink 04-06	

Cable Bay Marlborough Pinot Noir   (★★★☆)

Grown in the Brancott Valley and French oak-matured, the debut 2003 vintage (★★★☆) is vibrantly fruity and smooth. It's an easy-drinking style with full, ruby colour, good depth of cherry, herb and plum flavours, some toasty, savoury complexity and gentle, well-rounded tannins.

Vintage 03	DRY $33 -V
WR 6	
Drink 04-08	

Cairnbrae Marlborough Pinot Noir   ★★★

The 2003 vintage (★★★), grown in the Wairau Valley and American oak-aged for six months, has raspberryish aromas leading into a youthful, clearly varietal, plum and spice-flavoured wine, not highly complex but enjoyable. The 2002 (★★★) is also a middleweight, with moderate complexity in a forward, smooth, easy-drinking style.

Vintage 03	DRY $23 AV
WR 6	
Drink 04-06	

Canterbury House Pinot Noir   ★★☆

The Pinot Noirs from this Waipara producer have typically been solid but plain, with crisp, strawberryish, green-edged flavours, lacking real weight, ripeness and depth.

DRY $20 -V

Carrick Central Otago Pinot Noir ★★★★★

The densely flavoured 2003 vintage (★★★★★) was grown at Bannockburn, low-cropped (5.5 tonnes per hectare) and matured in French oak barriques (30 per cent new). Dark and richly scented, it has deep, ripe, spicy flavours and savoury characters adding complexity. Fleshy and still very youthful, it shows excellent potential.

Vintage	03	02	01
WR	6	7	7
Drink	04-10+	05+	04+

DRY $38 V+

Chard Farm Finla Mor Pinot Noir ★★★☆

Rob Hay's second-tier Central Otago red typically has strong raspberry and cherry flavours, with finely integrated wood. The 2002 vintage (★★★☆) was grown in three districts in the Cromwell Basin – Cairnmuir, Bannockburn and Parkburn – and matured for 11 months in French oak barriques. A sweetly fruited, richly coloured and fragrant wine, it offers good depth of ripe cherry, raspberry and spice flavours, seasoned with toasty oak. The 2003 (tasted as a barrel sample, and so not rated), was ruby-hued, fresh and crisp, but slightly lighter than the 2002.

Vintage	02	01	00	99
WR	7	6	5	6
Drink	04-08	04-05	P	P

DRY $38 -V

Chard Farm Red Gate Vineyard Pinot Noir ★★★★

This single-vineyard Central Otago red is grown at Parkburn, in the Cromwell Basin. Bottled unfined and unfiltered, the 2002 vintage (★★★★) is dark and exuberantly fruity. Crammed with sweet, ripe-fruit flavours of plums and cherries, it's a supple, deliciously well-rounded, slightly savoury wine, moderately complex at this stage but still fresh and youthful. Open 2005 onwards.

DRY $57 -V

Chard Farm River Run Pinot Noir ★★★☆

This is a floral, fruit-driven style with great drink-young charm. The 2003 vintage (★★★☆) was grown at Gibbston and in the Cromwell Basin, and matured for 10 months in French oak casks (20 per cent new). An elegant, medium-bodied Central Otago wine, it is soft and fruity, with sweet fruit characters, an attractively smooth texture and good depth of plum, cherry and spice flavours.

Vintage	03	02	01	00
WR	6	7	6	5
Drink	04-07	04-05	P	P

DRY $28 AV

Churton Marlborough Pinot Noir (★★★★)

The spicy, warm and generous 2002 vintage (★★★★) was low-cropped (5 tonnes/hectare) and matured for a year in French oak barriques (25 per cent new). The palate is lush, with considerable complexity, a firm foundation of tannin and a long finish.

DRY $25 V+

Cirrus Martinborough Pinot Noir (★★☆)

The light, pleasant 2003 vintage (★★☆), based on young (three-year-old) vines, was matured for nine months in French oak casks (30 per cent new). Raspberryish aromas lead into an uncomplicated, berry and plum-flavoured wine with gentle tannins.

DRY $30 -V

Clifford Bay Marlborough Pinot Noir   (★★★)

The ruby-hued 2003 vintage (★★★) is a charming, fruit-driven style with strong plum and cherry flavours, fresh and vibrant, but no real complexity, at least in its youth.

DRY $30 ·V

Clos Henri Marlborough Pinot Noir   (★★★★)

From Henri Bourgeois, a leading Loire Valley producer with a site near Renwick, the debut 2003 vintage (★★★★) was made from the first crop off young vines and matured in French oak barriques (30 per cent new). Deep and youthful in colour, it is supple and vibrantly fruity, with raspberry, spicy oak and plum flavours. Delicious in its youth, with warmth, structure and a persistent finish, it should unfold well during 2005–06.

DRY $38 AV

Cloudy Bay Pinot Noir   ★★★★☆

Cloudy Bay a few years ago successfully switched its red-wine focus from Cabernet/Merlot blends to Pinot Noir. The 2002 vintage (★★★★★), grown in the lower Brancott and Fairhall districts of the Wairau Valley, is a blend of seven Pinot Noir clones, harvested at 24.1 brix (average) and matured for 10 months in French oak barriques (45 per cent new). Full ruby, with a warm, smoky fragrance, it's a finely textured wine, mouthfilling (14 per cent alcohol) and complex, with sweet fruit delights, rich cherry, plum, herb, spice and nut flavours and a lasting finish. Immensely pleasurable already, it's a finely scented, very graceful and supple wine; arguably the best since 1999.

Vintage	02	01	00	99	98	97	96	95	94
WR	6	6	6	6	5	6	5	NM	4
Drink	04-06	04-05	P	P	P	P	P	NM	P

DRY $40 AV

Collards Queen Charlotte Marlborough Pinot Noir   ★★★

The 2000 vintage (★★★☆) is an elegant, supple wine with fragrant, strawberry/spice aromas leading into a full-bodied, lightly wooded wine with gentle tannins. It's now savoury and mellow. (There are no subsequent vintages.)

Vintage	03	02	01	00	99
WR	NM	NM	NM	7	6
Drink	NM	NM	NM	P	P

DRY $19 AV

Coney Pizzicato Pinot Noir   ★★★★

The 2002 vintage (★★★) of this Martinborough red is a silky middleweight with good depth of cherryish, plummy, green-edged flavours, spicy oak and a rounded finish. Not released until early 2005, the bolder 2003 (★★★★) was matured in French oak casks (30 per cent new). More concentrated than past vintages, it is deep ruby, weighty and generous, with sweet fruit characters and firm cherry, plum and spice flavours, seasoned with toasty oak. Open mid-2005+.

Vintage	03	02	01
WR	5	5	6
Drink	05-09	04-06	04-06

DRY $34 AV

Coopers Creek Marlborough Pinot Noir   ★★★☆

The 2003 vintage (★★★☆) was matured in French oak casks (one-third new). Delicious in its youth, it has floral, berryish aromas leading into a supple, charming wine with plum, cherry and spice flavours showing some gamey, savoury complexity. It's a drink-young style, offering good value.

Vintage	03	02	01
WR	5	6	6
Drink	04-06	04-05	P

DRY $20 V+

Coopers Creek Reserve Marlborough Pinot Noir (★★★★☆)

The lovely 2002 vintage (★★★★☆) is a single-vineyard wine, grown near Blenheim and matured for 10 months in new and one-year-old French oak barriques. Ruby-hued, with a delicious spread of raspberry, cherry and plum flavours, it's a ripe and supple, notably harmonious wine, with smoky oak adding complexity. Winemaker Simon Nunns likens it to a premier cru of Burgundy – and fair enough.

Vintage	03	02
WR	NM	6
Drink	NM	04-07

DRY $27 V+

Corbans Cottage Block Marlborough Pinot Noir (★★★★☆)

The deep ruby 2002 vintage (★★★★☆) is one of Allied Domecq's finest Pinot Noirs to date. Hand-picked at 24 brix from 'very low-yielding' vines in the Rapaura and Renwick districts, it was matured for a year in French oak barriques (40 per cent new). The richly fragrant bouquet of cherries and spice leads into a serious, concentrated yet supple wine with lovely fruit sweetness and notable complexity. Very savoury, spicy and nutty, it's already delicious, yet also has good cellaring potential.

Vintage	02
WR	6
Drink	04-06

DRY $35 V+

Corbans Private Bin Marlborough Pinot Noir ★★★☆

Showing good complexity, the 2002 vintage (★★★☆) was matured in French oak barriques (40 per cent new). Full-coloured, it's a firm, flavoursome wine, savoury and spicy, with a lingering finish.

Vintage	02	01
WR	6	5
Drink	04-07	04-06

DRY $25 V+

Cornish Point Central Otago Pinot Noir (★★★☆)

From a Cromwell Basin site owned by Nigel Greening, who also controls Felton Road, the 2003 vintage (★★★☆) is a full-bodied, moderately complex wine offering strong cherry, plum and herb flavours.

DRY $40 -V

Cottle Hill Pinot Noir ★★

The light, green-edged 2002 vintage (★★) was grown at Kerikeri, in Northland, and French oak-aged for 18 months. Lacking real fragrance, freshness, ripeness and depth, it doesn't make a convincing case for growing Pinot Noir in the north.

Vintage	02
WR	7
Drink	04-08

DRY $26 -V

Covell Estate Pinot Noir ★☆

Grown organically against the flanks of the Ureweras at Galatea, near Murupara, in the inland Bay of Plenty, this has typically been a light, mellow wine, lacking real richness and stuffing. Some vintages on sale have been well past their best, but Bob and Des Covell deserve respect for their pioneering spirit.

DRY $20 -V

Crab Farm Pinot Noir   ★★★

The characterful, slightly rustic 2002 vintage (★★★) was grown in Hawke's Bay and matured for 18 months in French oak casks (30 per cent new). It's a distinctive expression of Pinot Noir – firm and flavoursome, earthy, plummy, spicy and peppery, with overtones of Syrah and slightly chewy tannins.

DRY $25 -V

Craggy Range Te Muna Road Vineyard Pinot Noir   ★★★★

The 2002 vintage (★★★★) is an elegant, sweet-fruited Martinborough wine with ripe plum and spice flavours, savoury and complex, and a firm foundation of tannin. The 2003 (★★★★) was fermented with indigenous yeasts and matured for over a year in French oak barriques. Deep and youthful in colour, with a floral bouquet, it's an elegant, savoury and supple wine with good richness, complexity and structure.

DRY $40 AV

Crossings, The, Marlborough Pinot Noir   ★★★☆

Grown in the Medway River vineyard, at elevation in the Awatere Valley, the 2003 vintage (★★★☆) was low-cropped (5 tonnes/hectare) and matured for 10 months in French oak barriques (one-third new). Deep and youthful in colour, with a spicy, toasty bouquet, it offers strong plum and spice flavours, warm and supple. It's not a highly complex style, but very enjoyable in its youth.

Vintage	03
WR	6
Drink	04-08

DRY $24 V+

Crossroads Collectors Edition Pinot Noir   (★★☆)

Grown in Hawke's Bay and French oak-aged for seven months, the 2002 vintage (★★☆) is mature and soft, gamey, savoury and mellow. It tastes fully developed; drink now.

DRY $29 -V

Crossroads Destination Series Pinot Noir   (★★☆)

The debut 2002 vintage (★★☆) of this Hawke's Bay red was oak-matured for seven months. It's a lightish wine with raspberry, cherry and herb flavours, some savoury, spicy notes and gentle tannins. Ready.

Vintage	02
WR	6
Drink	P

DRY $25 -V

Crossroads Reserve Pinot Noir   (★★★★)

The 2000 vintage (★★★★) is a bold, mouthfilling Hawke's Bay red with good colour and well-defined varietal character. Based on young vines and matured in French oak casks (25 per cent new), it has warm, sweet fruit flavours of cherry and spice and a lasting, rounded finish. Has to be one of the best Hawke's Bay Pinots yet.

Vintage	00
WR	6
Drink	04

DRY $32 AV

Daniel Schuster
Omihi Hills Vineyard Selection Pinot Noir   ★★★★

Canterbury winemaker Danny Schuster's pride and joy is made from a 'selection of the best fruit from the Omihi Vineyard at Waipara, aged in a mixture of new and older Tronçais oak'. The powerful 2001 vintage (★★★★★) is the star wine to date. Based on 16-year-old, unirrigated, very low-yielding vines (2.5 to 3.5

tonnes/hectare), it was matured for 15 months in French oak barriques (30 per cent new) and bottled without fining or filtration. Deeply coloured, it is very generous, sweet-fruited and savoury, with deep plum, berry and spice flavours and impressive complexity. A substantial (14 per cent alcohol) wine with a winning richness and softness, it is probably now at its peak. The 2002 (★★★☆) is a forward, moderately complex and savoury wine with lightish colour, a smooth entry and attractive cherry, bacon and spice flavours, let down on the back palate by slightly green, tough tannins. There is no 2003.

Vintage	04	03	02	01	00	99	98	DRY $60 -V
WR	7	NM	6	7	6	NM	7	
Drink	09-11	NM	05-08	06-09	04-06	NM	04-06	

Daniel Schuster Twin Vineyards Pinot Noir   ★★★☆

Danny Schuster's regional blend is designed for earlier drinking than the top label (above). The 2002 vintage (★★★☆) is a blend of grapes from the Petrie vineyard near Rakaia, south of Christchurch, and the Omihi Hills vineyard at Waipara. Matured for a year in seasoned French oak casks, it's a ruby-hued wine with fresh raspberry, cherry and spice aromas leading into a middleweight palate, sweet-fruited, ripe and supple, with some savoury complexity. Drink now on.

Vintage	04	03	02	01	00	DRY $27 AV
WR	6	6	6	6	6	
Drink	05-06	04-06	04-06	04-05	P	

Dashwood Marlborough Pinot Noir   ★★★

Designed for early drinking, the 2003 vintage (★★★☆) from Vavasour was hand-picked, 60 per cent in the Wairau Valley and 40 per cent in the Awatere Valley. Matured in small and large French oak barrels, it is full-coloured, buoyantly fruity and supple, with very good depth of ripe, plummy, spicy flavour, subtle oak and gentle tannins. In its youth, it's a real charmer.

DRY $20 AV

Delta Marlborough Pinot Noir   (★★★★)

Sold by mail-order wine clubs, the 2002 vintage (★★★★) is a richly coloured wine with fresh, deep cherry and raspberry flavours, a strong but not excessive oak influence and good mouthfeel and length.

DRY $29 V+

Dog Point Vineyard Marlborough Pinot Noir   (★★★★☆)

The seductive 2002 vintage (★★★★☆) is a blend of six Pinot Noir clones, matured for 18 months in French oak casks (60 per cent new). Ruby-hued, it is full-bodied, warm and generous, with strawberry, plum and cherry flavours that caress the mouth in a very harmonious, ripe and supple style. Best drinking 2005+.

Vintage	02	DRY $40 AV
WR	5	
Drink	04-07	

Domaine Georges Michel Golden Mile Pinot Noir   ★★

The 2002 vintage (★★) was grown in the Rapaura district of Marlborough and French oak-aged for eight months. It's a lean wine with raspberry and cherry flavours and a green, stalky finish.

Vintage	02	01	DRY $25 -V
WR	5	5	
Drink	04-07	04-06	

Domaine Georges Michel La Reserve Pinot Noir   (★★)

Why the 2002 vintage (★☆) deserves to be designated 'La Reserve', I'm not sure. Matured for 13 months in French oak, it's a thin, green Marlborough red, developed in colour and going nowhere.

Vintage	02		DRY $34 -V
WR	5		
Drink	04-08		

Domaine Georges Michel Petit Pinot   ★★

Designed as a Beaujolais-style red for easy, luncheon drinking, the 2003 vintage (★★) of this Marlborough red was French oak-matured for four months. Light and developed in colour, it lacks ripeness and richness, offering shallow plum and berry flavours.

DRY $19 -V

Dry Gully Pinot Noir   ★★★☆

From Alexandra, in Central Otago, the 2003 vintage (★★★) was fermented with indigenous yeasts and matured for 10 months in French oak barriques (30 per cent new). Light ruby, it's a charming, medium-bodied wine with cherry, herb and plum aromas and flavours and gentle tannins, but lacks the richness and stuffing of the excellent 2002 (★★★★☆).

DRY $34 -V

Drylands Marlborough Pinot Noir   ★★☆

The 2003 vintage (★★★) from Nobilo is a drink-young style. Matured in new and seasoned French and 'European' oak casks for nine months, it's a ruby-hued, smooth wine with gentle tannins and vibrantly fruity, plum and spice flavours. It lacks a bit of stuffing, but offers enough flavour to be interesting.

Vintage	03	02	01	DRY $20 -V
WR	7	7	7	
Drink	04-06	04-06	P	

Dry River Pinot Noir   ★★★★★

Dark, robust and densely flavoured, this Martinborough red ranks among New Zealand's greatest Pinot Noirs. Its striking depth, says winemaker Neil McCallum, comes from 'getting the grapes really ripe' and 'keeping the vines' crops below 2.5 tonnes per acre'. Matured for a year in French oak barriques (25 to 30 per cent new), it is a slower developing wine than other New Zealand Pinot Noirs, but matures superbly. The 1996 vintage is lovely now – beautifully fragrant and rich, with highly concentrated plum, cherry and spice flavours – and should drink memorably for several more years. The 2003 vintage (★★★★★) is a wine of great power from an ultra low-cropping (below 3 tonnes/hectare) vintage. Dense purple/black, it is crammed with plum, spice and blackberry flavours, with its ample tannins and quality oak buried in lush, opulent fruit. Exuberantly fruity in its youth, but needing at least five years to break into full stride, it's still a baby.

Vintage	03	02	01	00	99	98	97	96	DRY $65 AV
WR	7	7	7	7	7	6	7	7	
Drink	05-12	04-10	04-09	04-08	04-07	04-08	P	P	🍇🍇🍇

Drystone Pinot Noir   ★★★★

From Berridge Vineyard Estates, at Gibbston in Central Otago, the 2003 vintage (★★★★) is an elegant, supple wine, French oak-aged for nine months. Worth cellaring, it is full-bodied (14 per cent alcohol) and harmonious, with ripe, sweet fruit characters, very good depth of youthful cherry and plum flavours and finely balanced tannins.

Vintage	03	02	DRY $40 AV
WR	6	5	
Drink	05-10	04-08	

Escarpment Vineyard Martinborough Pinot Noir ★★★★☆

Still in its infancy, the 2003 vintage (★★★★☆) was grown in the Te Muna Road district and matured in French oak casks (30 per cent new). Deeply coloured, it is muscular and dense, with sweet fruit characters and firmly structured flavours of cherry, plum, spice and toasty oak. It's a serious wine for cellaring; open 2006+. (I have also tasted an even bolder, vineyard-designated Pinot Noir from 2003, showing exceptional concentration.)

Vintage	03	02	01
WR	7	6	5
Drink	07-09	06-07	05-06

DRY $45 AV

Fairhall Downs Marlborough Pinot Noir ★★★☆

Grown in the Brancott Valley, the 2002 vintage (★★★☆) is a powerful, generous red with rich plum/spice flavours seasoned with toasty oak. It's a full-bodied wine with sweet fruit characters, some earthy, truffley complexities and a strong, charred oak influence. The 2003 (★★★) was less impressive in its youth. Matured for a year in French oak casks (new and seasoned), it has mouthfilling body and smooth raspberry/plum flavours showing some complexity, but lacks the richness of the 2002.

Vintage	03	02
WR	7	7
Drink	05-08	04-09

DRY $29 AV

Fairmont Estate Block One Pinot Noir ★★★★

The 2003 vintage (★★★★), like the 2001 (★★★★☆), is one of the finest wines I've tasted from this small producer at Gladstone, in the Wairarapa. Matured in French oak barriques (50 per cent new), it's a youthful wine showing good varietal character and complexity. Full-bodied and supple, it has excellent density of cherry, spice and nutty oak flavours.

DRY $40 AV

Felton Road Block 3 Pinot Noir ★★★★★

Grown at Bannockburn, this is a majestic Central Otago wine, among the finest Pinot Noirs in the country. Cultivated in a section of the vineyard where the clay content is relatively high, giving 'dried herbs and ripe fruit' characters, in barrel tastings the wine from Block 3 'always shows greater concentration and complexity', says winemaker Blair Walter. French oak-aged for a year (in 45 per cent new barriques), the powerful, tightly built 2003 vintage (★★★★★) is deep in colour, with lovely concentration and poise. Offering an abundance of ripe, sweet cherry and spice flavours, it is savoury and complex, with a firm backbone of tannin. It should unfold superbly over the next few years.

Vintage	03	02	01	00	99	98	97
WR	6	7	7	7	7	7	7
Drink	04-11	04-10	04-07	04-06	P	P	P

DRY $60 AV

🍇🍇

Felton Road Block 5 Pinot Noir ★★★★★

The 2002 vintage (★★★★★) was grown in a single block of the vineyard at Bannockburn, in Central Otago, and matured in French oak barriques (30 per cent new). Bold and savoury, it is deeply coloured, with a complex, spicy bouquet showing the lifted aromatics so typical of the region. Mouthfilling (14 per cent alcohol), rich and ripe, with cherry, plum and spice flavours showing great concentration, harmony and complexity, it's a supple, layered wine, coupling power and beauty.

Vintage	02	01	00	99
WR	7	7	7	7
Drink	04-10	04-09	04-08	04-05

DRY $60 AV

Felton Road Pinot Noir   ★★★★☆

The Bannockburn, Central Otago winery's 'standard' Pinot Noir is made with 'restrained' use of oak, but the 2003 vintage (★★★★☆) is impressive. Matured in French oak casks (30 per cent new), it is generous and supple, with deep colour and fragrant raspberry and spice aromas. Bursting with ripe, sweet fruit characters, it's a mouthfilling wine (14 per cent alcohol), still youthful, with good concentration and a tight structure, suggesting plenty of cellaring potential.

Vintage	03	02	01	00	99	98	97
WR	6	7	6	7	6	6	6
Drink	04-10	04-09	04-06	04-06	04	P	P

DRY $45 AV

Fiddler's Green Waipara Pinot Noir   ★★★★

The 2003 vintage (★★★★) is one of the best. Matured for nine months in French oak barriques (30 per cent new), it is deep and youthful in colour, with fresh, rich flavours of plums, cherries and spice. Fruit-packed, it's a powerful, supple wine, very promising in its youth and worth cellaring to mid-2005+.

Vintage	03	02	01	00
WR	6	6	6	6
Drink	05-07	04-07	04-06	P

DRY $35 AV

Floating Mountain Nelson/Waipara Pinot Noir   (★★★)

Grown in Nelson and North Canterbury and matured for 10 months in French oak casks (25 per cent new), the 2003 vintage (★★★) is a middleweight style, ruby-hued, with slightly herbal aromas and a supple palate with good but not great depth of cherry, raspberry and spice flavours.

Vintage	03
WR	5
Drink	05-07

DRY $25 -V

Forrest Estate Vineyard Selection Pinot Noir   (★★★★)

Showing good richness, the 2002 vintage (★★★★) is warm and graceful, with smooth, strong cherry and plum flavours and savoury, spicy, nutty complexities. It's a deliciously supple Marlborough red, for drinking now onwards.

Vintage	02
WR	5
Drink	04-08

DRY $35 AV

Forrest Marlborough Pinot Noir   ★★★☆

The 2002 vintage (★★★☆), grown at several sites in the Wairau Valley, is a harmonious wine with fresh, raspberry, strawberry and spice flavours and subtle oak. Ruby-hued, with gentle tannins, it's a moderately complex but highly attractive wine, for drinking now onwards.

Vintage	03	02	01	00
WR	6	5	4	4
Drink	04-08	04-05	P	P

DRY $24 V+

Foxes Island Pinot Noir ★★★★☆

Showing significant quality advances in recent vintages, John Belsham's Marlborough red is grown in the 'Home Block' at Rapaura and matured in French oak barriques (60 per cent new). The elegant, full-coloured 2002 vintage (★★★★) has a fragrant, gently oaked bouquet. It's a mouthfilling (14 per cent alcohol), graceful wine with smooth, ripe cherry, plum, raspberry and spice flavours, finely balanced and supple. An elegant wine with good complexity, it offers excellent drinking now to 2006.

Vintage	02	01	00	99	DRY $40 AV
WR	7	6	6	5	
Drink	04-06	04-06	04-05	P	

Framingham Marlborough Pinot Noir ★★★☆

The youthful 2003 vintage (★★★☆) has strong drink-young appeal. Matured in French oak casks (25 per cent new), it is scented and supple, with ripe cherry, plum and spice flavours, showing good complexity. It should open out well during 2005–06.

Vintage	03	02	01	00	99	DRY $29 AV
WR	6	6	5	4	6	
Drink	04-08	04-06	P	P	P	

Fromm La Strada Clayvin Vineyard Pinot Noir ★★★★★

This powerful, muscular but not tough Marlborough red is grown at the hillside Clayvin site in the Brancott Valley. Matured for 14 months in French oak barriques (20 per cent new), and bottled without fining or filtering, the 2001 vintage (★★★★★) is notably sturdy, warm and concentrated, with rich red-berry and plum flavours, savoury, spicy, nutty complexities and firm underlying tannins. It's a wine of great depth and structure, likely to reward lengthy cellaring.

Vintage	03	02	01	00	DRY $53 AV
WR	6	6	6	6	
Drink	05-11	04-10	04-09	04-08	

Fromm La Strada Fromm Vineyard Pinot Noir ★★★★★

Winemaker Hatsch Kalberer describes this majestic Marlborough red, first made in 1996, as 'not a typical New World style, but the truest expression of terroir you could find'. Estate-grown between Woodbourne and Renwick, in the heart of the Wairau Valley, it is matured in French oak barriques (25 per cent new). In a vertical tasting of the 1997 (labelled Reserve) to 2002 vintages, held in mid-2004, the 1999 (★★★★★) was a star – powerful and complex, with very rich, firm coffee and spice flavours. Matured for 16 months in French oak barriques (25 per cent new), the 2002 vintage (★★★★★) is still very youthful, with impressive weight and spicy, savoury, nutty flavours, dense and tight-knit. Open 2006+.

Vintage	03	02	01	00	99	98	DRY $60 AV
WR	6	6	7	6	7	6	
Drink	06-13	05-12	04-11	04-08	04-07	04-06	🍇🍇

Fromm La Strada Pinot Noir ★★★★☆

The Fromm Pinot Noir style is distinctive – powerful, warm, meaty and firm. Grown at two sites (one is the Clayvin vineyard) in the Brancott Valley of Marlborough and matured in French oak casks (only 10 per cent new), the 2001 vintage (★★★★★) is arguably the best yet, and superior to most producers' top labels. It's a very weighty and generous wine with rich, complex flavours, subtle oak, firm but not grippy tannins and great mouthfeel. It's less of a crime to drink this wine young than its stablemates (above), but it still shows obvious cellaring potential.

Vintage	03	02	01	00	99	98	97	96	95	94	DRY $40 AV
WR	6	6	7	6	6	6	5	5	6	5	
Drink	05-10	04-08	04-07	04-06	04-06	04-05	P	P	P	P	

Gibbston Valley Central Otago Pinot Noir ★★★★

The powerful, densely packed 2002 (★★★★☆) and 2003 (★★★★) vintages are by far the best yet. Matured for 11 months in French oak barriques (30 per cent new), the 2003 is an elegant, richly varietal wine, bright ruby, with concentrated cherry, raspberry and spice flavours and finely balanced toasty oak. It's a youthful, well-structured red with plenty of charm and upfront appeal.

Vintage	03	02	01	00	99	98	97	96
WR	6	7	6	6	6	6	5	5
Drink	04-10	05-12	04-09	04-08	04-05	P	P	P

DRY $39 AV

Gibbston Valley Gold River Pinot Noir ★★☆

This is the Central Otago winery's 'lighter' red. The floral 2003 vintage (★★★), oak-aged for six months, is light ruby, with fresh, berryish, plummy, slightly toasty flavours and gentle tannins. It's a middleweight style with an easy-drinking appeal.

Vintage	03
WR	5
Drink	04-08

DRY $26 -V

Gibbston Valley Reserve Pinot Noir ★★★★★

This multiple gold medal and trophy-winning Central Otago red is typically mouthfilling and savoury, with a superb concentration of sweet-tasting, plummy fruit and lovely harmony. Winemaker Grant Taylor is after a 'tannic, powerful style'. The wine is typically matured in French oak barriques, 100 per cent new, for between 12 and 18 months. The 1998 vintage sold at $48; the 1999 at $55, the 2000 at $65, the 2001 at $75 and the 2002 has been released at $90. The 2002 vintage (★★★★★) is richly fragrant, with red-berry and herb aromas, and deep, purple-flushed colour. Bursting with ripe-plum and cherry flavours, it's a beautifully harmonious, exceptionally rich wine with silky tannins. A fruit bomb in its youth, it needs time; open 2006+.

Vintage	02	01	00	99	98	97	96
WR	7	7	7	6	7	6	6
Drink	06-15	04-15	04-12	04-10	04-15	04-10	04-05

DRY $90 -V

Giesen Canterbury/Marlborough Pinot Noir ★★☆

The 2002 vintage (★★) is light and rustic, with vegetative characters on the nose and palate and green tannins, indicating a lack of full ripeness.

Vintage	03	02	01
WR	6	4	5
Drink	04-06	04-05	P

DRY $22 -V

Giesen Reserve Barrel Selection Canterbury Pinot Noir ★★★★

The 2001 vintage (★★★★) is a strong candidate for cellaring. Boldly coloured, it is packed with cherryish, plummy flavour, seasoned with spicy oak. A youthful, firmly structured wine, it should be at its best from 2005 onwards.

Vintage	01	00	99
WR	7	7	7
Drink	04-08	04-07	04-05

DRY $50 -V

Giesen Reserve Barrel Selection Marlborough Pinot Noir ★★★☆

Still fresh and youthful, the 2001 vintage (★★★☆) reveals deep, bright colour and strong raspberry, strawberry and spice flavours. It's a moderately complex wine with cellaring potential.

Vintage	01	00	DRY $35 -V
WR	7	7	
Drink	05-09	04-05	

Gifford Road Marlborough Pinot Noir ★★☆

The 2003 vintage (★★☆) is medium ruby, with plum and herb flavours showing moderate ripeness and depth, and a fresh, crisp finish. The 2002 (★★☆) is very similar, with green-edged, berryish flavours that lack complexity.

DRY $25 -V

Gladstone Atavar Pinot Noir (★★☆)

The unusual 2003 vintage (★★☆) was grown in the Atavar ('manifestation of a deity') vineyard at Te Horo, on the Kapiti Coast. Matured for nine months in new French oak casks, it is ruby-hued and herbaceous, with plum, spice and green-leaf flavours and noticeably high alcohol (around 15 per cent). It's a powerful wine, but lacks finesse.

DRY $39 -V

Gladstone Wairarapa Pinot Noir ★★★

The 2002 vintage (★★★) is fresh and lively, but not highly complex, with cherry, plum and herb flavours and light tannins in a forward, easy-drinking style.

DRY $32 -V

Glamour Puss Pinot Noir (★★☆)

From Coopers Creek, the flavoursome, easy-drinking 2004 vintage (★★☆) is a 2:1 blend of Marlborough and Hawke's Bay grapes. Ruby-hued, it is plummy, spicy and slightly earthy, with gentle tannins and a very smooth finish.

DRY $13 V+

Glover's Moutere Pinot Noir Front Block ★★★

Upper Moutere winemaker Dave Glover keeps to one side the grapes from the cooler block in front of the winery, which he finds gives a slightly more floral and supple style than the wine from the hotter Back Block. The wines tend to be rustic and tannin-laden, lacking real fragrance and finesse, but are also sturdy, honest and characterful, with loads of flavour.

DRY $40 -V

Greenhough Hope Vineyard Pinot Noir ★★★★★

One of Nelson's greatest wines. In a vertical tasting of the 1997 to 2002 vintages, held in late 2003, the star was the beautifully scented and rich, notably complete 2001. The refined and harmonious 2002 vintage (★★★★★) is savoury, spicy, gamey and nutty, in a firmly structured, highly complex style. The stylish 2003 (★★★★) was fermented with indigenous and cultured yeasts and matured for a year in French oak barriques (37 per cent new). It's a powerful yet exceptionally elegant wine, notably concentrated, vibrant and youthful, with layers of flavour and a finely poised, lasting finish. Open 2006+.

Vintage	03	02	01	00	99	98	97	DRY $42 V+
WR	5	7	6	6	6	5	6	
Drink	04-08	04-07	04-06	04-05	P	P	P	

Greenhough Nelson Vineyards Pinot Noir   ★★★☆

This wine is handled in a similar way to its Hope Vineyard stablemate (above), but without the contribution of as much new oak or fruit from the oldest vines. The 2003 vintage (★★★★) was hand-harvested from a range of sites, including the estate vineyard. Two-thirds of the wine was barrel-aged, and the final blend has a 23 per cent new French oak component. Deep and youthful in colour, it has a fragrant, spicy, plummy bouquet and mouthfilling, warm and generous palate, crammed with flavour. Moderately firm, with a seasoning of toasty oak, it's an unexpectedly good wine for a second label, offering very satisfying drinking now to 2006.

Vintage	03
WR	6
Drink	04-06

DRY $26 AV

Grove Mill Marlborough Pinot Noir   ★★★★

From a low-yielding season (4 tonnes/hectare), the 2002 vintage (★★★★) is deeply coloured, with a complex, ripe bouquet. Matured for a year in French oak casks (40 per cent new), it is robust (14.5 per cent alcohol) and rounded, with deep plum and spice flavours, earthy, gamey characters, gentle acidity and a solid underlay of tannins. It's a bold style, for drinking now or cellaring.

Vintage	02	01	00	99
WR	7	6	5	5
Drink	04-09	04-06	P	P

DRY $40 AV

Gypsy Dancer Central Otago Pinot Noir   (★★★★)

The 2003 vintage (★★★★) has fragrant, slightly herbal aromas leading into a substantial, weighty, concentrated wine with deep, plummy, spicy, toasty flavours, showing good complexity and firm tannins. It needs time; open mid-2005+.

DRY $50 -V

Hanmer Junction, The, Waipara Pinot Noir   (★★☆)

The 2002 vintage (★★☆) has a leafy, green-edged bouquet but the palate is supple, with some fruit sweetness and decent flavour depth. Verging on three stars.

DRY $19 -V

Hawkdun Rise Redbarnais Pinot Noir   ★★★☆

Grown on the northern outskirts of Alexandra, in Central Otago, the 2002 vintage (★★★★) is a single-vineyard red, full-coloured, with a scented bouquet of raspberries and herbs. Elegant, with strong, sweet cherry, plum and spice flavours and smooth, ripe tannins, it shows good warmth, depth and complexity.

Vintage	02
WR	6
Drink	05-07

DRY $36 -V

Herzog Marlborough Pinot Noir   ★★★★

The powerful 2003 vintage (★★★★) was hand-picked at 24.5 brix, fermented with indigenous yeasts, matured for 15 months in French oak barriques (half new), and bottled without fining or filtration. Deep and youthful in colour, it is very warm, rich and rounded, although not highly fragrant, with concentrated, sweet fruit characters and bold plum, cherry and spice flavours, well-seasoned with toasty oak. It's still very youthful; open 2006+.

DRY $48 -V

Highfield Marlborough Pinot Noir ★★★☆

The 2002 vintage (★★★★) was blended from three sites and French oak-aged for 11 months. Fragrant and fleshy, it has a gamey, spicy bouquet and smooth, concentrated flavours, ripe, plummy, cherryish and nutty. A mouthfilling wine (14 per cent alcohol), it is generous, complex and drinking well now.

Vintage	02	01	00	99	
WR	6	7	6	6	DRY $37 -V
Drink	04-06	04-06	P	04-05	

Hinton Estate Central Otago Pinot Noir (★★★★)

The 2002 vintage (★★★★) is an elegant middleweight with a seasoning of quality French oak. Ruby-hued, fresh and lively, it has ripe, red-berry and plum flavours, tightly structured and youthful, with a long finish.

DRY $38 AV

Huia Marlborough Pinot Noir ★★★★

The elegant 2002 vintage (★★★★) was grown in four vineyards, from Rapaura, on the north side of the Wairau Valley, to the Brancott Valley in the south, and French oak-aged for a year. Fragrant and supple, with ripe-cherry and plum flavours showing some savoury complexity, it's a full-bodied, harmonious, finely textured wine, maturing well.

Vintage	02	01	00	99	
WR	6	6	6	5	DRY $35 AV
Drink	04-07	04-05	04-05	04	

Hunter's Flaxmill Marlborough Pinot Noir (★★★)

Sold by mail-order wine clubs, the 2003 vintage (★★★) is bright ruby, with a fragrant, spicy bouquet. It's a middleweight style with clearly varietal flavours of plums and cherries, showing good depth.

DRY $23 AV

Hunter's Marlborough Pinot Noir ★★★☆

Easy to enjoy, the 2002 vintage (★★★☆) was harvested in the Wairau Valley at 24.5 brix and matured for nine months in French oak casks (20 per cent new). Ruby-hued, it's a graceful, middleweight style with ripe raspberry and spice flavours, some savoury, spicy complexity, finely integrated oak and fairly firm tannins.

Vintage	02	01	00	99	98	97	96	
WR	6	6	6	6	6	6	6	DRY $24 AV
Drink	04-06	04-05	P	P	P	P	P	

Hyperion Eos Pinot Noir ★★☆

Estate-grown at Matakana, north of Auckland, and French oak-matured for a year, this is one of New Zealand's northernmost Pinot Noirs. The 2002 vintage (★★) was enjoyably fresh and supple in its youth, but lacks flavour depth and is now past its best.

Vintage	03	
WR	4	DRY $27 -V
Drink	05-07	

Isabel Marlborough Pinot Noir   ★★★★★

This outstanding red is grown in the close-planted Tiller vineyard near Renwick and matured in French oak casks (20 per cent new). In a vertical tasting of selected vintages, held in May 2004, the debut 1994 was beautifully perfumed and savoury, and the 2000 was intense and youthful, with outstanding potential. The 2002 vintage (★★★★★), released after one year in French oak barrels and another year of bottle-age, is a blend of nine clones, harvested at 23.5 to 27 brix. It's a generous, warm, spicy and earthy wine, with a deliciously soft texture and impressive concentration and complexity.

Vintage	03	02	01	00	99	98	97	96	95	94	DRY $40 V+
WR		5	6	7	6	6	5	5	4	NM	6	
Drink		05-07	04-10	04-09	04-08	04-06	04-05	P	P	NM	P	

Jackson Estate Marlborough Pinot Noir   ★★★

The 2003 vintage (★★★), French oak-aged for seven months, is ruby-hued, with a floral bouquet and plum/cherry flavours gently seasoned with toasty oak. It's a middleweight style, not concentrated but supple and enjoyable.

Vintage	03	02	01	00	99	98	DRY $25 -V
WR		5	6	5	6	6	5	
Drink	04-08	04-05	04	04-05	04	P	

Judge Rock Pinot Noir   ★★★☆

The 2002 vintage (★★★★) of this Central Otago red is boldly coloured, with substantial body, generous cherry, plum and rhubarb flavours, some savoury complexity and a firm foundation of tannin. The 2003 (★★★) is ruby-hued, with plummy, slightly earthy aromas and flavours and a positive tannin grip.

DRY $28 AV

Jules Taylor Marlborough Pinot Noir   (★★★)

Showing a Beaujolais-like freshness, fruitiness and charm, the debut 2002 vintage (★★★) was hand-picked in the Omaka Valley and matured for 11 months in French oak casks (40 per cent new). It's a vibrantly fruity wine with gentle tannins and attractive raspberry/plum flavours, fresh and smooth.

DRY $28 -V

Julicher Martinborough Pinot Noir   ★★★☆

The 2002 (★★★★), grown on the Te Muna Terraces and matured in new French oak casks, is full-coloured, mouthfilling and supple, with ripe-cherry, plum and spice flavours, warm, savoury, toasty and complex. The 2003 vintage (★★★) is a floral, middleweight style with ripe-cherry/plum flavours showing moderate complexity and some drink-young charm.

Vintage	03	02	DRY $36 -V
WR	5	5	
Drink	05-10	04-09	

Kahurangi Estate Nelson Pinot Noir   ★★☆

Grown in the Moutere hills and on the Waimea Plains, the 2003 vintage (★★★) is a boldly coloured, gutsy wine (14 per cent alcohol), with slightly green tannins but plenty of plummy, spicy, moderately complex flavour. The 2002 (★★☆) is developed in colour, with spicy, green-edged flavours.

Vintage	03	DRY $23 -V
WR	4	
Drink	05-07	

Kaikoura Pinot Noir   (★★★)

There's no region stated on the label, but the 2002 vintage (★★★) was grown in Canterbury. Matured in new to four-year-old French oak casks, it's a fruity, easy-drinking style with ripe raspberry and cherry characters, a restrained wood influence and a smooth finish.

DRY $25 -V

Kaimira Estate Nelson Pinot Noir   (★★☆)

Priced right, the 2003 vintage (★★☆) was grown on several sites and lightly oaked. Made 'to accentuate its fresh, fruity characters', it's an easy-drinking, light wine with strawberry, spice and herb aromas and flavours and gentle tannins. It's probably at its best during late 2004 and early 2005.

Vintage	03
WR	5
Drink	04-07

DRY $16 AV

Kaituna Valley The Awatere Vineyard Pinot Noir   ★★★★☆

This Marlborough wine is typically powerful, robust and crammed with flavour. The 2002 (★★★★☆) is deeply coloured, with generous, upfront fruit characters and concentrated plum, coffee, herb and spice flavours showing excellent complexity and length. The 2003 vintage (★★★★☆) was ultra low-cropped (2.4 tonnes/hectare), harvested at 23.8 to 25 brix, and matured for 14 months in French oak barriques (half new). Still unfolding, it's a muscular (14 per cent alcohol), richly coloured wine with warm, plummy, spicy flavours, smooth and generous, good texture and mouthfeel.

Vintage	03	02	01	00
WR	7	7	7	7
Drink	04-10	04-08	04-06	04-05

DRY $46 -V

Kaituna Valley The Kaituna Vineyard Pinot Noir   ★★★★★

This consistently striking Canterbury red flows from a close-planted, low-yielding vineyard on Banks Peninsula, first planted in the late 1970s, and is matured for over a year in French oak casks (60 to 70 per cent new). The 2003 (★★★★★) is dark, opulent and densely flavoured. In the winery's words, it's a 'bold and dramatic' style, with hugely concentrated berry, plum and spice characters and hints of liquorice. It's a very ripe, richly alcoholic wine (14.5 per cent), but there's no denying its majestic body and richness.

Vintage	03	02	01	00	99	98	97	96	95	94
WR	7	7	7	7	7	7	6	6	NM	6
Drink	04-10	04-09	04-08	04-06	04-07	04-06	P	P	NM	P

DRY $46 AV

Kawarau Estate Pinot Noir   ★★★

A fresh, lightly oaked style, grown organically at Lowburn, near Cromwell in Central Otago. Typically medium-bodied, ripe and smooth, it's a drink-young style. The 2003 vintage (★★★☆), only 10 per cent barrel-aged, is fragrant, vibrant and supple, with sweet fruit characters, very good depth of cherryish, plummy flavour, and a well-rounded finish.

DRY $26 -V

Kawarau Estate Reserve Pinot Noir   ★★★★

Grown organically at Lowburn in Central Otago, at its best this is a notably classy, powerful and complex wine. The 2002 vintage (★★★★☆) is highly impressive. Matured in French oak barriques (20 per cent new), it offers lovely depth of cherry, raspberry and spice flavours, with finely integrated oak. The 2003 (★★★☆) is ruby-hued, with sweet fruit characters, fresh, tight cherry and plum flavours, some savoury, spicy complexity and supple tannins.

Vintage	03	02	01	00	99	98
WR	6	6	6	6	5	5
Drink	04-07	04-06	04-05	P	P	P

DRY $36 AV

Kim Crawford Anderson Vineyard
Marlborough Pinot Noir   ★★★

Grown in the Anderson vineyard, in the Brancott Valley, the 2001 vintage (★★★★) is richly flavoured, with ripe, plummy fruit seasoned with toasty oak (French, one-third new). However, the deeply coloured 2002 (★★) is green-edged, with raspberry and herb flavours that lack fragrance and charm.

Vintage	02		DRY $40 -V
WR	5		
Drink	07-09		

Kim Crawford Marlborough Pinot Noir   ★★★

A fruit-driven style, only 40 per cent wood-aged (in older American oak barrels). The 2003 vintage (★★☆) is deep ruby in hue, in a medium to full-bodied style with finely balanced tannins and plummy, slightly herbal flavours that lack real complexity, but offer decent depth. Verging on three stars.

Vintage	03		DRY $20 AV
WR	5		
Drink	05-07		

Kim Crawford Nelson Pinot Noir   (★★★★)

The 2003 vintage (★★★★) is a great buy. Only partly barrel-aged (in seasoned oak barrels), it is deeply coloured, muscular (14 per cent alcohol) and generous, with firm, ripe tannins and rich, spicy flavours, showing a stronger toasty oak influence than you'd expect. Best drinking 2005-06.

DRY $20 V+

Kina Beach Vineyard Reserve Pinot Noir   (★★★★☆)

Estate-grown on the Nelson coast and picked at 26.5 brix, the debut 2003 vintage (★★★★☆) was matured for 11 months in new, one and two-year-old French oak barriques. Deep and youthful in colour, with strawberryish, spicy, slightly earthy aromas, it's a powerful wine with sweet fruit delights and concentrated cherry, plum and spice flavours. Savoury and complex, it's a bold style of Pinot Noir, already delicious, but likely to unfold really well during 2005-06.

DRY $40 AV

Konrad Pinot Noir   ★★★☆

The 2003 vintage (★★★☆) was grown in the Wairau and Waihopai valleys and matured for 10 months in French oak casks (new and old). Full-bodied, supple and vibrantly fruity, it's a fruit-driven style with ripe-plum, cherry and spice flavours showing very good depth, finely integrated oak and some aging potential.

Vintage	03	02	DRY $30 AV
WR	6	5	
Drink	04-09	04-08	

Koura Bay Blue Duck Pinot Noir   ★★★★

Estate-grown in the Awatere Valley and French oak-aged, the graceful 2003 vintage (★★★★) of this Marlborough red offers fresh, ripe, raspberry and plum fruit flavours, long and well-rounded. It's a sensuous, vibrant, fruit-driven but not simple style, offering excellent drinking through 2005.

Vintage	03		DRY $36 AV
WR	7		
Drink	04-08		

Kumeu River Kumeu Pinot Noir   ★★★☆

This West Auckland red is typically markedly different to the perfumed, vibrantly fruity reds grown in the south – less intensely varietal, more earthy and 'red-winey'. The 2002 (tasted just prior to bottling, and so not rated), is fragrant, with strong, vibrant cherry, plum and spice flavours, a distinctly gamey character and a firm tannin underlay. The 2003 vintage (★★★☆) is youthful, firm and tight, with cherryish, nutty, savoury characters. It should mature well; open mid-2005+.

Vintage	04	03	02	01	00	DRY $30 AV
WR	5	6	4	6	5	
Drink	05-07	06-08	P	05-10	P	

Kumeu River Village Pinot Noir   ★★★

The 2003 vintage (★★★) was grown at Kumeu, in West Auckland, and matured for a year in seasoned French oak casks. It offers firm strawberry and spice flavours, good depth and plenty of character. Best drinking 2005.

DRY $18 V+

Lake Chalice Marlborough Pinot Noir   ★★★

The youthful 2003 vintage (★★★) was grown in the Rapaura district and matured for 11 months in French oak barriques (25 per cent new). Ruby-hued, it is fresh and supple, in a charming, middleweight style with good depth of berry, plum and spice flavours and moderate cellar potential.

DRY $23 AV

Lake Hayes Central Otago Pinot Noir   (★★☆)

From Amisfield, the 2003 vintage (★★☆) was grown at Lowburn, in the Cromwell Basin, and Alexandra, and matured in French oak barriques (15 per cent new). Designed for early drinking ('usually before the sun goes down'), it's ruby-hued, with raspberry, plum and spice flavours, fresh, vibrant and simple.

Vintage	03	DRY $30 -V
WR	5	
Drink	04-06	

Lawson's Dry Hills Marlborough Pinot Noir   ★★★

The latest releases are the best. Grown at several sites around the Wairau Valley, the 2002 vintage (★★★) was fermented mainly with indigenous ('wild', rather than cultured) yeasts and matured in new to four-year-old French oak casks. Ruby-hued, with fragrant raspberry and spice aromas, it's full-bodied, fresh and supple, with well-ripened, vibrant fruit characters, gentle tannins and some savoury complexity. It's not highly concentrated, but instantly appealing.

Vintage	03	02	01	00	DRY $28 -V
WR	5	6	6	5	
Drink	04-06	04-07	04-06	P	

Leaning Rock Central Otago Pinot Noir   ★★★★

Grown on the outskirts of Alexandra and French oak-matured, the 2002 vintage (★★★★☆) is a powerful (14.5 per cent alcohol) wine, delicious in its youth, with ripe, sweet fruit characters of plums and spice, good, savoury complexity and supple tannins. The 2003 (★★★☆) is floral, fresh and vibrant, with fresh acidity and attractive raspberry, plum and spice flavours. It's less ripe and concentrated than the 2002, but moderately complex and worth cellaring.

Vintage	03	02	01	00	DRY $37 AV
WR	6	7	5	6	
Drink	05-10	04-12	04-05	04-10	

Leaning Rock Obelisk Pinot Noir ★★★☆

The 2003 vintage (★★★☆) was made from nine to 13-year-old vines at Alexandra, in Central Otago, and matured for 11 months in French oak casks. Ruby-hued and smooth, with cherry, plum and spice flavours, it's only moderately complex, but weighty (13.8 per cent alcohol), with ripe-fruit characters and a deliciously soft texture.

Vintage	03	02	01	00	DRY $24 V+
WR	6	6	NM	NM	
Drink	04-07	04-06	NM	NM	

Leaning Rock Rise and Shine Pinot Noir ★★★☆

Named after a gold reef, the 2003 vintage (★★★★) was grown at Alexandra, in Central Otago, and matured in French oak barriques (60 per cent new). Richly scented, it's a very charming wine with sweet fruit delights, rich raspberry, cherry and spicy oak flavours and more muscle (14.4 per cent alcohol) than its ruby hue suggests. It's a finely textured wine, delicious young, but also worth cellaring.

Vintage	03	02	DRY $40 -V
WR	7	NM	
Drink	05-13	NM	

Lincoln Heritage Pinot Noir ★★☆

Pinot Noir is a rare beast in the Waikato, but the 2002 vintage (★★★) of this Te Kauwhata red shows decent varietal character. Blended with 10 per cent Malbec and matured in French oak casks (30 per cent new), it's a full-coloured wine with strong, raspberryish, spicy, slightly raisined and nutty flavours.

Vintage	03	02	01	DRY $17 AV
WR	5	6	5	
Drink	04-08	04-06	P	

Loopline Vineyard Wairarapa Pinot Noir ★★★☆

Grown on the Opaki Plains, north of Masterton, the 2002 vintage (★★★☆) was matured for 10 months in French oak barriques (50 per cent new). Light/medium ruby, with fresh, berryish aromas, it shows good ripeness, with raspberry/cherry flavours, some savoury complexity and a well-rounded finish.

Vintage	02	01	00	DRY $29 AV
WR	7	6	5	
Drink	04-09	04-06	04-05	

Loopline Vineyard Wairarapa Reserve Pinot Noir ★★★☆

Grown north of Masterton and matured for 10 months in French oak barriques (50 per cent new), the 2002 vintage (★★★☆) is full ruby, with a spicy, raspberryish bouquet. Full-bodied and sweet-fruited, it offers youthful cherry and plum flavours, showing some toasty complexity.

Vintage	02	01	DRY $39 -V
WR	7	6	
Drink	04-09	04-08	

Lowburn Ferry Central Otago Pinot Noir (★★★★)

This single-vineyard wine is grown at Lowburn, in the Cromwell Basin. The debut 2003 vintage (★★★★) was harvested at 24.2 brix and matured in French oak barriques (half new). Deeply coloured, with an attractively scented, berryish, spicy bouquet, it's a warm, generous wine, mouthfilling and supple, with sweet fruit delights, gentle tannins and concentrated, slightly nutty flavours. Open mid-2005+.

DRY $33 AV

Lynskey's Wairau Peaks Marlborough Pinot Noir ★★★☆

Matured in French oak barriques (half new), the easy-drinking 2002 vintage (★★★) is smooth and fruity, with slightly earthy aromas and plenty of berryish, moderately complex flavour.

Vintage	02	01	00	99	98
WR	7	7	6	7	7
Drink	04-06	04-05	P	P	P

DRY $38 -V

Mahi Byrne Vineyard Pinot Noir ★★★★☆

Mahi is the personal label of Brian Bicknell, winemaker at Seresin Estate. The fragrant and richly coloured 2002 vintage (★★★★★) was grown in a single vineyard at Conders Bend, near Renwick, in Marlborough. Fermented with indigenous yeasts, it was French oak-aged for 15 months and bottled unfiltered. It possesses lovely richness, structure and harmony, with concentrated plum, cherry and spice flavours, savoury characters adding complexity and firm, ripe tannins. One of the region's most multi-faceted reds, it can be cellared with confidence.

Vintage	02	01
WR	6	6
Drink	04-08	04-09

DRY $35 V+

Main Divide Pinot Noir ★★★☆

A good buy. The 2003 vintage (★★★☆), grown in Canterbury and matured in seasoned French oak casks, is a graceful, supple red with cherry, spice and plum flavours showing good depth. Mouthfilling, with a deliciously soft texture, it's a forward style, already enjoyable.

Vintage	03	02	01	00
WR	5	5	7	6
Drink	04-08	P	04-05	P

DRY $24 V+

Maison Esquilat Marlborough Pinot Noir (★★★)

Still youthful, the 2002 vintage (★★★) is a deeply coloured, middleweight wine with vibrant, plummy, slightly herbal flavours and smooth tannins.

DRY $40 -V

Margrain Martinborough Pinot Noir ★★★★

This is typically an impressive red. The youthful 2003 vintage (★★★★★) is full-coloured and sweet-fruited, with concentrated plum, cherry, spice and nut flavours and savoury, earthy complexities. A powerful, weighty, well-structured wine with a firm tannin backbone, it should be at its best 2006+.

Vintage	03	02	01	00	99	98	97	96	95
WR	7	6	6	6	7	7	5	6	4
Drink	05-10	04-08	04-08	04-06	04-05	P	P	P	P

DRY $49 -V

Margrain Petit Pinot Noir (★★☆)

Barrel selected for its smoothness and early drinking charm', the 2002 vintage (★★☆) was grown in Martinborough and oak-aged for eight months. Ruby-hued, it lacks real fruit sweetness and depth, with a slightly high-acid finish.

Vintage	02
WR	5
Drink	04-06

DRY $30 -V

Marlborough Wines Marlborough/Nelson Pinot Noir   (★★★)

The moderately priced 2003 vintage (★★★) shows good freshness and clearcut varietal characters. Full ruby in hue, it is crisp, berryish and spicy, with solid depth and a slight lack of softness on the finish.

DRY $19 AV

Martinborough Vineyard Pinot Noir   ★★★★★

This was the first consistently distinguished Pinot Noir made in New Zealand. An intensely varietal wine, it is typically fragrant, with sweet-tasting fruit and cherryish, spicy, slightly smoky flavours. In the past, it impressed principally with fragrance and finesse, rather than sheer scale, but in recent years (especially since the phasing out of the magisterial Reserve Pinot Noir, last seen from the 1998 vintage), the wine has become markedly bolder. Grown on the shingly Martinborough Terrace, with vines ranging up to 23 years old, it is matured for a year in French oak barriques (30 per cent new, the rest one and two-year-old). The 2003 vintage (★★★★★) promises to be a classic, with deep, noble colour and a beautifully fragrant bouquet. Concentrated, rich and supple, with sweet fruit delights, it has dense plum, cherry and spice flavours, highly complex and very youthful. Open 2006+.

Vintage	01	00	99	98	97	96	95	94
WR	7	7	7	7	6	7	7	7
Drink	04-07	04-07	04-06	04-05	P	P	P	P

DRY $60 AV

Martinborough Vineyard Te Tera Pinot Noir   ★★★☆

Te Tera ('the other') is designed as 'a more accessible wine, approachable earlier' than its famous big brother (above). Based on young and old vines grown in Martinborough and matured in French oak casks (30 per cent new), the 2003 vintage (★★★) is ruby-hued, with toasty aromas, mouthfilling body and plummy, slightly herbal, moderately ripe flavours showing some savoury complexity.

DRY $28 AV

Martinus Estate Martinborough Pinot Noir   ★★★☆

The richly coloured 2003 vintage (★★★☆) was matured in French oak casks (25 per cent new). Vibrantly fruity and supple, it possesses ripe, sweet plum and cherry flavours in a moderately complex style with subtle oak and very good depth. Drink mid-2005+.

Vintage	03	02	01
WR	6	4	6
Drink	05+	04-06	04-06

DRY $35 -V

Matariki Pinot Noir   ★★★

Although grown in the siltiest (coolest) soils in the company's vineyard in Gimblett Road, Hawke's Bay and matured in French oak casks (50 per cent new), the 2002 vintage (★★) is disappointing, with light green-edged flavours that lack ripeness and depth.

Vintage	02	01
WR	6	5
Drink	04-07	04-06

DRY $30 -V

Matariki Reserve Pinot Noir   ★★★

The disappointing 2002 vintage (★★☆), grown in the Gimblett Gravels district of Hawke's Bay, was harvested at 24.5 to 25 brix, and matured in French oak barriques (73 per cent new). It offers simple plum and spice flavours that lack real complexity and richness.

Vintage	02
WR	6
Drink	04-09

DRY $48 -V

Matua Valley Innovator Pinot Noir   (★★★★)

Deeply coloured for a Pinot Noir, the 2003 vintage (★★★★) was grown in Marlborough and matured for a year in French oak casks (one-third new). Crammed with plum, cherry and spice flavours, coated with toasty oak, it's a real fruit bomb in its youth. Fresh and vibrant, it shows plenty of potential; open mid-2005+.

Vintage	03
WR	6
Drink	04-08

DRY $29 V+

Matua Valley Wairarapa Vineyard Pinot Noir   ★★★★

Here's proof you don't have to pay $35 or more for an excellent New Zealand Pinot Noir. Grown in the Petrie vineyard, south of Masterton, the 2003 vintage (★★★★☆) is from an ultra low-cropping season (below 2.5 tonnes/hectare). Fermented with indigenous yeasts and matured for 14 months in French oak barriques (one-third new), it is bold and youthful in colour, with rich flavours of dark cherries, plums and spice and even a hint of liquorice. A very ripe style, firm and youthful, with impressive density, it's best cellared to 2006 onwards.

Vintage	03	02	01	00	99	98
WR	6	6	6	6	NM	5
Drink	04-10	04-07	P	04-06	NM	P

DRY $29 V+

Melness Pinot Noir   ★★★☆

Grown at three North Canterbury sites (including the Melness estate vineyard) and French oak-aged for 10 months, the 2003 vintage (★★★☆) is ruby-hued, with sweet fruit characters, strong plum, herb and spice flavours and good complexity. It's a supple, well-rounded wine with drink-young charm, but also worth cellaring.

Vintage	03	02	01
WR	7	6	7
Drink	04-09	04-08	04-06

DRY $29 AV

Mills Reef Pinot Noir   (★★☆)

Designed for early drinking, the modestly priced 2003 vintage (★★☆) is a 50/50 blend of Marlborough and Waipara grapes. A middleweight style, it is supple, with ripe raspberry, cherry and spice flavours, a touch of toasty oak and smooth tannins. It's not intense, but priced right. Verging on three stars.

DRY $16 AV

Millton Clos de Ste Anne Naboth's Vineyard Pinot Noir   ★★★★

This single-vineyard Gisborne red is one of the country's northernmost quality Pinot Noirs. The 2003 vintage (★★★☆) was fermented with indigenous yeasts, matured for 14 months in French oak barriques (20 per cent new) and bottled without filtration. Full-coloured, it is robust and tannic, with strong plum, raspberry and spice flavours and lots of personality. Tasting slightly raw and tough in mid to late 2004, it needs time; open 2006+.

Vintage	03	02	01	00	99	98
WR	6	6	NM	NM	5	5
Drink	04-08	04-09	NM	NM	04-05	P

DRY $45 -V

Montana Marlborough Pinot Noir   ★★★

As an 'entry level' Pinot Noir, this large-volume red works well, smelling and tasting like Pinot Noir in a medium-bodied style that offers very easy drinking. The 2003 vintage (★★★) was harvested at 23 to 24 brix and matured for 10 months in a mix of French oak barriques and 10,000-litre oak cuves. It shows good depth and varietal character, with smooth cherry, plum and raspberry flavours, a touch of smoky, toasty oak and moderately firm tannins. At $16, great value.

Vintage	03	02	01	00
WR	5	5	6	6
Drink	04-06	04-06	P	P

DRY $16 V+

Montana Reserve Marlborough Pinot Noir   ★★★★

This is consistently a finely structured, harmonious wine, bargain-priced. The 2003 vintage (★★★★), matured in French oak barriques (40 per cent new), is full and bright in colour, with warm, spicy, slightly smoky aromas. The palate is weighty and warm, with plum, cherry and spice flavours showing good complexity and a tight finish, promising good cellar potential. The 2002 (★★★★) is also very satisfying, with deep, well-ripened, cherry and spice flavours and a savoury, nutty complexity.

Vintage	03
WR	5
Drink	04-07

DRY $24 V+

Montana Terraces Estate Marlborough Pinot Noir   (★★★★)

The debut 2002 vintage (★★★★) was blended from grapes grown at Terraces Estate (a young 8-hectare vineyard on 'a small spur adjacent to Brancott Estate'), and older Pinot Noir vines from nearby Fairhall Estate. (As the Terrace Estate vineyard matures, the proportion of grapes from this site will rise.) Matured for a year in French oak barriques (40 per cent new), it is floral and fleshy, with generous plum and spice flavours, good savoury complexity and firm tannins. The deep ruby-hued 2003 (★★★★☆) is warm and mouthfilling, with rich, plummy, spicy flavours and firm underlying tannins. It's a youthful wine, best cellared to mid-2005+.

DRY $33 AV

Morton Estate Stone Creek Marlborough Pinot Noir   ★★★

Released at three years old, the 2001 vintage (★★★) was French oak-aged for a year. Built to last, it's a full-bodied wine (14 per cent alcohol) with a slight lack of fruit sweetness but good depth of cherry, spice and nut flavours, some savoury complexity and firm tannins.

Vintage	02	01
WR	6	6
Drink	04-07	04-06

DRY $22 AV

Morton Estate White Label Hawke's Bay Pinot Noir   ★★★

French oak-matured for a year, the 2002 vintage (★★★☆) is arguably the best yet. Grown in the company's coolest vineyards, Riverview and Colefield, it's full-coloured, with a spicy, smoky bouquet. Warm and weighty (14 per cent alcohol), it is firm and concentrated, with ripe cherry and plum flavours in a sturdy, meaty style, offering aging potential and fine value.

Vintage	03	02	01	00	99	98
WR	5	7	6	7	5	5
Drink	04-05	04-07	04-06	04-06	P	P

DRY $19 AV

Morton Estate White Label Marlborough Pinot Noir (★★★)

The 2001 vintage (★★★) is a ruby-hued, full-bodied wine with good depth of raspberry, plum and spice flavours and a firm backbone of tannin.

Vintage	02	01
WR	6	6
Drink	04-06	04-06

DRY $20 AV

Morworth Estate Barrel Selection Marlborough Pinot Noir (★★★☆)

The charming 2002 vintage (★★★☆) was harvested at 23.4 brix from low-cropped vines (5 tonnes/hectare), and matured for a year in French oak casks. Ruby-hued, with floral, raspberryish aromas, it's an elegant middleweight with ripe, cherryish fruit characters, a subtle oak influence and gentle tannins.

DRY $33 -V·

Mount Edward Central Otago Pinot Noir ★★★★☆

Alan Brady aims for 'elegance, fine texture and an enduring structure'. In a vertical tasting of the 1998 to 2003 vintages, staged in early 2004, the star was the powerful, generous and complex 1999, followed closely by the perfumed and savoury 2001 and 2002. Grown in the Gibbston (70 per cent) and Alexandra sub-regions, and aged for 11 months in French oak barriques (30 per cent new), the 2003 vintage (★★★★☆) shows impressive body and structure. Mouthfilling, warm, spicy, earthy and nutty, it's a complex wine, built for cellaring.

Vintage	03	02	01	00
WR	6	7	6	6
Drink	05-10	04-10	04-08	04-07

DRY $42 AV

Mount Edward Susan's Vineyard Pinot Noir (★★★★)

An 'early drinking' style, based on young vines, the 2003 vintage (★★★★) was grown just 200 metres from the Mount Edward winery, in a tiny, 1-hectare vineyard in the Gibbston Valley owned by Susan and Terry Stevens. Matured for 11 months in French oak casks (50 per cent new), it is deep ruby, enticingly floral and supple, with good body and warmth. Impressively complex for such a young wine, it is savoury and seamless, with ripe-cherry, raspberry, herb and spice flavours showing excellent depth and harmony. Drink now onwards.

Vintage	03
WR	6
Drink	05-07

DRY $38 AV

Mountford Pinot Noir ★★★★☆

From a small hillside vineyard at Waipara, Mountford produces bold, rich Pinot Noirs, full of personality. The outstanding 2001 vintage (★★★★★) is a voluptuous, silky red. Richly coloured, it is plump, deeply flavoured and supple, with intense cherry and plum characters, good savoury, mushroomy complexity, a backbone of ripe tannins and a lasting finish. The 2002 (★★★★☆) is slightly lighter, but beautifully fragrant and savoury, with moderately firm tannins and impressive warmth, depth and complexity.

DRY $52 -V

Mount Maude Central Otago Pinot Noir ★★★☆

Grown on steep slopes in the Maungawera Valley, between Lakes Wanaka and Hawea, the 2002 vintage (★★★☆) has strong plum, cherry and spice flavours, braced by firm tannins. The 2003 (★★★☆), from 10-year-old vines, is a fresh, youthful wine with raspberry, plum and spice flavours showing good depth, some savoury, nutty complexity and a firm finish.

DRY $38 -V

Mount Michael Pinot Noir   ★★★☆

Grown at Cromwell, in Central Otago, and matured in French oak casks (30 per cent new), the 2003 vintage (★★★☆) is an elegant, middleweight style, ruby-hued, fruity and smooth, with vibrant, cherryish, spicy flavours, delicate, fresh and intensely varietal.

DRY $32 -V

Mount Riley Nelson/Marlborough Pinot Noir   ★★★☆

The 2003 vintage (★★★) is a good, drink-young style. Grown in Nelson, the Wairau Valley and the Seventeen Valley vineyard, south of Blenheim, and matured for eight months in French and American oak casks (20 per cent new), it is ruby-hued and smooth, with plummy, spicy flavours and some nutty, savoury complexity.

Vintage	03
WR	5
Drink	04-06

DRY $21 V+

Mount Riley Seventeen Valley Marlborough Pinot Noir   ★★★★

A single-vineyard wine, grown south of Blenheim, the 2001 vintage (★★★★) is deep and still youthful in colour, with sweet fruit delights. Its strong, spicy, plummy, cherryish flavours are well seasoned with smoky oak (French and American, 80 per cent new), in a generous, supple style with good but not great complexity.

Vintage	01
WR	6
Drink	04-06

DRY $35 AV

Mount Riley Winemakers Selection Pinot Noir   (★★★☆)

The vibrantly fruity 2003 vintage (★★★☆) was grown in Marlborough and matured for eight months in oak casks (60 per cent new). Deep ruby, it is mouthfilling and supple, with fresh, strong plum and cherry flavours, finely integrated oak and a tight finish. It's still unfolding; drink 2005–06.

Vintage	03
WR	6
Drink	06-08

DRY $28 AV

Moutere Hills Nelson Pinot Noir   ★★☆

The 2002 vintage (★★★), estate-grown and matured in French oak casks, is a light wine with raspberry and plum flavours and a very restrained wood influence. It's an easy-drinking style, with a Beaujolais-like freshness and simplicity.

Vintage	02	01	00	99	98
WR	5	5	5	6	4
Drink	04-07	04-06	P	04-05	P

DRY $25 -V

Mt Difficulty Pinot Noir   ★★★★

Grown at Bannockburn, in Central Otago, the 2002 vintage (★★★★☆) is deeply coloured, with concentrated, ripe cherry and plum flavours. A muscular wine (14.5 per cent alcohol), it is vibrantly fruity with finely integrated oak and a firm, long finish. The tightly structured 2003 (★★★☆) is robust (14.5 per cent alcohol), with full ruby colour, fresh plum, herb and spice flavours, moderate complexity and firm tannins. It needs time; open mid-2005+.

DRY $40 AV

Mt Difficulty Single Vineyard Pipeclay Terrace Pinot Noir (★★★★★)

The outstanding 2002 vintage (★★★★★), French oak-matured for 18 months, is a powerful Central Otago wine, lush and concentrated, with densely packed, cherryish, plummy flavours, spicy and long. It's a classy, firmly structured wine with a long future ahead.

DRY $60 AV

Mt Rosa Pinot Noir (★★★☆)

Grown at Gibbston, in Central Otago, the ruby-hued 2003 vintage (★★★☆) is an elegant wine with scented cherry and spice aromas. Supple and ripe, with good depth of flavour and some nutty, savoury complexity, it should be at its best from mid-2005 onwards.

DRY $32 -V

Muddy Water Reloaded Pinot Noir (★★★★)

As a barrel-aging trial, the 2002 vintage (★★★★) was matured for three months longer than usual (15 months, instead of one year). Light ruby, with a fragrant bouquet of cherries, spices and herbs, it is elegant, supple and complex, although not powerful or highly concentrated.

Vintage	02
WR	6
Drink	04-06

DRY $42 -V

Muddy Water Waipara Pinot Noir ★★★★

The 2003 vintage (★★★★) was fermented with indigenous yeasts, matured for a year in French oak barriques (25 per cent new) and bottled without filtration. Seducing with grace, charm and suppleness, rather than sheer power, it is fragrant, with berry and spice aromas and a subtle oak influence. An intensely varietal red with gentle tannins and sweet fruit flavours of raspberries, plums and spice, it's already delicious.

Vintage	03	02	01	00	99	98	97
WR	6	5	5	6	5	5	5
Drink	05-08	04-06	04-08	04-05	P	P	P

DRY $39 AV

Mud House Marlborough Vineyard Selection Pinot Noir (★★★)

The 2002 vintage (★★★) was French oak-aged for 10 months. Bright ruby-red, with fresh raspberry, cherry and plum flavours, slightly spicy and nutty, and firm tannins, it's a moderately complex style, priced right.

DRY $20 AV

Murdoch James Blue Rock Pinot Noir ★★★★

Estate-grown just south of Martinborough, the 2003 vintage (★★★★) is a full-coloured, sweet-fruited wine, fresh and supple, with cherry and raspberry flavours, slightly toasty, nutty and spicy. It shows good richness, in a more floral and vibrantly fruity style than its Fraser stablemate (below).

Vintage	03	02	01	00	99
WR	7	6	7	6	5
Drink	04-08	04-06	04-06	04-05	P

DRY $53 -V

Murdoch James Fraser Pinot Noir   ★★★★

Grown in the Fraser vineyard, on the Martinborough Terrace, the 2003 vintage (★★★★☆) is full-coloured, warm, nutty and spicy, with a firm underlay of tannin. Mouthfilling, fleshy and savoury, it is concentrated and complex, with obvious cellaring potential.

Vintage	03	02	01	00	99	98	97	96	DRY $65 -V
WR	7	6	7	6	6	5	6	6	
Drink	04-10	04-08	04-07	04-06	04-06	P	P	P	

Nautilus Marlborough Pinot Noir   ★★★★

Deeply coloured and robust (14.5 per cent alcohol), the savoury, firm and nutty 2002 vintage (★★★★☆) is a blend of six clones grown at five sites, hand-picked and matured for 11 months in French oak barriques (30 per cent new). An impressively complex style with smoky, earthy characters adding interest to sweet, raspberry and plum fruit flavours, it's a powerful, serious wine, offering lovely drinking from now onwards.

Vintage	02	01	00	99	DRY $37 AV
WR	7	6	6	5	
Drink	04-07	04-05	04-06	P	

Neudorf Moutere Home Vineyard Pinot Noir   ★★★★★

Neudorf's flagship Pinot Noir. Estate-grown at Upper Moutere, in Nelson, the 2002 vintage (★★★★★) was harvested at over 24 brix, matured in French oak barriques (44 per cent new) and bottled without fining or filtration. A muscular wine (over 14 per cent alcohol) with a very complex, savoury, spicy bouquet, it shows great personality, with rich, cherryish, spicy, savoury, earthy flavours, building to a lasting finish. Showing lovely weight, texture and harmony, it's still evolving; open 2005+.

Vintage	03	02	01	DRY $62 AV
WR	6	6	6	
Drink	04-13	04-12	04-08	🍇

Neudorf Moutere Pinot Noir   ★★★★★

Typically a very classy Nelson red. The 2002 (★★★★★) is a blend of grapes harvested at over 24 brix in the home vineyard and from mature, low-cropping vines in the Neudorf-managed Pomona vineyard, overlooking Tasman Bay. Fermented with indigenous yeasts, matured for a year in French oak barriques (44 per cent new) and bottled without fining or filtering, it's a highly complex wine with substantial body, very concentrated flavours, cherryish, nutty and spicy, and a firm tannin grip. The 2003 (★★★★★) is fragrant and muscular (14.5 per cent alcohol), with advanced ripeness and very rich cherry, plum, spice and roasted nut flavours. Weighty and complex, with deep, youthful colour, it's a serious, densely structured wine, with firm tannins. Open 2006+.

Vintage	03	02	01	00	99	98	97	96	DRY $52 AV
WR	6	6	7	6	6	NM	7	6	
Drink	04-13	05-12	04-08	04-05	P	NM	P	P	🍇 🍇

Neudorf Nelson Pinot Noir   ★★★★

Still unfolding, the 2003 vintage (★★★★) was matured in French oak casks (25 per cent new). Richly coloured, with fresh plum and spice aromas, it's a sturdy (14 per cent alcohol) wine with excellent ripeness and flavour depth, considerable complexity and finely balanced tannins. Best drinking mid-2005+.

Vintage	03	DRY $32 AV
WR	6	
Drink	04-10	

Nevis Bluff Pinot Noir   ★★★☆

Grown in the Nevis Bluff estate vineyard and the neighbouring Pociecha block at Gibbston, and matured in French oak casks (20 per cent new), the 2002 vintage (★★★★) of this Central Otago red is one of the best yet. Boldly coloured, it is fragrant and exuberantly fruity, with concentrated, ripe flavours of cherries and plums and finely integrated oak. A powerful, youthful wine, it's worth cellaring.

Vintage	03	02	01	00	
WR	6	6	5	5	DRY $36 -V
Drink	05-09	04-07	04-06	P	

Nga Waka Pinot Noir   ★★★☆

Typically a graceful Martinborough red, very scented and supple. Delicious now, the 2002 vintage (★★★☆) was harvested from low-cropping vines (4.25 tonnes/hectare) at 24.9 to 25.4 brix, matured for 11 months in French oak barriques (one-third new), and bottled unfined and unfiltered. Charmingly fragrant and supple, it's a forward wine with gentle tannins, sweet fruit delights and a lot more depth of cherryish, plummy, silky-smooth flavour than its light colour suggests.

Vintage	02	01	00	
WR	5	6	6	DRY $35 -V
Drink	04+	04-06	04-05	

Nobilo Fall Harvest Pinot Noir   (★★)

A blend of Australian and New Zealand wine, the 2002 vintage (★★) is a ripe, slightly raisiny red with plum and raspberry flavours and a very smooth finish. It's a solid quaffer, but shows limited varietal character.

DRY $12 AV

Nobilo Icon Marlborough Pinot Noir   ★★★

The 2003 vintage (★★★) is a charming middleweight style, grown in the Wairau and Awatere valleys and matured for a year in new and seasoned French oak casks. With its fresh cherry, plum and spice flavours that show good but not great depth and gentle tannins, it delivers lots of drink-young pleasure.

Vintage	03	02	
WR	7	7	DRY $24 AV
Drink	04-05	P	

Northrow Marlborough Pinot Noir   ★★★☆

Northrow is a range from Villa Maria, aimed at the restaurant trade. The 2002 vintage (★★★☆) was grown in the Wairau, Waihopai and Awatere valleys and French oak-aged. Full-coloured and fragrant, with cherry and spice aromas, ripe-fruit characters and good complexity, it's an intensely varietal wine with moderate tannins and strong drink-young appeal. The 2003 (★★★☆) is an elegant wine, fragrant and vibrantly fruity, with fresh raspberry/plum flavours gently seasoned with toasty oak.

DRY $30 AV

Odyssey Marlborough Pinot Noir   (★★★)

The 2003 vintage (★★★) is a single-vineyard wine, grown in the Omaka Valley and matured in French oak barriques (60 per cent new). Full and youthful in colour, it offers plum and red-berry aromas and flavours in an attractively fresh and vibrantly fruity, but not intense, style.

Vintage	03	
WR	5	DRY $30 -V
Drink	04-08	

Old Coach Road Pinot Noir   (★★)

Grown in Nelson and aged for nine months in seasoned French oak casks, the 2003 vintage (★★) is a very light style, with green-edged, strawberry and spice flavours that lack richness and roundness.

Vintage	03	DRY $17 -V
WR	6	
Drink	04-07	

Old Weka Pass Road Canterbury Pinot Noir   (★★★★)

A North Canterbury wine of substance and personality, the 2001 vintage (★★★★) was grown in Marcel Giesen's and Sherwyn Veldhuizen's Bell Hill Vineyard at Waikari, in the Weka Pass. Matured in French oak barriques (44 per cent new), it is deeply coloured, weighty and concentrated, with a core of sweet, cherryish fruit, slight herbal touches and spicy, earthy, savoury complexities. A delicious, harmonious wine with substantial tannins beneath, it bodes well for the inaugural release under the top Bell Hill label from 2003.

Vintage	01	DRY $35 AV
WR	7	
Drink	04-09	

Olssen's Jackson Barry Pinot Noir   ★★★★

Named after the first mayor of Cromwell, this is the Bannockburn, Central Otago winery's 'mainstream' red; Slapjack Creek (below) is the reserve. The 2002 (★★★★☆) is enticingly fragrant, with concentrated cherry and spice flavours in a weighty, softly structured style, savoury and complex. Estate-grown in The Garden vineyard, picked at 24 to over 26 brix and matured in French oak barriques (35 per cent new), the 2003 vintage (★★★★) is fresh and floral, with ripe, sweet fruit characters and cherry/plum flavours in a vibrantly fruity, supple style with some savoury complexity. It's slightly less intense than the 2002, but delicious young.

Vintage	03	02	01	DRY $35 AV
WR	6	7	5	
Drink	05-10	04-10	04-08	

Olssen's Slapjack Creek Reserve Pinot Noir   ★★★★☆

The top label from the Bannockburn, Central Otago winery is 'made from a careful selection of barrels in those years when the wine is of distinctly superior quality'. The 2002 vintage (★★★★★) is boldly coloured, with lovely concentration and warmth, a firm foundation of tannin and a lasting finish. The 2003 (★★★★☆), matured in French oak barriques (50 per cent new), is nearly as good – densely packed, with substantial body and rich berry, plum, spice and liquorice flavours. A powerful and complex wine, it's still youthful; open mid-2005+.

Vintage	03	02	01	00	99	98	DRY $48 -V
WR	6	7	6	NM	6	5	
Drink	05-10	04-08	04-06	NM	04-05	P	

Omaka Springs Marlborough Pinot Noir   ★★★

French oak-aged for a year, the 2003 vintage (★★☆) is fairly developed for its age. A green-edged, plum and cherry-flavoured wine, it lacks real fruit sweetness and richness, with a spicy, firm finish.

DRY $20 AV

Omaka Springs Winemakers Selection Pinot Noir   (★★

The 2002 vintage (★★) is a ruby-hued Marlborough wine. Showing a lot of development for its age, it distinctly rustic, lacking ripeness and fragrance.

DRY $20 -V

Opihi Pinot Noir   ★★☆

Grown in South Canterbury, the 2002 vintage (★★) was low-cropped (2.4 tonnes/hectare), picked at 25 brix and matured for 13 months in French oak casks. Yet the wine is disappointing. Medium ruby, with some colour development showing, it has strongly leafy aromas in a vegetal, stalky style, full-bodied but rustic.

Vintage	02	01
WR	6	5
Drink	04-05	P

DRY $31 -V

Oyster Bay Marlborough Pinot Noir   ★★★★

Matured for 10 months in French oak barriques (25 per cent new), the 2002 vintage (★★★★) from Delegat's offers cherryish, sweet fruit flavours in a supple, elegant, richly varietal style. The 2003 (★★★☆) has fresh cherry and raspberry aromas leading into a supple, sweet-fruited wine, not highly concentrated but very charming and harmonious, with some savoury touches and gentle tannins.

Vintage	03	02	01
WR	6	7	7
Drink	04-05	04-05	04-06

DRY $30 AV

Palliser Estate Pinot Noir   ★★★★★

A richly perfumed, notably elegant and harmonious Martinborough red, concentrated, supple and attractively priced (reflecting its relatively large volume). Wood maturation is for a year in French oak barriques (25 per cent new). The 2001 vintage (★★★★★) is a generous wine (14 per cent alcohol), full-coloured and ripely fragrant, with sweet fruit delights, rich raspberry, plum and spice flavours, smoky oak adding complexity, firm underlying tannins and a lasting finish. The 2002 (★★★★) is medium-full ruby, with sweet, ripe-plum and cherry flavours and firm tannins. It's an impressively complex wine with savoury, spicy, nutty characters, but less lush and concentrated than most recent vintages, and more forward; drink now onwards.

Vintage	02	01	00	99	98	97	96	95	94
WR	5	7	7	7	7	7	7	5	5
Drink	04-06	04-08	04-07	04-06	04-05	04-05	P	P	P

DRY $38 V+

Palliser Pencarrow Martinborough Pinot Noir –
see Pencarrow Martinborough Pinot Noir

Pegasus Bay Pinot Noir   ★★★★★

This Waipara red is one of Canterbury's greatest Pinot Noirs, typically very rich in body and flavour. Matured in French oak barriques (30 per cent new), the 2002 (★★★★) is fragrant, mouthfilling and rich, but lacks the opulence of top years. A generous, supple wine with some muscle (14 per cent alcohol) and fresh plum, spice, herb and nut flavours, it's still developing; open mid-2005+.

Vintage	02	01	00	99
WR	6	7	5	7
Drink	04-10	04-10	04-05	04-08

DRY $43 V+

Pegasus Bay Prima Donna Pinot Noir   ★★★★★

For its reserve Waipara Pinot Noir, Pegasus Bay wants 'a heavenly voice, a shapely body and a velvety nose'. Harvested 'after an amazing Indian summer', the 2001 vintage (★★★★★) was matured for 18 months in Burgundy oak barriques (30 per cent new). Powerful and weighty, with rich colour, it is firm and highly concentrated, with bold, warm cherry, plum and spice flavours that build to a rich, tightly structured, lasting finish.

Vintage	01	00	99	98	97	96
WR	7	NM	6	7	NM	5
Drink	04-12	NM	04-10	04-10	NM	P

DRY $75 AV

Pencarrow Martinborough Pinot Noir   ★★★★

This is Palliser Estate's second-tier label, but in favourable vintages it's an impressive wine, better than some companies' top reds. The 2002 (★★★) has smooth cherry and spice flavours of greater depth than its lightish colour suggests, but is a relatively early-maturing vintage, for current consumption.

DRY $26 V+

Peregrine Central Otago Pinot Noir   ★★★★★

This consistently outstanding red is also a great buy. A deeply coloured, sophisticated wine with sweet fruit delights, the 2003 vintage (★★★★★) was grown in the Lowburn, Northburn and Bendigo districts (all in the Cromwell Basin), and French oak-matured for almost a year. Rich, charming and intensely varietal, it offers dense raspberry, plum and spice flavours, warm and complex, that build across the palate to a firm, harmonious finish.

Vintage	03	02
WR	6	7
Drink	04-08	04-08

DRY $35 V+

Peregrine Wentworth Pinot Noir   (★★★★☆)

Estate-grown in the Wentworth vineyard, at Gibbston, in Central Otago, the debut 2002 vintage (★★★★☆) was matured for 10 months in French oak barriques (30 per cent new). Boldly coloured, it's deliciously mouthfilling and supple, with concentrated plum, cherry and spice flavours, hints of coffee and herbs, firm tannins and a long, rich finish. In its infancy, it was more restrained than its lower-priced stablemate (above), but looked full of potential.

Vintage	02
WR	7
Drink	04-10

DRY $50 -V

Pisa Moorings Pinot Noir   ★★☆

Grown at Cromwell, in Central Otago, the 2002 vintage (★★★) is a fruity and supple red with raspberry/plum flavours showing moderate complexity. The 2003 (★★☆) is full ruby, with berry and plum flavours, fresh and light.

DRY $30 -V

Pisa Range Estate Black Poplar Block Pinot Noir   ★★★★

Grown at Pisa Flats, north of Cromwell, in Central Otago, this is an enticingly scented and supple wine. Retasted in mid-2004, the 2001 vintage (★★★★) is maturing into a very graceful, savoury, supple wine with excellent richness and harmony. The 2003 (★★★☆), matured for a year in French oak casks (one-third new), is full-coloured and perfumed, with substantial body (14.5 per cent alcohol) and good but not great depth of raspberry, cherry, spice and herb flavours, fresh, vibrant and well-rounded.

DRY $37 AV

Pond Paddock Martinborough Pinot Noir   (★★★☆)

The attractive 2003 vintage (★★★☆) was grown in Te Muna Road and matured in French oak casks (25 per cent new). Medium-full ruby, it is mouthfilling and vibrant, with sweet fruit characters and good depth of cherry, plum and spice flavours. It's a moderately complex style with balanced tannins and some aging potential.

Vintage	03
WR	5
Drink	04-07

DRY $28 AV

Porters Martinborough Pinot Noir   ★★★★

The 2003 vintage (★★★★) is an elegant, complex wine, French oak-aged for a year. Full ruby, it is mouthfilling, with ripe-fruit characters and spicy, plummy flavours seasoned with toasty oak. Firm, with good complexity, it needs time and is worth cellaring to 2006 onwards.

Vintage	03	02	01	00	99	98
WR	6	6	7	7	7	6
Drink	04+	04-06	04-07	04-06	P	P

DRY $39 AV

Pukawa Lake Taupo Pinot Noir   ★★★

Grown on the southern shores of the lake and French oak-matured for 10 months, the 2002 vintage (★★★☆) is full-coloured, with a spicy, almost peppery fragrance. Tightly structured, with strong cherry and spice flavours and nutty oak, it's a serious wine for cellaring. There's a slight lack of ripeness here, but it's a quality wine nevertheless.

DRY $30 ·V

Quartz Reef Bendigo Estate Vineyard Pinot Noir   ★★★★★

An emerging Central Otago star. Sold only in 1.5-litre magnums, the 2002 vintage (★★★★★) of Rudi Bauer's red was grown in the company's 'seriously warm' hillside vineyard at the north-east end of Lake Dunstan, at Bendigo Station. It's crammed with cherry and spice flavours in an opulent style with noticeably high alcohol and great length. The youthful 2003 (★★★★★) is muscular, with densely packed plum, cherry, spice and nut flavours seasoned with quality oak. An exceptionally powerful, ripe, complex and savoury wine with a firm foundation of tannin, it's best cellared to 2006 onwards. (The debut 2001 (★★★★), tasted in mid-late 2004, is finely scented and weighty, with very good ripeness and depth, but less concentrated than the later releases.)

Vintage	03	02
WR	6	7
Drink	06-09	05-08

DRY $150 (1.5L) AV

Quartz Reef Pinot Noir   ★★★★☆

A classy Central Otago red, always very graceful and complex. The 2003 vintage (★★★★) is youthful, full-coloured and sturdy (14.5 per cent alcohol), with a scented bouquet of spices and herbs. Generous and vibrantly fruity, it possesses rich, finely balanced plum and spice flavours, savoury, complex characters and smooth, ripe tannins. It's enjoyable now, but well worth cellaring.

Vintage	03	02	01	00	99	98
WR	6	7	6	6	7	6
Drink	05-08	04-09	04-06	04-07	04-07	04-05

DRY $42 AV

Rabbit Ranch Central Otago Pinot Noir   (★★★☆)

The 2003 vintage (★★★☆) from Chard Farm introduced a 'new breed of Pinot Noir from Central Otago – affordable, early-drinking, fruit-driven'. Grown in the Cromwell Basin, at Lowburn, and French oak-aged for 10 months, it's like a quality Beaujolais, with sweet fruit delights, fresh, vibrant plum/cherry flavours and gentle tannins. A skilfully made wine, fragrant and softly seductive, it's not hugely complex, but a delightful mouthful.

Vintage	03	DRY $24 V+
WR	6	
Drink	04-07	

Rimu Grove Nelson Pinot Noir   ★★★★

Estate-grown near Mapua, on the Nelson coast, this is a firm, characterful and concentrated wine, built to last. The sturdy, full-coloured 2003 vintage (★★★★) was harvested at 22.6 to 24.2 brix and matured for 10 months in French oak barriques (34 per cent new) A youthful red, it is mouthfilling, rich and ripe, with firm tannins, sweet fruit characters and strong raspberry, plum and spice flavours, with obvious aging potential.

DRY $38 AV

Rippon Pinot Noir   ★★★☆

A scented, vibrantly fruity Lake Wanaka, Central Otago red with plenty of body and smooth, cherryish flavours (leafy in cool seasons). The charming 2001 vintage (★★★★) is one of the best. Ruby-hued, it's a middleweight style but elegant, intensely varietal and supple, with cherry and spice flavours showing good complexity, gentle tannins and a finely balanced, lingering finish. The 2003 (★★★☆) is ruby-hued, with good but not great depth of spicy, nutty, slightly herbal flavour and some complexity.

Vintage	02	01	00	99	98	DRY $39 -V
WR	7	7	6	5	5	
Drink	04-08	04-07	04-06	P	P	

Riverby Estate Marlborough Pinot Noir   (★★★)

Deeply coloured, the 2001 vintage (★★★) has strong raspberry, dark cherry and plum flavours and a firm finish.

DRY $29 -V

Roaring Meg Pinot Noir   (★★★)

From Mt Difficulty, the 2003 vintage (★★★) was grown in Central Otago and oak-matured for nine months. It's a full-bodied, youthful wine with some fruit sweetness, decent depth of raspberry, herb and plum flavours and moderately firm tannins.

DRY $28 -V

Rockburn Central Otago Pinot Noir   ★★★★

The 2003 vintage (★★★★) is a blend of Lowburn, Cromwell Basin (79 per cent), Gibbston (15 per cent) and Lake Hayes (6 per cent) grapes, matured in French oak barriques (30 per cent new). Supple and mouthfilling (14.5 per cent alcohol), with full, ruby colour, it's a fragrant, richly varietal wine with gentle tannins and excellent depth of plum, spice, herb and nut flavours, showing considerable complexity.

DRY $35 AV

Rossendale Canterbury Pinot Noir   ★★☆

The 2002 vintage (★★☆) has slightly herbal aromas, light, plummy flavours and a slightly high-acid finish

DRY $20 -V

St Helena Canterbury Pinot Noir ★★☆

Robin Mundy's Belfast red set the Canterbury wine scene on fire with the 1982's gold medal success, but the wine now lacks its old notable power and flavour richness. French and American oak-aged, at its best it has cherryish, savoury, spicy, nutty characters and decent depth, but other years are smooth, strawberryish, green-edged and simple.

Vintage 02
WR   5
Drink 04-06

DRY $19 -V

St Helena Reserve Pinot Noir ★★★

The 2002 vintage (★★★) is labelled as being of South Island, rather than entirely Canterbury, origin. French oak-aged, it is lightish in colour, with spicy, slightly leafy flavours showing good depth. It's not especially ripe or concentrated, but offers some savoury complexity.

Vintage 02
WR   6
Drink 04-07

DRY $28 -V

Sacred Hill Central Otago Pinot Noir (★★★★)

Priced right, the 2003 vintage (★★★★) was grown in the Cromwell Basin and French oak-aged for eight months. It's a supple, sweet-fruited charmer with good body and strong cherry and spice flavours. Soft and long, it shows good persistence and personality, and can only get better during 2005–06.

Vintage 03
WR   7
Drink 04-06

DRY $30 V+

Saddleback Central Otago Pinot Noir (★★★☆)

From Peregrine, the debut 2003 vintage (★★★☆) is a great buy. Grown at Lowburn, in the Cromwell Basin, and Gibbston, and matured for 10 months in French oak barriques (10 per cent new), it has promisingly deep colour and very good body, flavour depth and roundness. Smooth and fruit-crammed, it's not highly complex but fresh and vibrant, with plenty of drink-young charm.

DRY $25 V+

Saint Clair Doctor's Creek Marlborough Pinot Noir ★★★☆

Grown mainly in the company's Doctors Creek vineyard in the Wairau Valley, the 2002 vintage (★★★★) was matured for 10 months in French oak casks. A tightly structured red with lovely colour and bright fruit characters, it has substantial body, with plum, cherry and spice flavours developing considerable complexity.

Vintage 02 01
WR   6   6
Drink 04-05 04-05

DRY $25 V+

Saint Clair Marlborough Pinot Noir (★★☆)

The light 2003 vintage (★★☆) was mostly handled in tanks, but 40 per cent of the blend was oak-aged for eight months. It's a green-edged wine with moderate depth of plum, raspberry and herb flavours.

Vintage 03
WR   6
Drink 04-06

DRY $20 -V

Saint Clair Omaka Reserve Marlborough Pinot Noir   ★★★★

The deeply coloured 2001 vintage (★★★★) was grown in the Omaka Valley, hand-picked and matured for 12 months in a mix of new French (35 per cent) and older American oak casks. It's a warm, generous wine with a strong bouquet of cherries and smoky bacon and plummy, spicy flavours, firm and youthful. The 2002 (★★★★) is full-coloured and firmly structured, with generous depth of ripe-fruit flavours and good, savoury complexity.

Vintage	02	01	00	DRY $30 AV
WR	6	6	6	
Drink	04-07	04-06	04-05	

Saint Clair Vicar's Choice Marlborough Pinot Noir   ★★☆

Designed as Saint Clair's 'entry level' Pinot Noir, the 2003 vintage (★★☆) was handled mostly in tanks, but 30 per cent of the blend spent eight months in French oak casks. An easy-drinking, middleweight style with berryish aromas, ripe berry/plum flavours and gentle tannins, it lacks richness, but is priced right.

Vintage	02	DRY $17 AV
WR	6	
Drink	04-05	

Schubert Marion's Vineyard Pinot Noir   ★★★

Schubert's lower-priced red is based on a selection of clones (mostly Abel and Pommard) designed to produce 'a more fruit-driven style with a softer tannin structure'. The 2003 vintage (★★★) was grown in the Wairarapa and matured for over a year in French oak barriques (50 per cent new). Full-bodied (14 per cent alcohol), with strawberry, spice and toast flavours showing a distinctly herbal edge, it's a substantial, supple wine, ready for drinking.

Vintage	02	DRY $30 -V
WR	5	
Drink	04-07	

Schubert Wairarapa Pinot Noir   ★★★☆

The 2003 vintage (★★★☆) was grown mostly at East Taratahi, near Masterton, and matured for over a year in French oak casks (75 per cent new). It shows some colour development, with strawberry, spice and herb aromas in a muscular (14.5 per cent alcohol), savoury, firm style with good complexity and harmony. Quite advanced for a 2003, it's drinking well already.

Vintage	02	01	DRY $45 -V
WR	6	6	
Drink	04-12	04-11	

Seifried Nelson Pinot Noir   ★★★

Traditionally a light style, but the latest releases are more generous. Matured for a year in new and one-year-old French oak barriques, the 2003 vintage (★★★) is a substantial wine (14 per cent alcohol) with firm tannins and ripe-fruit characters. Robust and spicy, it's a flavoursome wine, still unfolding.

Vintage	03	DRY $23 AV
WR	6	
Drink	04-08	

Seifried Winemakers Collection Pinot Noir ★★★★

The 2003 vintage (★★★★) was grown in Nelson, and matured for a year in new and three-year-old French oak casks. It's a bold (14.5 per cent alcohol), sweet-fruited wine with concentrated cherry, herb and nut flavours, considerable complexity and firm tannins. The 2002 (★★★★) also shows excellent depth and complexity, with plum, coffee, spice and nut flavours, rich and rounded.

Vintage	03
WR	6
Drink	04-07

DRY $35 AV

Selaks Founders Reserve Marlborough Pinot Noir (★★★☆)

Strongly wood-influenced, the 2002 vintage (★★★☆) is a single-vineyard red, harvested at over 24 brix and matured for 14 months in all-new French oak barriques. Ready now, it's warm, spicy and supple, with ripe-plum and spice flavours, gentle tannins and a smooth finish.

Vintage	02
WR	7
Drink	04-06

DRY $33 -V

Seresin Marlborough Pinot Noir ★★★★★

Top vintages are crammed with dark cherry, spice and nut flavours, very warm, complex and rich. Fermented with indigenous yeasts, matured for 15 months in French oak barriques and bottled unfiltered, the 2002 (★★★★★) is deeply coloured and impressively concentrated, with cherry, raspberry and spice flavours and finely integrated oak. Still youthful, it's a firmly structured wine showing excellent complexity, but needs more time; open 2006+.

Vintage	02	01	00	99	98
WR	6	6	6	6	6
Drink	04-11	04-10	04-09	04-08	04-07

DRY $38 V+

Shepherds Ridge Marlborough Pinot Noir (★★★☆)

From Wither Hills, the debut 2002 vintage (★★★☆) was harvested at 25 brix and matured for a year in French oak casks. Ruby-hued, with a smoky, spicy bouquet, it shows greater complexity than many $30 Pinot Noirs, with firm tannins and satisfying depth of cherry, plum and herb flavours, slightly nutty and savoury. Good drinking now onwards.

Vintage	03
WR	7
Drink	05-09

DRY $30 AV

Sherwood Estate Marlborough Pinot Noir (★★)

The 2003 vintage (★★), oak-aged for three months, has light, slightly developed colour and simple, berryish, green-edged flavours.

DRY $19 -V

Shingle Peak Marlborough Pinot Noir ★★★

The 2003 vintage (★★★) from Matua Valley was matured for 10 months in French oak casks (20 per cent new). Strawberry and spice aromas lead into a middleweight wine, fresh, lively and supple, with a gentle seasoning of toasty oak and plenty of drink-young charm.

Vintage	03	02	01	00
WR	5	6	5	5
Drink	04-06	04-06	P	P

DRY $19 AV

Sileni Cellar Selection Hawke's Bay Pinot Noir ★★☆

The 2003 vintage (★★☆) is a Beaujolais-style red, light in colour, flavour and body. French oak-aged for nine months, it is lean (only 11 per cent alcohol), with uncomplicated raspberry and plum, slightly spicy flavours that lack real warmth and intensity, but offer pleasant, early drinking.

Vintage	03	02
WR	5	5
Drink	04-07	04-07

DRY $25 -V

Sleeping Dogs Pinot Noir ★★★☆

Grown on the slopes of Mount Rosa, in the Gibbston district, the 2002 vintage (★★★☆) of Roger Donaldson's Central Otago red is rich in colour, with fresh, strong plum and spice flavours. An exuberantly fruity, moderately complex wine with firm tannins, it's worth cellaring. The 2003 (★★★) is mouthfilling and full-coloured, with some complexity and depth of plum and herb flavours.

DRY $30 AV

Solstone Wairarapa Pinot Noir ★★★

Grown at Masterton, the 2001 (★★★) is a middleweight style, ruby-hued, with strawberry and spice flavours, some savoury complexity and a fresh, crisp finish. The 2002 (★★☆), matured for a year in French oak casks (50 per cent new), has light, slightly developed colour and green-edged flavours that lack real ripeness and stuffing.

Vintage	03	02	01
WR	5	6	4
Drink	05-11	05-10	05-06

DRY $32 -V

Spencer Hill Coastal Ridge Nelson Pinot Noir (★★★)

Grown a few kilometres north of Nelson city, on a ridge overlooking Tasman Bay, the 2003 vintage (★★★) was fermented with indigenous yeasts and matured in contact with French oak in small tanks (rather than barrel-aged). Ruby-hued, with leafy aromas, it's a medium-bodied wine with smooth cherry, raspberry and herb flavours and gentle tannins in a moderately complex, forward style. Overpriced.

Vintage	03
WR	6
Drink	04-10

DRY $39 -V

Springvale Estate Pinot Noir ★★★☆

The 2002 vintage (★★★★) is a youthful, ruby-hued Alexandra, Central Otago red with earthy, herbal, forest-floor notes on the nose. It's a middleweight style, savoury and warm, with oak complexity, firm tannins and good length.

DRY $34 -V

Spy Valley Marlborough Pinot Noir ★★★☆

Grown in the Waihopai Valley, the full-bodied 2002 vintage (★★★★) was matured for a year in French oak barriques (30 per cent new). Full-flavoured and warm, with firm tannins, it has ripe, sweet fruit characters of plums and spice, showing some bottle-aged complexity.

Vintage	03	02	01	00
WR	7	6	6	6
Drink	04-08	04-07	04-06	04-05

DRY $29 AV

Squawking Magpie The Mudlark
Martinborough Pinot Noir   (★★☆)

Described as a 'notably bold style', the 2002 vintage (★★☆) is a single-vineyard red, French oak-aged. Lightish in colour, with mellow, cherryish flavours and a hint of herbs, it's a forward style with moderate depth.

DRY $27 -V

Staete Landt Marlborough Pinot Noir   ★★★☆

In the graceful mould of Volnay or Santenay, the single-vineyard 2002 vintage (★★★☆) was harvested at 24 to 25 brix and matured in French oak barriques (25 per cent new). Only moderately concentrated but very charming, it displays ripe cherry and raspberry flavours mingled with spicy oak and a well-rounded finish. Drink 2004–05.

Vintage	02
WR	6
Drink	04-06

DRY $36 -V

Stonecutter Martinborough Pinot Noir   ★★★

The 2003 vintage (★★★), French oak-aged for 10 months, is a middleweight style with firm plum, spice and herb flavours, fresh, slightly savoury and youthful. It shows a slight lack of flesh and ripeness, but some potential; open mid-2005+.

DRY $33 -V

Stoneleigh Marlborough Pinot Noir   ★★★☆

Gone are the days when you couldn't buy a decent Pinot Noir for under $20. The 2002 vintage (★★★☆) from Allied Domecq was grown at Rapaura, harvested at 23 to 24 brix, and matured for 10 months in French oak casks (30 per cent new). Deep ruby, with a smoky, toasty bouquet, it is warm, spicy and flavoursome, with fairly firm tannins. The 2003 (★★★) is ruby-hued and floral, with plum, herb and raspberry flavours, a touch of toasty oak and gentle tannins.

Vintage	02	01	00	99	98	97
WR	6	6	7	6	5	4
Drink	04-10	04+	03+	P	P	P

DRY $18 V+

Stoneleigh Vineyards Rapaura Series
Marlborough Pinot Noir   ★★★★

The fine-value 2002 vintage (★★★★) from Allied Domecq was hand-picked at 23.5 to 24.5 brix and matured for 10 months in French oak barriques (30 per cent new). Full ruby, with strong fruit flavours of cherry and spice, it shows good fruit sweetness, depth and complexity, and should mature well. The 2003 (★★★☆) is full ruby, with fresh, ripe-plum, cherry and spice flavours, slightly nutty, savoury and supple, but less concentrated than the 2002.

Vintage	02	01	00
WR	6	7	7
Drink	04-10	04+	P

DRY $27 V+

Stratford Martinborough Pinot Noir   ★★★★

The 2003 vintage (★★★★☆) is full-coloured, with a spicy bouquet. Sturdy and youthful, it is tight, vibrantly fruity and concentrated, with dense cherry, plum and roasted nut flavours and a firm framework of tannin. It's built for cellaring; open 2006+.

Vintage	03	02	01	00	99	98	97
WR	6	5	6	6	7	6	5
Drink	05-10	04-10	04-07	04-06	04-06	04-05	P

DRY $40 AV

Strugglers Flat Martinborough Pinot Noir   (★★★★)

From Capricorn Estates, a division of Craggy Range, the 2002 vintage (★★★★) is a cherryish, plummy, nutty red with impressive colour, body and complexity. Richly flavoured, it shows a strong oak influence, with savoury, spicy characters adding interest. Fine value.

DRY $25 V+

Sunset Valley Vineyard Nelson Pinot Noir   ★★★

Grown organically, the 2003 vintage (★★★) is full-coloured and mouthfilling, with firm, plummy, spicy flavours, moderately complex. It shows some density and aging potential, but only moderate varietal character.

DRY $24 AV

Sunset Valley Vineyard Reserve Pinot Noir   ★★★

Grown organically in the Upper Moutere hills, the 2003 vintage (★★☆) was matured in new oak casks for a year. It's a light ruby, firmly structured but slightly rustic wine, lacking real fragrance and complexity.

Vintage	02
WR	6
Drink	04+

DRY $28 -V

Tasman Bay Nelson Pinot Noir   ★★☆

The 2002 vintage (★★☆) is a ruby-hued, medium-bodied wine with strawberryish, green-edged flavours and a slightly crisp finish. It's a drink-young style, lacking any real complexity.

DRY $20 -V

Tasman Bay Vintage Special Selection Pinot Noir   (★★☆)

Designed as a 'soft, fruit-driven' style, the 2002 vintage (★★☆) is a blend of grapes from five regions – Hawke's Bay, Martinborough, Nelson, Marlborough and Canterbury. Ruby-hued, with strawberry and spice flavours, it's an easy-drinking, light to medium-bodied wine, quite developed for its age, with some savoury characters and gentle tannins. Drink now.

DRY $19 -V

Te Hera Estate Martinborough Pinot Noir   ★★★

First planted in 1996, Te Hera ('The Sail') Estate was the first commercial vineyard founded in the Te Muna Road district, a few kilometres south of Martinborough. The 2003 vintage (★★★☆) has deep, youthful colour and strong plum/cherry flavours, delicately seasoned with toasty oak. Vibrantly fruity and supple, it shows some elegance and potential; open 2006+.

DRY $29 -V

Te Kairanga Martinborough Pinot Noir   ★★★☆

This Martinborough red is a consistently attractive drink-young style. Picked at an average of 24 brix and matured for 10 months in French oak barriques (20 per cent new), the 2002 (★★★☆) is medium ruby, with cherry and spice flavours and gentle tannins. It shows good but not great flavour depth, with some complexity. There is no 2003.

Vintage	03	02	01	00	99	98
WR	NM	7	7	7	7	7
Drink	NM	04-07	04-06	04-05	04-05	P

DRY $35 -V

Te Kairanga Reserve Pinot Noir ★★★★

Based on a vineyard selection by 'vine age and specific flavours', this is typically a bold style of Martinborough red. The 2003 vintage (★★★★), harvested at 24 brix and matured for 10 months in French oak barriques (20 per cent new), is deeply coloured, with rich plum, spice and herb flavours, nutty and savoury, some funky, earthy elements and firm tannins beneath. Mouthfilling but less strapping than in some past years, it shows obvious aging potential; open 2006.

Vintage	03	02	01	00	99	98
WR	7	NM	7	7	6	6
Drink	04-10	NM	04-08	04-06	04-06	04-05

DRY $55 -V

Te Mania Nelson Pinot Noir ★★★☆

From a small winery on the Waimea Plains, this wine offers good value. The 2003 vintage (★★★), French oak-aged, is a full-coloured wine with strong raspberry, spice and herb flavours, firm and youthful.

Vintage	03	02	01	00	99	98
WR	6	6	6	5	6	5
Drink	04-07	04-06	04-05	P	P	P

DRY $20 V+

Te Mania Reserve Pinot Noir ★★★☆

The 2002 vintage (★★★☆) is a scented, youthful Nelson red with lively plum, spice and herb flavours. Matured for 10 months in French oak casks (40 per cent new), the 2003 (★★★) is a ruby-hued, supple wine with moderately complex cherry/plum flavours and a smooth finish.

Vintage	03	02	01
WR	6	6	7
Drink	05-08	04-07	04-06

DRY $30 AV

Terrace Heights Estate Marlborough Pinot Noir (★★★★)

The densely coloured, fruit-packed 2003 vintage (★★★★) is a single-vineyard wine, French oak-aged for 11 months. It's a bold, supple wine with fresh, strong cherry, plum and spice flavours, subtle oak and considerable power and length.

Vintage	03
WR	6
Drink	04-07

DRY $27 V+

Terrace Road Marlborough Pinot Noir ★★★

Past vintages were plain, but Cellier Le Brun's red took a giant step forward in 2002 (★★★★), offering outstanding value. The less impressive 2003 (★★☆) has strawberry and spice aromas and flavours in a fruity, gently oaked style that lacks real warmth, richness and roundness.

DRY $20 AV

Terravin Marlborough Pinot Noir ★★★★

Grown on the slopes of the upper Omaka Valley, the 2002 vintage (★★★★) is a supple, vibrant red with a beguiling fragrance and excellent depth of plum, spice and red-berry flavours. It's an elegant wine with mouthfilling body, ripe-fruit characters and a well-rounded finish. The 2003 (★★★★) is less fragrant, but more concentrated and spicy, than the 2002, with rich colour and flavour.

DRY $38 AV

Thornbury Marlborough Pinot Noir   ★★★

The mouthfilling, fruit-crammed 2001 (★★★☆), made from young vines at Rapaura and oak-aged for a year, is a moderately complex wine with subtle oak, fairly firm tannins and strong, vibrant cherry/plum flavours. The 2002 vintage (★★☆) is disappointing. Deeply coloured, it's a gutsy, powerful wine, but slightly rustic, with hard tannins, and lacks charm and finesse.

Vintage	03	02	01	DRY $28 -V
WR	6	4	6	
Drink	05-09	04-07	04-07	

Three Miners Pinot Noir   (★★★)

A promising debut, the 2003 vintage (★★★) was grown in the Earnscleugh Valley of Central Otago. Bright, medium ruby, with red-berry and herb aromas, it's not a concentrated wine but offers plum and herb flavours, showing some warmth and complexity, and a well-rounded finish. Drink 2005.

DRY $28 -V

Tohu Marlborough Pinot Noir   ★★★☆

Hand-picked and French oak-matured, the 2003 vintage (★★★) is a finely balanced wine, not concentrated but enjoyable. Ruby-hued, with plum, berry, herb and spice flavours gently seasoned with toasty oak, it's a moderately complex red, for drinking now or short-term cellaring.

Vintage	03	02	DRY $25 AV
WR	5	4	
Drink	04-07	04-05	

Torlesse Canterbury Pinot Noir   ★★☆

Grown in Waipara and other parts of Canterbury, the 2003 vintage (★★☆) is a drink-young style with berryish, leafy flavours, light, green-edged and crisp.

Vintage	02	DRY $20 -V
WR	7	
Drink	03-06	

Torlesse Waipara Pinot Noir   ★★★☆

The 2002 vintage (★★★) of this North Canterbury red, matured in French oak barriques for a year, is an enjoyable, clearly varietal wine with berry, plum and herb flavours showing solid but not great depth.

Vintage	01	DRY $29 AV
WR	7	
Drink	04-06	

Trinity Hill Hawke's Bay Pinot Noir   (★★★)

Priced right, the 2002 vintage (★★★) is an attractive drink-young style. Grown at two sites, at Te Awanga and in the hill country south of the Heretaunga Plains, it was matured for eight months in one-year-old French oak casks and bottled without filtration. Ruby-hued, with clearly varietal, strawberry and spice aromas and flavours, it's not highly concentrated but warm, spicy and savoury, with a rounded finish.

Vintage	04	03	02	01	DRY $20 AV
WR	5	4	6	4	
Drink	05-08	04-06	04-05	04-05	

Trinity Hill High Country Pinot Noir ★★★★

Grown at three vineyards (on Oban, Glencoe and Mangaorapa stations) in the relatively cool hills south of the Heretaunga Plains, the 2003 vintage (★★★★) was matured for 10 months in new French oak barriques, and bottled unfined and lightly filtered. A mouthfilling, generous red with a fragrant, toasty bouquet, it's still very youthful, but shows elegant, sweet fruit characters seasoned with new oak, a firm foundation of tannin and good, gamey complexity.

Vintage	04	03	02
WR	5	4	6
Drink	05-08	04-07	04-06

DRY $40 AV

Twin Islands Marlborough Pinot Noir ★★★

Negociants' red offers solid value in an easy-drinking style. The gently oaked 2003 vintage (★★☆) is light ruby, with decent depth of strawberryish, slightly herbal flavours and a fresh, crisp finish, but less ripe and complex than the 2002 (★★★).

Vintage	03	02	01	00
WR	6	7	6	6
Drink	04-06	04-05	P	P

DRY $20 AV

Two Paddocks First Paddock Pinot Noir (★★★)

Grown in Sam Neill's original Central Otago vineyard, planted in the Gibbston Back Road in 1993, the 2003 vintage (★★★) was matured in French oak barriques (30 per cent new). It's a moderately ripe but full-flavoured wine with a strong herbal influence and earthy, spicy, savoury complexities.

Vintage	03	02
WR	6	6
Drink	04-07	04-07

DRY $37 -V

Two Paddocks Last Chance Pinot Noir (★★★)

This Central Otago red is grown in Sam Neill's second vineyard, established at Earnscleugh, near Alexandra. Matured in French oak barriques (20 per cent new), the 2003 vintage (★★★) is flavoursome, berryish and plummy, with a distinctly herbal streak and moderate complexity.

Vintage	03	02
WR	6	6
Drink	05-09	04-09

DRY $37 -V

Valli Bannockburn Vineyard Pinot Noir ★★★★☆

The power-packed 2002 vintage (★★★★★) is deeply coloured and sturdy, bold and ripe, with a rich array of cherry, spice and nut flavours and a lasting finish. French oak-aged for a year, the lighter but still full-bodied 2003 (★★★★) is a scented and stylish Central Otago wine, highly attractive in its youth, with very good depth of ripe-cherry, herb and spice flavours, nutty oak and moderately firm tannins. It should age well; open 2006+.

Vintage	03	02
WR	7	6
Drink	06-12	04-10

DRY $45 AV

Valli Gibbston Vineyard Pinot Noir   ★★★★★

The youthful, finely scented 2002 vintage (★★★★★) is dark, rich and complex, with an abundance of sweet, ripe-cherry, plum and spice flavours and firm tannins. The 2003 (★★★★★), French oak-aged for a year, is a generous, ruby-hued Central Otago red with rich, sweet fruit characters and aromas of wild herbs. It has strong plum/spice flavours, savoury and complex, with silky tannins giving excellent texture and a lasting finish.

Vintage	03	02		
WR	7	7		
Drink	05-10	04-10		

DRY $45 AV

Vavasour Marlborough Pinot Noir   ★★★☆

The 2002 vintage (★★★☆) is a blend of Wairau Valley (57 per cent) and Awatere Valley (43 per cent) grapes, matured for nine months in French oak casks (35 per cent new). Harvested at 24 to 25 brix, it is full and fresh, with smoky, toasty aromas and strong raspberry, cherry and spice flavours. Showing finely balanced tannins and good complexity, it's worth cellaring for a year or two.

Vintage	02	01	00	99
WR	7	7	6	6
Drink	04-07	P	P	P

DRY $30 AV

Vidal Estate Hawke's Bay Pinot Noir   (★★★★)

Robust (14.5 per cent alcohol), with excellent flavour depth, the 2002 vintage (★★★★) was matured for 10 months in French oak casks. Dark and concentrated, with cherry and spice characters, it is warm and savoury, with good complexity and moderately firm tannins. A good buy.

Vintage	03	02	01	
WR	NM	6	NM	
Drink	NM	04-06	NM	

DRY $25 V+

Vidal Estate Marlborough Pinot Noir   ★★★★

A consistently good buy. Harvested from four-year-old vines in the Awatere Valley and French oak-matured for nine months, the 2003 vintage (★★★★) has generous, youthful colour and a fragrant bouquet. Sturdy and supple, with rich, ripe flavours of plums and cherries, seasoned with toasty oak, it should age well; open mid-2005 onwards.

Vintage	03	02	01	00	99
WR	6	6	6	6	5
Drink	05-07	04-06	04-05	P	P

DRY $25 V+

Vidal Estate Stopbank Pinot Noir   (★★★★☆)

Richly coloured and highly fragrant, the 2002 vintage (★★★★☆) was grown in the Keltern Vineyard in Hawke's Bay. It's a mouthfilling wine with lovely softness through the palate, warm, ripe-cherry and spice flavours and savoury, slightly earthy and chocolatey characters adding complexity.

Vintage	03	02		
WR	NM	7		
Drink	NM	04-07		

DRY $30 V+

Villa Maria Cellar Selection Marlborough Pinot Noir   ★★★★

At just under $30, this consistently attractive wine is a match for many much higher priced Pinot Noirs. The 2003 vintage (★★★★☆) was grown in the Awatere and Wairau valleys and matured for nine months in French oak casks (60 per cent new). Fragrant, full-bodied and finely balanced, with cellaring potential, it's a youthful, concentrated wine with rich colour, ripe, sweet fruit characters and fresh, strong cherry, plum and spice flavours.

Vintage	03	02	01	00	99
WR	6	7	6	7	5
Drink	04-07	04-07	04-06	04-06	P

`DRY $30 V+`

Villa Maria Private Bin Marlborough Pinot Noir   (★★★)

Full-bodied, flavoursome and supple, the debut 2003 vintage (★★★) was grown in the Wairau and Awetere valleys, hand-picked and matured for 10 months in French oak barriques. Ruby-hued, cherryish, plummy and spicy, with fresh acidity on the finish, it's a good but not great Pinot Noir, priced right.

Vintage	03
WR	6
Drink	04-07

`DRY $22 AV`

Villa Maria Reserve Marlborough Pinot Noir   ★★★★★

Launched from 2000, this label has swiftly won recognition as one of the region's boldest, lushest reds. The 2002 vintage (★★★★★) is richly coloured and highly fragrant. Substantial, with lovely, sweet fruit characters and complex cherry and spice flavours, it shows greater finesse than the super-charged (15 per cent alcohol) 2001 (★★★★☆). Matured for 11 months in French oak barriques (40 per cent), the 2003 vintage (★★★★★) is again a powerful style, nutty, savoury and complex. Richly coloured and intensely varietal, it offers vivid plum, cherry and spice flavours, bold and youthful.

Vintage	03	02	01	00
WR	7	7	6	7
Drink	05-10	04-09	04-06	04-06

`DRY $50 AV`

Villa Maria Single Vineyard Seddon Pinot Noir   (★★★★☆)

The densely coloured 2002 vintage (★★★★☆) was grown in the Awatere Valley and matured for nine months in French oak barriques (60 per cent new). Supple and crammed with plum, spice and herb flavours, it's a generous, complex and voluptuous Marlborough wine that flows across the palate to a rich, silky-smooth finish.

Vintage	02
WR	7
Drink	04-08

`DRY $55 -V`

Villa Maria Single Vineyard Taylors Pass Pinot Noir   (★★★★)

The 2003 vintage (★★★★) was grown in Marlborough's Awatere Valley and matured for 11 months in French oak barriques. Deeply coloured, it's a powerful wine with bold plum, berry and herb flavours, concentrated and youthful, and firm tannins.

Vintage	03
WR	7
Drink	05-10

`DRY $55 -V`

Voss Estate Pinot Noir   ★★★★

Voss is a small Martinborough winery with a big, instantly likeable, reasonably priced Pinot Noir. The 2003 vintage (★★★★) was matured for a year in French oak barriques (30 per cent new – a stronger new oak influence than usual). It's a graceful wine with an array of plum, cherry, herb and spice flavours, ripe and rich, a silky elegance and attractively scented bouquet.

Vintage	03	02	01	00	99	98	97	96	DRY $34 AV
WR	7	5	6	6	7	7	6	6	
Drink	06-09	04-06	04-06	04-05	P	P	P	P	

Vynfields Martinborough Pinot Noir   ★★★

Mouthfilling, plummy, spicy and slightly herbal, the 2003 vintage (★★★) is a powerful, full-bodied wine with some savoury complexity and a soft finish.

Vintage	03	02	DRY $39 ·V
WR	6	5	
Drink	04-08	04-06	

Waimea Estates Bolitho Reserve Pinot Noir   ★★★☆

Fragrant and rich, the 2001 (★★★★) is a powerful wine, bold, spicy, complex and firm. The 2002 vintage (★★☆), grown at Tasman and Lower Moutere, was low-cropped (below 5 tonnes/hectare), picked at 25 brix and matured in French oak barriques (50 per cent new). It's a strapping (14.5 per cent alcohol), tannic, raisiny, spicy wine, but rustic, lacking the fruit intensity, fragrance and finesse of the 2002.

Vintage	02	01	DRY $35 ·V
WR	5	6	
Drink	05-06	04-06	

Waimea Estates Nelson Pinot Noir   ★★★☆

The 2003 vintage (★★★★) is a great buy. Grown at four sites on the Waimea Plains and in the Moutere hills, picked at an average of 24.7 brix and matured in French and American oak casks (old and new), it is fragrant and full-flavoured, plummy, spicy and nutty. Exuberantly fruity, rich and substantial (14 per cent alcohol), it has a solid foundation of tannin and impressive complexity.

Vintage	03	02	01	00	99	DRY $24 V+
WR	7	6	5	4	4	
Drink	06-09	05-07	04-05	P	P	

Waipara Downs Pinot Noir   ★★★

The latest vintages of this North Canterbury red are the best. Matured in French oak barriques (25 per cent new), the 2002 vintage (★★★) has a floral, berryish bouquet, leading into a fresh, vibrantly fruity palate with raspberry and plum flavours and moderately firm tannins. Priced right.

DRY $19 AV

Waipara Hills Canterbury/Marlborough Pinot Noir   (★★☆)

French oak-matured for six months, the 2003 vintage (★★☆) is a middleweight style that slightly lacks fruit sweetness, but offers decent depth of spicy, slightly herbal and toasty flavour.

Vintage	03	DRY $21 ·V
WR	5	
Drink	04-05	

Waipara Hills
Marlborough Simmonds Vineyard Pinot Noir   ★★★★

The 2003 vintage (★★★★) is a single-vineyard, Wairau Valley wine, matured for a year in all-new French oak casks. It's a powerful, concentrated, muscular red, richly coloured, with very ripe, sweet fruit characters and bold plum, spice and slight liquorice flavours. Vibrantly fruity, with noticeably high alcohol (15.5 per cent), it's a firmly structured wine, best cellared to 2006+.

Vintage	02
WR	7
Drink	04-14

DRY $50 -V

Waipara Springs Pinot Noir   ★★★☆

Grown at Waipara and matured for nine months in French oak barrels, the 2003 vintage (★★★) is an easy-drinking, silky-smooth wine in a moderately ripe, middleweight style with delicate plum, spice and herb flavours.

Vintage	03	02	01
WR	7	6	7
Drink	04-07	04-05	04-06

DRY $25 AV

Waipara Springs Reserve Pinot Noir   ★★★★

Made from mature Waipara vines, the 2002 vintage (★★★★) is a concentrated, complex red with good colour and a welcoming, spicy, toasty bouquet. Finely balanced, with good aging potential, it possesses rich, ripe-plum, red-berry and spice flavours, seasoned with quality French oak (20 per cent new).

Vintage	02	01
WR	6	6
Drink	04-05	04-06

DRY $38 AV

Waipara West Pinot Noir   ★★★★

This small-volume red is mostly shipped to the UK. The ruby-hued, floral 2003 vintage (★★★☆), matured for 10 months in French oak barriques (30 per cent new), has moderately concentrated, sweet fruit characters and ripe-plum/spice flavours, seasoned with toasty oak. A pretty, finely crafted wine with rounded tannins, good texture and considerable complexity, it's worth cellaring to 2005–06. Verging on four stars.

Vintage	03
WR	6
Drink	06-07

DRY $39 AV

Waipipi Reserve Basket Press Pinot Noir   (★★☆)

Grown at Opaki, near Masterton, in the Wairarapa, and French oak-aged, the 2002 vintage (★★☆) is a berryish, plummy wine, still youthful in colour, with fresh acidity and a Beaujolais-like simplicity.

DRY $32 -V

Waitiri Creek Pinot Noir   ★★★

This red typically shows the herbal character of Pinot Noirs from Gibbston, one of the cooler sub-regions of Central Otago. Matured in French oak barriques (20 per cent new), the 2003 vintage (★★★) is full-coloured, with plum, raspberry and herb flavours showing decent depth and firm tannins. Open mid-2005+.

DRY $35 -V

Waiwera Estate Pinot Noir   ★★★☆

The 2001 vintage (★★★★) is a generous Nelson wine with concentrated plum/spice flavours, oak complexity and loads of character. The 2002 (★★★), grown at Tasman Bay and Golden Bay, and matured for 15 months in French oak barriques (new and two-year-old), has good colour and depth. Full-coloured, it's a warm, generous wine with plummy, spicy flavours but slightly grippy, tough tannins.

DRY $26 AV

Walnut Ridge Pinot Noir   ★★★☆

Ata Rangi's second label, designed to be 'soft and approachable, even when young' is a blend of fruit from several Martinborough sites, including the award-winning Walnut Ridge vineyard and younger blocks. Matured in French oak barriques (25 per cent new), the 2003 vintage (★★★☆) is deeply coloured, with loads of plum, slightly herbal, spicy, nutty flavours, smooth and generous.

Vintage	03
WR	6
Drink	04-06

DRY $26 AV

Whitehaven Pinot Noir   ★★★

French oak-aged, the 2002 vintage (★★★) is ruby-hued, with plummy, slightly herbal flavours showing some charm and depth.

Vintage	02
WR	5
Drink	04-05

DRY $28 -V

William Hill Pinot Noir   ★★★

The 2003 vintage (★★★★) from this Central Otago winery is the best yet. Estate-grown at Alexandra and French oak-matured for 11 months, it's a deep ruby, fleshy wine (14 per cent alcohol), with ripe, sweet fruit characters, strong, vibrant plum, cherry and toasty oak flavours and firm tannins. It should age well for several years.

Vintage	03	02	01	00	99
WR	6	6	5	6	5
Drink	04-08	04-07	04-07	04-06	04-06

DRY $35 -V

William Hill Reserve Pinot Noir   ★★★

The reserve red from William Hill is not necessarily better than the cheaper label (above). Estate-grown at Alexandra and French oak-aged for 11 months, the 2002 vintage (★★☆) is a slightly confectionery wine with advanced colour and simple raspberry/plum flavours. The 2003 (★★★) shows some development, with concentrated plum, cherry, spice and herb flavours seasoned with nutty oak.

Vintage	03	02
WR	7	6
Drink	05-11	04-10

DRY $46 -V

William Hill Shaky Bridge Pinot Noir   (★★★★)

The 2003 vintage (★★★★) is a full ruby, slightly herbal Central Otago wine from Alexandra, French oak-aged for 11 months. It's a generous, complex wine showing cherry and plum flavours with very good depth and a firm finish.

Vintage	03
WR	6
Drink	04-10

DRY $39 AV

Winslow Colton Reserve Pinot Noir   ★★☆

The 2003 vintage (★★☆) of this Martinborough red was French oak-matured for 11 months. Light in colour, with some development showing, it's a lean, slightly hard wine, lacking real freshness and delicacy.

DRY $32 -V

Wishart Basket Press Pinot Noir   (★★★)

The fresh, supple 2002 vintage (★★★) was grown in Hawke's Bay, harvested at 23 brix and matured for eight months in seasoned French oak casks. It's a full-bodied wine with good varietal character and depth of raspberry, plum and spice flavours in a slightly earthy, moderately complex style.

DRY $25 -V

Wishart Reserve Pinot Noir   (★★★)

The warm, spicy 2001 vintage (★★★☆) was grown at Bay View, on the Hawke's Bay coast, and matured for 18 months in French oak casks. It is sturdy and supple, with good intensity of cherryish, plummy, slightly earthy flavours, savoury and nutty, but now slightly past its best.

DRY $39 -V

Wither Hills Marlborough Pinot Noir   ★★★★★

One of the region's most multi-faceted reds, this is now the star of the Wither Hills range. The 2003 vintage (★★★★★), French oak-aged for 14 months, is deeply coloured and perfumed, with lovely fruit sweetness, concentration and body (14 per cent alcohol). Already delicious, it offers ripe-raspberry, spice and nut flavours, savoury, complex and firm.

Vintage	03	02	01	00	99	98	97
WR	7	7	7	7	7	7	6
Drink	05-11	04-07	04-07	04-06	04-05	P	P

DRY $47 AV

Woollaston Estates Nelson Pinot Noir   (★★★★)

The bold, chewy 2002 vintage (★★★★) was based on extremely low-yielding vines (below 2.5 tonnes/hectare) and matured for 10 months in French oak barriques. Deeply coloured, it's a powerful wine with very ripe, almost Syrah-like flavours of raspberry and spice. It needs cellaring and could be very long-lived.

DRY $29 V+

Sangiovese

Sangiovese is Italy's most extensively planted red-wine variety, but a rarity in New Zealand. Cultivated as a workhorse grape throughout central Italy, in Tuscany it is the foundation of such famous reds as Chianti and Brunello di Montalcino. Here, Sangiovese is sometimes confused with Montepulciano, and the 5 hectares of bearing vines in 2003 are only projected to expand to 6 hectares by 2006.

Black Barn Sangiovese/Cabernet   (★★★)

The skilfully made 2002 vintage (★★★) is a Hawke's Bay blend of Sangiovese (78 per cent) and Cabernet Sauvignon (22 per cent). It's a full-coloured wine with satisfying depth of blackcurrant and spice flavours and oak complexity, but a slightly high-acid finish.

DRY $29 -V

Heron's Flight Matakana Sangiovese   ★★★★

North of Auckland, David Hoskins and Mary Evans have staked their future on Sangiovese. The 2002 vintage (★★★★), matured for a year in new French oak barriques, has deep, purple-flushed colour and spicy, new oak aromas. A powerful wine (13.5 per cent alcohol), fresh, vibrant, plummy, spicy, firm and high-flavoured, it should be long-lived. In terms of varietal character, it doesn't remind me of Italian Sangiovese, but judged simply as a red wine, shows impressive power and concentration.

DRY $50 -V

Matariki Sangiovese   (★★★☆)

The promising 2001 vintage (★★★☆) was picked at 24 brix in the Gimblett Gravels district of Hawke's Bay, blended with 16 per cent Cabernet Sauvignon and 2 per cent Merlot, and matured for 21 months in one-year-old French oak casks. It tastes like Sangiovese, with fresh, vibrant cherry, plum and spice flavours and a crisp but not over-acid finish. Deeply coloured and mouthfilling, with well-integrated oak, it's an attractive wine, drinking well now.

Vintage	01
WR	5
Drink	04-08

DRY $40 -V

Vin Alto Sangiovese   (★★☆)

Grown at Clevedon, in South Auckland, and oak-matured for two years, the 1999 vintage (★★☆) has fullish colour, showing some development. It's a firmly structured wine with cherry, raspberry and spice flavours and oak complexity, but lacks real ripeness and roundness.

Vintage	99
WR	4
Drink	06

DRY $28 -V

Syrah (Shiraz)

Suddenly, Hawke's Bay has a hot new red-wine variety. At the Tri Nations Wine Challenge, a taste-off between the best of Australia, New Zealand and South Africa, staged in Sydney in late 2003, the top Syrah (Shiraz) was Kingsley Estate Gimblett Gravels Syrah 2001, with Craggy Range Block 14 Syrah 2001 in second place. After heading off the far higher profile Aussie Shirazes, the Kingsley Estate Syrah was subsequently voted the best wine of the entire tasting.

Confirming the exciting quality advances of New Zealand (notably Hawke's Bay) Syrah, at the 2004 Sydney International Wine Competition, the trophy for Best Red Table Wine was awarded to Brookfields Hillside Syrah 2002 – a result show director Warren Mason predicted would 'send a ripple through the Australian wine industry'.

The classic 'Syrah' of the Rhône Valley, in France, and Australian 'Shiraz' are in fact the same variety. On the rocky, baking slopes of the upper Rhône Valley, and in several Australian states, this noble grape yields red wines renowned for their outstanding depth of cassis, plum and black-pepper flavours.

In New Zealand, interest in the variety has been stirring for a decade. Dozens of labels are now on the market, and the results from the favourable 2002 vintage are exceptional. After judging at the 2003 New Zealand Wine Society Royal Easter Wine Show, Australian wine writer James Halliday declared that the 'outstanding class of the show was undoubtedly Syrah/Shiraz ... The great thing about this [Hawke's Bay] style is that it is ripe. There's no hint of green or minty or other unripe flavours, yet it also keeps those wonderful spice, liquorice, black pepper characters which are at the riper end of the cool-climate spectrum. So it beautifully straddles the two. It is definitely different in style from Australian Shiraz, notwithstanding its diversity within Australia.'

Syrah was well known in New Zealand a century ago. Government viticulturist S.F. Anderson wrote in 1917 that Shiraz was being 'grown in nearly all our vineyards [but] the trouble with this variety has been an unevenness in ripening its fruit'. For today's winemakers, the problem has not changed: Syrah has never favoured a too-cool growing environment. Having said that, it thrives in poor soils and ripens ahead of Cabernet Sauvignon.

The latest national vineyard survey showed that 225 hectares of Syrah will be bearing by 2006 – a steep rise from 62 hectares in 2000. Syrah is now New Zealand's fourth most widely planted red-wine variety, ahead of Cabernet Franc and Malbec. Over 75 per cent of the vines are in Hawke's Bay, with smaller pockets in Auckland and Marlborough. Syrah's potential in this country's warmer vineyard sites is finally being tapped.

Artisan Fantail Island Vineyard Syrah ★★★☆

Grown in Rex and Maria Sunde's vineyard at Oratia, in West Auckland, the 2002 vintage (★★★★) is a richly coloured wine with strong black pepper aromas and very good depth of berry and spice flavours, fresh, ripe and smooth. A medium to full-bodied wine, warm and slightly earthy, it's a characterful wine, likely to age well. The lighter 2003 (★★★) is fullish in colour, peppery, slightly savoury and earthy, in a firm, middleweight style with some complexity.

Vintage	03	02
WR	5	6
Drink	05-06	05-08

DRY $25 AV

Ata Rangi Syrah   ★★★★☆

After repeated urgings by its customers to release Syrah (a key component of its blended red, Célèbre) as a varietal wine, Ata Rangi leased a block of Syrah in the Arapoff vineyard, at Martinborough. The second release, from the 2002 vintage (★★★★☆) was matured for 18 months in French and American oak barriques (25 per cent new). It's a weighty, warm wine with deep, youthful colour and bold, black pepper aromas, unmistakably Syrah. It shows good aging potential, with very concentrated cassis, plum and black pepper flavours, complexity and a very persistent finish. There is no 2003.

Vintage	03	02	01
WR	NM	6	6
Drink	NM	04-06	04-06

DRY $40 AV

Babich Winemakers Reserve Syrah   ★★★☆

Grown in Gimblett Road, Hawke's Bay, and matured for a year in American oak casks (old and new), the 2002 vintage (★★★☆) is deeply coloured, with a peppery, toasty bouquet. It's an elegant, tightly structured wine with strong plum, spice and green pepper flavours, finely integrated oak and firm tannins.

Vintage	03	02	01
WR	5	7	6
Drink	04-07	04-09	04-07

DRY $25 AV

Bilancia Hawke's Bay Syrah/Viognier   ★★★★

The 2002 (★★★★☆), labelled as a straight Syrah, is a blend of grapes from vineyards in the Gimblett Gravels district (80 per cent) and the company's own block, La Collina, on Roy's Hill. Matured for 17 months in French (predominantly) and American oak barriques, it's a dark, weighty wine with black pepper aromas and powerful, plummy, spicy flavours, intense and chewy. The 2003 vintage (★★★★), which includes 2 per cent Viognier, is a lighter style than the 2002, with a pungent, peppery bouquet, showing intense varietal character. Fresh and well-spiced, it's still very youthful, with good intensity and structure, some earthy, savoury notes and a firm finish.

Vintage	03	02	01
WR	6	7	6
Drink	04-08	04-10	04-08

DRY $34 -V

Brookfields Reserve Vintage Hillside Syrah   ★★★★☆

Grown on a sheltered slope between Maraekakaho and Bridge Pa in Hawke's Bay (described by winemaker Peter Robertson as 'surreal – a chosen site'), the 2002 vintage (★★★★★) bursts with plum and black pepper flavours. Dark and spicy, with game and liquorice elements, very ripe, sweet fruit characters and a voluminous bouquet of plums, pepper and toasty oak, it's a deliciously refined and supple wine approachable now, but best cellared to 2006+.

Vintage	02	01	00
WR	7	7	7
Drink	04-10	07-10	04-12

DRY $40 AV

C.J. Pask Gimblett Road Syrah   ★★★☆

The 2002 vintage (★★★☆) is a Hawke's Bay wine, matured for a year in French oak casks. A dark, intense red with strong, spicy, peppery characters and good fruit sweetness, it is finely balanced and firmly structured, with good concentration and aging potential.

Vintage	02	01
WR	7	5
Drink	04-07	04-05

DRY $25 AV

C.J. Pask Reserve Syrah (★★★★)

The 2000 vintage (★★★★) was based on first-crop vines in Gimblett Road and matured for 16 months in all-new French oak barriques. Deeply coloured, with an assertive, toasty oak influence, it has ripe, concentrated plum and black-pepper fruit flavours and firm tannins. There is no 2001, but the label returns from the 2002 vintage.

Vintage	02	01	00	
WR	7	NM	7	
Drink	04-08	NM	04-06	DRY $50 -V

Coopers Creek Hawke's Bay Syrah (★★★☆)

The full-coloured 2003 vintage (★★★☆) was grown near Havelock North, in Hawke's Bay, and matured in French oak casks (50 per cent new). Strong, peppery, slightly earthy aromas lead into a full-bodied (13.5 per cent alcohol) wine with generous plum and spice, slightly earthy and toasty flavours.

DRY $18 V+

Corazon The Collective Syrah (★★★)

A forward style, for drinking now onwards, the 2003 vintage (★★★) is a single-vineyard wine, grown at Mangatawhiri, in the Waikato, and matured for 10 months in seasoned French and American oak barriques. Fullish and youthful in colour, with peppery, earthy aromas, it's a medium-bodied wine with plum/spice flavours that show a slight lack of warmth, but good balance and drinkability.

Vintage	03	
WR	5	
Drink	04-06	DRY $23 -V

Craggy Range Gimblett Gravels Vineyard Block 14 Syrah ★★★★☆

Dense, purple/black in colour, the pungently varietal 2002 vintage (★★★★) was fermented with indigenous yeasts and matured for 18 months in French oak barriques (35 per cent new). A very complete Hawke's Bay wine with a lovely, creamy-rich texture, it has super-ripe flavours of black pepper, prunes, plums, dark chocolate and liquorice, showing exceptional fruit sweetness and depth.

Vintage	02	01	
WR	6	7	
Drink	04-08+	05-09	DRY $32 AV

Craggy Range Le Sol Syrah – see Craggy Range Le Sol in the Branded and Other Reds section

Crossroads Destination Series Syrah ★★★

Grown in Hawke's Bay, the 2002 vintage (★★★☆) is full-bodied and smooth, with purple-flushed colour and a peppery, earthy bouquet. It's a strongly varietal wine with sweet fruit characters, raspberry, plum and pepper flavours showing very good depth, a seasoning of toasty oak and a lasting finish. The 2003 (★★☆) is slightly rustic, with green-edged flavours, spicy and firm.

DRY $17 AV

Delegat's Gimblett Gravels Syrah (★★★☆)

The refined 2000 vintage (★★★☆) was made from Hawke's Bay vines that have since been replaced with a superior clone of Syrah. Barrique-aged for two years, it's a warm, rounded wine, not hugely concentrated, but ripe and clearly varietal, with great drinkability.

DRY $35 -V

Dry River Syrah   ★★★★☆

In a vertical tasting of the 1996 to 2002 vintages, staged in March 2004, the 1998 (★★★★★) was impressively power-packed and youthful, and the 2000 (★★★★★) was highly fragrant, intense and refined. The 2002 vintage (★★★★☆), grown in the Lovat vineyard (previously called Arapoff) in Martinborough, is densely coloured, with pungent black pepper aromas and fresh acidity woven through its highly concentrated plum, berry and spice flavours. A distinctly cool-climate, intensely varietal style with a long, peppery finish, it needs time; open 2006+.

Vintage	02	01	00	99	98	97
WR	7	7	7	6	7	7
Drink	05-10	04-11	04-11	04-10	04-05	04-10

DRY $55 -V

Esk Valley Reserve Syrah   (★★★★★)

The lovely, silky, rich 2002 vintage (★★★★★) was grown in a single vineyard in the Gimblett Gravels of Hawke's Bay and matured for 18 months in French oak barriques (100 per cent new). It has dense, purple-flushed colour and a perfumed bouquet of blackpepper and toasty oak. With its striking power, intensity and structure, bold, sweet but not jammy fruit characters and ripe, supple tannins, it's an exciting mouthful.

Vintage	02
WR	7
Drink	04-10

DRY $40 AV

Fromm La Strada Reserve Syrah   ★★★★☆

Still youthful, the 2002 vintage (★★★★☆) was blended with 6 per cent Viognier and matured in French oak casks (25 per cent new). Deeply coloured, with intense black pepper aromas, it's a distinctly cool-climate Marlborough red with fresh, vivid varietal characters of plums and spice, savoury, earthy complexities, excellent concentration and a long, supple finish. Open 2006+.

Vintage	03	02	01	00	99	98	97	96
WR	6	6	7	NM	6	7	7	6
Drink	05-11	04-10	04-09	NM	04-07	04-10	04-09	04-06

DRY $48 -V

Karikari Estate Syrah   (★★★)

Grown on Northland's Karikari Peninsula, the debut 2003 vintage (★★★) is a blend of Syrah (91 per cent) and Viognier (9 per cent), matured for a year in new American oak casks. Deeply coloured, with a peppery, toasty bouquet, it's a medium-bodied wine (12.6 per cent alcohol), with good intensity and complexity of fresh, vibrant, plum and black pepper flavours, firm and strongly spicy, but also a slight lack of warmth and softness. From a challenging season, it's a very promising debut, worth cellaring to mid-2005+.

DRY $27 -V

Kingsley Estate Gimblett Gravels Syrah/Malbec/Cabernet Sauvignon   ★★★★★

The classy 2002 vintage (★★★★★) was grown at two sites, including the estate vineyard, in the Gimblett Gravels district of Hawke's Bay. A blend of Syrah (86 per cent), Cabernet Sauvignon (7 per cent) and Malbec (7 per cent), it was matured in French oak barriques (45 per cent new). Boldly coloured, it's a flavour-crammed red, fragrant and mouthfilling, with intense, beautifully ripe blackcurrant and spice characters and lovely texture. It's an opulent wine, still youthful.

Vintage	02	01
WR	6	7
Drink	04-08	04-08

DRY $46 AV

Longlands Syrah ★★★☆

From Te Awa winery, the excellent-value 2003 vintage (★★★☆) was grown in the Gimblett Gravels district and matured for 14 months in French oak barriques (15 per cent new). Like a minor Côtes-du-Rhône, it's a skilfully made, charming Hawke's Bay wine, full-coloured, with fresh, smooth plum and black pepper flavours, vibrant and lightly oaked, and gentle tannins.

Vintage	03	02	01	00	99
WR	6	NM	6	6	6
Drink	04-07	NM	04-06	04-05	P

DRY $20 V+

Longview Estate Syrah (NR)

Like a decent Côtes-du-Rhône, the 2002 vintage (tasted prior to bottling, and so not rated) offers good depth of warm, plum and spice flavours. Matured in a 50/50 split of French and American oak casks, it's a full-coloured Northland red with a fragrant, clearly varietal bouquet of plums and pepper. Ripely flavoured, with a toasty oak influence and gentle acidity and tannins, it's a very promising debut.

DRY $25 V?

Lucknow Estate Lomond Bridge Vineyard Syrah (★★★)

A drink-young style, the 2003 vintage (★★★) is a vibrantly fruity, middleweight Hawke's Bay red with fresh plum and pepper flavours, easy tannins and a distinctly spicy finish.

Vintage	03
WR	5
Drink	04-05

DRY $20 AV

Mahurangi Estate Syrah (★★★☆)

Grown near Warkworth, north of Auckland, the 2002 vintage (★★★☆) includes a splash of Malbec (2 per cent). It's a fresh, full-coloured wine with good varietal character, offering plenty of gently oaked, plummy, spicy flavour.

DRY $24 AV

Matakana Estate Syrah ★★★★

The stylish, estate-grown 2002 vintage (★★★★) is full but not dense in colour, with a fragrant, peppery bouquet and spicy, earthy flavours in a Rhône-like style with good complexity and firm tannins. The 1999 (★★★★) and 2000 (★★★★) vintages were also very successful.

DRY $35 -V

Matariki Aspire Syrah (★★★☆)

The sharply priced 2002 vintage (★★★☆) was picked at 23.5 to 24.2 brix in the Gimblett Gravels district of Hawke's Bay and matured for 15 months in seasoned oak casks. Deeply coloured, with a peppery, slightly earthy, intensely varietal bouquet, it's a youthful, vibrant wine with plummy, spicy flavours, ripe, strong and firm.

Vintage	02
WR	7
Drink	04-08

DRY $20 V+

Matariki Hawke's Bay Syrah ★★★☆

Showing some earthy rusticity, the 2001 vintage (★★★) is a full-coloured Hawke's Bay red, weighty and moderately ripe, with firm tannins, fresh acidity and good depth of plum and spice flavours.

Vintage	01
WR	6
Drink	04-08

DRY $30 -V

Matua Valley Innovator Bullrush Vineyard Syrah   ★★★★☆

Concentrated by the 'saignee' (bleeding) technique, whereby a portion of the juice is drawn off at the start of ferment to concentrate the remaining juice, the 2002 vintage (★★★★☆) is a densely coloured, powerful Hawke's Bay red with substantial body and warm plum, black pepper and dark chocolate flavours, nutty, tannic and notably concentrated. The 2003 (★★★★☆) was matured for a year in French and American oak barriques (55 per cent new). Dark, with lovely depth of plummy, peppery, slightly earthy flavour, it is bold, vibrant and firm, with impressive complexity and structure.

Vintage	03	02
WR	6	6
Drink	04-09	04-07

DRY $29 V+

Matua Valley Matheson Syrah   ★★★☆

Grown at the Matheson Vineyard, in the 'Ngatarawa Triangle', the 2002 vintage (★★★☆) is a boldly coloured Hawke's Bay wine. Matured in American and French oak casks (50 per cent new), it shows good varietal character, with gentle tannins and a distinctly spicy finish. The 2003 (★★★☆) is similar – dark and mouthfilling, with strong plum and black pepper flavours, fresh, vibrant and smooth.

Vintage	03	02
WR	5	5
Drink	04-07	04-06

DRY $19 V+

Mills Reef Elspeth Syrah   ★★★★★

One of New Zealand's greatest Syrahs. Estate-grown in the company's Mere Road vineyard, near Hastings, in Hawke's Bay, the 2002 vintage (★★★★★) is a super-rich, purple/black wine, overflowing with ripe cassis, black pepper, liquorice and nut flavours. Strapping, with bold (slightly grippy) tannins and enormously concentrated fruit, it demands cellaring until at least 2006 onwards, maybe 2010 onwards.

Vintage	02	01	00	99	98
WR	7	7	7	7	7
Drink	04-08	04-06	04-05	P	P

DRY $45 AV

Mills Reef Reserve Syrah   (★★★☆)

The youthful 2003 vintage (★★★☆) is a Hawke's Bay red with deep, purple-flushed colour and strong black pepper aromas. Vibrant, with strong flavours of blackcurrants, spice and toasty oak, balanced tannins and fresh acidity, it should be at its best during 2005–06.

DRY $25 AV

Mission Hawke's Bay Reserve Syrah   ★★★☆

The 2002 vintage (★★★★) was grown in the Gimblett Gravels district of Hawke's Bay and matured for 15 months in French oak barriques (30 per cent new). Rich and youthful in colour, with a fragrant, peppery, slightly earthy bouquet, it flows smoothly across the palate, with strong, brambly, plummy, spicy flavours, finely balanced and lingering.

Vintage	02	01	00
WR	5	NM	6
Drink	04-08	NM	04-10

DRY $22 AV

Mission Jewelstone Syrah ★★★★☆

The classy 2002 vintage (★★★★☆) was hand-picked in Gimblett Road, Hawke's Bay, and matured for 15 months in French oak barriques (half new). Densely coloured, it's still youthful, with generous plum, dark chocolate and black pepper flavours, showing excellent ripeness and complexity, gentle tannins and a well-rounded, long finish. Drink now or cellar.

Vintage	02	01	00	99
WR	5	5	NM	7
Drink	04-10	04-08	NM	04-10

DRY $32 AV

Moana Park Vineyard Tribute Syrah (★★★★)

Drinking well now, the rich, soft 2002 vintage (★★★★) was grown in the Dartmoor Valley, Hawke's Bay, and matured in American oak casks. It's a deeply coloured wine with ripe, sweet fruit characters and very good density of blackcurrant, plum, herb and sweet oak flavours.

Vintage	02
WR	6
Drink	06-07

DRY $25 V+

Morton Estate Black Label Hawke's Bay Syrah ★★★

The 2002 vintage (★★☆), matured for a year in American and French oak casks, is fullish but not deep in colour, with some spicy complexity. Slightly herbaceous, it lacks real richness and roundness.

Vintage	02	01
WR	6	6
Drink	04-06	04-08

DRY $34 -V

Mudbrick Vineyard Reserve Syrah ★★★

The 2002 vintage (★★☆) of this Waiheke Island red was matured for a year in French oak barriques (30 per cent new). It's a full-coloured wine with firm acidity woven through its plum and black pepper flavours. When tasted in mid-2003, it lacked real warmth and softness, but will probably improve with time.

DRY $38 -V

Muddy Water Waipara Syrah ★★★☆

Picked at 24.9 brix, fermented with indigenous yeasts and matured in oak casks (20 per cent new), the 2002 vintage (★★★☆) is full-coloured and peppery, with strong plum/spice flavours and good complexity, but a slight lack of softness on the finish. The 2003 (★★★☆) is similar – spicy and slightly earthy, with vibrant plum and black pepper flavours that need a bit more warmth and roundness, but show excellent depth.

Vintage	03	02
WR	5	5
Drink	05-08	04-07

DRY $27 -V

Murdoch James Estate Syrah ★★★☆

The 2003 vintage (★★★) is a boldly coloured, French oak-aged Martinborough red with strong, plummy, peppery aromas and flavours, fresh, crisp and vibrant. It shows a slight lack of warmth, but is still very youthful; open 2006+.

DRY $30 -V

Newton Forrest Estate Cornerstone Syrah ★★★★☆

The dense, inky, potent 2002 vintage (★★★★★) is a muscular (14.5 per cent alcohol), complex Hawke's Bay red with sweet fruit characters. Crammed with very ripe, highly concentrated blackcurrant, plum, liquorice and black pepper flavours, framed by soft tannins, it's still very fresh and well worth cellaring to 2006+. There is no 2003.

Vintage	03	02	01	
WR	NM	6	5	**DRY $40 AV**
Drink	NM	04-10	05-07	

Ngaruroro Estate Rockhill Syrah (★★★☆)

The youthful 2002 vintage (★★★☆), grown on north-facing limestone terraces in Hawke's Bay, was matured in new French and old American oak casks for 14 months. Full and purple-flushed in colour, with cracked pepper aromas, it is fresh and vibrant, with good depth of plum and black pepper flavours in a strongly varietal style, showing some complexity.

DRY $27 -V

Okahu Estate Kaz Shiraz ★★★★

Estate-grown at Kaitaia, this is a typically impressive Northland wine, richly varietal and highly concentrated in top years. The 2000 vintage (★★★☆), matured for 18 months in American (60 per cent) and French oak casks (half new), is full-coloured, with a hint of development, and perfumed, sweet oak aromas. The palate is spicy and strongly wood-influenced, with some fruit sweetness and firm tannins. Ready.

Vintage	00	99	98	
WR	7	NM	7	**DRY $50 -V**
Drink	04-12	NM	04-10	

Okahu Estate Ninety Mile Reserve Shiraz/Cabernet ★★★☆

Estate-grown near Kaitaia, the 2002 vintage (★★★☆) is a blend of 60 per cent Shiraz and 40 per cent Cabernet Sauvignon, matured for 15 months in seasoned French and American oak casks. Drinking well now, but also worth cellaring, it's a full-coloured wine with strong, ripe, blackcurrant and spice flavours, leathery, earthy, savoury complexities and a well-rounded finish.

Vintage	02	01	
WR	7	6	**DRY $28 -V**
Drink	04-08	04-07	

Passage Rock Syrah ★★★★

A robust Waiheke Island red, dark and complex, with a powerful presence in the mouth. Matured in French and American oak barriques (60 per cent new), the 2002 vintage (★★★★☆) is an intensely varietal wine with fragrant, black pepper aromas leading into a warm, spicy, nutty, firm palate with excellent depth and structure and a lasting finish. The 2003 (★★★☆) is deeply coloured, with sweet oak aromas, and a concentrated, youthful palate with peppery, oaky flavours showing very good depth.

DRY $40 -V

Peninsula Estate Zeno Syrah ★★★☆

Named after a rock in Auckland's Hauraki Gulf, the 2001 vintage (★★★) is a characterful Waiheke Island red, French oak-aged for a year. Fullish but not deep in colour, with a mellow, slightly earthy, spicy and nutty bouquet, it lacks real richness but shows some complexity, with a firm finish. Drink 2004–05.

Vintage	01	
WR	6	**DRY $40 -V**
Drink	04-08	

Red Rock The Under Arm Syrah   (★★★★★)

The bargain-priced, densely coloured 2002 vintage (★★★★★) overflows with richly varietal, cassis and black pepper flavours. Made by Capricorn Estates, a division of Craggy Range, it's a muscular Hawke's Bay wine with bold, sweet fruit characters and a firm underlay of tannin.

DRY $22 V+

Schubert Syrah   ★★★★

The transition from Hawke's Bay as the region of origin (and source of the outstanding 2000 vintage) to the Wairarapa is not proving easy. The 2002 (★★☆), matured for 25 months in French oak barriques (half new), is fullish in colour and lean, with under-ripe, green-edged flavours and a firm, spicy, slightly high-acid finish.

Vintage	01	00	99
WR	7	7	6
Drink	04-11	04-10	04-09

DRY $45 -V

Seifried Syrah   (★★★☆)

The floral, full-coloured 2003 vintage (★★★☆) was grown at Brightwater, in Nelson, and matured for a year in new and one-year-old French oak barriques. It's a vibrant, spicy wine with good varietal character, sweet, ripe-fruit flavours of plums and pepper and gentle tannins.

Vintage	03
WR	6
Drink	04-08

DRY $23 AV

Seifried Winemakers Collection Syrah   (★★★☆)

Pungently peppery on the nose, the 2003 vintage (★★★☆) was grown at Brightwater and matured for over a year in new and one-year-old casks. It's a full-coloured Nelson red, mouthfilling, with strong, plummy, spicy, slightly earthy flavours showing good balance and complexity.

DRY $30 -V

Selaks Founders Reserve Hawke's Bay Syrah   (★★★★★)

Grown in the Pykes Flat block, on the banks of the Mohaka River, in northern Hawke's Bay, the delicious 2002 vintage (★★★★★) was harvested at over 24 brix and matured for 14 months in one-year-old French oak barriques (70 per cent) and new American oak barriques (30 per cent). It's a deeply coloured wine with a fragrant, peppery bouquet, deep blackcurrant, plum and spice flavours and a well-rounded finish. A forward style, it shows lovely ripeness, richness and varietal definition.

DRY $28 V+

Stonecroft Syrah   ★★★★★

With an arresting series of bold, dark, flavour-drenched reds, Alan Limmer was the first winemaker in this country to consistently produce a top-flight Syrah. The early vintages were grown entirely in Stonecroft's stony, arid vineyard in Mere Road, west of Hastings, but the 1998 introduced grapes from the newer Tokarahi vineyard at the foot of Roys Hill, which is contributing 'denser, more intense flavours'. Maturation is for 18 months in French oak barriques (50 per cent new). Deeply coloured, with a perfumed, peppery bouquet, the 2002 vintage (★★★★☆) is an elegant, rather than blockbuster, wine with excellent depth of plum and spice flavours, ripe and rounded.

Vintage	02	01	00	99	98	97	96
WR	5	6	NM	6	6	6	6
Drink	05+	04-10	NM	04-10	04-10	04-08	04-06

DRY $38 V+

Te Awa Syrah   (★★★★)

The tightly focused and complex 2002 vintage (★★★★) was grown in the Gimblett Gravels district of Hawke's Bay and matured for 14 months in French oak barriques (20 per cent new). Richly coloured, it shows good structure and potential, with distinctly peppery, plummy, spicy, nutty flavours of excellent ripeness and depth and a firm finish.

Vintage	02	**DRY $30 AV**
WR	6	
Drink	04-08	

Te Kairanga Syrah   (★★★★☆)

Grown in the Gimblett Gravels district, the 2002 vintage (★★★★☆) is a dark, elegant Hawke's Bay red with intense cassis and blackberry aromas and a rich palate showing lovely structure and persistence.

DRY $45 -V

Te Mata Estate Bullnose Syrah   ★★★★★

Grown in the Bullnose vineyard, in the Ngatarawa district of Hawke's Bay, this classy red is matured for 16 months in French oak barriques, new and seasoned. The 2002 vintage (★★★★★), rated by the winery as 'the best yet', is richly scented, with impressive weight (14.5 per cent alcohol) and intensity of berryish, strongly spiced, lingering flavours. It's a very refined, tight-knit and intensely varietal wine, showing great elegance.

Vintage	03	02	01	00	99	98	97	96	95	**DRY $36 V+**
WR	6	7	7	7	6	7	7	6	6	
Drink	06-08	05-09	04-07	04-06	04-05	P	P	P	P	

Te Mata Estate Woodthorpe Syrah/Viognier   ★★★★

Attractive drinking from now on, the 2003 vintage (★★★☆) was made by co-fermenting Syrah with a tiny amount (2 per cent of the blend) of Viognier (a traditional technique of the northern Rhône Valley, designed to add 'a perfumed, floral aroma'). French oak-aged for 15 months, it's a full-coloured Hawke's Bay wine with a spicy bouquet and good depth of fresh, vibrant plum/pepper flavours, showing some earthy, spicy, nutty complexity.

Vintage	03	02	**DRY $25 AV**
WR	6	6	
Drink	05-07	04-06	

Trinity Hill Gimblett Rd Syrah   ★★★★

Winemaker John Hancock is after a 'savoury, earthy Rhône style'. The 2002 vintage (★★★★), grown in the Gimblett Gravels and matured for 16 months in French and American oak barriques, is an elegant yet powerful Hawke's Bay red with impressive colour, spicy aromatics and ripe, clearly delineated varietal flavours of plum and black pepper, underpinned by firm tannins.

Vintage	03	02	01	00	99	98	97	**DRY $30 AV**
WR	NM	6	5	5	6	5	5	
Drink	NM	06-12	04-10	04-08	04-09	04-08	04-06	

Unison Hawke's Bay Syrah (★★★★★)

Following the consistent success of Syrah as a vital ingredient in its blended red, Unison, the Hawke's Bay winery top-grafted some of its Merlot vines to Syrah. Barrel-aged for 20 months (mostly in American oak), the debut 2002 vintage (★★★★★) is densely coloured, with highly concentrated, sweet fruit flavours of plums, pepper, dark chocolate and liquorice. It's less alcoholic (13.5 per cent) and overtly oaky than some Hawke's Bay Syrahs, but still power-packed, with firm tannins and great structure for aging.

DRY $36 V+

Vidal Estate Soler Syrah ★★★★☆

The powerful, splendidly ripe 2002 vintage (★★★★★) was grown in the Gimblett Gravels district of Hawke's Bay and matured for 18 months in French (95 per cent) and American oak barriques. Delicious in its youth, it's an enticingly fragrant, muscular wine (14.8 per cent alcohol), with densely packed blackcurrant, plum and spice flavours, deliciously rich and rounded. Drink now or cellar.

Vintage	03	02	01
WR	NM	6	6
Drink	NM	04-10	04-05

DRY $30 AV

Vidal Estate Syrah (★★★★★)

The bargain-priced 2002 vintage (★★★★★) is a Hawke's Bay red, grown in the Gimblett Gravels district and matured for 16 months in French (95 per cent) and American oak barriques. Floral and elegant, with dense colour and generous, ripe and persistent flavours of plums, pepper and dark chocolate, it's a well-structured wine with a long future.

Vintage	03	02
WR	6	6
Drink	05-08	04-08

DRY $25 V+

Wishart Reserve Hawke's Bay Syrah ★★★★

Grown on the beach gravels at Bay View, the 2001 vintage (★★★★) is an excellent debut. French oak-aged for a year, it is dark and fragrant, with highly concentrated flavours of blackcurrants, plums and spice and oak complexity. Rich and fairly ripe, yet with firm acidity, it's a sophisticated wine, maturing well.

Vintage	01
WR	6
Drink	04-08

DRY $45 -V

Zinfandel

In California, where it is extensively planted, Zinfandel produces muscular, heady reds that can approach a dry port style. It is believed to be identical to the Primitivo variety, which yields highly characterful, warm, spicy reds in southern Italy. There are only 4 hectares of bearing Zinfandel vines in New Zealand (with no growth projected from 2004 to 2006), but Alan Limmer, of the Stonecroft winery in Hawke's Bay, believes 'Zin' has potential here, 'if you can stand the stress of growing a grape that falls apart at the first sign of a dubious weather map!'

Kemblefield The Reserve Zinfandel   ★★★☆

One of the few commercial releases of 'Zin' in New Zealand, the 2002 vintage (★★★☆) of this Hawke's Bay red was estate-grown at Mangatahi and matured for 18 months in French oak casks. Richly coloured, it's a robust red (14.5 per cent alcohol) with brambly, plummy, spicy flavours showing very good depth. A concentrated but green-edged wine, it needs a tad more warmth and ripeness.

DRY $50 ·V

Stonecroft Zinfandel   ★★★☆

The first commercial release of Zinfandel in New Zealand was the 1999 vintage (★★★☆), a Hawke's Bay red with moderately ripe, plummy, spicy flavours and firm acidity. The 2002 (★★★) is 'not the greatest Zin we'll make', reports winemaker Alan Limmer. 'It was knocked around by the rain.' Light in colour, it's a high-alcohol wine (14 per cent) with plum, strawberry and spice flavours that lack real stuffing, but some peppery, drink-young charm.

Vintage 02
WR 4
Drink 04+

DRY $25 AV

Index of Wine Brands

This index should be especially useful when you are visiting wineries as a quick way to find the reviews of each company's range of wines. It also provides links between different wine brands made by the same producer (for example, Matua Valley and Shingle Peak).